# Honda
# XL/XR600R &
# XR650L/R
# Service and Repair Manual

## by Alan Ahlstrand and Bob Henderson

**Models covered**

XL600R, 1983 through 1987
XR600R, 1985 through 2000
XR650L, 1993 through 2014
XR650R, 2000 through 2007

*(2183-3S4-2)*

ABCDE
FGHIJ
KLMN

ISBN-13: **978-1-62092-097-8**
ISBN-10: **1-62092-097-2**

**Library of Congress Control Number 2014936157**
Printed in the USA

**Haynes Publishing**
Sparkford, Nr Yeovil, Somerset BA22 7JJ, England

**Haynes North America, Inc**
861 Lawrence Drive, Newbury Park, California 91320, USA

© Haynes North America, Inc. 2008, 2014
With permission from J.H. Haynes & Co. Ltd.

A book in the **Haynes Service and Repair Manual Series**

14-320

# Contents

## LIVING WITH YOUR HONDA

### Introduction

### Daily (pre-ride) checks

## MAINTENANCE

### Routine maintenance and servicing

# Contents

# The Birth of a Dream

by Julian Ryder

There is no better example of the Japanese post-War industrial miracle than Honda. Like other companies which have become household names, it started with one man's vision. In this case the man was the 40-year old Soichiro Honda, who had sold his piston-ring manufacturing business to Toyota in 1945 and was happily spending the proceeds on prolonged parties for his friends. However, the difficulties of getting around in the chaos of post-War Japan irked Honda, so when he came across a job lot of generator engines he realised that here was a way of getting people mobile again at low cost.

A 12 by 18-foot shack in Hamamatsu became his first bike factory, fitting the generator motors into pushbikes. Before long he'd used up all 500 generator motors and started manufacturing his own engine, known as the "chimney," either because of the elongated cylinder head or the smoky exhaust

or perhaps both. The chimney made all of half a horsepower from its 50 cc engine, but it was a major success and became the Honda A-type. Less than two years after he'd set up in Hamamatsu, Soichiro Honda founded the Honda Motor Company in September 1948. By then, the A-type had been developed into the 90 cc B-type engine, which Mr. Honda decided deserved its own chassis, not a bicycle frame. Honda was about to become Japan's first post-War manufacturer of complete motorcycles. In August 1949, the first prototype was ready. With an output of three horsepower, the 98 cc D-type was still a simple two-stroke but it had a two-speed transmission and, most importantly, a pressed steel frame with telescopic forks and hard tail rear end. The frame was almost triangular in profile, with the top rail going in a straight line from the massively braced steering head to the rear axle. Legend has it that after the D-type's first tests, the entire workforce went

for a drink to celebrate and try and think of a name for the bike. One man broke one of those silences you get when people are thinking, exclaiming "This is like a dream!" "That's it!" shouted Honda, and so the Honda Dream was christened.

Mr. Honda was a brilliant, intuitive engineer and designer, but he did not bother himself with the marketing side of his business. With hindsight, it is possible to see that employing Takeo Fujisawa - who would both sort out the home market and plan the eventual expansion into overseas markets - was a masterstroke. He arrived in October 1949, and in 1950 was made Sales Director. Another vital new name was Kiyoshi Kawashima, who along with Honda himself, designed the company's first four-stroke - after Kawashima had told them that the four-stroke opposition to Honda's two-strokes sounded nicer and therefore sold better. The result of that statement was the overhead-valve 148 cc E-type which first ran in July 1951, just two months after the first drawings were made. Kawashima was made a director of the Honda Company at 34 years old.

The E-type was a massive success, over 32,000 were made in 1953 alone, but Honda's lifelong pursuit of technical innovation sometimes distracted him from commercial reality. Fujisawa pointed out that they were in danger of ignoring their core business, the motorised bicycles that still formed Japan's main means of transport. In May 1952 the F-type Cub appeared, another two-stroke despite the top men's reservations. You could buy a complete machine or just the motor to attach to your own bicycle. The result was certainly distinctive, a white fuel tank with a circular profile went just below and behind the saddle on the left of the bike, and the motor with its horizontal cylinder and bright red cover just below the rear axle on the same side of the bike. This machine turned Honda into the biggest bike maker in Japan with 70% of the market for bolt-on bicycle motors. The F-type was also the first Honda to be exported. Next came the machine that would turn Honda into the biggest motorcycle manufacturer in the world.

The C100 Super Cub was a typically audacious piece of Honda engineering and marketing. For the first time, but not the last, Honda invented a completely new type of motorcycle. The term "scooterette" was coined to describe the new bike which had many of the characteristics of a scooter but

**Honda C70 and C90 OHV-engined models**

the large wheels, and therefore stability, of a motorcycle. The first one was sold in August 1958; fifteen years later over nine-million of them were on the roads of the world. If ever a machine can be said to have brought mobility to the masses, it is the Super Cub. If you add in the electric starter that was added for the C102 model of 1961, the design of the Super Cub has remained substantially unchanged ever since - testament to how right Honda got it the first time. The Super Cub made Honda the world's biggest manufacturer after just two years of production.

Honda's export drive started in earnest in 1957 when Britain and Holland got their first bikes, America got just two bikes the next year. By 1962 Honda had half the American market with 65,000 sales. But Soichiro Honda had already travelled abroad to Europe and the USA, making a special point of going to the Isle of Man TT, then the most important race in the GP calendar. He realised that no matter how advanced his products were, only racing success would convince overseas markets for whom "Made in Japan" still meant cheap and nasty. It took five years from Soichiro Honda's first visit to the Island before his bikes were ready for the TT. In 1959 the factory entered five riders in the 125. They did not have a massive impact on the event, being benevolently regarded as a curiosity, but sixth, seventh and eighth were good enough for the team prize. The bikes were off the pace, but they were well engineered and very reliable.

The TT was the only time the West saw the Hondas in '59, but they came back for more the following year with the first of a generation of bikes which shaped the future of motorcycling - the double-overhead-cam four-cylinder 250. It was fast and reliable - it revved to 14,000 rpm - but didn't handle anywhere near as well as the opposition. However, Honda had now signed up non-Japanese riders to lead

The CB250N Super Dream became a favorite with UK learner riders of the late seventies and early eighties

their challenge. The first win didn't come until 1962 (Aussie Tom Phillis in the Spanish 125 GP) and was followed up with a world-shaking performance at the TT. Twenty-one year old Mike Hailwood won both 125 and 250 cc TTs and Hondas filled the top five positions in both races. Soichiro Honda's master plan was starting to come to fruition; Hailwood and Honda won the 1961 250 cc World Championship. Next year Honda won three titles. The other Japanese factories fought back and inspired Honda to produce some of the most fascinating racers ever seen: the awesome six-cylinder 250, the five-cylinder 125, and the 500 four, with which the immortal Hailwood battled Agostini and the MV Agusta.

When Honda pulled out of racing in '67 they had won sixteen rider's titles, eighteen manufacturer's titles, and 137 GPs - including 18 TTs - and introduced the concept of the modern works team to motorcycle racing. Sales success followed racing victory as Soichiro Honda had predicted, but only because the products advanced as rapidly as the racing machinery. The Hondas that came to Britain in the early '60s were incredibly sophisticated. They had overhead cams where the British bikes had pushrods, they had electric starters when the Brits relied on the kickstart, they had 12V electrics when even the biggest British bike used a 6V system. There seemed no end to the technical wizardry and when, in 1968, the first four-cylinder CB750 road bike arrived, the world changed forever. They even had to invent a new word for it: superbike. Honda raced again with the CB750 at Daytona and won the World Endurance title with a prototype DOHC version that became the CB900 roadster. There was the six-cylinder CBX, the first turbocharged production bike, they invented the full-dress tourer with the Goldwing and came back to GPs with the revolutionary oval-pistoned NR500 four-stroke - a much-misunderstood bike that was more rolling experiment than racer. It was true, though, that Mr. Honda was not keen on two-strokes - early motocross engines had to be explained away to him as lawnmower motors! However, in 1982 Honda raced the NS500, an agile three-cylinder lightweight against the big four-cylinder opposition in 500 GPs. The bike won in the first year and in '83 took the world title for Freddie Spencer. In four-stroke racing, the V4 layout took over from the straight four, dominating TT, F1 and Endurance championships, and when

The GL1000 introduced in 1975, was the first in Honda's line of Goldwings

Carl Fogarty in action at the Suzuka 8 Hour on the RC45

An early CB750 Four

Superbike arrived, Honda was ready with the RC30. On the roads, the VFR V4 became an instant classic while the CBR600 invented another new class of bike on its way to becoming a best-seller.

And then there was the NR750. This limited-edition technological tour-de-force embodied many of Soichiro Honda's ideals. It used the latest techniques and materials in every component, from the oval-piston, 32-valve V4 motor to the titanium coating on the windscreen, it was - as Mr. Honda would have wanted - the best it could possibly be. A fitting memorial to the man who has shaped the motorcycle industry and motorcycles as we know them today.

## The Dream Continues

No one, when in the middle of a good dream, wants to awaken. To Honda's way of thinking, that's not necessary at all. They know that the only thing that's necessary to prolong the "Dream" is to offer the best possible machine required for its intended purpose and their core customers will never stray. This book deals with dual-sport and off-road bikes, so let's venture back a few years (quite a few) and look at the off-road landscape way back when dirt bikes first started to become popular.

First of all, the landscape - there was a *lot* more of it! Land usage rights and access issues were almost non-existent. Enthusiasts

wishing to ride off-road usually didn't have to travel very far to do so - sometimes only right down the street. Motorcycle parks and tracks were abundant, and those willing to put up with a longer trek could venture out to the desert or woods and enjoy a day or weekend having their way with whatever terrain they chose to ride. Dirt bikes gained almost a cult status, but definitely in a good way. Camaraderie was the name of the game and everyone was after only one thing: a good time.

Early dirt competition (excluding, perhaps, flat-tracking and hillclimbs) was dominated by British iron. Riders of Triumph, Norton, BSA, Matchless, CCM, and hybrid combinations of custom frames and of any of the above marques usually wound up on the podium. These heavy, converted road-going machines, stripped of everything unnecessary for dirt riding, couldn't be beaten at the time. Then came the two strokes. Husqvarna, CZ, Bultaco and Suzuki were some of the first to turn the tide, but it wasn't long until Honda joined the fray and introduced the two-stroke Elsinore line and began to fight back.

And fight back they did. As everyone eventually jumped off the four-stroke dirt-bike ship and hopped on two stroke steeds for competition, Honda and its Elsinore models, later to become known as simply the "CR," enjoyed incredible success, both on the professional level and in the weekly "On Any Sunday" world of amateur racing. These were awesome bikes for racing, and even for play riding. But not everyone needed, or even wanted, the alarming "hit" of a powerful two stroke when it comes into its powerband.

Honda realized another market existed, so they introduced the XL and XR line of bikes. Many displacements were offered over the years, both street-legal (XL) and off-road (XR) models. They gained a following of faithful owners who appreciated the simplicity and ease-of-use of these bikes. With regular maintenance and the occasional repair, they'd

1996 Honda XR600R

2003 Honda XR650R

2007 Honda XR650L

pretty much last forever. There are those who say that these bikes will pretty much last forever with NO maintenance, too! Although neglecting a machine is never a good bet, it IS a good testimony to the reliability of these bikes.

Most of these bikes, though, were of small displacement and not really suited to racing of any type (save for the XR75 in mini-cross and, in some forums of competition, the XR250). Eventually, Honda came out with the XR500 and, through a series of modifications became very competitive, winning some of the most grueling desert races, such as those held in Baja, Mexico.

In 1983, a punched-out version was unveiled as a dual-sport model - the XL600R. With more horsepower on tap it was better suited for use on the highway, but was still reasonably rideable off the road. This model continued until 1987. Beginning in 1985 the

bike was also offered as a dirt-only model - the XR600R - and enjoyed much success in the world of long distance desert racing, just like its older brother, the XR500.

In 1993, the dual-sport model was reintroduced, with the displacement increased to 650cc and offered as the XR650L. At the time of publication, this bike remained largely unchanged; further evidence of Honda's keen intuition of its customers' needs and desires.

Fast-forward to the year 2000. This would be the last year for the XR600R, which was (and still is) a great bike - as indestructible as a bowling ball and very competitive in its day - but its nemesis in the desert, the two-stroke Kawasaki KX500 (a.k.a. the world's scariest dirt bike), was a bit too much for it to deal with. Honda had a new secret weapon in its arsenal and unleashed it in the form of the 2000 XR650R. This bike wasn't a just a 600R with a 650L engine - it was a completely

redesigned machine.

The XR650R was a purpose-built competition machine designed to dominate the world of high-speed, long distance off-road competition, which it did. During its reign it was considered almost unbeatable. It features an aluminum (rather than steel) frame, and a considerably more powerful liquid-cooled engine than its predecessor. It has enjoyed legendary status in the desert racing world, up until the end of its model run in 2007. That's when Honda's CRF450X took over the 650R's spot in the winner's circle, and then in 2008, on the showroom floor as well. The 450X is lighter, therefore more nimble, and almost as fast (in some setups *as* fast) as the 650R, so now it gets to bask in the limelight. But the reputation and reliability of the 650R will continue to ensure that the bike will have a loyal following for years to come. It's not time to wake up yet . . .

## Acknowledgements

Thanks are due to Honda of Milpitas, Milpitas, California, for providing some of the motorcycles shown in these photographs; to Pete Sirett, service manager, for arranging the facilities and fitting many of the procedures into his shop's busy schedule; and to Steve Van Horn, service technician, for performing many of the mechanical procedures and for providing valuable technical information. Kolbe Honda of Woodland Hills, California, provided the XR600R shown on the cover.

Our thanks are also due to Craig Adams of Cal Coast Motorsports, Ventura, California, for supplying the 2007 XR650L shown on the cover and in certain mechanical procedures throughout the book. Special thanks to Cal Northrop of Full Travel Innovations, LLC, Wendy, Bobby and Mark Henderson, Jill Cook,

Kent Reppert, John Wegmann and Jennifer Bulger; without their help this book would not have been possible.

## About this manual

The aim of this manual is to help you get the best value from your motorcycle. It can do so in several ways. It can help you decide what work must be done, even if you choose to have it done by a dealer; it provides information and procedures for routine maintenance and servicing; and it offers diagnostic and repair procedures to follow when trouble occurs.

We hope you use the manual to tackle the work yourself. For many simpler jobs, doing it yourself may be quicker than arranging an appointment to get the motorcycle into a dealer and making the trips to leave it and pick it up. More importantly, a lot of money

can be saved by avoiding the expense the shop must pass on to you to cover its labor and overhead costs. An added benefit is the sense of satisfaction and accomplishment that you feel after doing the job yourself.

References to the left or right side of the motorcycle assume you are sitting on the seat, facing forward.

**We take great pride in the accuracy of information given in this manual, but motorcycle manufacturers make alterations and design changes during the production run of a particular motorcycle of which they do not inform us. No liability can be accepted by the authors or publishers for loss, damage or injury caused by any errors in, or omissions from, the information given.**

## Identification numbers

The frame serial number is stamped into the front of the frame. The engine number is stamped into the left side of the crankcase. Both of these numbers should be recorded and kept in a safe place so they can be furnished to law enforcement officials in the event of a theft.

The frame serial number, engine serial number and carburetor identification number should also be kept in a handy place so they are always available when purchasing or ordering parts for your motorcycle.

The models covered by this manual are as follows:
XL600R, 1983 through 1987
XR600R, 1985 through 2000
XR650L, 1993 through 2014
XR650R, 2000 through 2007

### Identifying model years

#### XL600R

| Year | Initial engine number | Initial frame number |
|---|---|---|
| 1983 | PD03E-5000053 | PD030-DM000027 |
| 1984 | | |
| 49 states | PD03E-5100007 | PD030-EM100006 |
| California | PD03E-5100214 | PD031-EM100007 |
| 1985 | | |
| 49 states | PD03E-5200004 | PD030-FK200003 |
| California | PD03E-5200008 | PD031-FK200002 |
| 1986 | | |
| 49 states | PD03E-5300004 | PD030-GK300002 |
| California | PD03E-5300002 | PD031-GK300001 |
| 1987 | | |
| 49 states | PD03E-5400003 | PD030-HK400002 |
| California | PD03E-5400008 | PD031-HK400001 |

#### XR600R

| Year | Initial engine number | Initial frame number |
|---|---|---|
| 1985 | PE04E-5000038 | PE040-FK000024 |
| 1986 | PE04E-5100003 | PE040-GK100003 |
| 1987 | PE04E-5200003 | PE040-HK200003 |
| 1988 | PE04E-5300014 | PE040-JK300009 |
| 1989 | PE04E-5400001 | PE040-KK400001 |
| 1990 | PE04E-5500011 | PE040-LK500001 |
| 1991 | PE04E-5600011 | PE040-MK600008 |
| 1992 | PE04E-5700007 | PE040-NM700004 |
| 1993 | PE04E-5800005 | PE040-PM800002 |
| 1994 | PE04E-5900001 | PE040-RM900001 |
| 1995 | PE04E-5950001 | PE040-SM000001 |
| 1996 | PE04E-6000001 | PE040-TM000001 |
| 1997 | PE04E-7000001 | PE040-VM200001 |
| 1998 | | |
| 49 states | PE04E-8100001 (1) | PE040-WM300001 (2) |
| California | PE04E-8000001 | PE041-WM300001 (3) |
| 1999 | | |
| 49 states | PE04E-8100001 | PE040-XK500001 |
| California | PE04E-8100001 | PE041-XK500001 |
| 2000 | | |
| 49 states | PE04E-8100001 | PE040-YK600001 |
| California | PE04E-8100001 | PE041-YK600001 |

(1) Or PE04E-8000001.
(2) Or PE040-WK4000001.
(3) Or PE041-WK4000001.

## XR650L

| Year | Initial engine number | Initial frame number |
|---|---|---|
| 1993 | | |
|     49 states | RD06E-2000009 | JH2RD060*PM000004 |
|     California | RD06E-2000014 | JH2RD061*PM000005 |
| 1994 | | |
|     49 states | RD06E-2000016 | JH2RD060*RM100007 |
|     California | RD06E-2000451 | JH2RD061*RM100010 |
| 1995 | | |
|     49 states | RD06E-2200001 | JH2RD060*SM200001 |
|     California | RD06E-2200001 | JH2RD061*RM000010 |
| 1996 | | |
|     49 states | RD06E-2300001 | JH2RD060*TM300001 |
|     California | RD06E-2300001 | JH2RD061*TM000001 |
| 1997 | | |
|     49 states | RD06E-2400001 | JH2RD060*VM400001 |
|     California | RD06E-2400001 | JH2RD061*VM400001 |
| 1998 | | |
|     49 states | RD06E-2600001 | JH2RD060*WK600001 |
|     or | RD06E-2500001 | JH2RD060*WM500001 |
|     California | RD06E-2500001 | JH2RD061*WM500001 |
|     or | RD06E-2600001 | JH2RD061*WK600001 |
| 1999 | | |
|     49 states | RD06E-2600001 | JH2RD060*XK700001 |
|     California | RD06E-2600001 | JH2RD061*XK700001 |
| 2000 | | |
|     49 states | RD06E-2600001 | JH2RD060*YK800001 |
|     California | RD06E-2600001 | JH2RD061*YK800001 |
| 2001 | | |
|     49 states | RD06E-2600001 | JH2RD060*1K900001 |
|     California | RD06E-2600001 | JH2RD061*1K900001 |
| 2002 | | |
|     49 states | RD06E-2600001 | JH2RD060*2K000001 |
|     California | RD06E-2600001 | JH2RD061*2K000001 |
| 2003 | | |
|     49 states | RD06E-2700001 | JH2RD060*3M100001 |
|     California | RD06E-2700001 | JH2RD061*3M100001 |
| 2004 | | |
|     49 states | RD06E-2800001 | JH2RD060*4K200001 |
|     or | RD06E-2850001 | JH2RD060*4K210001 |
|     or | RD06E-2900001 | JH2RD060*4K250001 |
|     California | RD06E-2800001 | JH2RD061*4K200001 |
|     or | RD06E-2850001 | JH2RD061*4M210001 |
|     or | RD06E-2900001 | JH2RD061*4K250001 |
| 2005 | | |
|     49 states | RD06E-2910001 | JH2RD060*5M300001 |
|     or | RD06E-2920001 | JH2RD060*5K310001 |
|     California | RD06E-2910001 | JH2RD061*5M300001 |
|     or | RD06E-2920001 | JH2RD061*5K310001 |
|     or | RD06E-2900001 | JH2RD061*4K250001 |
| 2006 | | |
|     49 states | RD06E-2920001 | JH2RD060*6K400001 |
|     California | RD06E-2920001 | JH2RD061*6K400001 |

## XR650L (continued)

| Year | Initial engine number | Initial frame number |
|------|----------------------|---------------------|
| 2007 | | |
| 49 states | RD06E-2920001 | JH2RD060-7K500001 |
| California | RD06E-2920001 | JH2RD061-7K500001 |
| 2008 | | |
| 49 states | RD06E-2920001 | JH2RD060-8K600001 |
| California | RD06E-2920001 | JH2RD061-8K600001 |
| 2009 | | |
| 49 states | RD06E-2920001 | JH2RD060-9K700001 |
| California | RD06E-2920001 | JH2RD061-9K700001 |
| 2010 | | |
| Not produced | | |
| 2011 | | |
| Not produced | | |
| 2012 | | |
| 49 states | RD06E-2920001 | JH2RD060-CK900001 |
| California | RD06E-2920001 | JH2RD061-CK900001 |
| 2013 | | |
| 49 states | RD06E-3000001 | JH2RD060-DK100001 |
| California | RD06E-3000001 | JH2RD061-DK100001 |
| 2014 | | |
| 49 states | RD06E-3000001 | JH2RD060-EK200001 |
| California | RD06E-3000001 | JH2RD061-EK200001 |

## XR650R

| Year | Initial engine number | Initial frame number |
|------|----------------------|---------------------|
| 2000 | | |
| 49 states | RE01E-5100001 | JH2RE010*YK100001 |
| California | RE01E-5100001 | JH2RE011*YK100001 |
| 2001 | | |
| 49 states | RE01E-5100001 | JH2RE010*1K200001 |
| California | RE01E-5100001 | JH2RE011*1K200001 |
| 2002 | | |
| 49 states | RE01E-5100001 | JH2RE010*2K300001 |
| California | RE01E-5100001 | JH2RE011*2K300001 |
| 2003 | | |
| 49 states | RE01E-5200001 | JH2RE010*3M400001 |
| or | RE01E-5300001 | JH2RE010*3K450001 |
| California | RE01E-5200001 | JH2RE012*3M400001 |
| or | RE01E-5300001 | JH2RE011*3K450001 |
| 2004 | | |
| 49 states | RE01E-5300001 | JH2RE010*4K500001 |
| California | RE01E-5300001 | JH2RE011*4K500001 |
| 2005 | | |
| 49 states | RE01E-5300001 | JH2RE010*5K600001 |
| or | RE01E-5310001 | JH2RE010*5M610001 |
| or | RE01E-5320001 | JH2RE010*5K620001 |
| California | RE01E-5300001 | JH2RE011*5K600001 |
| or | RE01E-5310001 | JH2RE011*5M610001 |
| or | RE01E-5320001 | JH2RE011*5K620001 |
| 2006 | | |
| 49 states | RE01E-5320001 | JH2RE010*6K700001 |
| California | RE01E-5320001 | JH2RE011*6K700001 |
| 2007 | Not available | |

## Buying spare parts

Once you have found all the identification numbers, record them for reference when buying parts. Since the manufacturers change specifications, parts and vendors (companies that manufacture various components on the machine), providing the ID numbers is the only way to be reasonably sure that you are buying the correct parts.

Whenever possible, take the worn part to the dealer so direct comparison with the new component can be made. Along the trail from the manufacturer to the parts shelf, there are

numerous places that the part can end up with the wrong number or be listed incorrectly.

The two places to purchase new parts for your motorcycle – the accessory store and the franchised dealer – differ in the type of parts they carry. While dealers can obtain virtually every part for your motorcycle, the accessory dealer is usually limited to normal high wear items such as shock absorbers, tune-up parts, various engine gaskets, cables, chains, brake parts, etc. Rarely will an accessory outlet have major suspension components, cylinders,

transmission gears, or cases.

Used parts can be obtained for considerably less than new ones, but you can't always be sure of what you're getting. Once again, take your worn part to the salvage yard for direct comparison.

Whether buying new, used or rebuilt parts, the best course is to deal directly with someone who specializes in parts for your particular make.

The engine number is stamped into the right side of the crankcase

The carburetor identification number is located on the right side of the carburetor on XR650R models. On all other models it's on the left side

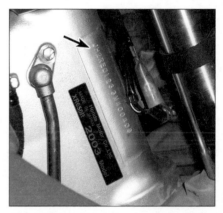
The frame serial number is stamped into the right side of the steering head

(on left side)

Professional mechanics are trained in safe working procedures. However enthusiastic you may be about getting on with the job at hand, take the time to ensure that your safety is not put at risk. A moment's lack of attention can result in an accident, as can failure to observe simple precautions.

There will always be new ways of having accidents, and the following is not a comprehensive list of all dangers; it is intended rather to make you aware of the risks and to encourage a safe approach to all work you carry out on your bike.

## Asbestos

● Certain friction, insulating, sealing and other products - such as brake pads, clutch linings, gaskets, etc. - contain asbestos. Extreme care must be taken to avoid inhalation of dust from such products since it is hazardous to health. If in doubt, assume that they do contain asbestos.

## Fire

● Remember at all times that gasoline is highly flammable. Never smoke or have any kind of naked flame around, when working on the vehicle. But the risk does not end there - a spark caused by an electrical short-circuit, by two metal surfaces contacting each other, by careless use of tools, or even by static electricity built up in your body under certain conditions, can ignite gasoline vapor, which in a confined space is highly explosive. Never use gasoline as a cleaning solvent. Use an approved safety solvent.

● Always disconnect the battery ground terminal before working on any part of the fuel or electrical system, and never risk spilling fuel on to a hot engine or exhaust.

● It is recommended that a fire extinguisher of a type suitable for fuel and electrical fires is kept handy in the garage or workplace at all times. Never try to extinguish a fuel or electrical fire with water.

## Fumes

● Certain fumes are highly toxic and can quickly cause unconsciousness and even death if inhaled to any extent. Gasoline vapor comes into this category, as do the vapors from certain solvents such as trichloro-ethylene. Any draining or pouring of such volatile fluids should be done in a well ventilated area.

● When using cleaning fluids and solvents, read the instructions carefully. Never use materials from unmarked containers - they may give off poisonous vapors.

● Never run the engine of a motor vehicle in an enclosed space such as a garage. Exhaust fumes contain carbon monoxide which is extremely poisonous; if you need to run the engine, always do so in the open air or at least have the rear of the vehicle outside the workplace.

## The battery

● Never cause a spark, or allow a naked light near the vehicle's battery. It will normally be giving off a certain amount of hydrogen gas, which is highly explosive.

● Always disconnect the battery ground terminal before working on the fuel or electrical systems (except where noted).

● If possible, loosen the filler plugs or cover when charging the battery from an external source. Do not charge at an excessive rate or the battery may burst.

● Take care when topping up, cleaning or carrying the battery. The acid electrolyte, even when diluted, is very corrosive and should not be allowed to contact the eyes or skin. Always wear rubber gloves and goggles or a face shield. If you ever need to prepare electrolyte yourself, always add the acid slowly to the water; never add the water to the acid.

## Electricity

● When using an electric power tool, inspection light etc., always ensure that the appliance is correctly connected to its plug and that, where necessary, it is properly grounded. Do not use such appliances in damp conditions and, again, beware of creating a spark or applying excessive heat in the vicinity of fuel or fuel vapor. Also ensure that the appliances meet national safety standards.

● A severe electric shock can result from touching certain parts of the electrical system, such as the spark plug wires (HT leads), when the engine is running or being cranked, particularly if components are damp or the insulation is defective. Where an electronic ignition system is used, the secondary (HT) voltage is much higher and could prove fatal.

## Remember...

✗ **Don't** start the engine without first ascertaining that the transmission is in neutral.

✗ **Don't** suddenly remove the pressure cap from a hot cooling system - cover it with a cloth and release the pressure gradually first, or you may get scalded by escaping coolant.

✗ **Don't** attempt to drain oil until you are sure it has cooled sufficiently to avoid scalding you.

✗ **Don't** grasp any part of the engine or exhaust system without first ascertaining that it is cool enough not to burn you.

✗ **Don't** allow brake fluid or antifreeze to contact the machine's paintwork or plastic components.

✗ **Don't** siphon toxic liquids such as fuel, hydraulic fluid or antifreeze by mouth, or allow them to remain on your skin.

✗ **Don't** inhale dust - it may be injurious to health (see Asbestos heading).

✗ **Don't** allow any spilled oil or grease to remain on the floor - wipe it up right away, before someone slips on it.

✗ **Don't** use ill-fitting wrenches or other tools which may slip and cause injury.

✗ **Don't** lift a heavy component which may be beyond your capability - get assistance.

✗ **Don't** rush to finish a job or take unverified short cuts.

✗ **Don't** allow children or animals in or around an unattended vehicle.

✗ **Don't** inflate a tire above the recommended pressure. Apart from overstressing the carcass, in extreme cases the tire may blow off forcibly.

✔ **Do** ensure that the machine is supported securely at all times. This is especially important when the machine is blocked up to aid wheel or fork removal.

✔ **Do** take care when attempting to loosen a stubborn nut or bolt. It is generally better to pull on a wrench, rather than push, so that if you slip, you fall away from the machine rather than onto it.

✔ **Do** wear eye protection when using power tools such as drill, sander, bench grinder etc.

✔ **Do** use a barrier cream on your hands prior to undertaking dirty jobs - it will protect your skin from infection as well as making the dirt easier to remove afterwards; but make sure your hands aren't left slippery. Note that long-term contact with used engine oil can be a health hazard.

✔ **Do** keep loose clothing (cuffs, ties etc. and long hair) well out of the way of moving mechanical parts.

✔ **Do** remove rings, wristwatch etc., before working on the vehicle - especially the electrical system.

✔ **Do** keep your work area tidy - it is only too easy to fall over articles left lying around.

✔ **Do** exercise caution when compressing springs for removal or installation. Ensure that the tension is applied and released in a controlled manner, using suitable tools which preclude the possibility of the spring escaping violently.

✔ **Do** ensure that any lifting tackle used has a safe working load rating adequate for the job.

✔ **Do** get someone to check periodically that all is well, when working alone on the vehicle.

✔ **Do** carry out work in a logical sequence and check that everything is correctly assembled and tightened afterwards.

✔ **Do** remember that your vehicle's safety affects that of yourself and others. If in doubt on any point, get professional advice.

● If in spite of following these precautions, you are unfortunate enough to injure yourself, seek medical attention as soon as possible.

# 1 Engine/transmission oil level check

## Before you start:
✔ Park the motorcycle outside or in some other well-ventilated area.
✔ Start the engine and let it idle for five minutes. If the air temperature is less than 50-degrees F (10-degrees C), allow it to run for five more minutes.

✔ After the bike has idled for the specified amount of time, turn it off. Support the bike in an upright position. The easiest way to do this when by yourself is to simply sit on the seat while checking the oil level. Immediately proceed to check the oil level.

## Bike care:
● If you have to add oil frequently, you should check whether you have any oil leaks. If there is no sign of oil leakage from the joints and gaskets the engine could be burning oil (see *Troubleshooting*).

## The correct oil
● Modern, high-revving engines place great demands on their oil. It is very important that the correct oil for your bike is used.
● Always top up with a good quality oil of the specified type and viscosity and do not overfill the engine.

### Oil type
API grade SG or higher meeting JASO standard MA - the MA standard is required to prevent clutch slippage. See Chapter 1 for viscosity ratings.

1 These bikes have a dipstick at the top of the frame, between the steering head and the fuel tank. Unscrew the dipstick, lift it out and wipe it clean, then reinsert it, but don't screw it in (just let it rest on the threads).

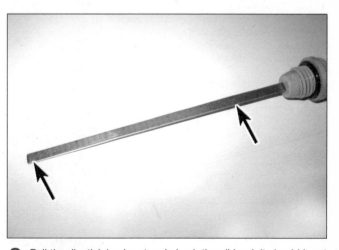

2 Pull the dipstick back out and check the oil level; it should be at or near the upper level mark. If it's nearer to the lower level mark, or below it, add oil a little at a time until it's near the upper mark. **Note:** *Use a funnel to prevent spills. Also, when reinstalling the dipstick, be sure the O-ring is in place and, when inserting it in its hole, angle the bottom end of it slightly to the right.* **Caution:** *Don't overfill the oil tank. This is a dry-sump system and doing so could cause too much oil to build up in the crankcase and transmission, and the resulting pressure could blow out the countershaft oil seal.*

## 2 Coolant level check (XR650R models)

 **Warning: Never remove the radiator cap while the engine is warm or scalding coolant will spray out. Let the engine cool down before removing the cap.**

 **Warning: Antifreeze is poisonous. Do not leave open containers of coolant lying around.**

 **Warning: Do not run the engine in an enclosed space such as a garage or workshop.**

### Before you start:

✔ Make sure you have a supply of coolant available. A mixture of 50% distilled water and 50% corrosion inhibited ethylene glycol antifreeze is needed. Keep in mind that many brands of motorcycle coolant are pre-mixed, so be sure to check the container. Do not add water to pre-mixed coolant, as this would dilute the mixture.
✔ Always check the coolant level when the engine is cold.
✔ Ensure the motorcycle is held vertical while checking the coolant level. Make sure the motorcycle is on level ground.

### Bike care:

● Use only the specified coolant mixture. It is important that antifreeze is used in the system all year round, and not just in the winter. Do not top the system up using only water, as the system will become too diluted.
● Do not overfill the reservoir tank. If the coolant is significantly above the F (full) level line at any time, the surplus should be siphoned or drained off to prevent the possibility of it being expelled out of the overflow hose.
● If the coolant level falls steadily, check the system for leaks (see Chapter 1). If no leaks are found and the level continues to fall, it is recommended that the machine is taken to a dealer or other repair shop for a pressure test.

Check the coolant level in the reservoir located at the bottom left side of the frame. If it's below the lower mark with the engine cold, add the specified coolant.

# 3 Brake fluid level check

> ⚠ **Warning: Brake fluid can harm your eyes and damage painted or some plastic surfaces, so use extreme caution when handling and pouring it and cover surrounding surfaces with rag. Do not use fluid that has been standing open for some time, as it absorbs moisture from the air which can cause a dangerous loss of braking effectiveness.**

## Before you start:

✔ Ensure the motorcycle is held vertical while checking the levels. Make sure the motorcycle is on level ground.

✔ Make sure you have the correct brake fluid. DOT 4 is recommended. Never reuse old fluid.

✔ Wrap a rag around the reservoir being worked on to ensure that any spillage does not come into contact with painted surfaces.

## Bike care:

● The fluid in the front and rear brake master cylinder reservoirs will drop slightly as the brake pads wear down.

● If any fluid reservoir requires repeated topping-up, this is an indication of a hydraulic leak somewhere in the system, which should be investigated immediately.

● Check for signs of fluid leakage from the hydraulic hoses and components – if found, rectify immediately.

● Check the operation of both brakes before taking the machine on the road; if there is evidence of air in the system (spongy feel to lever or pedal), it must be bled as described in Chapter 7.

**1** With the front brake fluid reservoir as level as possible, check that the fluid level is above the LOWER level line on the inspection window.

**2** If the level is below the LOWER level line, remove the cover screws and lift off the cover and diaphragm.

**3** Top up fluid to the upper level line; don't overfill the reservoir, and take care to avoid spills (see WARNING above). Reinstall the diaphragm and cover and tighten the screws securely.

**4** The level in the rear master cylinder can be seen through the translucent reservoir - keep the fluid level between the upper and lower marks.

# 4 Tire checks

## The correct pressures:

● The tires must be checked when **cold**, not immediately after riding. Note that low tire pressures may cause the tire to slip on the rim or come off. High tire pressures will cause abnormal tread wear and unsafe handling.

● Use an accurate pressure gauge.

● Proper air pressure will increase tire life and provide maximum stability and ride comfort.

## Tire care:

● Check the tires carefully for cuts, tears, embedded nails or other sharp objects and excessive wear. Operation of the motorcycle with excessively worn tires is extremely hazardous, as traction and handling are directly affected.

● Check the condition of the tire valve and ensure the dust cap is in place.

● Pick out any stones or nails which may have become embedded in the tire tread. If left, they will eventually penetrate through the casing and cause a puncture.

● If tire damage is apparent, or unexplained loss of pressure is experienced, seek the advice of a tire fitting specialist without delay.

## Tire tread depth:

● On dual-sport models, periodically check the tread depth. When the tread depth wears down to 3 mm, (1/8-inch), it's time to replace the tire.

● Honda doesn't specify a minimum tread depth for motocross or off-road tires, but to maintain good performance and handling, check the profile of the knobs on the tires. When the knobs begin to get excessively rounded on their edges, the tire should be replaced (this usually happens far before the height of the knobs wears down very far).

## Final drive checks:

● Make sure the drive chain slack isn't excessive and adjust it if necessary (see Chapter 1).

● Lubricate the chain if it looks dry (see Chapter 1).

| Tire pressures | | |
|---|---|---|
| Dual-sport models | | |
| XL600R, XR650L | 21 psi front | and rear |
| XR650Ry | | |
| Front | | 25 psi |
| Rear | | 18 psi |
| Off-road models | | |
| (XR600R, XR650R) | 15 psi front | and rear |

**1** Check the tire pressures when the tires are **cold** and keep them properly inflated.

**2** Honda doesn't specify a minimum tread depth for dirt bikes. A typical new tire looks like this. Bear in mind that a worn tire's poor traction can be dangerous, not just annoying - a sudden loss of traction can lead to loss of control and a fall.

# Chapter 1
# Tune-up and routine maintenance

## Contents

## Degrees of difficulty

| **Easy,** suitable for novice with little experience |  | **Fairly easy,** suitable for beginner with some experience |  | **Fairly difficult,** suitable for competent DIY mechanic |  | **Difficult,** suitable for experienced DIY mechanic | | **Very difficult,** suitable for expert DIY or professional |  |

## Specifications

**Engine**

Spark plugs
  XL600R, XR600R and XR650L
    Type

| | |
|---|---|
| Standard | NGK DPR8EA-9 or ND X24EPR-U9 |
| Extended high speed riding | NGK DPR9EA-9 or ND X27EPR-U9 |
| Cold climates (below 5-degrees C/41-degrees F) | NGK DPR7EA-9 or ND X22EPR-U9 |
| Gap | 0.8 to 0.9 mm (0.031 to 0.035 inch) |

  XR650R
    Type

| | |
|---|---|
| Standard | NGK BKR7E-11 or ND K22PR-U11 |
| Extended high speed riding | NGK BKR8E-11 or ND K24PR-U11 |
| Gap | 1.0 to 1.1 mm (0.039 to 0.043 inch) |

Ignition timing full advance

| | |
|---|---|
| XL600R | 31-degrees BTDC @ 4000 rpm |
| XR600R | 31-degrees BTDC @ 3500 rpm |
| XR650L | 28-degrees BTDC @ 4000 rpm |
| XR650R | 31-degrees BTDC @ 3500 rpm |

Engine idle speed

| | |
|---|---|
| XL600R | |
|   1983 models | 1200 +/- 100 rpm |
|   1984 on | 1300 +/- 100 rpm |
| XR600R | 1300 +/- 100 rpm |
| XR650L | 1300 +/- 100 rpm |
| XR650R | 1400 +/- 100 rpm |

## Engine (continued)

Valve clearance (COLD engine)
XL600R
    Intake .................................................................................. 0.05 mm (0.002 inch)
    Exhaust ................................................................................ 0.10 mm (0.004 inch)
XR600R
    Intake .................................................................................. 0.10 mm (0.004 inch)
    Exhaust ................................................................................ 0.12 mm (0.005 inch)
XR650L
    Intake .................................................................................. 0.10 +/- 0.02 mm (0.004 +/- 0.001 inch)
    Exhaust ................................................................................ 0.12 +/- 0.02 mm (0.005 +/- 0.001 inch)
XR650R
    Intake .................................................................................. 0.15 +/- 0.02 mm (0.006 +/- 0.001 inch)
    Exhaust ................................................................................ 0.20 +/- 0.02 mm (0.008 +/- 0.001 inch)
Cylinder compression (standard)
XL600R .................................................................................... 12.5 kg/cm2 (175 psi)
XR600R
    1985 through 1987 .............................................................. 12.5 +/- 1.5 kg/cm2 (175 +/- 21 psi)
    1988 on
        Decompressor applied ................................................... 5 +/- 1 kg/cm2 (71 +/- 14.2 psi)
        Decompressor not applied ............................................. 14 +/- 1 kg/cm2 (200 +/- 14.2 psi)
XR650L
    Decompressor applied ........................................................ 6.5 +/- 1 kg/cm2 (92 psi)
    Decompressor not applied .................................................. 14 +/- 1 kg/cm2 (200 psi)
XR650R
    Decompressor applied ........................................................ 6.12 kg/cm2 (87 psi)
    Decompressor not applied .................................................. 11.22 kg/cm2 (160 psi)

## Miscellaneous

Brake pad lining thickness limit ................................................ See text (Section 3)
Rear brake shoe lining thickness limit ...................................... 2 mm (0.08 inch)
Front brake lever freeplay
    XL600R, 1985 XR600R ........................................................ See text (Section 4)
    1986 and 1987 XR600R ....................................................... 1 to 8 mm (1/8 to 5/16 inch)
    1988 and later XR600R ........................................................ 0.6 to 8.0 mm (1/32 to 5/16 inch)
    XR650L ................................................................................ Not specified
    XR650R ................................................................................ 10 to 20 mm (3/8 to 3/4 inch)
Rear brake pedal freeplay (drum brake models) ...................... 20 to 30 mm (3/4 to 1-1/4 inch)
Rear master cylinder pushrod length (disc brake models)
    XR600R, XR650L ................................................................. 71 mm (2.8 inch)
    XR650R ................................................................................ 68 mm (2.68 inch)
Rear brake light switch adjustment
    XL600R ................................................................................ 10 mm (3/8 inch)
    XR650L ................................................................................ Not available
Clutch lever freeplay .................................................................. 10 to 20 mm (3/8 to 3/4 inch)
Throttle grip freeplay ................................................................. 2 to 6 mm (3/32 to 1/4 inch)
Choke valve stroke (XL600R) ................................................... 5 to 7 mm (3/16 to 9/32 inch)
Decompressor freeplay
XL600R
    1983 through 1987
        Kickstarter decompressor ............................................. 1 to 3 mm (1/32 to 1/8 inch)
        Manual decompressor .................................................. 1 to 2 mm (1/32 to 3/32 inch)
XR600R
    1985 through 1987
        Kickstarter decompressor ............................................. 1 to 2 mm (1/32 to 3/32 inch)
        Manual decompressor .................................................. 5 to 8 mm (3/16 to 5/16 inch)
    1988 on (manual) ................................................................ 5 to 8 mm (3/16 to 5/16 inch)
XR650L ................................................................................... Not adjustable
XR650R ................................................................................... 5 to 8 mm (3/16 to 5/16 inch)
Minimum tire tread depth
    Dual-sport models (XL600R, XR650L) ................................ 3 mm (1/8 inch)
    Off-road models (XR600R, XR650R) ................................... Not specified

Tire pressures (cold)
  Dual-sport models
    XL600R, XR650L ................................................................ 21 psi front and rear
    XR650Ry
      Front .................................................................................... 25 psi
      Rear ..................................................................................... 18 psi
  Off-road models (XR600R, XR650R) ........................................ 15 psi front and rear
Tire sizes
  XL600R
    Front .......................................................................................... 3.00-21-4PR
    Rear ........................................................................................... 5.10-17-4PR
  XR600R
    1985
      Front ................................................................................... 3.00-21-6PR
      Rear .................................................................................... 5.10-17-6PR
    1986 and 1987
      Front ................................................................................... 80/100-21 51M
      Rear .................................................................................... 110/100-17 63M
    1988 on
      Front ................................................................................... 80/100-21 51M
      Rear .................................................................................... 110/100-18 64M
  XR650L
    Front .......................................................................................... 3.00-21-4PR
    Rear ........................................................................................... 4.60-18-4PR
  XR650R
    Front .......................................................................................... 80/100-21 51M
    Rear ........................................................................................... 110/100-18 64M
  XR650Ry
    Front .......................................................................................... 3.00-21 51P
    Rear ........................................................................................... 4.50-18 70P
Drive chain slack
  XL600R ......................................................................................... 30 to 40 mm (1-1/4 to 1-5/8 inch)
  XR600R ......................................................................................... 35 to 45 mm (1-3/8 to 1-3/4 inch)
  XR650L ......................................................................................... 35 to 45 mm (1-3/8 to 1-3/4 inch)
  XR650R ......................................................................................... 20 to 30 mm (13/16 to 1-3/16 inch)

## Torque specifications

**Note:** *One foot-pound (ft-lb) of torque is equivalent to 12 inch-pounds (in-lbs) of torque. Torque values below approximately 15 ft-lbs are expressed in inch-pounds, since most foot-pound torque wrenches are not accurate at these smaller values.*

Coolant drain bolt (XR650R models) ........................................... 12 Nm (108 in-lbs)
Oil drain plug in frame
  XL600R ......................................................................................... 25 to 32 Nm (18 to 23 ft-lbs)
  XR600R
    1985 through 1987 .................................................................. 35 to 45 Nm (25 to 33 ft-lbs)
    1988 and later.......................................................................... 40 Nm (29 ft-lbs)
  XR650L, XR650R ......................................................................... 25 Nm (18 ft-lbs)
Oil drain plug in crankcase
  1983 through 1987 models ......................................................... 30 to 40 Nm (22 to 29 ft-lbs)
  1988 and later .............................................................................. 25 Nm (18 ft-lbs)
Oil filter cover bolts
  1983 through 1987 models ......................................................... 8 to 10 Nm (60 to 84 in-lbs)
  1988 and later .............................................................................. 12 Nm (108 in-lbs)
Oil strainer screen to frame
  XL600R ......................................................................................... 35 to 45 Nm (25 to 32 ft-lbs)
  XR600R, XR650L, XR650R ......................................................... 55 Nm (40 ft-lbs)
Hose fitting to oil strainer screen................................................. 40 Nm (29 ft-lbs)
Crankcase oil strainer screen bolt
  XL600R ......................................................................................... 35 to 45 Nm (25 to 32 ft-lbs)
  XR600R, XR650L ......................................................................... 40 Nm (29 ft-lbs)
  XR650R ......................................................................................... 37 Nm (27 ft-lbs)
Spark plug
  All except XR650L ....................................................................... 18 Nm (156 in-lbs)
  XR650L ......................................................................................... 17 Nm (144 in-lbs)
Valve adjusting screw locknut ..................................................... 25 Nm (18 ft-lbs)
Valve adjusting hole cover
  Through 1997 ............................................................................... Not specified
  1998 and later XR600R ................................................................ 15 Nm (132 in-lbs)
  XR650L ......................................................................................... Not specified
  XR650R ......................................................................................... 12 Nm (108 in-lbs)

## Torque specifications (continued)

Crankshaft hole cap (exc. XR650R)
    Through 1997 .......................................................................... Not specified
    1998 and later ........................................................................ 15 Nm (132 in-lbs)
Timing hole cap
    XL600R, XR600R
        Through 1997 .................................................................. Not specified
        1998 and later ................................................................ 10 Nm (84 in-lbs)
    XR650L ..................................................................................... Not specified
    XR650R ..................................................................................... 10 Nm (84 in-lbs)
Wheel spokes ................................................................................... 4.0 Nm (36 in-lbs)
Rim lock locknut ................................................................................ 13 Nm (108 in-lbs)
Steering stem adjusting nut
    Initial torque (to seat bearings) ............................................... 20 to 30 Nm (14 to 22 ft-lbs)
    Final torque
        1983 through 1987 ........................................................ 1 to 2 Nm (9 to 16 in-lbs)
        1988 through 1990 ........................................................ 3 Nm (24 in-lbs)
        1991 and 1992 .............................................................. 1 Nm (9 in-lbs)
        1993 and later
            XR600R ................................................................. 1.5 Nm (13 in-lbs)
            XR650L ................................................................. 1 Nm (9 in-lbs)
    XR650R ..................................................................................... 8 Nm (69.5 in-lbs)
Steering stem nut
    XL600R ..................................................................................... 80 to 120 Nm (58 to 87 ft-lbs)
    XR600R
        1985 to 1987 ................................................................ 95 to 140 Nm (69 to 101 ft-lbs)
        1988 and later .............................................................. 118 Nm (85 ft-lbs)
    XR650L ..................................................................................... 118 Nm (85 ft-lbs)
    XR650R ..................................................................................... 98 Nm (72 ft-lbs)

## Recommended lubricants and fluids

Engine/transmission oil
    Type ......................................................................................... Pro Honda GN4, HP4 (without moly additives) four-stroke motor oil, or equivalent
    Viscosity
        Standard .......................................................................... 10W-40
        Optional
            10 to 90-degrees F ................................................... 20W-40 or 20W-50
            0 to 80-degrees F ..................................................... 10W-30
    Capacity (approximate - add as necessary to bring to appropriate level)
        Oil change
            XL600R ................................................................. 2.0 liters (2.1 US qts)
            XR600R, XR650L ................................................... 1.9 liters (2.0 US qts)
            XR650R ................................................................. 1.5 liters (1.6 US qts)
        After engine overhaul
            XL600R ................................................................. 2.5 liters (2.6 US qts)
            XR600R, XR650L ................................................... 2.3 liters (2.4 US qts)
            XR650R ................................................................. 2.0 liters (2.1 US qts)
Coolant (XR650R)
    Type ......................................................................................... Pro Honda HP coolant or 50/50 mixture of equivalent ethylene glycol-based, silicate-free antifreeze and distilled water*
    Capacity
        Engine/radiator .............................................................. 1.5 liters (1.6 US qts)
        Reserve tank ................................................................... 0.2 liters (0.21 US qts)
Air filter oil (for foam filters) ........................................................... Honda Foam Filter Oil or SAE 80 or 90 gear oil
Brake fluid ........................................................................................ DOT 4
Drive chain lubricant ....................................................................... Chain lube formulated for O-ring chains, or SAE 80 to 90 gear oil
Miscellaneous
    Wheel bearings ........................................................................ Medium weight, lithium-based multi-purpose grease (NLGI no. 3)
    Swingarm pivot bushings .......................................................... Molybdenum disulfide paste grease containing 40 percent or more molybdenum disulfide
    Cables and lever pivots ............................................................ Medium weight, lithium-based multi-purpose grease (NLGI no. 3)
    Brake pedal/shift lever/throttle lever pivots ............................. Medium weight, lithium-based multi-purpose grease (NLGI no. 3)

*Many brands of antifreeze do not require mixing with water. Check the instructions on the container carefully.*

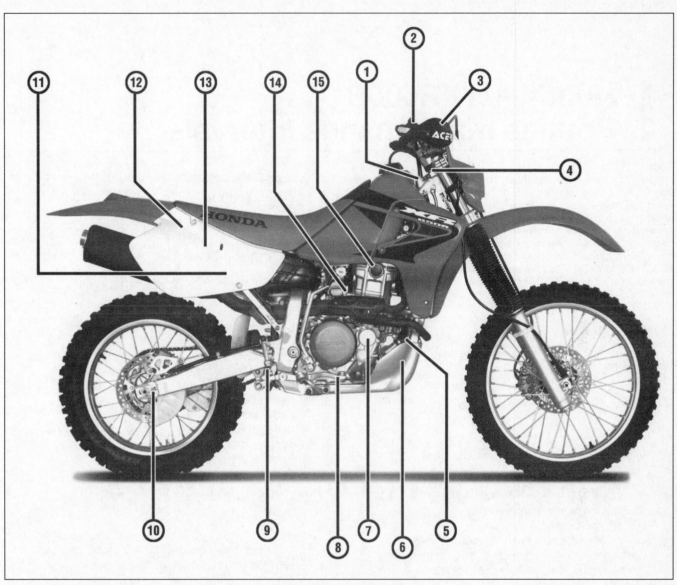

**Honda XR maintenance points**

1  Engine oil dipstick
2  Clutch cable adjuster
3  Front brake fluid reservoir
4  Steering head bearing adjuster
5  Coolant reservoir (left side) - XR650R only
6  Coolant drain bolt (behind skid plate) - XR650R only
7  Engine oil filter
8  Engine oil drain plug (left side)
9  Rear brake pedal adjuster

10  Drive chain adjuster
11  Rear brake fluid reservoir (disc brake models only)
12  Battery/fuses (behind left side cover) -
    XR600L/XL650R models only
13  Air filter (behind left side cover)
14  Throttle stop screw (on left side)
15  Spark plug location (XR650R, left side; all others,
    front of cylinder head)

# 1 Honda XL/XR600R Routine maintenance intervals

**Note 1:** *The pre-ride inspection outlined in the owner's manual covers checks and maintenance that should be carried out on a daily basis. It's condensed and included here to remind you of its importance. Always perform the pre-ride inspection at every maintenance interval (in addition to the procedures listed). The intervals listed below are the shortest intervals recommended by the manufacturer for each particular operation during the model years covered in this manual. Your owner's manual may have different intervals for your model.*

**Note 2:** *The following schedules are for motorcycles given normal use (including off-road riding). If the bike is used in competition, perform the entire maintenance schedule before every race.*

## Daily or before riding
- [ ] See *Daily (pre-ride) checks* at the beginning of this manual.

## Every 300 miles
- [ ] Lubricate and inspect the drive chain and sliders*

## Every 4,000 miles on XR600L or every 30 operating days (approximately 1,000 miles) on XR600R through 1997
*Perform all of the daily checks plus:*
- [ ] Inspect the brakes
- [ ] Check the brake pads and shoes for wear
- [ ] Check the brake fluid level
- [ ] Check and adjust the valve clearances
- [ ] Check the decompressor system
- [ ] Clean the air filter element*
- [ ] Clean the air cleaner housing drain tube
- [ ] Check the crankcase breather (XL600R)
- [ ] Check the evaporative emission control system (XL600R California models)
- [ ] Inspect the battery (XL600R)
- [ ] Check/adjust the throttle lever freeplay
- [ ] Check choke operation
- [ ] Check/adjust the idle speed
- [ ] Change the engine oil and filter and clean the strainer screen (in the frame downtube)
- [ ] Check the tightness of all fasteners
- [ ] Inspect the suspension
- [ ] Clean and gap the spark plug
- [ ] Check/adjust the clutch
- [ ] Check the exhaust system for leaks and check fastener tightness; clean the spark arrester
- [ ] Inspect the wheels and tires
- [ ] Check the cleanliness of the fuel system and the condition of the fuel line

- [ ] Clean the fuel tap strainer screen
- [ ] Inspect the steering system and steering head bearings
- [ ] Check the sidestand operation

## Every 600 miles or 6 months on 1998 and later models
*Perform all of the daily checks plus:*
- [ ] Inspect the brakes
- [ ] Check the brakes pads and shoes for wear
- [ ] Check the brake fluid level
- [ ] Clean the air filter element*
- [ ] Clean and gap the spark plug
- [ ] Check the decompressor system
- [ ] Check and adjust the valve clearance
- [ ] Check engine idle speed
- [ ] Change the engine oil and filter
- [ ] Check/adjust the clutch
- [ ] Inspect the wheels and tires

## Every 1,200 miles or 12 months on 1998 and later models
*Perform all of the daily and 600-mile checks plus:*
- [ ] Check the cleanliness of the fuel system
- [ ] Clean the fuel tap strainer screen
- [ ] Check/adjust the throttle lever freeplay
- [ ] Check choke operation
- [ ] Clean the engine oil strainer screen (in the frame down-tube)
- [ ] Check the tightness of all fasteners
- [ ] Inspect the steering system and steering head bearings
- [ ] Inspect the suspension
- [ ] Inspect the sidestand
- [ ] Check headlight aim

## Every two years or 2,400 miles
- [ ] Replace the brake fluid
- [ ] Replace the fork oil**

 * *More often in dusty, sandy or wet conditions.*

** *Honda doesn't give a service interval for this operation, but changing the fork oil on a regular basis will ensure conitinued good handling of the bike and reduce wear to the internal fork components.*

# 1 Honda XL/XR650L
# Routine maintenance intervals

**Note:** *The pre-ride inspection outlined in the owner's manual covers checks and maintenance that should be carried out on a daily basis. It's condensed and included here to remind you of its importance. Always perform the pre-ride inspection at every maintenance interval (in addition to the procedures listed). The intervals listed below are the shortest intervals recommended by the manufacturer for each particular operation during the model years covered in this manual. Your owner's manual may have different intervals for your model.*

## Daily or before riding
☐ See *Daily (pre-ride)* checks at the beginning of this manual.

## Every 500 miles
☐ Lubricate and inspect the drive chain and sliders*

## After the first 600 miles
☐ Change the engine oil and filter and clean the strainer screen (in the frame downtube)
☐ Check and adjust the valve clearances

## Every 2,000 miles
☐ Change the engine oil and filter and clean the strainer screen (in the frame downtube)

## Every 4,000 miles
☐ Check the cleanliness of the fuel system and the condition of the fuel line
☐ Clean the fuel tap strainer screen
☐ Clean and gap the spark plug
☐ Check the air filter element*
☐ Check and adjust the valve clearances
☐ Check/adjust the idle speed
☐ Check the brake pads for wear
☐ Check the brake fluid level

☐ Check the operation of the brake light switch
☐ Check/adjust the clutch
☐ Check the exhaust system for leaks and check fastener tightness; clean the spark arrester
☐ Check the tightness of all fasteners
☐ Inspect the wheels and tires

## Every 8,000 miles
☐ Perform everything listed under the 4,000 mile interval, plus the following:
☐ Check the throttle operation
☐ Check the choke operation
☐ Replace the spark plug
☐ Check the secondary air supply system, if equipped (PAIR valve and hoses; see Chapter 4)
☐ Check the headlight aim
☐ Check the sidestand operation
☐ Inspect the suspension
☐ Inspect the steering system and steering head bearings
☐ Replace the fork oil**

## Every 12,000 miles
☐ Perform everything listed under the 4,000 mile interval, plus the following:
☐ Replace the air filter element
☐ Inspect the evaporative emissions control system
☐ Replace the brake fluid

\* *More often in dusty, sandy or wet conditions.*
\*\* *Honda doesn't give a service interval for this operation, but changing the fork oil on a regular basis will ensure coninitued good handling of the bike and reduce wear to the internal fork components.*

# 1 Honda XR650R Routine maintenance intervals

**Note 1:** *The pre-ride inspection outlined in the owner's manual covers checks and maintenance that should be carried out on a daily basis. It's condensed and included here to remind you of its importance. Always perform the pre-ride inspection at every maintenance interval (in addition to the procedures listed). The intervals listed below are the shortest intervals recommended by the manufacturer for each particular operation during the model years covered in this manual. Your owner's manual may have different intervals for your model.*
**Note 2:** *The following maintenance schedule is for recreational riding. If the bike is used for competition, perform all of the items before each race (with the exception of the fork oil change, which can be performed less frequently if desired.*

## Daily or before riding
☐ See *Daily (pre-ride) checks* at the beginning of this manual.

## After the first 100 miles or first month
☐ Check and adjust the valve clearances
☐ Change the engine oil and filter and clean the strainer screen (in the frame downtube)
☐ Check the decompressor system
☐ Check/adjust the idle speed
☐ Check the coolant level and inspect the cooling system
☐ Lubricate and inspect the drive chain and sliders*
☐ Check the brake pads for wear
☐ Check the brake fluid level
☐ Check/adjust the clutch
☐ Check the exhaust system for leaks and check fastener tightness; clean the spark arrester
☐ Check the tightness of all fasteners
☐ Inspect the steering system and steering head bearings
☐ Inspect the wheels and tires

## Every 300 miles or three months
☐ Lubricate and inspect the drive chain and sliders*
☐ Check the tightness of all fasteners
☐ Inspect the wheels and tires

## Every 600 miles or 6 months
*Perform everything listed under the 300 mile interval, plus the following:*
☐ Clean the air filter element*
☐ Change the engine oil and filter and clean the strainer screen (in the frame downtube)
☐ Clean and gap the spark plug
☐ Check and adjust the valve clearances
☐ Check the decompressor system
☐ Check/adjust the idle speed
☐ Inspect the cooling system
☐ Check the brake pads for wear
☐ Check/adjust the clutch

## Every 1,000 miles or 100 operating hours
☐ Check the exhaust system for leaks and check fastener tightness; clean the spark arrester

## Every 1,200 miles or 12 months
*Perform everything listed under the 600 mile interval, plus the following:*
☐ Check the cleanliness of the fuel system and the condition of the fuel line
☐ Clean the fuel tap strainer screen
☐ Check the throttle operation
☐ Check the choke operation
☐ Check the decompressor system
☐ Check the secondary air supply system, if equipped (PAIR valve and hoses; see Chapter 4)
☐ Check the headlight aim

## Every two years or 2,400 miles
☐ Replace the brake fluid
☐ Replace the engine coolant
☐ Replace the fork oil**

　* *More often in dusty, sandy or wet conditions.*
　** *Honda doesn't give a service interval for this operation, but changing the fork oil on a regular basis will ensure coninitued good handling of the bike and reduce wear to the internal fork components.*

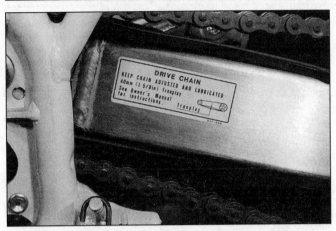

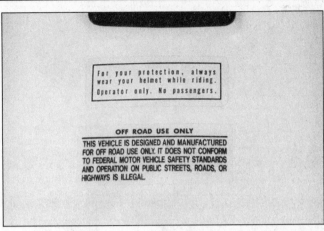

**2.1a  Decals on the motorcycle include maintenance information such as drive chain adjustment . . .**

**2.1b  . . . as well as certification and safety information**

## 2  Introduction to tune-up and routine maintenance

This Chapter covers in detail the checks and procedures necessary for the tune-up and routine maintenance of your motorcycle. Section 1 includes the routine maintenance schedule, which is designed to keep the machine in proper running condition and prevent possible problems. The remaining Sections contain detailed procedures for carrying out the items listed on the maintenance schedule, as well as additional maintenance information designed to increase reliability. Maintenance, certification and safety information is also printed on decals, which are mounted in various locations on the motorcycle **(see illustrations)**. Where information on the decals differs from that presented in this Chapter, use the decal information.

Since routine maintenance plays such an important role in the safe and efficient operation of your motorcycle, it is presented here as a comprehensive check list. For the rider who does all his own maintenance, these lists outline the procedures and checks that should be done on a routine basis.

Deciding where to start or plug into the routine maintenance schedule depends on several factors. If you have a motorcycle whose warranty has recently expired, and if it has been maintained according to the warranty standards, you may want to pick up routine maintenance as it coincides with the next mileage or calendar interval. If you have owned the machine for some time but have never performed any maintenance on it, then you may want to start at the nearest interval and include some additional procedures to ensure that nothing important is overlooked. If you have just had a major engine overhaul, then you may want to start the maintenance routine from the beginning. If you have a used machine and have no knowledge of its history or maintenance record, you may desire to combine all the checks into one large service

initially and then settle into the maintenance schedule prescribed.

The Sections which actually outline the inspection and maintenance procedures are written as step-by-step comprehensive guides to the actual performance of the work. They explain in detail each of the routine inspections and maintenance procedures on the check list. References to additional information in applicable Chapters is also included and should not be overlooked.

Before beginning any actual maintenance or repair, the machine should be cleaned thoroughly, especially around the oil filter housing, spark plug, valve cover, side covers, carburetor, etc. Cleaning will help ensure that dirt does not contaminate the engine and will allow you to detect wear and damage that could otherwise easily go unnoticed.

## 3  Brake system - general check

1   A routine general check of the brakes will ensure that any problems are discovered and remedied before the rider's safety

is jeopardized.
2   Check the brake lever and pedal for loose connections, excessive play, bends, and other damage. Replace any damaged parts with new ones (see Chapter 7).
3   Make sure all brake fasteners are tight. Check the brakes for wear as described below.

### Brake fluid

3   Refer to *Daily (pre-ride) checks* at the front of this manual.

### Disc Brakes

4   Look into the caliper from either the front or the rear. Each brake pad has either a notch or a wear line marked on the pad material - if either pad has worn down to this notch or mark (or approximately 1 mm [0.040 inch]), replace the pads as a set (see Chapter 7).

### Rear drum brakes

5   Operate the brake pedal. If operation is rough or sticky, refer to Section 9 and lubricate the cable.
6   With the rear brake lever and pedal free-play properly adjusted (see Section 4), check the wear indicator on the brake panel **(see illustration)**. If the pointer lines up with the

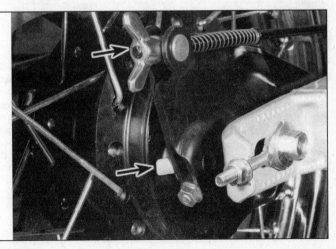

**3.6 The wear indicator on rear drum brakes is at the rear of the panel (lower arrow); adjustments are made with the wingnut (upper arrow)**

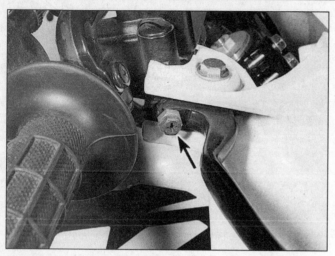

**4.3 Front brake lever freeplay on later models is adjusted by loosening the locknut and turning the screw**

**4.4 Drum brake pedal height is adjusted by loosening the locknut and turning the bolt**

indicator when the pedal is pressed, refer to Chapter 7 and replace the brake shoes.

---

**4 Brake lever and pedal freeplay - check and adjustment**

### *Front brake lever*
#### XL600R and 1985 XR600R models
1 These models don't have a specified amount of freeplay. There are only two free-play settings, which can be selected by turn-ing the adjuster on the brake lever. Align the single dot on the adjuster with the pointer for maximum freeplay; align the double dots for minimum freeplay. Be sure not to place the adjuster in any but the two specified posi-tions.

#### 1986 and later XR600R, all XR650L and XR650R models
2 Squeeze the front brake lever and note how far the lever travels (measure at the tip of the lever). If it exceeds the limit listed in

this Chapter's Specifications, adjust the front brake as described below.
3 If lever travel needs to be adjusted, loosen the locknut and turn the adjusting screw **(see illustration)**. Tighten the locknut after making the adjustment.

### *Rear brake pedal*
#### Drum brake models
4 To adjust brake pedal height, loosen the locknut and turn the adjusting bolt **(see illustration)**. Honda doesn't specify pedal height.
5 Check the play of the brake pedal. If it exceeds the limit listed in this Chapter's Specifications, adjust it with the wingnut at the rear end of the brake rod **(see illustra-tion 3.6)**.

#### Disc brake models
6 To adjust pedal height, loosen the lock-nut and turn the adjusting bolt on the rear master cylinder **(see illustration)**. Although pedal height isn't specified, a dimension for the length of the clevis assembly is listed in this Chapter's Specifications.
7 Pedal freeplay on disc brake models is

automatic and no means of manual adjust-ment is provided.

### *Brake light switches (XL600R, XR650L and XR650Ry models)*
#### Front brake light switch
8 The front brake light switch isn't adjust-able, but it should activate the brake light when pulled in just a few millimeters. If it doesn't, check the continuity of the switch as described in Chapter 5.

#### Rear brake light switch
9 The rear brake light should illuminate when the pedal is pressed 10 mm (3/8 inch) from its resting position. If it comes on too soon or too late, turn the plastic nut that secures the switch to the bracket (on the frame member above and behind the brake pedal). Don't try to turn the switch itself.

---

**5 Tires/wheels - general check**

1 Routine tire and wheel checks should be made with the realization that your safety depends to a great extent on their condition.
2 Check the tires carefully for cuts, tears, embedded nails or other sharp objects and excessive wear. Operation of the motorcycle with excessively worn tires is extremely haz-ardous, as traction and handling are directly affected. Check the tread depth at the center of the tire and compare it to the value listed in this Chapter's Specifications. Honda doesn't specify a minimum tread depth for off-road models, but as a general rule, tires should be replaced with new ones when the tread knobs are considerably rounded on the drive side of the knobs. A new, sharp tire changes the entire riding characteristics of the bike.
3 Repair or replace punctured tires as

**4.6 Rear disc brake pedal height is adjusted by loosening the locknut (lower arrow) and turning the adjusting bolt (upper arrow); pushrod length is measured from the center of the lower mounting bolt to the center of the clevis pin**

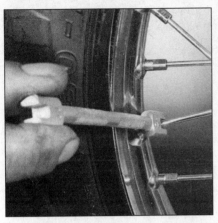

5.5 Make sure the spokes are tight, but don't overtighten them

5.7 Tighten the locknut on the rim lock to the specified torque

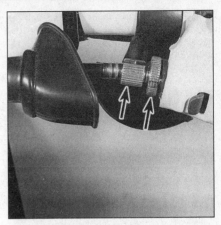

6.2 Loosen the lockwheel (right arrow) and turn the adjuster (left arrow) to make minor adjustments in clutch lever freeplay

soon as damage is noted. Do not try to patch a torn tire, as wheel balance and tire reliability may be impaired.

4 Check the tire pressures as described in *Daily (pre-ride) checks* at the front of this manual.

5 The wheels should be kept clean and checked periodically for cracks, bending, loose spokes and rust. Never attempt to repair damaged wheels; they must be replaced with new ones. Loose spokes can be tightened with a spoke wrench **(see illustration)**, but be careful not to overtighten and distort the wheel rim.

6 Check the valve stem locknuts to make sure they're tight. Also, make sure the valve stem cap is in place and tight. If it is missing, install a new one made of metal or hard plastic.

7 Check the tightness of the locknut on the rim lock **(see illustration)**. Tighten it if necessary to the torque listed in this Chapter's Specifications.

## 6 Clutch - check and freeplay adjustment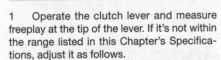

1 Operate the clutch lever and measure freeplay at the tip of the lever. If it's not within the range listed in this Chapter's Specifications, adjust it as follows.

2 Pull back the rubber cover from the adjuster at the handlebar **(see illustration)**. Loosen the lockwheel and turn the adjuster to change freeplay.

3 If freeplay can't be brought within specifications by using the handlebar adjuster, turn the handlebar adjuster in all the way, then back it out one turn.

4 Loosen the locknut on the lower cable adjuster and turn the adjusting nut to set freeplay **(see illustrations)**. Tighten the locknut and adjusting nut securely.

5 If freeplay still can't be adjusted to within the specified range, the cable is probably stretched and should be replaced with a new one.

## 7 Throttle operation/grip freeplay - check and adjustment

### Check

1 Make sure the throttle twistgrip moves easily from fully closed to fully open with the front wheel turned at various angles. The grip should return automatically from fully open to fully closed when released. If the throttle sticks, check the throttle cable for cracks or kinks in the housings. Also, make sure the inner cable is clean and well-lubricated.

2 Check for a small amount of freeplay at the twistgrip and compare the freeplay to the value listed in this Chapter's Specifications.

### Adjustment

3 Minor adjustments are made at the throttle lever end of the accelerator cable. Major adjustments are made at the carburetor end of the cable.

6.4a Major adjustments are made at the adjuster near the lower end of the clutch cable. This is an air-cooled model . . .

6.4b . . . and this is an XR650R

4    Pull back the rubber cover from the adjuster and loosen the lockwheel on the cable **(see illustration)**. Turn the adjuster until the desired freeplay is obtained, then retighten the lockwheel.

5    If the freeplay can't be adjusted at the grip end, loosen the locknuts at the carburetor end of the cable **(see illustrations)**. Turn the adjuster to set freeplay, then tighten the locknuts securely.

## 8  Choke - operation check

### XL600R models

1    Check that the choke lever on the left handlebar moves smoothly. If not, refer to Section 9 and lubricate the cable.

2    Remove the seat and fuel tank (see Chapters 8 and 4). Locate the choke cable at its connection to the carburetor. Move the choke lever through its full stroke and measure the distance that the cable fitting at the carburetor moves. Compare this to the value

listed in this Chapter's Specifications.

3    If the choke valve stroke is not within the specified range, loosen the cable fitting at the carburetor and relocate the cable housing within the fitting.

### XR600R and XR650R models

4    Operate the choke lever on the carburetor while you feel for smooth operation.

5    If the lever doesn't move smoothly, refer to Chapter 4 and check the choke mechanism for worn or damaged parts.

### XR650L models

6    Unscrew the choke cable fitting from the carburetor **(see illustration)**. Check the condition of the choke valve piston; it should be smooth and free of scratches **(see illustration)**.

7    Place the choke lever on the handlebar in the On position and measure the distance between the top of the choke valve piston and the bottom of the nut; it should be 1 to 2 mm (0.04 to 0.08 inch). If it isn't, adjust the choke cable at the handlebar end.

8    When reinstalling the choke cable fitting to the carburetor, tighten it finger tight, then

just a little bit more with a wrench to secure it; it's plastic and breaks easily.

## 9  Lubrication - general

1    Since the controls, cables and various other components of a motorcycle are exposed to the elements, they should be lubricated periodically to ensure safe and trouble-free operation.

2    The throttle twistgrip, brake lever, brake pedal, kickstarter pedal pivot and sidestand pivot should be lubricated frequently. In order for the lubricant to be applied where it will do the most good, the component should be disassembled. However, if chain and cable lubricant is being used, it can be applied to the pivot joint gaps and will usually work its way into the areas where friction occurs. If motor oil or light grease is being used, apply it sparingly as it may attract dirt (which could cause the controls to bind or wear at an accelerated rate). **Note:** *One of the best lubricants for the control lever pivots is a dry-*

7.4  Loosen the locknut and turn the adjuster to make minor throttle freeplay adjustments

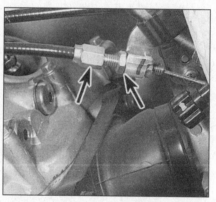

7.5a  Major throttle cable adjustments are made at the adjuster near the carburetor. This is an XR600R . . .

7.5b  . . . and this is an XR650R

8.6a  On XR650L models, unscrew the choke cable fitting from the left side of the carburetor . . .

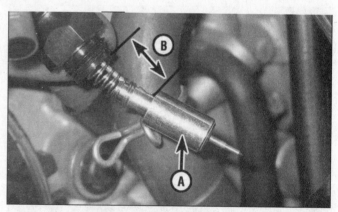

8.6b  . . . and check the choke valve piston (A) - it shouldn't have any scratches on it. Then, place the choke lever on the handlebar in the on position and measure the distance between the top of the piston and the bottom of the plastic nut (B) (the choke has not been actuated in this photo; that's why the clearance is greater than specified)

film lubricant (available from many sources by different names).

3  The throttle and clutch cables (and the brake and choke cables, if equipped) should be removed and treated with a commercially available cable lubricant which is specially formulated for use on motorcycle control cables. **Note:** *Honda states that lubrication of the throttle and clutch cables (except for the end pivots) is not necessary on XR600R models. They recommend replacing these cables if their operation is sticky.* Small adapters for pressure lubricating the cables with spray can lubricants are available and ensure that the cable is lubricated along its entire length **(see illustration)**. When attaching the cable to the lever, be sure to lubricate the barrel-shaped fitting at the end with multi-purpose grease.

4  To lubricate the cables, disconnect them at the upper end, then lubricate the cable with a pressure lube adapter **(see illustration 9.3)**. See Chapter 4 (throttle cable) or Chapter 2A or 2B (clutch cable).

5  On all models except the XR650R, the

swingarm and rear suspension linkage pivots can be lubricated with a grease gun through the grease fittings **(see illustrations)**.

6  Refer to Chapter 6 for the following lubrication procedures:

a) Swingarm bearings and dust seals
b) Steering head bearings

7  Refer to Chapter 7 for the following lubrication procedures:

a) Front and rear wheel bearings
b) Brake pedal pivot

## 10  Engine oil change and filter screen cleaning

1  Consistent routine oil changes and filter screen cleaning are the single most important maintenance procedure you can perform on these models. The oil not only lubricates the internal parts of the engine, transmission and clutch, but it also acts as a coolant, a cleaner, a sealant, and a protectant.

Because of these demands, the oil takes a terrific amount of abuse and should be replaced often with new oil of the recommended grade and type. Saving a little money on the difference in cost between a good oil and a cheap oil won't pay off if the engine is damaged. Honda recommends against using the following:

a) Oils with graphite or molybdenum additives (they will make the clutch slip and wear)
b) Non-detergent oils
c) Castor or vegetable based oils
d) Oil additives

2  Before changing the oil and cleaning the filter screen, warm up the engine so the oil will drain easily. Be careful when draining the oil, as the exhaust pipe, the engine and the oil itself can cause severe burns.

3  Park the motorcycle over a drain pan.

4  Remove the dipstick/oil filler cap to vent the frame and crankcase, and to act as a reminder that there is no oil in the engine.

5  Next, remove the drain plugs from the frame and crankcase **(see illustrations)** and

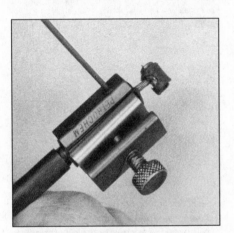

**9.3  Lubricating a cable with a pressure lube adapter (make sure the tool seats around the inner cable)**

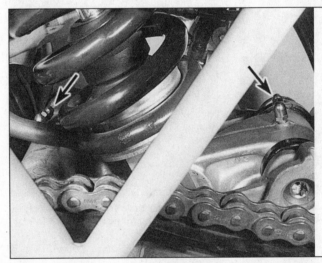

**9.5a  There's a grease fitting on the swingarm (left arrow) and on the shock arm pivot (right arrow) - all except XR650R models**

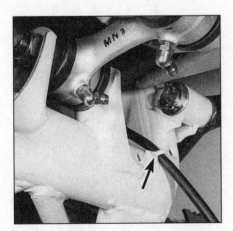

**9.5b  Lubricate the suspension linkage relay arm through the two grease fittings (all except XR650R models); the carburetor vent hose on XR600R models fits through a bracket on the swingarm**

**10.5a  The oil tank drain plug is located in the bottom of the front frame member (XR650R shown)**

**10.5b  There's another oil drain plug in the left side of the crankcase**

10.6a  Remove the bolts . . .

10.6b  . . . then pull off the oil filter cover, filter element and spring - this is an air-cooled model . . .

10.6c  . . . and this is an XR650R . . .

10.6d  . . . removing the cover from an XR650R also exposes the outer half of the oil pump

10.7  Unscrew the oil hose strainer screen from the frame and clean it

10.8a  The right engine cover must be removed for access to the oil strainer screen; remove its bolt (XR650R models don't have a bolt) . . .

10.8b  . . . and slide the screen out of the crankcase (it isn't necessary to clean this screen during a routine oil change)

10.11a  It's important to install the filter in the right direction; the side labeled THIS SIDE AND SPRING TOWARD ENGINE goes into the engine first . . .

10.11b  . . . while the side labeled OUT SIDE TOWARD FILTER COVER faces out when the filter is installed

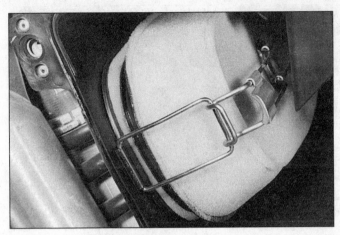

11.4a  Unclip the filter retaining band . . .

11.4b  . . . and pull the filter out of the case (this is a paper filter element on an XR650L; if it's dirty it must be replaced with a new one)

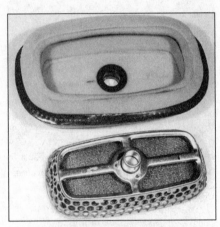

11.4c  Separate the foam element from the core for cleaning and re-oiling

allow the oil to drain into the pan. Don't lose the sealing washers on the drain plugs.

6   Remove the filter cover from the right side of the crankcase, then pull out the filter and spring **(see illustrations)**.

7   As the oil is draining, unscrew the hose fitting from the frame oil screen, then unscrew the strainer screen from the bottom of the oil tank **(see illustration)**. Note: On XR650R models, remove the skid plate for access to the screen (see Chapter 8). If additional maintenance is planned for this time period, check or service another component while the oil is allowed to drain completely.

8   Although it's not required at periodic oil changes, Honda recommends that the strainer screen in the bottom of the crankcase be removed and cleaned whenever the right engine cover is removed. For access, remove the right engine cover (air-cooled models, see Chapter 2A, Section 16; liquid-cooled models, see Chapter 2B, Section 18). Remove the mounting bolt and pull the filter screen out of its slot in the crankcase **(see illustrations)**.

9   Clean the strainer screen(s) thoroughly

with a high flash point solvent, then dry them completely (blow dry with compressed air, if available).

10   Check the condition of the drain plug threads. Replace the plug if the threads are damaged.

11   Install the spring and a new oil filter in the engine **(see illustrations)**.

*Caution: Be sure to install the filter facing in the proper direction, referring to the instructions stamped on the filter.*

12   Install the filter screen in its slot (if it was removed) and install the mounting bolt, then refer to Chapter 2 and install the right engine cover.

13   Place a new O-ring on the strainer fitting in the frame. Place the frame strainer screen in the frame, tightening it to the torque listed in this Chapter's Specifications, then install the hose fitting, tightening the fitting bolt to the torque listed in this Chapter's Specifications. Note: *Use new sealing washers on either side of the hose fitting.*

14   Slip a new sealing washer over each drain plug, then install and tighten the plugs to the torque listed in this Chapter's Specifications. Avoid overtightening, as damage to the threads or engine case will result.

15   Before refilling the engine, check the old oil carefully. If the oil was drained into a clean pan, small pieces of metal or other material can be easily detected. If the oil is very metallic colored, then the engine is experiencing wear from break-in (new engine) or from insufficient lubrication. If there are flakes or chips of metal in the oil, then something is drastically wrong internally and the engine will have to be disassembled for inspection and repair.

16   If there are pieces of fiber-like material in the oil, the clutch is experiencing excessive wear and should be checked.

17   If the inspection of the oil turns up nothing unusual, add one quart of the recommended oil to the frame oil tank and install the dipstick/filler cap (there isn't room in the frame oil tank for the full amount at this time). Start

the engine and let it idle (don't rev it up) for two or three minutes.

18   Shut the engine off, wait a few minutes, then add the remaining oil. Approximate capacity is listed in this Chapter's Specifications. Use the dipstick to determine the exact amount to add. Check around the drain plugs and filter cover for leaks.

19   The old oil drained from the engine cannot be reused in its present state and should be disposed of. Check with your local refuse disposal company, disposal facility, auto parts store or environmental agency to see if they will accept the oil for recycling. Don't pour used oil into drains or onto the ground. After the oil has cooled, it can be drained into a suitable container (capped plastic jugs, topped bottles, milk cartons, etc.) for transport to one of these disposal sites.

## 11  Air cleaner - filter element and drain tube cleaning

### *Element cleaning/replacement*

Note: *XR650L models use a paper filter element that can't be cleaned; if it's dirty, replace it with a new one.*

1   Remove the left side cover (see Chapter 8).

2   If you're working on an XL600R, remove three cover screws and take the cover off the air cleaner case. Grasp the holder tab, pull out the holder together with the foam element and separate the element from the holder.

3   If you're working on an XR600R and the air cleaner duct is attached to the case, remove the seat (see Chapter 8) and the air cleaner duct (see Chapter 4).

4   Unclip the retaining band that secures the filter, pull the filter out and separate the foam element from the metal core **(see illustrations)**.

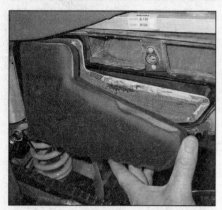

11.5 The filter element on an XR650R practically falls out of the airbox after the left side cover is removed

11.10 Open the drain tube to release accumulated oil and water; if it's clogged, remove it for cleaning

12.1a The fuel tap on XR600R and XR650R models is bolted to the tank

12.1b There's a drain hose and a vent hose connected to the bottom of the float chamber

12.6a On XL600R and XR650L models, turn the hex (lower arrow) counterclockwise to unscrew the cup from the fuel tap; drain the fuel tank and remove the fuel tap nut (upper arrow) if it's necessary to remove the in-tank strainer

12.6b Pull the O-ring and plastic strainer from the fuel tap; on installation, line up the match mark on the strainer with the mark on the fuel tap - XL600R and XR650L models

5    If you're working on an XR650R, remove the filter elelment from the airbox **(see illustration)**.
6    On models with a foam filter element, clean the element and holder or core in a high flash point solvent, squeeze the solvent out of the foam and let the core and element dry completely.
7    Soak the foam element in the type of oil listed in this Chapter's Specifications, then squeeze it firmly to remove the excess oil.
8    Place the element on the holder or core.
9    The remainder of installation is the reverse of the removal steps.

### Drain tube cleaning

10    Squeeze the drain tube to let accumulated water and oil run out **(see illustration)**. If the tube is clogged, squeeze its clamp, remove it from the air cleaner housing and clean it out. Install the drain tube on the housing and secure it with the clamp.

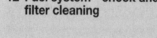

## 12 Fuel system - check and filter cleaning

⚠️ *Warning: Gasoline is extremely flammable, so take extra precautions when you work on any part of the fuel system. Don't smoke or allow open flames or bare light bulbs near the work area, and don't work in a garage where a gas-type appliance (such as a water heater or clothes dryer) is present. Since gasoline is carcinogenic, wear latex gloves when there's a possibility of being exposed to fuel, and if you spill any fuel on your skin, rinse it off immediately with soap and water. Mop up any fuel spills immediately and do not store fuel-soaked rags where they could ignite. When you perform any kind of work on the fuel system, wear safety glasses and have a Class B type fire extinguisher (flammable liquids) on hand.*

1    Check the carburetor, fuel tank, the fuel tap and line and the carburetor hoses for leaks and evidence of damage **(see illustrations)**.
2    If carburetor gaskets/O-rings are leaking, the carburetor should be disassembled and rebuilt (see Chapter 4).
3    If the fuel tap is leaking at the gasket, tightening the screws may help. If leakage persists, the tap should be removed and a new gasket installed. The tap can't be disassembled, so if it's leaking around the handle, it should be replaced with a new one.
4    If the fuel line or drain hose is cracked or otherwise deteriorated, replace it with a new one.

### XL600R and XR650L models

5    Place the fuel tap lever in the Off position.
6    Place a wrench on the hex at the bottom of the fuel tap and remove the cup, strainer and O-ring **(see illustrations)**.
7    Clean the strainer. If it's heavily clogged, remove the fuel tank (see Chapter 4). Unscrew the fuel valve nut **(see illustration 12.6a)**, then remove the fuel tank and clean the in-tank strainer.

12.10 Fuel tap strainer (XR650R model shown, XR600R similar)

13.3a Unbolt the plate(s) (XR650L models have two) ...

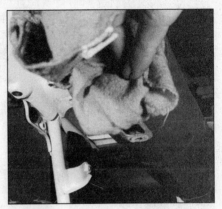

13.3b ... then hold a rag against the muffler opening and rev the engine a few times to blow carbon out of the spark arrester

## XR600R and XR650R models

8  Drain the fuel from the fuel tank. This can be done by removing the tank and pouring the fuel into an approved fuel container, or by turning the fuel tap lever to the Off position, detaching the fuel line from the tap and attaching a hose to the tap, then directing the hose into an approved fuel container and turning the fuel tap On.

9  Disconnect and plug the fuel line, remove the bolts and take the tap out of the fuel tank (see illustration 12.1a).

10  Clean the strainer (see illustration). If it's too heavily clogged to clean, replace the fuel tap.

11  Installation is the reverse of the removal steps. Tighten the fuel tap screws securely, but don't overtighten them and strip out the threads.

12  After installation, run the engine and check for fuel leaks.

13  If the motorcycle will be stored for a month or more, remove and drain the fuel tank. Also loosen the float chamber drain screw and drain the fuel from the carburetor (see Chapter 4).

## 13 Exhaust system - inspection and spark arrester cleaning

**Warning: Operating the bike with a defective spark arrester could result in a fire, and you could be held responsible for any damages to the environment and people affected by it.**

**Warning: Make sure the exhaust system is cool before performing this procedure.**

## XL600R, XR600R and XR650L

1  Periodically check the exhaust system for leaks and loose fasteners (see Chapter 4). If tightening the holder nuts at the cylinder head fails to stop any leaks, replace the gasket with a new one (a procedure which requires removal of the system).

2  The exhaust pipe flange nuts at the cylinder head are especially prone to loosening, which could cause damage to the head. Check them frequently and keep them tight.

3  At the specified interval, remove the plate(s) from under the muffler (see illustration). Fold up a thick rag and hold it firmly over the normal exhaust outlet at the rear end of the muffler (see illustration). Have an assistant start the engine and rev it a few times to blow carbon out of the plate hole, then shut the engine off.

4  After the exhaust system has cooled, install the plate and gasket. Tighten the bolts securely.

## XR650R

5  Remove the bolts from the end of the spark arrester and pull the spark arrester out of the muffler (see illustration).

6  Clean the spark arrester with a soft brush, then inspect it for damage (see illustration). If there are any holes or cracks, it must be replaced.

7  Check the condition of the spark arrester gasket, replacing it if necessary.

8  Reinstall the spark arrester and tighten the bolts securely.

13.5 Remove the bolts securing the spark arrester ...

13.6 ... then remove the spark arrester, clean it with a brush and check it for damage. Performance and safety will benefit!

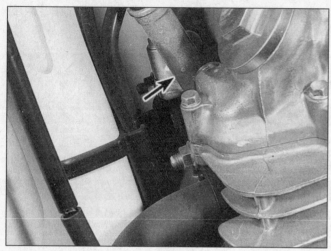

14.1a Twist the spark plug cap back and forth to free it, then pull it off the plug. This is an XR600R (other air cooled models similar) . . .

14.1b . . . and this is an XR650R

## 14 Spark plug - replacement

1    Twist the spark plug cap to break it free from the plug, then pull it off (see illustrations). Note: Although not absolutely necessary, removing the fuel tank makes it easier to get to the spark plug.
2    If available, use compressed air to blow any accumulated debris from around the spark plug. Remove the plug with a spark plug socket.
3    Inspect the electrodes for wear. Both the center and side electrodes should have square edges and the side electrode should be of uniform thickness. Look for excessive deposits and evidence of a cracked or chipped insulator around the center electrode. Compare your spark plugs to the color

spark plug chart on the inside back cover of this manual. Check the threads, the washer and the ceramic insulator body for cracks and other damage.
4    If the electrodes are not excessively worn, and if the deposits can be easily removed with a wire brush, the plug can be regapped and reused (if no cracks or chips are visible in the insulator). If in doubt concerning the condition of the plug, replace it with a new one, as the expense is minimal.
5    Cleaning the spark plug by sandblasting is permitted, provided you clean the plug with a high flash-point solvent afterwards. Note: This only applies to standard, non-platinum or non-iridium spark plugs. Platinum and iridium spark plugs should not be cleaned.
6    Before installing a new plug, make sure it is the correct type and heat range. Check the gap between the electrodes, as it is not preset. For best results, use a wire-type

gauge rather than a flat gauge to check the gap (see illustration). If the gap must be adjusted, bend the side electrode only and be very careful not to chip or crack the insulator nose (see illustration). Make sure the washer is in place before installing the plug.
7    Since the cylinder head is made of aluminum, which is soft and easily damaged, thread the plug into the head by hand. Slip a short length of hose over the end of the plug to use as a tool to thread it into place (see illustration). The hose will grip the plug well enough to turn it, but will start to slip if the plug begins to cross-thread in the hole - this will prevent damaged threads and the accompanying repair costs.
8    Once the plug is finger tight, the job can be finished with a socket, tightening the plug to the torque listed in this Chapter's Specifications.
9    Reconnect the spark plug cap.

14.6a Spark plug manufacturers recommend using a wire type gauge when checking the gap - if the wire doesn't slide between the electrodes with a slight drag, adjustment is required

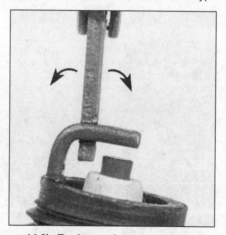

14.6b To change the gap, bend the side electrode only, as indicated by the arrows, and be very careful not to crack or chip the ceramic insulator surrounding the center electrode

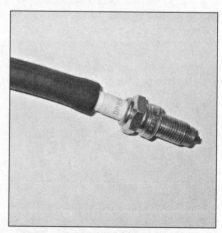

14.7 A length of snug-fitting hose will prevent damaged threads when installing the spark plug

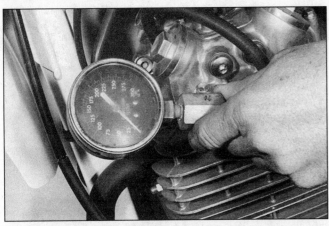

15.5 A compression gauge with a threaded fitting for the spark plug hole is preferred over the type that requires hand pressure to maintain the seal

16.3a On air-cooled models, unscrew the valve adjuster hole covers

## 15 Cylinder compression - check

1 Among other things, poor engine performance may be caused by leaking valves, incorrect valve clearances, a leaking head gasket, or a worn piston, rings and/or cylinder wall. A cylinder compression check will help pinpoint these conditions and can also indicate the presence of excessive carbon deposits in the cylinder head.
2 The only tools required are a compression gauge and a spark plug wrench. Depending on the outcome of the initial test, a squirt-type oil can may also be needed.
3 Start the engine and allow it to reach normal operating temperature, then remove the spark plug. Work carefully - don't strip the spark plug hole threads and don't burn your hands.
4 Remove the fuel tank (see Chapter 4), then disable the ignition by disconnecting the primary (low tension) wires from the coil (see Chapter 5). Be sure to mark the locations of the wires before detaching them.
5 Install the compression gauge in the spark plug hole **(see illustration)**. Hold or block the throttle wide open.
6 Kick the engine over a minimum of four or five revolutions (or until the gauge reading stops increasing) and observe the initial movement of the compression gauge needle as well as the final total gauge reading. Compare the results to the value listed in this Chapter's Specifications (use the *"Decompressor applied"* value on 1988 and later models).
7 If the compression built up quickly and evenly to the specified amount, you can assume the engine upper end is in reasonably good mechanical condition. Worn or sticking piston rings and worn cylinders will produce very little initial movement of the gauge needle, but compression will tend to build up gradually as the engine spins over. Valve and valve seat leakage, or head gasket

leakage, is indicated by low initial compression which does not tend to build up.
8 To further confirm your findings, add a small amount of engine oil to the cylinder by inserting the nozzle of a squirt-type oil can through the spark plug hole. The oil will tend to seal the piston rings if they are leaking.
9 If the compression increases significantly after the addition of the oil, the piston rings and/or cylinder are definitely worn. If the compression does not increase, the pressure is leaking past the valves or the head gasket. Leakage past the valves may be due to insufficient valve clearances, burned, warped or cracked valves or valve seats or valves that are hanging up in the guides.
10 **1988 and later models:** If the compression is still not within specification, loosen the right exhaust valve adjuster locknut (air-cooled models) or the left exhaust valve adjuster locknut (XR650R models) and back off the adjuster so the clearance is about 1 mm (0.04 inch), then repeat the test, comparing your findings with the *"Decompressor not applied"* value. Be sure to readjust the valve clearance after the test (see Section 16).
11 If compression readings are considerably higher than specified, the combustion chamber might be coated with excessive carbon deposits, or the decompressor system might not be working properly. It is pos-

sible (but not very likely) for carbon deposits to raise the compression enough to compensate for the effects of leakage past rings or valves. Referring to Chapter 2, remove the cylinder head and carefully decarbonize the combustion chamber.

## 16 Valve clearances - check and adjustment

1 The engine must be completely cool for this procedure (below 35-degrees C/95-degrees F), so if possible let the machine sit overnight before beginning.
2 Refer to Section 14 and remove the spark plug. This will make it easier to turn the engine. If you're working on an XR650R, drain the cooling system (see Section 29) and remove the radiators (see Chapter 3). **Note:** *It's possible to measure the exhaust valve clearances without removing the radiators, but trying to actually adjust the exhaust valves with the radiators in place isn't worth the effort; it's easier and quicker to remove the radiators.*
3 Remove the valve adjusting hole plugs (air-cooled models) or covers (XR650R models) from the cylinder head cover **(see illustrations)**.

16.3b On XR650R models, remove the two bolts from each access cover, then remove the covers (exhaust valve cover shown)

**16.4 On air-cooled models, unscrew the timing hole cover to look at the timing marks (don't forget to inspect its O-ring); the center cover (arrow) provides access to the alternator rotor bolt, which you can use to turn the engine**

**16.5a The line next to the T on the alternator rotor should be aligned with the timing hole notch for valve adjustment**

**16.5b The line next to the T indicates top dead center; the line next to the F is the ignition timing mark at idle speed; the two parallel lines form the advance timing mark (left engine cover removed for clarity)**

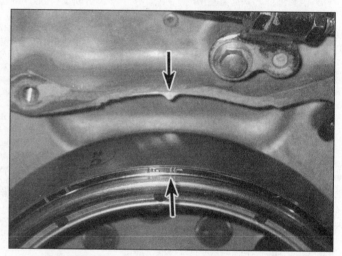

**16.5c XR650R models don't have an access plug for the crankshaft bolt, so it's easier to remove the left engine cover; align the T mark with the pointer on the crankcase**

**16.7 Slip a feeler gauge between the rocker arm and valve stem to measure the clearance (XR650R shown)**

4    On air-cooled models, remove the timing hole plug and the center access plug from the left engine cover (see illustration). On XR650R models, remove the left crankcase cover (see Chapter 5, Section 14).

5    Position the piston at Top Dead Center (TDC) on the compression stroke. Do this by turning the crankshaft until the T mark on the rotor is aligned with the notch in the left engine cover (air-cooled models) or with the timing pointer on the crankcase (see illustrations). Reach through the access holes and try to wiggle the rocker arms. They should have some play. If they don't, the piston is on the exhaust stroke; rotate the crankshaft one full turn to bring the marks into alignment again, and recheck to make sure there's now some play in the rocker arms.

*Caution: Be sure the engine is on the compression stroke, not the exhaust stroke; engine damage may occur if the*

*valves are adjusted with the piston on the exhaust stroke.*

If you're still in doubt, place a finger over the spark plug hole while you turn the engine. As the piston rises on its compression stroke, you'll feel the compression build up.

6    With the engine in this position, all four of the valves can be checked.

7    To check, insert a feeler gauge of the thickness listed in this Chapter's Specifications between the valve stem and rocker arm (see illustration). Pull the feeler gauge out slowly - you should feel a slight drag. If there's no drag, the clearance is too loose. If there's a heavy drag, the clearance is too tight.

8    If the clearance is incorrect, loosen the adjuster locknut with a box-end wrench. Turn the adjusting screw until the correct clearance is achieved, then tighten the locknut while holding the screw to prevent the adjust-

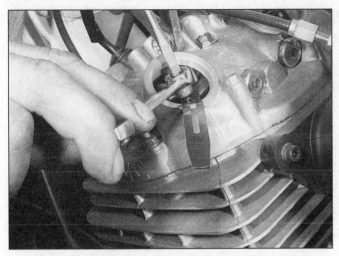

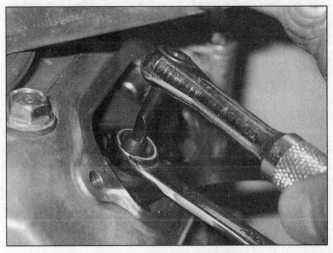

16.8a  To change the clearance, loosen the locknut and turn the adjuster with a screwdriver. This is an XR600R (other air-cooled models similar) . . .

16.8b  . . . and this is an XR650R

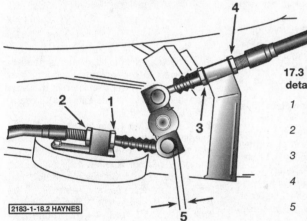

2183-1-18.2 HAYNES

17.3  Kickstarter decompressor details (1986 and 1987 models)

1   Locknut (kickstarter decompressor)
2   Adjusting nut (kickstarter decompressor)
3   Locknut (manual decompressor)
4   Adjusting nut (manual decompressor)
5   Freeplay (kickstarter decompressor)

17.4a  On 1988 and later models, loosen the locknuts (left arrow) and turn the adjusting nut (right arrow) to set decompressor lever freeplay. On air-cooled models like this XR600R it's on the right side of the engine . . .

ment from changing (see illustrations).
9   After adjusting, recheck the clearance with the feeler gauge to make sure it wasn't changed when the locknut was tightened.
10   Now measure the other valves, following the same procedure you used for the first valve. Make sure to use a feeler gauge of the specified thickness.
11   With all of the clearances within the Specifications, install the adjusting hole plugs, center access cover and the timing hole plug.
12   Always check the adjustment of the decompressor after adjusting the valve clearances (see Section 17).

**17  Decompressor freeplay - check and adjustment**

1   Make sure the engine is at top dead center on its compression stroke (see Section 16), then remove the fuel tank (see Chapter 4) Make the adjustments in the following order.

### 1983 through 1985 models

2   Measure freeplay at the tip of the decompressor lever on the rear side of the cylinder head. If it's not within the range listed in this Chapter's Specifications, loosen the locknut, turn the adjusting nut to obtain the correct freeplay and tighten the locknut.

### 1986 and 1987 models

3   Measure play at the end of the kickstarter decompressor cable (see illustration). If it's not within the range listed in this Chapter's Specifications, loosen the locknut, turn the adjusting nut to obtain the correct freeplay and tighten the locknut.

### All models

4   Operate the decompressor lever on the left handlebar and note the amount of freeplay at the outer end of the lever (how far the lever travels before it starts to pull the decompressor). If it's not within the range listed in this Chapter's Specifications, loosen the locknut and adjuster nut at the engine (see illustrations). Turn the adjuster nut to obtain correct freeplay and tighten the locknut.

17.4b  . . . and on XR650R models it's on the left side of the engine

19.3a Turn the throttle stop screw to set idle speed. This is an XR600R . . .

19.3b . . . this is an XR650L . . .

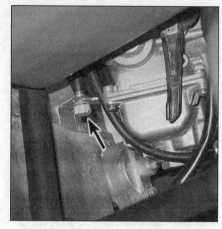

19.3c . . . and this is an XR650R

## 18 Ignition timing

1    Ignition timing is fixed and can't be adjusted. It only needs to be checked if you suspect the CDI unit is faulty (not advancing properly), or to confirm proper operation of a new CDI unit.
2    See Chapter 5 for the ignition timing check procedure.

## 19 Idle speed - check and adjustment

1    Before adjusting the idle speed, make sure the valve clearances and spark plug gap are correct. Also, turn the handlebars back-and-forth and see if the idle speed changes as this is done. If it does, the throttle cable might not be adjusted correctly, might not be

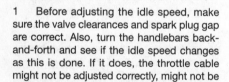

routed correctly, or it may be worn out. Be sure to correct this problem before proceeding.
2    The engine should be at normal operating temperature, which is usually reached after 10 to 15 minutes of stop and go riding. Make sure the transmission is in Neutral. Connect an inductive-type tachometer to the spark plug wire.
3    Turn the throttle stop screw (see illustrations) until the idle speed listed in this Chapter's Specifications is obtained.
4    Snap the throttle open and shut a few times, then recheck the idle speed. If necessary, repeat the adjustment procedure.
5    If a smooth, steady idle can't be achieved, the fuel/air mixture may be incorrect. Refer to Chapter 4 for additional carburetor information.

## 20 Fasteners - check

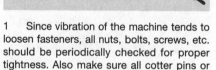

1    Since vibration of the machine tends to loosen fasteners, all nuts, bolts, screws, etc. should be periodically checked for proper tightness. Also make sure all cotter pins or other safety fasteners are correctly installed.
2    Pay particular attention to the following:

    Spark plug
    Engine oil drain plugs
    Gearshift pedal
    Brake lever and pedal
    Kickstarter pedal
    Footpegs
    Engine mounting bolts
    Steering stem locknut
    Triple clamp bolts (upper and lower)
    Front axle and clamp nuts
    Rear axle nut
    Skid bar/plate bolts

3    If a torque wrench is available, use it along with the torque specifications at the beginning of this, or other, Chapters.

## 21 Suspension - check

1    The suspension components must be maintained in top operating condition to ensure rider safety. Loose, worn or damaged suspension parts decrease the motorcycle's stability and control.
2    Lock the front brake and push on the handlebars to compress the front forks several times. See if they move up-and-down smoothly without binding. If binding is felt, the forks should be disassembled and inspected as described in Chapter 6.
3    Check the tightness of all front suspension nuts and bolts to be sure none have worked loose.
4    With the front forks cold and fully extended, remove the air valve caps (models with Schrader valves) and depress the valve core or unscrew the air relief screw and allow the pressure to equalize (the pressure in the forks should be zero) (see illustrations).

21.4a On early models, remove the air valve cap and depress the valve core to relieve any pressure built up in the fork

21.4b On later models, unscrew the air relief screw from each fork to allow built up pressure in the fork to escape

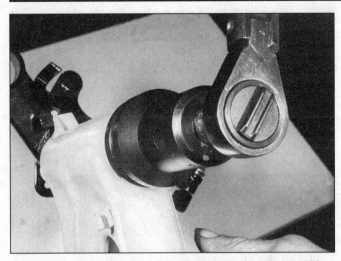

22.6  The best way to adjust the steering stem bearings is with a torque wrench and a special socket . . .

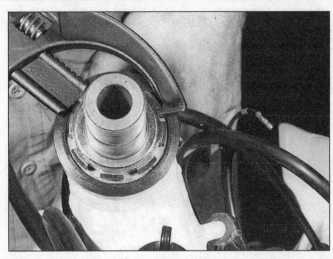

22.9  . . . but an adjustable spanner can also be used; be very sure there's no binding or looseness in the bearings

5    Inspect the rear shock absorber for fluid leakage and tightness of the mounting nuts and bolts. If leakage is found, the shock should be replaced, or rebuilt by a suspension specialist.

6    Support the motorcycle securely upright with its rear wheel off the ground. Grab the swingarm on each side, just ahead of the axle. Rock the swingarm from side to side - there should be no discernible movement at the rear. If there's a little movement or a slight clicking can be heard, make sure the swingarm pivot shaft is tight. If the pivot shaft is tight but movement is still noticeable, the swingarm will have to be removed and the bearings replaced as described in Chapter 6.

7    Inspect the tightness of the rear suspension nuts and bolts.

**22  Steering head bearings - check and adjustment**

### Inspection

1    These motorcycles are equipped with ball-and-cone or roller-and-cone type steering head bearings, which can become dented, rough or loose during normal use of the machine. In extreme cases, worn or loose steering head bearings can cause steering wobble that is potentially dangerous.

2    To check the bearings, lift up the front end of the motorcycle and place a secure support beneath the engine so the front wheel is off the ground.

3    Point the wheel straight ahead and slowly move the handlebars from side-to-side. Dents or roughness in the bearing will be felt and the bars will not move smoothly.

**Note:** *Make sure any hesitation in movement is not being caused by the cables and wiring harnesses that run to the handlebars.*

4    Next, grasp the fork legs and try to move the wheel forward and backward. Any looseness in the steering head bearings will be felt. If play is felt in the bearings, adjust the steering head as follows.

### Adjustment

5    Remove the handlebars and upper triple clamp (see Chapter 6).

6    Loosen the bearing adjusting nut, then tighten it to the torque listed in this Chapter's Specifications **(see illustration)**.

7    Turn the lower triple clamp from lock-to-lock (all the way to the left and all the way back to the right) four or five times to seat the bearings.

8    Unscrew the adjusting nut until it's loose, then tighten it to the final torque listed in this Chapter's Specifications.

23.3  Check drive chain freeplay midway along the lower chain run

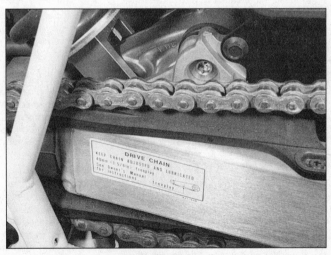

23.6  Inspect the slider at the front of the swingarm and replace it if it's worn

23.8a Turn the chain adjuster to tighten or loosen the chain (all except XR650R models shown)

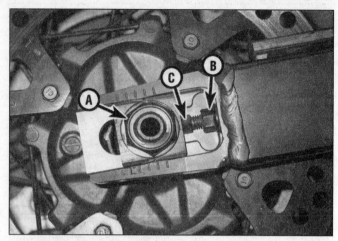

23.8b XR650R models: After loosening the axle nut (A), loosen the locknut (B) and turn the bolt (C) to make adjustments (do this equally on each side)

9    An adjustable spanner wrench can be used to adjust the bearings if you don't have the special socket (see illustration). Since this tool can't be used with a torque wrench, it will be necessary to estimate the tightness of the nut. Be sure the final result is that the steering stem turns from side-to-side freely, but there is no side-to-side or vertical play of the steering stem in the bearings.

## 23 Drive chain and sprockets - check, adjustment and lubrication

1    A neglected drive chain won't last long and can quickly damage the sprockets. Routine chain adjustment isn't difficult and will ensure maximum chain and sprocket life.
2    To check the chain, support the bike securely with the rear wheel off the ground. Place the transmission in neutral.
3    Push up on the bottom run of the chain and measure the slack midway between the two sprockets (see illustration), then compare the measurements to the value listed in this Chapter's Specifications. As wear occurs, the chain will actually stretch, which means it must be adjusted by removing some slack from the chain. In some cases where lubrication has been neglected, corrosion and galling may cause the links to bind and kink, which effectively shortens the chain's length. If the chain is tight between the sprockets, rusty or kinked, it's time to replace it with a new one. Note: Repeat the chain slack measurement along the length of the chain - ideally, every inch or so. If you find a tight area, mark it with a felt pen or paint and repeat the measurement after the bike has been ridden. If the chain is still tight in the same areas, it may be damaged or worn. Because a tight or kinked chain can damage the transmission countershaft bearing, it's a good idea to replace it.
4    Check the entire length of the chain for

damaged rollers, loose links and loose pins.
5    Look through the slots in the engine sprocket cover and inspect the engine sprocket. Check the teeth on the engine sprocket and the rear sprocket for wear (see illustration 11.3 in Chapter 6). Refer to Chapter 6 for the sprocket replacement procedure if the sprockets appear to be worn excessively.
6    Check the chain slider on the swingarm near the front (see illustration). If it's worn, measure its thickness. If it's less than the value listed in the Chapter 6 Specifications, replace it (see Chapter 6).

### Adjustment
7    Rotate the rear wheel until the chain is positioned with the least amount of slack present.
8    Loosen the rear axle nut. Turn the adjuster on each side of the swingarm evenly until the proper chain tension is obtained (get the adjuster on the chain side close, then set the adjuster on the opposite side) (see illustrations). Be sure to turn the adjusters evenly to keep the wheel in alignment. If the adjusters reach the end of their travel, the chain is excessively worn and should be replaced with a new one (see Chapter 6).
9    When the chain has the correct amount of slack, make sure the marks on the adjusters or axle blocks correspond to the same relative marks on each side of the swingarm (see illustrations 23.8a and 23.8b). Tighten the axle nut to the torque listed in the Chapter 7 Specifications.

### Lubrication
Note: If the chain is dirty, it should be removed and cleaned before it's lubricated (see Chapter 6).
10    Use a good quality chain lubricant of the type listed in this Chapter's Specifications. Be sure the lubricant is intended for use with O-ring chains - if the lubricant causes the O-rings to deteriorate, the chain will lose its internal lubricant and dirt will find its way

into the rollers. Apply the lubricant along the top of the lower chain run, so that when the bike is ridden, centrifugal force will move the lubricant into the chain, rather than throwing it off.
11    After applying the lubricant, let it soak in a few minutes before wiping off any excess.

## 24 Crankcase breather system - check

1    Check the breather hoses for damage, deterioration and loose connections (see illustration). On 1998 and later California models, make sure the breather separator unit is securely mounted in the hoses.
2    On all except 1998 and later California models, at the bottom end of the drain hose, either remove the plug (XL600R) or squeeze the fitting (XR600R) to open it so any breather deposits can drain out (see illustration). If the hose is clogged, remove it and clean out the deposits.

24.1 Inspect the breather hoses (XR600R except 1998 and later California models shown)

**24.2 Squeeze the fitting at the bottom end of the drain hose to let out accumulated oil and water**

**28.5 If coolant is leaking from the small hole under the water pump, it's time for a new pump**

## 25 Evaporative emission control system - check

1   This system is used on XL600R and XR650L models first sold in California. It stores gasoline vapor from the fuel system in a canister filled with activated charcoal. The stored vapor is pulled into the engine for combustion when the engine is run.
2   To inspect the system, check the hoses for misconnection, cracks and general deterioration and connect or replace them as necessary.
3   Remove the canister from the hoses and turn it upside down. If gasoline runs out, the canister should be replaced and the cause of gas entering the canister should be diagnosed (check for a sunken float in the carburetor).
4   See Chapter 4 for more information.

## 26 Front fork oil change

1   Although fork oil changes are not a regularly scheduled maintenance procedure, the oil should be changed if it becomes contaminated. The following steps apply to models equipped with fork drain screws. If you're working on a bike that doesn't have a drain screw, you'll need to disassemble the forks part-way to drain the oil (see Chapter 6). However, the best way to change the fork oil on *any* model is to remove the forks, disassemble and clean the components, then reassemble them and fill them with new fork oil of the specified type.
2   Support the motorcycle securely upright.
3   Remove the handlebars (see Chapter 6).
4   Remove the fork cap bolts.

5   Wrap a rag around the top of the fork to catch dripping oil, then lift out the fork spring from each fork.
6   Place a pan under the fork drain bolt and remove the drain bolt and gasket.

⚠️ *Warning: Do not allow the fork oil to drip onto the tire or brake disc. If it does, wash it off with soap and water before riding the motorcycle.*

7   After most of the oil has drained, slowly compress and release the forks to pump out the rest of the oil. An assistant may be needed to do this.
8   Check the drain bolt gasket for damage and replace it if necessary. Clean the threads of the drain bolt with solvent and let it dry, then reinstall the bolt and gasket, tightening it securely.
9   Pour the type and amount of fork oil listed in the Chapter 6 Specifications into the fork tube through the opening at the top. Slowly pump the forks a few times to purge air from the upper and lower chambers.
10   Fully compress the front forks (you may need an assistant to do this). Insert a stiff tape measure into the fork tube and measure the distance from the oil to the top of the fork tube **(see illustration 4.15b in Chapter 6)**. Compare your measurement to the value listed in the Chapter 6 Specifications. Drain or add oil as necessary until the level is correct.
11   Check the O-ring on the fork cap bolt and replace it with a new one if it's deteriorated, broken or otherwise damaged. Install the fork spring. Install the cap bolt and tighten it to the torque listed in the Chapter 6 Specifications.
12   Repeat the procedure for the other fork. It is essential that the oil level is identical in each fork.
13   Install the handlebar, being sure to locate it correctly in the brackets, and tighten the handlebar bracket bolts to the torque listed in the Chapter 6 Specifications.

## 27 Sidestand - check

The sidestand should be checked to make sure it stays down when extended and up when retracted. Refer to Chapter 8 and check tightness of the sidestand mounting bolts. Check the spring for cracks or rust and replace it if any problems are found.

## 28 Cooling system (XR650R models) - inspection

1   Remove the radiator shrouds (see Chapter 8) and grilles (see Chapter 3). Clean mud, leaves or other obstructions out of the radiator fins with low-pressure water or compressed air, from the back to the front.
2   If any fins are bent, carefully straighten them with a small screwdriver, taking care not to puncture the coolant tubes in the radiator.
3   If more than about 20 percent of the radiator's surface area is blocked, replace the radiator.
4   Check the coolant hoses for swelling, cracks, burns, cuts or other defects. Replace the hoses if their condition is doubtful. Make sure the hose clamps are tight and free of corrosion. Tighten loose clamps and replace corroded or damaged ones.
5   Check for leaks at the water pump weep hole **(see illustration)** and gaskets. Also check for leaks at the coolant drain bolt, which is the lower bolt on the water pump cover. Replace water pump or drain plug gaskets if they've been leaking. If coolant or oil has been leaking from the weep hole, it's time for new water pump seals (see Chapter 3).

29.1a  Unscrew the coolant drain bolt . . .

29.1b  . . . and let the coolant drain into a container

## 29  Coolant (XR650R models) - change

 Warning 1: Do not allow antifreeze to come in contact with your skin or painted surfaces of the vehicle. Rinse off spills immediately with plenty of water. Antifreeze is highly toxic if ingested. Never leave antifreeze lying around in an open container or in puddles on the floor; children and pets are attracted by its sweet smell and may drink it. Check with local authorities about disposing of used antifreeze. Many communities have collection centers which will see that antifreeze is disposed of safely.

Warning 2: Wait until the engine is completely cool before beginning this procedure. Don't remove the radiator cap when the engine and radiator are hot.

Scalding coolant and steam may be blown out under pressure, which could cause serious injury. To open the radiator cap, place a thick rag, like a towel, over the radiator cap; slowly rotate the cap counterclockwise to the first stop. This procedure allows any residual pressure to escape. When the steam has stopped escaping, press down on the cap while turning it counterclockwise and remove it.

1    Remove the skid plate (see Chapter 8). Remove the radiator cap, place a drain pan beneath the coolant drain bolt, then unscrew the bolt and allow the coolant to drain (see illustrations). When the flow of coolant stops, tilt the bike side-to-side to drain any remaining coolant.

2    Once the coolant has drained completely, place a new sealing washer on the drain bolt. Install the drain bolt and tighten it to the torque listed in this Chapter's Specifications.

3    Remove the coolant reserve tank and drain the coolant from it (see Chapter 3).

4    Fill the cooling system with the proper antifreeze mixture listed in this Chapter's Specifications.

5    Lean the bike about twenty-degrees to one side, then the other, several times. This will allow air trapped in the coolant passages to make its way to the top of the coolant.

6    Check the coolant level. It should be up to the bottom of the radiator filler neck. Add more antifreeze mixture if necessary.

7    Fill the coolant reserve tank up to the upper level line.

8    Start the engine and let it idle for about three minutes, then rev up the engine three or four times. This will help bleed air out of the system.

9    Turn off the engine and re-check the coolant level in the radiator. If it's not up to the bottom of the radiator filler neck, add some until it is.

10    Check the coolant level in the reserve tank again, adding as necessary to bring it to the upper level line.

11    Reinstall the skid plate.

# Chapter 2 Part A
## Engine (air-cooled), clutch and transmission

## Contents

## Degrees of difficulty

| | | | | |
|---|---|---|---|---|
| **Easy,** suitable for novice with little experience  | **Fairly easy,** suitable for beginner with some experience  | **Fairly difficult,** suitable for competent DIY mechanic  | **Difficult,** suitable for experienced DIY mechanic  | **Very difficult,** suitable for expert DIY or professional  |

## Specifications

### Main rocker arms
Rocker arm inside diameter
Standard .......................................................................... 11.500 to 11.518 mm (0.4528 to 0.4535 inch)
Limit .............................................................................. 11.55 mm (0.455 inch)
Rocker shaft outside diameter
Standard .......................................................................... 11.466 to 11.484 mm (0.4514 to 0.4521 inch)
Limit .............................................................................. 11.41 mm (0.449 inch)
Shaft-to-arm clearance
Standard .......................................................................... 0.016 to 0.052 mm (0.0006 to 0.0020 inch)
Limit .............................................................................. 0.14 mm (0.006 inch)

### Sub-rocker arms
Rocker arm inside diameter
Intake
Standard .......................................................................... 8.000 to 8.015 mm (0.3150 to 0.3156 inch)
Limit .............................................................................. 8.05 mm (0.317 inch)
Exhaust
Standard .......................................................................... 7.000 to 7.015 mm (0.2756 to 0.2762 inch)
Limit .............................................................................. 7.05 mm (0.278 inch)

## Sub-rocker arms (continued)

Rocker shaft outside diameter
  Intake
    Standard .................................................................................... 7.969 to 7.972 mm (0.3137 to 0.3138 inch)
    Limit .......................................................................................... 7.92 mm (0.312 inch)
Shaft-to-arm clearance
  All except XR650L
    Standard .................................................................................... 0.033 to 0.043 mm (0.0013 to 0.0017 inch)
    Limit .......................................................................................... 0.08 mm (0.003 inch)
  XR650L
    Standard .................................................................................... 0.028 to 0.046 mm (0.0011 to 0.0018 inch)
    Limit .......................................................................................... 0.01 mm (0.004 inch)

## Camshaft

Lobe height
  XL600R
    Intake
      Standard ................................................................................ 31.023 mm (1.2214 inches)
      Limit ...................................................................................... 30.85 mm (1.215 inches)
    Exhaust
      Standard ................................................................................ 30.976 mm (1.2195 inches)
      Limit ...................................................................................... 30.81 mm (1.213 inches)
  XR600R
    Intake
      Standard ................................................................................ 31.155 to 31.315 mm (1.2266 to 1.2329 inches)
      Limit ...................................................................................... 31.05 mm (1.222 inches)
    Exhaust
      Standard ................................................................................ 31.091 to 31.251 mm (1.2241 to 1.2304 inches)
      Limit ...................................................................................... 31.00 mm (1.220 inches)
  XR650L
    Intake
      Standard ................................................................................ 31.101 to 31.341 mm (1.2244 to 1.2339 inches)
      Limit ...................................................................................... 30.48 mm (1.200 inches)
    Exhaust
      Standard ................................................................................ 31.072 to 31.312 mm (1.2233 to 1.2328 inches)
      Limit ...................................................................................... 30.45 mm (1.199 inches)
Journal diameter ............................................................................... Not specified
Bearing journal inside diameter........................................................ Not specified
Camshaft runout limit
  All except XR650L............................................................................ 0.04 mm (0.002 inch)
  XR650L ............................................................................................ 0.03 mm (0.001 inch)
Camshaft side clearance (endplay)
  XL600R
    Standard .................................................................................... 0.05 to 0.25 mm (0.002 to 0.010 inch)
    Limit .......................................................................................... 0.40 mm (0.016 inch)
  XR600R, XR650L ............................................................................ Not specified

## Cylinder head, valves and valve springs

Cylinder head warpage limit............................................................. 0.10 mm (0.004 inch)
Valve stem runout............................................................................. Not specified
Valve stem diameter
  Intake
    Standard .................................................................................... 6.575 to 6.590 mm (0.2589 to 0.2594 inch)
    Limit .......................................................................................... 6.56 mm (0.258 inch)
  Exhaust
    All except XR650L
      Standard ................................................................................ 6.560 to 6.575 mm (0.2583 to 0.2589 inch)
      Limit ...................................................................................... 6.55 mm (0.257 inch)
    XR650L
      Standard ................................................................................ 6.565 to 6.575 mm (0.2585 to 0.2589 inch)
      Limit ...................................................................................... 6.55 mm (0.257 inch)
Valve guide inside diameter (intake and exhaust)
  Standard ........................................................................................ 6.600 to 6.615 mm (0.2589 to 0.2604 inch)
  Limit .............................................................................................. 6.63 mm (0.261 inch)

Stem-to-guide clearance
  Intake
    Standard ............................................................................... 0.010 to 0.040 mm (0.0004 to 0.0016 inch)
    Limit ..................................................................................... 0.065 mm (0.0026 inch)
  Exhaust
    XL600R
      Standard ........................................................................... 0.030 to 0.055 mm (0.0012 to 0.0022 inch)
      Limit ................................................................................. 0.08 mm (0.0031 inch)
    XR600R
      1985 through 1987
        Standard ....................................................................... 0.025 to 0.050 mm (0.0010 to 0.0020 inch)
        Limit ............................................................................. 0.08 mm (0.0031 inch)
      1988 and later
        Standard ....................................................................... 0.025 to 0.055 mm (0.0010 to 0.0022 inch)
        Limit ............................................................................. 0.08 mm (0.0031 inch)
    XR650L
      Standard ........................................................................... 0.030 to 0.055 mm (0.0012 to 0.0022 inch)
      Limit ................................................................................. 0.08 mm (0.0031 inch)
Valve spring free length
  Inner spring
    Standard ............................................................................... 35.1 mm (1.240 inches)
    Limit ..................................................................................... 34.1 mm (1.34 inches)
  Outer spring
    Standard ............................................................................... 36.0 mm (1.42 inches)
    Limit ..................................................................................... 35.0 mm (1.38 inches)
Valve seat width (intake and exhaust)
  Standard ................................................................................... 1.2 to 1.4 mm (0.05 to 0.06 inch)
  Limit ......................................................................................... 2.0 mm (0.08 inch)
Valve face width
  Intake
    Standard ............................................................................... 1.20 to 1.85 mm (0.047 to 0.071 inch)
    Limit ..................................................................................... 2.6 mm (0.10 inch)
  Exhaust
    Standard ............................................................................... 0.9 to 1.7 mm (0.04 to 0.67 inch)
    Limit ..................................................................................... 2.4 mm (0.09 inch)
Sub-chamber valve (1983 through 1985 XL600R)
  Stem runout .............................................................................. Not specified
  Stem diameter
    Standard ............................................................................... 4.970 to 4.985 mm (0.1957 to 0.1963 inch)
    Limit ..................................................................................... 4.96 mm (0.195 inch)
  Guide inside diameter
    Standard ............................................................................... 5.010 to 5.028 mm (0.1972 to 0.1980 inch)
    Limit ..................................................................................... 5.02 mm (0.199 inch)
  Stem to guide clearance .......................................................... Not specified
  Seat width limit ........................................................................ 1.5 mm (0.059 inch)
  Face width
    Standard ............................................................................... 1.00 to 1.40 mm (0.039 to 0.0551 inch)
    Limit ..................................................................................... 2.0 mm (0.08 inch)
  Spring free length
    Standard ............................................................................... 40.5 mm (1.594 inches)
    Limit ..................................................................................... 39.3 mm (1.55 inches)

## Cylinder

Bore
  XL600R
    Standard ............................................................................... 100.00 to 100.01 mm (3.934 to 3.940 inches)
    Limit ..................................................................................... 100.12 mm (3.942 inches)
  XR600R (1985 through 1990)
    Standard ............................................................................... 97.000 to 97.010 mm (3.8189 to 3.8193 inches)
    Limit ..................................................................................... 97.12 mm (3.823 inches)
  XR600R (1991 and later)
    Standard ............................................................................... 97.010 to 97.020 mm (3.8193 to 3.8197 inches)
    Limit ..................................................................................... 97.13 mm (3.824 inches)
  XR650L
    Standard ............................................................................... 100.00 to 100.01 mm (3.934 to 3.940 inches)
    Limit ..................................................................................... 100.12 mm (3.942 inches)
Taper and out-of-round limits ........................................................ 0.05 mm (0.002 inch)
Surface warpage limit .................................................................... 0.10 mm (0.004 inch)

## Piston

Piston diameter
  XL600R
    Standard ............................................................................. 99.95 to 99.98 (3.935 to 3.936 inches)
    Limit ................................................................................... 99.85 mm (3.93 inches)
  XR600R
    Standard ............................................................................. 96.96 to 96.99 mm (3.8173 to 3.8284 inches)
    Limit ................................................................................... 96.96 mm (3.813 inches)
  XR650L
    Standard ............................................................................. 99.96 to 99.99 mm (3.9354 to 3.9362 inches)
    Limit ................................................................................... 99.85 mm (3.931 inches)
Piston diameter measuring point (above bottom of piston)
  All except XR650L.................................................................. 10 mm (0.40 inch)
  XR650L .................................................................................. 25 mm (1.0 inch)
Piston-to-cylinder clearance
  Standard
    XL600R................................................................................ 0.01 to 0.06 mm (0.0004 to 0.002 inch)
    XR600R
      1985 through 1987 ......................................................... 0.02 to 0.06 mm (0.001 to 0.002 inch)
      1988 on .......................................................................... 0.01 to 0.06 mm (0.0004 to 0.002 inch)
    XR650R................................................................................ 0.02 to 0.05 mm (0.0008 to 0.002 inch)
  Limit
    All except XR650L .............................................................. 0.10 mm (0.004 inch)
    XR650L ............................................................................... 0.12 mm (0.005 inch)
Piston pin bore in piston
  Standard ............................................................................. 24.002 to 24.008 mm (0.9450 to 0.9452 inch)
  Limit ................................................................................... 24.03 mm (0.946 inch)
Piston pin bore in connecting rod
  Standard ............................................................................. 24.020 to 24.041 mm (0.9457 to 0.9465 inch)
  Limit ................................................................................... 24.07 mm (0.948 inch)
Piston pin outer diameter
  All except XR650L
    Standard ............................................................................. 23.989 to 23.995 mm (0.9444 to 0.9447 inch)
    Limit ................................................................................... 23.96 mm (0.943 inch)
  XR650L
    Standard ............................................................................. 23.992 to 23.996 mm (0.9446 to 0.9447 inch)
    Limit ................................................................................... 23.96 mm (0.943 inch)
Piston pin-to-piston clearance
  Standard
    XL600R ............................................................................... 0.002 to 0.014 mm (0.0001 to 0.0006 inch)
    XR600R ............................................................................... 0.007 to 0.019 mm (0.0003 to 0.0007 inch)
  Limit ................................................................................... 0.07 mm (0.003 inch)
Piston pin-to-connecting rod clearance
  All except XR650L.................................................................. Not specified
  XR650L .................................................................................. 0.024 to 0.149 mm (0.0009 to 0.0019 inch)
Top ring side clearance
  Standard
    1983 through 1987 ............................................................. 0.030 to 0.065 mm (0.0012 to 0.0026 inch)
    1988 on............................................................................... 0.015 to 0.045 mm (0.0006 to 0.0018 inch)
  Limit ................................................................................... 0.12 mm (0.006 inch)
Second ring side clearance
  Standard ............................................................................. 0.015 to 0.045 mm (0.0006 to 0.0018 inch)
  Limit ................................................................................... 0.12 mm (0.006 inch)
Oil ring side clearance................................................................ Not specified
Ring end gap (XL600R)
  Top and second
    Standard ............................................................................. 0.20 to 0.40 mm (0.008 to 0.016 inch)
    Limit ................................................................................... 0.5 mm (0.02 inch)
  Oil ring side rails
    Standard ............................................................................. 0.20 to 0.90 mm (0.010 to 0.030 inch)
    Limit ................................................................................... Not specified
Ring end gap (XR600R)
  Top
    Standard ............................................................................. 0.20 to 0.40 mm (0.008 to 0.016 inch)
    Limit ................................................................................... 0.5 mm (0.020 inch)
  Second
    Standard ............................................................................. 0.35 to 0.55 mm (0.014 to 0.022 inch)
    Limit ................................................................................... 0.65 mm (0.026 inch)

Oil ring side rails
    Standard ............................................................................. 0.20 to 0.90 mm (0.008 to 0.040 inch)
    Limit .................................................................................. Not specified
Ring end gap (XR650L)
  Top
    1993 through 1996 ............................................................ 0.20 to 0.40 mm (0.008 to 0.016 inch)
    1997 and later .................................................................. 0.20 to 0.35 mm (0.008 to 0.014 inch)
  Second
    1993 through 1996 ............................................................ 0.35 to 0.55 mm (0.014 to 0.022 inch)
    1997 and later .................................................................. 0.35 to 0.50 mm (0.014 to 0.020 inch)
  Oil ring side rails
    Standard ............................................................................. 0.20 to 0.70 mm (0.008 to 0.030 inch)
    Limit .................................................................................. Not specified

## Clutch

Spring free length
  XL600R
    Standard ............................................................................. 44.3 mm (1.744 inches)
    Limit .................................................................................. 42.7 mm (1.68 inches)
  XR600R, XR650L
    Standard ............................................................................. 44.7 mm (1.76 inches)
    Limit .................................................................................. 43.1 mm (1.70 inches)
Friction plate thickness
  Standard ............................................................................. 2.92 to 3.08 mm (0.115 to 0.121 inch)
  Limit .................................................................................. 2.6 mm (0.10 inch)
Friction and metal plate warpage limit ..................................... 0.15 mm (0.006 inch)
Clutch housing bushing inside diameter
  XL600R, XR600R
    Standard ............................................................................. 21.99 to 22.035 mm (0.8657 to 0.8675 inch)
    Limit .................................................................................. 22.05 mm (0.868 inch)
  XR650L ................................................................................. Not specified
Clutch housing bushing outside diameter
  XL600R, XR600R
    Standard ............................................................................. 26.959 to 26.980 mm (1.0614 to 1.0622 inch)
    Limit .................................................................................. 26.91 mm (1.059 inch)
  XR650L ................................................................................. Not specified
Clutch housing bushing clearance to crankshaft
  XL600R ................................................................................. Not specified
  XR600R (limit)...................................................................... 0.14 mm (0.006 inch)
  XR650L ................................................................................. Not specified
Clutch housing inside diameter
  XR650L ................................................................................. Not specified
    Standard ............................................................................. 27.00 to 27.021 mm (1.0630 to 1.0638 inches)
    Limit .................................................................................. 27.05 mm (1.065 inches)
  XR650L ................................................................................. Not specified

## Oil pump

Outer rotor-to-body clearance
  Standard ............................................................................. 0.15 to 0.21 mm (0.006 to 0.008 inch)
  Limit .................................................................................. 0.25 mm (0.010 inch)
Inner-to-outer rotor clearance
  Standard ............................................................................. 0.15 mm (0.006 inch) or less
  Limit .................................................................................. 0.20 mm (0.008 inch)
Side clearance (rotors-to-straightedge)
  Standard ............................................................................. 0.02 to 0.08 mm (0.001 to 0.003 inch)
  Limit .................................................................................. 0.12 mm (0.005 inch)

## Kickstarter

Shaft outside diameter
  Standard ............................................................................. 21.959 to 21.980 mm (0.8645 to 0.8654 inch)
  Limit .................................................................................. 21.90 mm (0.862 inch)
Pinion gear inside diameter
  1983 through 1986
    Standard ............................................................................. 22.00 to 22.033 mm (0.8661 to 0.8674 inch)
    Limit .................................................................................. 22.12 mm (0.871 inch)
  1987 on
    Standard ............................................................................. 25.500 to 25.521 mm (1.0039 to 1.0048 inches)
    Limit .................................................................................. 25.58 mm (1.007 inches)

## Kickstarter (continued)

Pinion bushing inside diameter
    Standard .................................................................... 21.995 to 22.015 mm (0.8660 to 0.8667 inch)
    Limit ........................................................................... 22.07 mm (0.869 inch)
Pinion bushing outside diameter
    Standard .................................................................... 25.465 to 25.485 mm (1.0026 to 1.0033 inches)
    Limit ........................................................................... 25.41 mm (1.004 inches)
Idler gear inside diameter
    Standard .................................................................... 20.00 to 20.021 mm (0.7874 to 0.7822 inch)
    Limit ........................................................................... 20.11 mm (0.792 inch)
Idler gear bushing inside diameter
    Standard .................................................................... 16.00 to 16.018 mm 0.6299 to 0.6366 inch)
    Limit ........................................................................... 16.03 mm (0.631 inch)
Idler gear bushing outside diameter
    Standard .................................................................... 19.959 to 19.980 mm (0.7858 to 0.7866 inch)
    Limit ........................................................................... 19.90 mm (0.783 inch)

## Shift drum and forks

Fork inside diameter
    XL600R, XR600R
        Standard .............................................................. 14.000 to 14.018 mm (0.5512 to 0.5519 inch)
        Limit ..................................................................... 14.05 mm (0.553 inch)
    XR650L
        Standard
            Left ................................................................ 14.000 to 14.018 mm (0.5512 to 0.5519 inch)
            Center ............................................................ 14.000 to 14.015 mm (0.5512 to 0.5518 inch)
            Right .............................................................. 14.000 to 14.018 mm (0.5512 to 0.5519 inch)
        Limit ..................................................................... 14.05 mm (0.553 inch)
Fork shaft outside diameter
    Standard .................................................................... 13.966 to 13.984 mm (0.5498 to 0.5506 inch)
    Limit ........................................................................... 13.90 mm (0.547 inch)
Fork ear thickness
    Standard .................................................................... 4.93 to 5.00 mm (0.194 to 0.197 inch)
    Limit ........................................................................... 4.50 mm (0.18 inch)
Shift drum groove width limit ............................................... Not specified

## Transmission

Gear inside diameters
    Mainshaft fourth (XL600R)
        Standard .............................................................. 25.020 to 25.041 mm (0.9850 to 0.9859 inch)
        Limit ..................................................................... 25.10 mm (0.988 inch)
    Mainshaft fourth (XR600R, XR650L)
        Standard .............................................................. 28.020 to 28.041 mm (1.1031 to 1.1040 inches)
        Limit ..................................................................... 28.10 mm (1.106 inches)
    Mainshaft fifth
        Standard .............................................................. 28.000 to 28.021 mm (1.1024 to 1.1032 inches)
        Limit ..................................................................... 28.08 mm (1.106 inches)
    Countershaft first
        Standard .............................................................. 25.020 to 25.041 mm (0.9850 to 0.9859 inch)
        Limit ..................................................................... 25.10 mm (0.988 inch)
    Countershaft second
        Standard .............................................................. 28.020 to 28.041 mm (1.1031 to 1.1040 inches)
        Limit ..................................................................... 28.10 mm (1.106 inches)
    Countershaft third
        1983 through 1987
            Standard ........................................................ 25.020 to 25.041 mm (0.9850 to 0.9859 inch)
            Limit ............................................................. 25.10 mm (0.988 inch)
        1988 and later
            Standard ........................................................ 28.020 to 28.041 mm (1.1031 to 1.1040 inches)
            Limit ............................................................. 25.10 mm (0.988 inch)
Bushing inside diameters
    Countershaft first
        Standard .............................................................. 20.020 to 20.041 mm (0.7882 to 0.7890 inch)
        Limit ..................................................................... 20.01 mm (0.791 inch)

Countershaft second, countershaft third (XR650L), mainshaft fourth
  Standard ................................................................................. 25.020 to 25.041 mm (0.9850 to 0.9859 inch)
  Limit ...................................................................................... 25.10 mm (0.988 inch)
Bushing outside diameters
  Mainshaft fifth
    Standard ............................................................................. 27.949 to 27.980 mm (1.1004 to 1.1016 inch)
    Limit .................................................................................. 27.90 mm (1.098 inches)
  Countershaft first
    Standard ............................................................................. 24.984 to 25.005 mm (0.9836 to 0.9844 inch)
    Limit .................................................................................. 24.93 mm (0.981 inch)
  Countershaft second, countershaft third (XR650L)
    Standard ............................................................................. 27.979 to 28.000 mm (1.1015 to 1.1024 inches)
    Limit .................................................................................. 27.93 mm (1.100 inches)
Gear-to-bushing clearances
  Mainshaft fifth
    Standard ............................................................................. 0.020 to 0.072 mm (0.0008 to 0.0028 inch)
    Limit .................................................................................. 0.10 mm (0.004 inch)
  Mainshaft fourth, countershaft second
    Standard ............................................................................. 0.020 to 0.062 mm (0.0008 to 0.0024 inch)
    Limit .................................................................................. 0.10 mm (0.004 inch)
  Countershaft first
    Standard ............................................................................. 0.015 to 0.057 mm (0.0006 to 0.0022 inch)
    Limit .................................................................................. 0.10 mm (0.004 inch)
Mainshaft diameter (at fourth gear)
  Standard ................................................................................. 24.972 to 24.993 mm (0.9831 to 0.9840 inch)
  Limit ...................................................................................... 24.92 mm (0.981 inch)
Mainshaft diameter (at clutch housing bushing)
  XL600R ................................................................................... Not specified
  XR600R (limit) ........................................................................ 21.91 mm (0.863 inch)
Countershaft diameter (at kickstarter idler gear)
  Standard ................................................................................. 15.966 to 15.984 mm (0.6286 to 0.6293 inch)
  Limit ...................................................................................... 15.93 mm (0.627 inch)
Countershaft diameter (at first gear)
  Standard ................................................................................. 19.980 to 19.993 mm (0.7866 to 0.7871 inch)
  Limit ...................................................................................... 19.94 mm (0.785 inch)
Countershaft diameter (at second gear)
  Standard ................................................................................. 24.972 to 24.993 mm (0.9831 to 0.9840 inch)
  Limit ...................................................................................... 24.92 mm (0.981 inch)
Countershaft diameter (at third gear)
  Standard ................................................................................. 24.959 to 24.980 mm (0.9826 to 0.9835 inch)
  Limit  ..................................................................................... 24.92 mm (0.981 inch)
Shaft-to-gear clearance
  XL600R, XR600R
    Mainshaft fourth
      Standard .......................................................................... 0.027 to 0.068 mm (0.0011 to 0.0027 inch)
      Limit ............................................................................... 0.10 mm (0.004 inch)
    Countershaft third
      Standard .......................................................................... 0.041 to 0.082 mm (0.0016 to 0.0032 inch)
      Limit ............................................................................... 0.15 mm (0.006 inch)
  XR650L .................................................................................. Not specified
Shaft-to-bushing clearance
  Countershaft first
    Standard ............................................................................. 0.027 to 0.061 mm (0.0011 to 0.0024 inch)
    Limit .................................................................................. 0.10 mm (0.004 inch)
  Countershaft second (and countershaft third, mainshaft fourth on XR650L models)
    Standard ............................................................................. 0.027 to 0.069 mm (0.0011 to 0.0027 inch)
    Limit .................................................................................. 0.10 mm (0.004 inch)

## Crankshaft and balancer

Connecting rod side clearance
  XL600R, XR600R
    Standard ............................................................................. 0.050 to 0.650 mm (0.0020 to 0.0256 inch)
    Limit .................................................................................. 0.80 mm (0.031 inch)
  XR650L .................................................................................. 0.050 to 0.450 mm (0.002 to 0.0177)
Connecting rod big end radial clearance
  Standard ................................................................................. 0.006 to 0.018 mm (0.0002 to 0.0007 inch)
  Limit ...................................................................................... 0.05 mm (0.002 inch)
Runout limit ................................................................................ 0.10 mm (0.004 inch)

## Crankshaft and balancer

Balancer shaft diameter
  XL600R
    Standard ............................................................................ 16.977 to 16.995 mm (0.6684 to 0.6691 inch)
    Limit ................................................................................... 16.95 mm (0.667 inch)
  XR600R, XR650L ...................................................................... Not specified

## Torque specifications

**Note:** *One foot-pound (ft-lb) of torque is equivalent to 12 inch-pounds (in-lbs) of torque. Torque values below approximately 15 ft-lbs are expressed in inch-pounds, since most foot-pound torque wrenches are not accurate at these smaller values.*

Engine mounting bolts
  XL600R
    8 mm bolts............................................................................ 30 to 37 Nm (22 to 27 ft-lbs)
    Front 10 mm mounting bracket bolts ......................................... 35 to 45 Nm (25 to 33 ft-lbs)
    Rear and top 10 mm mounting bolts........................................... 55 to 65 Nm (40 to 47 ft-lbs)
  XR600R
    8 mm bolts............................................................................ 27 Nm (20 ft-lbs)
    10 mm bolts.......................................................................... 40 Nm (29 ft-lbs)
  XR650L
    8 mm bolts............................................................................ 27 Nm (20 ft-lbs)
    10 mm bolts.......................................................................... 50 Nm (30 ft-lbs)
External oil hose and pipe nuts ....................................................... 40 Nm (29 ft-lbs)
Cylinder head cover bolts
  6 mm small head bolt ................................................................ 10 Nm (84 in-lbs)
  6 mm regular head bolts ............................................................ 12 Nm (108 in-lbs)
  8 mm bolt ................................................................................ 23 Nm (17 ft-lbs) (1)
Cam sprocket bolts ....................................................................... 20 Nm (14 ft-lbs)
Main rocker shafts........................................................................ 27 Nm (20 ft-lbs)
Sub-rocker shafts (2)
  Intake .................................................................................... 27 Nm (20 ft-lbs)
  Exhaust .................................................................................. 23 Nm (17 ft-lbs)
Cam chain tensioner bolt
  XL600R, XR600R
    Through 1997 ......................................................................... Not specified
    1998 and later......................................................................... 12 Nm (108 inch-lbs) (2)
  XR650L ................................................................................... Not specified
Cylinder head main bolts
  1983 through 1987 models......................................................... 27 to 32 Nm (20 to 23 ft-lbs)
  1988 and later .......................................................................... 36 Nm (26 ft-lbs)
Cylinder head small nuts/bolts
  Through 1997............................................................................ Not specified
  1998 and later .......................................................................... 12 Nm (108 inch-lbs)
Cylinder main bolts........................................................................ 50 Nm (36 ft-lbs)
Cylinder small bolts ....................................................................... Not specified
Intake manifold (carburetor insulator) bolts....................................... Not specified
Right and left engine cover bolts..................................................... 12 Nm (108 in-lbs)
Clutch spring bolts
  XL600R ................................................................................... 8 to 12 Nm (72 to 108 in-lbs)
  XR600R
    Through 1997 ......................................................................... Not specified
    1998 and later......................................................................... 12 Nm (108 in-lbs)
  XR650L ................................................................................... Not specified
Primary drive gear locknut
  XL600R ................................................................................... 50 to Nm (36 to 43 ft-lbs)
  XR600R
    1985 through 1987 .................................................................. 70 to 80 Nm (50 to 58 ft-lbs)
    1988 and later......................................................................... 110 Nm (80 ft-lbs)
  XR650L ................................................................................... 110 Nm (80 ft-lbs)
Clutch locknut
  XL600R ................................................................................... 50 to Nm (36 to 43 ft-lbs)
  XR600R
    1985 through 1987 .................................................................. 70 to 80 Nm (50 to 58 ft-lbs)
    1988 and later......................................................................... 110 Nm (80 ft-lbs)
  XR650L ................................................................................... 120 Nm (87 ft-lbs)
Shift cam plate to shift drum bolt.................................................... 12 Nm (108 in-lbs)
Shift drum stopper arm bolt ........................................................... 25 Nm (18 ft-lbs)

Shift pedal pinch bolt
    XL600R ................................................................. 8 to 12 Nm (72 to 108 in-lbs)
    XR600R ................................................................. Not specified
    XR650L ................................................................. 12 Nm (108 in-lbs)
Crankcase bolts .......................................................... 12 Nm (108 in-lbs)
Crankshaft bearing retainer bolt
    XL600R, XR600R
        Through 1997 ................................................. Not specified
        1998 and later.................................................. 25 Nm (18 ft-lbs)
    XR650L ................................................................. Not specified
Center shift fork-to-shaft bolt........................................ 15 Nm (132 in-lbs)

*(1) On 1998 and later models, apply clean engine oil to the bolt threads.*
*(2) On 1998 and later models, apply non-permanent thread locking agent to the bolt threads.*

## 1  General information

The engine/transmission unit is of the air-cooled, single-cylinder four-stroke design. The four valves are operated by an overhead camshaft which is chain driven off the crankshaft. The valves are arranged in a circle, rather than in the parallel pairs more commonly used in four-valves-per-cylinder engines. To accommodate this arrangement, the camshaft operates four main rocker arms, each of which in turn operates its valve through a sub-rocker arm rather than directly. Honda refers to this design as Radial Four Valve Combustion (RFVC).

The engine/transmission assembly is constructed from aluminum alloy. The crankcase is divided vertically.

The crankcase incorporates a dry sump, pressure-fed lubrication system which uses a gear-driven rotor-type oil pump, an oil filter and separate strainer screen (or more than one screen, depending on model). Oil not circulating through the engine is stored inside the upper and front frame member, which acts as an oil tank. The oil pump has two sets of rotors, one to circulate oil under pressure to the engine and the other to scavenge oil from the engine.

Power from the crankshaft is routed to the transmission via a wet, multi-plate type clutch. The transmission has five forward gears.

A decompressor reduces the effort required to kick start the engine. On 1988 and later models, there are two decompressor cams; one to reduce starting effort and the other to reduce engine kickback during starting.

## 2  Operations possible with the engine in the frame

The components and assemblies listed below can be removed without having to remove the engine from the frame. If, however, a number of areas require attention at the same time, removal of the engine is recommended.

*Camshaft, rocker arms and cylinder head (1988 and later models only)*
*External shift mechanism*
*Clutch*
*External oil hoses*
*Oil pump and pipe*
*Kickstarter*
*Starter motor/starter gear/starter clutch (XR650L models)*

## 3  Operations requiring engine removal

It is necessary to remove the engine/transmission assembly from the frame to gain access to the following components:

*Camshaft, rocker arms and cylinder head (1983 through 1987 models)*
*Cylinder and piston (1983 through 1987 models)*
*Crankshaft, balancer and connecting rod*
*Transmission shafts*
*Internal shift mechanism (shift shaft, shift drum and forks)*
*Crankcase bearings*

## 4  Major engine repair - general note

1  It is not always easy to determine when or if an engine should be completely overhauled, as a number of factors must be considered.
2  High mileage is not necessarily an indication that an overhaul is needed, while low mileage, on the other hand, does not preclude the need for an overhaul. Frequency of servicing is probably the single most important consideration. An engine that has regular and frequent oil and filter changes, as well as other required maintenance, will most likely give many miles of reliable service. Conversely, a neglected engine, or one which has not been broken in properly, may require an overhaul very early in its life.
3  Exhaust smoke and excessive oil consumption are both indications that piston rings and/or valve guides are in need of attention. Make sure oil leaks are not responsible before deciding that the rings and guides are bad. Refer to Chapter 1 and perform a cylinder compression check to determine for certain the nature and extent of the work required.
4  If the engine is making obvious knocking or rumbling noises, the connecting rod and/or main bearings are probably at fault.
5  Loss of power, rough running, excessive valve train noise and high fuel consumption rates may also point to the need for an overhaul, especially if they are all present at the same time. If a complete tune-up does not remedy the situation, major mechanical work is the only solution.
6  An engine overhaul generally involves restoring the internal parts to the specifica-

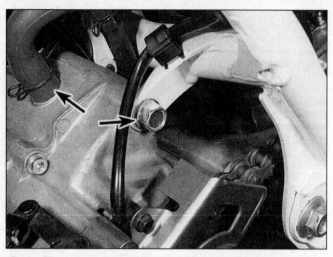

**5.11a Disconnect the breather hose (left arrow) and remove the upper rear mounting bolt (right arrow)**

**5.11b Disconnect the oil overflow hose and pull back the rubber cover from the upper mount nuts; pull off the cover on the other side for access to the bolt heads**

tions of a new engine. During an overhaul the piston rings are replaced and the cylinder walls are bored and/or honed. If a rebore is done, then a new piston is also required. The crankshaft and connecting rod are permanently assembled, so if one of these components needs to be replaced, both must be. Generally the valves are serviced as well, since they are usually in less than perfect condition at this point. While the engine is being overhauled, other components such as the carburetor(s) can be rebuilt also. The end result should be a like-new engine that will give as many trouble-free miles as the original.

7   Before beginning the engine overhaul, read through all of the related procedures to familiarize yourself with the scope and requirements of the job. Overhauling an engine is not all that difficult, but it is time consuming. Check on the availability of parts and make sure that any necessary special tools, equipment and supplies are obtained in advance.

8   Most work can be done with typical shop hand tools, although a number of precision measuring tools are required for inspecting parts to determine if they must be replaced. Often a dealer service department or repair shop will handle the inspection of parts and offer advice concerning reconditioning and replacement. As a general rule, time is the primary cost of an overhaul so it doesn't pay to install worn or substandard parts.

9   As a final note, to ensure maximum life and minimum trouble from a rebuilt engine, everything must be assembled with care in a spotlessly clean environment.

## 5  Engine - removal and installation

**Note:** *Engine removal and installation should be done with the aid of an assistant to avoid damage or injury that could occur if the engine is dropped. A hydraulic floor jack should be used to support and lower the*

*engine if possible (they can be rented at low cost).*

### Removal

1   Drain the engine oil (see Chapter 1).
2   Remove the seat, both side covers and the left footpeg (see Chapter 8). If you're working on an XL600R, remove the right footpeg as well.
3   Remove the fuel tank, exhaust system and carburetor (see Chapter 4).
4   Disconnect the spark plug wire (see Chapter 1).
5   Label and disconnect the alternator and pulse generator wires (refer to Chapter 5 for component location if necessary). Detach the wires from their retainers.
6   Remove the drive chain (see Chapter 6). If you're working on a XR650L model, remove the secondary air (PAIR) valve and hoses (see Chapter 4).
7   Remove the skid plate/bars from beneath the engine (see Chapter 8).
8   Disconnect the clutch cable (see Section 16).

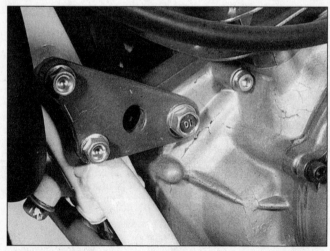

**5.13a Remove the front engine mounting bolts and bracket**

**5.13b Remove the upper rear engine mounting bolts and bracket**

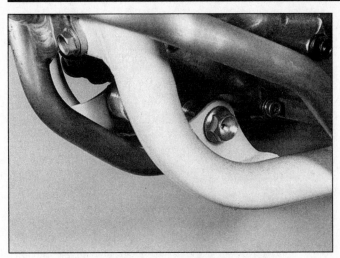

5.13c Remove the lower front through-bolt . . .

5.13d . . . and its spacers

9    Remove the kickstarter pedal (see Section 21).

10    Disconnect the decompressor cable(s) from the engine (see Section 20).

11    Disconnect the crankcase breather tube and oil overflow hose from the top of the engine **(see illustrations)**. If you're working on an XL600R, remove the oil separator. On all models, refer to Section 22 and disconnect the oil hoses from the engine.

12    Support the bike securely upright so it can't fall over during the remainder of this procedure. Support the engine with a jack, using a block of wood between the jack and the engine to protect the crankcase.

13    Remove the engine mounting bolts, nuts and brackets at the top, upper front, upper rear, lower front and lower rear **(see illustration 5.11a and the accompanying illustrations). Note:** *Raise and lower the jack as needed to relieve strain on the mounting bolts.*

14    Have an assistant help you lift the engine out of the right side of the frame.

15    Slowly lower the engine to a suitable work surface.

## Installation

16    Have an assistant help lift the engine into the frame so it rests on the jack and block of wood. Use the jack to align the mounting bolt holes, then install the brackets, bolts and nuts. Tighten them to the torque values listed in this Chapter's Specifications.

17    The remainder of installation is the reverse of the removal steps, with the following additions:

a)  *Use new gaskets at all exhaust pipe connections.*

b)  *Adjust the throttle cable, decompression cable and clutch cable following the procedures in Chapter 1.*

c)  *Fill the engine with oil, also following the procedures in Chapter 1.*

d)  *Run the engine and check for oil and exhaust leaks.*

## 6   Engine disassembly and reassembly - general information

1    Before disassembling the engine, clean the exterior with a degreaser and rinse it with water. A clean engine will make the job easier and prevent the possibility of getting dirt into the internal areas of the engine.

2    In addition to the precision measuring tools mentioned earlier, you will need a torque wrench, a valve spring compressor, oil gallery brushes **(see illustration)**, a piston ring removal and installation tool and a piston ring compressor. Some new, clean engine oil of the correct grade and type, some engine assembly lube (or moly-based grease) and a tube of liquid gasket will also be required.

3    An engine support stand made from short lengths of two-by-fours bolted together will facilitate the disassembly and reassem-

5.13e Remove the lower rear mounting bolt

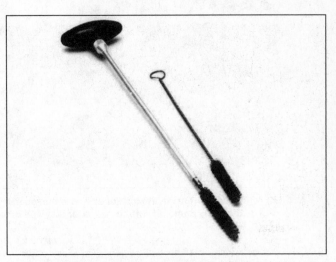

6.2 A selection of brushes is required for cleaning holes and passages in the engine components

6.3 An engine stand can be made from short lengths
of lumber and lag bolts or nails

7.7 Loosen the cover bolts evenly in two or three stages

bly procedures (see illustration). If you have an automotive-type engine stand, an adapter plate can be made from a piece of plate, some angle iron and some nuts and bolts.

4    When disassembling the engine, keep "mated" parts together (including gears, rocker arms and shafts, etc.) that have been in contact with each other during engine operation. These "mated" parts must be reused or replaced as an assembly.

5    Engine/transmission disassembly should be done in the following general order with reference to the appropriate Sections.

*Remove the cylinder head cover and rocker arm assembly*
*Remove the cam sprocket and camshaft*
*Remove the cylinder head and cam chain tensioner*

*Remove the cylinder*
*Remove the piston*
*Remove the primary drive gear*
*Remove the clutch*
*Remove the kickstarter*
*Remove the oil pump*
*Remove the external shift mechanism*
*Remove the alternator rotor (flywheel)*
*Remove the starter clutch and driven gear (see Chapter 5)*
*Separate the crankcase halves*
*Remove the internal shift mechanism*
*Remove the transmission shafts/gears*
*Remove the crankshaft, connecting rod and balancer*

6    Reassembly is accomplished by reversing the general disassembly sequence.

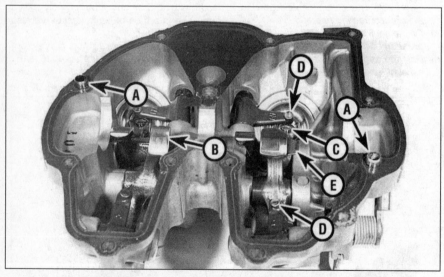

7.10 Lift off the cover, remove the gasket and note the locations of the dowels;
they may come off with the cover or stay in the head

A    Dowels
B    Main rocker arm camshaft contact surfaces
C    Main rocker arm to sub-rocker arm

    contact surfaces
D    Sub-rocker arm valve stem contact surfaces
E    Decompressor lever contact surface

---

### 7    Cylinder head cover and rocker arms - removal, inspection and installation

### Removal

**Note:** *The cylinder head cover on 1988 and later models can be removed with the engine in the frame. If the engine has been removed, ignore the steps which don't apply.*

#### 1983 through 1987 models

1    Remove the engine from the frame (see Section 5).

#### 1988 and later models

2    Remove the seat, fuel tank and carburetor (see Chapters 8 and 4).
3    Disconnect the oil overflow tube from the cover **(see illustration 5.11b)**.
4    Disconnect the decompressor cable from the cover and lever (see Section 20).

#### All models

5    Remove the external oil line (see Section 22).
6    Refer to the valve adjustment procedure in Chapter 1 and place the piston at Top Dead Center on its compression stroke. Remove the valve adjusting hole covers from the cylinder head cover.
7    Unscrew the cylinder head cover bolts **(see illustration)**. On 1983 through 1987 models, remove all of the bolts. On 1988 and later models, loosen the two center bolts for now and remove them after the cover is removed.
8    If you're working on a 1988 or later model, pull the cover toward the carburetor side of the engine to provide removal clearance.
9    Lift the cover off the engine. If it's stuck, don't attempt to pry it off - tap around its sides with a plastic hammer to dislodge it.
10   Remove the gasket from the cylinder head cover **(see illustration)**. Use a new gasket whenever the cover is removed.

7.12a  Pull out the decompressor shaft retaining pin

7.12b  Note how the cable bracket secures the spring, then remove the bracket bolt

## Inspection

11   Refer to Section 9 and check the cam bearing surfaces in the cylinder head and its cover for wear or damage. Check the rocker arms for wear at the cam contact surfaces and at the tips of the valve adjusting screws (see illustration 7.10). Also check the decompressor shaft for wear at the point where it contacts the exhaust rocker arm. Try to twist the rocker arms from side-to-side on the shafts. If they're loose on the shafts or if there's visible wear, remove them as described below.

12   Pull out the decompressor shaft retaining pin (see illustration). If you're working on a 1983 through 1985 XL600R, remove the kickstarter decompressor lever. On all models, unbolt the cable bracket/spring retainer and pull the decompressor shaft out of the cover (see illustration).

13   Unscrew the rocker shafts and sub-rocker shafts and pull them out of the cover, making careful notes as to the locations of all the components (see illustration). Remove the sealing washers, wave washers (sub-rocker arms only) and the rocker arms. Note:

*Some of the rocker arms (all of the rocker arms on some models) have identification marks so they can be returned to their original positions. Look for the marks, and make your own if they aren't clearly visible. It's a good idea to label all of the rocker arms and sub-rocker arms so they can be reinstalled in their original locations. In addition to developing wear patterns with their shafts, some of the rocker arms are shaped differently from the others and won't work in the wrong location.*

14   Check the decompressor lever and its shaft for wear, damage or a broken spring. If any problems are found, replace the shaft or spring. Pry the shaft oil seal out of its bore.

15   Measure the outer diameter of each rocker shaft and the inner diameter of the rocker arms with a micrometer and compare the measurements to the values listed in this Chapter's Specifications. If rocker arm-to-shaft clearance is excessive, replace the rocker arm or shaft, whichever is worn.

## Installation

16   Press a new decompressor shaft oil seal into the bore with a seal driver or a socket the

same diameter as the seal. Install the shaft, securing its spring with the cable bracket (see illustration 7.12b). Install the retaining pin.

17   Coat the main rocker shafts and rocker arm bores with moly-based grease containing 40-percent or more molybdenum disulfide. Apply non-hardening gasket sealant to the threads of the main rocker shafts. Install the rocker shafts and rocker arms in the cylinder head cover, using new copper sealing washers on the shafts. Depending on model, the main rocker arms will be marked as follows:

a) No marks
b) A and B
c) A, B, C and D

18   If the rocker arms are unmarked, you'll need to refer to the labels made on disassembly. Note that the exhaust rocker arm with the lug for the decompressor goes next to the decompressor shaft bore.

19   If the rocker arms have factory labels, install them in the specified locations (see illustration).

20   Coat new sub-rocker shaft sealing rings

7.13  Remove the rocker shafts

7.19  The exhaust sub-rocker arms are labeled A and B (upper arrows); both intake sub-rocker arms are labeled IN (lower arrows)

**7.20a  Intake sub-rocker shaft wave washer locations**

**7.20b  Exhaust sub-rocker shaft wave washer locations**

with clean engine oil and install them on the shafts. Coat the shaft threads with non-hardening gasket sealant. Install the sub-rocker arms and their wave washers in the correct locations in the cylinder head cover, then install the shafts and sealing washers **(see illustrations)**.

21   Install the decompressor shaft in the cylinder head cover. Align the groove in the shaft with the retaining pin, then install the retaining pin through the groove.

22   Clean the mating surfaces of the cylinder head and cover with lacquer thinner, acetone or brake system cleaner. Install a new gasket, taking care not to damage its silicone coating.

23   Make sure the piston is still at top dead center on its compression stroke (both cam lobes pointing downward). Fill the oil pockets in the top of the cylinder head with clean engine oil so the oil covers the cam lobes.

24   Loosen the valve adjusting screws all the way, then install the cover on the cylinder head. Install the bolts and tighten them evenly in two or three stages to the torque

values listed in this Chapter's Specifications. Note that there are three types of bolts with different torque settings.

25   Adjust the valve clearances (see Chapter 1).

26   Install the oil pipe, using new sealing washers (see Section 22).

27   Refer to Section 20 and reconnect the decompressor cable.

28   The remainder of installation is the reverse of the removal steps.

29   Refer to Chapter 1 and adjust the decompressor cable.

## 8   Cam chain tensioner - removal, inspection and installation

### Removal

1   Refer to Section 7 and remove the cylinder head cover.

2   If you're working on a 1983 through 1986 model, pull out the tensioner retaining

pin with pliers. If you're working on a 1987 or later model, unscrew the tensioner bolt **(see illustration)**.

3   Pull the tensioner shaft out of the cylinder head and lift out the tensioner **(see illustration)**.

### Inspection

4   Check the tensioner shaft and bushing for wear **(see illustration)**. Check for wear or damage at the tensioner tip and check the spring for breakage. Replace any worn or damaged parts. It's a good idea to replace the O-ring whenever the tensioner is removed.

5   Insert the shaft into the tensioner and try to rotate it **(see illustration)**. The shaft should turn freely clockwise and not at all counterclockwise. If not, replace the tensioner.

### Installation

6   You'll need a way to hold the tensioner lever against its spring tension while you install the tensioner in the cylinder head. Honda manufactures a special tool that's

**8.2  Remove the cam chain tensioner bolt (upper arrow) and pull out the shaft (lower arrow)**

**8.3  Lift the tensioner out of the cylinder head**

**8.4  Pull the shaft out of the tensioner and inspect its O-ring**

**8.5  The tensioner shaft should rotate clockwise, but not counterclockwise**

curved to fit the tensioner body, with a pin that fits into the hole in the tensioner **(see illustrations)**. If you don't have the special tool, you may be able to fabricate a substitute, but be sure it holds the tensioner securely - the spring is powerful and can cause injury if it's released suddenly.

7   Coat a new O-ring with clean engine oil and install it on the tensioner shaft.

8   Place the spring on the tensioner, then position them in the cylinder head and insert the shaft.

9   Push the tensioner lever straight down, so the hole in the tensioner is facing up **(see illustration)**. Insert the special holding tool (Honda part no. 07973-MG30001 or 07973-MG30002) into the hole in the tensioner, then carefully release the lever **(see illustration 8.6b)**. The holder will rotate with the tensioner until it rests against the cylinder head.

10   If the camshaft has been removed, leave the holder in position until the camshaft is reinstalled.

**8.6a  This tool holds the tensioner spring compressed . . .**

## 9   Camshaft, guides and chain - removal and installation

### Removal

1   Remove the cylinder head cover and cam chain tensioner (see Sections 7 and 8).

2   Stuff rags into the cam chain opening so the camshaft bolts won't fall into the crankcase.

**8.6b  . . . its pin fits into the hole in the tensioner and its curved portion fits over the tensioner body**

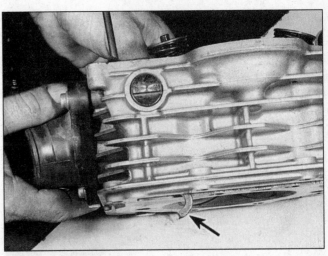

**8.9  Pull the end of the cam chain tensioner down and secure it in this position with the holder (cylinder head removed for clarity)**

9.3 Rotate the camshaft sprocket so one bolt is accessible, then remove the bolt; rotate the engine to remove the other bolt, then turn the engine back so the sprocket marks are even with the cylinder head surface and the sprocket timing mark is straight up

9.5 Pull the decompressor pin and spring out of the cylinder head

9.6 Check the cam bearing surfaces for scoring or wear

3   Turn the engine so one of the cam sprocket bolts is accessible, then remove it. Next, turn the engine so the other bolt is accessible, remove it and turn the engine back to TDC compression **(see illustration)**.
4   Disengage the sprocket from the cam chain. Support the cam chain so it won't drop into the engine, then remove the sprocket.
5   Lift the camshaft out of the cylinder head, then remove the decompressor pin and spring **(see illustration)**.

### Inspection
**Note:** *Before replacing the cylinder head cover and cylinder head because of damage, check with local machine shops specializing in motorcycle engine work. If the bearing surfaces in the center of the cylinder head or cover are damaged, it may be possible for them to be bored out to accept bearing inserts. Due to the cost of a new cylinder*

*head it is recommended that all options be explored before condemning it as trash!*
6   Inspect the cam bearing surfaces of the cylinder head and cover **(see illustration)**. Look for score marks, deep scratches and evidence of spalling (a pitted appearance). The bearing surfaces that support the ends of the camshaft contain ball bearings, so the surfaces shouldn't be scored or worn. If they are, the bearings may have spun in their bores due to seizure or a loose cylinder head cover.
7   Check the camshaft lobes for heat dis-coloration (blue appearance), score marks, chipped areas, flat spots and spalling **(see illustration)**. Measure the height of each lobe with a micrometer **(see illustration)** and compare the results to the minimum lobe height listed in this Chapter's Specifications. If damage is noted or wear is excessive, the camshaft must be replaced. Also, be sure to check the condition of the rocker arms as

9.7a Check the cam lobes for wear - here's a good example of lobe damage which will require replacement of the camshaft

9.7b Measure the height of the cam lobes with a micrometer

**9.8a The front chain guide fits in notches in the cylinder head**

**9.8b The rear chain guide is secured by a shouldered bolt (left arrow); the front chain guide fits in a pocket cast in the crankcase (right arrow)**

**9.8c There's an O-ring between the rear chain guide and the crankcase**

**9.9 Lower the chain and take it off the sprocket**

described in Section 7.

8    Check the chain guides for wear or damage. If they are worn or damaged, replace them. To remove the exhaust side (front) chain guide, you'll need to remove the cylinder head (see Section 10), then lift the guide out of its notches **(see illustration)**. To remove the intake side guide, you'll need to remove the right engine cover (see Section 16), then unscrew the shouldered bolt and take off the chain guide and O-ring **(see illustrations)**.

9    Except in cases of oil starvation, the camshaft chain wears very little. If the chain has stretched excessively, which makes it difficult to maintain proper tension, replace it with a new one. To remove the chain from the crankshaft sprocket, it's necessary to remove the chain guides as described above. Once this is done, the chain can be lowered away from the sprocket **(see illustration)**. If necessary, slide the cam chain sprocket off the crankshaft.

10    Check the sprocket for wear, cracks and other damage, replacing it if necessary. If

the sprocket is worn, the chain is also worn, and possibly the sprocket on the crankshaft. If wear this severe is apparent, the entire engine should be disassembled for inspection.

11    Slip the ball bearings off the ends of the

camshaft **(see illustration)**. Hold the center race of each bearing with fingers and turn the outer race. The bearing should spin freely without roughness, looseness or noise. If it has obvious problems, or if you aren't sure it's in good condition, replace the bearing.

**9.11 There's a ball bearing on each end of the camshaft; the sealed side of the bearing at the sprocket end faces away from the camshaft**

9.14a  Coat the cam lobes with moly-based grease

9.14b  Position the bearing in its saddle and make sure the dowel is in position, then do the same at the other end of the camshaft

## Installation

12   Install the cam chain guides, cylinder head and right side cover if they were removed.

13   Make sure the bearing surfaces in the cylinder head and cylinder head cover are clean. Install the ball bearings on the ends of the camshaft (see illustration 9.11). If there's only one sealed bearing, install it on the sprocket end of the camshaft with its sealed side facing away from the center of the engine. If both bearings are sealed, install both with their sealed sides facing away from the center of the engine.

14   Lubricate the cam bearing journals with moly-based grease. Lay the camshaft in the cylinder head with the lobes downward (see illustration). Install the bearing retaining dowels in the cylinder head at each end of the camshaft (see illustration).

15   Engage the sprocket with the chain so its timing mark will be straight up and its OUT mark faces away from the center of the engine (see illustration 9.3). Place the sprocket on the camshaft so its bolt holes

align with the camshaft bolt holes. Rotate the sprocket as needed for access, install the bolts and tighten them to the torque listed in this Chapter's Specifications.

16   Turn the sprocket so its timing mark is straight up and the marks are aligned with the cylinder head gasket surface (see illustration 9.3).

17   Recheck the crankshaft timing mark on the alternator rotor to make sure it's still at the TDC position (see *Valve clearance - check and adjustment* in Chapter 1). If it's out of position and the camshaft sprocket is aligned as described in Step 16, you'll need to remove the chain from the sprocket and reposition it. Don't run the engine with the marks out of alignment or severe engine damage could occur.

18   Remove the holder from the cam chain tensioner.

19   Adjust the valve clearances (see Chapter 1).

20   The remainder of installation is the reverse of removal.

## 10 Cylinder head - removal and installation

*Caution: The engine must be completely cool before beginning this procedure, or the cylinder head may become warped.*

## Removal

1   If you're working on a 1987 or earlier model, remove the engine from the frame (see Section 5).

2   Remove the cylinder head cover, cam chain tensioner and camshaft (see Sections 7, 8 and 9).

3   Remove the two nuts that secure the cylinder head to the cylinder (see illustration).

4   Loosen the main cylinder head bolts in two or three stages, in a criss-cross pattern (see illustration).

5   Lift the cylinder head off the cylinder. If the head is stuck, tap around the side of the head with a rubber mallet to jar it loose, or

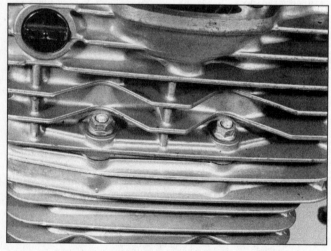

10.3  Remove the two small cylinder head nuts

10.4  Loosen the head bolts evenly, in a criss-cross pattern, in two or three stages

10.6 Lift the head off, remove the gasket and locate the dowels (arrows); they may come off with the head or stay in the cylinder

12.7a Install a valve spring compressor and compress the valve springs, then remove the keepers, the valve spring retainer, springs, spring seat and valve

use wooden dowels inserted into the intake or exhaust ports to lever the head off. Don't attempt to pry the head off by inserting a screwdriver between the head and the cylinder - you'll damage the sealing surfaces.

6   Support the cam chain so it won't drop into the cam chain tunnel, and stuff a clean rag into the tunnel to prevent the entry of debris. Once this is done, remove the gasket and two dowel pins from the cylinder (see illustration).

7   If the front (exhaust) side chain guide is worn, lift it out of its notches (see illustration 9.8a).

8   Check the cylinder head gasket and the mating surfaces on the cylinder head and cylinder for leakage, which could indicate warpage. Refer to Section 12 and check the flatness of the cylinder head.

9   Clean all traces of old gasket material from the cylinder head and cylinder. Be careful not to let any of the gasket material fall into the crankcase, the cylinder bore or the bolt holes.

## Installation

10   Install the two dowel pins, then lay the new gasket in place on the cylinder block. Never reuse the old gasket and don't use any type of gasket sealant.

11   Make sure the cam chain front guide fits in its notches (see illustration 9.8b).

12   Carefully lower the cylinder head over the dowels. It's helpful to have an assistant support the camshaft chain with a piece of wire so it doesn't fall and become kinked or detached from the crankshaft. When the head is resting on the cylinder, wire the cam chain to another component to keep tension on it.

13   Install the head bolts and their washers in the proper holes (they're different lengths). Tighten the bolts in two or three stages, in a criss-cross pattern, to the torque listed in this Chapter's Specifications.

14   Install the cylinder head nuts and tighten them securely, but don't overtighten them

and strip the threads.

15   The remainder of installation is the reverse of the removal steps.

16   Change the engine oil (see Chapter 1).

## 11 Valves/valve seats/valve guides - servicing

1   Because of the complex nature of this job and the special tools and equipment required, servicing of the valves, the valve seats and the valve guides (commonly known as a valve job) is best left to a professional.

2   The home mechanic can, however, remove and disassemble the head, do the initial cleaning and inspection, then reassemble and deliver the head to a dealer service department or properly equipped motorcycle repair shop for the actual valve servicing. Refer to Section 12 for those procedures.

3   The service department will remove the valves and springs, recondition or replace the valves and valve seats, replace the valve guides, check and replace the valve springs, spring retainers and keepers (as necessary), replace the valve seals with new ones and reassemble the valve components.

4   After the valve job has been performed, the head will be in like-new condition. When the head is returned, be sure to clean it again very thoroughly before installation on the engine to remove any metal particles or abrasive grit that may still be present from the valve service operations. Use compressed air, if available, to blow out all the holes and passages.

## 12 Cylinder head and valves - disassembly, inspection and reassembly

1   As mentioned in Section 11, valve servicing and valve guide replacement should

be left to a dealer service department or motorcycle repair shop. However, disassembly, cleaning and inspection of the valves and related components can be done (if the necessary special tools are available) by the home mechanic. This way no expense is incurred if the inspection reveals that service work is not required at this time.

2   To properly disassemble the valve components without the risk of damaging them, a valve spring compressor is absolutely necessary. If the special tool is not available, have a dealer service department or motorcycle repair shop handle the entire process of disassembly, inspection, service or repair (if required) and reassembly of the valves.

## Disassembly

3   Remove the intake manifold (carburetor insulator) from the cylinder head.

4   Before the valves are removed, scrape away any traces of gasket material from the head gasket sealing surface. Work slowly and do not nick or gouge the soft aluminum of the head. Gasket removing solvents, which work very well, are available at most motorcycle shops and auto parts stores.

5   Carefully scrape all carbon deposits out of the combustion chamber area. A handheld wire brush or a piece of fine emery cloth can be used once most of the deposits have been scraped away. Do not use a wire brush mounted in a drill motor, or one with extremely stiff bristles, as the head material is soft and may be eroded away or scratched by the wire brush.

6   Before proceeding, arrange to label and store the valves along with their related components so they can be kept separate and reinstalled in the same valve guides they are removed from (plastic bags work well for this).

7   Compress the valve spring(s) on the first valve with a spring compressor, then remove the keepers and the retainer from the valve assembly (see illustrations). Do not compress the spring(s) any more than is abso-

lutely necessary. Carefully release the valve spring compressor and remove the spring(s), spring seat and valve from the head. If the valve binds in the guide (won't pull through), push it back into the head and deburr the area around the keeper groove with a very fine file or whetstone **(see illustration)**.

8    Repeat the procedure for the remaining valves. Remember to keep the parts for each valve together so they can be reinstalled in the same location.

9    Once the valves have been removed and labeled, pull off the valve stem seals with pliers and discard them (the old seals should never be reused).

10    Next, clean the cylinder head with solvent and dry it thoroughly. Compressed air will speed the drying process and ensure that all holes and recessed areas are clean.

11    Clean all of the valve springs, keepers, retainers and spring seats with solvent and dry them thoroughly. Clean the parts from one valve at a time so that no mixing of parts between valves occurs.

12    Scrape off any deposits that may have formed on the valve, then use a motorized wire brush to remove deposits from the valve heads and stems. Again, make sure the valves do not get mixed up.

### Inspection

13    Inspect the head very carefully for cracks and other damage. If cracks are found, a new head will be required. Check the cam bearing surfaces for wear and evidence of seizure. Check the camshaft for wear as well (see Section 9).

14    Using a precision straightedge and a feeler gauge, check the head gasket mating surface for warpage. Lay the straightedge lengthwise, across the head and diagonally (corner-to-corner), intersecting the head bolt holes, and try to slip a feeler gauge under it, on either side of the combustion chamber **(see illustration)**. The feeler gauge thickness should be the same as the cylinder head warpage limit listed in this Chapter's Speci-

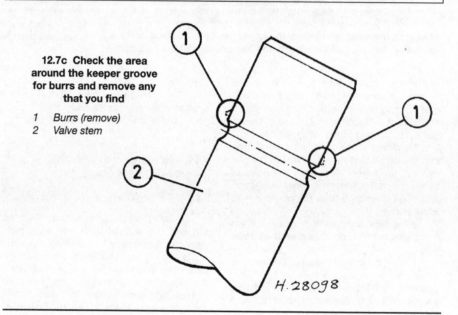

**12.7b Valve and related components**

A    Valve
B    Oil seal
C    Spring seat
D    Inner valve spring
E    Outer valve spring
F    Valve spring retainer
G    Keepers
H    Tightly wound coils

**12.7c Check the area around the keeper groove for burrs and remove any that you find**

1    Burrs (remove)
2    Valve stem

H.28098

fications. If the feeler gauge can be inserted between the head and the straightedge, the head is warped and must either be machined or, if warpage is excessive, replaced with a new one.

15    Examine the valve seats in each of the combustion chambers. If they are pitted, cracked or burned, the head will require valve service that is beyond the scope of the home mechanic. Measure the valve seat width **(see**

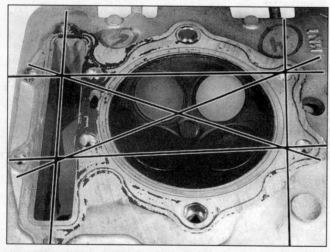

**12.14 Check the gasket surface for flatness with a straightedge and feeler gauge in the directions shown**

**12.15 Measuring valve seat width**

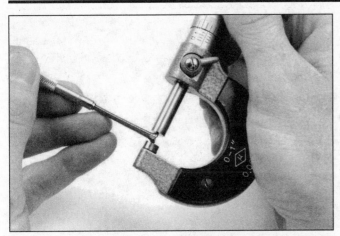

12.16 Measure the valve guide inside diameter with a hole gauge,
then measure the gauge with a micrometer

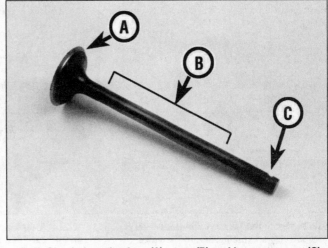

12.17 Check the valve face (A), stem (B) and keeper groove (C)
for wear and damage

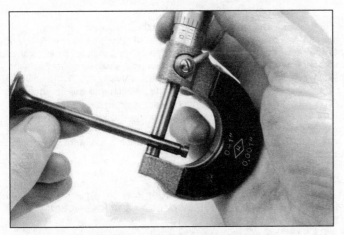

12.18a Measuring valve stem diameter

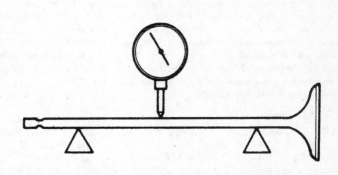

12.18b Check the valve stem for bends with a V-block (or
V-blocks, as shown here) and a dial indicator

illustration) and compare it to this Chapter's Specifications. If it is not within the specified range, or if it varies around its circumference, valve service work is required.

16   Clean the valve guides to remove any carbon buildup, then measure the inside diameters of the guides (at both ends and the center of the guide) with a small hole gauge and a micrometer (see illustration). Record the measurements for future reference. The guides are measured at the ends and at the center to determine if they are worn in a bell-mouth pattern (more wear at the ends). If they are, guide replacement is an absolute must.

17   Carefully inspect each valve face for cracks, pits and burned spots. Check the valve stem and the keeper groove area for cracks (see illustration). Rotate the valve and check for any obvious indication that it is bent. Check the end of the stem for pitting and excessive wear. The presence of any of the above conditions indicates the need for valve servicing.

18   Measure the valve stem diameter (see illustration). If the diameter is less than listed in this Chapter's Specifications, the valves will have to be replaced with new ones. Also

check the valve stem for bending. Set the valve in a V-block with a dial indicator touching the middle of the stem (see illustration). Rotate the valve and look for a reading on the gauge (which indicates a bent stem). If the stem is bent, replace the valve.

19   Check the end of each valve spring for

wear and pitting. Measure the free length (see illustration) and compare it to this Chapter's Specifications. Any springs that are shorter than specified have sagged and should not be reused. Stand the spring on a flat surface and check it for squareness (see illustration).

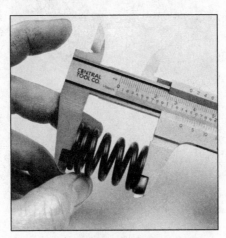

12.19a Measuring the free length of
the valve springs

12.19b Checking the valve springs
for squareness

**12.23 Apply the lapping compound very sparingly, in small dabs, to the valve face only**

**12.24a After lapping, the valve face should exhibit a uniform, unbroken contact pattern . . .**

**12.24b . . . and the seat should be the specified width with a smooth, unbroken appearance**

20  Check the spring retainers and keepers for obvious wear and cracks. Any questionable parts should not be reused, as extensive damage will occur in the event of failure during engine operation.

21  If the inspection indicates that no service work is required, the valve components can be reinstalled in the head.

## Reassembly

22  If the valve seats have been ground, the valves and seats should be lapped before installing the valves in the head to ensure a positive seal between the valves and seats. This procedure requires coarse and fine valve lapping compound (available at auto parts stores) and a valve lapping tool. If a lapping tool is not available, a piece of rubber or plastic hose can be slipped over the valve stem (after the valve has been installed in the guide) and used to turn the valve.

23  Apply a small amount of coarse lapping compound to the valve face **(see illustration)**, then slip the valve into the guide. **Note:** *Make sure the valve is installed in the correct guide and be careful not to get any lapping compound on the valve stem.*

24  Attach the lapping tool (or hose) to the valve and rotate the tool between the palms of your hands. Use a back-and-forth motion rather than a circular motion. Lift the valve off the seat and turn it at regular intervals to distribute the lapping compound properly. Continue the lapping procedure until the valve face and seat contact area is of uniform width and unbroken around the entire circumference of the valve face and seat **(see illustrations)**. Once this is accomplished, lap the valves again with fine lapping compound.

25  Carefully remove the valve from the guide and wipe off all traces of lapping compound. Use solvent to clean the valve and wipe the seat area thoroughly with a solvent soaked cloth. Repeat the procedure for the remaining valves.

26  Lay the spring seat in place in the cylinder head, then install a new valve stem

seal on the guide **(see illustration)**. Use a deep socket of the appropriate size to push the seals into place until they are properly seated. Don't twist or cock them, or they will not seal properly against the valve stems. Also, don't remove them again or they will be damaged.

27  Coat the valve stems with assembly lube or moly-based grease, then install one of them into its guide. Next, install the spring seat, springs and retainers, compress the springs and install the keepers. **Note:** *Install the springs with the tightly wound coils at the bottom (next to the spring seat). When compressing the springs with the valve spring compressor, depress them only as far as is absolutely necessary to slip the keepers into place.* Apply a small amount of grease to the keepers **(see illustration)** to help hold them in place as the pressure is released from the springs. Make certain that the keepers are securely locked in their retaining grooves.

28  Support the cylinder head on blocks so the valves can't contact the workbench top, then very gently tap each of the valve stems with a soft-faced hammer. This will help seat

the keepers in their grooves.

29  Once all of the valves have been installed in the head, check for proper valve sealing by pouring a small amount of solvent into each of the valve ports. If the solvent leaks past the valve(s) into the combustion chamber area, disassemble the valve(s) and repeat the lapping procedure, then reinstall the valve(s) and repeat the check. Repeat the procedure until a satisfactory seal is obtained.

## 13 Cylinder - removal, inspection and installation

## Removal

1  Remove the cylinder head cover, camshaft and cylinder head (see Sections 7, 9 and 10). Make sure the crankshaft is positioned at Top Dead Center (TDC).

2  Remove two small bolts securing the cylinder to the crankcase **(see illustration)**.

**12.26 Push the oil seal onto the valve guide**

**12.27 A small dab of grease will help hold the keepers in place on the valve while the spring compressor is released**

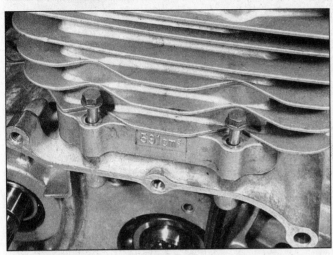

13.2 Remove the two small bolts that secure the cylinder to the crankcase . . .

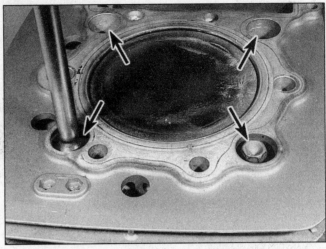

13.3 . . . then loosen the main bolts evenly, in a criss-cross pattern; you'll need an extension to reach the shorter bolts

3    Loosen the main cylinder attaching bolts in two or three stages in a criss-cross pattern (see illustration).
4    Lift the cylinder straight up, off the pis-

13.4 Lift the cylinder off the crankcase; if you're very careful, the cylinder can be installed over the rings without a ring compressor, but a compressor is recommended

ton and the rear cam chain guide (see illustration). If it's stuck, tap around its perimeter with a soft-faced hammer (but don't tap on the cooling fins or they may break). Don't

attempt to pry between the cylinder and the crankcase, as you'll ruin the sealing surfaces.
5    Locate the dowel pins (they may have come off with the cylinder or still be in the crankcase) (see illustration). Be careful not to let these drop into the engine. Stuff rags around the piston and remove the gasket and all traces of old gasket material from the surfaces of the cylinder and the crankcase.

## Inspection

Caution: Don't attempt to separate the liner from the cylinder.

6    Check the top surface of the cylinder for warpage, using the same method as for the cylinder head (see Section 12) (see illustration).
7    Check the cylinder walls carefully for scratches and score marks.
8    Using the appropriate precision measuring tools, check the cylinder's diameter at the top, center and bottom of the cylinder bore,

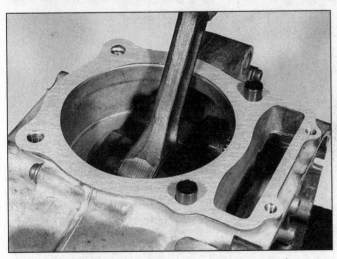

13.5  Locate the dowels and remove the base gasket

13.6  Check the cylinder top surface for warpage in the directions shown

parallel to the crankshaft axis **(see illustration)**. Next, measure the cylinder's diameter at the same three locations across the crankshaft axis. Compare the results to this Chapter's Specifications. If the cylinder walls are tapered, out-of-round, worn beyond the specified limits, or badly scuffed or scored, have the cylinder rebored and honed by a dealer service department or other motorcycle repair shop. If a rebore is done, oversize pistons and rings will be required as well. **Note:** *Honda supplies pistons in two oversizes.*

9    As an alternative, if the precision measuring tools are not available, a dealer service department or other repair shop will make the measurements and offer advice concerning servicing of the cylinder.

10    If it's in reasonably good condition and not worn to the outside of the limits, and if the piston-to-cylinder clearance can be maintained properly, then the cylinder does not have to be rebored; honing is all that is necessary.

11    To perform the honing operation you will need the proper size flexible hone with fine stones as shown in *Maintenance techniques, tools and working facilities* at the front of this book, or a "bottle brush" type hone, plenty of light oil or honing oil, some shop towels and an electric drill motor. Hold the cylinder in a vise (cushioned with soft jaws or wood blocks) when performing the honing operation. Mount the hone in the drill motor, compress the stones and slip the hone into the cylinder. Lubricate the cylinder thoroughly, turn on the drill and move the hone up and down in the cylinder at a pace which will produce a fine crosshatch pattern on the cylinder wall with the crosshatch lines intersecting at approximately a 60-degree angle. Be sure to use plenty of lubricant and do not take off any more material than is absolutely necessary to produce the desired effect. Do not withdraw the hone from the cylinder while it is running. Instead, shut off the drill and continue moving the hone up and down in the cylinder until it comes to a complete

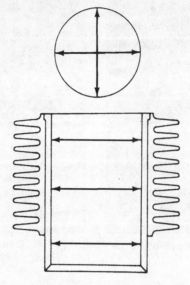

**13.8 Measure the cylinder diameter in two directions, at top, center and bottom of the ring travel**

stop, then compress the stones and withdraw the hone. Wipe the oil out of the cylinder. Remember, do not remove too much material from the cylinder wall. If you do not have the tools, or do not desire to perform the honing operation, a dealer service department or other repair shop will generally do it for a reasonable fee.

12    Next, the cylinder must be thoroughly washed with warm soapy water to remove all traces of the abrasive grit produced during the honing operation. Be sure to run a brush through the bolt holes and flush them with running water. After rinsing, dry the cylinder thoroughly and apply a coat of light, rust-preventative oil to all machined surfaces.

## Installation

13    Lubricate the cylinder bore with plenty of clean engine oil. Apply a thin film of moly-

based grease to the piston skirt.

14    Install the dowel pins, then lower a new cylinder base gasket over them **(see illustration 13.5)**.

15    Install the cylinder over the studs and carefully lower it down until the piston crown fits into the cylinder liner **(see illustration 13.4)**. Squeeze the piston rings with your fingers to compress them enough to slip into the cylinder as it's lowered. If necessary, use a large hose clamp to compress the rings. While doing this, pull the camshaft chain up, using a hooked tool or a piece of stiff wire. Push down on the cylinder, making sure the piston doesn't get cocked sideways, until the bottom of the cylinder liner slides down past the piston rings. A wood or plastic hammer handle can be used to gently tap the cylinder down, but don't use too much force or the piston will be damaged.

16    Remove the piston ring compressor or hose clamp, being careful not to scratch the piston.

17    The remainder of installation is the reverse of the removal steps.

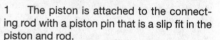

### 14 Piston - removal, inspection and installation

1    The piston is attached to the connecting rod with a piston pin that is a slip fit in the piston and rod.

2    Before removing the piston from the rod, stuff a clean shop towel into the crankcase hole, around the connecting rod. This will prevent the circlips from falling into the crankcase if they are inadvertently dropped.

## Removal

3    The piston should have an IN mark on its crown that goes toward the intake (rear) side of the engine **(see illustration)**. If this mark is not visible due to carbon buildup, scribe an arrow into the piston crown before

**14.3a  The IN mark on top of the piston faces the intake (rear) side of the engine**

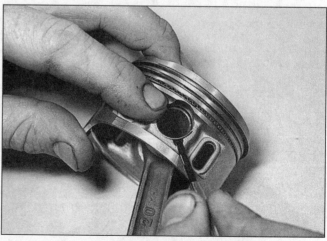

**14.3b  Wear eye protection and pry the circlip out of its groove with a pointed tool**

14.4a Push the piston pin part way out, then pull it the rest of the way

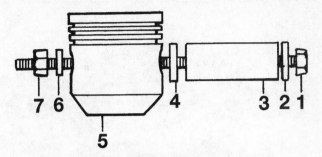

14.4b The piston pin should come out with hand pressure - if it doesn't, this removal tool can be fabricated from readily available parts

| 1 | Bolt | 4 | Padding * | 6 | Washer ** |
|---|------|---|-----------|---|-----------|
| 2 | Washer | 5 | Piston | 7 | Nut ** |
| 3 | Pipe * | | | | |

*   Large enough for piston pin to fit inside
**  Small enough to fit through the pin bore in the piston

removal. Support the piston and pry the circlip out with a pointed tool (see illustration).

 **Warning: Wear eye protection.**

4    Push the piston pin out from the opposite end to free the piston from the rod (see illustration). You may have to deburr the area around the groove to enable the pin to slide out (use a triangular file for this procedure). If the pin won't come out, you can fabricate a piston pin removal tool from a long bolt, a nut, a piece of tubing and washers (see illustration).

## Inspection

5    Before the inspection process can be carried out, the pistons must be cleaned and the old piston rings removed.
6    Using a piston ring removal and installation tool, carefully remove the rings from the pistons (see illustration). Do not nick or gouge the pistons in the process.
7    Scrape all traces of carbon from the

tops of the pistons. A hand-held wire brush or a piece of fine emery cloth can be used once the majority of the deposits have been scraped away. Do not, under any circumstances, use a wire brush mounted in a drill motor to remove deposits from the pistons; the piston material is soft and will be eroded away by the wire brush.
8    Use a piston ring groove cleaning tool to remove any carbon deposits from the ring grooves. If a tool is not available, a piece broken off the old ring will do the job. Be very careful to remove only the carbon deposits. Do not remove any metal and do not nick or gouge the sides of the ring grooves.
9    Once the deposits have been removed, clean the pistons with solvent and dry them thoroughly. Make sure the oil return holes below the oil ring grooves are clear.
10   If the pistons are not damaged or worn excessively and if the cylinders are not rebored, new pistons will not be necessary. Normal piston wear appears as even, vertical wear on the thrust surfaces of the piston and slight looseness of the top ring in its groove. New piston rings, on the other hand, should

always be used when an engine is rebuilt.
11   Carefully inspect each piston for cracks around the skirt, at the pin bosses and at the ring lands.
12   Look for scoring and scuffing on the thrust faces of the skirt, holes in the piston crown and burned areas at the edge of the crown. If the skirt is scored or scuffed, the engine may have been suffering from overheating and/or abnormal combustion, which caused excessively high operating temperatures. The oil pump should be checked thoroughly. A hole in the piston crown, an extreme to be sure, is an indication that abnormal combustion (pre-ignition) was occurring. Burned areas at the edge of the piston crown are usually evidence of spark knock (detonation). If any of the above problems exist, the causes must be corrected or the damage will occur again.
13   Measure the piston ring-to-groove clearance (side clearance) by laying a new piston ring in the ring groove and slipping a feeler gauge in beside it (see illustration). Check the clearance at three or four locations around the groove. Be sure to use the

14.6 Remove the piston rings with a ring removal and installation tool

14.13 Measure the piston ring-to-groove clearance with a feeler gauge

14.14 Measure the piston diameter with a micrometer

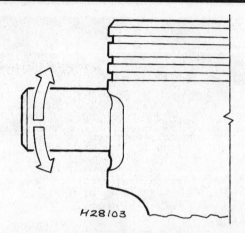

H28103

14.15 Slip the pin into the piston and try to wiggle it back-and-forth; if it's loose, replace the piston and pin

correct ring for each groove; they are different. If the clearance is greater than specified, a new piston will have to be used when the engine is reassembled.

14    Check the piston-to-bore clearance by measuring the bore (see Section 13) and the piston diameter **(see illustration)**. Measure the piston across the skirt on the thrust faces at a 90-degree angle to the piston pin, at the specified distance up from the bottom of the skirt. Subtract the piston diameter from the bore diameter to obtain the clearance. If it is greater than specified, the cylinder will have to be rebored and a new oversized piston and rings installed. If the appropriate precision measuring tools are not available, the piston-to-cylinder clearance can be obtained, though not quite as accurately, using feeler gauge stock. Feeler gauge stock comes in 12-inch lengths and various thicknesses and is generally available at auto parts stores. To check the clearance, slip a piece of feeler gauge stock of the same thickness as the specified piston clearance into the cylinder along with the appropriate piston. The cylinder should be upside down and the piston must be positioned exactly as

it normally would be. Place the feeler gauge between the piston and cylinder on one of the thrust faces (90-degrees to the piston pin bore). The piston should slip through the cylinder (with the feeler gauge in place) with moderate pressure. If it falls through, or slides through easily, the clearance is excessive and a new piston will be required. If the piston binds at the lower end of the cylinder and is loose toward the top, the cylinder is tapered, and if tight spots are encountered as the piston/feeler gauge is rotated in the cylinder, the cylinder is out-of-round. Be sure to have the cylinder and piston checked by a dealer service department or a repair shop to confirm your findings before purchasing new parts.

15    Apply clean engine oil to the pin, insert it into the piston and check for freeplay by rocking the pin back-and-forth **(see illustration)**. If the pin is loose, a new piston and possibly a new pin must be installed.

16    Repeat Step 15, this time inserting the piston pin into the connecting rod **(see illustration)**. If the pin is loose, measure the pin diameter and the pin bore in the rod (or have this done by a dealer service depart-

ment or other repair shop). A worn pin can be replaced separately; if the rod bore is worn, the rod and crankshaft must be replaced as an assembly.

17    Refer to Section 15 and install the rings on the pistons.

### Installation

18    Install the piston with its IN mark toward the intake side (rear) of the engine. Lubricate the pin and the rod bore with moly-based grease. Install a new circlips in the groove in one side of the piston (don't reuse the old circlips). Push the pin into position from the opposite side and install another new circlip. Compress the circlips only enough for them to fit in the piston. Make sure the clips are properly seated in the grooves **(see illustration)**.

### 15 Piston rings - installation

1    Before installing the new piston rings, the ring end gaps must be checked.

2    Insert the top (No. 1) ring into the bottom of the cylinder and square it up with the cylinder walls by pushing it in with the top of the piston. The ring should be about one-half inch above the bottom edge of the cylinder. To measure the end gap, slip a feeler gauge between the ends of the ring **(see illustration)** and compare the measurement to the Specifications.

3    If the gap is larger or smaller than specified, double check to make sure that you have the correct rings before proceeding.

4    If the gap is too small, it must be enlarged or the ring ends may come in contact with each other during engine operation, which can cause serious damage. The end gap can be increased by filing the ring ends very carefully with a fine file **(see illustration)**. When performing this operation, file only from the outside in.

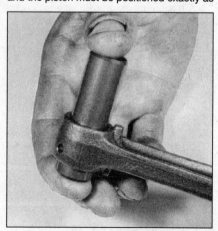

14.16 Slip the piston pin into the rod and try to rock it back-and-forth to check for looseness

14.18 Make sure both piston pin circlips are securely seated in their grooves

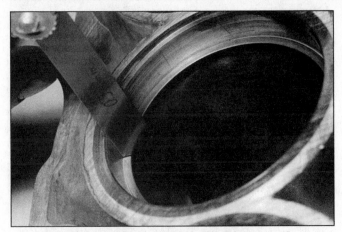

15.2  Check the piston ring end gap with a feeler gauge at the bottom of the cylinder

15.4  If the end gap is too small, clamp a file in a vise and file the ring ends (from the outside in only) to enlarge the gap slightly

15.7a  Installing the oil ring expander - make sure the ends don't overlap

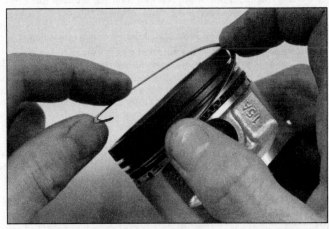

15.7b  Installing an oil ring side rail - don't use a ring installation tool to do this

5   Repeat the procedure for the second compression ring and oil ring.

6   Once the ring end gaps have been checked/corrected, the rings can be installed on the piston.

7   The oil control ring (lowest on the piston) is installed first. It is composed of three separate components. Slip the spacer into the groove, then install the upper side rail **(see illustrations)**. Do not use a piston ring installation tool on the oil ring side rails as they may be damaged. Instead, place one end of the side rail into the groove between the spacer expander and the ring land. Hold it firmly in place and slide a finger around the piston while pushing the rail into the groove (taking care not to cut your fingers on the sharp edges). Next, install the lower side rail in the same manner.

8   After the three oil ring components have been installed, check to make sure that both the upper and lower side rails can be turned smoothly in the ring groove.

9   Install the no. 2 (middle) ring next. It can be readily distinguished from the top ring by its cross-section shape **(see illustration 15.7c)**. Do not mix the top and middle rings.

15.7c  Ring details

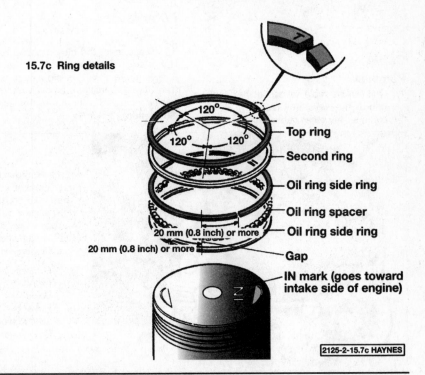

Top ring
Second ring
Oil ring side ring
Oil ring spacer
Oil ring side ring
Gap
IN mark (goes toward intake side of engine)

20 mm (0.8 inch) or more
20 mm (0.8 inch) or more

2125-2-15.7c HAYNES

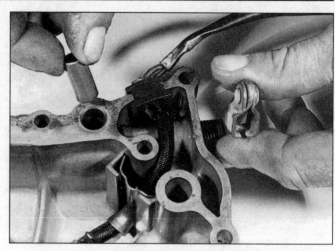

**16.2 Loosen the locknut and adjusting nut (left arrow) and slip the cable out of the bracket, then slip it out of the lifter lever (right arrow)**

**16.6 Pull out the retaining pin and slide the lifter lever out of the engine cover**

10   To avoid breaking the ring, use a piston ring installation tool and make sure that the identification mark is facing up **(see illustration 15.7c)**. Fit the ring into the middle groove on the piston. Do not expand the ring any more than is necessary to slide it into place.

11   Finally, install the no. 1 (top) ring in the same manner. Make sure the identifying mark is facing up. Be very careful not to confuse the top and second rings.

12   Once the rings have been properly installed, stagger the end gaps, including those of the oil ring side rails **(see illustration 15.7c)**.

## 16 Clutch - removal, inspection and installation

### Cable

#### Removal

1   Loosen the cable adjuster at the handlebar grip all the way (see Chapter 1). Rotate the cable so the inner cable aligns with the slot in the lever, then slip the cable end fitting out of the lever.

2   Loosen the locknut and adjusting nut at the engine bracket **(see illustration)**. Slip the cable out of the bracket, then disengage it from the lifter lever in the left engine cover.

#### Inspection

3   Slide the inner cable back and forth in the housing and make sure it moves freely. If it doesn't, try lubricating it as described in Chapter 1. If that doesn't help, replace the cable.

#### Installation

4   Installation is the reverse of the removal steps. Refer to Chapter 1 and adjust clutch freeplay.

### Lifter lever

#### Removal

5   Disconnect the clutch cable from the lifter lever as described above.

6   Remove the right-side engine cover (see Step 11). Inside the cover, remove the retaining pin and pull out the lifter lever **(see illustration)**.

#### Inspection

7   Check for visible wear or damage at the contact points of the lifter lever and push-rod. Replace any parts that show problems. Replace the lifter shaft O-ring in the engine cover whenever it's removed.

#### Installation

8   Installation is the reverse of the removal steps. Refill the engine oil and adjust the clutch (see Chapter 1).

### Clutch

#### Removal

9   Remove the kickstarter pedal (all except XR650L models, see Section 21) and the lower oil pipe bolt (see Section 22).

10   Remove the right footpeg (600R models) and the skid bars (see Chapter 8) and the brake pedal (see Chapter 7).

11   Remove the bolts and nuts and take off the right-side engine cover **(see illustration)**.

12   Refer to the accompanying illustrations to remove the clutch components **(see illustrations)**.

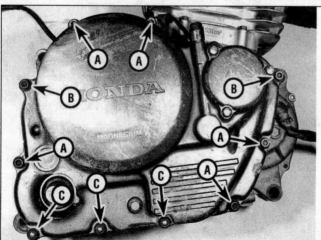

**16.11 Remove the cover bolts and nuts and take off the right engine cover to expose the clutch (600R model shown, 650L similar)**

a)   Cover bolts (without dowels)
b)   Cover bolts (with dowels)
c)   Cover nuts

**16.12a Remove the spring bolts, washers, springs and pressure plate . . .**

16.12b . . . lift out the push piece . . .

16.12c . . . the clutch pushrod and the outermost friction plate . . .

16.12d . . . the outermost metal plate, then the remaining friction and metal plates

16.12e If you're working on a 1985 through 1987 model, bend back the lockwasher tab; If you're working on a 1988 or later model (shown), bend back the staked portion of the locknut . . .

16.12f . . . then unscrew the locknut and remove the washer; if there's an OUT SIDE mark on the washer, it faces away from the engine on installation

16.12g Pull off the clutch center . . .

16.12h . . . the thrust washer . . .

16.12i . . . the clutch housing . . .

16.12j . . . and the clutch housing bushing (600R model shown)

16.13 Check the ball bearing in the center of the pressure plate for roughness, looseness or noise; check the friction surface (arrow) for scoring

## Inspection

13   Check the friction surface on the pressure plate for scoring or wear (see illustration). Replace the pressure plate if any defects are found. Rotate the release bearing and check it for rough, loose or noisy operation. If the bearing's condition is in doubt, push it out of the pressure plate and push in a new one.

14   Check the edges of the slots in the clutch housing for indentations made by the friction plate tabs (see illustration). If the indentations are deep they can prevent clutch release, so the housing should be replaced with a new one. If the indentations can be removed easily with a file, the life of the housing can be prolonged to an extent. Also, check the driven gear teeth for cracks, chips and excessive wear and the springs on the back side (if equipped) for breakage. If the gear is worn or damaged or the springs are broken, the clutch housing must be replaced with a new one.

15   Check the bearing surface in the center of the clutch housing for score marks, scratches and excessive wear (see illustration 16.14). Measure the inside diameter of the bearing surface, the inside and outside diameters of the clutch housing bushing and the bushing's mounting surface on the transmission mainshaft. Compare these to the values listed in this Chapter's Specifications. Replace any parts worn beyond the service

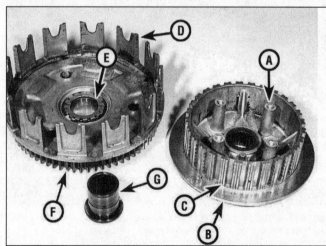

16.14 Clutch inspection points

A   Clutch center posts
B   Clutch center friction surface
C   Clutch center splines
D   Clutch housing slots
E   Clutch housing bushing surface
F   Driven gear
G   Clutch housing bushing

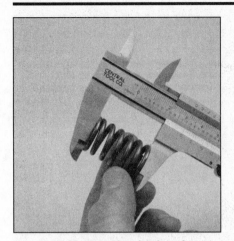

**16.17  Measure the clutch spring free length**

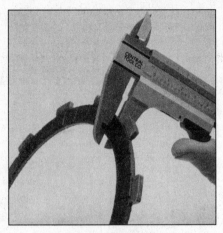

**16.18  Measure the thickness of the friction plates**

**16.19  Check the metal plates for warpage**

limits. If the bushing mounting surface is worn excessively, the mainshaft will have to be replaced.

16   Check the clutch center's friction surface and slots for scoring, wear and indentations **(see illustration 16.14)**. Also check the splines in the middle of the clutch center. Replace the clutch center if problems are found.

17   Measure the free length of the clutch springs **(see illustration)** and compare the results to this Chapter's Specifications. If the springs have sagged, or if cracks are noted, replace them with new ones as a set.

18   If the lining material of the friction plates smells burnt or if it is glazed, new parts are required. If the metal clutch plates are scored or discolored, they must be replaced with new ones. Measure the thickness of the friction plates **(see illustration)** and replace with new parts any friction plates that are worn.

19   Lay the metal plates, one at a time, on a perfectly flat surface (such as a piece of plate glass) and check for warpage by trying to slip a feeler gauge between the flat surface and the plate **(see illustration)**. The feeler gauge

should be the same thickness as the maximum warp listed in this Chapter's Specifications. Do this at several places around the plate's circumference. If the feeler gauge can be slipped under the plate, it is warped and should be replaced with a new one.

20   Check the tabs on the friction plates for excessive wear and mushroomed edges. They can be cleaned up with a file if the deformation is not severe. Check the friction plates for warpage as described in Step 19.

21   Inside the right engine cover, remove the thrust washer (if it didn't stay on the kickstarter shaft) and check the kickstarter shaft needle bearing and seal **(see illustration)**. Replace the seal if it has been leaking and replace the needle bearing if it's worn or damaged. If you're working on a bike equipped with a kickstarter decompressor cable, you'll need to remove the snap-ring, lifter lever, spring and lifter cam (mounted inside the cover) for access to the seal.

22   Also inside the right engine cover, check the primary drive gear shaft seal for wear **(see illustration)**. If necessary, remove the snap-ring and replace it. The oil passage

O-ring should be replaced whenever the cover is removed (it may have come off with the cover or stayed on the oil pump sleeve).

**Installation**

23   Installation is the reverse of the removal steps, with the following additions:

a) *If you're working on a 1983 or 1984 model, install the lockwasher with its OUT SIDE mark facing away from the engine, then install the clutch nut and tighten it to the torque listed in this Chapter's Specifications.*

b) *If you're working on a 1985 through 1987 model, install a new lockwasher with its small round hole over the post on the clutch housing. Install the clutch nut and tighten it to the torque listed in this Chapter's Specifications, then bend a lockwasher tab up against one of the flats on the nut.*

c) *If you're working on a 1988 or later model, install a new clutch nut and stake it into the notch on the mainshaft* **(see illustration)**.

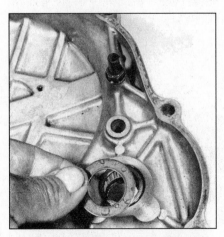

**16.21  Remove the thrust washer and inspect the kickstarter shaft bearing**

**16.22  Inspect the seal for the primary drive gear shaft and replace the oil passage O-ring**

**16.23a  Stake the locknut with a hammer and punch**

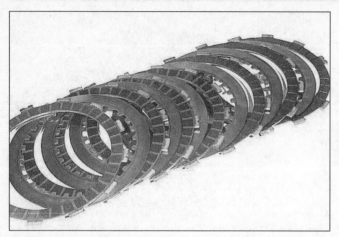

16.23b  There's a metal plate between each pair of friction plates; friction plates go on first and last

17.2  Remove the oil pump gear

17.3a  Remove the oil pipe nut (A) and bolt (B); the two remaining bolts (C) secure the oil pump to the crankcase

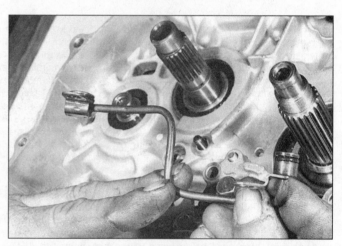

17.3b  Work the fittings free of the engine and take the pipe off; there's an O-ring at each end that should be replaced whenever the pipe is removed

d)  Coat the friction plates with clean engine oil before you install them.
e)  Install a friction plate, then alternate the remaining metal and friction plates until they're all installed. Friction plates go on first and last, so the friction material contacts the metal surfaces of the clutch center and the pressure plate (see illustration).

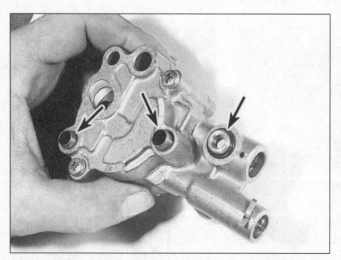

17.4  Pull the oil pipe off the engine and locate the dowels (left arrows) and the sleeve and O-ring (right arrow)

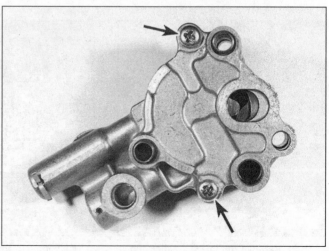

17.5a  Remove the oil pump cover screws . . .

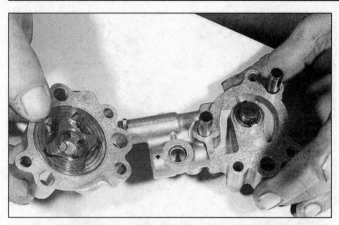

17.5b  . . . then lift off the housing and scavenge rotors

17.6a  Push out the drive pin and remove the washer . . .

## 17 Oil pump and internal pipe - removal, inspection and installation

**Note:** *The oil pump can be removed with the engine in the frame.*

### Removal

1  Remove the right engine cover and clutch (see Section 16). On XR650L models, remove the oil pump drive gear, pulse generator rotor and the primary drive gear (see Section 18).

2  Slide the oil pump gear off its shaft **(see illustration)**.

3  Remove the oil pipe mounting nut and bolt and take the pipe off the engine, together with the O-rings **(see illustrations)**.

4  Remove the two remaining mounting bolts, then pull the pump out of the engine and remove the sleeve and O-ring **(see illustration)**. Note the locations of the two dowels.

### Inspection

5  Remove the screws (1983 through 1992 models) or bolts (1993 and later models) and lift off the pump cover with its rotors

17.6b  . . . then remove the remaining housing and rotors

**(see illustrations).**

6  Pull the drive pin and remove the washer and shaft, then remove the remaining set of rotors **(see illustrations)**.

7  Wash all the components in solvent, then dry them off. Check the pump body, the rotors, the drive gear and the covers for scoring and wear. If any damage or uneven or excessive wear is evident, replace the pump. If you are rebuilding the engine, it's a good idea to install a new oil pump.

8  Place the rotors in the pump body. Measure the clearance between the outer rotor and body, and between the inner and outer rotors, with a feeler gauge **(see illustrations)**. If any of the clearances are beyond the limits listed in this Chapter's Specifications, replace the pump.

9  Place a straightedge across the outer pump body and rotors and measure the gap with a feeler gauge **(see illustration)**. If the clearance is beyond the limits listed in this

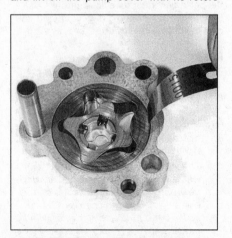

17.8a  Measure the clearance between the outer rotor and body . . .

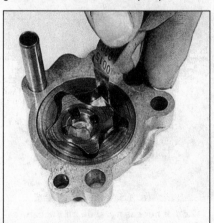

17.8b  . . . between the inner and outer rotors . . .

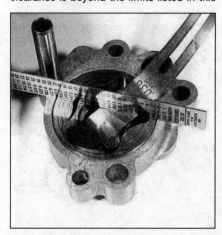

17.9  . . . and between the thin rotors and a straightedge laid across the pump body

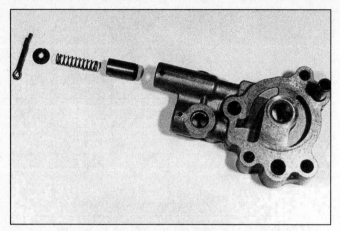

**17.11 Remove the cotter pin, washer, spring and check valve**

**18.2 Wedge a rag between the primary drive and driven gears and loosen the locknut**

Chapter's Specifications, replace the pump.
10   To check the end clearance of the inner rotors and pump, you'll need some Plastigage. Place the rotors in the pump. Cut a strip of Plastigage, lay it across the rotors, then install the pump cover and tighten the screws or bolts. Remove the screws or bolts, lift off the cover, and measure the width of

**18.5 Remove the pulse generator rotor and the pulse generator**

**18.6a Slide the primary drive gear off**

the crushed Plastigage with the scale on the envelope it comes in. If the end clearance is beyond the limit listed in this Chapter's Specifications, replace the pump.
11   Remove the cotter pin, washer, spring and relief valve **(see illustration)**. If any of the parts are damaged or if the relief valve or its bore are scored, replace the pump. If you're planning to reuse the pump, use a new cotter pin when you install the relief valve.
12   Reassemble the pump by reversing the disassembly steps, with the following additions:

a) *Before installing the covers, pack the cavities between the rotors with petroleum jelly - this will ensure the pump develops suction quickly and begins oil circulation as soon as the engine is started.*
b) *Tighten the cover screws or bolts securely.*

### Installation

13   Installation is the reverse of removal, with the following additions:

**18.6b  If necessary, slide off the cam chain sprocket; the wide notch in the sprocket aligns with the wide spline on the crankshaft**

a) *Install new O-rings on the pump sleeve and pipe fittings* **(see illustration 17.3b and 17.4)**.
b) *Tighten the oil pump mounting screws or bolts securely, but don't overtighten them.*

## 18 Primary drive gear - removal, inspection and installation

### Removal

1   Remove the right engine cover (see Section 16).
2   Wedge a rag between the teeth of the primary drive gear and the primary driven gear on the clutch housing. Loosen the primary drive gear locknut **(see illustration)**, Remove the clutch (see Section 16).
3   On 600R models, remove the oil pump (see Section 17).
4   Remove the locknut, the dished washer and the oil pump drive gear.
5   Remove the pulse generator rotor and the pulse generator **(see illustration)**.
6   Slide the primary drive gear off the crankshaft **(see illustrations)**.

### Inspection

7   Check the drive gear for obvious damage such as chipped or broken teeth. Replace it if any of these problems are found.

### Installation

8   Installation is the reverse of the removal steps, with the following additions:

a) *The wide spline on the crankshaft aligns with a wide groove on the primary drive gear and pulse generator rotor so they can only be installed one way.*
b) *Install the pulse generator rotor with its tab outward (away from the engine)* **(see illustration)**.

**18.8  The tab on the pulse generator rotor faces away from the engine**

**19.1  If you don't see a punch mark on the pedal and the end of the spindle, make your own**

c) *Install the lockwasher with its OUT SIDE mark away from the engine.*
d) *Tighten the locknut to the torque listed in this Chapter's Specifications.*
e) *Check the engine oil level and add some, if necessary (see Chapter 1).*

**19.4  The smaller seal in the left engine cover is for the shift shaft; the other is for the transmission countershaft**

## 19 External shift mechanism - removal, inspection and installation

### Shift pedal
#### Removal
1    Look for alignment marks on the end of the shift pedal and shift shaft **(see illustration)**. If they aren't visible, make your own marks with a sharp punch.
2    Remove the shift pedal pinch bolt and slide the pedal off the shaft.

#### Inspection
3    Check the shift pedal for wear or damage such as bending. Check the splines on the shift pedal and shaft for stripping or step wear. Replace the pedal or shaft if these problems are found.
4    Check the shift shaft seal for signs of oil leakage **(see illustration)**. If it has been leaking, refer to Chapter 5 and remove the left engine cover. Pry the seal out of the cover and install a new one. You may be able to push the seal in with your thumbs; if not, tap

it in with a hammer and block of wood or a socket the same diameter as the seal.

#### Installation
5    Line up the punch marks, install the shift pedal and tighten the pinch bolt securely.

### External shift linkage
6    Shift linkage components accessible without splitting the crankcase include the stopper arm and cam plate.

#### Removal
7    Remove the shift pedal as previously described.
8    If you're working on a 600R model, remove the clutch (see Section 16).
9    Note how the stopper arm spring presses against the case and hooks around the stopper arm **(see illustration)**. Pull the stopper arm away from the shift drum cam, then loosen the stopper arm bolt and release the spring tension **(see illustration)**. Remove the bolt and take the stopper arm and spring off the crankcase.
10    Remove the bolt from the shift drum cam and take the cam off the drum **(see illustration 19.9b)**.

**19.9a  Note how the ends of the spring are positioned (A), then loosen the stopper arm bolt (B) . . .**

**19.9b  . . . release the spring tension and remove the bolt; the shift drum cam bolt can then be removed**

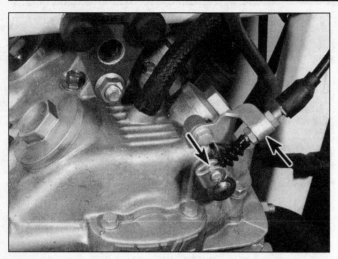

20.1 Loosen the locknuts and slip the cable out of the bracket (right arrow), then rotate the cable to align it with the slot in the lever (left arrow) and slide it sideways out of the lever

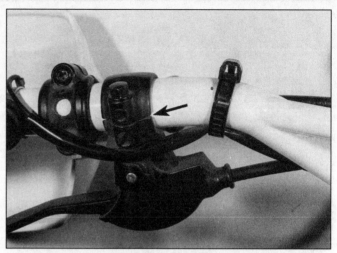

20.2 The decompressor lever is secured to the handlebar by a clamp; on installation, align the split in the clamp with the punch mark on the handlebar

## Inspection

11   Check all parts for visible wear or damage and replace any parts that show problems.

## Installation

12   Position the shift drum cam on the shift drum, aligning the hole in the back of the cam with the pin on the shift drum. Apply non-permanent thread locking agent to the threads of the bolt, then tighten it to the torque listed in this Chapter's Specifications.
13   Position the spring on the stopper arm, then install the stopper arm on the engine and tighten its bolt loosely (see illustration 19.9b). Pull up the stopper arm and engage its roller end with the neutral notch in the shift drum cam (see illustration 19.9a). Tighten the bolt to the torque listed in this Chapter's Specifications.
14   The remainder of installation is the reverse of the removal steps.
15   Check the engine oil level and add some, if necessary (see Chapter 1).

### 20  Decompressor lever and cable - removal and installation

1    At the engine, loosen the cable locknuts and slip the cable out of the bracket (see illustration). Turn the cable end to align the cable with the groove in the decompression lever, then slip it sideways out of the lever.
2    At the left handlebar, loosen the pinch bolt on the decompressor lever (see illustration). Slide the lever toward the center of the bike to create slack in the cable. Pull back the rubber boot, rotate the cable to align it with the slot in the lever and detach the cable from the lever.
3    Note carefully how the cable is routed and detach it from any retainers.
4    To remove the lever, remove the left handgrip and clutch lever (see Chapter 6) and the engine stop button or switch (see Chapter 5).
5    Installation is the reverse of the removal

steps, with the following additions:
a)  Align the parting line of the decompressor lever bracket with the punch mark on the handlebar (see illustration 20.2).
b)  Adjust the decompressor lever freeplay (see Chapter 1).

### 21  Kickstarter - removal, inspection and installation

## Removal

### Pedal

1    The kickstarter pedal is accessible from outside the engine. The kickstarter mechanism can be reached by removing the right engine cover (see Section 16).
2    To remove the pedal from the shaft, remove its mounting screw and slip the pedal off (see illustration).
3    Look for a punch mark on the end of the

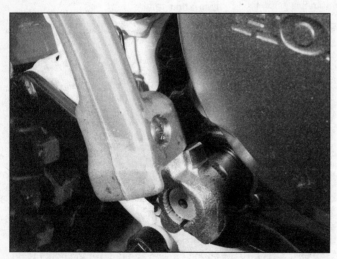

21.2  The pedal is secured to the lever by a screw

21.3  Look for alignment marks on the pedal and shaft; if you don't see them, make a punch mark on the end of the shaft that aligns with the slit in the pedal

21.5a  With the clutch removed, the kickstarter idler gear can be pulled off its shaft . . .

21.5b . . . followed by the bushing

kickstarter spindle **(see illustration)**. If you can't see one, make your own to align with the slit in the pedal shaft. Loosen the pinch bolt and slide the pedal off the spindle.

## Kickstarter mechanism

4    Remove the kickstarter pedal (see Step 3) and the right engine cover (see Section 16). If you're planning to remove the kickstarter idler gear, you'll need to remove the clutch (see Section 16).

5    Slide the kickstarter idler gear off its shaft, then remove its bushing **(see illustrations)**.

6    Slip the kickstarter pedal back onto the shaft. Turn the pedal counterclockwise until the ratchet pawl clears the guide, then pull the kickstarter out of the engine **(see illustrations)**. Pull the kickstarter out until the pawl clears the guide, then slowly release the spring tension and pull the pedal off the shaft.

7    If the thrust washer for the needle bearing in the right engine cover didn't come off the cover, remove it from the kickstarter shaft **(see illustration)**. If you're working on an XL600R, remove the decompressor

21.6a  Turn the kickstarter so the tab . . .

21.6b  . . . clears the guide on the crankcase (kickstarter removed for clarity)

cam, cam spring, spring seat and snap-ring, carefully noting how the parts are arranged. If you're working on an XR600R, note the position of the remaining washer; it can be removed now or left where it is for the time being.

8    Unhook the return spring from its lug on the crankcase casting and pull the kickstarter assembly out of the engine **(see illustration)**.

21.7  Slide the washer off the shaft; on installation, its OUT SIDE mark faces away from the engine

21.8  The return spring hooks into the crankcase

21.9a  The straight end of the return spring . . .

21.9b  . . . fits into this hole in the shaft

21.10  Remove the snap-ring (arrow), washer or bushing and the kickstarter gear from the shaft

9    Disengage the return spring from the hole in the shaft (see illustrations). Slide off the return spring and collar, spring seat, ratchet spring and ratchet.
10   Remove the snap-ring (see illustration). Slide off the washer (early models) or

flange bushing (later models) and the pinion gear.

### Inspection
11   Check all parts for wear or damage, paying special attention to the teeth on the ratchet and the matching teeth on the pinion gear. Replace worn or damaged parts.
12   Measure the inside diameter of the pinion gear (early models) or the bushing (later models) and the outside diameter of the shaft where the pinion rides. Replace any parts that are worn beyond the limit listed in this Chapter's Specifications.

### Installation
#### Kickstarter mechanism
13   Installation is the reverse of the removal steps, with the following additions:
 a) Use a new snap-ring (two new snap-rings on XL600R models).
 b) Align the punch marks on the ratchet and shaft (see illustration).
 c) Place the end of the return spring in the notch of the collar (see illustration).

### Pedal
14   Slip the pedal onto the kickstarter spindle, aligning the marks. Install the pinch bolt and tighten it securely.

## 22 External oil line and hoses - removal and installation

### External oil line
1    Loosen the union bolt at the upper rear corner of the cylinder head (see illustration). Unbolt the retainer, then remove the union bolt and its two sealing washers.
2    Unbolt the bracket from the cylinder head (see illustration 22.1).
3    Follow the oil line to the lower union bolt, then remove the bolt and its two sealing washers (see illustration). Lift the oil line off the engine.
4    Installation is the reverse of the removal

21.13a  Align the punch marks on the shaft and ratchet

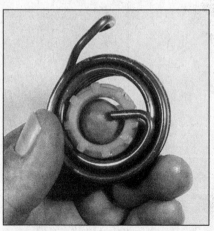

21.13b  The straight end of the return spring fits into this notch in the collar

22.1  At the upper end of the pipe, remove the union bolt and sealing washers (upper arrow) and the bracket (lower arrow) . . .

22.3  . . . and at the lower end of the pipe, remove the union bolt - on installation, use new sealing washers on both union bolts and place the lower end of the pipe against the stop on the crankcase (arrow); this prevents the pipe from being twisted when the union bolt is tightened

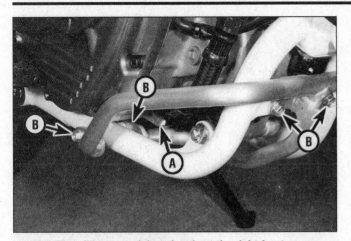

**22.7  The oil hose retaining plate is at the right front corner of the crankcase**

| A | Oil hose retaining plate | B | Skid bar bolts |

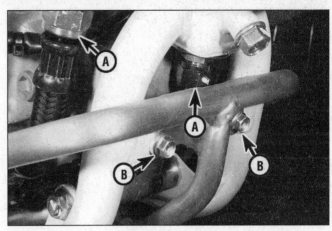

**22.8  Unscrew the fittings to detach the upper ends of the oil hoses**

| A | Oil hose fittings | B | Skid bar bolts |

steps, with the following additions:

a) *Install the light-colored union bolt (with the small oil hole) at the upper end of the oil line. Install the dark-colored union bolt (with the large oil hole) at the lower end of the oil line.*

b) *Use a new sealing washer on each side of the union bolt fittings.*

c) *Tighten the union bolts to the torque listed in this Chapter's Specifications.*

## Oil hoses

5    There are two oil hoses connected to the lower front of the engine. The shorter hose is the inlet from the oil reservoir (in the upper frame member) to the engine. The longer hose returns oil from the engine to the oil tank.

6    Drain the engine oil (see Chapter 1).

7    Unbolt the hose mounting plate at the crankcase **(see illustration)**. Pull out the two hoses and their O-rings.

8    Unscrew the fitting at the upper end of each hose from the frame **(see illustration)**.

9    Installation is the reverse of the removal steps, with the following addition:

a) *Use new O-rings at the lower ends of the hoses.*

b) *Tighten the nuts at the upper ends of the hoses to the torque listed in this Chapter's Specifications.*

### 23  Crankcase - disassembly and reassembly

1    To examine and repair or replace the crankshaft, connecting rod, balancer, bearings and transmission components, the crankcase must be split into two parts.

## Disassembly

2    Remove the engine from the motorcycle (see Section 5).

3    Remove the alternator rotor (see Chapter 5). If you're working on a 650L model,

remove the starter motor, reduction gear and shaft and the starter idler gear and shaft (see Chapter 5)

4    Loosen the primary drive gear locknut (see Section 18), then remove the clutch (see Section 16).

5    Remove the external shift mechanism (see Section 19).

6    Remove the oil pump (see Section 17).

7    Remove the cylinder head cover, cam chain tensioner, camshaft, cylinder head, cylinder, primary drive gear, cam chain and sprocket, chain guides and piston (see Sections 7, 8, 9, 10, 13, 14 and 18).

8    Remove the kickstarter (see Section 21).

9    Check carefully to make sure there aren't any remaining components that attach the halves of the crankcase together.

10    Loosen the crankcase bolts in the right side of the crankcase evenly in two or three stages, then remove them **(see illustration)**. Do the same to remove the bolts from the other side of the crankcase **(see illustration)**.

**23.10a  Remove two bolts from the right side of the crankcase . . .**

**23.10b  . . . and remove the remaining bolts from the left side**

| A | Crankcase bolts | B | Dowel locations |

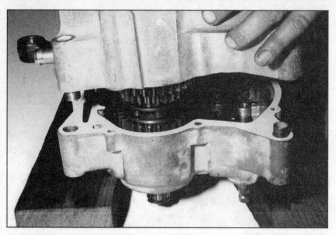

**23.11 Support the crankcase on wood blocks so it isn't resting on the shift or transmission shafts, then lift the right case half off the left half**

**23.17a Coat the mating surfaces with sealant . . .**

11   Place the crankcase with its left side down on a pair of wood blocks so the shift pedal shaft and transmission countershaft can extend downward. Carefully pry the crankcase apart and lift the right half off the left half **(see illustration)**. Don't pry against the mating surfaces or they'll develop leaks.

12   Locate the three crankcase dowels **(see illustration 23.10b)**.

13   Refer to Sections 24 through 27 for information on the internal components of the crankcase.

## *Reassembly*

14   Remove all traces of old gasket and sealant from the crankcase mating surfaces. Be careful not to let any fall into the case as this is done and be careful not to damage the mating surfaces.

15   Check to make sure the three dowel pins are in place in their holes in the mating surface of the left crankcase half **(see illustration 23.10b)**.

16   Pour some engine oil over the transmission and balancer gears, the right crankshaft bearing and the shift drum. Don't get any oil on the crankcase mating surface.

17   Coat the crankcase mating surfaces with gasket sealant, then install a new gasket on the crankcase mating surface **(see illustrations)**. Cut out the portion of the gasket that crosses the cylinder opening.

18   Carefully place the right crankcase half onto the left crankcase half. While doing this, make sure the transmission shafts, shift drum, crankshaft and balancer fit into their bearings in the right crankcase half.

19   Install the crankcase bolts and tighten them so they are just snug. Then tighten them evenly in two or three stages to the torque listed in this Chapter's Specifications.

20   Turn the transmission mainshaft to make sure it turns freely. Also make sure the crankshaft turns freely.

21   The remainder of assembly is the reverse of disassembly.

## 24 Crankcase components - inspection and servicing

1   Separate the crankcase and remove the following:

a) *Balancer*
b) *Transmission shafts and gears*
c) *Crankshaft*
d) *Shift drum and forks*

2   Clean the crankcase halves thoroughly with new solvent and dry them with compressed air. All oil passages should be blown out with compressed air and all traces of old gasket should be removed from the mating surfaces.

*Caution: Be very careful not to nick or gouge the crankcase mating surfaces or leaks will result. Check both crankcase halves very carefully for cracks and other damage.*

3   Check the bearings in the case halves

**23.17b . . . then install the gasket (cut away the portion that spans the cylinder opening)**

**24.3a Check the bearings in the right case half for roughness, looseness or noise**

24.3b To remove the retainer, bend back its lockwasher tab and unscrew the bolt

(see illustrations). For details of the transmission and balancer bearings in the left side of the crankcase, see Sections 26 and 27. If the bearings don't turn smoothly, replace

them. For bearings which aren't accessible from the outside, a blind hole puller will be needed for removal (see illustration). Drive the remaining bearing out with a bearing driver or a socket having an outside diameter slightly smaller than that of the bearing outer race. Before installing the bearings, allow them to sit in the freezer overnight, and about fifteen minutes before installation, place the case half in an oven, set to about 200-degrees F, and allow it to heat up. The bearings are an interference fit, and this will ease installation.

⚠ Warning: Before heating the case, wash it thoroughly with soap and water so no explosive fumes are present. Also, don't use a flame to heat the case. Install the ball bearings with a socket or bearing driver that bears against the bearing outer race.

4   If any damage is found that can't be repaired, replace the crankcase halves as a set.

5   Assemble the case halves (see Section 23) and check to make sure the crankshaft and the transmission shafts turn freely.

### 25 Internal shift mechanism - removal, inspection and installation

1   Refer to Section 23 and separate the crankcase halves.

## Shift shaft
### Removal
2   Pull the pawls of the gearshift plate back against spring pressure until they clear the shift drum, then lift the shift shaft out of the crankcase (see illustration).

### Inspection
3   Check the shift shaft for bends and damage to the splines (see illustration). If the shaft is bent, you can attempt to straighten it, but if the splines are damaged,

24.3c The left half contains needle roller bearings (one held by a retainer), as well as ball bearings for the transmission, crankshaft and balancer

24.3d A blind hole puller like this one is needed to remove bearings which are only accessible from one side

25.2 Push the shift shaft pawls in the direction of the arrow to disengage them from the shift drum and pull the shift shaft out of the crankcase

25.3a The return spring is installed like this . . .

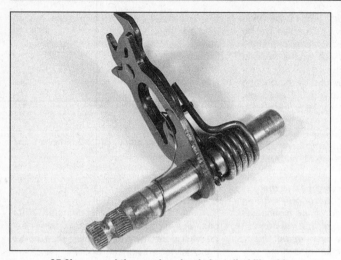

25.3b . . . and the pawl spring is installed like this

25.4 The return spring post (lower arrow) should be tight; the center fork is secured to the shift shaft by a bolt and lockwasher (upper arrow)

25.5 One end of the return spring should be on each side of the post and the pawls should engage the shift drum

25.7 Lift out the shift drum

25.8a With the shift shaft removed from the forks, disengage the right fork; on installation, its letter R goes upward . . .

25.8b . . . the center fork, identified by the letter C . . .

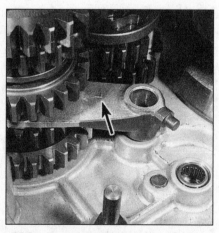

25.8c . . . and the left fork, identified by the letter L

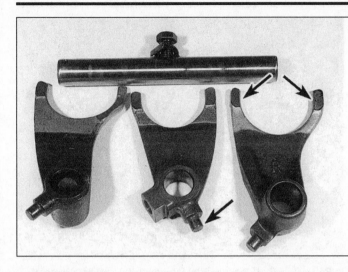

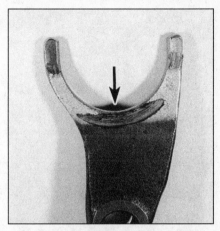

**25.11a The fork ears and pins (arrows) are common wear points**

**25.11b An arc-shaped burn mark like this means the fork was rubbing against a gear, probably due to bending or worn fork ears**

it will have to be replaced. Check the condition of the gearshift plate and the pawl spring **(see illustration)**. Replace them if they're worn, cracked or distorted.

4 Make sure the return spring post isn't loose **(see illustration)**. If it is, unscrew it, apply a non-hardening locking compound to the threads, then reinstall it and tighten it securely.

### Installation

5 Pull back the pawls of the gearshift plate, slide the shaft into its bore and release the claws. Make sure the return spring fits over the post and the pawls engage the shift drum pins **(see illustration)**.

## Shift drum and forks

### Removal

6 Bend back the lockplate and unbolt the center shift fork from the fork shaft **(see illustration 25.4)**.

7 Note how the forks fit in the gear and shift drum grooves, then pull the fork shaft out of the forks and lift out the shift drum **(see illustration)**.

8 Disengage the forks from the gears and lift them out **(see illustrations)**.

### Inspection

9 Wash all of the components in clean solvent and dry them off.

10 Inspect the shift fork grooves in the gears. If a groove is worn or scored, replace the affected gear (see Section 26) and inspect its corresponding shift fork.

11 Check the shift forks for distortion and wear, especially at the fork ears **(see illustrations)**. Measure the thickness of the fork ears and compare your findings with this Chapter's Specifications. If they are discolored or severely worn they are probably bent. Inspect the guide pins for excessive wear and distortion and replace any defective parts with new ones.

12 Measure the inside diameter of the forks and the outside diameter of the fork shaft and compare to the values listed in this Chapter's Specifications. Replace any parts that are worn beyond the limits. Check the shift fork shaft for evidence of wear, galling and other damage. Make sure the shift forks

move smoothly on the shaft. If the shaft is worn or bent, replace it with a new one.

13 Check the edges of the grooves in the drum for signs of excessive wear **(see illustration)**.

14 Spin the shift drum bearing with your fingers and replace it if it's rough, loose or noisy.

15 Check the shift drum bearing in the transmission case **(see illustration)**. If it's worn or damaged, lift it out. If it won't come easily, use a blind hole puller **(see illustration 24.3d)**.

### Installation

16 Installation is the reverse of the removal steps, with the following additions:

a) Refer to the identifying letters on the forks and make sure they're installed in the correct positions.

b) Use a new lockplate on the center shift fork bolt. Tighten the bolt to the torque listed in this Chapter's Specifications.

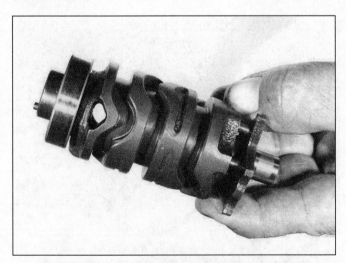

**25.13 Check the shift drum grooves for wear, especially at the points**

**25.15 Wear on the shift drum needle roller bearing is hard to see, so it should be replaced if there's any doubt about its condition**

26.4a Lift off the thrust washer and countershaft first gear . . .

26.4b . . . lift off the bushing, thrust washer and countershaft fourth gear . . .

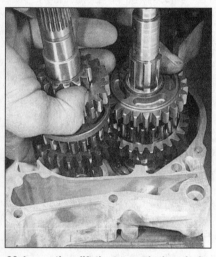

26.4c . . . then lift the transmission shafts out of the case

26.4d Lift the thrust washer off the needle roller bearing . . .

## 26 Transmission shafts - removal, inspection and installation

**Note:** *When disassembling the transmission shafts, place the parts on a long rod or thread a wire through them to keep them in order and facing the proper direction.*

### Removal

1    Remove the engine, then separate the case halves (see Sections 5 and 23).
2    The transmission components remain in the left case half when the case is separated.
3    Refer to Section 25 and remove the shift shaft, shift drum and forks.
4    Lift the transmission shafts out of the case together. This will be easier if two of the gears are removed from the countershaft first **(see illustrations)**.

26.4e . . . lift the bearing out of the housing . . .

26.4f . . . then unbolt the retainer and lift the housing out of the case

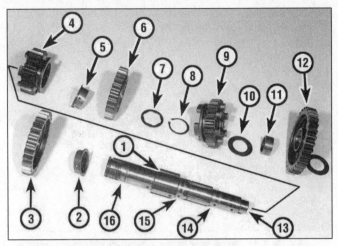

**26.6a  Countershaft details**

| | | | |
|---|---|---|---|
| 1 | Countershaft | 11 | Bushing |
| 2 | Flanged bushing | 12 | Countershaft first gear |
| 3 | Countershaft second gear | 13 | Measuring point (kickstarter idler gear) |
| 4 | Countershaft fifth gear | 14 | Measuring point (countershaft first gear) |
| 5 | Flanged bushing | | |
| 6 | Countershaft third gear | 15 | Measuring point (countershaft third gear) |
| 7 | Splined thrust washer | | |
| 8 | Snap-ring | 16 | Measuring point (countershaft second gear) |
| 9 | Countershaft fourth gear | | |
| 10 | Thrust washer | | |

**26.6b  Mainshaft details**

| | | | |
|---|---|---|---|
| 1 | Thrust washer | 11 | Snap-ring |
| 2 | Mainshaft second gear | 12 | Splined thrust washer |
| 3 | Thrust washer (some models) | 13 | Flanged bushing (install on mainshaft first, flange toward integral first gear) |
| 4 | Snap-ring | | |
| 5 | Thrust washer | 14 | Mainshaft fourth gear (install after flanged bushing) |
| 6 | Mainshaft fifth gear | | |
| 7 | Bushing | 15 | Mainshaft with integral first gear |
| 8 | Thrust washer | | |
| 9 | Snap-ring | | |
| 10 | Mainshaft third gear | | |

5    Separate the shafts once they're lifted out. If you're not planning to disassemble them right away, reinstall the removed components and place a large rubber band over both ends of each shaft so the gears won't slide off.

## Disassembly

6    To disassemble the shafts, remove the snap-rings and slide the gears, bushings and thrust washers off (see illustrations).

## Inspection

7    Wash all of the components in clean solvent and dry them off.

8    Inspect the shift fork grooves in the countershaft fifth gear, countershaft fourth gear and mainshaft third gear. If a groove is worn or scored, replace the affected gear and inspect its corresponding shift fork.

9    Check the gear teeth for cracking and other obvious damage. Check the bushing or surface in the inner diameter of the free-wheeling gears for scoring or heat discoloration. Measure the inside diameters of the gears and compare them to the values listed in this Chapter's Specifications. Replace parts that are damaged or worn beyond the limits.

10    Inspect the engagement dogs and dog holes on gears so equipped for excessive wear or rounding off (see illustration). Replace the paired gears as a set if necessary.

11    Measure the transmission shaft diameters at the points shown (see illustrations 26.6a and 26.6b). If they're worn beyond the limits listed in this Chapter's Specifications, replace the shaft(s).

12    Measure the inner and outer diameters of the gear bushings and replace any that are worn beyond the limit listed in this Chapter's Specifications.

13    Inspect the thrust washers. Honda doesn't specify wear limits, but they should be replaced if they show any visible wear or scoring. It's a good idea to replace them whenever the transmission is disassembled.

14    Check the transmission shaft bearings in the crankcase for roughness, looseness or noise and replace them if necessary ([see illustrations 26.4d, 26.4e and 26.4f] [left side bearings] or Section 24 [right side bearings]).

15    Discard the snap-rings and use new ones on reassembly.

## Assembly and installation

16    Assembly and installation are the reverse of the removal procedure, but take note of the following points:

a)  If you're working on an XR600R or an XR650L, install the flanged bushing on the mainshaft, wide side first, then install fourth gear (see illustration).

**26.10 Check the slots (left arrow) and dogs (right arrow) for wear, especially at the edges; rounded corners cause the transmission to jump out of gear - new gears (bottom) have sharp edges**

**26.16a Install the flanged bushing on the mainshaft first with its wide side toward the integral first gear**

**26.16b Be sure the oil hole in the mainshaft fifth gear bushing aligns with the oil hole in the mainshaft**

**26.16c The assembled shafts and gears should fit together like this**

d) Lubricate the components with engine oil before assembling them.
e) After assembly, check the gears to make sure they're installed correctly (see illustration).

---

**27 Crankshaft and balancer - removal, inspection and installation**

### *Balancer*
**Removal**

1    Remove the engine and separate the crankcase halves (see Sections 5 and 23).
2    Turn the crankshaft so the punch marks on the balancer and crankshaft are aligned (see illustration). The marks must be aligned like this on installation to prevent severe engine vibration. On XR650L models, insert a nail or Allen wrench into the holes in the balancer gears to hold them together, then turn the crankshaft until the balancer

---

b) Install the splined bushing so its oil hole is aligned with the oil hole in the main-shaft (see illustration).
c) Install thrust washers and snap-rings with their chamfered (rolled) edges facing the gears they hold onto the shaft

(thrust load). Be sure to align the gap in the snap-ring with a spline groove. Make sure each snap-ring is fully seated in its groove by opening it slightly and rotating it in its groove

**27.2 The timing marks on the balancer and crankshaft must be aligned to prevent severe engine vibration**

**27.3 Lift the balancer shaft out of the case and inspect the bearing**

27.5 The outer and inner portions of the balancer gear are slightly offset; be sure to align the marks on the inner and outer gears as described in Step 17

27.6a Press the crankshaft out of the crankcase (be careful not to let it drop)

weight clears the crankshaft counterweight and make a paint mark on the balancer gear to the drive gear on the crankshaft. **Note:** *It may be necessary to use a screwdriver to pry the gear teeth together to align the holes in the gears.*
3    Lift the balancer shaft out of its bearing **(see illustration)**. If you're working on an XR650L, remove the nail from the gears.

## Inspection
4    Check the balancer gear teeth and its bearing surface for wear or damage. Replace the balancer if problems can be seen in these areas.
5    The balancer gear on 1983 through 1990 600R models and all 650L models is made in two parts, with the teeth of each part held slightly offset from each other by springs.

This spring-loaded offset eliminates backlash between the balancer and crankshaft gears. To check the springs, first note the alignment of the punch mark on the outer gear between the lines on two of the teeth of the inner gear. Remove the snap-ring and washer from the balancer gear and lift the outer portion of the gear off **(see illustration)**. Check the four springs for wear or damage, replacing them if their condition is in doubt.

## *Crankshaft*
### Removal
**Note:** *Removal and installation of the crankshaft requires a press and some special tools. If you don't have the necessary equipment or suitable substitutes, have the crankshaft removed and installed by a Honda dealer or other qualified repair shop.*

6    Place the left crankcase half in a press and press out the crankshaft **(see illustration)**. The ball bearing may remain in the crankcase or come out with the crankshaft. If it stays on the crankshaft, remove it with the press and a bearing splitter **(see illustration)**. Discard the bearing, no matter what its apparent condition, and use a new one on installation.

## Inspection
7    Measure the side clearance between connecting rod and crankshaft with a feeler gauge **(see illustration)**. If it's more than the limit listed in this Chapter's Specifications, replace the crankshaft and connecting rod as an assembly.
8    Set up the crankshaft in V-blocks with a dial indicator contacting the big end of the

27.6b If the bearing stays on the crankshaft, remove it with the press and a bearing splitter

27.7 Check the connecting rod side clearance with a feeler gauge

**27.8 Check the connecting rod radial clearance with a dial indicator**

**27.13 Thread the adapter into the end of the crankshaft . . .**

connecting rod **(see illustration)**. Move the connecting rod up-and-down against the indicator pointer and compare the reading to the value listed in this Chapter's Specifications. If it's beyond the limit, replace the crankshaft and connecting rod as an assembly.

9    Check the crankshaft, gear and splines for visible wear or damage, such as chipped teeth or scoring. If any of these conditions are found, replace the crankshaft and connecting rod as an assembly.

10    Set the crankshaft in a pair of V-blocks, with a dial indicator contacting the bearing surface on each end. Rotate the crankshaft and note the runout. If the runout at either end is beyond the limit listed in this Chapter's Specifications, replace the crankshaft and connecting rod as an assembly.

### Installation

11    Install the crankshaft bearing in the left crankcase half.

12    Install the crankshaft in the left crankcase half.

13    Thread a puller adapter (Honda part no. 07931-KF00200) into the end of the crankshaft **(see illustration)**.

14    Install a crankshaft puller (Honda part no. 07931-ME4000A) and collar (07931-KF00100) on the end of the crankshaft **(see illustration)**.

15    Hold the puller shaft with one wrench and turn the nut with another wrench to pull the crankshaft into the center race of the ball bearing.

16    Remove the special tools from the crankshaft.

17    Install the balancer shaft in the crankcase: **Note:** *It's important to align the timing marks exactly throughout this procedure. Severe engine vibration will occur if the crankshaft and balancer are out of time.*

a) *On 600R models, assemble the inner and outer balancer gears so the punch*

mark on the outer gear is centered between the punch marks on the inner gear. Install the washer and snap-ring, making sure the snap-ring seats properly. Install the balancer shaft, making sure its punch mark is aligned with the punch mark on the crankshaft **(see illustration 27.2)**.

b) *On 650L models, assemble the inner and outer balancer gears so the punch mark on the outer gear is aligned with the left punch mark on the inner gear **(see illustration)**. Using a screwdriver, pry the gears against the spring tension and insert the nail or Allen wrench through the holes in the gears. Install the dished washer (with the convex side facing outward) and the snap-ring, making sure it seats properly. Install the balancer shaft, aligning the previously made paint marks, then rotate the crankshaft and verify that the alignment marks on the crankshaft gear and the*

**27.14 . . . and attach the puller to the adapter**

2183-2A-27.17 HAYNES

**27.17 When assembling the balancer shaft gears on an XR650L, the mark on the outer gear must line up with the left mark on the inner gear**

*balancer shaft gear line up properly* **(see illustration 27.2).**

18   Installation is the reverse of the removal steps.

## 28  Initial start-up after overhaul

 **Warning: Have a fire extinguisher handy when starting the engine for the first time.**

1   Make sure the engine oil level is correct, then remove the spark plug from the engine. Unplug the primary wires from the coil.
2   Crank the engine over with the kick-starter (600R and models) or the electric starter (XR650L models) several times to build up oil pressure. Reinstall the spark plug and connect the wires to the coil.
3   Make sure there is fuel in the tank, then operate the choke.

4   Start the engine and allow it to run at a moderately fast idle. Let the engine continue running until it reaches operating temperature.
5   Check carefully for oil leaks and make sure the transmission and controls, especially the brakes, function properly before riding the machine. Refer to Section 29 for the recommended break-in procedure.

## 29  Recommended break-in procedure

1   Any rebuilt engine needs time to break-in, even if parts have been installed in their original locations. For this reason, treat the machine gently for the first few miles to make sure oil has circulated throughout the engine and any new parts installed have started to seat.
2   Even greater care is necessary if the cylinder has been rebored or a new crankshaft has been installed. In the case of a rebore,

the engine will have to be broken in as if the machine were new. This means greater use of the transmission and a restraining hand on the throttle for the first few operating days. There's no point in keeping to any set speed limit - the main idea is to vary the engine speed, keep from lugging the engine and to avoid full-throttle operation. These recommendations can be lessened to an extent when only a new crankshaft is installed. Experience is the best guide, since it's easy to tell when an engine is running freely.
3   If a lubrication failure is suspected, stop the engine immediately and try to find the cause. If an engine is run without oil, even for a short period of time, irreparable damage will occur.
4   After riding the bike conservatively for about an hour, change the engine oil and filter, and after the engine has cooled down completely, recheck the valve clearances (see Chapter 1).

# Notes

# Chapter 2  Part B
# Engine (liquid-cooled), clutch and transmission

## Contents

## Degrees of difficulty

| **Easy,** suitable for novice with little experience |  | **Fairly easy,** suitable for beginner with some experience |  | **Fairly difficult,** suitable for competent DIY mechanic |  | **Difficult,** suitable for experienced DIY mechanic |  | **Very difficult,** suitable for expert DIY or professional |  |

## Specifications

### General

| | |
|---|---|
| Bore | 100.0 mm (3.94 inches) |
| Stroke | 82.6 mm (3.25 inches) |
| Displacement | 649 cc (39.6 cubic inches) |
| Cylinder compression | |
|   Decompressor applied | 600 kPa (87 psi) at 400 rpm |
|   Decompressor not applied | 1,100 kPa (160 psi) at 400 rpm |

## Rocker arms

| | |
|---|---|
| Rocker arm inside diameter | |
|    Standard | 14.000 to 14.018 mm (0.5512 to 0.5519 inch) |
|    Limit | 14.05 mm (0.553 inch) |
| Rocker shaft outside diameter | |
|    Standard | 13.966 to 13.984 mm (0.5498 to 0.5506 inch) |
|    Limit | 13.91 mm (0.548 inch) |
| Shaft-to-arm clearance | |
|    Standard | 0.016 to 0.052 mm (0.0006 to 0.0020 inch) |
|    Limit | 0.14 mm (0.006 inch) |

## Camshaft

| | |
|---|---|
| Lobe height | |
|    Intake | |
|       Standard | 41.158 to 41.398 mm (1.6024 to 1.6298 inches) |
|       Limit | 41.00 mm (1.614 inches) |
|    Exhaust | |
|       Standard | 41.196 to 41.436 mm (1.6219 to 1.6313 inches) |
|       Limit | 41.05 mm (1.616 inches) |
| Journal diameter | Not specified |
| Camshaft runout limit | 0.03 mm (0.001 inch) |

## Cylinder head, valves and valve springs

| | |
|---|---|
| Cylinder head warpage limit | 0.10 mm (0.004 inch) |
| Valve stem runout | Not specified |
| Valve stem diameter | |
|    Intake | |
|       Standard | 6.575 to 6.590 mm (0.2589 to 0.2594 inch) |
|       Limit | 6.56 mm (0.258 inch) |
|    Exhaust | |
|       Standard | 6.555 to 6.570 mm (0.2581 to 0.2587 inch) |
|       Limit | 6.55 mm (0.258 inch) |
| Valve guide inside diameter (intake and exhaust) | |
|    Standard | 6.600 to 6.615 mm (0.2589 to 0.2604 inch) |
|    Limit | 6.63 mm (0.261 inch) |
| Stem-to-guide clearance | |
|    Intake | |
|       Standard | 0.010 to 0.040 mm (0.0004 to 0.0016 inch) |
|       Limit | Not specified |
|    Exhaust | |
|       Standard | 0.030 to 0.060 mm (0.0012 to 0.0024 inch) |
|       Limit | Not specified |
| Valve guide projection from cylinder head (intake and exhaust) | 16.3 to 16.5 mm (0.64 to 0.65 inch) |
| Valve seat width | |
|    Intake | |
|       Standard | 1.1 to 1.3 mm (0.04 to 0.05 inch) |
|       Limit | 2.0 mm (0.08 inch) |
|    Exhaust | |
|       Standard | 1.3 to 1.5 mm (0.05 to 0.06 inch) |
|       Limit | 2.0 mm (0.08 inch) |
| Valve face width | Not specified |
| Valve spring free length | |
|    Inner spring | |
|       Standard | 44.0 mm (1.73 inches) |
|       Limit | 43.0 mm (1.69 inches) |
|    Outer spring | |
|       Standard | 45.2 mm (1.78 inches) |
|       Limit | 44.2 mm (1.74 inches) |

## Cylinder

| | |
|---|---|
| Bore diameter | |
|    Standard | 100.00 to 100.015 mm (3.9370 to 3.9376 inches) |
|    Limit | 100.05 mm (3.939 inches) |
| Taper and out-of-round limits | 0.05 mm (0.002 inch) |
| Surface warpage limit | 0.05 mm (0.002 inch) |

## Piston

Piston diameter
    Standard ................................................................................ 99.96 to 99.99 mm (3.935 to 3.937 inches)
    Limit ..................................................................................... 99.86 mm (3.931 inches)
Piston diameter measuring point (above bottom of piston) .................... 20 mm (0.8 inch)
Piston-to-cylinder clearance
    Standard ................................................................................ 0.010 to 0.055 mm (0.0004 to 0.0022 inch)
    Limit ..................................................................................... 0.19 mm (0.007 inch)
Piston pin bore in piston
    Standard ................................................................................ 23.002 to 23.008 mm (0.9056 to 0.9058 inch)
    Limit ..................................................................................... 23.03 mm (0.907 inch)
Piston pin bore in connecting rod
    Standard ................................................................................ 23.020 to 23.041 mm (0.9063 to 0.9071 inch)
    Limit ..................................................................................... 23.05 mm (0.907 inch)
Piston pin outer diameter
    Standard ................................................................................ 22.994 to 23.000 mm (0.9053 to 0.9055 inch)
    Limit ..................................................................................... 22.98 mm (0.905 inch)
Piston pin-to-piston clearance
    Standard ................................................................................ 0.002 to 0.014 mm (0.0001 to 0.0006 inch)
    Limit ..................................................................................... 0.070 mm (0.003 inch)
Piston pin-to-connecting rod clearance
    Standard ................................................................................ 0.020 to 0.047 mm (0.0008 to 0.0019 inch)
    Limit ..................................................................................... 0.067 mm (0.0026)
Piston ring markings
    Top ....................................................................................... R
    Second.................................................................................. RN
Top ring side clearance
    Standard ................................................................................ 0.045 to 0.080 mm (0.0018 to 0.0031 inch)
    Limit ..................................................................................... 0.095 mm (0.037 inch)
Second ring side clearance
    Standard ................................................................................ 0.025 to 0.060 mm (0.0010 to 0.0024 inch)
    Limit ..................................................................................... 0.075 mm (0.003 inch)
Oil ring side clearance................................................................ Not specified
Ring end gap
    Top
        Standard .......................................................................... 0.25 to 0.40 mm (0.010 to 0.016 inch)
        Limit ............................................................................... 0.55 mm (0.022 inch)
    Second
        Standard .......................................................................... 0.40 to 0.55 mm (0.016 to 0.022 inch)
        Limit ............................................................................... 0.70 mm (0.028 inch)
    Oil ring side rails
        Standard .......................................................................... 0.20 to 0.70 mm (0.008 to 0.028 inch)
        Limit ............................................................................... 0.90 mm (0.035 inch)

## Clutch

Spring free length
    Standard ................................................................................ 49.0 mm (1.93 inches)
    Limit ..................................................................................... 46.0 mm (1.81 inches)
Friction plate thickness
    Discs "A" (outer six friction plates)
        Standard .......................................................................... 3.22 to 3.38 mm (0.127 to 0.133 inch)
        Limit ............................................................................... 3.0 mm (0.118 inch)
    Disc "B" (innermost friction plate)
        Standard .......................................................................... 2.92 to 3.08 mm (0.115 to 0.121 inch)
        Limit ............................................................................... 2.69 mm (0.106 inch)
Friction and metal plate warpage limit ........................................ 0.30 mm (0.012 inch)
Clutch housing inside diameter
    Standard ................................................................................ 29.000 to 29.021 mm (1.1417 to 1.1426 inch)
    Limit ..................................................................................... 29.05 mm (1.144 inch)
Clutch housing bushing (guide)
    Inside diameter
        Standard .......................................................................... 21.990 to 22.035 mm (0.8657 to 0.8675 inch)
        Limit ............................................................................... 22.05 mm (0.868 inch)
    Outside diameter
        Standard .......................................................................... 28.959 to 28.980 mm (1.1401 to 1.1409 inch)
        Limit ............................................................................... 28.91 mm (1.138 inch)
Mainshaft outside diameter at clutch housing bushing (guide)
    Standard ................................................................................ 21.967 to 21.980 mm (0.8648 to 0.8654 inch)
    Limit ..................................................................................... 21.94 mm (0.864 inch)

## Oil pump

Outer rotor-to-body clearance
    Standard ........................................................................... 0.15 to 0.22 mm (0.006 to 0.009 inch)
    Limit ................................................................................. 0.35 mm (0.014 inch)
Inner-to-outer rotor clearance
    Standard ........................................................................... 0.15 mm (0.006 inch)
    Limit ................................................................................. 0.20 mm (0.008 inch)
Side clearance (rotors-to-straightedge)
    Standard ........................................................................... 0.03 to 0.08 mm (0.001 to 0.003 inch)
    Limit ................................................................................. 0.10 mm (0.004 inch)

## Kickstarter

Shaft outside diameter
    Standard ........................................................................... 21.959 to 21.980 mm (0.8645 to 0.8654 inch)
    Limit ................................................................................. 21.91 mm (0.863 inch)
Pinion gear inside diameter
    Standard ........................................................................... 22.020 to 22.041 mm (0.8669 to 0.8678 inch)
    Limit ................................................................................. 22.09 mm (0.870 inch)
Idler gear inside diameter
    Standard ........................................................................... 23.000 to 23.021 mm (0.9055 to 0.9063 inch)
    Limit ................................................................................. 23.11 mm (0.910 inch)
Idler gear bushing inside diameter
    Standard ........................................................................... 20.013 to 20.031 mm 0.7879 to 0.7886 inch)
    Limit ................................................................................. 20.05 mm (0.789 inch)
Idler gear bushing outside diameter
    Standard ........................................................................... 22.959 to 22.980 mm (0.9039 to 0.9047 inch)
    Limit ................................................................................. 22.90 mm (0.902 inch)
Countershaft outside diameter at idler gear
    Standard ........................................................................... 19.980 to 19.993 mm (0.7866 to 0.7871 inch)
    Limit ................................................................................. 19.94 mm (0.785 inch)

## Shift drum and forks

Fork inside diameter
    Standard ........................................................................... 14.000 to 14.021 mm (0.5512 to 0.5520 inch)
    Limit ................................................................................. 14.03 mm (0.552 inch)
Fork shaft outside diameter
    Standard ........................................................................... 13.957 to 13.968 mm (0.5495 to 0.5499 inch)
    Limit ................................................................................. 13.95 mm (0.549 inch)
Fork ear thickness
    Standard ........................................................................... 5.93 to 6.00 mm (0.233 to 0.236 inch)
    Limit ................................................................................. 5.90 mm (0.23 inch)
Shift drum outside diameter
    Right side .......................................................................... 19.959 to 19.980 mm (0.7858 to 0.7866 inch)
    Left side ............................................................................ 11.966 to 11.984 mm (0.4711 to 0.4718 inch)
Shift drum groove width .......................................................... Not specified

## Transmission

Gear inside diameters
    Mainshaft fourth, fifth
        Standard ...................................................................... 28.000 to 28.021 mm (1.1024 to 1.1032 inches)
        Limit ............................................................................ 28.08 mm (1.104 inches)
    Countershaft first
        Standard ...................................................................... 23.000 to 23.021 mm (0.9055 to 0.9063 inch)
        Limit ............................................................................ 23.04 mm (0.907 inch)
    Countershaft second
        Standard ...................................................................... 28.000 to 28.021 mm (1.1024 to 1.1032 inches)
        Limit ............................................................................ 28.08 mm (1.104 inches)
    Countershaft third
        Standard ...................................................................... 31.000 to 31.025 mm (1.2205 to 1.2215 inches)
        Limit ............................................................................ 31.05 mm (1.222 inch)
Bushing inside diameters
    Mainshaft fourth
        Standard ...................................................................... 24.985 to 25.006 mm (0.9837 to 0.9845 inch)
        Limit ............................................................................ 25.02 (0.985 inch)
    Countershaft first
        Standard ...................................................................... 20.000 to 20.021 mm (0.7874 to 0.7882 inch)
        Limit ............................................................................ 20.04 (0.789 inch)

Countershaft second
    Standard ......................................................................... 25.000 to 25.021 mm (0.9843 to 0.9851 inch)
    Limit ............................................................................... 25.04 (0.986 inch)
Countershaft third
    Standard ......................................................................... 27.995 to 28.016 mm (1.1022 to 1.1030 inch)
    Limit ............................................................................... 28.04 (1.104 inch)
Bushing outside diameters
  Mainshaft fourth, fifth
    Standard ......................................................................... 27.959 to 27.980 mm (1.1007 to 1.1016 inch)
    Limit ............................................................................... 27.93 mm (1.100 inches)
  Countershaft first
    Standard ......................................................................... 22.959 to 22.979 mm (0.9039 to 0.9047 inch)
    Limit ............................................................................... 22.93 mm (0.903 inch)
  Countershaft second
    Standard ......................................................................... 27.959 to 27.980 mm (1.1007 to 1.1016 inch)
    Limit ............................................................................... 27.93 mm (1.100 inches)
  Countershaft third
    Standard ......................................................................... 30.950 to 30.975 mm (1.2185 to 1.2195 inch)
    Limit ............................................................................... 30.92 mm (1.217 inches)
Gear-to-bushing clearances
  Mainshaft fourth, fifth, countershaft second
    Standard ......................................................................... 0.020 to 0.062 mm (0.0008 to 0.0024 inch)
    Limit ............................................................................... 0.10 mm (0.004 inch)
  Countershaft first
    Standard ......................................................................... 0.021 to 0.062 mm (0.0008 to 0.0024 inch)
    Limit ............................................................................... 0.10 mm (0.004 inch)
  Countershaft third
    Standard ......................................................................... 0.025 to 0.075 mm (0.0010 to 0.0030 inch)
    Limit ............................................................................... 0.13 mm (0.005 inch)
Mainshaft diameter (at fourth gear)
    Standard ......................................................................... 24.967 to 24.980 mm (0.9830 to 0.9835 inch)
    Limit ............................................................................... 24.94 mm (0.982 inch)
Mainshaft diameter (at clutch housing bushing)
    Standard ......................................................................... 21.967 to 21.980 mm (0.8648 to 0.8654 inch)
    Limit ............................................................................... 21.94 mm (0.864 inch)
Countershaft diameter (at kickstarter idler gear)
    Standard ......................................................................... 19.980 to 19.993 mm (0.7866 to 0.7871 inch)
    Limit ............................................................................... 19.94 mm (0.785 inch)
Countershaft diameter (at first gear)
    Standard ......................................................................... 19.980 to 19.993 mm (0.7866 to 0.7871 inch)
    Limit ............................................................................... 19.94 mm (0.785 inch)
Countershaft diameter (at second gear)
    Standard ......................................................................... 24.972 to 24.993 mm (0.9831 to 0.9840 inch)
    Limit ............................................................................... 24.95 mm (0.982 inch)
Countershaft diameter (at third gear)
    Standard ......................................................................... 27.959 to 27.980 mm (1.1007 to 1.1016 inch)
    Limit ............................................................................... 27.93 mm (1.100 inch)
Shaft-to-bushing clearance
  Mainshaft fourth
    Standard ......................................................................... 0.005 to 0.039 mm (0.0002 to 0.0015 inch)
    Limit ............................................................................... 0.06 mm (0.002 inch)
  Countershaft first
    Standard ......................................................................... 0.007 to 0.041 mm (0.000 to 0.0016 inch)
    Limit ............................................................................... 0.06 mm (0.002 inch)
  Countershaft second
    Standard ......................................................................... 0.007 to 0.049 mm (0.0003 to 0.0019 inch)
    Limit ............................................................................... 0.06 mm (0.002 inch)
  Countershaft third
    Standard ......................................................................... 0.015 to 0.057 mm (0.0006 to 0.0022 inch)
    Limit ............................................................................... 0.06 mm (0.002 inch)

## Crankshaft and balancer

Connecting rod side clearance .............................................. 0.050 to 0.650 mm (0.002 to 0.026 inch)
Connecting rod big end radial clearance (limit) ..................... 0.05 mm (0.002 inch)
Crankshaft runout limit .......................................................... 0.05 mm (0.002 inch)
Balancer shaft journal diameter ............................................ Not specified

## Torque specifications

**Note:** *One foot-pound (ft-lb) of torque is equivalent to 12 inch-pounds (in-lbs) of torque. Torque values below approximately 15 ft-lbs are expressed in inch-pounds, since most foot-pound torque wrenches are not accurate at these smaller values.*

| | |
|---|---|
| Engine mounting fasteners | |
|   Hanger plate nuts | |
|     8 mm | 26 Nm (20 ft-lbs) |
|     10 mm | 54 Nm (40 ft-lbs) |
|   Hanger plate bolt (at rear of transmission) | 26 Nm (20 ft-lbs) |
| External oil hose and pipe bolt | |
|   Upper (at steering head) | Not specified (tighten securely) |
|   Lower (at bottom of frame downtube) | 37 Nm (27 ft-lbs) |
|   At engine | Not specified (tighten securely) |
| Cylinder head cover bolts | |
|   6 mm bolts | 12 Nm (108 in-lbs) |
|   8 mm bolts | 23 Nm (17 ft-lbs) |
| Cam sprocket bolts | 20 Nm (14 ft-lbs) (2) |
| Decompressor lifter lever bolt | 12 Nm (108 in-lbs) (2) |
| Cam chain tensioner lifter bolts (on back of cylinder) | 12 Nm (108 inch-lbs) |
| Cam chain tensioner bolt (behind right crankcase cover) | 12 Nm (108 inch-lbs) (2) |
| Cylinder head nuts (10 mm) | 67 Nm (49 ft-lbs) (1) |
| Cylinder-to-crankcase bolts | 12 Nm (108 in-lbs) |
| Crankcase cover bolts (right and left) | 12 Nm (108 in-lbs) |
| Clutch lever perch bolts | 10 Nm (84 in-lbs) |
| Clutch spring bolts | 12 Nm (108 in-lbs) |
| Clutch locknut | 118 Nm (87 ft-lbs) (1) |
| Flywheel (alternator rotor) bolt | See Chapter 5 |
| Primary drive gear locknut | 118 Nm (87 ft-lbs) (1) |
| Engine sprocket bolts | See Chapter 6 |
| Mainshaft bearing set plate bolt | 12 Nm (108 in-lbs) |
| Oil pump stopper plate screw | Securely |
| Oil pump plate bolts | 12 Nm (108 in-lbs) |
| Shift cam-to-shift drum bolt | 12 Nm (108 in-lbs) (2) |
| Shift cam stopper arm bolt | 12 Nm (108 in-lbs) |
| Shift pedal pinch bolt | Not specified |
| Kickstarter bolt | 26 Nm (20 ft-lbs) |
| Crankcase bolts | 12 Nm (108 in-lbs) |
| Mainshaft bearing retainer bolt | 12 Nm (108 in-lbs) (2) |

*(1) Apply clean engine oil to the bolt threads and underside of bolt head.*
*(2) Apply non-permanent thread locking agent to the bolt threads.*

## 1  General information

The engine/transmission unit is of the liquid-cooled, single-cylinder four-stroke design. The four valves are operated by an overhead camshaft which is chain driven off the crankshaft. The valves are operated by rocker arms mounted in the cylinder head cover. Valve clearances are adjusted with screw and locknut type valve adjusters. The engine/transmission assembly is constructed from aluminum alloy. The crankcase is divided vertically.

The crankcase incorporates a dry sump, pressure-fed lubrication system which uses a gear-driven rotor-type oil pump and an oil filter. The engine, transmission and clutch share the same oil.

Power from the crankshaft is routed to the transmission via a wet multi-plate clutch. The transmission has five forward speeds.

## 2  Operations possible with the engine in the frame/ operations requiring engine removal

### Operations possible with the engine in the frame

The components and assemblies listed below can be removed without having to remove the engine from the frame. If, however, a number of areas require attention at the same time, removal of the engine is recommended.

*Carburetor*
*Cylinder head cover*
*Rocker arm assembly*
*Cam chain tensioner*
*Camshaft*
*Cylinder head*
*Cylinder and piston*
*Alternator rotor and stator*
*Gear selector mechanism external components*
*Clutch assembly*
*Primary drive gear*
*Oil pump*
*Water pump*

### Operations requiring engine removal

It is necessary to remove the engine/ transmission assembly from the frame and separate the crankcase halves to gain access to the following components:

*Crankshaft and connecting rod*
*Transmission shafts*
*Shift drum and forks*
*Balancer shaft*

## 3  Major engine repair - general note

1    It is not always easy to determine when or if an engine should be completely overhauled, as a number of factors must be considered.

2    High mileage or running time is not necessarily an indication that an overhaul is needed, while low mileage or running time, on the other hand, does not preclude the need for an overhaul. Frequency of servicing is probably the single most important consideration. An engine that has regular and frequent oil and filter changes, as well as other required maintenance, will most likely give many miles of reliable service. Conversely, a neglected engine, or one which has not been broken in properly, may require an overhaul very early in its life.

3    Exhaust smoke and excessive oil consumption are both indications that piston rings and/or valve guides are in need of attention. Make sure oil leaks are not responsible before deciding that the rings and guides are bad. Refer to Chapter 1 and perform a cylinder compression check to determine for certain the nature and extent of the work required.

4    If the engine is making obvious knocking or rumbling noises, the connecting rod and/or main bearings are probably at fault.

5    Loss of power, rough running, excessive valve train noise and high fuel consumption rates may also point to the need for an overhaul, especially if they are all present at the same time. If a complete tune-up does not remedy the situation, major mechanical work is the only solution.

6    An engine overhaul generally involves restoring the internal parts to the specifications of a new engine. During an overhaul the piston rings are replaced and the cylinder walls are bored and/or honed. If a rebore is done, then a new piston is also required.

The crankshaft and connecting rod are permanently assembled, so if one of these components needs to be replaced both must be. Generally the valves are serviced as well, since they are usually in less than perfect condition at this point. While the engine is being overhauled, other components such as the carburetor and the starter motor can be rebuilt also. The end result should be a like-new engine that will give as many trouble-free miles as the original.

7    Before beginning the engine overhaul, read through all of the related procedures to familiarize yourself with the scope and requirements of the job. Overhauling an engine is not all that difficult, but it is time consuming. Check on the availability of parts and make sure that any necessary special tools, equipment and supplies are obtained in advance.

8    Most work can be done with typical shop hand tools, although a number of precision measuring tools are required for inspecting parts to determine if they must be replaced. Often a dealer service department or repair shop will handle the inspection of parts and offer advice concerning reconditioning and replacement. As a general rule, time is the primary cost of an overhaul so it doesn't pay to install worn or substandard parts.

9    As a final note, to ensure maximum life and minimum trouble from a rebuilt engine, everything must be assembled with care in a spotlessly clean environment.

## 4  Engine - removal and installation

!  **Warning: Wait until the engine is completely cool before beginning this procedure.**

**Note:** *Engine removal and installation should be done with the aid of an assistant to avoid* damage or injury that could occur if the engine is dropped.

### Removal

1    Loosen the rear axle nut and back off the chain adjusters to provide some slack in the drive chain.

2    Drain the engine oil and coolant (see Chapter 1).

3    Remove the seat (see Chapter 8) and the fuel tank (see Chapter 4).

4    Remove the skid plate and the radiator reserve tank (see Chapter 3).

5    Disconnect the crankcase breather tube from the cylinder head cover and from the rear of the crankcase **(see illustrations)**. Also, on California models, detach the fresh air hose from the PAIR valve and disconnect it from the wire clips at the rear of the crankcase.

6    Remove the carburetor and the exhaust system (see Chapter 4). Plug the intake and exhaust openings in the cylinder head with a rag or cover them with duct tape.

7    Disconnect the radiator hoses from the water pump and the cylinder head (see Chapter 3).

8    Label and disconnect the following wires:

   *Spark plug wire (see Chapter 1)*
   *Alternator and pulse generator electrical connectors (see Chapter 5)*

9    Remove the shift pedal (see Section 23) and the brake pedal (see Chapter 7). Also remove the right-side footpeg and bracket (see Chapter 8).

10    Disconnect the clutch cable from the lifter arm and detach the cable bracket from the crankcase (see Section 15). Set the clutch cable aside.

11    Disconnect the decompressor cable from the lever on the cylinder head (see Section 6).

12    Remove the drive sprocket cover, remove the drive sprocket and pull the drive chain back so that it doesn't interfere with engine removal (see Chapter 6).

4.5a  Squeeze the clamp and slide it up the breather hose, then disconnect the hose from the cylinder head cover . . .

4.5b  . . . and from the crankcase

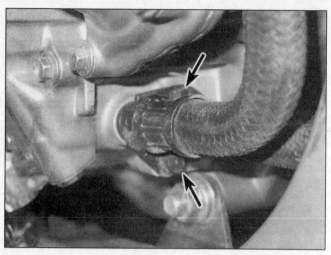

**4.13 Remove the bolts and the retainer plate and detach the oil pipes from the engine**

**4.15a Remove the hanger plate bolts at the top of the engine . . .**

13 Remove the bolts and detach the oil pipes from the engine **(see illustration)**.
14 Remove the swingarm pivot bolt (see Chapter 6).

**4.15b . . . the front of the engine . . .**

15 Remove the engine mounting bolts, nuts and hanger plates at the top, front, rear and lower front of the engine **(see illustrations)**. You'll have to pry between the engine and the frame to relieve the engine weight from the bolts in order to get them out. If the bike is being supported on a motorcycle lift (the kind that the entire bike is wheeled up onto), a floor jack and block of wood can be used to support the engine.
16 Lift the engine and maneuver it out from the right side of the frame. If necessary, have an assistant help you.
17 Carefully place the engine on a suitable work surface.
18 Reinstall the swingarm pivot bolt so the bike can be rolled, if desired.

## Installation

19 Maneuver the engine back into the frame by reversing the removal sequence.
20 Align the mounting bolt holes, then install the hanger plates, bolts and nuts. Tighten the fasteners to the torque values listed in this Chapter's Specifications.

21 The remainder of installation is the reverse of the removal steps, with the following additions:

a) *Use new gaskets at all exhaust pipe connections.*
b) *Adjust the clutch cable, decompressor cable and throttle cable (see Chapter 1).*
c) *Adjust the drive chain slack (see Chapter 1).*
d) *Fill the engine with oil and the cooling system with coolant (see Chapter 1). Run the engine and check for leaks.*

## 5 Engine disassembly and reassembly - general information

1 Before disassembling the engine, clean the exterior with a degreaser and rinse it with water. A clean engine will make the job easier and prevent the possibility of getting dirt into the internal areas of the engine.

**4.15c . . . the rear of the engine . . .**

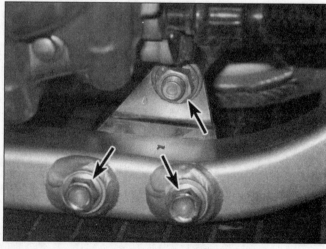

**4.15d . . . and the bottom of the engine**

2   In addition to the precision measuring tools mentioned earlier, you will need a torque wrench, a valve spring compressor, oil gallery brushes (see illustration), a piston ring removal and installation tool, a piston ring compressor and a clutch holder tool (shown in Section 16). Some new, clean engine oil of the correct grade and type, some engine assembly lube (or moly-based grease) and a tube of liquid gasket sealant will also be required.
3   An engine support stand made from short lengths of 2 x 4's bolted together will facilitate the disassembly and reassembly procedures (see illustration).
4   When disassembling the engine, keep mated parts together (including gears, drum shifter pawls, etc.) that have been in contact with each other during engine operation. These mated parts must be reused or replaced as an assembly.
5   Engine/transmission disassembly should be done in the following general order with reference to the appropriate Sections.

*Remove the cylinder head cover and rocker arms*
*Remove the cam chain tensioner lifter*
*Remove the camshaft*
*Remove the cylinder head*
*Remove the cylinder*
*Remove the piston*
*Remove the clutch*
*Remove the gearshift cam and stopper arm*
*Remove the alternator rotor*
*Remove the primary drive gear*
*Remove the cam chain tensioner and guide*
*Remove the cam chain and sprocket*
*Separate the crankcase halves*
*Remove the shift drum/forks*
*Remove the transmission shafts/gears*
*Remove the crankshaft, connecting rod and balancer shaft*

6   Reassembly is accomplished by reversing the general disassembly sequence.

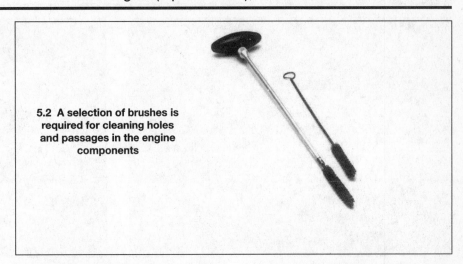

**5.2  A selection of brushes is required for cleaning holes and passages in the engine components**

### 6   Decompressor lever and cable - removal and installation

1   Remove the seat (see Chapter 8) and the fuel tank (see Chapter 4).
2   At the engine, loosen the cable locknuts and slip the cable out of the bracket (see illustration). If you're just detaching the cable to remove the cylinder head cover or engine, unbolt the cable bracket from the cylinder head cover instead. Turn the cable end to align the cable with the slot in the decompression lever, then slip it sideways out of the lever.
3   At the left handlebar, rotate the cable to align it with the slot in the lever and detach the cable from the lever.
4   Note carefully how the cable is routed and detach it from any retainers.
5   To remove the lever, remove the decompressor lever/clutch lever pivot bolt (see Section 15).
6   Installation is the reverse of removal. Adjust the decompressor lever freeplay (see Chapter 1).

### 7   Cylinder head cover and rocker arms - removal, disassembly, inspection, reassembly and installation

**Warning: Wait until the engine is completely cool before beginning this procedure.**

**Note:** *The cylinder head cover can be removed with the engine in the frame. If the engine has been removed, ignore the steps that don't apply.*

### Removal

1   Drain the engine coolant (see Chapter 1).
2   Remove the fuel tank (see Chapter 4). Disconnect the spark plug wire.
3   Disconnect the breather hose from the cylinder head cover (see illustration 4.5a).
4   Unbolt the decompressor cable bracket from the cylinder head cover and disconnect the cable from the lever (see Section 6).

**5.3  A simple engine stand can be made from short lengths of wood**

**6.2  Decompressor cable locknuts (A) and bracket-to-cylinder head cover bolt (B)**

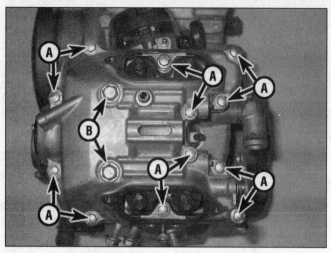

7.8 Cylinder head cover bolts

*A    6 mm bolts*          *B    8 mm bolts*

7.10 Cylinder head cover dowel pins and camshaft hole cap

7.11 Check the O-ring on the dowel pin near the camshaft sprocket, replacing it if necessary

5    Remove the left crankcase cover (see Chapter 5, Section 14) and set the engine at TDC on the compression stroke (see Chapter 1, Section 16).

6    Remove the engine hanger plate from the cylinder head cover and the frame **(see illustration 4.15a)**

7    Remove the valve adjusting covers from the cylinder head cover (see Chapter 1, Section 16).

8    Working in a criss-cross pattern, loosen the 6 mm cylinder head cover bolts in two or three steps, then remove them. Then remove the 8 mm cylinder head cover bolts and washers **(see illustration)**.

9    Lift the cover off. If the cover is stuck, don't try to pry it off; tap around the sides of it with a plastic hammer to dislodge it.

10    Note the locations of the dowel pins; remove the dowel pins and the camshaft hole cap **(see illustration)**.

11    Check the condition of the O-ring on the dowel pin near the camshaft sprocket, replacing it if necessary **(see illustration)**.

12    Thoroughly clean the mating surfaces of the cylinder head and cylinder head cover of all gasket sealant material.

## Disassembly

13    Remove the bolt that secures the decompressor lever, then remove the lever, spring, and washer **(see illustrations)**. Remove the lever shaft oil seal from the bore.

14    Remove the rocker arm shafts from the cylinder head cover **(see illustration)**. Don't mix them up - they must be returned to their original locations.

15    Remove the rocker arms and wave washers from the cylinder head cover, noting the arrangement of the components **(see illustration)**.

## Inspection

16    Check the rocker arms and adjuster screws for wear on the screw tips and where the rocker arms ride on the camshaft **(see illustration)**.

17    Measure the inside diameter of the rocker arms and the outside diameter of the rocker arm shafts, comparing your readings to the values listed in this Chapter's Specifications **(see illustrations)**.

7.13a  Remove this bolt . . .

7.13b  . . . and pull out the decompressor lever, spring and washer

7.14  Pull out the rocker arm shafts . . .

7.15 . . . then remove the rocker arms and wave washers, noting their locations

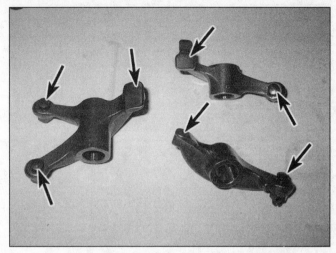

7.16 Check the rocker arms for wear at these points

18  Replace any parts that are not within specification.

## Reassembly

19  Lubricate the rocker arm shafts and the bores of the rocker arms with clean engine oil.

20  Lubricate the camshaft contact surfaces of the rocker arms and the adjuster screw tips with a mixture of clean engine oil and moly-based grease.

21  Reinstall the rocker arms and wave washers, in their original locations, into the cylinder head cover. **Note 1:** *The wave washers are inserted next to the small triangular marks on the cylinder head cover* **(see illustration). Note 2:** *The left exhaust rocker arm is the one with the lug for the decompressor lever.*

22  Lubricate two new O-rings for the rocker arm shafts and install them on the shafts, then install the shafts, in their original locations, into the cylinder head cover. Twist the shafts so the grooves in the shafts align with

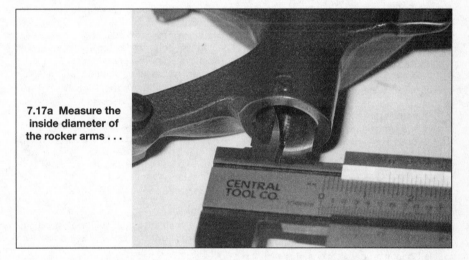

7.17a  Measure the inside diameter of the rocker arms . . .

the bolt holes in the cylinder head cover.

23  Press in a new decompressor lever shaft oil seal, then install the decompressor lever, spring and washer. Apply a non-hard-

ening thread locking agent to the threads of the bolt, then install the bolt, tightening it securely (just be careful not to strip the threads).

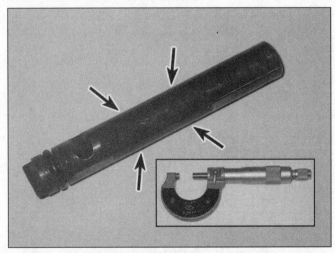

7.17b  . . . and the outside diameter of the rocker arm shafts, in the areas where the rocker arms ride

7.21  The wave washers are inserted next to the small triangular casting marks in the cylinder head cover

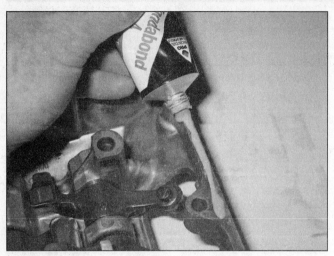

7.28 Apply liquid gasket sealant to the mating surface of the cylinder head cover

8.6 Remove the camshaft sprocket bolts (remove the exposed bolt, then turn the crankshaft one full turn and remove the other one); hold the alternator rotor with a wrench to prevent the camshaft from turning

## Installation

24 Lubricate the camshaft lobes and valve stems with clean engine oil. Coat the rocker arms with a mixture of clean engine oil and moly-based grease.

25 Install the dowel pins (and O-ring on the dowel pin near the cam sprocket) and the camshaft hole cap.

26 Turn the crankshaft until all of the camshaft lobes are pointing down.

27 Loosen the locknuts and back off the valve adjusting screws.

28 Apply a thin film of liquid gasket sealant to the mating surface of the cylinder head cover **(see illustration)**.

29 Install the cover on the engine. Install new sealing washers on the 8 mm bolts. Install the 8 mm bolts and the 6 mm bolts. Tighten the 8 mm bolts to the torque listed in this Chapter's Specifications, then tighten the 6 mm bolts to the torque listed in this Chapter's Specifications. Tighten the bolts a little at a time, working in a criss-cross pattern.

30 Set the engine to TDC compression,

then adjust the valve clearances (see Chapter 1, Section 16).

31 Install the valve adjusting covers, tightening the bolts to the torque listed in this Chapter's Specifications.

32 The remainder of installation is the reverse of the removal steps.

<table>
<tr><td>8</td><td>Camshaft and timing chain - removal, inspection and installation</td><td></td></tr>
</table>

## Removal

### Camshaft

1 Remove the spark plug (see Chapter 1).

2 Remove the left crankcase cover (see Chapter 5, Section 14).

3 Set the engine at TDC on the compression stroke (see Chapter 1, Section 16).

4 Remove the cylinder head cover (see Section 7).

5 Remove the cam chain tensioner lifter

and gasket (see Section 9).

6 Remove the camshaft sprocket bolts **(see illustration)**. Only one bolt can be removed at a time; remove the bolt that is accessible, then rotate the crankshaft one complete revolution and remove the other bolt.

7 Free the sprocket from the camshaft flange and disengage the chain from the sprocket, then remove the sprocket **(see illustration)**.

8 Remove the camshaft from the cylinder head.

9 Tie the chain to the engine (or frame, if the engine hasn't been removed) with a piece of wire so it doesn't drop down into the cam chain tunnel. Engine damage could occur if the engine is rotated with the chain bunched up around the crank sprocket.

10 Remove the camshaft bearing set pin, stopper ring, plunger and spring from the cylinder head **(see illustration)**.

11 Cover the top of the cylinder head with a rag to prevent foreign objects from falling into the engine.

8.7 Disengage the sprocket from the camshaft and remove it from the chain

8.10 Camshaft bearing set pin (A), stopper ring (B), plunger (C) and spring (under plunger)

8.17a  Check the cam lobes for wear - here's a good example of lobe damage which will require replacement of the camshaft (typical)

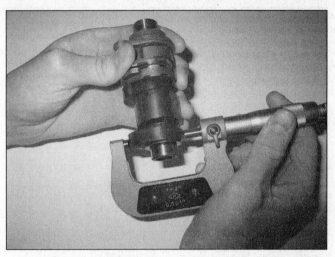

8.17b  Measure the height of the cam lobes with a micrometer

8.18  Make sure the decompressor turns smoothly, in one direction only

### Timing chain and crankshaft sprocket

12  Remove the right crankcase cover (see Section 18) and the primary drive gear (see Section 22).
13  Disengage the chain from the crankshaft sprocket and pull it up through the slot in the side of the cylinder.
14  Remove the sprocket from the crankshaft.
15  The timing chain guide can be removed after the cylinder head has been removed (see Section 10). The chain tensioner guide can be removed after the cylinder has been removed (see Section 13).

### *Inspection*

### Camshaft, bearings and decompressor

16  Inspect the cam bearings for wear by rotating them with your fingers. If either bearing is blue (overheated due to lack of lubrica-

tion), stiff or noisy, replace the bearings as a set.
17  Check the camshaft lobes for heat discoloration (blue appearance), score marks, chipped areas, flat spots and spalling **(see illustration)**. Measure the height of each lobe with a micrometer and compare the results to the minimum lobe height listed in this Chapter's Specifications **(see illustration)**. If damage is noted or wear is excessive, the camshaft must be replaced.
18  Turn the decompressor one-way clutch, making sure it turns smoothly, and only in one direction **(see illustration)**.
19  If the decompressor has to be disassembled, use a two jaw puller to remove the cam sprocket flange from the camshaft **(see illustration)**.
20  Remove the washer, one-way clutch (with the springs and rollers), the stopper pin, the reverse decompressor cam, the decompressor cam and the spring from the camshaft **(see illustrations)**.

8.19  Remove the cam sprocket flange with a two-jaw puller . . .

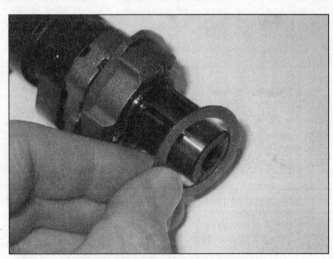

8.20a  . . . then remove the thrust washer . . .

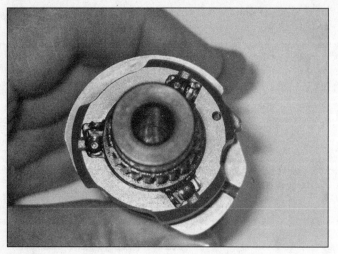

8.20b . . . the clutch outer (be careful not to let the rollers and springs fly out) . . .

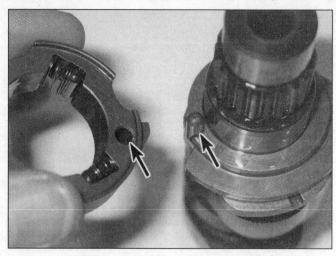

8.20c . . . the stopper pin (note how it engages with the hole in the clutch outer) . . .

8.20d . . . the reverse decompressor cam . . .

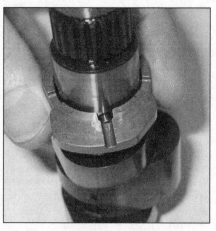

8.20e . . . the decompressor cam . . .

8.20f . . . and the spring

21  Check all of the contact surfaces of the removed components for wear.
22  To assemble the decompressor:

a) Lubricate the decompressor cams, one way clutch and washer with clean engine oil.
b) Insert the spring into the hole in the camshaft, then install the decompressor cam onto the camshaft while holding the spring in place.
c) Slide the reverse decompressor cam onto the camshaft, followed by the stopper pin (see illustration).
d) If removed, install the one-way clutch springs and rollers into the outer portion of the one-way clutch. Install the clutch

assembly onto the camshaft, rotating it as you do, then align the hole in the clutch outer with the stopper pin (see illustration).
e) Install the camshaft sprocket flange onto the camshaft, aligning the wide groove in the flange with the wide teeth on the camshaft splines (see illustration). Use a hydraulic press and a properly sized driver to push the flange into place. Push it onto the camshaft so the distance between the outer end of the flange and the thrust surface on the other end of the camshaft is 88.8 to 89.1 mm (3.49 to 3.51 inches) (see illustration).

## Timing chain, sprockets and guides

23  Inspect the sprocket for wear, cracks and other damage, replacing it if necessary. If the sprocket is worn, the chain is also worn, and possibly the sprocket on the crankshaft is, too. If wear this severe is apparent, the entire engine should be disassembled for inspection.

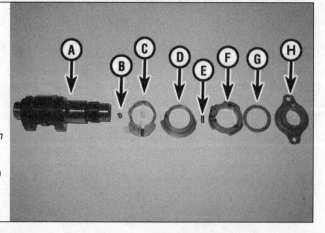

8.20g Exploded view of the decompressor system

A  Camshaft
B  Spring
C  Decompressor cam
D  Reverse decompressor cam
E  Stopper pin
F  Clutch outer (with springs and rollers)
G  Washer
H  Sprocket flange

8.22a Install the decompressor cam, aligning its slot with the pin on the camshaft, then depress the spring and slide the cam over it

8.22b Install the reverse decompressor cam and the stopper pin

8.22c One-way clutch spring and roller details

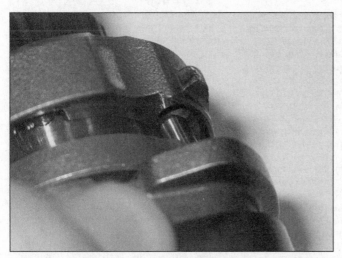

8.22d Align the hole in the clutch outer with the stopper pin

8.22e When installing the cam sprocket flange, align the wide tooth in the flange with the wide tooth on the camshaft

24   Except in cases of oil starvation, the camshaft chain wears very little (provided the sprockets are in good shape). If the chain has stretched excessively, the cam chain tensioner will be unable to maintain correct tension. If the chain has stretched excessively, replace it.

25   Using a flashlight, inspect the chain guides for wear or damage. If they're worn or damaged, replace them.

26   Wash all parts in clean solvent and lay them out for inspection.

### Installation

27   Lubricate the lobes of the camshaft with a moly-based oil or camshaft installation lube. Lubricate the bearings with clean engine oil and install them on the camshaft. **Note:** *The bearing with the rubber shield goes on the sprocket end of the camshaft, and the bearing's rubber shield faces outward. Also, the markings on both bearings face outward.*

28   Install the spring, plunger and stopper ring into the bore in the cylinder head **(see illustration 8.10)**

29   Turn the crankshaft and align the "T" mark on the alternator rotor with the pointer on the crankcase (see Chapter 1, Section 16).

30   If removed, install the timing chain, crankshaft sprocket and guides. When

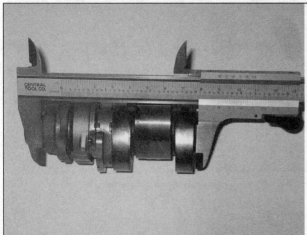

8.22f Press the cam sprocket flange onto the camshaft so the distance between the outer end of the flange and the thrust surface on the other end of the camshaft is 88.8 to 89.1 mm (3.49 to 3.51 inches)

8.30a When installing the cam chain crankshaft sprocket, align the wide spline in the sprocket . . .

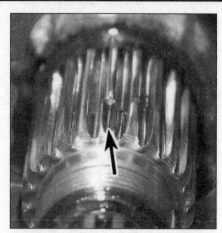

8.30b . . . with the "different" spline on the crankshaft

# 9 Cam chain tensioner lifter - removal and installation

## Removal

1   Break loose the center bolt of the tensioner, then unscrew the tensioner lifter mounting bolts, a little at a time, and remove the tensioner lifter (see illustration).
2   Remove all traces of gasket material from the tensioner and the cylinder.
3   Check that the tensioner plunger doesn't depress when force is applied to it.
4   Insert a screwdriver into the tensioner and turn it clockwise; the plunger should be retracted. When the screwdriver is released, the plunger should spring back out.

## Installation

5   The cam chain tensioner lifter shaft must be retracted and locked into place before installing the tensioner. Fabricate a tool from a piece of 1 mm thick sheet steel, to the proper dimensions (see illustration). This tool can easily be made with a hacksaw and a file.
6   Lubricate the shaft of the plunger with moly-based grease.
7   Using a small screwdriver, turn the tensioner shaft clockwise until the plunger is retracted, then hold the plunger in position, insert the tool into the tensioner and push it in so it engages with the slots in the shaft and the tensioner body and keeps the plunger in the retracted position (see illustrations).
8   Install a new gasket on the tensioner lifter. Position the tensioner lifter on the cylinder, install the tensioner bolts and tighten them to the torque listed in this Chapter's Specifications.
9   Remove the tensioner tool. When

installing the sprocket, align the wide spline in the gear with the "different" or "relieved" spline on the crankshaft (see illustrations).
31   Lower the camshaft sprocket into place, aligning the "EX" mark line with the front of the cylinder head-to-cylinder head cover mating surface, and the other line with the rear of the cylinder head-to-cylinder head cover mating surface (see illustration).
32   While keeping the sprocket in this attitude, loop the chain up and over it, engaging it with the sprocket teeth. Pull up on the sprocket and make sure the timing marks are still aligned with the top surface of the cylinder head.
33   Guide the camshaft into place and through the sprocket, making sure it seats properly on the shoulder of the camshaft. Apply a non-hardening thread-locking compound to the threads of the sprocket bolts, then install one of the bolts into the exposed bolt hole, but don't tighten it completely yet.

34   Turn the crankshaft counterclockwise so that the other bolt hole is exposed. Install the other bolt and tighten it to the torque listed in this Chapter's Specifications. Then turn the crankshaft counterclockwise to expose the first bolt and tighten it to the torque listed in this Chapter's Specifications.
35   Align the "T" mark on the alternator rotor with the pointer on the crankcase and make sure the timing marks are properly aligned with the top surface of the cylinder head (see illustration 8.31).
36   Install the dowel pin and O-ring into the hole near the camshaft sprocket (see illustration 7.10).
37   Retract the cam chain tensioner lifter as described in the next Section then install it, using a new gasket, tightening the bolts to the torque listed in this Chapter's Specifications.
38   The remainder of installation is the reverse of removal.

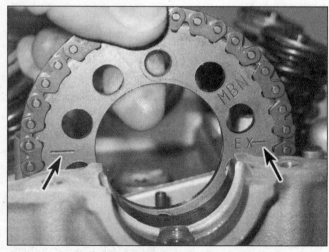

8.31 Align these timing marks with the cylinder head top mating surface

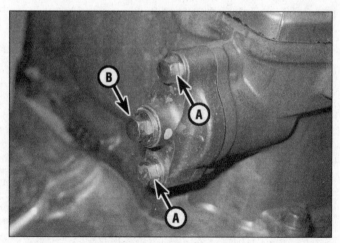

9.1 Cam chain tensioner lifter

A   Mounting bolts
B   Center bolt and sealing washer

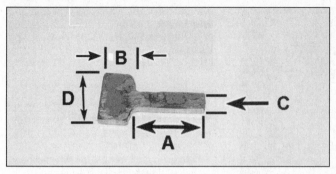

**9.5  Cam chain tensioner tool dimensions**

A   9.5 mm
B   At least 8.5 mm (but
    longer will make the tool
    easier to hold and turn)
C   3.5 mm
D   8.5 mm

**9.7a  Using a small screwdriver, turn the tensioner shaft clockwise until the plunger is retracted . . .**

released, the lifter shaft will automatically extend.

10   Install the tensioner center bolt with a new sealing washer and tighten the bolt to the torque listed in this Chapter's Specifications.

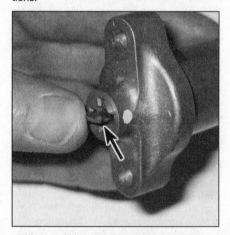

**9.7b  . . . then hold the tensioner plunger and insert the tool into the tensioner to lock the plunger in the retracted position**

## 10  Cylinder head - removal and installation

**Caution: The engine must be completely cool before beginning this procedure, or the cylinder head may become warped.**

**Note:** *This procedure assumes that the engine is still in the vehicle. If it has been removed, ignore the Steps which don't apply.*

### Removal

1   Drain the engine oil and coolant (see Chapter 1).
2   Remove the carburetor and the exhaust system (see Chapter 4). Also disconnect the water hose from the cylinder head.
3   Remove the cylinder head cover and camshaft (see Sections 7 and 8).
4   Remove the upper engine hanger plates.
5   Loosen the cylinder head nuts in three or four stages in a criss-cross pattern **(see illustration)**. Remove the nuts and washers (use

needle-nose pliers to remove the washers if necessary).
6   Lift the cylinder head off the cylinder. If the head is stuck, tap around the side of the head with a rubber mallet to jar it loose, or use two wooden dowels inserted into the intake or exhaust ports to lever the head off. Don't attempt to pry the head off by inserting a screwdriver between the head and the cylinder - you'll damage the sealing surfaces.
7   Remove the head gasket and the two dowel pins from the cylinder **(see illustration)**. (The dowel pins might be in the cylinder head or in the cylinder.) Support the cam chain so it won't drop into the cam chain tunnel, and stuff a clean rag into the cam chain tunnel to prevent the entry of debris.
8   Check the cylinder head gasket and the mating surfaces on the cylinder head and cylinder for leakage, which could indicate warpage. Check the flatness of the cylinder head (see Section 12).
9   Clean all traces of old gasket material from the cylinder head and cylinder. Be careful not to let any of the gasket material fall into the crankcase, the cylinder bore or the bolt holes.

**10.5  Cylinder head nuts**

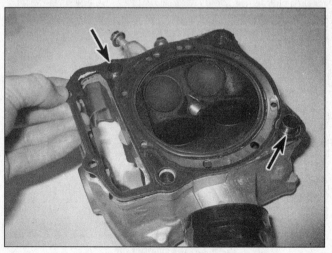

**10.7  Remove the head gasket and the two dowel pins from the head (or the cylinder - wherever it sticks)**

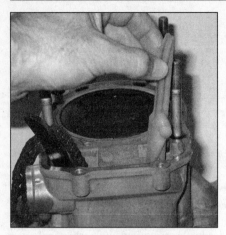

**13.2 Remove the front cam chain guide from the cam chain tunnel**

**13.3 Remove the bolts that attach the base of the cylinder to the crankcase**

sive grit that may still be present from the valve servicing operations. Use compressed air, if available, to blow out all the holes and passages.

## 12 Cylinder head and valves - disassembly, inspection and reassembly

Refer to Chapter 2A for cylinder head and valves disassembly, inspection and reassembly. Although the XR650R engine is liquid cooled, these procedures are essentially the same as for the air-cooled models. Just be sure to use the values listed in this Chapter's specifications when performing the checks.

## Installation

10   Install the two dowel pins, then lay the new gasket in place on the cylinder block. Never re-use the old gasket and don't use any type of gasket sealant.

11   Carefully lower the cylinder head over the studs and dowels. It is helpful to have an assistant support the camshaft chain with a piece of wire so it doesn't fall and become kinked or detached from the crankshaft. When the head is resting on the cylinder, wire the cam chain to another component to prevent it from falling into the tunnel.

12   Lubricate the threads of the cylinder head studs with clean engine oil. Install the washers and nuts on the studs.

13   Tighten the nuts in three or four stages, working in a criss-cross pattern, to the torque listed in this Chapter's Specifications.

14   The remainder of installation is the reverse of removal. Be sure to adjust the valve clearances (see Chapter 1).

15   Change the engine oil and fill the cooling system (see Chapter 1).

## 11 Valves/valve seats/valve guides - servicing

1   Because of the complex nature of this job and the special tools and equipment required, servicing of the valves, the valve seats and the valve guides (commonly known as a valve job) is best left to a professional.

2   The dealer service department or motorcycle repair shop will remove the valves and springs, recondition or replace the valves and valve seats, replace the valve guides, check and replace the valve springs, spring retainers and keepers (as necessary), replace the valve seals with new ones and reassemble the valve components.

3   After the valve job has been performed, the head will be in like-new condition. When the head is returned, be sure to clean it again very thoroughly before installation on the engine to remove any metal particles or abra-

## 13 Cylinder - removal, inspection and installation

## Removal

1   Remove the cylinder head (see Section 10).

2   Lift out the cam chain front guide **(see illustration)**.

3   Remove the bolts that secure the base of the cylinder to the crankcase **(see illustration)**.

4   Lift the cylinder straight up to remove it **(see illustration)**. If it's stuck, tap around its perimeter with a soft-faced hammer. Do NOT try to pry between the cylinder and the crankcase; this will ruin the sealing surfaces. Look for the dowel pins and collar. If they didn't come off with the cylinder, they may still be in the crankcase **(see illustration)**.

5   Be careful not to let the dowel pins drop

**13.4a Lift the cylinder off . . .**

**13.4b . . . and note the location of the dowel pins and O-ring**

14.3a The IN mark on the piston crown faces the rear (intake side) of the engine

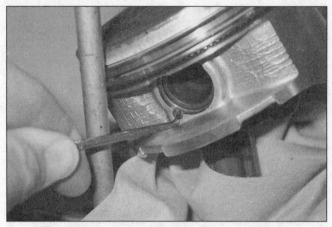

14.3b Wear eye protection and pry the circlip out of its groove with a pointed tool

into the engine. Stuff rags around the piston and remove the cylinder base gasket and all traces of old gasket material from the surfaces of the cylinder and the crankcase.

## Inspection

6   Refer to Chapter 2, Part A, for the inspection procedures.

## Installation

7   Lubricate the cylinder bore and piston rings with plenty of clean engine oil. Apply a thin film of moly-based grease to the piston skirt.

8   Install the dowel pins and O-ring (see illustration 13.4b), then lower a new cylinder base gasket over them.

9   Install the cylinder over the studs and carefully lower it down until the piston crown fits into the cylinder liner. While doing this, compress the piston rings with your fingers and simultaneously pull the camshaft timing chain up, using a hooked tool or a piece

of stiff wire (an assistant would be helpful). Push down on the cylinder, making sure the piston doesn't get cocked sideways, until the bottom of the cylinder liner slides down past the piston rings. If you feel any resistance, stop and find out what's hanging up

10   The remainder of installation is the reverse of the removal steps. Fit the cam chain guide securely into its pocket in the crankcase.

---

### 14 Piston - removal, inspection and installation

1   The piston is attached to the connecting rod with a piston pin that is a slip fit in the piston and rod.

2   Before removing the piston from the rod, stuff a clean shop towel into the crank-

case hole, around the connecting rod. This will prevent the circlips from falling into the crankcase if they are inadvertently dropped.

## Removal

3   The piston should have an IN mark on its crown that goes toward the intake (rear) side of the engine (see illustration). If this mark is not visible due to carbon buildup, scribe an arrow into the piston crown before removal. Support the piston and remove the circlip (see illustration).

4   Push the piston pin out from the opposite end to free the piston from the rod (see illustration). You may have to deburr the area around the groove to enable the pin to slide out (use a triangular file for this procedure). If the pin won't come out, you can fabricate a piston pin removal tool from a long bolt, a nut, and a piece of tubing and washers (see illustration), or use a piston pin removal tool available from aftermarket tool suppliers.

14.4a Push the piston pin part-way out, then pull it the rest of the way

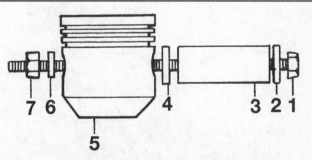

14.4b The piston pin should come out with hand pressure - if it doesn't, this removal tool can be fabricated from readily available parts

| 1 | Bolt | 4 | Padding * | 6 | Washer ** |
|---|------|---|-----------|---|-----------|
| 2 | Washer | 5 | Piston | 7 | Nut ** |
| 3 | Pipe * | | | | |

*   Large enough for piston pin to fit inside
**   Small enough to fit through the pin bore in the piston

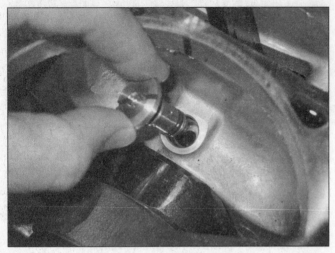

14.5  Remove the oil jet and O-rings

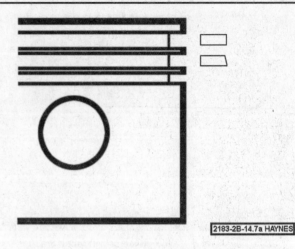

2183-2B-14.7a HAYNES

14.7a  Be sure to install the top and second compression rings in the proper order - they have different profiles

14.7b  Ring end gap positioning. Don't align the ring end gaps with the piston pin hole or 90-degrees from the piston pin hole

120°

120°     120°

Top ring
Second ring
Oil ring side ring
Oil ring spacer
40 mm (1.6 inch) or more — Oil ring side ring
40 mm (1.6 inch) or more — Gap

IN mark (goes toward intake side of engine)

2125-2-15.7c HAYNES

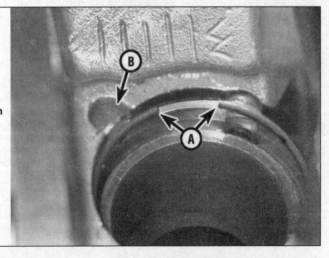

14.9  Seat both piston pin circlips securely in the piston grooves and make sure that their ends (A) are not aligned with the removal notch (B)

5    Remove the oil jet and its O-rings from the right half of the crankcase (see illustration). Check the orifice in the oil jet for clogging, cleaning it as necessary. Replace the O-rings if they show signs of wear or deterioration.

### Inspection

6    Refer to Chapter 2 Part A for the piston inspection and ring end gap checking procedures (Chapter 2A, Sections 14 and 15).

### Installation

7    Refer to Chapter 2A, Section 15, and install the rings on the piston, but use the ring profile illustration shown here to ensure the rings are installed in their proper grooves (see illustration). Be sure to stagger the ring end gaps (see illustration).
8    Lubricate the oil jet O-rings with clean engine oil and install the jet into its bore.
9    Install the piston with its IN mark toward the intake side (rear) of the engine. Lubricate the pin and the rod bore with moly-based grease. Install a new circlip in the groove in one side of the piston (don't reuse the old circlips). Push the pin into position from the opposite side and install another new circlip. Compress the circlips only enough for them to fit in the piston. Make sure the circlips are fully seated in their grooves in the piston pin bore, and make sure that the end gaps of the circlips are not aligned with the notch in the pin bore (see illustration).
10   Install the cylinder (see Section 13).
11   The remainder of installation is the reverse of the removal procedure.

---

## 15  Clutch cable and lever - removal and installation

### Cable

1    Remove the fuel tank (see Chapter 4).
2    At the handlebar, peel back the rubber

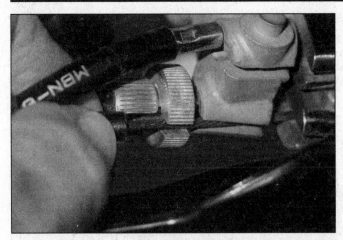

15.2a  Align the slot in the cable adjuster with the slot in the lever perch, then pass the cable through . . .

15.2b  . . . and detach the cable end from the lever

dust cover, back off the locknut and screw the clutch cable adjuster in completely. To disengage the upper end of the cable from the clutch lever, rotate the cable adjuster and locknut so that the slots in both are aligned with the cable, then slip the cable out of the adjuster and locknut **(see illustration)** and disengage the end from the lever **(see illustration)**.

3    Trace the clutch cable down to the cable guide on top of the crankcase **(see illustration)**. If you're removing the cable for access to other components, unbolt the cable guide from the engine. If you're planning to replace the cable, loosen the front nut and unscrew the rear nut, then free the cable from the bracket.

4    Disengage the lower end of the cable

from the clutch lifter arm **(see illustration)**. Note the routing of the clutch cable, then remove the cable.

5    Slide the cable back and forth in the housing and make sure it moves freely. If it doesn't, try lubricating it as described in Chapter 1. If that doesn't help, replace the cable.

6    If the lifter arm seal has been leaking or the bearings seem to be worn, remove the lifter arm (see Section 17). Replace the seal and bearings as needed.

7    Installation is the reverse of removal. Adjust the cable as described in Chapter 1.

### Lever

8    Loosen the clutch cable adjuster to provide some slack (see Chapter 1, if necessary).

9    If just the lever is being replaced, unscrew the nut from the bottom of the lever pivot bolt **(see illustration)**, then unscrew the bolt, swing the lever out and detach the cable from the lever.

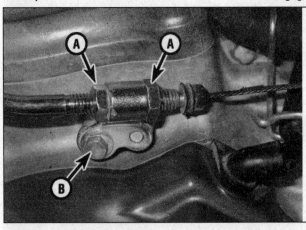

15.3  If you're replacing the cable, loosen the nuts (A) at the clutch cable guide and remove the rear nut. If you're detaching the cable to remove the engine, remove the bracket bolt (B)

15.4  Disengage the cable end plug from the lifter arm clevis

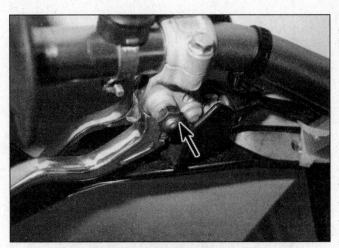

15.9  Don't try to unscrew the clutch lever bolt until the nut on the underside is removed

15.11 When installing the clutch lever perch, make sure the mark on the clamp faces up

16.2a Loosen the clutch cover bolts in a criss-cross pattern, then remove them

10   If the perch is being removed, remove the pivot bolt, clutch lever and decompressor lever, then remove the perch clamp bolts.

11   Installation is the reverse of removal. If you removed the lever perch, make sure that the small dot on the clamp faces up **(see illustration)** and the edge of the bracket aligns with the mark on the handlebar (although the angle of the clutch lever is largely a matter of personal preference). Tighten the bolts to the torque listed in this Chapter's Specifications (upper first, then lower) and be sure to adjust the cable (see Chapter 1).

16.2b Remove the cover and its O-ring

16.3a Remove the bolts, springs . . .

16.3b . . . and pressure plate and bearing

16.4a Remove the lifter piece . . .

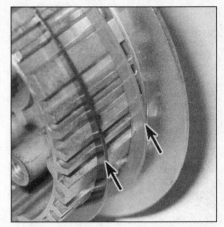

**16.4b** . . . then pull out the pushrod (actuate the clutch lifter arm to push it out far enough to grab). Note: *The rounded end of the pushrod contacts the lifter piece*

**16.5a** Remove the clutch plates from the center (a wide friction plate comes off first, then alternating metal and friction plates) . . .

**16.5b** . . . then remove the judder spring and spring seat (the concave side of the judder spring faces away from the engine)

**16 Clutch - removal, inspection and installation**

## Removal

1    Drain the engine oil (see Chapter 1).
2    Loosen the clutch cover bolts evenly, then remove the cover and its O-ring **(see illustrations)**.
3    Loosen the pressure plate bolts evenly, then remove the bolts, springs, pressure plate and bearing **(see illustrations)**.
4    Remove the lifter piece and pushrod **(see illustrations)**.
5    Remove the friction plates and metal plates from the clutch center. Remove the final, narrow friction plate, judder spring and spring seat **(see illustrations)**.
6    **Note:** *If you're just changing the clutch plates, this, and the next two steps can be skipped.* Unstake the clutch center locknut **(see illustration)**. Note: *A punch or chisel*

**16.5c** The last friction plate is narrower than the others

*will sometimes work, but if the stake is very stubborn, a die grinder might have to be used to remove it. Hold the clutch center with a tool designed for the purpose and loosen the locknut* **(see illustration)**. Remove the lock-

**16.6a** Unstake the locknut . . .

nut, lockwasher and thrust washer, then slide the clutch center off **(see illustration)**. Note: *Obtain a new locknut and discard the old one. A new locknut should always be used whenever the clutch center is removed.*

**16.6b** . . . and unscrew the locknut; use a tool like this one to prevent the clutch center from turning (if you have an impact wrench, use it instead of a breaker bar) . . .

**16.6c** . . . then remove the lockwasher, thrust washer and clutch center

**16.7 Remove the thrust washer from the clutch housing . . .**

7    Remove the thrust washer (see illustration).

8    Pull the clutch housing off, then slide the bushing off the mainshaft (see illustrations).

## Inspection

9    Inspect the outer end of the lifter piece (the disc-shaped friction face that pushes against the bearing in the pressure plate) and the inner end. If either end of the lifter piece is excessively worn, replace it.

10   If the inner end of the lifter piece is worn, carefully inspect the clutch pushrod for visible wear or damage at the contact point with the lifter piece.

11   If the friction face of the lifter piece is excessively worn, look closely at the clutch pressure plate bearing, which is probably also worn.

12   Inspect the bolt posts and the friction surface on the pressure plate for damaged threads, scoring or wear (see illustration). Replace the pressure plate if any defects are found.

13   Inspect the edges of the slots in the clutch housing for indentations made by the friction plate tabs. If the indentations are deep they can prevent clutch release, so the housing should be replaced with a new one. If the indentations can be removed easily with a file, the life of the housing can be prolonged

to an extent. Also, check the driven gear teeth for cracks, chips and excessive wear and the springs on the back side for breakage. If the gear is worn or damaged or the springs are broken, the clutch housing must be replaced with a new one. Check the bearing surface in the center of the clutch housing for score marks, scratches and excessive wear.

14   Measure the free length of the clutch springs (see illustration) and compare the results to this Chapter's Specifications. If the springs have sagged, or if cracks are noted, replace them with new ones as a set.

15   If the lining material of the friction plates smells burnt or if it is glazed, new parts are required. If the metal clutch plates are scored or discolored, they must be replaced with new ones. Measure the thickness of the friction plates (see illustration) and replace any friction plates that are worn with new parts. Note: If any friction plates are worn beyond the minimum thickness, it's a good idea to replace them all.

16   Lay the metal plates, one at a time, on a perfectly flat surface (such as a piece of plate glass) and check for warpage by trying to slip

**16.8a . . . remove the clutch housing . . .**

**16.8b . . . then remove the bushing from the mainshaft**

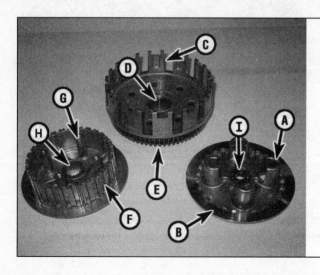

**16.12 Clutch inspection points**

A    Pressure plate posts
B    Pressure plate friction surface
C    Clutch housing slots
D    Clutch housing bushing surface
E    Primary driven gear
F    Clutch center slots and raised portions
G    Clutch center posts
H    Clutch center splines
I    Pressure plate bearing

**16.14 Measure the clutch spring free length**

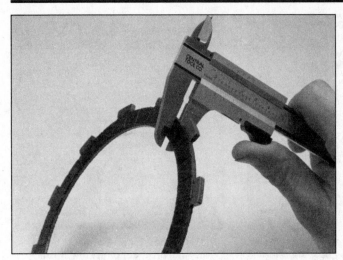

**16.15  Measure the thickness of the friction plates**

**16.16  Check the metal plates for warpage**

a feeler gauge between the flat surface and the plate **(see illustration)**. The feeler gauge should be the same thickness as the maximum warpage listed in this Chapter's Specifications. Do this at several places around the plate's circumference. If the feeler gauge can be slipped under the plate, it is warped and should be replaced with a new one.

17   Inspect the tabs on the friction plates for excessive wear and mushroomed edges. They can be cleaned up with a file if the deformation is not severe. Check the friction plates for warpage as described in Step 16.

18   Inspect the clutch housing guide bushing for score marks, heat discoloration and evidence of excessive wear. Replace the guide bushing if it appears worn.

19   Inspect the splines of the clutch center for wear or damage and replace the clutch center if problems are found.

### Installation

20   If you removed the guide bushing that supports the clutch housing, install it **(see illustration 16.8b)**. Apply moly-based grease to the bushing contact surface on the transmission shaft before installing the bushing. Also apply the lubricant to the outer surface of the bushing.

21   Install the clutch housing and its thrust washer, followed by the clutch center, thrust washer, lockwasher and a **new** locknut **(see illustration)**. **Note:** *Make sure the housing seats completely, engaging with the primary drive gear and the kickstarter idle gear.* Hold the clutch center with the tool used during removal, then tighten the clutch locknut to the torque listed in this Chapter's Specifications. Stake the collar of the new locknut into the groove in the countershaft

22   Install the spring seat in the clutch housing, then install the judder spring with its concave side facing away from the engine **(see illustration 16.5b)**.

23   Dip the friction plates in engine oil (see the Chapter 1 Specifications for the proper type of oil).

24   Install the narrow friction plate in the clutch housing.

25   Install a metal plate, then a friction plate, alternating them until they are all installed. When installing the final friction plate, seat the tabs of the plate with the cutouts in the housing fingers **(see illustration)**.

26   Insert the clutch pushrod into its bore in the mainshaft. Coat the lifter piece with engine oil and install it over the pushrod.

27   Install the pressure plate, bearing and springs, then thread the bolts into their holes. Tighten the bolts in a criss-cross pattern to the torque listed in this Chapter's Specifications.

28   Lubricate a new clutch cover O-ring with engine oil, then work it into the cover groove. Install the cover and tighten its bolts in a criss-cross pattern. Tighten the bolts securely, but don't overtighten them and crack the cover or strip the threads.

29   Installation is otherwise the reverse of removal.

30   Refill the engine with oil and adjust the clutch cable (see Chapter 1).

**16.21  Arrangement of the clutch housing, thrust washer, clutch center, thrust washer, lock washer and nut**

**16.25  The outer clutch friction plate is installed with its tabs in the cutouts of the clutch housing fingers**

## 17 Clutch lifter arm - removal, inspection and installation

1   Remove the clutch pressure plate, lifter piece and pushrod (see Section 16).
2   Disconnect the clutch cable from the lifter arm (see Section 15).
3   Pull the lifter arm out of the engine, noting how the return spring is oriented **(see illustration)**. Also remove the washer.
4   If the lifter arm seal has been leaking, pry it out of the engine **(see illustration)**. Inspect the lifter arm needle bearings. If they are worn or damaged, remove them with a slide hammer and puller. Drive in new bearings with a shouldered drift that fits inside the bearings, with a shoulder the same diameter as the outside of the bearing. Take care not to collapse the bearing cages.
5   Press in a new seal with a socket the same diameter as the seal.
6   Check the lifter arm for wear and damage, especially where it contacts the pushrod **(see illustration)**. Replace it if necessary.
7   Installation is the reverse of the removal steps.

## 18 Right crankcase cover - removal and installation

### Removal

1   Remove the skid plate, then drain the engine oil (see Chapter 1).
2   Remove the brake pedal (see Chapter 7).
3   Remove the kickstarter pedal (see Section 21).
4   Loosen the cover bolts evenly, a little at a time, in a criss-cross pattern **(see illustration)**. The bolts are of different lengths, so keep track of their locations.

**17.3 Remove the lifter arm, return spring and washer, observing how the return spring is oriented**

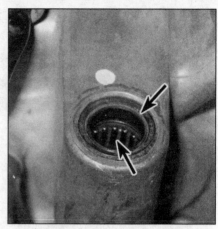

**17.4 If the lifter arm seal has been leaking, pry it out of the engine and press in a new one. Also check the needle bearing**

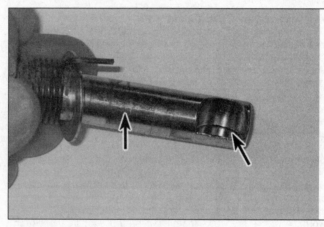

**17.6 Check the lifter arm shaft and pushrod pocket for wear**

5   Take the cover off **(see illustration)**. Tap it gently with a soft-faced mallet if it's stuck. Don't pry between the cover and engine or the gasket surface will be damaged.
6   Note the locations of the cover dow-

els and the orifice/O-ring **(see illustration)**. Remove the orifice and O-ring, then carefully clean all old gasket material from the cover and engine.
7   Check the cover for cracks or other

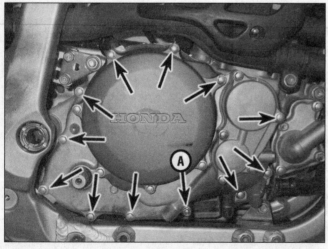

**18.4 Loosen the cover fasteners evenly, in two or three stages, in a criss-cross pattern - note that the top three bolts also secure the clutch cover. (A) is a nut . . .**

**18.5 . . . then remove the cover**

**18.6 Note the locations of the dowels (A), the orifice/O-ring (B), the oil passage dowels/O-rings (C), and the relief valve/ O-rings (D)**

**18.8 If the kickstarter bearing is defective, tap it out with an appropriately sized driver, then install a new one**

**18.10 Pull out the oil strainer screen and clean it**

**18.9 If the seal has been leaking, pry it out and press in a new one**

damage. Small depressions in the gasket surface can be filled in with sealant.

8    Check the kickstarter bearing for wear and damage **(see illustration)**. If necessary, remove it, then drive in a new one with a socket or bearing driver the same diameter as the bearing.

9    If the kickstarter seal has been leaking **(see illustration)**, pry it out, then press a new one in with a seal driver or a socket the same diameter as the seal.

10    Whenever the right crankcase cover is removed, remove and clean the oil strainer screen **(see illustration)**.

## Installation

11    Installation is the reverse of the removal steps, with the following additions:

a) *Lubricate the kickstarter seal with multi-purpose grease and the kickstarter bearing with engine oil.*

b) *Use a new gasket and orifice O-ring.*

c) *Tighten the bolts in two or three stages, in a criss-cross pattern, to the torque listed in this Chapter's Specifications.*

d) *Refill the engine with proper type and quantity of oil (see Chapter 1).*

## 19  Oil pump - removal, inspection and installation

## Removal

1    Remove the oil filter/oil pump cover (see Chapter 1).

2    Remove the right crankcase cover (see Section 18).

3    Remove the circlip and the inner rotor from the outer side of the right crankcase **(see illustrations)**. The oil pump shaft will probably drop out from the inner side.

**19.3a  Pry out the circlip . . .**

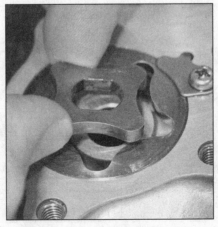

**19.3b  . . . then remove the inner rotor**

4 Remove the screw and the stopper plate, then remove the outer rotor **(see illustration)**.

5 Turn the right crankcase cover over, remove the bolts and the plate from the inner half of the oil pump, then remove the pump rotors **(see illustrations)**.

## Inspection

6 Wash all the components in solvent or brake cleaner, then dry them off. Check the pump body, the rotors and the cover for scoring and wear **(see illustrations)**. If any damage or uneven or excessive wear is evident, replace the pump (and right crankcase cover, if necessary).

7 Reassemble the pump rotors and shaft in the right crankcase cover. Measure the clearance of each set of rotors between the outer rotor and body, and between the inner and outer rotors, with a feeler gauge. Place a straightedge across the pump body and rotors and measure the gap with a feeler gauge **(see illustrations)**. If any of the clearances are beyond the limits listed in this Chapter's Specifications, replace the pump.

**19.4 Remove the screw, stopper plate, and the outer rotor**

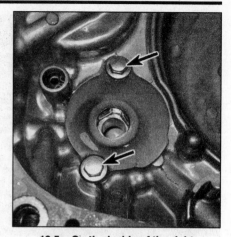

**19.5a On the inside of the right crankcase cover, remove the bolts and cover plate . . .**

8 Reassemble the pump by reversing the disassembly steps, with the following additions:

a) *When installing the pump rotors, align the dimples* **(see illustration)**.

b) *Before installing the cover, pack the cavities between the rotors with petroleum jelly* **(see illustration)** - *this will ensure the pump develops suction quickly and begins oil circulation as soon as the*

**19.5b . . . and the inner and outer rotors**

**19.6a Check the oil pump cover for excessive wear**

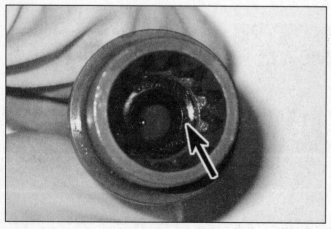

**19.6b Check the seal on the inner end of the oil pump driveshaft, replacing it if it isn't in good condition**

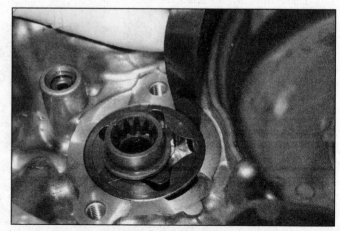

**19.7a Measure the clearance between the outer rotor and housing . . .**

19.7b . . . the inner and outer rotor tips . . .

19.7c . . . and between the rotors and a precision straightedge laid across the surface of the cover (do this for each set of rotors)

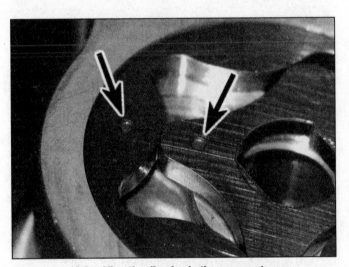

19.8a Align the dimples in the pump rotors

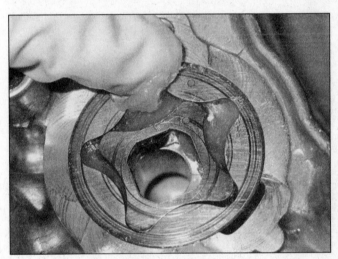

19.8b Pack the cavities between the pump rotors with petroleum jelly

engine is started. Tighten the stopper plate screw securely, and tighten the oil pump cover plate bolts to the torque listed in this Chapter's Specifications.

## Installation

9   Installation is the reverse of removal. Tighten all fasteners to the torque values listed in this Chapter's Specifications.

## 20 Oil pressure relief valve - removal and installation

⚠ **Warning: The oil pressure relief valve is under spring pressure. Wear eye protection when removing the snap-ring.**

1   Remove the right crankcase cover (see Section 18).
2   Depress the relief valve with a punch, then remove the snap-ring and pull the retainer, spring and relief valve out of the cover **(see illustration)**. Check the valve for scoring, and the spring for distortion. Replace parts as necessary.
3   Installation is the reverse of the removal steps.

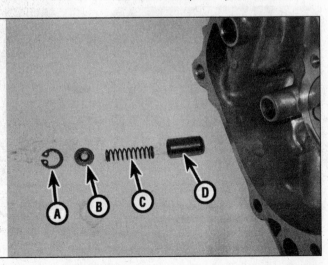

20.2 Oil pressure relief valve details

A   Snap-ring
B   Retainer
C   Spring
D   Relief valve

21.2 Remove the kickstarter pedal bolt and look for alignment
marks - make your own marks if necessary

21.6a Remove the idle gear . . .

21.6b . . . and the bushing

21.7 Unhook the return spring from its hole in the crankcase
and carefully let it unwind . . .

## 21 Kickstarter - removal, inspection and installation

### Pedal

1   Remove the kickstarter pedal bolt.
2   Look for alignment marks on the kick-starter pedal and spindle (see illustration). Make your own marks if they aren't visible, then pull the pedal off the spindle. If it's stuck, use a small two-jaw puller to remove it.
3   Installation is the reverse of the removal steps. Tighten the pedal bolt to the torque listed in this Chapter's Specifications.

### Mechanism

#### Removal

4   Remove the right crankcase cover (see Section 18).
5   Remove the clutch, including the hous-

ing (see Section 16).
6   Remove the idle gear and bushing (see illustrations).
7   Note how the return spring fits into the

hole in the crankcase, then unhook it (see illustration).
8   Remove the kickstarter mechanism from the engine (see illustrations).

21.8a . . . then remove the washer . . .

21.8b . . . the kickstarter spindle, pinion
gear and return spring, ratchet spring . . .

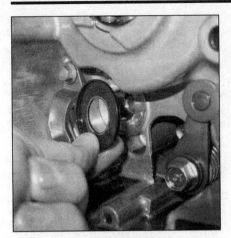

**21.8c . . . and spring seat**

**21.9a Pull the end of the spring out of its hole, then remove it and the collar**

**21.9b Remove the snap-ring and thrust washer from the back side of the starter pinion gear**

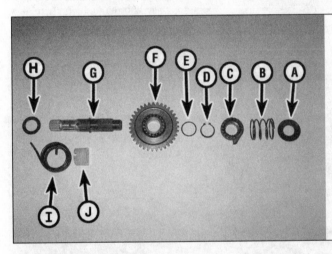

**21.9c Exploded view of the kickstarter mechanism**

A   Spring seat
B   Ratchet spring
C   Ratchet
D   Snap-ring
E   Thrust washer
F   Pinion gear
G   Spindle
H   Thrust washer
I   Return spring
J   Collar

## Inspection

9   Remove the spring seat, ratchet spring and ratchet from the spindle, then remove the snap-ring **(see illustrations)**. Lay the parts in order on a clean workbench **(see illustration)**. **Note:** *Sometimes the outer thrust washer sticks to the inside of the right crankcase cover.*

10   Check all parts for wear or damage and replace them as needed.

11   Measure the inner diameter of the pinion gear and idle gear and compare them to the values listed in this Chapter's Specifications. Replace the gears if they're worn beyond the limits.

12   Measure the inner and outer diameter of the idle gear bushing and compare them to the values listed in this Chapter's Specifications. Replace the bushing if it's beyond the limits.

13   Measure the outer diameter of the kickstarter spindle (where the pinion gear rides) and the transmission countershaft where the idle gear rides on it. Replace either part if it's worn. **Note:** *Replacing the countershaft will require disassembly of the crankcase and transmission.*

14   Apply moly-based grease to all of the friction surfaces. Assemble the mechanism by reversing Step 9. Install the snap-ring with its rounded edge toward the pinion gear and its sharp edge away from it. Place the inner end of the return spring in the spindle hole and align the collar notch with the spring end. Align the punch marks on the ratchet and spindle **(see illustration)**.

15   Check the kickstarter seal and bearing in the right crankcase cover and replace them if necessary.

16   Install the ratchet spring and spring seat on the inner end of the spindle, and the thrust washer on the outer end.

## Installation

17   Installation is the reverse of the removal steps. Lubricate all friction surfaces with molybdenum disulfide oil.

### 22 Primary drive gear - removal and installation

1   Remove the clutch and right crankcase cover (see Sections 16 and 18).

2   Temporarily install the clutch housing. To prevent the primary drive gear from turning when the locknut is loosened, use a gear-jamming tool or jam a copper washer or penny between the teeth of the primary drive gear and the driven gear on the back of the clutch housing **(see illustration)**.

**21.14 Align the punch marks on the ratchet and spindle**

**22.2 Wedge a penny or copper washer into the gear teeth and unscrew the primary drive gear nut. Note:** *The penny will probably fold, but that's no cause for alarm*

**22.4  Remove the nut, washer and primary drive gear**

3    Remove the clutch housing.
4    Unscrew the primary drive gear nut and remove the washer **(see illustration)**.
5    Slide the primary drive gear off the crankshaft.
6    Installation is the reverse of removal,

with the following additions:

a) *Align the wide tooth in the gear splines with the "different," or "relieved" spline on the crankshaft* **(see illustrations)**, *and make sure the OUT SIDE mark on the washer faces out.*
b) *Prevent the gear from turning with the same copper washer or penny used for removal, but wedge it in the top side of the gears.*
c) *Lubricate the threads and the underside of the nut with clean engine oil. Install the lockwasher and nut. Tighten the nut to the torque listed in this Chapter's Specifications.*

**23  Shift pedal, gearshift cam and stopper arm - removal, inspection and installation**

### Shift pedal
#### Removal
1    Look for punch marks on the shift pedal and the end of the shift shaft. If there aren't any, make your own marks with a

sharp punch.
2    Remove the shift pedal pinch bolt and slide the pedal off the shaft.

#### Inspection
3    Inspect the shift pedal for wear or damage such as bending.
4    Check the splines on the shift pedal and shaft for stripping or step wear. Replace the pedal or shaft if these problems are found.

#### Installation
5    Install the shift pedal. Line up the punch marks and tighten the pinch bolt securely.

### *Gearshift cam and stopper arm*
#### Removal
6    Remove the clutch (see Section 16) and right crankcase cover (see Section 18).
7    Unscrew the bolt and remove the stopper arm, collar and return spring **(see illustration)**. **Note:** *The collar is part of the arm.*
8    Unscrew the bolt and remove the gearshift cam and its dowel pin **(see illustration)**. **Note:** *The dowel pin might stay in the shift drum.*

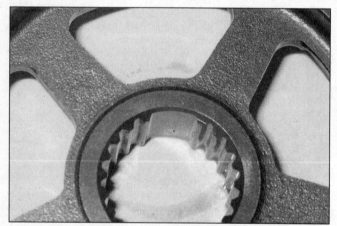

**22.6a  On installation, align the wide spline in the gear . . .**

**22.6b  . . . with the "different" spline on the shaft (it's the only way it'll fit)**

**23.7  Remove the stopper arm and return spring**

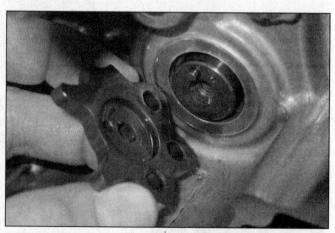

**23.8  Unscrew the bolt and remove the gearshift cam and dowel pin, noting which side of the cam faces out**

24.13 Locations of the left-side crankcase bolts

24.14 Locations of the right-side crankcase bolts

## Inspection

9    Inspect the parts and replace any that are worn or damaged.

## Installation

10    Install the dowel pin into its hole in the shift drum.

11    Install the gearshift cam onto the shift drum, aligning the hole in the cam with the dowel pin. Make sure the stepped side of the cam faces out.

12    Apply a non-hardening thread-locking agent to the threads of the cam bolt, but don't get any sealant within 6.5 mm (1/4-inch) of the tip of the bolt. Install the bolt and tighten it to the torque listed in this Chapter's Specifications.

13    Install the stopper arm spring, collar, stopper arm and bolt. Tighten the bolt to the torque listed in this Chapter's Specifications.

14    The remainder of installation is the reverse of removal.

15    Refill the engine with oil (see Chapter 1).

16    Run the engine for a few minutes, then shut it off. Check the engine oil level and add some, if necessary (see Chapter 1).

## 24  Crankcase - disassembly and reassembly

1    To examine and repair or replace the crankshaft, connecting rod, bearings and transmission components, the crankcase must be split into two parts.

## Disassembly

2    Remove the engine (see Section 4).

3    Remove the clutch (see Section 16).

4    Remove the water pump (see Chapter 3).

5    Remove the right crankcase cover (see Section 18).

6    Remove the primary drive gear (see Section 22).

7    Remove the gearshift cam and stopper arm (see Section 23).

8    Remove the left crankcase cover and the alternator rotor (see Chapter 5).

9    Remove the cylinder head, cylinder and piston (see Sections 10, 13 and 14).

10    Remove the relief valve and O-rings, orifice and its O-ring, and the dowel pins from the right side of the crankcase (see illustration 18.6).

11    Remove the cam chain guides, chain and crankshaft sprocket (see Section 8).

12    Look over the crankcase carefully to make sure there aren't any remaining components that attach the two halves of the crankcase together.

13    Loosen the left-side crankcase bolts evenly, in two or three stages, then remove them (see illustration).

14    Place the crankcase on its left side and loosen the right-side crankcase bolts evenly, in two or three stages, then remove them (see illustration).

15    Remove the right crankcase half from the left half. If they don't come apart easily, use a three-legged puller or tap them apart with a plastic mallet (see illustrations).

*Caution: Don't pry the case halves apart - oil leaks will develop.*

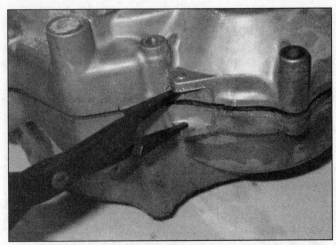

24.15a A pair of large snap-ring pliers will sometimes work to separate the crankcase halves

25.15b Lift the right case half off the left half

24.16 Note the locations of the dowels and orifice/O-ring. The inner race of the crankshaft right-side bearing might stay in the right case half. The thrust washer on the countershaft might stick to the countershaft bearing, too

24.17 Remove the reed valve from the crankcase

16   Remove the two crankcase dowels and the orifice and its O-ring (see illustration).

17   Remove the reed valve from the left half of the crankcase (see illustration). Check the valve for wear or damage and replace it if necessary.

18   Refer to Sections 25 through 27 for information on the internal components of the crankcase.

## Reassembly

19   Remove all traces of old gasket and sealant from the crankcase mating surfaces. Be careful not to let any fall into the case as this is done and be careful not to damage the mating surfaces.

20   Install the crankshaft, balancer shaft, transmission shafts, shift drum and any other parts that were removed. Be sure to lubricate and install the right main bearing inner race on the crankshaft.

21   Pour some oil over the transmission gears, the crankshaft bearing surface and the shift drum. Don't get any oil on the crankcase mating surface.

22   Apply a light film of liquid gasket to the

sealing surfaces of the crankcase, except in the area of the oil passage. Wipe off any excess sealant from the inside of the crankcase.

23   Install the two dowel pins and the orifice/O-ring in their holes in the mating surface of the left crankcase half (see illustration 24.16).

24   Install the reed valve into the left crankcase half.

25   Carefully place the right crankcase half onto the left crankcase half. While doing this, make sure the transmission shafts, shift drum, balancer shaft and crankshaft fit into their ball bearings in the right crankcase half.

26   Install the crankcase half bolts in the correct holes and tighten them so they are just snug, then tighten the crankcase bolts in two or three stages, in a criss-cross pattern, to the torque listed in this Chapter's Specifications.

27   Install a new countershaft seal and its snap-ring (see illustration).

28   The remainder of installation is the reverse of removal.

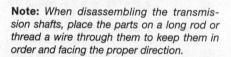

## 25 Transmission shafts and shift drum - removal, inspection and installation

Note: When disassembling the transmission shafts, place the parts on a long rod or thread a wire through them to keep them in order and facing the proper direction.

## Removal

1   Separate the case halves (see Section 24).

2   The transmission components and shift drum remain in the left case half when the case is separated. To remove the components, refer to the accompanying photo sequence (see illustrations).

## Inspection

3   Remove the shaft components with snap-ring pliers and place them in order on a wire or a long rod (see illustrations).

4   Wash all of the components in clean solvent or brake cleaner and dry them off.

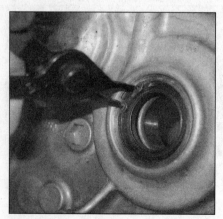

24.27 Drive the countershaft seal into its bore just past the snap-ring groove, then install the snap-ring, making sure it seats completely

25.2a Pull out the shift fork shaft

25.2b Pull the shift plate back and remove the gearshift drum . . .

25.2c . . . then remove the shift forks

25.2d  Remove the gearshift spindle and gearshift plate

25.2e  Lift out the mainshaft and countershaft together

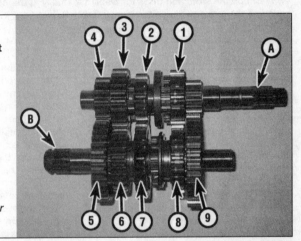

**25.2f  This is how the mainshaft and countershaft gears mesh**

A   Mainshaft
B   Countershaft
1   Mainshaft fourth gear
2   Mainshaft third gear
3   Mainshaft fifth gear
4   Mainshaft second gear
5   Countershaft second gear
6   Countershaft fifth gear
7   Countershaft third gear
8   Countershaft fourth gear
9   Countershaft first gear

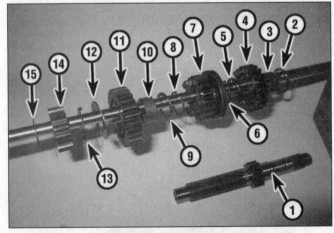

25.3a  Disassemble the shafts with snap-ring pliers and place the parts in order on a long rod or coat hanger - this is the mainshaft . . .

1   Mainshaft
2   Thrust washer
3   Mainshaft fourth gear bushing
4   Mainshaft fourth gear
5   Spline washer
6   Snap-ring
7   Mainshaft third gear
8   Snap-ring
9   Spline washer
10  Mainshaft fifth gear bushing
11  Mainshaft fifth gear
12  Spline washer
13  Lock washer
14  Mainshaft second gear
15  Thrust washer

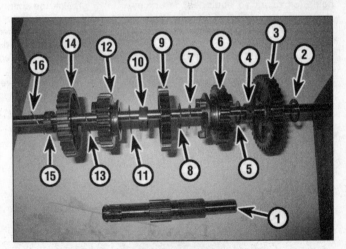

25.3b . . . and this is the countershaft

1   Countershaft
2   Thrust washer
3   Countershaft first gear
4   Countershaft first gear bushing
5   Thrust washer
6   Countershaft fourth gear
7   Snap-ring
8   Spline washer
9   Countershaft third gear
10  Countershaft third gear bushing
11  Thrust washer
12  Countershaft fifth gear
13  Thrust washer
14  Countershaft second gear
15  Countershaft second gear bushing
16  Thrust washer

25.7 Check the slots and dogs for wear, especially at the edges; rounded corners can cause the transmission to jump out of gear

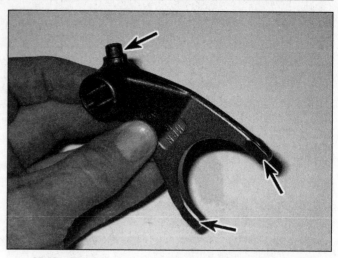

25.13a The fork ears and pins are common wear points

5    Inspect the shift fork grooves in gears so equipped. If a groove is worn or scored, replace the affected gear and inspect its corresponding shift fork.

6    Check the gear teeth for cracking and other obvious damage. Check the bushing or surface in the inner diameter of the freewheeling gears for scoring or heat discoloration. Measure the inside diameters of the gears and compare them to the values listed in this Chapter's Specifications. Replace parts that are damaged or worn beyond the limits.

7    Inspect the engagement dogs and dog holes (on gears so equipped) for excessive wear or rounding off (see illustration). Replace the paired gears as a set if necessary.

8    Measure the transmission shaft diameters at the points listed in this Chapter's Specifications. If they're worn beyond the limits, replace the shaft(s).

9    Measure the inner and outer diameters of the gear bushings and replace any that are worn beyond the limit listed in this Chapter's Specifications.

10   Inspect the thrust washers. Honda doesn't specify wear limits, but they should be replaced if they show any visible wear or scoring. It's a good idea to replace them whenever the transmission is disassembled.

11   Check the transmission shaft bearings in the crankcase for roughness, looseness or noise and replace them if necessary.

12   Discard the snap-rings and use new ones on reassembly.

13   Check the shift forks for distortion and wear, especially at the fork ears (see illustrations). Measure the thickness of the fork ears and compare your findings with this Chapter's Specifications. If they are discolored or severely worn they are probably bent. Inspect the guide pins for excessive wear and distortion and replace any defective parts with new ones.

14   Measure the inside diameter of the forks and the outside diameter of the fork shaft and compare to the values listed in this Chapter's Specifications. Replace any parts that are worn beyond the limits. Check the shift fork shaft for evidence of wear, galling and other damage. Make sure the shift forks move smoothly on the shaft. If the shaft is worn or bent, replace it with a new one.

15   Check the edges of the grooves in the drum for signs of excessive wear (see illustration).

16   Spin the shift drum bearing with your fingers and replace it if it's rough, loose or noisy.

### Installation

17   Installation is basically the reverse of the removal procedure, but take note of the following points:

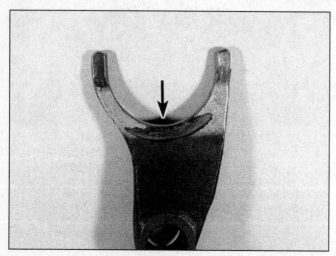

25.13b An arc-shaped burn mark like this means the fork was rubbing against a gear, probably due to bending or worn fork ears

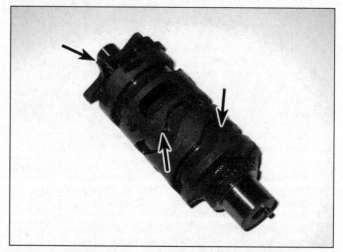

25.15 Check the shift drum grooves for wear, especially at the points

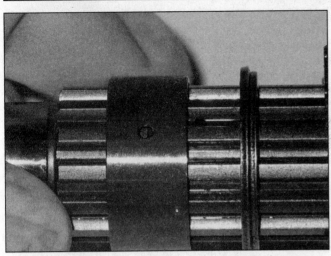

25.17a Align the mainshaft fifth gear bushing with the hole in the mainshaft (actually, it'll be one tooth off)

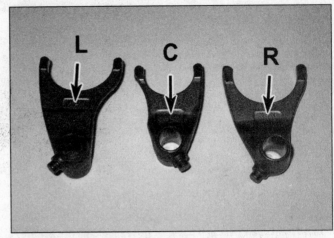

25.17b Install the shift forks with the marks facing up (towards the right side of the engine) - they're marked as to where they go (L = left, C = center, R = right)

26.2 Removing the crankshaft with a press

26.3 Check the connecting rod side clearance with a feeler gauge

a) Lubricate each part with engine oil before installing it.
b) Use new snap-rings (worn snap-rings can easily turn in their grooves).
c) Install snap-rings with their chamfered (rolled) edges facing the thrust load (the sharp edge of the snap-ring must face away from the load, or toward the outside of the shaft). Be sure to align the gap in the snap-ring with a spline groove. Make sure each snap-ring is fully seated in its groove by opening it slightly and rotating it in the groove.
d) Thrust washers, too, must be installed with their chamfered edges facing the thrust load.
e) When installing the mainshaft fifth gear bushing, align its oil hole with the hole in the mainshaft (see illustration).
f) When installing the shift forks, make sure that the R, C and L marks are facing up (see illustration).

## 26 Crankshaft and balancer - removal, inspection and installation

### Removal

1   Remove the engine, separate the crankcase halves and remove the transmission shafts (see Sections 4, 24 and 25).
2   Using a press, remove the crankshaft from the crankcase (see illustration). Be sure to support the crankshaft and the balancer as this is done; they will come out together. Be careful not to let them drop.

### Inspection

3   Measure the clearance between the connecting rod and crankshaft with a feeler gauge (see illustration). If it's more than the limit listed in this Chapter's Specifications, replace the crankshaft and connecting rod as an assembly.
4   Set up the crankshaft in V-blocks with

26.4 Check the connecting rod radial clearance with a dial indicator

a dial indicator contacting the big end of the connecting rod (see illustration). Move the connecting rod up-and-down against the indicator pointer and compare the reading

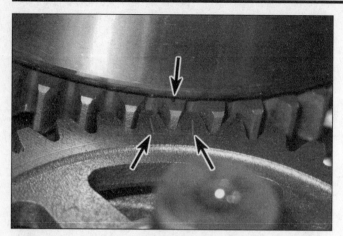

26.9 Crankshaft gear and balancer gear alignment marks (the bearing came out with the crankshaft and makes the mark on the crankshaft gear hard to see, but there's no need to remove the bearing if it's in good condition)

26.10a Thread the adapter of the puller into the crankshaft ...

to the value listed in this Chapter's Specifications. If it's beyond the limit, replace the crankshaft and connecting rod as an assembly.

5    Check the crankshaft gear and bearing journals for visible wear or damage, such as chipped teeth or scoring. If any of these conditions are found, replace the crankshaft and connecting rod as an assembly.

6    Set the crankshaft in a pair of V-blocks, with a dial indicator contacting each end. Rotate the crankshaft and note the runout. If the runout at either end is beyond the limit listed in this Chapter's Specifications, replace the crankshaft and connecting rod as an assembly.

### Installation

7    Make sure both crankcase halves are clean, and the mating surfaces are free of any old gasket material or sealant.

8    Lubricate the bearings in the crankcase

and the big end of the connecting rod with a mixture of clean engine oil and moly-based grease.

9    Assemble the balance shaft and crankshaft together, making sure the marks on their gears are aligned **(see illustration)**.

10    Insert the crankshaft and balancer shaft into the left crankcase half, then pull the crankshaft into its bearing using an adapter on the threads of the crankshaft and a collar that bears against the bearing **(see illustrations)**.

*Caution: Don't try to hammer the crankshaft into its bearing. Also, don't attempt to use a press to push the crankshaft into the bearing in the left case half; the force exerted through the crankshaft/crank pin could "scissors" the crankshaft counterweights on the crank pin, which would ruin it.*

Note: *If the crankshaft's left bearing came out with the crankshaft, and it it's in good*

condition and doesn't need to be replaced, place the crankshaft and bearing in a freezer for a few hours before installing it. Also, heat the left-side crankcase in an oven for awhile (at around 250-degrees F) or use a heat gun to heat it up (DO NOT use a torch), then install the crankshaft and bearing (and balance shaft) into the left-side crankcase.

 **Warning: Make sure the crankcase is completely clean and free of petroleum products before placing it in an oven.**

11    Install a new crankshaft seal in the left case half.

12    Lubricate the inner race of the right crankshaft bearing with a mixture of clean engine oil and moly-based grease, then install it on the crankshaft **(see illustration)**.

13    Install the transmission and related components following Section 25, then reassemble the crankcase halves (see Section 24).

26.10b ... then install the puller and tighten the bolt to draw the crankshaft into the bearing in the left case half (typical)

26.12 Lubricate the inner race of the right crankshaft bearing, then install it on the crankshaft

**27.3 A blind-hole puller like this one is needed to remove bearings which are only accessible from one side**

## 27 Crankcase components - inspection and servicing

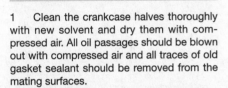

1    Clean the crankcase halves thoroughly with new solvent and dry them with compressed air. All oil passages should be blown out with compressed air and all traces of old gasket sealant should be removed from the mating surfaces.

*Caution: Be very careful not to nick or gouge the crankcase mating surfaces, or leaks will result. Check both crankcase sections very carefully for cracks and other damage.*

2    Inspect the bearings in the case halves. If they don't turn smoothly, replace them.

3    You'll need a blind-hole puller to remove bearings that are accessible from only one side **(see illustration)**. Drive out the other bearings with a bearing driver or a socket having an outside diameter slightly smaller than that of the bearing outer race.

4    Remove the old oil seals from the case halves using a seal removal tool.

5    Before installing the bearings, allow them to sit in the freezer overnight, and about fifteen-minutes before installation, place the case half in an oven, set to about 200-degrees F, and allow it to heat up. The bearings are an interference fit, and this will ease installation.

 *Warning: Before heating the case, wash it thoroughly with soap and water so no explosive fumes are present. Also, don't use a flame to heat the case. Install ball bearings with a socket or bearing driver that contacts the bearing outer race. Install needle roller bearings with a shouldered drift that fits inside the bearing to keep it from collapsing while the shoulder applies force to the outer race.*

**Note:** *Install the bearings with the marked side toward the inside of the case.*

6    Install the new seals in the case with a seal driver, with the lips of the seal facing the inner side of the case.

7    If any damage is found that can't be repaired, replace the crankcase halves as a set.

8    Assemble the case halves (see Section 24) and check to make sure the crankshaft and the transmission shafts turn freely.

## 28 Initial start-up after overhaul

1    Make sure the engine is filled with coolant and the oil level is correct, then remove the spark plug from the engine. Unplug the primary (low tension) wires from the coil.

2    Kick over the engine several times to build up oil pressure. Reinstall the spark plug and connect the wires to the coil.

3    Make sure there is fuel in the tank, then turn the fuel valve On and pull up the choke lever.

4    Start the engine and allow it to run at a moderately fast idle until it reaches operating temperature.

5    Check carefully for oil leaks and make sure the transmission and controls, especially the brakes, function properly before road testing the machine. Refer to Section 29 for the recommended break-in procedure.

6    After riding the bike conservatively for about an hour, and after the engine has cooled down completely, change the engine oil and recheck the valve clearances (see Chapter 1).

## 29 Recommended break-in procedure

1    Any rebuilt engine needs time to break-in, even if parts have been installed in their original locations. For this reason, treat the machine gently for the first few miles to make sure oil has circulated throughout the engine and any new parts installed have started to seat.

2    Even greater care is necessary if the cylinder has been rebored or a new crankshaft has been installed. In the case of a rebore, the engine will have to be broken in as if the machine were new. This means greater use of the transmission and a restraining hand on the throttle for the first few operating days. There's no point in keeping to any set speed limit - the main idea is to vary the engine speed, keep from lugging (laboring) the engine and to avoid full-throttle operation. These recommendations can be lessened to an extent when only a new crankshaft is installed. Experience is the best guide, since it's easy to tell when an engine is running freely.

3    If a lubrication failure is suspected, stop the engine immediately and try to find the cause. If an engine is run without oil, even for a short period of time, irreparable damage will occur.

4    Change the engine oil and oil filter after the first hour of operation (see Chapter 1).

# Notes

# Chapter 3
## Cooling system (XR650R models)

## Contents

## Degrees of difficulty

| Easy, suitable for novice with little experience  | Fairly easy, suitable for beginner with some experience  | Fairly difficult, suitable for competent DIY mechanic  | Difficult, suitable for experienced DIY mechanic  | Very difficult, suitable for expert DIY or professional  |
|---|---|---|---|---|

## Specifications

### General
| | |
|---|---|
| Radiator cap relief pressure | 16 to 20 psi |
| Coolant typs | See Chapter 1 |

### Torque specifications
**Note:** *One foot-pound (ft-lb) of torque is equivalent to 12 inch-pounds (in-lbs) of torque. Torque values below approximately 15 ft-lbs are expressed in inch-pounds, since most foot-pound torque wrenches are not accurate at these smaller values.*

| | |
|---|---|
| Thermostat housing cover bolts | 12 Nm (108 in-lbs) |
| Water pump impeller | 12 Nm (108 in-lbs) |
| Water pump bolts | 12 Nm (108 in-lbs) |

### 1 General information

The XR650R equipped with a liquid cooling system which utilizes a water/anti-freeze mixture to carry away excess heat produced during the combustion process. The cylinder is surrounded by a water jacket, through which the coolant is circulated by the water pump. The pump is mounted to the right side of the crankcase and is driven by the balancer shaft driven gear. The coolant is pumped through the cylinder and cylinder head, then up through the thermostat and into the left and right radiators where it is cooled, then out of the right-side radiator and back to the water pump.

The XR650R has a coolant recovery system that saves coolant that escapes past the radiator cap when the pressure in the system exceeds the radiator cap value. When the engine cools down, coolant is automatically drawn back into the system from the reserve tank.

### 2 Radiator cap - check

If problems such as overheating or loss of coolant occur, check the entire system as described in Chapter 1. The radiator cap opening pressure should be checked by a dealer service department or service station equipped with the special tester required to do the job. If the cap is defective, replace it with a new one.

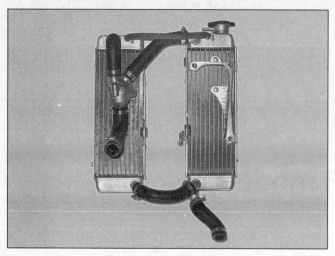

3.1 Coolant hose routing details

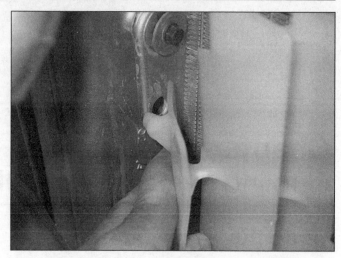

4.2a Flex the grille to disengage the mounting pins from the radiator . . .

## 3 Coolant hoses - removal and installation

**Warning: The engine must be completely cool before beginning this procedure.**

1 The coolant hoses are all secured by screw-type clamps to fittings on the engine, thermostat housing and radiators **(see illustration)**.

2 Before removing a hose, drain the cooling system (see Chapter 1).

3 To remove a hose, loosen its clamp and carefully detach it from the fitting.

4 If the hose is stuck, pry the edge up slightly with a pointed tool and spray WD40 (or equivalent) into the gap. Work the tool around the fitting, lifting the edge of the hose and spraying into the gap until the hose comes free of the fitting.

5 In extreme cases, you may have to slit the hose and cut it off the fitting with a knife. Make sure you can get a replacement hose before doing this.

6 Tighten the hose clamps securely, but not so tight as to cause them to cut into the hose.

7 Refill the cooling system with the proper type of coolant and perform the air bleeding procedure as described in Chapter 1, then check for leaks.

## 4 Radiator(s) - removal and installation

**Warning: The engine must be completely cool before beginning this procedure.**

1 Support the bike securely upright.

Remove the fuel tank (see Chapter 4) and drain the cooling system (see Chapter 1).

2 Remove the grille from the radiator **(see illustrations)**. **Note:** *It isn't absolutely necessary to remove the grill from the radiator, but doing so makes access to the upper mounting bolt easier.*

3 Disconnect the hoses at the top and bottom of the radiator.

4 Remove the radiator mounting bolts **(see illustration)**. Note the arrangement of the washers, grommets and collars.

5 Lift the radiator away from the frame. Inspect the mounting bolt grommets and replace them of they're worn or deteriorated.

6 Installation is the reverse of the removal steps, with the following additions:

a) Tighten the mounting bolts securely, but don't overtighten them and distort the grommets.

b) Fill the cooling system and bleed it of air (see Chapter 1).

c) Check for coolant leaks.

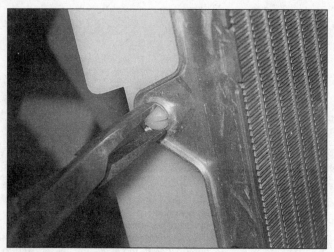

4.2b . . . then squeeze the outer mounting pins and push them from their holes

4.4 Radiator mounting bolts

**5.2  Thermostat housing cover bolts**

**5.3  The spring end of the thermostat goes into the housing. Be sure to replace the housing cover O-ring with a new one**

## 5  Thermostat - removal and installation

 **Warning: The engine must be completely cool before beginning this procedure.**

1    Remove the fuel tank (see Chapter 4) and drain the cooling system (see Chapter 1).
2    Remove the bolts from the thermostat housing cover, then remove the cover **(see illustration)**.
3    Remove the thermostat, noting its installed direction (the spring end goes down into the housing) **(see illustration)**.
4    Installation is the reverse of removal, with the following additions:

a)  *Install a new O-ring on the thermostat housing cover.*

b)  *Tighten the thermostat housing cover bolts to the torque listed in this Chapter's Specifications.*
c)  *Fill the cooling system and bleed it of air (see Chapter 1).*
d)  *Check for coolant leaks.*

## 6  Water pump - removal and installation

1    The water pump is made up of a pump cover, and an impeller and seal housed in the water pump assembly, mounted on the right side of the crankcase. The water pump drive shaft is driven by the balancer shaft.
2    Failure of the water seal will result in coolant dripping from the weep hole in the underside of the pump (see Chapter 1, Section 28). Failure of the oil seal will result in oil in the cooling system. The water pump is not

rebuildable; if it fails, it must be replaced as a unit.

### Removal

 **Warning: The engine must be completely cool before beginning this procedure.**

3    Drain the cooling system (see Chapter 1).
4    Remove the water pump cover-to-water pump assembly bolts and the water pump-to-crankcase bolts and detach the water pump cover, leaving the hose attached **(see illustration)**. The hose can be removed if desired, but it isn't necessary to remove it to remove the water pump assembly. **Note:** *The bolts are different lengths, so note their locations for reinstallation. Also note that the forward lower bolt (the drain bolt) is equipped with a copper washer.*
5    Remove the water pump assembly from the crankcase **(see illustration)**.

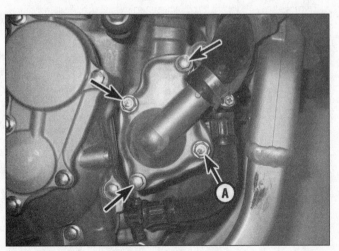

**6.4  Water pump mounting bolts ("A" is the coolant drain bolt)**

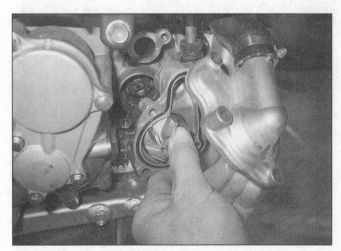

**6.5  Remove the water pump assembly from the crankcase**

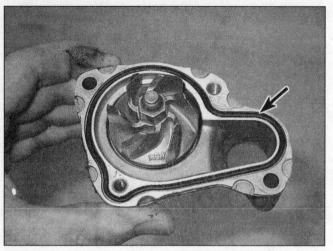

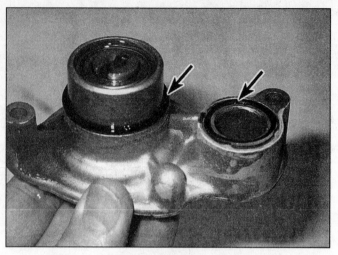

6.6a Remove the O-ring from the front of the water pump . . .

6.6b . . . and the two O-rings on the back of the water pump assembly

6    Remove the O-ring gasket from the pump cover and the two O-rings on the water pump assembly **(see illustrations)**.

## Installation

7    Installation is the reverse of the removal steps, with the following additions:

a) *Use a new water pump cover O-ring if it isn't in perfect condition. Lubricate the O-ring with a thin coat of multi-purpose grease before installing it.*

b) *Install new O-rings, lubricated with a thin coat of multi-purpose grease, to the*

backside of the pump before installing it

c) *Align the slot in the water pump shaft with the tang on the end of the balancer gear shaft, then carefully slide the pump into place.*

d) *Tighten the water pump bolts to the torque listed in this Chapter's Specifications.*

e) *Refill and bleed the cooling system (see Chapter 1).*

f) *Run the engine and check for coolant and oil leaks.*

## 7    Radiator reserve tank - removal and installation

⚠ ***Warning: The engine must be completely cool before beginning this procedure.***

1    Remove the skid plate (see Chapter 8).
2    Place a container under the reserve tank.
3    Remove the bolt and detach the tab on the bottom of the tank from the frame **(see illustration)**. Remove the cap and drain the coolant from the tank.
4    Detach the hoses from the tank.
5    Installation is the reverse of removal.
6    Fill the tank with the proper coolant to between the UPPER and LOWER marks.

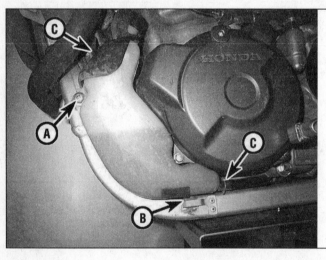

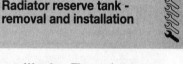

**7.3 Radiator reserve tank mounting details**

A    Mounting bolt
B    Tang
C    Hoses

# Chapter 4
# Fuel, exhaust and emission control systems

## Contents

## Degrees of difficulty

| | | | | |
|---|---|---|---|---|
| **Easy,** suitable for novice with little experience  | **Fairly easy,** suitable for beginner with some experience  | **Fairly difficult,** suitable for competent DIY mechanic  | **Difficult,** suitable for experienced DIY mechanic  | **Very difficult,** suitable for expert DIY or professional  |

## Specifications

### General
| | |
|---|---|
| Fuel type | Unleaded, 91 octane or higher |
| Engine idle speed | See Chapter 1 |

### Carburetor (XL600R)
Identification mark
| | |
|---|---|
| 1983 | PH60A |
| 1984 49 states | PH64A |
| 1984 California | PH66A |
| 1985 49 states | PH68A-B |
| 1985 California | PH68B-B |
| 1986 and later 49 states | PH68G |
| 1986 and later California | PH68H |

Jet sizes and settings
Standard main jet (sea level to 5000 ft)
| | |
|---|---|
| 1983 | |
|     Primary | 125 |
|     Secondary | 112 |
| 1984 49 states (primary and secondary) | 120 |
| 1984 California (primary and secondary) | 118 |
| 1985 and later | |
|     Primary | 118 |
|     Secondary | 115 |

## Carburetor (XL600R) (continued)

| | |
|---|---|
| High altitude main jet (5000 ft to 6500 ft) | Same as standard |
| High altitude main jet (above 6500 ft) | |
| 1983 | Same as standard |
| 1984 49 states (primary and secondary) | 112 |
| 1984 California (primary and secondary) | 110 |
| 1985 and later | |
|     Primary | 115 |
|     Secondary | 112 |
| Slow jet | |
| 1983 | 55 |
| 1984 and 1985 | 65 |
| 1986 and later | 62 |
| Jet needle clip position | Not specified |
| Mixture screw setting (turns out from lightly seated position) - see Section 4 | |
| Sea level to 5000 ft | |
| 1983 | 1 |
| 1984 and 1985 | 2 |
| 1986 on | 1-1/2 |
| Above 5000 ft | |
| 1983 | 1/2 |
| 1984 | 1-1/2 |
| 1985 and later | 1-3/8 |
| Float level | |
| 1983 and 1984 | 20.0 mm (0.79 inch) |
| 1985 and later | 18.0 mm (0.71 inch) |

## Carburetor (XR600R)

| | |
|---|---|
| Identification mark | |
| 1985 through 1987 | PH52A |
| 1988 | PD8AA |
| 1989 and 1990 | PD8AD |
| 1991 and later (except 1998 and later California) | PD8AF |
| 1998 and later California | PDM18 |
| Jet sizes and settings | |
| Standard main jet (sea level to 5000 ft) | |
| 1983 through 1987 (primary and secondary) | 122 |
| 1988 through 1990 | 165 |
| 1991 and later (except 1998 and later California) | 152 |
| 1998 and later California | 128 |
| Slow jet | |
| 1983 through 1987 | 45 |
| 1988 | 60 |
| 1989 and later (except 1998 and later California) | 62 |
| 1998 and later California | 58 |
| Jet needle clip position | |
| 1983 through 1987 | |
|     Primary | 4th groove from top |
|     Secondary | 2nd groove from top |
| 1988 and later | 3rd groove from top |
| Mixture screw setting (turns out from lightly seated position) - see Section 4 | |
| Standard | |
| 1983 through 1987 | 1-3/8 |
| 1988 | 2-5/8 |
| 1989 through 1997 | 2 |
| 1998 and later (except California) | |
|     Initial setting | 2 |
|     Final setting | 3/4 |
| 1998 and later California | |
|     Initial setting | 1-1/8 |
|     Final setting | 1/2 in from standard final setting (see Section 4) |
| High altitude | 1/2-turn in from standard final setting (see Section 4) |
| Float level | |
| 1983 through 1987 | 18.0 mm (0.71 inch) |
| 1988 and later | 14.5 mm (0.57 inch) |

## Carburetor (XR650L)

Identification mark
    1993 and 1994
        Except California ......................................................... VE85A
        California.................................................................... VE86A
    1995 and later
        49 state (and 2008 Canada) ........................................ VE85C
        California.................................................................... VE86B
        Canada (except 2008) ................................................ VE85D
Jet sizes and settings
    Standard main jet (sea level to 5000 ft)
        1993
            49 state
                Frame serial no. PM-000001 to PM-000958...................... 155
                Frame serial no. PM-000959 on.......................... 152
            California
                Frame serial no. PM-000001 to PM-000078...................... 155
                Frame serial no. PM-000079 on.......................... 152
            Canada..................................................................... 152
        1994 and later.............................................................. 152
    High altitude main jet (above 5000 ft)
        1993
            49 state
                 Frame serial no. PM-000001 to PM-000958...................... 152
                Frame serial no. PM-000959 on.......................... 150
            California
                Frame serial no. PM-000001 to PM-000078...................... 152
                Frame serial no. PM-000079 on.......................... 150
            Canada..................................................................... 150
        1994 and later.............................................................. 150
    Slow jet ............................................................................ 50
Jet needle clip position .......................................................... Not adjustable
Mixture (pilot) screw setting (turns out from lightly seated position) - see Section 4
    Initial setting
        1993 and 1994
            Standard
                49 state
                    Frame serial no. PM-000001 to PM-000958.................. 2-3/4
                    Frame serial no. PM-000959 on...................... 2-1/4
                California
                    Frame serial no. PM-000001 to PM-000078.................. 2-3/4
                    Frame serial no. PM-000079 on...................... 2-1/4
                Canada................................................................. 2-1/4
            High altitude .......................................................... 1/2-turn in from standard final setting (see Section 4)
        1995 and later
            Standard.............................................................. 2
            High altitude ......................................................... 1/2-turn in from standard final setting (see Section 4)
    Final setting (all) ............................................................... 3/4
Float level .............................................................................. 18.7 mm (0.73 inch)

## Carburetor (XR650R)

### North American models

Identification mark
    2000 to 2006
        Except California ......................................................... PE78A
        California.................................................................... PE78B
    2007 ................................................................................ PE78E
Jet sizes and settings
    Main jet
        Standard ...................................................................... 125
        High altitude ................................................................ 122
    Slow jet ............................................................................ 65
Jet needle clip position
    Standard ........................................................................... 2nd groove from top
    High altitude...................................................................... Top groove

## Carburetor (XR650R)

### North American models (continued)

Mixture (pilot) screw setting (turns out from lightly seated position) - see Section 4

    Initial setting

        Standard

| | |
|---|---|
| Except California and all 2007 USA models ........................... | 2 |
| California and after 2007 USA models ................................... | 1-1/5 |
| Final setting .................................................................... | 5/8 in from standard final setting (see Section 4) |
| High altitude ................................................................... | 1/4-turn in from standard final setting (see Section 4) |
| Float level ........................................................................... | 16.0 mm (0.63 inch) |

### Except North American models

| | |
|---|---|
| Identification mark | |
|     European and general export........................................... | PE78C |
|     Australia ........................................................................ | PE78D |
| Jet sizes and settings | |
|     Main jet | |
|         European and general export ...................................... | 175 |
|         Australia ................................................................. | 112 |
|     Slow jet ...................................................................... | 65 |
| Jet needle clip position ...................................................... | 3rd groove from top |
| Mixture (pilot) screw setting (turns out from lightly seated position) - see Section 4 | |
|     Initial setting................................................................. | 1-3/4 |
|     Final setting................................................................... | 3/4 in from standard final setting (see Section 4) |
| Float level ........................................................................... | 16.0 mm (0.63 inch) |

## Torque specifications

**Note:** *One foot-pound (ft-lb) of torque is equivalent to 12 inch-pounds (in-lbs) of torque. Torque values below approximately 15 ft-lbs are expressed in inch-pounds, since most foot-pound torque wrenches are not accurate at these smaller values.*

| | |
|---|---|
| Exhaust pipe-to-cylinder head nuts | |
|     XL600R ........................................................................... | 18 to 25 Nm (13 to 18 ft-lbs) |
|     XR600R | |
|         1985 through 1987 .................................................... | 8 to 12 Nm (72 to 108 in-lbs) |
|         1988 through 1990 .................................................... | 27 Nm (20 ft-lbs) |
|         1991 and later.......................................................... | 17 Nm (144 in-lbs) |
|     XR650L ........................................................................... | 17 Nm (144 in-lbs) |
|     XR650R ........................................................................... | 18 Nm (156 in-lbs) |
| Muffler clamp bolts | |
|     1983 through 1987........................................................... | 15 to 25 Nm (13 to 18 ft-lbs) |
|     1988 and later | |
|         XR600R................................................................... | 27 Nm (20 ft-lbs) |
|         XR650L, XR650R ...................................................... | 20 Nm (168 in-lbs) |
| Muffler mounting bolts | |
|     XL600R ........................................................................... | Not specified |
|     XR600R | |
|         1983 through 1987 .................................................... | 20 to 30 Nm (15 to 22 ft-lbs) |
|         1988 through 1990 .................................................... | 70 Nm (51 ft-lbs) |
|         1991 and later.......................................................... | 35 Nm (25 ft-lbs) |
|     XR650L/R......................................................................... | 32 Nm (24 ft-lbs) |

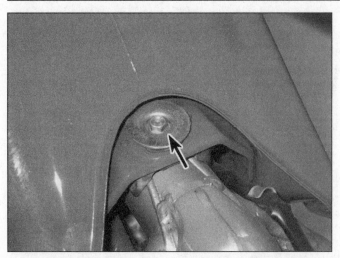

**2.3 Fuel tank mounting bolt - XL600R and XR650L models**

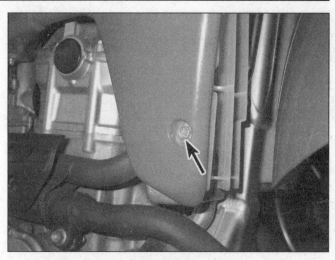

**2.5 Remove the radiator shroud-to-radiator bolts from each side (XR650R models)**

## 1  General information

The fuel system consists of the fuel tank, fuel tap, filter screen, carburetor and connecting lines, hoses and control cables.

All models except the XR650L use the slide carburetor design, in which the slide acts as the throttle valve. XR650L models use a Constant Vacuum (CV) type carburetor.

1983 through 1987 models use dual carburetors. The primary carburetor operates from idle to 1/3 throttle, which allows high mixture velocity at low speeds for efficient combustion. At about 1/3 to 1/2 throttle, the secondary carburetor begins to open, allowing increased fuel mixture flow to meet the needs of the large-displacement engine. A crossover port in the cylinder connects the intake tracts of the two carburetors. On 1983 models only, a reed valve in the crossover port closes as the primary carburetor starts to open.

For cold starting on all except XR650L models, a butterfly-type choke valve is actuated by a lever mounted on the carburetor. XR650L models use a piston-type starting enrichment or choke valve, controlled by a cable from the left handlebar.

The exhaust system consists of a pipe and muffler/silencer with a spark arrester function.

XL600R and XR650L models sold in California use an evaporative emission control system that routes fuel tank vapors to the engine for burning. All XR650L models sold in the U.S.A., and Canadian models beginning in 1997, use a Secondary Air Injection system which admits additional air into the exhaust stream to reduce the emission of unburned hydrocarbons.

Some of the fuel system service procedures are considered routine maintenance

items and for that reason are included in Chapter 1.

## 2  Fuel tank - removal and installation

⚠️ **Warning: Gasoline is extremely flammable, so take extra precautions when you work on any part of the fuel system. Don't smoke or allow open flames or bare light bulbs near the work area, and don't work in a garage where a gas-type appliance (such as a water heater or clothes dryer) is present. Since gasoline is carcinogenic, wear fuel-resistant gloves when there's a possibility of being exposed to fuel, and, if you spill any fuel on your skin, rinse it off immediately with soap and water. Mop up any spills immediately and do not store fuel-soaked rags where they could ignite. When you perform any kind of work on the fuel**

**system, wear safety glasses and have a Class B type fire extinguisher on hand.**

### Removal
1    Remove the seat (see Chapter 8). Turn the fuel tap to Off.

### XL600R and XR650L models
2    Disconnect the cable from the negative terminal of the battery (see Chapter 5). Disconnect the fuel line from the fuel tap. On XR650L models, remove the shrouds from the tank (see Chapter 8).
3    Remove the mounting bolt at the rear of the tank **(see illustration)**. Pull the tank backward so the cups clear the rubber mounts, then lift the tank off the machine.

### XR600R and XR650R models
4    Remove the seat (see Chapter 8).
5    If you're working on an XR650R, remove the radiator shroud-to-radiator bolts **(see illustration)**.
6    Unhook the strap from the rear of the tank **(see illustrations)**.

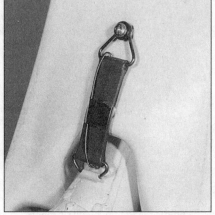

**2.6a  Unhook the retaining strap from the tank . . .**

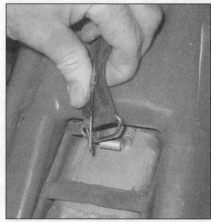

**2.6b  . . . or, on XR650R models, from the hook on the frame**

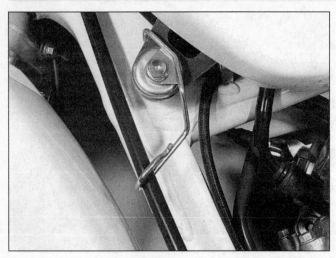

**2.7a Remove the mounting bolts at the front (there's one on each side) - this is an XR600R**

**2.7b The fuel tank mounting bolts on XR650R models are accessed through the openings between the radiator shroud and the tank**

7   Remove the fuel tank mounting bolts **(see illustrations)**.
8   Disconnect the fuel line from the fuel tap **(see illustration)**.
9   Lift the fuel tank off the bike together with the fuel tap.

## Installation

10   Before installing the tank, check the condition of the rubber mounting bushings at the front, the insulator on the frame and the rubber mount or strap at the rear - if they're hardened, cracked, or show any other signs of deterioration, replace them **(see illustrations)**.
11   When installing the tank, reverse the removal procedure. Make sure the tank does not pinch any wires. Tighten the tank mounting bolt(s) securely, but don't overtighten them and strip the threads.

## 3   Fuel tank - cleaning and repair

1   Metal fuel tanks can be repaired, depending on the extent of damage. All repairs to the fuel tank should be carried out by a professional who has experience in this critical and potentially dangerous work. Even after cleaning and flushing of the fuel system, explosive fumes can remain and ignite during repair of the tank.
2   Plastic tanks cannot be repaired. In the event of damage, a plastic tank must be replaced with a new one.
3   If the fuel tank is removed from the vehicle, it should not be placed in an area where sparks or open flames could ignite the fumes coming out of the tank. Be especially careful inside garages where a gas-type appliance is located, because it could cause an explosion.

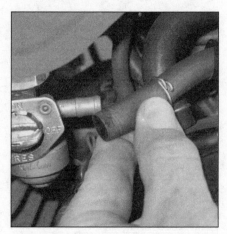

**2.8 Squeeze the clamp and slide it back on the fuel line, then disconnect the fuel line from the tap**

**2.10a XL600R and XR650L models have bushings on each side of the frame that engage with cups on the fuel tank. Replace them if they're not in good condition**

**2.10b Replace the mounting insulator on top of the frame if it's deteriorated (XR600R shown)**

## 4  Idle fuel/air mixture adjustment

**Note:** *The mixture screw is also known as the pilot screw.*

### Normal adjustment

1   Idle fuel/air mixture on these vehicles is preset at the factory and should not need adjustment unless the carburetor is over-hauled or the mixture adjustment screw is replaced. A limiter cap on XL600R and XR650L models prevents the mixture adjust-ment screw from being turned to enrichen the mixture. Because XR600R and XR650R models are off-road bikes, they are not required to have a limiter cap on the mixture screw.
2   On 1983 XL600R models and 1983 through 1987 XR600R models, mixture adjustment is controlled by an air screw mounted in the side of the carburetor **(see illustration)**.
3   On 1984 through 1987 XL600R models, 1988 and later XR600R models and XR650L models, mixture is controlled by a pilot screw mounted in the underside of the carburetor body **(see illustrations)**. On XR650R models the pilot screw is located on the right side of the carburetor body **(see illustration)**.
4   The engine must be properly tuned-up before making the adjustment (valve clear-ances set to specifications, spark plug in good condition and properly gapped). You'll also need a tune-up tachometer that can accurately indicate changes as small as 100 rpm.

### 1983 XL600R models

5   The air screw is covered by a limiter cap that allows it to be rotated only coun-terclockwise (leaner mixture) and prevents it from being rotated clockwise (richer mixture).

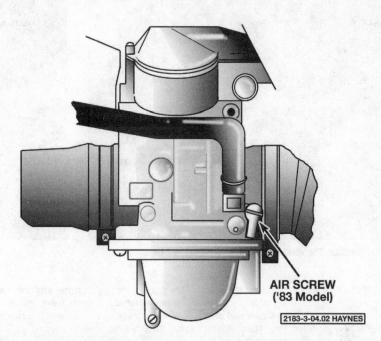

**AIR SCREW ('83 Model)**

2183-3-04.02 HAYNES

**4.2  Idle mixture on 1983 XL600R models and 1983 through 1987 XR600R models is adjusted with an air screw that may have a limiter cap . . .**

The limiter cap must be broken off with pliers to make initial mixture adjustments when the carburetor is overhauled.
6   Once the limiter cap is removed, back the air screw all the way out of the carbure-tor.
7   Install the new air screw in the carbure-tor and turn it clockwise until it seats lightly, then back it out the number of turns listed in this Chapter's Specifications **(see illustra-tion 4.2)**.

*Caution: Turn the screw just far enough to seat it lightly. If it's bottomed hard, the screw or its seat may be damaged, which will make accurate mixture adjustments impossible.*

8   Warm up the engine to normal operating temperature (10 minutes of stop-and-go rid-ing will do). Shut it off and connect a tune-up tachometer, following the tachometer manu-facturer's instructions.
9   Restart the engine and compare idle speed to the value listed in the Chapter 1 Specifications. Adjust it if necessary.
10   Turn the air screw in or out to obtain the highest possible idle speed.
11   Recheck idle speed on the tachometer and readjust it to the specified setting with the throttle stop screw.
12   Slowly turn the air screw clockwise until idle speed drops 100 rpm.
13   Back the air screw out one full turn,

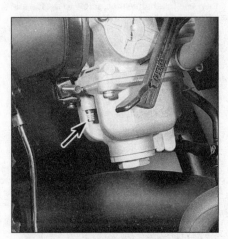

**4.3a  . . . on other models it's adjusted with a pilot screw; the pilot screw has a limiter cap on street-legal models. This is an XL600R model**

**4.3b  Pilot screw location - XR650L model**

**4.3c  Pilot screw location - XR650R model**

4.33a Throttle stop screw - XR650L models

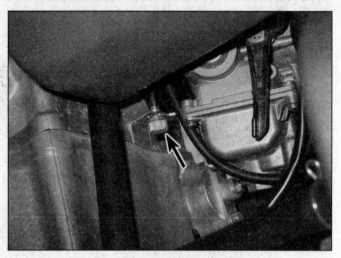

4.33b Throttle stop screw - XR650R models

then readjust idle speed with the throttle stop screw.

14   Coat the inside of a new limiter cap with Loctite 601 or equivalent, then install it with its tab resting against the stop on the carburetor body so the screw can be turned counterclockwise but not clockwise.

### 1984 through 1987 XL600R models

15   Remove the carburetor from the motorcycle, then remove the float chamber from the carburetor (see Sections 6 and 7).

16   If you're installing a new mixture screw, remove the old one from the carburetor. Install the new one without the limiter cap for now.

17   Turn the mixture screw clockwise until it seats lightly, then back it out the number of turns listed in this Chapter's Specifications (see illustration 4.3a).

*Caution: Turn the screw just far enough to seat it lightly. If it's bottomed hard, the screw or its seat may be damaged, which will make accurate mixture adjustments impossible.*

18   Warm up the engine to normal operating temperature (10 minutes of stop-and-go riding will do). Shut it off and connect a tune-up tachometer, following the tachometer manufacturer's instructions.

19   Restart the engine and compare idle speed to the value listed in the Chapter 1 Specifications. Adjust it if necessary.

20   Turn the mixture screw in or out to obtain the highest possible idle speed.

21   Recheck idle speed on the tachometer and readjust it to the specified setting with the throttle stop screw.

22   Slowly turn the mixture screw clockwise until idle speed drops 100 rpm. **Note:** *If the pilot screw bottoms before engine speed drops 100 rpm, go to the next step.*

23   Back the mixture screw out two full turns, then readjust idle speed with the throttle stop screw.

24   Coat the inside of a new limiter cap with Loctite 601 or equivalent, then install it so

its tab will rest against the stop on the float chamber (after the float chamber is installed) so the screw can be turned clockwise but not counterclockwise.

### XR600R models

25   Turn the mixture screw clockwise until it seats lightly, then back it out the number of turns listed in this Chapter's Specifications (on 1998 and later models, use the initial setting) (see illustration 4.2 or 4.3a).

26   Warm up the engine to normal operating temperature (10 minutes of stop-and-go riding will do). Shut it off and connect a tune-up tachometer, following the tachometer manufacturer's instructions.

27   Restart the engine and compare idle speed to the value listed in the Chapter 1 Specifications. Adjust it if necessary.

28   Turn the mixture screw in or out to obtain the highest possible idle speed.

a) *If you're working on a 1997 or earlier model, go to Step 29.*

b) *If you're working on a 1998 or later model, turn the mixture screw (not the throttle stop screw) slowly clockwise until idle speed drops 100 rpm from the highest speed. Then turn the mixture screw back out the number of turns listed under the Final setting in this Chapter's Specifications.*

29   Recheck idle speed on the tachometer and readjust it to the specified setting with the throttle stop screw.

### XR650L and XR650R models

30   Turn the mixture screw clockwise until it seats lightly, then back it out the number of turns listed in this Chapter's Specifications (use the initial setting) (see illustration 4.3b or 4.3c). **Note:** *On 2007 and later U.S market XR650R models, a "D"-shaped screw tool is required.*

31   If you're working on an XR650R model with a secondary air injection system, disconnect the PAIR valve vacuum hose and plug it (a golf tee works well). Connect a hand-held

vacuum pump to the port on the PAIR valve (see illustrations 12.2a and 12.2b). Apply a vacuum of at least 14.5 in-Hg (48 kPa).

32   Warm up the engine to normal operating temperature (10 minutes of stop-and-go riding will do). Shut it off and connect a tachometer, following the tachometer manufacturer's instructions.

33   Start the engine and adjust the idle speed with the throttle stop screw (see illustrations).

34   Turn the mixture screw in or out until the highest idle speed is obtained.

35   Turn the throttle stop screw to readjust the idle speed.

36   Crack the throttle open two or three times, then recheck the idle speed, adjusting it if necessary.

37   Slowly turn the mixture screw in until the idle speed decreases by 50 rpm (XR650L models) or 100 rpm (XR650R models).

38   From this point, turn the mixture screw out the number of turns given in the *Final setting* listed in this Chapter's Specifications, then use the throttle stop screw to set the idle speed.

### High altitude adjustment

39   If the motorcycle is normally used at altitudes from sea level to 5000 feet, use the normal main jets and mixture screw setting. If it's used regularly at altitudes above 5000 feet, the mixture screw setting, as well as the main jets on all except 1983 XL600R models, must be changed to compensate for the thinner air.

*Caution: Don't use the bike for sustained operation below 5000 feet with the main jets and mixture screw at the high altitude settings or the engine may overheat and be damaged.*

### 1983 XL600R models

40   Warm up the engine to normal operating temperature (10 minutes of stop-and-go riding will do). Shut it off and connect a tune-up

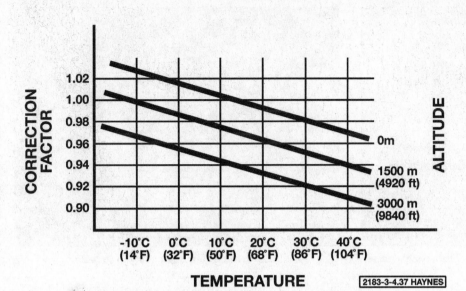

**4.46 Use this chart to determine the correction factor (XR600R models)**

[2183-3-4.37 HAYNES]

tachometer, following the tachometer manufacturer's instructions.
41 Turn the air screw 1/2 turn counterclockwise, then recheck idle speed on the tachometer and reset it, if necessary, to the value listed in this Chapter's Specifications.

### 1984 through 1987 XL600R models
42 Remove the carburetors (see Section 6). Replace the primary and secondary main jets with the high altitude jets listed in this Chapter's Specifications, then reinstall the carburetors.
43 Turn the mixture screw to the high altitude setting listed in this Chapter's Specifications.
44 Warm up the engine to normal operating temperature (10 minutes of stop-and-go riding will do). Shut it off and connect a tune-up tachometer, following the tachometer manufacturer's instructions.
45 Restart the engine and compare idle speed to the value listed in the Chapter 1 Specifications. Adjust it if necessary with the throttle stop screw.

### XR600R models
46 These models are rejetted to compensate for changes in temperature as well as altitude. This means you'll need a thermometer to determine the air temperature. To figure out whether you need to make any changes, find your altitude and the local air temperature on the accompanying chart (see illustration). Draw a line up from the temperature setting to the altitude line. From where the two lines meet, read across to the correction factor.
47 If the correction factor is above 0.95, leave the carburetor at the standard settings. If it's 0.95 or less, make changes as described below.
48 Turn the mixture adjusting screw in 1/2

turn from the standard setting. Raise the jet needle clip by one groove from the standard setting.
49 Multiply the standard main jet number by the correction factor to determine the proper size of main jet. For example, if your main jet is a no. 165 and the correction factor is 0.92, multiply 165 X 0.92 to get 151.8. Rounded off, the correct size main jet is 152.
50 Refer to Section 7 and change the main jet to the high altitude jet.
51 With the motorcycle at high altitude, adjust the idle speed with the throttle stop screw.

### XR650L and XR650R models
52 These models must also be rejetted to compensate for high altitude conditions. Remove the carburetor as described in Section 6, then remove the float bowl and change the main jet to the high-altitude jet listed in this Chapter's Specifications. Also change the needle clip to the groove listed in this Chapter's Specifications (XR650R models only).
53 With the motorcycle at high altitude, the mixture screw must be turned in the amount listed in this Chapter's Specifications under the *High altitude mixture (pilot) screw setting*.
54 Finally, adjust the idle speed with the throttle stop screw.

### 5 Carburetor overhaul - general information

1 Poor engine performance, hesitation, hard starting, stalling, flooding and backfiring are all signs that major carburetor maintenance may be required.
2 Keep in mind that many so-called car-

buretor problems are really not carburetor problems at all, but mechanical problems within the engine or ignition system malfunctions. Try to establish for certain that the carburetor is in need of maintenance before beginning a major overhaul.
3 Check the fuel tap and its strainer screen, the fuel lines, the intake manifold clamps, the O-ring between the intake manifold and cylinder head (XR600L, XR600R and XR650L models), the vacuum hoses, the air filter element, the cylinder compression, the spark plug and the ignition timing before assuming that a carburetor overhaul is required. If the bike has been unused for more than a month, drain the float chamber and refill the tank with fresh fuel (see illustrations 6.6a and 6.6b). Note: *A dirty mixture screw is a common source of trouble, especially if the bike hasn't been ridden in awhile.*
4 Most carburetor problems are caused by dirt particles, varnish and other deposits which build up in and block the fuel and air passages. Also, in time, gaskets and O-rings shrink or deteriorate and cause fuel and air leaks which lead to poor performance.
5 When the carburetor is overhauled, it is generally disassembled completely and the parts are cleaned thoroughly with a carburetor cleaning solvent and dried with filtered, unlubricated compressed air. The fuel and air passages are also blown through with compressed air to force out any dirt that may have been loosened but not removed by the solvent. Once the cleaning process is complete, the carburetor is reassembled using new gaskets, O-rings and, generally, a new inlet needle valve and seat.
6 Before disassembling the carburetor(s), make sure you have a carburetor rebuild kit (which will include all necessary O-rings and other parts), some carburetor cleaner, a supply of rags, some means of blowing out the carburetor passages and a clean place to work. Note: *If you don't have an air compressor, cans of compressed air (the kind used to blow dust from computer keyboards, etc.) will suffice.*

### 6 Carburetor - removal and installation

⚠ Warning: *Gasoline is extremely flammable, so take extra precautions when you work on any part of the fuel system. Don't smoke or allow open flames or bare light bulbs near the work area, and don't work in a garage where a gas-type appliance (such as a water heater or clothes dryer) is present. Since gasoline is carcinogenic, wear fuel-resistant gloves when there's a possibility of being exposed to fuel, and, if you spill any fuel on your skin, rinse it off immediately*

6.4  XR650R models: Remove the screw and throttle cable guide, then detach the cables from the throttle drum

6.5a  XR650L carburetor details - left side

A   PAIR valve vacuum hose
B   Starting enrichment (choke) valve/cable

with soap and water. Mop up any spills immediately and do not store fuel-soaked rags where they could ignite. When you perform any kind of work on the fuel system, wear safety glasses and have a Class B type fire extinguisher on hand.

### Removal

1   Remove the seat and both side covers (see Chapter 8).
2   Remove the fuel tank (see Section 2).
3   **XL600R:** Disconnect the throttle and choke cables at the carburetor (see Section 10).

4   **XR650R:** Remove the screw and detach the throttle cable guide from the side of the carburetor (see illustration), then detach the cable ends from the throttle drum.
5   **XR650L:** Remove the crankcase breather separator, the PAIR valve vacuum hose, the EVAP purge control valve hose (California models) (see Section 12) and the starting enrichment (choke) valve and cable from the left side of the carburetor (see illustrations). On the right side of the bike, unbolt the rear brake fluid reservoir from the frame and position it out of the way, but keep it upright to avoid spilling brake fluid. Loosen the throttle cable locknuts and detach the cables from the bracket, then detach the ends from the throttle drum (see Section 10).
6   Place a container under the carburetor drain hose, then loosen the fuel drain screw and allow the fuel in the float bowl to drain (see illustrations).
7   If you're working on a 1985 through 1987 XR600R, remove the mounting bands

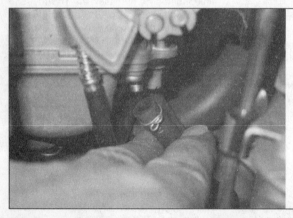

6.5b  Also detach the EVAP purge control valve hose from the right side of the carburetor (California XR650L models only)

6.6a  With a container placed under the carburetor drain hose . . .

6.6b  . . . loosen the drain screw and empty the float bowl

6.8 Loosen the clamping band screws

6.13 When reinstalling the carburetor, make sure the lug(s) on the carburetor body align with the tabs on the air filter housing duct and the intake manifold

from the rear shock reservoir and move the shock reservoir out of the way.

8    Loosen the clamping bands on the air filter duct and intake manifold **(see illustration)**. Work the carburetor free of the duct and manifold and lift it off, removing it from the right side of the bike.

9    **XR600R:** Disconnect the throttle cables from the carburetor (see Section 10).

10    Disconnect the vent and drain hoses from the carburetor.

11    Check the intake manifold tube for cracks, deterioration or other damage. If it has visible defects, or if there's reason to suspect its O-ring is leaking, remove it from the engine and inspect the O-ring (all except XR650R models, which have no O-ring). On 1983 through 1987 models, also remove the insulator spacer and inspect its O-rings.

12    After the carburetor has been removed, stuff clean rags into the intake manifold (or the intake port in the cylinder head, if the manifold has been removed) to prevent the entry of dirt or other objects.

## Installation

13    Installation is the reverse of the removal steps, with the following additions:

a) *When installing the carburetor, make sure the lugs on the carburetor body align with the tabs on the air filter housing duct and the intake manifold* **(see illustration)**.

b) *Adjust the throttle freeplay (see Chapter 1).*

c) *Adjust the idle speed (see Chapter 1).*

---

**7    Carburetor - disassembly, cleaning and inspection**

⚠️ *Warning: Gasoline is extremely flammable, so take extra precautions when you work on any part of the fuel system. Don't smoke or allow open flames or bare light bulbs near the work area, and don't work in a garage where a gas-type appliance (such as a water heater or clothes dryer) is present. Since gasoline is carcinogenic, wear fuel-resistant gloves when there's a possibility of being exposed to fuel, and, if you spill any fuel on your skin, rinse it off immediately with soap and water. Mop up any spills immediately and do not store fuel-soaked rags where they could ignite. When you perform any kind of work on the fuel system, wear safety glasses and have a Class B type fire extinguisher on hand.*

## Disassembly

1    Remove the carburetor(s) from the machine as described in Section 6. Set it on a clean working surface.

2    If it's necessary to separate the carburetors from each other on a dual carburetor model, remove the two assembly screws and detach the connecting hose. Remove the bracket for the throttle stop screw and separate the carburetors.

### All except XR650L models

3    To disassemble the carburetor(s), refer to the accompanying illustrations **(see illustrations)**.

7.3a  Remove the two screws . . .

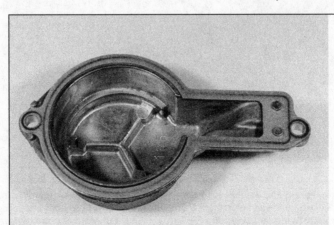

7.3b . . . and lift the top and gasket (or O-ring) off the carburetor

7.3c Remove the screw from the link arm

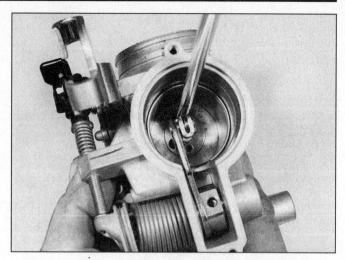

7.3d Remove the screws and lift out the link arm, link and jet needle retainer

7.3e Lift the jet needle out of the throttle valve and lift the throttle valve out of the carburetor

7.3f Remove the air cutoff valve cover screws; note the location of the air passage

7.3g Remove the O-ring, spring and diaphragm (some models use a U-ring instead of an O-ring. When installing a U-ring, install the flat side toward the carburetor body)

7.3h Remove the float chamber screws; the plug in the bottom of the float chamber allows the main jet to be changed without removing the carburetor from the engine. This is an XR600R . . .

7.3i  ... and this is an XR650R (screw "A" secures the throttle stop screw bracket)

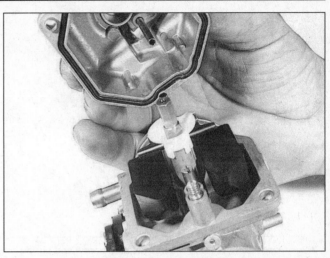

7.3j  Lift the float chamber and O-ring off the carburetor body

7.3k  Note the location of the notch in the baffle; push out the float pivot pin and remove the floats

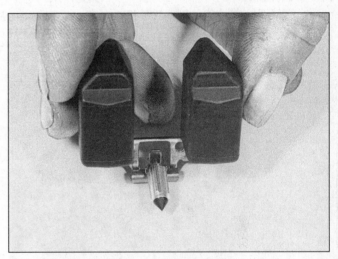

7.3l  Detach the needle valve from the floats

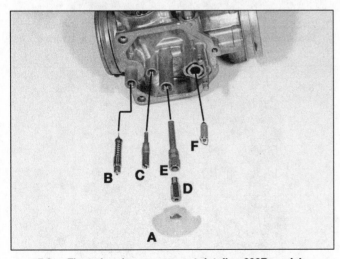

7.3m  Float chamber component details - 600R models

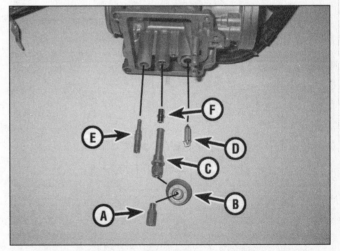

7.3n  Float chamber jets and needle valve - 650R models

| A | Baffle | D | Main jet |
| B | Pilot (mixture) screw | E | Needle jet holder |
|   | (if equipped) | F | Needle valve and clip |
| C | Slow jet | | |

| A | Main jet | D | Needle valve and clip |
| B | Jet holder | E | Slow jet |
| C | Needle jet holder | F | Needle jet |

7.3o If necessary, remove the throttle stop screw and spring

7.4a Remove the screws from the vacuum chamber cover . . .

## XR650L models

4    To disassemble the carburetor, refer to the accompanying illustrations (see illustrations).

## Cleaning

*Caution: Use only a carburetor cleaning solution that is safe for use with plastic parts (be sure to read the label on the container).*

4    Submerge the metal components in the carburetor cleaner for approximately thirty minutes (or longer, if the directions recommend it).

5    After the carburetor has soaked long

7.4b . . . then remove the cover, spring, diaphragm and vacuum piston/jet needle

7.4c Using an 8 mm socket (or, on later models a Phillips screwdriver), push down on the needle holder and turn it counterclockwise 1/4 -turn . . .

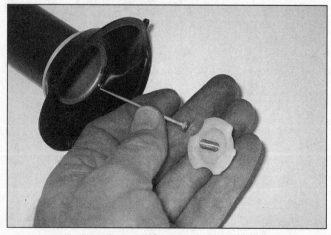

7.4d . . . then remove the jet needle and holder spring

7.4e Remove the float chamber screws, then lift off the float chamber and remove the O-ring

7.4f  Push out the float pivot pin . . .

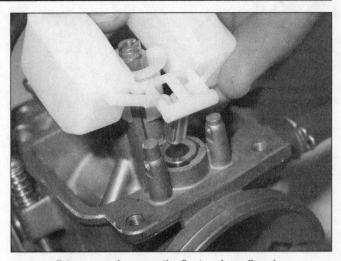

7.4g  . . . and remove the float and needle valve

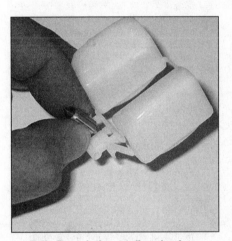

7.4h  Detach the needle valve from the float

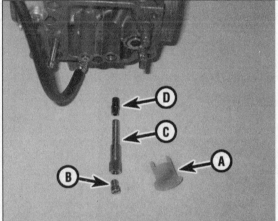

7.4i  Float chamber component details - XR650L models (remove and clean these components)

A   Baffle
B   Main jet
C   Needle jet holder
D   Needle jet

enough for the cleaner to loosen and dissolve most of the varnish and other deposits. Rinse it again, then dry it with compressed air. Blow out all of the fuel and air passages in the carburetor body.

*Caution: Never clean the jets or passages with a piece of wire or a drill bit, as they will be enlarged, causing the fuel and air metering rates to be upset.*

## Inspection

6   Check the operation of the choke valve (1983 through 1987), choke lever (1988 and later 600/650R models) or the starting enrichment (choke) valve (XR650L models). If it doesn't move smoothly, replace it.

7.4j  Remove the air cutoff valve screws . . .

7.4k  . . . and the cover, spring and diaphragm

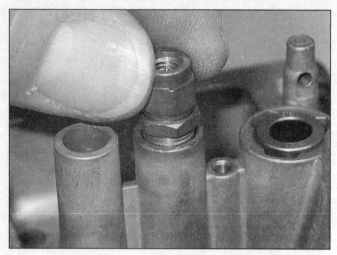

8.3a Thread the needle jet holder in until it seats . . .

8.3b . . . then tighten the locknut

7    Check the tapered portion of the air screw or pilot screw for wear or damage. Replace the screw if necessary.

8    Check the carburetor body, float chamber and carburetor top for cracks, distorted sealing surfaces and other damage. If any defects are found, replace the faulty component, although replacement of the entire carburetor will probably be necessary (check with your parts supplier for the availability of separate components).

9    Check the jet needle for straightness by rolling it on a flat surface (such as a piece of glass). Replace it if it's bent or if the tip is worn.

10    Check the tip of the fuel inlet valve needle. If it has grooves or scratches in it, it must be replaced. Push in on the rod in the other end of the needle, then release it - if it doesn't spring back, replace the valve needle.

11    Check the O-rings on the float chamber and the drain plug (in the float chamber). Replace them if they're damaged.

12    Check the floats for damage. This will usually be apparent by the presence of fuel

inside one of the floats. If the floats are damaged, they must be replaced.

13    Insert the throttle valve in the carburetor body and see that it moves up-and-down smoothly. Check the surface of the throttle valve for wear. If it's worn excessively or doesn't move smoothly in the bore, replace the carburetor.

14    On XR650L models, inspect the vacuum piston diaphragm for tears or cracking. Also make sure the vacuum piston moves up-and-down smoothly in its bore, and make sure its surface isn't worn excessively.

## 8    Carburetor - reassembly and float height check

**Caution: When installing the jets, be careful not to over-tighten them - they're made of soft material and can strip or shear easily.**

**Note:** When reassembling the carburetor,

be sure to use the new O-rings, gaskets and other parts supplied in the rebuild kit.

1    Install the clip on the jet needle if it was removed. Place it in the needle groove listed in this Chapter's Specifications. Install the needle and clip in the throttle valve.

2    Install the pilot screw along with its spring, washer and O-ring, turning it in until it seats lightly. Now, turn the screw out the number of turns listed in this Chapter's Specifications.

3    Reverse the disassembly steps to install the jets. On XR650R models, when installing the needle jet holder, screw it in until it's seated, then tighten the locknut **(see illustrations)**. Next, install the baffle, followed by the main jet holder and jet **(see illustrations)**.

4    Invert the carburetor. Attach the fuel inlet valve needle to the float. Set the float into position in the carburetor, making sure the valve needle seats correctly. Install the float pivot pin. To check the float height, hold the carburetor so the float hangs down, then tilt it back until the valve needle is just seated. Measure the distance from the float

8.3c Install the baffle and tighten the screw securely . . .

8.3d . . . then install the main jet and jet holder

chamber gasket surface to the top of the float and compare your measurement to the float height listed in this Chapter's Specifications. On models with a metal float tang, bend the float tang as necessary to change the adjustment. **Note:** *On models with a plastic float tang, the float height is not adjustable.*

5  Install the O-ring into the groove in the float chamber. Place the float chamber on the carburetor and install the screws, tightening them securely.

### 9  Air filter housing - removal and installation

#### XL600R and XR600R models

1  Remove the seat and both side covers (see Chapter 8). If you're working on an XR600R, remove the inner fender as well.
2  If you're working on an XL600R, remove the battery, regulator and regulator/rectifier (see Chapter 5). Remove the retainer for the wiring harness that runs across the top of the air cleaner case, then unplug the harness at the connector and position it out of the way.
3  If you're working on a 1985 through 1987 XR600R, remove the shock absorber reservoir mounting bands and position the reservoir out of the way. Remove the regulator and detach the wiring harness retainer from the top of the air cleaner case.
4  Loosen the clamp and detach the connecting tube(s) from the carburetor **(see illustration 6.5)**.
5  Lift the air duct out of the air cleaner housing **(see illustration)**.
6  Remove the air cleaner housing bolts (two on top of the case and one on the right side). Lift the air cleaner housing out of the frame, together with the intake duct.
7  Installation is the reverse of the removal steps.

**9.5  Lift the air duct out of the air filter housing (600R models)**

#### XR650L models

8  Remove both side covers, the seat and the mudguard at the front end of the rear fender (see Chapter 8).
9  Detach the breather tube and the air suction hose (if equipped) from the underside of the air filter housing **(see illustration)**.
10  Release the wire harness band clamps and free the harness from the clamps, then remove the mounting bolts **(see illustration)**.
11  Loosen the clamp and detach the connecting tube from the air filter housing duct to the carburetor.
12  Carefully maneuver the air filter housing out from the left side of the frame.
13  Installation is the reverse of removal.

#### XR650R models

14  Remove the subframe, then remove the mudguard from the air filter housing (see Chapter 8).
15  Remove the bolts and detach the air filter housing from the subframe.

**9.9  Squeeze the clamp(s) and slide them back on the hose(s), then detach the breather tube and air suction hose (if equipped) from the air filter housing (XR650L models)**

16  Check the connection between the air filter housing and the duct; if the seal has broken, remove the duct and apply new sealant to the duct's groove, then reinstall the duct.
17  Installation is the reverse of removal.

### 10  Throttle cables - removal, installation and adjustment

#### Removal and installation

1  Remove the fuel tank (see Section 2).
2  At the handlebar, loosen the throttle cable adjuster all the way (see Chapter 1).
3  Loosen the screw that secures the cover on the throttle cable roller (if equipped) **(see illustration)**. Separate the halves of the throttle cable housing, then slide the housing and throttle grip off the handlebar.

**9.10  Release the band clamps, detach the wiring harness from the housing and remove the mounting bolts (XR650L models)**

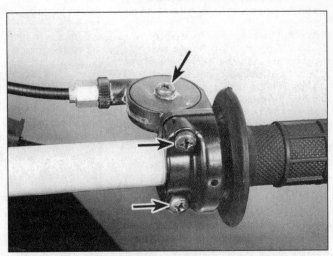
**10.3  Loosen the screw that secures the throttle roller cover (upper arrow) and remove the throttle housing screws (lower arrows) - 600R model shown, 650L/R models similar**

10.4a  Slide the throttle grip off the handlebar, then remove the throttle roller cover, gasket and throttle roller

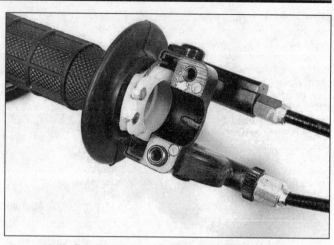

10.4b  Free the ends of the throttle cables from the throttle grip pulley

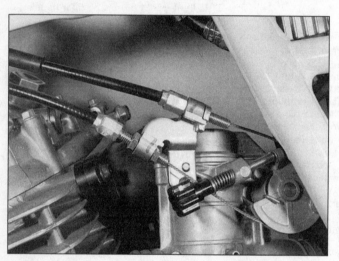

10.5a  At the carburetor, loosen the cable locknuts, detach the cables from the bracket and free the ends from the throttle pulley - this is a 600R . . .

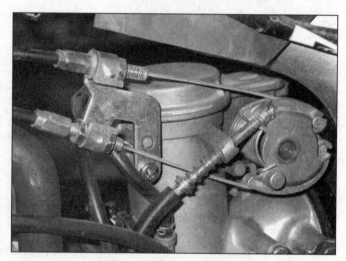

10.5b  . . . this is an XR650R . . .

4    Remove the cover, gasket and throttle cable roller (if equipped) **(see illustration)**. Rotate the cable ends to align them with the slots in the throttle grip pulley, then slip the ends out of the pulley **(see illustration)**.

5    At the carburetor(s), loosen the cable locknuts and slip the cables out of the bracket **(see illustrations)**. Rotate the cables to align with the slots in the throttle pulley and slide the cable ends sideways to detach them from the pulley.

6    Route the cables into place. Make sure they don't interfere with any other components and aren't kinked or bent sharply.

7    Lubricate the throttle pulley ends of the cables with multi-purpose grease. Reverse the disconnection steps to connect the throttle cables to the throttle grip pulley. If the bike has a throttle roller, install the roller, gasket and cover.

8    Coat the handlebar with silicone grease and slide the throttle housing and throttle grip on. Position the throttle housing so the parting line of the throttle housing and clamp is aligned with the punch mark on the handle-bar, then install the clamp **(see illustration)**. Tighten the clamp screws securely, then tighten the throttle roller screw (if equipped) securely.

9    Attach the cables to the throttle pulley at the carburetor and position them in

10.5c  . . . and this is an XR650L

the bracket.

10    Operate the throttle and make sure it returns to the idle position by itself under spring pressure.

10.8  The punch mark in the handlebar aligns with the parting line of the throttle housing halves upon installation

**11.1 Remove the holder nuts and slide the holders off the studs**

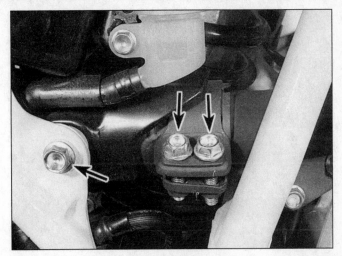

**11.2a Remove the forward mounting bolt (left arrow); to separate the muffler from the exhaust pipes, loosen the clamp bolts (right arrows)**

 *Warning: If the throttle doesn't return by itself, find and solve the problem before continuing with installation. A stuck throttle can lead to loss of control of the motorcycle.*

## Adjustment

11   Follow the procedure outlined in Chapter 1, *Throttle operation/grip freeplay - check and adjustment*, to adjust the cables.

12   Turn the handlebars back and forth to make sure the cables don't cause the steering to bind.

13   Once you're sure the cables operate properly, install the fuel tank.

14   With the engine idling, turn the handlebars through their full travel (full left lock to full right lock) and note whether idle speed increases. If it does, the cable is routed incorrectly. Correct this dangerous condition before riding the bike.

## 11 Exhaust system - removal and installation

1   Remove the exhaust pipe holder nuts and slide the holders off the mounting studs **(see illustration)**. **Note:** *If you're working on an XR650R, remove the radiator mounting fasteners and move them out of the way for access to the fasteners.*

2   Remove the muffler mounting bolts **(see illustrations)**.

3   Pull the exhaust system forward, separate the pipe from the cylinder head and remove the system from the machine. To detach the muffler, loosen the clamp and pull the pipes out of it **(see illustration 11.2a)**.

4   Installation is the reverse of removal, with the following additions:

a)  Be sure to install new gaskets at the cylinder head **(see illustration)**, and a new sleeve gasket where the muffler meets the exhaust pipe.

b)  Tighten the muffler mounting bolts, clamp bolts and holder nuts to the torque listed in this Chapter Specifications.

## 12 Emission control systems (XR650L and XR650R models)

### Secondary air supply system

**Description**

1   To reduce the amount of unburned hydrocarbons released in the exhaust gases, a pulse secondary air (PAIR) system is installed on all XR650L models destined for

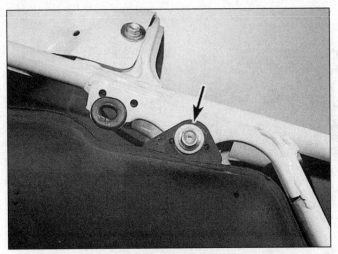

**11.2b Remove the rear mounting bolt to detach the muffler from the frame**

**11.4 Install new gaskets in the exhaust ports**

12.2a On XR650L models, the PAIR valve is located on the left side of the bike, above the left crankcase cover

12.2b On XR650R models, the PAIR control valve is mounted on a bracket attached to the right-side radiator

the U.S.A., 1996 and later XR650L models destined for Canada, and all XR650R models first sold in California. This system consists of the PAIR valve, and plumbing from the air filter housing to the valve, and from the valve to the exhaust ports. The PAIR valve allows fresh air to be drawn into the exhaust ports whenever negative pressure pulses are present in the exhaust system; this helps to complete combustion of the unburned hydrocarbons. Under periods of high intake manifold vacuum, the PAIR valve closes, which prevents exhaust from flowing backwards through the system. Cutting off fresh air to the exhaust system under deceleration also reduces backfiring.

### Check

2    Check the air supply hose and air injection pipes to and from the valve for deterioration and heat damage (see illustrations). Make sure the vacuum hose isn't cracked.
3    Disconnect the PAIR air supply hose from the air filter housing. Also detach the vacuum hose where it tees into the carburetor (XR650L) or the right side of the carburetor (XR650R) and connect a hand-held vacuum pump to the hose.
4    Start the engine and raise the engine speed a little and confirm that air is being sucked into the hose that was disconnected from the air filter housing.
5    Apply about 13 in-Hg of vacuum to the valve; air should no longer be sucked into the hose.
6    If air is still being sucked in, or if the PAIR valve doesn't hold vacuum, replace the PAIR valve with a new one.

### PAIR valve removal and installation

7    If you're working on an XR650R, remove the fuel tank (see Section 2).
8    Loosen the clamps and disconnect the hoses from the PAIR valve.
9    Remove the mounting fasteners and remove the PAIR valve.
10   Installation is the reverse of removal.

## Evaporative emission control (EVAP) system

### Description

11   XL600R and XR650L models first sold in California are equipped with an evaporative emission control (EVAP) system. This system stores vapors from the fuel tank and carburetors while the engine is not running. When the engine is running and the purge control valve is open, fuel vapors stored in the charcoal canister are drawn back into the intake tract and burned along with the air/fuel mixture.

### Check

12   Disconnect the vacuum hoses from the purge control valve, located on the left side of the bike, near the carburetor (see illustration). Connect a hand-held vacuum pump to each vacuum port one at a time) and apply vacuum. If the valve can't maintain the vacuum applied to it, replace the valve.
13   Check the hoses for loose connections and deterioration, replacing as necessary.
14   Check the charcoal canister for dam-

age and leaks, replacing if either condition is found. Note: If the canister has fuel in it, also be sure to check the carburetor float level and float. If the float level is too high, or if the float is defective and sinks, fuel will flow into the canister.

### Purge control valve removal and installation

15   Detach the valve from its rubber mount on the frame, then disconnect the hoses from the valve.
16   Installation is the reverse of removal.

### Canister removal and installation

17   On XL600R models the canister is located on the left side of the bike, above the left crankcase cover.
18   On XR650L models the canister is located on the left side of the bike, mounted to the frame downtube (see illustration).
19   On either model, disconnect the hoses from the canister, remove the mounting fasteners, then remove the canister from the bike.
20   Installation is the reverse of removal.

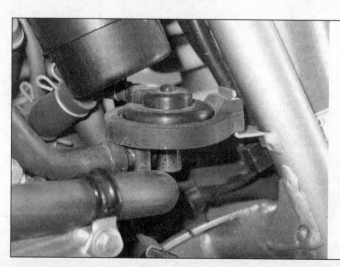

12.12 EVAP purge control valve (XR650L)

12.18 Charcoal canister mounting details (XR650L)

A    To purge control valve
B    To gas cap
C    Lower breather tube (to bracket on frame)
D    Upper breather tube (to bracket on cylinder head)
E    Mounting bolts

## Crankcase emission control system

21    XL600R and XR650L models first sold in California are equipped with a crankcase emission control system. This system routes blow-by gases and oil vapors back into the intake tract, where they are burned along with the normal air/fuel mixture.

22    The system consists of a breather/separator mounted on the left side of the bike (above the transmission) **(see illustration)**, a hose from the top of the crankcase to the valve, and a hose from the valve to the air filter housing.

23    Check the valve and hoses connected to the valve for cracks, hardening and other signs of deterioration, replacing as necessary.

12.22 Crankcase breather/separator (XR650L)

# Notes

# Chapter 5
# Ignition and electrical systems

## Contents

## Degrees of difficulty

| | | |
|---|---|---|
| **Easy,** suitable for novice with little experience  | **Fairly easy,** suitable for beginner with some experience  | **Fairly difficult,** suitable for competent DIY mechanic  |
| **Difficult,** suitable for experienced DIY mechanic 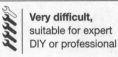 | **Very difficult,** suitable for expert DIY or professional  | |

## Specifications

### General
Battery
  XL600R
    Type ................................................................ 12V, 3Ah (amp-hours)
    Specific gravity ............................................... See Chapter 1
  XR650R
    Type ................................................................ 12V, 8Ah (amp-hours)
    Specific gravity ............................................... See Chapter 1
Fuse rating
  XL600R ............................................................ 10 amps
  XR650L
    Main fuse ......................................................... 20 amps
    Other three fuses (ignition, headlight, speedometer/tail/marker lights) ............ 10 amps
Charging system voltage
  XL600R, XR650R ............................................. 13.7 to 15.3 volts AC
AC regulator voltage
  XL600R
    1983 through 1986 ......................................... 13.5 to 14.5 volts at 5000 rpm
    1987 ............................................................... 13.7 to 14.2 volts at 5000 rpm
  XR600R ............................................................ 13.5 to 14.5 volts at 5000 rpm
  XR650L ............................................................ 14.7 to 15.5 volts at 5000 rpm
  XR650R ............................................................ 13.5 to 14.5 volts at 4500 rpm
AC regulator resistance (XR600R) ......................... 1 to 90 k-ohms

## Alternator stator coil resistance

XL600R
 Charging coil.................................................................. 0.95 to 1.29 ohms
 Lighting coil.................................................................. 0.4 to 0.55 ohms
 Exciter coil................................................................... 230 to 320 ohms
XR600R
 Exciter coil
  1985 through 1990................................................... 230 to 320 ohms
  1991 on.................................................................... 50 to 200 ohms
 Lighting coil
  1985 through 1987................................................... 0.44 to 0.60 ohms
  1988 on.................................................................... 0.1 to 1.0 ohms
XR650L
 Charging coil.................................................................. 0.2 to 1.2 ohms
 Lighting coil.................................................................. Not specified
 Exciter coil................................................................... Not specified
XR650R
 Exciter coil................................................................... 50 to 200 ohms
 Lighting coil.................................................................. 0.1 to 1.0 ohms
Pulse generator resistance
 XL600R, XR600R............................................................ 360 to 440 ohms
 XR650L.......................................................................... 423 to 517 ohms
 XR650R.......................................................................... 180 to 280 ohms

## Ignition coil resistance (at 20-degrees C/68-degrees F)

1983 through 1987 XL600R
 Primary resistance ........................................................ 0.1 to 0.3 ohms
 Secondary resistance
  With plug cap attached............................................. 8500 to 11,000 ohms
  With plug cap detached............................................ 3700 to 4500 ohms
XR600R
 Primary resistance ........................................................ 0.1 to 0.3 ohms
 Secondary resistance (with plug cap detached)
  1985 through 1987 (with plug cap connected)........... 7400 to 11,000 ohms
  1988 through 1990 (with plug cap detached)............. 7400 to 11,000 ohms
  1991 and later (with plug cap detached)................... 2000 to 4000 ohms
XR650L
 Primary resistance ........................................................ 0.19 to 0.23 ohms
 Secondary resistance (with plug cap detached)............... 6500 to 9700 ohms
XR650R ............................................................................. Not available

## Ignition timing

XL600R
 At idle (F mark aligned with index notch)
  1983 models............................................................ 6-degrees BTDC @ 1200 rpm
  1984 and later models.............................................. 11-degrees BTDC @ 1300 rpm
 At full advance ............................................................. 31-degrees BTDC @ 4000 rpm
XR600R
 1985 through 1987 models
  At idle (F mark aligned with index notch) ................. 11-degrees BTDC @ 1300 rpm
  At full advance......................................................... 31-degrees BTDC @ 4000 rpm
 1988 and later models
  At idle (F mark aligned with index notch) ................. 6-degrees BTDC @ 1300 rpm
  At full advance......................................................... 31-degrees BTDC @ 3500 rpm
XR650L
 At idle (F mark aligned with index notch)........................ 8-degrees BTDC @ 1300 rpm
 At full advance ............................................................. 28-degrees BTDC @ 4000 rpm
XR650R
 At idle (F mark aligned with index notch)........................ 6-degrees BTDC @ 1300 rpm
 At full advance ............................................................. 31-degrees BTDC @ 3500 rpm

## Torque specifications

**Note:** *One foot-pound (ft-lb) of torque is equivalent to 12 inch-pounds (in-lbs) of torque. Torque values below approximately 15 ft-lbs are expressed in inch-pounds, since most foot-pound torque wrenches are not accurate at these smaller values.*

Alternator rotor bolt
   XL600R, XR600R
      1983 through 1987 ........................................................... 100 to 120 Nm (72 to 87 ft-lbs)
      1988 and later................................................................ 125 Nm (90 ft-lbs)*
   XR650L .................................................................................. 125 Nm (90 ft-lbs)*
   XR650R .................................................................................. 125 Nm (90 ft-lbs)*
Starter gear cover bolts (XR650L) ........................................... 12 Nm (108 in-lbs)
Starter motor mounting bolts (XR650L)..................................... Not specified
Starter clutch housing-to-alternator rotor bolts ...................... 30 Nm (22 ft-lbs)
Timing hole cover ...................................................................... 84 in-lbs

*Apply clean engine oil to the threads and the underside of the bolt head.*

## 1 General information

All of the machines covered by this manual are equipped with a capacitive discharge ignition system (CDI), a headlight and a taillight. The engine is started with a kickstarter on all models except the XR650L, which has an electric starter.

XR600R and XR650R models do not have a battery, a fuse, turn signals or brake lights. Current generated by the alternator operates the ignition system and powers the lights.

XL600R, XR650L and XR650Ry models, which are street-legal, use a 12-volt electrical system with a battery. The components include a crankshaft-mounted permanent-magnet alternator and a solid state voltage regulator/rectifier unit.

The alternator consists of a multi-coil stator mounted inside the left engine cover and a permanent magnet rotor mounted on the end of the crankshaft. The regulator maintains the charging system output within the specified range to prevent overcharging. The rectifier converts the AC output of the alternator to DC current to power the lights and other components and to charge the battery. **Note:** *Keep in mind that electrical parts, once purchased, can't be returned. To avoid unnecessary expense, make very sure the faulty component has been positively identified before buying a replacement part.*

## 2 Electrical troubleshooting

A typical electrical circuit consists of an electrical component, the switches, relays, etc. related to that component and the wiring and connectors that hook the component to both the battery (if equipped) and the frame. To aid in locating a problem in any electrical circuit, wiring diagrams of each model are included in Chapter 9.

Before tackling any troublesome electrical circuit, first study the appropriate diagrams thoroughly to get a complete picture of what makes up that individual circuit. Trouble spots, for instance, can often be narrowed down by noting if other components related to that circuit are operating properly or not. If several components or circuits fail at one time, chances are the fault lies in the fuse (if equipped) or ground connection, as several circuits often are routed through the same fuse and ground connections.

Electrical problems often stem from simple causes, such as loose or corroded connections or a blown fuse. Prior to any electrical troubleshooting, always visually check the condition of the fuse (if equipped), wires and connections in the problem circuit.

If testing instruments are going to be utilized, use the diagrams to plan where you will make the necessary connections in order to accurately pinpoint the trouble spot.

The basic tools needed for electrical troubleshooting include a test light or voltmeter, an ohmmeter or a continuity tester (which includes a bulb, battery and set of test leads) and a jumper wire, preferably with a circuit breaker incorporated, which can be used to bypass electrical components. Specific checks described later in this Chapter may also require an ammeter.

On XL600R and XR650L models (which have a battery), voltage checks should be performed if a circuit is not functioning properly. Connect one lead of a test light or voltmeter to a known good ground. Connect the other lead to a connector in the circuit being tested, preferably nearest to the battery or fuse. If the bulb lights, voltage is reaching that point, which means the part of the circuit between that connector and the battery is problem-free. Continue checking the remainder of the circuit in the same manner. When you reach a point where no voltage is present, the problem lies between there and the last good test point. Most of the time the problem is due to a loose connection. Keep in mind that some circuits only receive voltage when the ignition key is in the On position.

One method of finding short circuits on XL600R and XR650L models is to remove the fuse (main fuse on XR650L models) and connect a test light or voltmeter in its place to the fuse terminals. There should be no load in the circuit. Move the wiring harness from side-to-side while watching the test light. If the bulb lights, there is a short to ground somewhere in that area, probably where insulation has rubbed off a wire. The same test can be performed on other components in the circuit, including the switch.

A ground check should be done on XL600R and XR650L models to see if a component is grounded properly. Disconnect the battery and connect one lead of a self-powered test light (such as a continuity tester) to a known good ground. Connect the other lead to the wire or ground connection being tested. If the bulb lights, the ground is good. If the bulb does not light, the ground is not good.

A continuity check is performed to see if a circuit, section of circuit or individual component is capable of passing electricity through it. Disconnect the battery and connect one lead of a self-powered test light (such as a continuity tester) to one end of the circuit being tested and the other lead to the other end of the circuit. If the bulb lights, there is continuity, which means the circuit is passing electricity through it properly. Switches can be checked in the same way.

Remember that all electrical circuits are designed to conduct electricity from the power source, through the wires, switches, etc. to the electrical component (light bulb, etc.). From there it is directed to the frame (ground) where it is passed back to the battery or alternator. Electrical problems are basically an interruption in the flow of electricity from the battery or back to it.

3.8 Battery mounting details - XR650L

A   Negative terminal
B   Positive terminal
C   Holder bracket bolts

## 3   Battery (XL600R and XR650L) - removal and installation

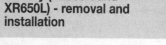

### XL600R

1   Remove the right side cover (see Chapter 8).
2   Remove the nut and lift off the battery holder bracket.
3   Disconnect the cables from the battery; negative cable first (evidenced by the minus sign), then the positive cable.
4   Detach the vent tube, if equipped.
5   Remove the battery.
6   Installation is the reverse of the removal procedure. Be sure to connect the positive cable first, followed by the negative cable.

### XR650L

7   Remove the left side cover (see Chapter 8).
8   Disconnect the cables from the battery; negative cable first (evidenced by the minus sign), then the positive cable (see illustration).
9   Detach the vent tube, if equipped.
10   Remove the bolts and take off the battery holder bracket, then remove the battery.
11   Installation is the reverse of the removal procedure. Be sure to connect the positive cable first, followed by the negative cable.

## 4   Battery (XL600R and XR650L) - check, maintenance and charging

 *Warning: Be extremely careful when handling or working around the battery. The electrolyte is very caustic and an explosive gas (hydrogen) is given off when the battery is charging. Wear eye protection and gloves when handling the battery.*

**Note:** *Parts of this section apply to fillable batteries. Maintenance-free batteries, which don't have cell caps, do not require periodic checks of the electrolyte level.*

### Check and maintenance
#### General

1   Most battery damage is caused by heat, vibration, and/or low electrolyte levels, so keep the battery securely mounted, check the electrolyte level frequently and make sure the charging system is functioning properly.
2   Check around the base inside of the battery for sediment, which is the result of sulfation caused by low electrolyte levels. These deposits will cause internal short circuits, which can quickly discharge the battery. Look for cracks in the case and replace the battery if either of these conditions is found.
3   Check the battery terminals and cable ends for tightness and corrosion. If corrosion is evident, remove the cables from the battery and clean the terminals and cable ends with a wire brush or knife and emery paper. Reconnect the cables and apply a thin coat of petroleum jelly to the connections to slow further corrosion.
4   The battery case should be kept clean to prevent current leakage, which can discharge the battery over a period of time (especially when it sits unused). Wash the outside of the case with a solution of baking soda and water. Do not get any baking soda

solution in the battery cells. Rinse the battery thoroughly, then dry it.
5   If acid has been spilled on the frame or battery box, neutralize it with the baking soda and water solution, dry it thoroughly, then touch up any damaged paint. Make sure the battery vent tube is directed away from the frame and is not kinked or pinched.
6   If the motorcycle sits unused for long periods of time, disconnect the cables from the battery terminals. It's also a good idea to charge the battery approximately once every month to keep it in good condition.

#### Electrolyte level check

7   If you're working on an XL600R, remove the right side cover. If you're working on an XR650L, remove the left side cover (see Chapter 8).
8   It may be possible to view the battery level marks without disconnecting its leads and lifting it out of its box. The electrolyte level is visible through the translucent battery case - it should be between the Upper and Lower level marks.
9   If the electrolyte level is low, remove the battery (see Section 3).
10   To top up the battery, remove the cell caps and fill each cell to the upper level mark with distilled water. Do not use tap water (except in an emergency), and do not overfill. If the level is within the marks on the case, additional water is not necessary. Reinstall the cell caps and wipe up any water spills.

 *The cell holes are quite small, so it may help to use a clean plastic squeeze bottle with a small spout to add the water.*

11   Reinstall the battery (see Section 3).

#### Specific gravity check

12   A specific gravity check measures the state of charge of the battery. If the specific gravity is low, the battery is not fully charged. This may be due to corroded battery termi-

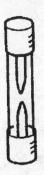

5.2a A blown fuse can be identified by its broken element - the fuse on the left is good; the fuse on the right is blown

5.2b XR650L models use fuses like this. A test light can be used to probe the exposed terminal tips; if voltage is present on one terminal but not the other, the fuse is blown

nals, a dirty battery case, a malfunctioning charging system, or loose or corroded wiring connections. On the other hand, it may be that the battery is worn out, especially if the machine is old, or that infrequent use of the motorcycle prevents normal charging from taking place.

13  You will need a battery hydrometer to measure specific gravity and the battery must be removed from the bike and cell caps removed as described above.

14  Refer to *Checking battery specific gravity* in the Fault Finding Equipment section of Reference at the end of this manual. Specific gravity should be 1.280 at 20°C (68°F) in a good condition charged battery.

## Charging

15  If the machine sits idle for extended periods or if the charging system malfunctions, the battery can be charged from an external source.

16  To properly charge the battery, you will need a charger of the correct rating, a hydrometer, a clean rag and a syringe for adding distilled water to the battery cells.

17  The maximum charging rate for any battery is 1/10 of the rated amp/hour capacity. As an example, the maximum charging rate for the 14 amp/hour battery would be 1.4 amps. If the battery is charged at a higher rate, it could be damaged.

18  Do not allow the battery to be subjected to a so-called quick charge (high rate of charge over a short period of time) unless you are prepared to buy a new battery.

19  When charging the battery, always remove it from the machine and be sure to check the electrolyte level before hooking up the charger. Add distilled water to any cells that are low.

20  Loosen the cell caps, hook up the battery charger leads (red to positive, black to negative), cover the top of the battery with a clean rag, then, and only then, plug in the battery charger.

⚠ *Warning: Remember, the gas escaping from a charging battery is explosive, so keep open flames and sparks well away from the area. Also, the electrolyte is extremely corrosive and will damage anything it comes in contact with.*

21  Allow the battery to charge until the specific gravity is as specified (see Step 14). The charger must be unplugged and disconnected from the battery when making specific gravity checks. If the battery overheats or gases excessively, the charging rate is too high. Either disconnect the charger or lower the charging rate to prevent damage to the battery.

22  If one or more of the cells do not show an increase in specific gravity after a long slow charge, or if the battery as a whole does not seem to want to take a charge, it is time for a new battery.

23  When the battery is fully charged, unplug the charger first, then disconnect the leads from the battery. Install the cell caps and wipe any electrolyte off the outside of the battery case.

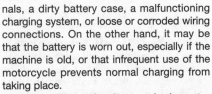

### 5  Fuse(s) (XL600R and XR650L) - check and replacement

1  On XL600R models, the fuse is located under the seat, next to the battery; the fuse is protected by a plastic cover. On XR650L models, the fuses are located behind the left side cover.

2  On XL600R models, a blown fuse is easily identified by a break in the element **(see illustration)**. On XR650L models, the best way to check for a blown fuse is with a test light. Probe the exposed terminal tips with a test light. If voltage is present on one side of the fuse but not the other, the fuse is blown **(see illustration)**.

3  If the fuse blows, be sure to check the wiring harnesses very carefully for evidence

of a short circuit. Look for bare wires and chafed, melted or burned insulation. If a fuse is replaced before the cause is located, the new fuse will blow immediately.

4  Never, under any circumstances, use a higher rated fuse or bridge the fuse holder terminals, as damage to the electrical system or a fire could result.

5  Occasionally a fuse will blow or cause an open circuit for no obvious reason. Corrosion of the fuse ends and fuse holder terminals may occur and cause poor fuse contact. If this happens, remove the corrosion with a wire brush or emery paper, then spray the fuse end and terminals with electrical contact cleaner.

### 6  Bulbs - replacement

1  Since most of these bikes are used off-road, it's a good idea to check the lens and bulb housing for built-up dirt and clean them thoroughly whenever a bulb is changed.

## Headlight bulbs

*Caution: Don't touch the bulb glass with your fingers; the oil from your skin could cause it to overheat and fail prematurely. If you do touch the glass, wipe the bulb off with a rag soaked with rubbing alcohol.*

### XL600R and XR650L models

2  Remove the two mounting bolts and take the headlight case off the motorcycle.

3  Pull off the rubber cover on the back of the headlight assembly.

4  Remove the bulb retaining clip or twist the bulb holder counterclockwise, as applicable, then pull the bulb out.

5  Installation is the reverse of the removal steps. Make sure the Top marks on the rubber cover and bulb are up.

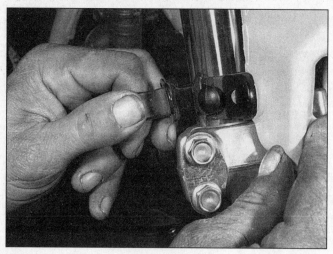

6.6 Unhook the retainer bands from the fork tubes to detach the headlight housing

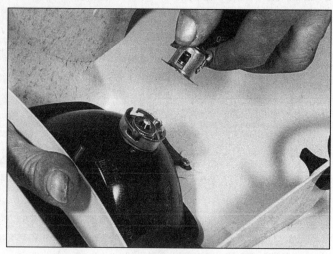

6.7 Press in the bulb socket and turn it counterclockwise, then pull it out

## XR600R and XR650R models

6 Unhook the rubber mounting bands and take the headlight case off (see illustration).
7 Twist the bulb socket counterclockwise and remove it from the headlight assembly (see illustration).
8 Twist the bulb counterclockwise and remove it (see illustration).
9 Installation is the reverse of the removal steps.

## All models

10 Refer to Section 7 and adjust headlight aim.

## Tail/brake/license plate light bulb (XL600R and XR650L models)

11 Remove the lens screws and take the lens off the tail light housing.
12 Press the bulb into its socket, turn it counterclockwise to align the bulb retaining pins with their grooves and pull the bulb out.

13 Installation is the reverse of the removal steps. The bulb pins are offset so the bulb can only go in one way.

## Tail light bulb (XR600R and XR650R models)

14 Remove the lens screws (they're accessible from underneath the fender) (see illustration).
15 Take the lens off, pull the bulb out of its socket and install a new one.

## Turn signal bulbs (XL600R and XR650L models)

16 Remove the lens screw(s) from the turn signal housing and take the lens and gasket off the housing.
17 Press the bulb into its socket, turn it counterclockwise to align the bulb retaining pins with their grooves and pull the bulb out.
18 Installation is the reverse of the removal steps.

## Instrument light bulbs (XL600R and XR650L models)

19 Pull the bulb socket out of the underside of the instrument housing. Pull the bulb out of the socket, push in a new one and push the socket back into the housing.

## 7 Headlight aim - check and adjustment

1 An improperly adjusted headlight may cause problems for oncoming traffic or provide poor, unsafe illumination of the terrain ahead. Before adjusting the headlight, be sure to consult with local traffic laws and regulations. Honda doesn't provide specifications for headlight adjustment.

## XL600R and XR650L models

2 Adjust the headlight vertically by loos-

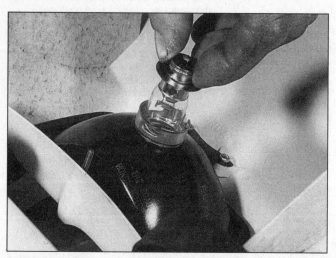

6.8 Rotate the bulb to align its tabs with the slots and pull it out

6.14 The XR600R and XR650R tail light lens screws are accessible from beneath the fender

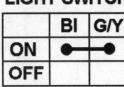

8.6 Brake light switch continuity charts (XL600R and XR650L models)

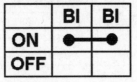

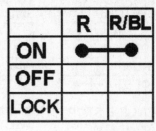

9.2 Ignition switch continuity chart

ening the headlight housing bolts, swiveling the housing and tightening the bolts.

3 Adjust the headlight horizontally by turning the screw in the underside of the headlight housing, to the right of center.

### XR600R and XR650R models

4 These bikes don't have a horizontal adjustment. Adjust the beam vertically by turning the screw in the lower front edge of the headlight housing.

### 8 Brake light switches (XL600R and XR650L) - check and replacement

1 Before checking any electrical circuit on an XL600R or XR650L model, check the fuse(s) (see Section 5).

2 The front brake light switch is mounted under the master cylinder. The rear brake light switch is mounted in a bracket behind the brake pedal.

### Test light check

3 Turn the ignition switch On. Using a test light connected to a good ground, check for voltage to the black wire at the front brake light switch or the black wire in the harness side of the connector at the rear brake light switch. Leave the connector at the rear brake light switch connected and insert the test light probe into the back of the terminal. If there's no voltage, check the wiring from the brake light switch to the ignition switch (see the wiring diagrams at the end of the book).

4 If voltage is available, connect the test light to the other terminal at the brake light switch, then pull the lever or push the pedal. If the test light comes on, the switch is good. If not, replace the switch.

### Ohmmeter check

5 This test can also be made with a self-powered test light (one that has its own battery).

6 Disconnect the wires from the switch. Connect the ohmmeter or test light between the switch terminals (if you're testing a rear

switch, connect the tester between the terminals in the switch side of the wiring harness) **(see illustration)**.

7 Pull the lever or press the pedal. The ohmmeter should show zero or near-zero; the test light should illuminate. If not, replace the switch.

### Replacement

8 To remove a front brake light switch, disconnect its wires, remove the switch mounting screw and take the switch off the master cylinder.

9 To remove a rear brake light switch, unhook the spring and disconnect the electrical connector. Loosen the adjusting nut until it comes off the switch threads, then pull the switch out of the bracket (don't turn the switch body).

10 Installation is the reverse of the removal steps. Refer to Chapter 1 to adjust the rear brake light switch. The front switch isn't adjustable.

### 9 Ignition switch (XL600R and XR650L) - check and replacement

### Check

1 Follow the wiring harness from the ignition switch to the connector and unplug the connector.

2 **XL600R:** Using an ohmmeter, check the continuity between the black wire and red wire terminals with the switch in the On position; continuity should exist **(see illustration)**. Next, check the continuity between the black/white wire and the green wire terminals with the switch in the Off position; continuity should exist.

3 **XR650L:** Using an ohmmeter, check the continuity between the red/black wire and red wire terminals with the switch in the On position; continuity should exist **(see illustration 9.2)**. Next, check the continuity between the same terminals with the switch in the Off and Lock positions; continuity should not exist.

4 If the switch fails either test, replace it.

### Replacement

5 Refer to Section 6 and remove the headlight housing.

6 Follow the switch wires to the connector and unplug it.

7 Place the key in the lock and turn it to a position halfway between On and Off.

8 If you're working on a 1986 or 1987 model, remove three screws that secure the switch to the lock cylinder.

9 Pry open the metal clip or cut off the plastic tie wrap that secures the wiring harness just below the switch.

10 Squeeze the plastic lugs that secure the switch in the lock cylinder housing and pull the switch out of the lock cylinder.

11 Installation is the reverse of the removal steps.

### 10 Handlebar switches - check and replacement

### Check

1 Generally speaking, the switches are reliable and trouble-free. Most troubles, when they do occur, are caused by dirty or corroded contacts, but wear and breakage of internal parts is a possibility that should not be overlooked. If breakage does occur, the entire switch and related wiring harness will have to be replaced with a new one, since individual parts are not usually available.

2 The switches can be checked for continuity with an ohmmeter or a continuity test light. If you're working on an XL600R or XR650L, always disconnect the battery negative cable, which will prevent the possibility of a short circuit, before making the checks.

3 Trace the wiring harness of the switch in question and unplug the electrical connectors.

4 Using the ohmmeter or test light, check for continuity between the terminals of the switch harness with the switch in the various positions **(see illustration)**. Refer to the continuity diagrams contained in the wiring diagrams at the end of the book. Continuity

**ENGINE STOP SWITCH (XL600R)**

|  | Bl/W | G |
|---|---|---|
| OFF | ●—● |  |
| RUN |  |  |
| OFF | ●—● |  |

**ENGINE STOP SWITCH (XR650L)**

|  | Bl/R | Bl/W |
|---|---|---|
| OFF | ●—● |  |
| RUN |  |  |

**HORN SWITCH**

|  | Lg | B |
|---|---|---|
| FREE |  |  |
| PUSH | ●—● |  |

**TURN SIGNAL SWITCH**

|  | Gr | Lb | O |
|---|---|---|---|
| R | ●—● |  |  |
| (N) |  |  |  |
| L |  | ●—● |  |

**DIMMER SWITCH (XL600R)**

|  | W/Y | W | Blu |
|---|---|---|---|
| Lo | ●—● |  |  |
| (N) | ●—●—● |  |  |
| Hi |  | ●—● |  |

**DIMMER SWITCH (XR650L)**

|  | Blu/W | W | Blu |
|---|---|---|---|
| Lo | ●—● |  |  |
| (N) | ●—●—● |  |  |
| Hi |  | ●—● |  |

**STARTER SWITCH (XR650L)**

|  | W/G | Y/R | Blu/W |
|---|---|---|---|
| FREE | ● |  | ●—● |
| PUSH | ●—● |  |  |

**SIDE STAND SWITCH (XR650L)**

|  | Y/Bl | G | G/W |
|---|---|---|---|
| UP |  | ●—● |  |
| (N) |  |  |  |
| DN | ●—● |  |  |

2183-5-10.4 HAYNES

**10.4 Handlebar switch continuity chart**

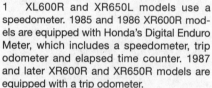

**10.8 Align the split in the switch housing or clamp with the punch mark in the handlebar (XR600R kill button shown)**

should exist between the terminals connected by a solid line when the switch is in the indicated position.

5    If the continuity check shows that a problem exists, disassemble the switch and spray the switch contacts with electrical contact cleaner. If they are accessible, the contacts can be scraped clean with a knife or polished with crocus cloth. If switch components are damaged or broken, it will be obvious when the switch is disassembled.

### Replacement

6    The handlebar switches, with the exception of the XR600R/XR650R kill switch, are composed of two halves that clamp around the bars (the XR600R/XR650R kill switch is a button that is secured to the left handlebar by a clamp). They are easily removed for cleaning or inspection by taking out the clamp screws and pulling the switch halves away from the handlebars.

7    To completely remove the switches, the electrical connectors in the wiring harness must be unplugged and the harness separated from the tie wraps and retainers.

8    When installing the switches, make sure the wiring harness is properly routed to avoid pinching or stretching the wires. Align the split in the switch housing or clamp with the punch mark on the handlebar (see illustration).

## 11 Speedometer/odometer and cable - removal and installation

1    XL600R and XR650L models use a speedometer. 1985 and 1986 XR600R models are equipped with Honda's Digital Enduro Meter, which includes a speedometer, trip odometer and elapsed time counter. 1987 and later XR600R and XR650R models are equipped with a trip odometer.

2    Unscrew the cable retaining bolt and pull the lower end of the cable out of the gear at the front wheel (see illustration).

3    Remove the retainer that secures the cable to the right fork leg (see illustration).

4    Unscrew the knurled nut and detach the cable from the instrument housing (see illustration). Note: *If you're removing the speedometer or odometer just for access to the components, you can leave the cable connected.*

**11.2 Remove the bolt and pull the speedometer cable out of the gear; on installation, position the gear lug in the notch on the fork leg**

**11.3 Detach the cable retainer from the fork leg**

**11.4 Unscrew the knurled nut and detach the cable from the meter (XR600R trip odometer shown)**

**11.5a Unbolt the bracket . . .**

5    Unbolt the bracket and take the speedometer or odometer off the triple clamp **(see illustrations)**.

6    Installation is the reverse of the removal steps.

---

**12  Charging system testing (XL600R and XR650L) - general information and precautions**

1    If the performance of the charging system is suspect, the system as a whole should be checked first, followed by testing of the individual components (the alternator and the regulator/rectifier). **Note:** *Before beginning the checks, make sure the battery is fully charged and that all system connections are clean and tight.*

2    Checking the output of the charging system and the performance of the various components within the charging system requires the use of a voltmeter, ammeter and ohmmeter or the equivalent multimeter.

3    When making the checks, follow the procedures carefully to prevent incorrect connections or short circuits, as irreparable damage to electrical system components may result if short circuits occur.

4    If the necessary test equipment is not available, it is recommended that charging system tests be left to a dealer service department or a reputable motorcycle repair shop.

---

**13  Charging system (XL600R and XR650L) - leakage and output test**

1    If a charging system problem is suspected, perform the following checks. Start by removing the right side cover (XL600R) or left side cover (XR650L) for access to the battery (see Chapter 8).

*Leakage test*

2    Turn the ignition switch Off and disconnect the cable from the battery negative terminal.

3    Set the multimeter to the mA (milliamps) function and connect its negative probe to the battery negative terminal, and the positive probe to the disconnected negative cable **(see illustration)**. Leakage should be very low - 1 milliamp or less.

4    If the reading is too high there is probably a short circuit in the wiring. Thoroughly check the wiring between the various components (see the wiring diagrams at the end of the book).

5    If the reading is satisfactory, disconnect the meter and connect the negative cable to the battery, tightening it securely. Proceed to the next Step.

**11.5b . . . and take the meter off (you can leave the cable connected if you're removing it for access to other components); remove the mounting nuts to detach the meter from the bracket**

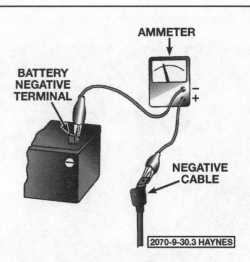

**13.3 Checking the charging system leakage rate with an ammeter**

14.4a Remove the bolts from the left-side engine cover; this is a 600R . . .

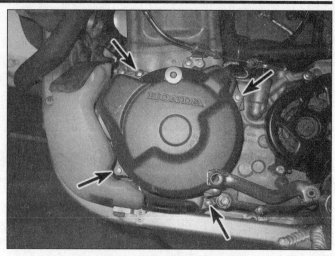

14.4b . . . and this is an XR650R

## Output test

6 Start the engine and let it warm up to normal operating temperature.

7 With the engine idling, attach the positive (red) voltmeter lead to the positive (+) battery terminal and the negative (black) lead to the battery negative (-) terminal. The voltmeter selector switch (if equipped) must be in the 0-20 DC volt range.

8 Slowly increase the engine speed until voltage reaches its maximum (don't exceed 8000 rpm) and compare the voltmeter reading to the value listed in this Chapter's Specifications.

9 If the output is as specified, the alternator is functioning properly.

10 Low voltage output may be the result of damaged windings in the alternator charging coil or wiring problems between the alternator and battery. Make sure all electrical connections are clean and tight, then refer to Section 14 to check the alternator charging coil. If the wiring and the charging coil are good, the problem may be a defective regulator/rectifier.

11 High voltage output (above the speci-fied range) indicates a defective voltage regulator/rectifier.

## 14 Alternator stator coils and rotor - check and replacement

## Stator coil check

1 Locate and disconnect the alternator coil connector on the left side of the vehicle frame (XL600R, XR650L) or under the seat (XR600R and XR650R - see Chapter 8 for seat removal).

2 To check the coils, connect an ohm-meter between the specified terminals in the side of the connector that runs back to the stator coils on the left side of the engine (in cases where ground is specified, connect the ohmmeter negative terminal to bare metal on the engine or frame). Wire colors and connections are as follows:

a) **XL600R** - *pink and yellow (charging coil), white/yellow and ground (light-ing coil), black/red and ground (ignition exciter coil)*

b) **XR600R** - *black/red and ground (igni-tion exciter coil), blue and ground (1985 through 1990 lighting coil), white/yellow and green (1991 and later lighting coil)*

c) **XR650L** - *yellow and yellow (charging coil).* **Note:** *No specifications are avail-able for the lighting coil or the exciter coil.*

d) **XR650R** - *brown and black/red (igni-tion exciter coil), white/yellow and green (lighting coil)*

If the readings are much outside the value listed in this Chapter's Specifications, replace the stator coils as described below.

## Stator coil replacement

3 If you're working on an XR650L, dis-connect the cable from the negative terminal of the battery, then remove the starter gear cover and reduction gears (see Section 24)

4 Remove the left engine cover **(see illus-trations).**

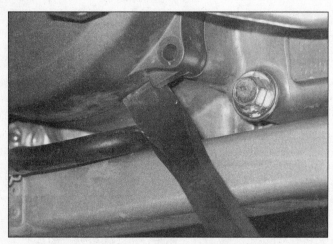

14.4c If the cover sticks, pry on a casting protrusion - not between the cover and the case (XR650R shown)

14.4d Remove the gasket and dowels

**14.5a  The harness grommet fits in a notch and the harness retainer fits in two slots**

**14.5b  Remove the bolts to detach the stator coils (XR600R shown)**

5    Peel the sealant away from the wiring harness grommet **(see illustration)**. Remove the stator coil bolts and take the stator coils out of the cover **(see illustration)**. If you're working on an XR650R, the ignition pulse generator must be removed along with the stator coils **(see illustration)**.

6    Installation is the reverse of the removal steps. Tighten the stator coil bolts securely, but don't overtighten them and strip the threads.

## Rotor replacement

### Removal

**Note:** *To remove the alternator rotor, the special Honda puller (part no. 07733-0020001 or 07933-3290001 [all except XR650R]/07933-3950000 [XR650R]) or an aftermarket equivalent will be required. Don't try to remove the rotor without the proper puller, as it's almost sure to be damaged. Pullers are readily available from motorcycle dealers and aftermarket tool suppliers.*

7    Remove the left engine cover (see

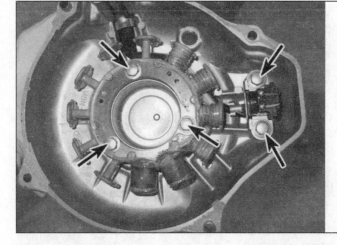

**14.5c  Stator coil and pulse generator mounting bolts - XR650R models**

Chapter 2A or 2B). If you're working on an XR650L, the starter gear cover and starter reduction gears will have to be removed first (see Section 24).

8    Hold the alternator rotor from turning. If it doesn't have flats for an open-end wrench,

use a strap wrench. If you don't have one and the engine is in the frame, the rotor can be locked by placing the transmission in gear and holding the rear brake on. Unscrew the rotor bolt **(see illustrations)**.

**14.8a  Hold the rotor and unscrew the bolt**

**14.8b  The rotor on XR650R models has flats for a wrench to prevent it from turning while the bolt is removed or the puller is tightened**

**14.9  Remove the rotor with a puller like this one (600 shown, 650 similar [but requires a different tool])**

14.11 Look for the Woodruff key - if it isn't secure in its slot, set it aside for safekeeping

14.12 Be sure there aren't any small metal objects stuck to the rotor magnets; an inconspicuous item like this Woodruff key can ruin the rotor and stator if the engine is run

9   Thread an alternator puller into the center of the rotor and use it to remove the rotor (see illustration). If the rotor doesn't come off easily, tap sharply on the end of the puller to release the rotor's grip on the tapered crankshaft end.

10   Pull the rotor off.

11   Check the Woodruff key (see illustration); if it's not secure in its slot, pull it out and set it aside for safekeeping.

## Installation

12   Take a look to make sure there isn't anything stuck to the inside of the rotor (see illustration).

13   Degrease the center of the rotor and the end of the crankshaft.

14   Make sure the Woodruff key is positioned securely in its slot (see illustration 14.11).

15   Align the rotor slot with the Woodruff key. Place the rotor on the crankshaft.

16   Lubricate the threads of the rotor bolt with clean engine oil, then install the rotor bolt and washer. Note: The washer on some models is chamfered; the chamfered side

should be facing out (toward the bolt head). Hold the rotor from turning with one of the methods described in Step 7 and tighten the bolt to the torque listed in this Chapter's Specifications.

17   Install the left engine cover (see Chapter 2A or 2B). Check the engine oil level and add, as necessary (see Daily (pre-ride) checks at the front of this manual).

## 15 AC regulator - check and replacement

### Check

1   If you're working on an XL600R or XR650L, test the charging system as described in Section 13 and correct any problems.

2   Refer to Section 6 and remove the headlight assembly.

3   Connect a voltmeter between the headlight wires. Set the voltmeter to the 0

to 20-volt range. Connect a tachometer to the motorcycle, following the manufacturer's instructions.

4   Start the engine. If you're working on an XL600R or XR650L, set the dimmer switch to Hi.

5   Slowly increase engine speed to 5,000 rpm and compare the voltmeter reading to the value listed in this Chapter's Specifications.

6   If voltage isn't within the specified range, shut off the engine and remove the seat (see Chapter 8).

### XL600R and XR650L models

7   If the voltage isn't within the specified range, check the dimmer switch (see Section 10). Check the dimmer switch wiring and AC regulator wiring for breaks or bad connections and make any necessary repairs.

8   If the switch and wiring are good, or if repairing them doesn't produce AC regulator voltage within the Specifications, the regulator itself is probably defective.

### XR600R models

9   Remove the seat (see Chapter 8). Set an ohmmeter at R x 1000 and connect it between the terminals of the AC regulator (white/yellow leads) (see illustration). If the reading is not within specifications, the AC regulator is probably defective.

### XR650L

10   Remove the right side cover (see Chapter 8), then unplug the two- and three-pin regulator/rectifier electrical connectors.

11   Using a voltmeter, measure the voltage between the red/white wire terminal and ground - battery voltage should be indicated on the meter.

12   Set the meter to the ohms scale, then measure the resistance between the two yellow wire terminals - the reading should be 0.2 to 1.2 ohms at 68-degrees F (20-degrees C).

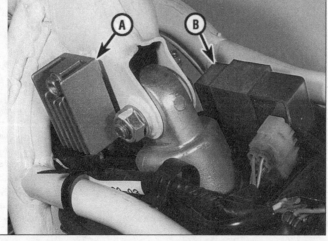

15.9 AC regulator and CDI unit locations - XR600R

A   AC regulator
B   CDI unit

| + Probe / − Probe | Black | Red/white | Yellow | Yellow | Yellow | Green |
|---|---|---|---|---|---|---|
| Black | | 20 to 100 kΩ | 15 to 80 kΩ | 15 to 80 kΩ | 15 to 80 kΩ | 10 to 50 kΩ |
| Red/white | ∞ | | ∞ | ∞ | ∞ | ∞ |
| Yellow | ∞ | 0.5 to 10 kΩ | | ∞ | ∞ | ∞ |
| Yellow | ∞ | 0.5 to 10 kΩ | ∞ | | ∞ | ∞ |
| Yellow | ∞ | 0.5 to 10 kΩ | ∞ | ∞ | | ∞ |
| Green | 1 to 20 kΩ | 1 to 20 kΩ | 0.5 to 10 kΩ | 0.5 to 10 kΩ | 0.5 to 10 kΩ | |

**15.13 Regulator/rectifier test details (XR650L)**

13   Set the ohmmeter to the K-ohms scale and measure the resistance between each of the terminals as indicated by the table **(see illustration)**. The readings should be within the range shown. Usually a fault is identifiable by the absence or presence of infinite or zero resistance when there should in fact be a measurable amount.

14   If the above checks do not provide the expected results, check the wiring and connectors between the battery, regulator/rectifier and alternator for shorts, breaks, and loose or corroded terminals (see the *wiring diagrams* at the end of this book).

15   If the wiring checks out, the regulator/rectifier unit is probably faulty. Take it to a Honda dealer for confirmation of its condi-tion before replacing it with a new one. Alternatively, obtain a known good one to use as a substitute, then check whether the fault has been corrected.

## Replacement

16   If you're working on an XR650L, remove the fuel tank (see Chapter 4). If you're working on an XL600R, XR600R or an XR650R, remove the seat (see Chapter 8). Follow the wiring harness from the AC regulator to the connector and unplug the connector. Remove the mounting bolt and lift the regulator off the motorcycle **(see illustrations)**.

17   Installation is the reverse of the removal steps.

### 16 Regulator/rectifier - replacement

1   On XL600R models, the regulator/rectifier is a plastic box mounted on the vehicle frame to the right of the AC regulator. On 650 models it's a finned metal unit; on XR650L models it's located under the fuel tank on the right side of the frame, near the steering head. On XR650R models it's located under the seat. XR600R models don't have a separate regulator/rectifier.

2   Follow the wiring harness from the regulator/rectifier to the six-pin connector and unplug the connectors. Remove the mount-

**15.16a  On XR650R models the AC regulator is mounted to the top of the air filter housing**

**15.16b  On XR650L models the regulator/rectifier is located on the right side of the frame, near the steering head**

18.5 Unscrew the spark plug cap from the plug wire and measure its resistance with an ohmmeter

18.12 A simple spark gap testing fixture can be made from a block of wood, two nails, a large alligator clip, a screw and a piece of wire

ing bolt and lift the regulator/rectifier off the bike.

3  Installation is the reverse of the removal steps.

## 17 Ignition system - general information

These motorcycles are equipped with a breakerless (CDI) ignition system. The CDI ignition system functions on the same principle as a breaker point ignition system with the pulse generator and CDI unit performing the tasks previously associated with the breaker points and mechanical advance system. As a result, adjustment and maintenance of breakerless ignition components is eliminated (with the exception of spark plug replacement).

Because of their nature, the individual ignition system components can be checked but not repaired. If ignition system troubles occur, and the faulty component can be isolated, the only cure for the problem is to replace the part with a new one. Keep in mind that most electrical parts, once purchased, can't be returned. To avoid unnecessary expense, make very sure the faulty component has been positively identified before buying a replacement part.

## 18 Ignition system - check

 **Warning: Because of the very high voltage generated by the ignition system, extreme care must be taken when these checks are performed.**

1  If the ignition system is the suspected

cause of poor engine performance or failure to start, a number of checks can be made to isolate the problem.

2  If you're working on an XL600R or XR650L model, make sure the ignition kill switch is in the Run or On position.

### Engine will not start

3  Refer to Chapter 1 and disconnect the spark plug wire. Connect the wire to a spare spark plug and lay the plug on the engine with the threads contacting the engine. If necessary, hold the spark plug with an insulated tool. Crank the engine over and make sure a well-defined, blue spark occurs between the spark plug electrodes.

 **Warning: Don't remove the spark plug from the engine to perform this check - atomized fuel being pumped out of the open spark plug hole could ignite, causing severe injury!**

4  If no spark occurs, the following checks should be made:

5  Unscrew the spark plug cap from the plug wire and check the cap resistance with an ohmmeter **(see illustration)**. If the resistance is infinite, replace it with a new one.

6  Make sure all electrical connectors are clean and tight. Check all wires for shorts, opens and correct installation.

7  If you're working on an XL600R or XR650L, check the battery voltage with a voltmeter. If the voltage is less than 12-volts, recharge the battery.

8  On all models, check the exciter coil and pulse generator (see Sections 14 and 20).

9  Refer to Section 19 and check the ignition coil primary and secondary resistance.

10  If the preceding checks produce positive results but there is still no spark at the plug, refer to Section 21 and check the CDI unit.

### Engine starts but misfires

11  If the engine starts but misfires, make the following checks before deciding that the ignition system is at fault.

12  The ignition system must be able to produce a spark across a seven millimeter (1/4-inch) gap (minimum). A simple test fixture **(see illustration)** can be constructed to make sure the minimum spark gap can be jumped. Make sure the fixture electrodes are positioned seven millimeters apart. Spark testers can also be obtained at motorcycle dealers and accessory shops.

13  Connect one of the spark plug wires to the protruding test fixture electrode, then attach the fixture's alligator clip to a good engine ground.

14  Crank the engine over with the kill switch in the Run position and see if well-defined, blue sparks occur between the test fixture electrodes. If the minimum spark gap test is positive, the ignition coil is functioning properly. If the spark will not jump the gap, or if it is weak (orange colored), refer to Steps 5 through 10 of this Section and perform the component checks described.

## 19 Ignition coil - check, removal and installation

### Check

1  In order to determine conclusively that the ignition coil is defective, it should be tested by an authorized Honda dealer service department or other qualified repair shop equipped with the special electrical tester required for this check.

2  However, the coil can be checked visually (for cracks and other damage) and the primary and secondary coil resistances can be measured with an ohmmeter. If the coil is undamaged, and if the resistances are as

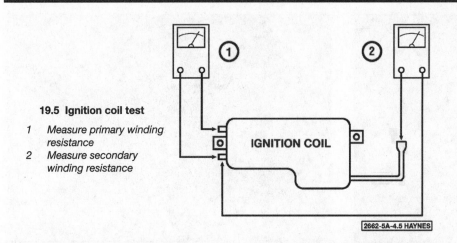

**19.5 Ignition coil test**

1  *Measure primary winding resistance*
2  *Measure secondary winding resistance*

green wire's primary terminal and the spark plug cap. Place the ohmmeter selector switch in the Rx100 position and compare the measured resistance to the values listed in this Chapter's Specifications.

7    If the resistances are not as specified, unscrew the spark plug cap from the plug wire and check the resistance between the green wire's primary terminal and the end of the spark plug wire. If it's now within specifications, the spark plug cap is bad. If it's still not as specified, the coil is probably defective and should be replaced with a new one.

### Removal and installation

8    To remove the coil, refer to Chapter 4 and remove the fuel tank, then disconnect the spark plug wire from the plug. After labeling them with tape to aid in reinstallation, unplug the coil primary circuit electrical connector(s).

9    Remove the coil mounting bolt, then lift the coil out **(see illustrations)**.

10    Installation is the reverse of removal.

---

specified, it is probably capable of proper operation.

3    To check the coil for physical damage, it must be removed (see Steps 8 and 9). To check the resistance, remove the fuel tank (see Chapter 4), unplug the primary circuit electrical connector(s) from the coil and remove the spark plug wire from the spark plug. Mark the locations of all wires before disconnecting them.

4    Label the primary terminal wires, then disconnect them from the ignition coil primary terminals.

5    Connect an ohmmeter between the primary terminals. Set the ohmmeter selector switch in the Rx1 position and compare the measured resistance to the value listed in this Chapter's Specifications **(see illustration)**.

6    Connect the ohmmeter between the

### 20 Pulse generator - check, removal and installation

### Check

1    Locate the pulse generator harness and follow it to its electrical connector. The pulse generator connector is a two-pin, white electrical connector. Follow the harness to the connector and unplug it.

- **XL600R AND XR600R:** Remove the fuel tank (see Chapter 4). The connector is located above the frame tube, right above the engine hanger plate.
- **XR650L:** The connector is located on the right side of the frame downtube **(see illustration)**.
- **XR650R:** Remove the seat (see Chapter 8). The connector is located near the CDI unit (ICM) **(see illustration)**.

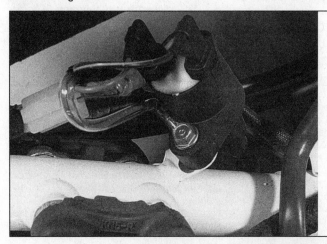

**19.9a The ignition coil is mounted beneath the fuel tank. This is an XR600R (XL600R and XR650L similar) . . .**

**19.9b . . . and this is an XR650R**

**20.1a Ignition pulse generator electrical connector - XR650L**

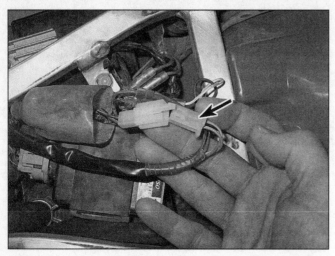

20.1b Ignition pulse generator electrical connector - XR650R

20.4 On XL600Rs, XR600Rs and XR650Ls, the pulse generator is bolted to the right side of the engine, inside the cover; coat the wiring harness grommet in the crankcase with a thin layer of sealant upon installation

2   Connect an ohmmeter between the wire terminals in the pulse generator side of the connector. Compare the reading to the value listed in this Chapter's Specifications. If it's outside the specified range, replace the pulse generator.

### Removal and installation

#### XL600R, XR600R and XL650R models

3   Remove the right engine cover (see Chapter 2). Disconnect the pulse generator wire at the connector above the engine.

4   Remove the pulse generator mounting bolts and take it off the engine (see illustration).

5   Installation is the reverse of the removal steps. Tighten the bolts securely, but don't overtighten them and strip the threads. Also, apply a film of RTV sealant to the wiring harness grommet to keep dirt and water out.

#### XR650R models

6   On 650R models, the pulse generator is removed along with the stator and is not available separately. See Section 14 for the stator/pulse generator replacement procedure.

### 21  CDI unit - harness check, removal and installation

1   The CDI unit is tested by process of elimination (when all other possible causes of ignition problems have been checked and eliminated, the CDI unit is at fault).

2   If you're working on an XL600R or a 1987 or earlier XR600R, remove the fuel tank (see Chapter 4). If you're working on an 1988 or later XR600R or an XR650R, remove the seat (see Chapter 8). If you're working on an XR650L, remove the left side cover (see

Chapter 8; the CDI unit is mounted to the rear of the battery) (see accompanying illustrations and illustration 15.9).

### Harness check

3   Follow the harness from the CDI unit to the two-pin and four-pin connectors and unplug them.

4   Set an ohmmeter at R x 1 and connect it between the black/yellow and green wire terminals in the harness. It should give the same reading as for ignition coil primary resistance, listed in this Chapter's Specifications. Note: No coil specifications are given for the XR650R, but on our project XR650R the resistance between the black/yellow and green wire terminals measured 0.7 ohms (and the bike runs perfectly). So as long as the reading is somewhere in that vicinity (not open or shorted), the harness (and coil primary windings) is most likely okay.

5   Disconnect the spark plug wire from the spark plug. If you're working on a 1988 or

21.2a  On XR650L models, the CDI unit is located in the battery box

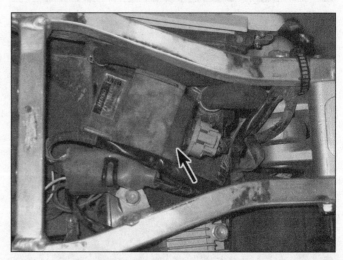

21.2b  On 1988 and later XR600R and all XR650R models, the CDI unit is located under the seat (XR650R model shown)

22.5  The timing hole cover is located on the left crankcase cover

22.8a  Point the timing light into the timing hole . . .

later model, remove the cap from the spark plug wire.

6   If you're working on an XL600R, set the ohmmeter to R x 1000 and connect it between the green wire terminal and the spark plug cap. It should give the same reading as for the secondary coil resistance, listed in this Chapter's Specifications.

7   If you're working on an XR600R, set the ohmmeter to R x 1000 and connect it between the black/yellow wire terminal and the spark plug cap (1985 through 1987) or the spark plug wire with the cap removed (1988 on). It should give the same reading as for the secondary coil resistance, listed in this Chapter's Specifications.

8   Set the ohmmeter at R x 100 and connect it between the green/white and blue/yellow wire terminals in the harness. It should give the same reading as for the pulse generator resistance, listed in this Chapter's Specifications.

9   Set the ohmmeter at R x 10 and connect the terminals between the black/red wire terminal in the harness and ground. It should give the same reading as for the alternator exciter coil resistance, listed in this Chapter's Specifications.

10   If you're working on an XL600R, turn the ignition switch to On. On all models, place the engine kill switch in the Run position. Connect the ohmmeter between the black/white and green terminals (1983 through 1987) or black/white and ground (1988 on). The ohmmeter should show infinite resistance (no continuity).

11   If the harness failed any of the preceding tests, check the affected wires for breaks or poor connections.

12   If the harness and all other system components tested good, the CDI unit may be defective. Before buying a new one, it's a good idea to substitute a known good CDI unit.

## Removal and installation

13   Locate the CDI unit (see Step 2). Unplug its connector and work the unit out of its

mounting band.
14   Installation is the reverse of the removal steps.

## 22  Ignition timing - general information and check

### General information

1   The ignition timing cannot be adjusted. Since none of the ignition system parts are subject to mechanical wear, there should be no need to check timing, unless you're troubleshooting a problem such as loss of power.

2   The ignition timing is checked with the engine running, at idle and at an accelerated engine speed, as indicated in this Chapter's Specifications.

3   A (less expensive) neon timing light is probably adequate, but it might produce such dim pulses that the timing marks are hard

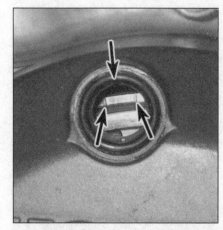

22.8b  . . . at idle, the line next to the F mark on the alternator rotor should align with the notch in the timing hole (note that there are two marks on the rotor; be sure the correct one lines up with the mark in the hole)

to see. An externally powered xenon timing light is more precise because it doesn't use the vehicle battery (on models so equipped), which can produce an incorrect reading because of stray electrical pulses in the system.

### Check

4   Warm the engine to normal operating temperature, make sure the transmission is in Neutral, then shut the engine off.

5   Remove the timing hole cover (see illustration).

6   Connect the timing light and a tachometer to the engine, following the tool manufacturer's instructions.

7   Start the engine. Make sure it idles at the speed listed in the Chapter 1 Specifications. Adjust if necessary.

8   Point the timing light into the timing hole (see illustration). At idle, the line next to the F mark on the alternator rotor should align with the notch in the timing hole (see illustration).

22.8c  When the engine speed is raised to the specified rpm, the advance marks should be aligned with the notch in the timing hole

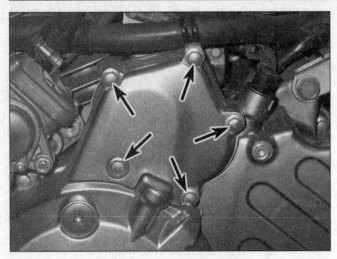

24.2a Starter gear cover bolts

24.2b Remove the starter gear cover. Note the locations of the dowel pins (the gears might come off with the cover)

9    If the timing is incorrect and all other ignition components have tested as good, the ICM is probably defective.
10    When the check is complete, grease the timing cover O-ring, then install the O-ring and cover and tighten the cover to the torque listed in this Chapter's Specifications. Disconnect the test equipment.

## 23 Starting system (XR650L) - check

1    If the starter won't crank the engine, make sure the battery has a full charge and that all of the fuses are good. Also check the cable connections at the battery terminals and at the starter motor.
2    Turn the ignition switch to the On position and push the starter button; you should hear a click coming from under the left side cover (the starter relay switch is located under the cover, just in front of the battery).
3    If the starter relay switch made a noise,

make sure the transmission is in Neutral, then connect a heavy-gauge jumper cable from the positive terminal of the battery to the terminal on the starter. If the starter motor doesn't operate, it's faulty. If it does operate, either the starter relay switch or the cable from the relay to the starter is faulty.
4    If the starter relay didn't make a noise in Step 2, unplug the connector from the starter relay switch.

   a) *Using an ohmmeter, check for continuity between the green/red wire terminal and ground (the transmission must still be in Neutral and the clutch lever must be released). There should be continuity.*
   b) *Also check the continuity between the same terminal, but with the transmission in gear, the side stand up and the clutch lever pulled in. There should be continuity.*

5    If there was no continuity, the side stand switch could be faulty, the clutch switch could be faulty, the neutral switch could be faulty, the clutch diode could be faulty, the neutral/

side stand diode could be faulty, one of the electrical connectors in the circuit might not be making good contact, or there could be a problem in the wiring harness between the components.
6    If there was continuity in Step 4, reconnect the electrical connector to the starter relay switch. Turn the ignition switch to the On position, push the starter switch and measure the voltage at the yellow/red wire of the starter switch connector. If no voltage is present, the starter switch could be faulty, the ignition switch could be faulty, there could be an open in the wiring harness between the components, or one of the electrical connectors in the circuit might not be making good contact.
7    If there was voltage present in Step 6, the starter relay switch is probably defective.

## 24 Starter reduction gears (XR650L) - removal, inspection and installation

### Removal

1    Disconnect the cable from the negative terminal of the battery (see Section 3).
2    Remove the starter gear cover **(see illustration)**. Locate the two dowel pins **(see illustration)** - be careful not to lose them.
3    Remove the washer(s) from the idle gear shaft and the reduction gear shaft **(see illustration)**. **Note:** *1996 and earlier models have two washers on the end of each shaft. 1997 and later models have one washer on the end of each shaft.*
4    Remove the reduction gear, shaft and, if you're working on a 1996 or earlier model, the washer between the gear and the engine case **(see illustration)**.
5    Remove the idle gear, shaft, and, if you're working on a 1996 or earlier model, the washer between the gear and the engine case **(see illustration)**.

24.3  Remove the washer from the idle gear shaft and, on 1996 and earlier models, the reduction gear shaft

24.4  Remove the reduction gear and shaft (and washer if you're working on a 1996 or earlier model)

24.5 Remove the idle gear shaft and gear (and washer if you're working on a 1996 or earlier model)

25.3 Remove the clutch cable bracket bolt

25.4 Pull back the boot and remove the nut securing the battery cable to the starter motor

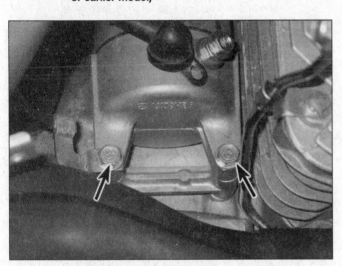

25.5 Starter motor mounting bolts

25.6 Remove the starter out the right side of the bike

## Inspection

6   Check the gears and their shafts for wear and damage. Replace as necessary.

25.7 Inspect the starter motor O-ring; if it's damaged, replace it

## Installation

7   Installation is the reverse of the removal steps. Apply clean engine oil to the gear shafts.

**Note:** *When installing the reduction gear, make sure the OUT marking is facing away from the engine.*

8   Install the starter gear cover, using a new gasket and making sure the dowel pins are in place, then tighten the bolts to the torque listed in this Chapter's Specifications.

### 25 Starter motor (XR650L) - removal and installation

## Removal

1   Disconnect the cable from the negative terminal of the battery (see Section 3).
2   Remove the carburetor (see Chap-

ter 4) and the starter reduction gear (see Section 24).
3   Remove the clutch cable bracket bolt and reposition the bracket and cable out of the way **(see illustration)**.
4   Pull back the rubber boot and remove the nut retaining the starter cable to the starter **(see illustration)**.
5   Remove the two starter mounting bolts and the spacer between the starter and the engine case **(see illustration)**.
6   Slide the starter out of the engine case, rotating it as necessary to maneuver it out of place **(see illustration)**.

*Caution: Don't drop or strike the starter; its magnets may be demagnetized, which will ruin it.*

7   Inspect the O-ring on the end of the starter and replace it if necessary **(see illustration)**. Note the location of the ground cable.
8   Remove any corrosion or dirt from the mounting lugs on the starter and the mounting points on the crankcase.

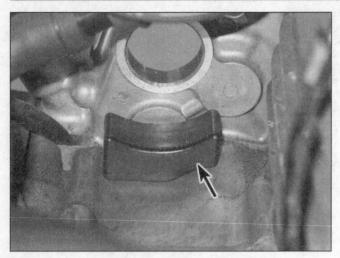

25.10 Starter motor spacer block

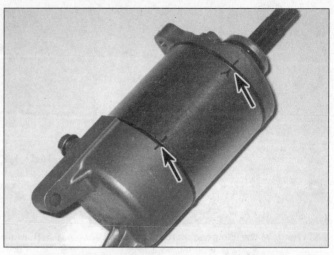

26.2 If there aren't any, make alignment marks between the housing and end covers before disassembly

26.3a Unscrew and remove the two bolts . . .

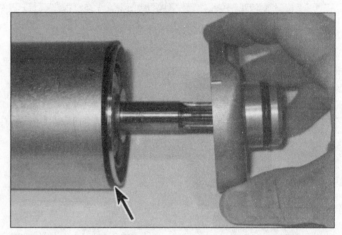

26.3b . . . then remove the front cover and sealing ring

## Installation

9    Before installing the starter motor, apply a little clean engine oil to the O-ring.
10    Installation is otherwise the reverse of removal. Be sure the spacer block is in position on top of the crankcase (see illustration).

---

**26 Starter motor (XR650L) - disassembly, inspection and reassembly**

## Disassembly

1    Remove the starter motor (see Section 25).
2    Note the alignment marks between the main housing and the front and rear covers, or make your own if they aren't clear (see illustration).
3    Unscrew the two long bolts, noting the washers, then remove the front cover from the motor along with its sealing ring (see illustrations). Discard the sealing ring as a new one should be used. Remove the tabbed

washer from the cover and slide the insulating washer and shim(s) from the front end of the armature, noting the number of shims and their correct fitted order (see illustrations).
4    Remove the rear cover from the motor along with its sealing ring (see illustration).

Discard the sealing ring, as a new one should be used. Remove the shims from the rear end of the armature, noting how many there are, and their correct installed positions (see illustration).
5    Withdraw the armature from the front of the main housing (see illustration).

26.3c Remove the tabbed washer . . .

26.3d . . . and the shims

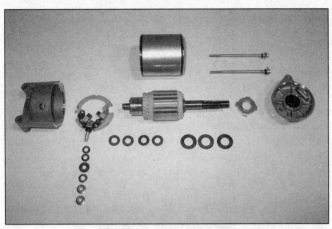

26.3e Exploded view of the starter motor

26.4a Remove the rear cover and its sealing ring . . .

26.4b . . . and remove the shims

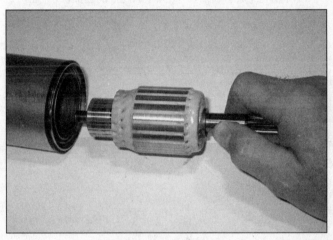

26.5 Withdraw the armature

6    Noting the correct installed location of each component, unscrew the nut from the terminal bolt and remove the plain washer, the one large and two small insulating washers and the rubber O-ring **(see illustration)**.

7    Remove the brush plate and terminal bolt from the main housing assembly **(see illustration)**.

8    Slide the brush plate brushes out of their holders.

### Inspection

9    The parts of the starter motor that are most likely to require attention are the brushes. Measure the length of each brush and compare the results to the Specifica-

tions at the beginning of the Chapter **(see illustration)**. If the brushes are worn beyond the service limit, replace the brush plate assembly and brush piece with new ones. If the brushes are not worn excessively, nor cracked, chipped, or otherwise damaged, they may be re-used.

10    Inspect the commutator bars on the

26.6 Unscrew the nut and remove the large and small insulating washers and the O-ring

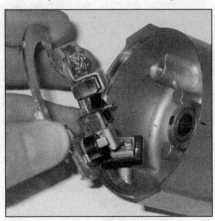

26.7 Remove the brush plate and terminal bolt assembly

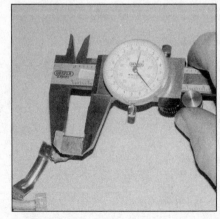

26.9 Measure the length of each brush

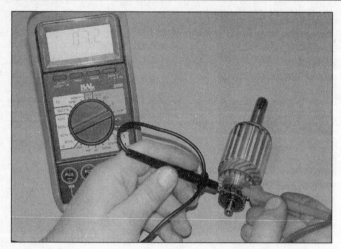

26.11 Continuity should exist between the commutator bars

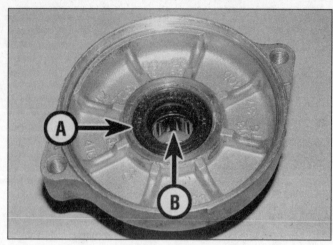

26.13 Check the seal (A) and needle bearing (B) in the front cover

armature for scoring, scratches and discoloration. The commutator can be cleaned and polished with crocus cloth, but do not use sandpaper or emery paper. After cleaning, wipe away any residue with a cloth soaked in electrical system cleaner or denatured alcohol.

11 Using an ohmmeter or a continuity tester, check for continuity between the commutator bars (see illustration). Continuity should exist between each bar and all of the others. Also, check for continuity between the commutator bars and the armature shaft. There should be no continuity (infinite resistance) between the commutator and the shaft. If the checks indicate otherwise, the armature is defective.

12 Check the starter pinion gear for worn, cracked, chipped and broken teeth. If the gear is damaged or worn, replace the starter motor.

13 Inspect the end covers for signs of cracks or wear. Check the needle bearing in the front cover and the bush in the rear cover for wear and damage (see illustration). Inspect the magnets in the main housing and the housing itself for cracks.

14 Inspect the insulating washers, O-ring, sealing rings and front cover oil seal for signs of damage, deformation and deterioration and replace them if necessary.

### Reassembly

15 Slide the brush plate brushes back into position in their housings and locate the brush spring ends onto the outer ends of the brushes (see illustration).

16 The remainder of assembly is the reverse of the disassembly procedure, noting the following points:

a) Lubricate the seal lips and ends of the armature with a thin film of multi-purpose grease.

b) When assembling the end covers, make sure the marks on the covers are aligned with the marks on the starter motor housing.

c) Fit new O-rings to the long bolts that hold the housing and covers together.

### 27 Starter clutch (XR650L) - removal, inspection and installation

### Removal and inspection

1 Remove the starter reduction gears (see Section 24), the left side engine cover and the alternator rotor (see Section 14).

2 Remove the washer, starter driven gear, needle bearing and washer. Lay the parts out in order so they don't get mixed up.

3 To check the operation of the starter clutch, assemble the starter driven gear (and its washer) to the back of the alternator rotor. It should be able to turn in one direction, but not the other.

4 Remove the Torx bolts securing the starter clutch housing to the backside of the alternator rotor. Note: These bolts are tight; an impact driver might be required to loosen them.

5 Lift off the starter clutch housing and remove the one-way clutch roller.

6 Check the one-way clutch roller, needle bearing, starter driven gear and thrust washers for wear and damage and replace as needed.

### Installation

7 Installation is basically the reverse of removal, noting the following points:

a) Lubricate the one-way clutch roller with clean engine oil.

b) Apply a non-hardening thread locking agent to the starter clutch housing bolts, then tighten them to the torque listed in this Chapter's Specifications.

c) Refer to Sections 14 and 24 to install the alternator rotor, left side engine cover, and the starter reduction gear and cover.

26.15 Slide each brush into its housing and place the spring end onto its outer end

# Chapter 6
# Steering, suspension and final drive

## Contents

## Degrees of difficulty

| | | | | |
|---|---|---|---|---|
| **Easy,** suitable for novice with little experience  | **Fairly easy,** suitable for beginner with some experience  | **Fairly difficult,** suitable for competent DIY mechanic 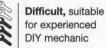 | **Difficult,** suitable for experienced DIY mechanic | **Very difficult,** suitable for expert DIY or professional |

## Specifications

### Front forks

Oil type
| | |
|---|---|
| 1983 through 1987 | Automatic transmission fluid |
| 1988 on, except XR650R models | Pro-Honda SS7 suspension fluid or equivalent |
| XR650R models | Pro Honda HP fork oil, 5W, or equivalent |

Oil capacity
| | |
|---|---|
| XL600R | 455 cc (15.4 fl oz) |
| XR600R | |
|   1985 through 1987 | 631 cc (21.3 fl oz) |
|   1988 through 1990 | 643 cc (21.74 fl oz) |
|   1991 and 1992 | 580 cc (19.61 fl oz) |
|   1993 on | 585 cc (19.78 fl oz) |
| XR650L | 564 cc (19.1 fl oz) |
| XR650R | 637 cc (21.5 fl oz) |

Oil level (fork fully compressed and spring removed)
| | |
|---|---|
| XL600R | 150 mm (5.9 inches) |
| XR600R | |
|   1985 through 1987 | 127 mm (5.0 inches) |
|   1988 through 1990 | 110 mm (4.3 inches) |
|   1991 on | |
|     Standard oil level | 125 mm (4.92 inches) |
|     Maximum oil level | 115 mm (4.53 inches) |
|     Minimum oil level | 135 mm (5.31 inches) |
| XR650L | 145 mm (5.70 inches) |
| XR650R | 120 mm (4.70 inches) |

## Front forks (continued)

Fork spring free length limit
  XL600R ............................................................ 557.0 mm (21.93 inch)
  XR600R
    1985 through 1987 .................................. 566.0 mm (22.28 inch)
    1988 and 1990 (short spring)................ 62.0 mm (2.441 inches)
    1988 and 1990 (long spring)................. 577.0 mm (22.717 inches)
    1991 on..................................................... 570.0 mm (22.441 inches)
  XR650L ............................................................ 576.0 mm (22.68 inches)
  XR650R ............................................................ 506 mm (19.9 inches)
Fork tube bend limit ........................................... 0.2 mm (0.008 inch)

## Rear suspension

Rear shock absorber spring free length
  XL600R
    Standard ................................................. 276.0 mm (10.87 inches)
    Limit........................................................ 273 mm (10.75 inches)
  XR600R
    1985 through 1987
      Standard............................................ 234.0 mm (9.2 inches)
      Limit................................................... 231 mm (9.1 inches)
    1988 through 1990
      Standard............................................ 242.3 mm (9.54 inches)
      Limit................................................... 240.0 mm (9.45 inches)
    1991 on
      Standard............................................ 215.5 mm (8.48 inches)
      Limit................................................... 213.3 mm (8.40 inches)
  XR650L
    Standard ................................................. 225.3 mm (8.87 inches)
    Limit ....................................................... Not available
  XR650R ............................................................ Not available
Rear shock absorber spring installed length
  XL600R (standard) ......................................... 265 mm (10.43 inches)
  XR600R
    1985
      Standard............................................ 225.2 mm (8.87 inches)
      Maximum .......................................... 230.2 mm (9.06 inches)
      Minimum ........................................... 220.2 mm (8.67 inches)
    1986 and 1987
      Standard............................................ 218.9 mm (8.62 inches)
      Maximum .......................................... 223.9 mm (8.81 inches)
      Minimum ........................................... 213.9 mm (8.42 inches)
    1988 through 1990
      Standard............................................ 234 mm (9.21 inches)
      Maximum .......................................... 229 mm (9.02 inches)
      Minimum ........................................... 239 mm (9.41 inches)
    1991 and later
      Standard............................................ 200 mm (7.87 inches)
      Maximum .......................................... 195 mm (7.68 inches)
      Minimum ........................................... 205 mm (8.07 inches)
  XR650L
    1993
      Standard............................................ 200.3 mm (7.89 inches)
      Maximum .......................................... 205 mm (8.1 inches)
      Minimum ........................................... 195 mm (7.7 inches)
    1994 and later
      Standard............................................ 206.5 +/- 3.6 mm (8.13 +/- 0.142 inches)
      Maximum .......................................... Not specified
  XR650R (standard) ........................................ 236.5 mm (9.31 inches)

## Drive chain

Drive chain frame slider minimum thickness.......... 6 mm (0.24 inch)
Drive chain length
  XL600R .......................................................... Not specified
  XR600R
    1985 through 1987 (109 pins)
      Standard............................................ 1730 mm (68.1 inches)
      Limit................................................... 1765 mm (69.5 inches)

1988 on (111 pins)
Standard ................................................... 1762 mm (69.4 inches)
Limit ........................................................ 1780 mm (59.7 inch)
XR650L ........................................................... Not specified
XR650R (41 pins) .......................................... 638 mm (25.1 inches)
Drive chain master link (XR650L and XR650R models)
Pin projection (from side plate, before staking) ............... 1.2 to 1.4 mm (0.05 to 0.06 inch)
Pin diameter (after staking) ........................................ 5.5 to 5.8 mm (0.217 to 0.228 inch)

## Torque specifications

**Note:** *One foot-pound (ft-lb) of torque is equivalent to 12 inch-pounds (in-lbs) of torque. Torque values below approximately 15 ft-lbs are expressed in inch-pounds, since most foot-pound torque wrenches are not accurate at these smaller values.*

Handlebar bracket bolts
XL600R ............................................................. 18 to 30 Nm (13 to 22 ft-lbs)
XR600R
1985 through 1987 ..................................... 22 to 30 Nm (16 to 22 ft-lbs)
1988 on ....................................................... 27 Nm (20 ft-lbs)
XR650L, XR650R ............................................ 27 Nm (20 ft-lbs)
Front axle nut ...................................................... See Chapter 7
Upper triple clamp bolts
XL600R ............................................................. 18 to 30 Nm (13 to 22 ft-lbs)
XR600R
1985 through 1987 ..................................... 25 to 30 Nm (18 to 22 ft-lbs)
1988 through 1990 ..................................... 33 Nm (24 ft-lbs)
1991 on ....................................................... 28 Nm (20 ft-lbs)
XR650L ........................................................... 28 Nm (20 ft-lbs)
XR650L ........................................................... 28 Nm (20 ft-lbs)
Lower triple clamp bolts
XL600R ............................................................. 30 to 35 Nm (22 to 25 ft-lbs)
XR600R
1985 through 1987 ..................................... 30 to 35 Nm (22 to 25 ft-lbs)
1988 on ....................................................... 35 Nm (25 ft-lbs)
XR650L, XR650R ............................................ 33 Nm (24 ft-lbs)
Front forks - XL600R, XR600R, XR650L
Damper rod Allen bolt (XL600R, 1985 through 1987 XR600R) .......... 15 to 25 Nm (11 to 18 ft-lbs)
Fork bottom bolt (1988 and later XR600R) ........................ 35 Nm (25 ft-lbs)
Fork cap-to-fork tube
XL600R, 1985 through 1987 XR600R ........................ 15 to 30 Nm (11 to 22 ft-lbs)
1988 and later XR600R ........................................ 23 Nm (17 ft-lbs)
Fork cap locknut (1991 and later XR600R) ....................... 60 Nm (43 ft-lbs)
Fork piston retainer (1991 on) ................................... 35 Nm (25 ft-lbs)
Front forks - XR650R
Fork bottom bolt .................................................. 54 Nm (40 ft-lbs)
Fork cap-to-damper rod ......................................... 15 Nm (132 in-lbs)
Fork cap-to-fork tube ............................................ 30 Nm (22 ft-lbs)
Steering stem bearing adjusting nut ........................... See Chapter 1
Steering stem nut
XL600R ............................................................. 80 to 120 Nm (58 to 87 ft-lbs)
XR600R
1985 through 1987 ..................................... 95 to 140 Nm (60 to 101 ft-lbs)
1988 on ....................................................... 118 Nm (85 ft-lbs)
XR650L ........................................................... 118 Nm (85 ft-lbs)
XR650R ........................................................... 98 Nm (72 ft-lbs)
Rear shock absorber upper mounting bolt
XL600R ............................................................. 40 to 50 Nm (29 to 36 ft-lbs)
XR600R
1985 through 1987 ..................................... 40 to 50 Nm (29 to 36 ft-lbs)
1988 on ....................................................... 45 Nm (33 ft-lbs)
XR650L, XR650R ............................................ 45 Nm (33 ft-lbs)
Rear shock absorber lower mounting bolt
XL600R ............................................................. 40 to 50 Nm (29 to 36 ft-lbs)
XR600R
1985 through 1987 ..................................... 25 to 35 Nm (14 to 25 ft-lbs)
1988 through 1990 ..................................... 30 Nm (22 ft-lbs)
1991 on ....................................................... 35 Nm (25 ft-lbs)
XR650L ........................................................... 35 Nm (25 ft-lbs)
XR650R ........................................................... 45 Nm (33 ft-lbs)

## Torque specifications (continued)

Shock arm-to-swingarm
    XL600R .......................................................................................... 90 to 120 Nm (65 to 87 ft-lbs)
    XR600R
        1985 through 1987 ........................................................... 60 to 80 Nm (43 to 57 ft-lbs)
        1988 on............................................................................ 70 Nm (51 ft-lbs)
    XR650L .......................................................................................... 70 Nm (51 ft-lbs)
    XR650R .......................................................................................... 78 Nm (58 ft-lbs)

Shock arm-to-shock link
    XL600R .......................................................................................... 40 to 50 Nm (29 to 36 ft-lbs)
    XR600R
        1985 through 1987 ........................................................... 40 to 50 Nm (29 to 36 ft-lbs)
        1988 on............................................................................ 45 Nm (33 ft-lbs)
    XR650L .......................................................................................... 45 Nm (33 ft-lbs)
    XR650R .......................................................................................... 69 Nm (51 ft-lbs)

Shock link-to-frame
    XL600R .......................................................................................... Not specified
    XR600R
        1985 through 1987 ........................................................... 40 to 50 Nm (29 to 36 ft-lbs)
        1988 on............................................................................ 45 Nm (33 ft-lbs)
    XR650L .......................................................................................... 55 Nm (40 ft-lbs)
    XR650R .......................................................................................... 69 Nm (51 ft-lbs)

Swingarm pivot bolt nut
    XL600R, 1985 through 1987 XR600R.............................................. 80 to 100 Nm (58 to 72 ft-lbs)
    1988 and later XR600R................................................................... 90 Nm (65 ft-lbs)
    XR650L .......................................................................................... 90 Nm (65 ft-lbs)
    XR650R .......................................................................................... 108 Nm (80 ft-lbs)

Swingarm pivot adjusting nut (XR650R)
    Stage 1.......................................................................................... 12 Nm (108 in-lbs)
    Stage 2.......................................................................................... Loosen until under no torque
    Stage 3.......................................................................................... 7 Nm (5.1 in-lbs)
    Adjusting nut locknut .................................................................... 64 Nm (47 ft-lbs)

Engine sprocket bolts
    All except XR650R ........................................................................ Not specified
    XR650R .......................................................................................... 12 Nm (108 in-lbs)

Rear sprocket bolts/nuts
    XL600R .......................................................................................... 32 to 35 Nm (23 to 25 ft-lbs)
    XR600R
        1985 through 1987 ........................................................... 34 to 40 Nm (24 to 29 ft-lbs)
        1988 on............................................................................ 44 Nm (32 ft-lbs)
    XR650L .......................................................................................... 64 Nm (46 ft-lbs)
    XR650R .......................................................................................... 42 Nm (31 ft-lbs)

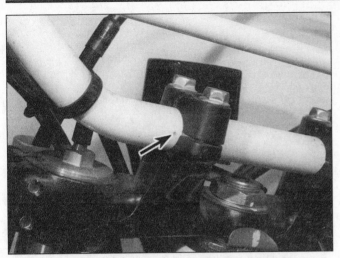

2.3 Remove the bolts and lift off the upper brackets; on installation, align the punch mark in the handlebar with the edge of the lower bracket

2.5 Install the upper brackets with their punch marks facing forward

## 1  General information

The steering system on these models consists of a one-piece handlebar and a tapered roller bearing steering head attached to the front portion of the frame. The front suspension consists of damper rod forks (early models), or cartridge forks (later models). The rear suspension consists of a single shock absorber with concentric coil spring, a swingarm and Honda's Pro-Link suspension linkage. The suspension linkage produces a progressive rising rate effect, where the suspension stiffens as its travel increases. This allows a softer ride over small bumps in the terrain, together with firmer suspension control over large irregularities.

## 2  Handlebars, control levers and handgrips - removal and installation

### Handlebars and control levers

1    The handlebars rest in a bracket integral with the upper triple clamp. If the handlebars must be removed for access to other components, such as the steering head bearings, simply remove the bolts and slip the handlebars off the bracket. It's not necessary to disconnect the throttle, clutch, or decompression cables, brake hose or the switch wiring, but it is a good idea to support the assembly with a piece of wire or rope, to avoid unnecessary strain on the cables.

2    If the handlebars are to be removed completely, remove the control lever clamp bolts and kill switch/switch housings, then detach the components from the handlebars.

3    Remove the upper bracket bolts, lift off the brackets and remove the handlebars (see illustration).
4    Place the handlebars in the lower brackets. Line up the punch mark on the handlebar with the parting line of the upper and lower brackets (see illustration 2.3).
5    Install the upper brackets with their punch marks facing forward (see illustration). Tighten the front bolts, then the rear bolts, to the torque listed in this Chapter's Specifications.

*Caution: If there's a gap between the upper and lower brackets at the rear after tightening the bolts, don't try to close it by tightening beyond the recommended torque. You'll only crack the brackets.*

6    If the control levers/switch(es) were removed, install them on the handlebars with the parting line of the lever holder and clamp aligned with the punch mark on the handlebar. Note: *This is largely a matter of personal preference; some riders feel more comfortable with the levers set at a different angle.*

### Handgrips

7    The easiest way to remove handgrips is to slit them with a utility knife and peel them off the handlebar and throttle tube.
8    Once the grips have been removed, clean the handlebar of all glue residue.
9    Apply grip glue (available at motorcycle dealers and accessory shops) to the surface of the handlebar or throttle tube and to the inside of the grip. Note: *The throttle grip has a larger inner diameter than the left side grip. Also, only apply glue and install one grip at a time.*
10    Slide the grip onto the handlebar or throttle tube, twisting it if necessary until it is fully in place. Note that some grips are asymmetrical and have to be aligned and matched so they're positioned the same from side-to-side. Also, some throttle tubes have a flange, which a groove in the grip must fit over.

3.3 If you're going to disassemble the forks, loosen the fork cap (upper arrow) while the fork is held in the triple clamps; loosen the upper triple clamp bolts (lower arrows) . . .

11    Allow the grip glue to dry (refer to the glue manufacturer's instructions for the specified amount of time) before riding the bike.

## 3  Front forks - removal and installation

### Removal

1    Support the bike securely upright so it can't fall over during this procedure.
2    Remove the front wheel, unbolt the brake caliper and detach the brake hose retainer from the left fork leg (see Chapter 7). If you're working on an XR600R or XR650R, remove the headlight assembly (see Chapter 4).
3    If you plan to disassemble the forks, loosen the fork caps now (see illustration). This can be done later, but it will be easier

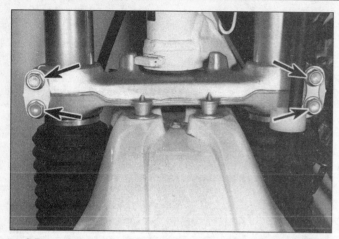

3.5 . . . and the lower triple clamp bolts to remove the forks

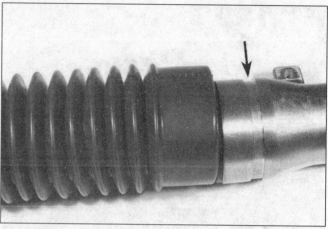

4.2a On 1988 and later models, slide the fork boot out of its groove and loosen the clamp at the top end to remove the boot

while the forks are securely held in the triple clamps.

4    Detach the speedometer cable and withdraw it from the retainer on the right fork leg.

5    Loosen the upper and lower triple clamp bolts **(see illustration 3.3 and the accompanying illustration)**.

6    Lower the fork leg out of the triple clamps, twisting it if necessary.

## *Installation*

7    Slide each fork leg into the lower triple clamp.

8    Slide the fork legs up, installing the tops of the tubes into the upper triple clamp.

Position the forks so the top of each tube is flush with the top surface of the upper triple clamp.

9    Tighten the triple clamp bolts to the torque listed in this Chapter's Specifications.

10    The remainder of installation is the reverse of the removal steps.

---

## 4    Front forks - disassembly, inspection and reassembly

1    Loosen the upper triple clamp bolts, then break loose (but do not remove) the fork cap. Then remove the forks following the procedure in Section 3. Work on one fork at a time to prevent mixing up the parts.

### *1983 through 1990 models*
#### Disassembly

2    To disassemble the forks, refer to the accompanying illustrations **(see illustrations)**.

4.2b Pry the dust seal out of the outer fork tube

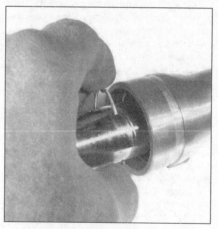

4.2c Pry the retaining ring out of its groove and slide it off the inner fork tube

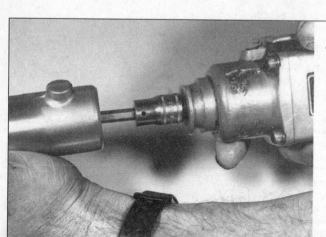

4.2d Loosen the Allen bolt in the bottom of the outer fork tube - an air wrench is the easiest way to do this if you have one, but if not, unscrew the bolt with an Allen wrench while the fork cap is still installed; the spring pressure will keep the damper rod from turning inside the fork

4.2e Remove the Allen bolt and its copper sealing washer; use a new washer on reassembly

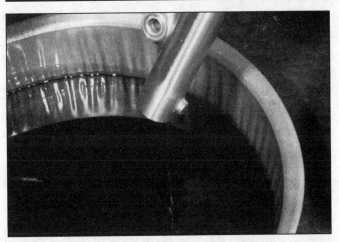

**4.2f  Let the oil drain from the bottom of the fork; pump the inner fork tube up and down to expel the oil**

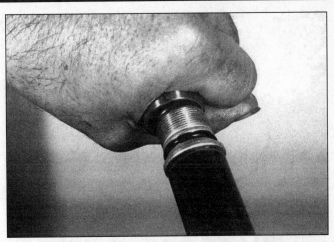

**4.2g  Unscrew the cap bolt and remove the O-ring - be careful of spring tension!**

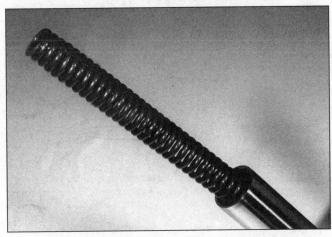

**4.2h  Pull the spring out of the fork; its narrow end faces into the fork tube on reassembly**

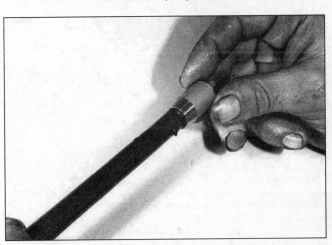

**4.2i  Take the oil lock piece off the end of the damper rod . . .**

## Inspection

3   Clean all parts in solvent and blow them dry with compressed air, if available. Check the inner and outer fork tubes and the damper rod for score marks, scratches, flaking of the chrome and excessive or abnormal wear. Look for dents in the tubes and replace them if any are found. Check the fork seal seat for nicks, gouges and scratches. If damage is evident, leaks will occur around the seal-to-outer tube junction. Replace worn or defective parts with new ones.

4   Using V-blocks and a dial indicator, check the inner fork tube for runout, or have it checked at a dealer service department or

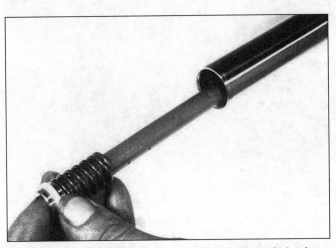

**4.2j  . . . and remove the damper rod from the inner fork tube**

**4.2k  Pry the oil seal out of its bore; be careful not to scratch the seal's seating area in the fork tube**

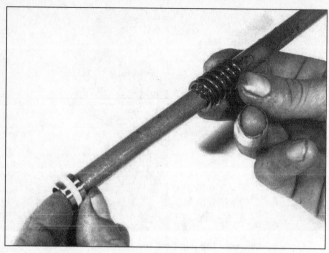

**4.6  Replace the Teflon ring on the damper rod if it's worn or damaged**

**4.8  Place the damper rod in the inner fork tube so it protrudes from the bottom . . .**

other repair shop. Compare your measurement with the limit listed in this Chapter's Specifications.

 **Warning: If the tube is bent, it should be replaced with a new one. Don't try to straighten it.**

5    Measure the overall length of the fork spring and check it for cracks or other damage. Compare the length to the minimum length listed in this Chapter's Specifications. If it's defective or sagged, replace both fork springs with new ones. Never replace only one spring.
6    Check the Teflon ring on the damper rod for wear or damage and replace it if problems are found **(see illustration)**. **Note:** *Don't remove the ring from the damper rod unless you plan to replace it.*
7    If you're working on a 1988 through 1990 model, check the fork slider bushing for wear and replace it if its condition is in doubt.

**Reassembly**

8    Place the rebound spring over the damper rod and slide the rod assembly into the inner fork tube until it protrudes from the lower end **(see illustration)**.
9    Place the oil lock piece on the base of the damper rod **(see illustration)**.
10   Insert the inner fork tube/damper rod assembly into the outer fork tube until the Allen-head bolt (with copper washer) can be threaded into the damper rod from the lower end of the outer tube **(see illustration 4.2e)**. **Note:** *Apply a non-permanent thread locking agent to the threads of the bolt. Keep the two tubes fairly horizontal so the oil lock piece doesn't fall off the damper rod inside the outer fork tube. Temporarily install the fork spring and cap to place tension on the damper rod so it won't spin inside the fork tube while you tighten the Allen bolt.*
11   Tighten the Allen bolt securely, then remove the fork cap and spring.
12   Lubricate the lips and outer diameter of

the fork seal with the recommended fork oil (see this Chapter's Specifications). Slide the seal down the inner tube with the lips facing down. Drive the seal into position with a fork seal driver (Honda part no. 07747-0010100 and 07447-0010300 or 07947-1180001). If you don't have access to one of these, it is recommended that you take the fork to a Honda dealer or other repair shop for seal installation. You can also make a substitute tool **(see illustration)**. If you're very careful, the seal can be driven in with a hammer and drift punch. Work around the circumference of the seal, tapping gently on the outer edge of the seal until it's seated **(see illustration 4.2k)**. Be careful - if you distort the seal, you'll have to disassemble the fork and end up taking it to a dealer anyway!
13   Install the retaining ring, making sure it's completely seated in its groove **(see illustration)**.
14   Install the dust seal, making sure it seats completely **(see illustration)**. Pull the

**4.9 . . . then place the oil lock piece on the end of the damper rod and install the assembly in the outer fork tube**

**4.12  If you don't have a seal driver, a section of pipe can be used the same way the seal driver would be used - as a slide hammer (be sure to tape the ends of the pipe so it doesn't scratch the fork tube)**

**4.13  Make sure the retaining ring seats in its groove**

**4.14  Push the dust seal down until it seats in the outer fork tube**

**4.15a  Pour the specified amount of oil into the fork**

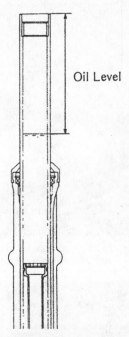

Oil Level

**4.15b  Measure the oil level in the fork with a stiff tape measure; add or drain oil to correct the level**

fork boot down into its groove on the outer fork tube and secure the upper end to the inner fork tube with the clamping band.
15   Compress the fork fully and add the recommended type and quantity of fork oil

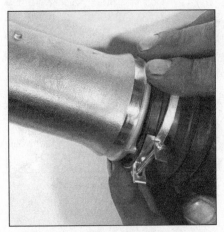

**4.18  Loosen the clamps and detach the fork boots**

listed in this Chapter's Specifications **(see illustration)**. Measure the fork oil level from the top of the fork tube **(see illustration)**. If necessary, add or remove oil to bring it to the proper level.
16   Install the fork spring, with the small-diameter end facing down. Install the O-ring and fork cap.
17   Install the fork, following the procedure outlined in Section 3. Tighten the fork cap after installation to the torque listed in this Chapter's Specifications.

### 1991 and later XR600R and all XR650L models

#### Disassembly
18   Loosen the boot clamps and slide the boot off the fork **(see illustration)**.

⚠️ *Warning: Air and spring pressure in the fork may cause the cap bolt to shoot out when it's unscrewed. Make sure the cap bolt is not pointed at yourself or anyone else.*

19   Release all air pressure from the fork

and unscrew the fork cap bolt.
20   Push the inner and outer fork tubes together to expose the spring. Hold the cap nut with one wrench and loosen the locknut away from the cap bolt with another wrench **(see illustration)**. Unscrew the cap bolt and locknut from the damper rod.
21   Take the washer off the spring, then lift the spring out of the fork.
22   Place the open (upper) end of the fork over a drain pan, then compress and extend the fork tubes several times to pump out the oil.
23   Pry the dust seal out of its bore, taking care not to scratch the fork tube **(see illustration)**.

**4.20  Hold the fork cap with one wrench and loosen the locknut with another**

**4.23  Pry the dust seal out of its bore**

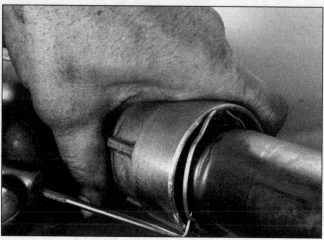

4.24 Pry the oil seal retainer out with a pointed tool; be careful not to scratch the seal bore or the fork tube

4.26a Remove the bottom cover from the fork leg

4.26b Unscrew the bottom bolt; use a new sealing washer on installation

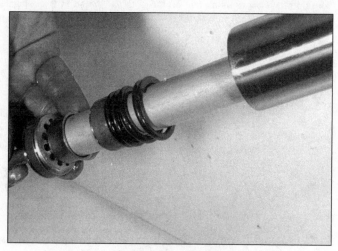

4.28 Pull the piston and rod out of the fork tube

24  Pry the oil seal retainer out of its groove, again taking care not to scratch the fork tube **(see illustration)**.

25  Place the outer fork tube in a padded vise. Tighten the vise just enough to keep the fork tube from rotating, but not tight enough to distort the fork tube.

26  Pry the bottom cover out of the fork tube **(see illustration)**. Unscrew the bottom bolt and remove the bolt with its sealing washer **(see illustration)**.

27  Unscrew the piston retainer from the piston cylinder with retainer wrench 07GMA-KS70100 and a box-end wrench. Take the bottom piece out of the cylinder.

28  Pull the piston and rod out of the inner fork tube **(see illustration)**.

29  Hold one fork tube in each hand and pull the tubes apart sharply several times (like a slide hammer) to separate them. Once they're separated, remove the oil lock piece from the inner fork tube.

### Inspection

30  Refer to Steps 3 through 5 to inspect the forks.

31  Check the fork tube bushings as well as the bushing on the fork piston for wear **(see illustrations)**. If the Teflon coating has worn off 3/4 or more of the surface, exposing the copper, replace the bushings. **Note:** *Don't remove the bushings unless they need to be replaced.*

32  Check the ring on the fork piston rod. If it's worn, replace it.

4.31a Don't remove the bushings unless they're worn

A  Oil seal
B  Backup ring
C  Bushings

4.31b There's a bushing on the piston (arrow) . . .

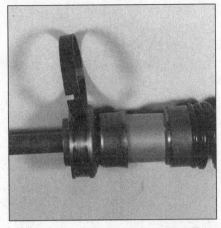

4.31c . . . to remove it, expand it at the slit and slip it off the fork

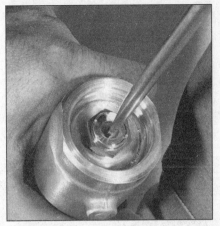

4.39 Turn the screw to adjust damping

## Reassembly

33   Insert the piston rod into the bottom end of the fork piston, then push the rod all the way in so its other end sticks out the top of the fork piston. Thread the fork cap locknut all the way onto the piston rod.

34   Install a new O-ring on the bottom piece and put the bottom piece in the fork piston with its hex downward. Thread the retainer into the bottom end of the fork piston and tighten it to the torque listed in this Chapter's Specifications, using the same special tool used for removal.

35   Pull the piston rod up to make sure it's all the way into the fork piston, then insert the fork piston into the inner fork tube.

36   Coat the lip of a new oil seal with the recommended fork oil. Install the bushings (if removed), backup ring and oil seal on the inner fork tube (see illustration 4.31a).

37   Install the oil lock piece on the bottom of the fork piston, then install the inner fork tube in the outer fork tube.

38   Place the outer fork tube in a padded vise, tightening it just enough to keep the fork tube from rotating but not tight enough to distort the fork tube.

39   Place a new sealing washer on the bottom bolt. Coat the threads of the bottom bolt with a non-permanent thread locking agent, then tighten it to the torque listed in this Chapter's Specifications. Set the damping adjuster to the desired setting (see illustration).

40   Seat the oil seal in its bore with a seal driver (see Step 12). Install the retaining ring in its groove, then seat the dust seal with the same tool used for the oil seal.

41   Compress the fork all the way. Pour half the amount of fork oil listed in this Chapter's Specifications into the inner fork tube. Pour the remaining fork oil slowly into the piston rod until it flows from the breather hole.

42   Slowly pump the piston rod up and down eight to ten times. Compress the fork all the way and leave it sitting upright for five minutes so the oil level can stabilize. Then measure the oil level and compare it to the values listed in this Chapter's Specifications. Add or drain oil as needed. **Note:** *When the air pressure in the fork is at the standard setting, a higher oil level (shorter distance from the top of the fork tube) will have the same effect as increasing the stiffness of the fork spring.*

 *Warning: To prevent unstable handling, make sure the oil level is exactly the same in both forks.*

43   Install the fork spring in the fork tube, tapered end first.

44   Dip a new fork cap O-ring in fork oil and place it on the fork cap. Install the washer on top of the spring, then install the fork cap and thread it down against the locknut. Hold the fork cap with one wrench, then tighten the locknut against the fork cap to the torque listed in this Chapter's Specifications.

45   Install the fork boot with its row of breather holes facing the rear of the fork.

## XR650R models

### Disassembly

46   Loosen the boot clamps and slide the boot off the fork (see illustration).

47   Pry out the dust cover from the bottom of the fork, then turn the compression adjuster screw counterclockwise all the way (see illustration). **Note:** *Record the number of clicks it takes to turn the screw all the way, and write this number down. That way you'll be able to return the compression adjustment*

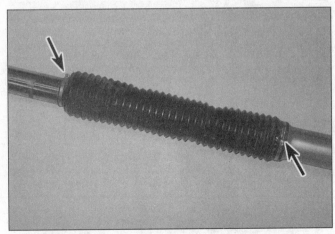

4.46 Loosen the clamp screws and slide the dust boot up and off the fork

4.47 Turn the compression adjuster screw counterclockwise all the way, counting the number of clicks it takes

4.49 Unscrew the fork cap bolt from the fork tube. Be careful - it's under spring pressure

4.50 Unscrew the fork cap bolt from the piston rod . . .

4.51 . . . remove the washers (if equipped), spring seat and spring . . .

*to its original setting.*

48 Unscrew the air bleed screw to release any built-up air pressure in the fork.

49 Unscrew the fork cap bolt (see illustration).

 *Warning: Wear eye protection - the cap bolt is under spring pressure. While unscrewing the cap bolt, keep some downward pressure on it so it doesn't pop out.*

50 Hold the lock nut on the piston rod with a wrench and unscrew the fork cap bolt from the piston rod (see illustration).

51 Remove the washers (if equipped) and spring seat from the top of the spring, then pull the spring out of the fork tube (see illustration).

52 Take the end plate off the bottom of the spring (see illustration).

53 Hold the end of the fork over a container and drain out the oil (see illustration). Pump the fork tube about ten times to help force the oil out.

54 Remove the adjuster collar and distance collar from the piston rod, then hold the fork

4.52 . . . then remove the end plate from the bottom of the spring

over the container and pump the piston rod about ten times to drain the oil from the fork damper (see illustrations).

55 Clamp the fork slider in a vise lined with soft jaws or rags, gripping on the caliper bracket or axle holder.

4.53 Drain the oil from the fork

*Caution: Do not overtighten the vise.*

Hold the fork damper with a special tool (available from specialty tool suppliers, or use Honda tool no. 07PMB-KZ4010A) and remove the center bolt (and its sealing washer) from the bottom of the fork using a

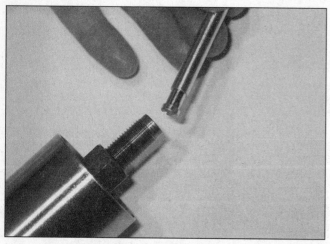

4.54a Remove the adjuster collar (noting the slotted end faces down into the piston rod) . . .

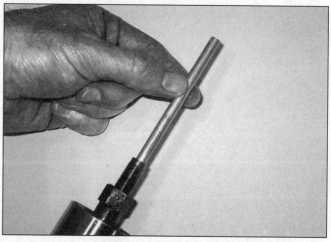

4.54b . . . and distance collar from the piston rod . . .

4.54c . . . then pump the piston rod a few times to force
the oil out of the fork damper

4.55a Hold the fork damper from turning using a special tool . . .

4.55b . . . and, using a 14 mm hex bit, unscrew the center
bolt from the bottom of the fork . . .

4.55c . . . be prepared for more oil to drain out

hex bit (see illustrations). Note: Depending on the diameter of the hole in your tool,
you might have to clamp the damper rod

in a soft-jaw vise and remove the lock nut,
then proceed with this Step (see illustration
4.57a).

56    Pull the fork damper out of the fork tube
and remove the oil lock piece from the end of
the damper (see illustrations).

4.56a Remove the damper . . .

4.56b . . . and oil lock piece from the fork tube
(note how it's oriented)

4.57a Clamp the damper rod in a soft-jaw vise, then remove the lock nut (if not already done) . . .

4.57b . . . and pull the piston rod from the fork damper.
**Note:** *The spring might stay in the damper (if so, that's OK)*

4.58a Being careful not to scratch the fork tube, pry out the stopper ring . . .

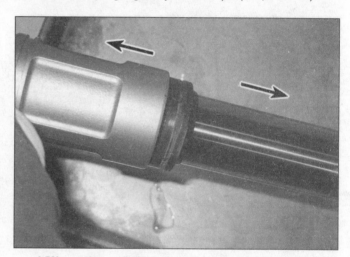

4.58b . . . then pull the fork tube sharply a few times, like a slide hammer, out of the fork slider

57  Unscrew the lock nut, then remove the rebound spring and piston rod from the fork damper **(see illustrations)**.

58  Carefully pry out the stopper ring, then pull the fork tube out of the slider **(see illus-** trations). This will require a few sharp pulls on the tube to remove the seals from the slider.

59  Remove the dust seal and oil seal by sliding them upward and off the top of the fork tube **(see illustration)**. Don't remove the bushings unless they're worn and need to be replaced.

### Inspection

60  Check the fork tube and spring as described in Steps 3 through 5.

61  Check the piston ring on the fork damper for damage or wear **(see illustra-tion)**. **Note:** *Don't remove the ring from the damper unless you plan to replace it.*

62  Check the piston rod and the ring and valve on the end of the rod for wear or dam-age **(see illustration)**. If wear or damage is found, the piston rod must be replaced as an assembly.

63  Check the fork center bolt for wear or damage. Also remove the O-rings and seal-ing washer from the center bolt and replace them with new ones **(see illustration)**.

64  Check the slider bushing and back-up bushing for wear; bushings should be replaced if they're worn so much that you can see copper extending from one edge to the other. To remove the bushings, insert the

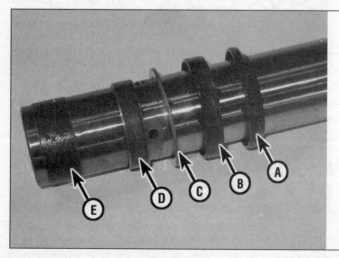

4.59 Fork seal and bushing details

A   Dust seal
B   Oil seal
C   Back-up ring
D   Guide bushing
E   Slider bushing

**4.61 Check the piston ring on the fork damper for wear**

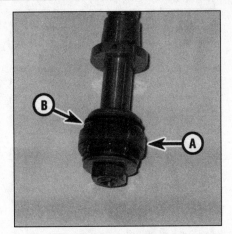

**4.62 Check the piston rod's ring (A) and valve (B) for damage**

**4.63 Fork center bolt details**

A   *Sealing washer*
B   *O-rings*

**4.68 Carefully drive the seals into the fork slider until the dust seal is just below the stopper ring groove, then install the stopper ring**

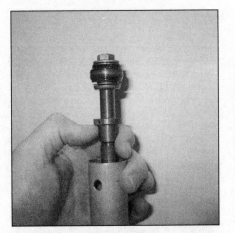

**4.69a Place the rebound spring onto the piston rod (if it came out) and insert the rod into the damper . . .**

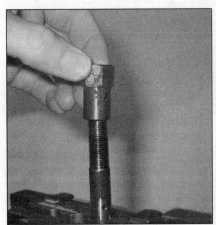

**4.69b . . . then install the lock nut**

blade of a screwdriver into the slot and twist it to expand the bushing. When installing the bushings, don't expand them any more than necessary.

65   Check the back-up ring for wear or distortion, replacing it if necessary.

### Reassembly

66   Install the back-up ring on the fork slider if it's not already in place. Lubricate the lips of the oil seal with clean fork oil and install it on the top of the fork tube, then slide it down. The marked side of the seal must face the top of the fork tube. **Note:** *Wrap electrical tape around the top of the fork tube to protect the lips of the seal as it's installed.*

67   Install the dust seal on the top of the fork tube, then slide it down.

68   Lubricate the bushings with clean fork oil and insert the fork tube into the slider. Using a fork seal driver, gently knock the seals into the slider until the dust seal is just below the groove for the stopper ring **(see illustration)**. Install the stopper ring in the groove, making sure it seats completely.

69   Slide the rebound spring over the end

of the piston rod (if it came out when the piston rod was removed), insert the piston rod into the fork damper, then install the lock nut onto the other end of the rod **(see illustrations)**. Tighten the nut so it's snug, but not too tight. **Note:** *If you had to remove the lock*

*nut before performing Step 55 (due to the diameter of the hole in the damper rod holding tool), install the lock nut after performing Step 71.*

70   Place the oil lock piece over the end of the damper **(see illustration)**, then install the damper into the fork tube

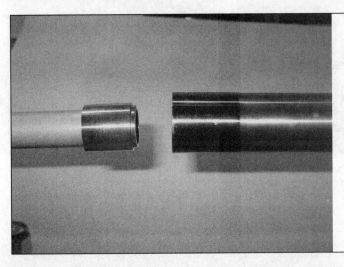

**4.70 Install the oil lock piece onto the damper, then install the damper into the fork tube, making sure the oil lock piece doesn't fall off (and that it engages properly with the bottom of the slider)**

**4.71 Install the center bolt and, while holding the damper rod with the special tool, tighten the center bolt to the torque listed in this Chapter's Specifications**

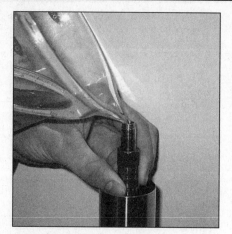

**4.72a Fill the piston rod until oil flows out the damper rod end, then compress the piston rod until it bottoms . . .**

**4.72b . . . then add half of the specified amount of fork oil listed in this Chapter's Specifications**

71   Clamp the fork slider back into the vise lined with soft jaws or rags, gripping on the caliper bracket or axle holder.

*Caution: Do not overtighten the vise.*

Install a new sealing washer on the center bolt, then apply a non-hardening thread locking agent to the threads of the center bolt. Install the center bolt and tighten it to the torque listed in this Chapter's Specifications, holding the fork damper with the tool described in Step 55 **(see illustration)**.

72   Support the fork upright. Push the piston rod all the way, then add half of the recommended type and quantity of fork oil listed in this Chapter's Specifications **(see illustrations)**. Cycle the fork tube and piston rod up-and-down about ten times, then wait five minutes to allow the oil level to stabilize.

73   Compress the piston rod and fork tube all the way down and measure the fork oil level from the top of the fork tube **(see illus-**

tration). If necessary, add or remove oil to bring it to the proper level.

74   Install the distance collar, followed by the adjuster collar, into the piston rod **(see illustration)**. **Note:** *The grooved end of the adjuster collar faces down, towards the distance collar.*

75   Thread the lock nut onto the piston rod, by hand only, to the end of the threads. Wrap a length of wire (about two feet long) to the underside of the lock nut **(see illustration)**.

76   Install the end plate to the fork's bottom coil **(see illustration 4.52)**, then thread the spring, spring seat and washers (if equipped) over the wire and down over the piston rod and into the fork tube.

77   Install a new O-ring on the fork cap, then hold the piston rod and remove the wire. Install the fork cap onto the lock nut, hold the lock nut with a wrench, and tighten the fork cap to the torque listed in this Chapter's Specifications.

78   Push the fork cap down into the fork tube and start the threads, being careful not to cross-thread them. Tighten the fork cap to the torque listed in this Chapter's Specifications. **Note:** *Tightening the fork cap is easier to do after the fork has been installed and the lower (but not the upper) triple clamp has been tightened; if you choose to do it that way, just don't forget.*

79   Referring to your notes made earlier, set the compression adjuster to its original setting, then push the dust cover into the hex of the center bolt.

80   Slide the dust boot down over the top of the fork and into place, with the holes in the boot at the bottom and facing the outside of the bike when the fork is installed, then tighten the bottom clamp.

81   Install the fork (see Section 3), slide the boot up against the lower triple clamp, then tighten the upper boot clamp screw securely.

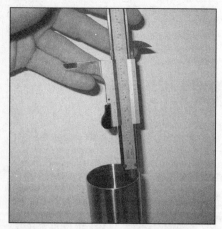

**4.73 Measure the fork oil level with the fork tube and piston rod compressed all the way (and without the distance collar and adjuster collar in place), then add oil as necessary to bring it to the level listed in this Chapter's Specifications**

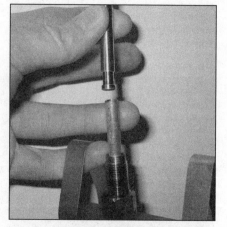

**4.74 Install the distance collar and rebound adjuster collar into the piston rod; the end of the adjuster collar with the groove points down**

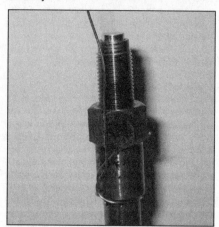

**4.75 After threading the lock nut onto the piston rod, wrap a length of wire around the nut (this will be used to prevent the piston rod from falling into the fork when the spring is installed)**

5.6a  Loosen the steering stem nut with a socket . . .

5.6b  . . . and unscrew it from the steering stem

## 5  Steering head bearings - replacement

1    If the steering head bearing check/adjustment (see Chapter 1) does not remedy excessive play or roughness in the steering head bearings, the entire front end must be disassembled and the bearings and races replaced with new ones.
2    Support the bike securely so it can't be knocked over during this procedure.
3    Remove the headlight assembly (see Chapter 5). If you're working on an XL600R or XR650L, remove the speedometer, its bracket and cable retainer and the horn (see Chapter 5). Unbolt the brake hose guide, where applicable.
4    If you're working on a 1985 or 1986 XR600R, remove the digital enduro meter and sensor. If you're working on a 1987 or later model XR600R or an XR650R, remove the odometer.
5    Remove the handlebars (see Section 2), the front wheel and brake caliper (see Chap-

5.6c  Lift off the washer . . .

ter 7), the front fender (see Chapter 8) and the forks (see Section 3).
6    Loosen the steering stem nut with a socket (see illustration). Remove the nut, washer, upper triple clamp and, on XR600R and XR650L models, the lockwasher

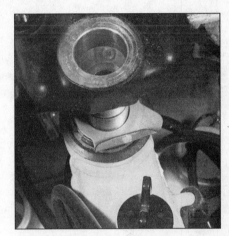

5.6d  . . . the upper triple clamp . . .

(see illustrations).
7    Using a socket or spanner wrench of the type described in Chapter 1, Section 22, remove the stem locknut and bearing cover (see illustrations) while supporting the steering head from the bottom.

5.6e  . . . and the lockwasher (XR600R and XR650L models)

5.7a  Remove the bearing adjusting nut . . .

5.7b  . . . and lift off the bearing cover

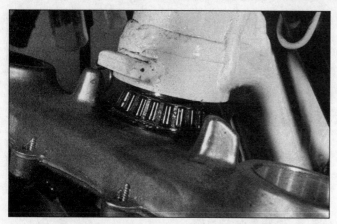

5.8 Lower the steering stem out of the steering head

5.9 Lift the upper bearing out of the steering head

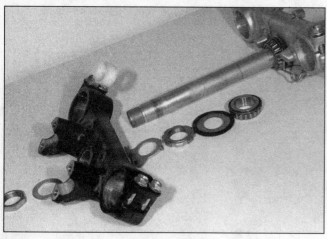

5.10 Steering stem and bearing details

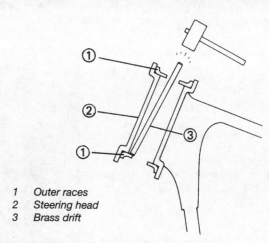

1   Outer races
2   Steering head
3   Brass drift

5.12a Drive out the bearing races with a hammer and brass drift

8   Remove the steering stem and lower triple clamp assembly **(see illustration)**. If it's stuck, gently tap on the top of the steering stem with a plastic mallet or a hammer and a wood block.

9   Remove the upper bearing **(see illustration)**.

10   Clean all the parts with solvent and dry them thoroughly, using compressed air, if available **(see illustration)**. If you do use compressed air, don't let the bearings spin as they're dried - it could ruin them. Wipe the old grease out of the steering head and bearing races.

11   Examine the races in the steering head for cracks, dents, and pits. If even the slightest amount of wear or damage is evident, the races should be replaced with new ones.

12   To remove the races, drive them out of the steering head with a hammer and drift punch **(see illustrations)**. A slide hammer

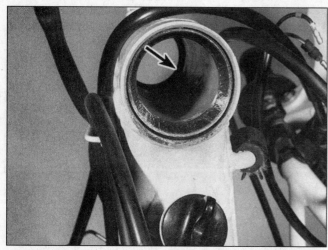

5.12b Place the drift against the edge of the lower bearing race (arrow) and tap evenly around it to drive the bearing out

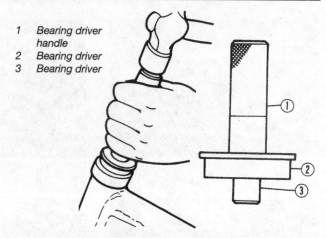

1   Bearing driver handle
2   Bearing driver
3   Bearing driver

5.12c Drive in the bearing races with a bearing driver or socket the same diameter as the bearing race

**5.14 Leave the lower bearing and grease seal (arrow) on the steering stem unless you plan to replace them**

**5.17 Work the grease completely into the rollers**

with the proper internal-jaw puller will also work. Since the races are an interference fit in the frame, installation will be easier if the new races are left overnight in a freezer. This will cause them to contract and slip into place in the frame with very little effort. When installing the races, use a bearing driver the same diameter as the outer race **(see illustration)**, or tap them gently into place with a hammer and punch or a large socket. Do not strike the bearing surface or the race will be damaged.

13   Check the bearings for wear. Look for cracks, dents, and pits in the races and flat spots on the bearings. Replace any defective parts with new ones. If a new bearing is required, replace both of them as a set.

14   Check the grease seal under the lower bearing and replace it with a new one if necessary **(see illustration)**.

15   To remove the lower bearing and grease seal from the steering stem, you may need to use a bearing puller, which can be rented. Don't remove this bearing unless it, or the grease seal underneath, must be replaced. Removal will damage the grease seal, so replace it whenever the bearing is removed.

16   Inspect the steering stem/lower triple clamp for cracks and other damage. Do not attempt to repair any steering components. Replace them with new parts if defects are found.

17   Pack the bearings with high-quality grease **(see illustration)**. Coat the outer races with grease also.

18   If removed, install the grease seal and lower bearing onto the steering stem. Drive the lower bearing onto the steering stem using a pipe the same diameter as the bearing inner race **(see illustration)**. Drive the bearing on until it's fully seated.

19   Insert the steering stem/lower triple clamp into the frame head. Install the upper bearing, bearing cover and adjusting nut. Refer to the adjustment procedure in Chapter 1 and tighten the adjusting nut to the torque listed in the Chapter 1 Specifications.

20   Make sure the steering head turns smoothly and that there's no play in the bearings.

21   Install a new lockwasher (XR600R and XR650L models) and the upper triple clamp. Install the washer and steering stem nut, but don't tighten the nut yet.

22   Install the fork tubes and tighten the lower triple clamp bolts to the torque listed in this Chapter's Specifications.

23   Tighten the steering stem nut to the torque listed in this Chapter's Specifications.

24   Check the alignment of the fork tubes with the upper triple clamp; the tops of the fork tubes should be even with the upper surface of the triple clamp. If necessary, loosen the lower triple clamp bolts and adjust the position of the fork tubes.

25   Tighten the triple clamp bolts to the torque listed in this Chapter's Specifications.

26   Bend the lockwasher against the upper triple clamp (XR600R and XR650L models).

27   The remainder of installation is the reverse of removal.

28   Check the alignment of the handlebars with the front wheel. If necessary, loosen the upper triple clamp bolts and align the handlebars with the front wheel, then tighten the upper triple clamp bolts to the torque listed in this Chapter's Specifications.

**6   Rear shock absorber - removal, inspection and installation**

1   Support the bike securely on a pit stand or lift so it can't be knocked over during this procedure. Support the rear wheel with a jack so the suspension can be raised or lowered as needed for access to the bolts.

2   Remove the seat, both side covers and the air filter housing (see Chapters 8 and 4). Cover the carburetor inlet with a rag to keep out dirt.

## *Removal*

### XL600R

3   Remove the upper mounting bolt.

4   Unbolt the shock link from the shock arm **(see illustration)**.

5   Unbolt the shock arm from the swingarm **(see illustration)**.

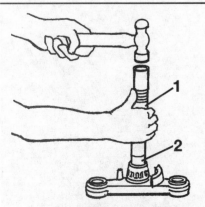

1   Driver
2   Bearing and grease seal

**5.18 Drive the grease seal and bearing lower race on with a hollow driver (or a piece of tubing of the same diameter as the bearing inner race)**

**6.4 Unbolt the shock link from the shock arm (right arrow); note the direction of the bolt head. The left arrow indicates the shock link-to-frame bolt**

6.5 Remove the nut and the bolt that secure the shock arm to the swingarm

6.18 Shock link-to-shock arm bolt/nut (XR650R)

6    Pull the top of the shock absorber to the rear, then lift the shock and link arm up and out from the frame.
7    The link arm can now be removed from the shock.

### XR600R

8    If you're working on a 1985 through 1990 XR600R, remove the shock reservoir's retaining bands and detach the reservoir from the bike. **Note:** *On later models, the shock reservoir is solidly attached to the shock, rather than being connected by a hose.*
9    If you're working on a 1988 or later XR600R, remove the CDI unit (see Chapter 5).
10    Remove the upper mounting bolt.
11    Raise the rear wheel with the jack and remove the shock absorber lower mounting bolt.
12    Lift the shock absorber up and out from the frame.

### XR650L

13    Remove the upper mounting bolt.
14    Remove the shock link-to-shock arm bolt.
15    Raise the rear wheel with the jack and

remove the shock absorber lower mounting bolt.
16    Remove the shock absorber out from the left side of the frame.

### XR650R

17    Remove the subframe (see Chapter 8).
18    Remove the shock link-to-shock arm bolt **(see illustration)**.
19    Remove the shock absorber lower mounting bolt **(see illustration)**.
20    Remove the shock absorber upper mounting bolt **(see illustration)**. Tilt the top of the shock back and lift it from the bike.

### *Inspection*

21    The shock absorber can be overhauled, but it's a complicated procedure that requires special tools not readily available to the typical owner. If inspection reveals problems, have the shock rebuilt by a dealer or motorcycle repair shop.
22    Check the shock absorber for damage and oil leaks. If these can be seen, have the shock overhauled.
23    Check the bearing at the upper end of the shock for leaking grease, looseness or signs of damage **(see illustration)**. If any of

these problems can be seen, have the bearing pressed out and a new one pressed in by a dealer or motorcycle repair shop.

### *Installation*

24    Installation is the reverse of the removal steps. Tighten the fasteners to the torque values listed in this Chapter's Specifications.

### 7    Rear shock linkage - removal, inspection and installation

1    Support the bike securely on a pit stand or lift. **Note:** *Place a floor jack under the rear wheel to raise it as necessary for access to the shock lower mounting bolt and the linkage bolts.*

### *Removal*

### XL600R

2    Remove the rear shock absorber (with the linkage - see Section 6), then remove the nut and bolt and separate the linkage from the shock absorber.

6.19 Shock absorber lower mounting bolt/nut (XR650R)

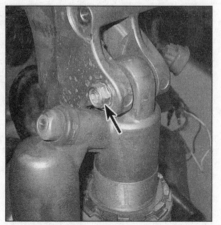

6.20 Rear shock absorber upper mounting bolt/nut (XR650R)

6.23 Check the bearing at the top of the shock absorber

7.9 Remove the bolt cover, then unscrew the shock arm-to-swingarm bolt (XR650L)

7.14 Shock arm-to-swingarm bolt/nut (XR650R)

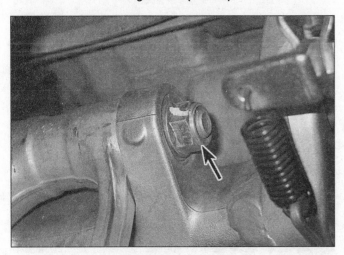

7.15 Remove the nut and pull out the bolt to detach the shock link from the frame (XR650R)

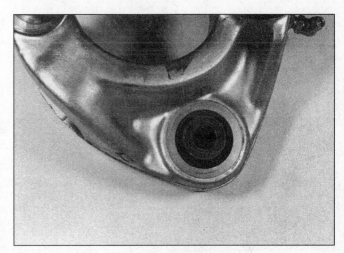

7.17a Check the bearing in the shock arm

## XR600R

3   Remove the shock absorber (see Section 6).
4   Loosen the link-to-shock arm bolt.
5   Remove the shock arm-to-swingarm bolt.
6   Remove the link-to-frame bolt.
7   Detach the arm and link, then remove the bolt and separate the two components.

## XR650L

8   Remove the rear shock absorber (see Section 6).
9   Remove the bolt and bolt cover, remove the shock arm-to-swingarm bolt **(see illustration)**, then detach the shock arm from the swingarm.
10   Remove the shock link-to-frame bolt and remove the shock link.

## XR650R

11   Unscrew the sidestand mounting bolts and detach the bolt and sidestand from the frame (see Chapter 8).
12   Remove the shock arm-to-shock link

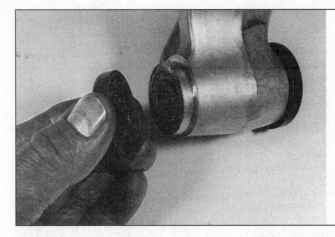

7.17b Pull the covers off the shock arm end pivots . . .

nut/bolt **(see illustration 6.18)**.
13   Remove the shock absorber lower mounting bolt **(see illustration 6.19)**.
14   Remove the shock arm-to-swingarm nut/bolt **(see illustration)**.
15   Remove the shock link-to-frame nut/bolt and remove the shock link **(see illustration)**.

## Inspection

16   The pivots at the ends of the shock link and the shock arm consist of needle bearings, sleeves and grease seals.
17   Clean all parts thoroughly with solvent and dry them with compressed air, if available **(see illustrations)**. Check all parts for scoring, damage or heavy corrosion and

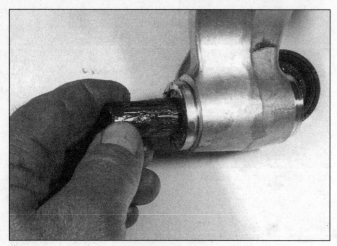

7.17c ... withdraw the pivot collars ...

7.17d ... and inspect the needle bearings

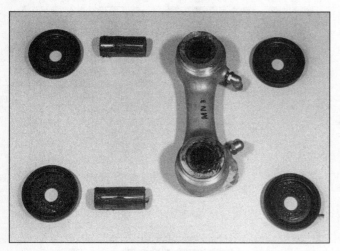

7.17e Shock link details

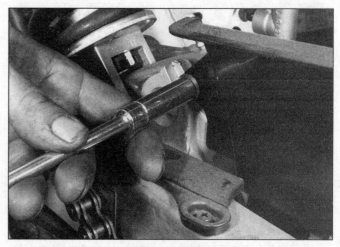

8.4a Unbolt the upper chain guard from the swingarm ...

replace them as necessary. Needle and spherical bearing replacement requires a press and a shouldered drift. If you don't have these, have the bearings replaced by a Honda dealer or motorcycle repair shop. Before removing the bearings, measure their installed depth; press the new ones in to the same depth. **Note:** *On XR650R models, the paired needle bearings in the shock arm and the shock link should be installed to a depth of 6.0 mm (0.24 inch) from the outside edge of the link.*

18    Apply grease to the needle bearings and a thin coat of grease to the sleeves, then install them in the needle bearings.

19    Install the dust seals.

### Installation

20    Installation is the reverse of the removal procedure. Be sure to tighten all of the fasteners to the torque values listed in this Chapter's Specifications.

## 8  Swingarm - removal and installation

1    Support the bike securely on a pit stand or lift, then remove the rear wheel (see Chapter 7).

2    If you're working on a drum brake model, unhook the brake pedal return spring from the swingarm, then remove the brake pedal (see Chapter 7). If you're working on a bike with a rear disc brake, detach the brake hose retainers from the swingarm. Remove the caliper and suspend it with a piece of wire.

### All models except the XR650R

3    If you're working on an XL600R, remove the shock absorber and shock linkage (see Sections 6 and 7).

4    Remove the chain cover/guard from the swingarm **(see illustrations)**. On 1988

8.4b ... and slip it off its post (XR600R)

and later XR600R models, remove the chain guide slider and chain guide.

5    Remove the shock arm-to-swingarm bolt and the shock link-to-frame bolt, then

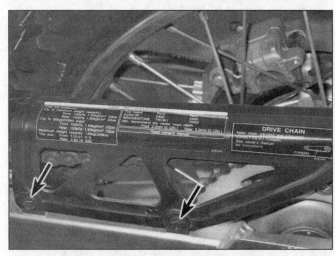

8.4c  XR650L upper chain guard bolts

8.4d  Unbolt the lower chain guide

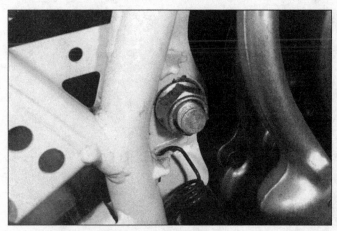

8.6a  Remove the locknut . . .

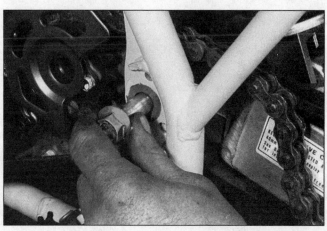

8.6b  . . . support the swingarm and pull the pivot bolt out

remove the shock absorber lower mounting bolt (see Section 7).

6    Support the swingarm from below, then unscrew its pivot bolt nut and pull the bolt out (see illustrations).

7    Check the chain slider, chain adjuster plates and brake disc guard for wear or damage (see illustration). Also check the adjuster plates at the wheel dropouts for wear (see illustration). Replace them as necessary.

8    Installation is the reverse of the removal

8.7a  Remove the chain slider if it's worn

8.7b  Check the adjuster plates for wear or damage

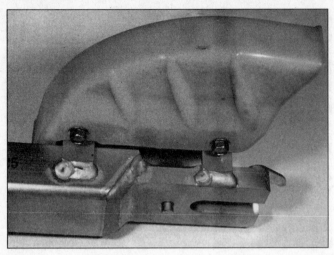

8.7c  Unbolt the brake disc guard

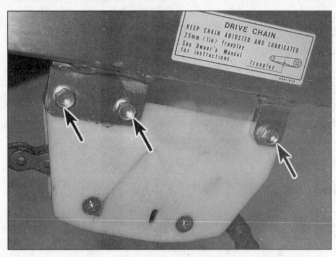

8.11  Chain guide mounting bolts

steps, with the following additions:

a) Tighten the swingarm pivot bolt and nut to the torque listed in this Chapter's Specifications.
b) Refer to Chapter 1 and adjust the drive chain. On drum brake models adjust the rear brake pedal.
c) Bleeding of the brakes won't be necessary, unless the brake hose was disconnected from the caliper. If it was, refer to Chapter 7 and bleed the brakes.
d) Lubricate the swingarm bearings through the grease fittings (see Chapter 1).

## XR650R models

### Removal

9    Unbolt the shock arm from the shock link and the swingarm (see Section 7).
10   Remove the caliper from the slide rail on the swing arm, then suspend the caliper with a piece of wire - don't let it hang by the hose.
11   Detach the chain guide from the swing-

8.12a  Remove the swingarm pivot bolt nut and washer . . .

8.12b  . . . then pull out the pivot bolt (you'll probably have to tap it out from the other side)

arm (see illustration).
12   Unscrew the nut from the swingarm pivot bolt, then pull out the bolt (see illustrations).

13   Remove the swingarm pivot locknut, followed by the swingarm pivot adjusting nut (see illustrations). This requires a couple

8.13a  Remove the locknut . . .

8.13b  . . . and the adjusting nut

8.13c  These are the special tools required to remove the swingarm pivot adjusting nut and locknut (and to install the swingarm properly)

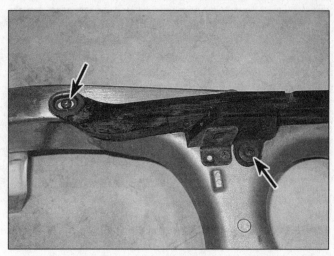

8.15a  The chain slider is retained by a screw on the top and on the inside of the swingarm . . .

of special tools (Honda tool nos. 07KMA-KAB0100 and 07VMA-MBB0101, or equivalent tools obtained from an aftermarket supplier). An alternative to purchasing these special tools would be to fabricate them from sockets of the appropriate size and some strap steel. The sockets would have to be cut or ground to fit the notches in the locknut and adjusting nut, and the strap steel would have to be cut and welded to the sockets to be used as handles.

14  Remove the swingarm from the frame.

15  Remove the chain slider from the swingarm if it's worn (see illustrations).

## Installation

16  Lubricate the swingarm bearings with a moly-based grease. Guide the swingarm up into position, then slide the pivot shaft in from the left side.

17  Install the adjusting nut and tighten it to the Stage 1 torque listed in this Chapter's Specifications using the special tool.

18  Loosen the nut completely, then tighten it to the stage 3 torque listed in this Chapter's Specifications.

19  Hold the adjusting nut from turning with the special tool, then tighten the locknut to the torque listed in this Chapter's Specifications using the other special tool (see illustration).

20  Remove the pivot bolt from the left side, then lubricate it with a light film of grease and install it from the right side.

21  Install the washer and pivot bolt nut, tightening the nut to the torque listed in this Chapter's Specifications.

22  The remainder of installation is the reverse of removal. If the drive chain was properly adjusted before swingarm removal, adjustment won't be necessary; otherwise, refer to Chapter 1 for adjustment.

23  Bleeding of the brakes won't be necessary, unless the brake hose was disconnected from the caliper. If it was, refer to Chapter 7 and bleed the brakes.

## 9  Swingarm bearings - check and replacement

### Check

1  Refer to Chapter 7 and remove the rear wheel.

2  Grasp the rear of the swingarm with one hand and place your other hand at the junction of the swingarm and frame. Try to move the rear of the swingarm from side-to-side. Any wear (play) in the bushings should be felt as movement between the swingarm and the frame at the front. The swingarm will actually be felt to move forward and backward at the front (not from side-to-side). If any play is noted, the bearings should be replaced with new ones.

3  Next, remove the rear shock absorber (see Section 6) and move the swingarm up-

8.15b  . . . and by one on the underside of the swingarm

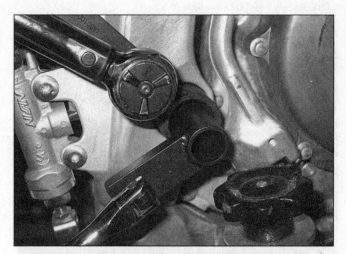

8.19  Hold the adjusting nut (inner) while tightening the locknut (outer) to the torque listed in this Chapter's Specifications

9.5 Pull the dust covers off the swingarm

9.6 Slide the pivot collar(s) out (XR650R models have two)

9.7 Have the needle bearings pressed out and new ones pressed in if they're worn

and-down through its full travel. It should move freely, without any binding or rough spots.

## Replacement

4    Refer to Section 8 and remove the swing-arm.
5    Pull the dust covers off the swingarm (see illustration).

6    Pull the pivot collar(s) out of the swing-arm (see illustration).
7    Check the needle bearings for wear or damage (see illustration). Needle bearing replacement requires a slide hammer with an internal bearing remover attachment, a press and a drift the same diameter as the bear-ings. If you don't have these, have the bear-ings replaced by a Honda dealer or motor-

cycle repair shop. On XR650L and XR650R models, install the bearings to the proper depth:

**XR650L:** 2 to 3 mm (0.08 to 0.12 inch) from the surface of the swing-arm.

**XR650R:**
Right side: 4 mm (0.16 inch) from the surface of the swingarm.
Left side: 5 mm (0.20 inch) from the surface of the swingarm.

8    Coat the bearings and pivot collar with moly-based grease and slip the collar(s) into the swingarm. Install the dust covers.
9    Install the swingarm (see Section 8).

10.1 Remove the clip from the master link; its open end faces rearward when the chain is on the top run

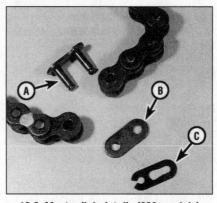

10.2 Master link details (600 models)

A  Link          C  Clip
B  Plate

---

**10 Drive chain - removal, cleaning, inspection and installation**

### XL600R and XR600R models
#### Removal
1    Turn the rear wheel to place the drive chain master link where it's easily accessible (see illustration).
2    Remove the clip and pull the master link out of the chain (see illustration).

10.3a Remove the bolts . . .

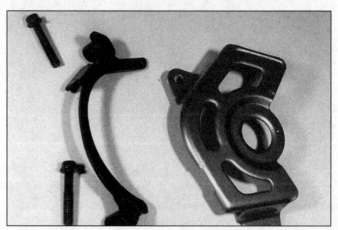

10.3b . . . and take off the engine sprocket cover and case guard

3    Remove the engine sprocket cover and case guard **(see illustrations)**.
4    Lift the chain off the sprockets and remove it from the bike.
5    Check the chain guards on the swingarm and frame for wear or damage and replace them as necessary (see Section 8).

### Cleaning and inspection

6    Soak the chain in a high flash point solvent for approximately five or six minutes. Use a brush to work the solvent into the spaces between the links and plates.
7    Wipe the chain dry, then check it carefully for worn or damaged links. Replace the chain if wear or damage is found at any point.
8    Stretch the chain taut and measure its length between the number of pins listed in this Chapter's Specifications. Compare the measured length to the specified value, and replace the chain if it's beyond the limit. If the chain needs to be replaced, refer to Section 11 and check the sprockets. If they're worn, replace them also. If a new chain is installed on worn sprockets, it will wear out quickly.
9    Lubricate the chain with a good quality chain lubricant or SAE 80 or 90 gear oil.

### Installation

10    Installation is the reverse of the removal steps, with the following additions:

  a)  *Install the master link clip so its opening faces the back of the motorcycle when the master link is in the upper chain run.*
  b)  *Refer to Chapter 1 and adjust the chain.*

## XR650L and XR650R models

**Note:** *The chain on these models should only be removed if it is necessary to replace it.*

### Cleaning and inspection

11    Clean the chain with kerosene or a chain cleaning solvent that's compatible with O-ring chains. A brush can be used to remove dirt and contaminated lubricant, but

10.18  Master link and
O-ring details
(650 models)

only from the outside of the chain; the manufacturer states that brushing the O-rings will damage them.
12    Check the chain carefully for worn, loose or damaged links and rollers. Measure the width of the chain inner plates at several points around the chain. Replace the chain if wear or damage is found at any point.

### Removal and installation

13    Loosen the rear axle nut and chain adjuster bolt locknuts, then back-off the chain adjuster bolts to provide more slack in the chain.
14    Find the master link, which will be evidenced by the two staked chain pins. Place it in a position where it's easy to install a chain tool (along the bottom run is the easiest). **Note:** *If you can't locate the master link, and you'll be replacing the chain with a new one anyway, you can grind off the ends from the pins on one of the links, then drive the pins out with a chain tool (if it won't come out by hand).*
15    Remove the engine sprocket cover and case guard **(see illustrations 10.3a and 10.3b)**.
16    Using an O-ring compatible chain tool,

drive the pins out of the master link and remove the chain.
17    Using the chain tool, cut the new chain to the specified length (see this Chapter's Specifications).
18    Place the new chain over the sprockets, then join the ends with the master link. Be sure to install the new O-rings on each pin of the master link, on each side of the chain **(see illustration)**. Press the link plate into place with the chain tool.
19    Make sure the master link pins protrude from the side plate the length listed in this Chapter's Specifications. If they don't, something's wrong; make sure the O-rings are the proper size and the master link is the proper part and installed completely.
20    Following the chain tool manufacturer's instructions, stake the pins of the master link **(see illustration)**. They must be staked so they expand to the dimension given in this Chapter's Specifications **(see illustration)**. **Note:** *Stake the link pins gradually so you don't over-stake them.*
21    Check your staking job; the staked ends of the master link pins must not only be the proper diameter, they must also be free of cracks around their circumference. If there

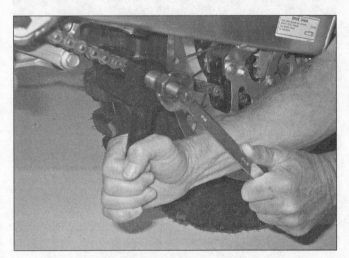

10.20a  Using a chain tool to stake the master link pins

10.20b  Measure the diameter of the staked master link pins and compare your measurement to the value listed in this Chapter's Specifications

are any cracks in the pins, use the chain tool to drive the master link pins out, then try again with a new master link.

22   Adjust the chain slack (see Chapter 1) and tighten the rear axle nut to the torque listed in the Chapter 7 Specifications. Install the case guard and engine sprocket cover, tightening the bolts securely.

23   Lubricate the chain with a good quality O-ring compatible chain lubricant or SAE 80 or 90 gear oil.

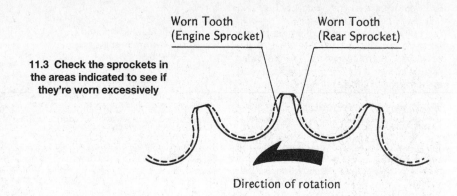

**11.3 Check the sprockets in the areas indicated to see if they're worn excessively**

Worn Tooth (Engine Sprocket)   Worn Tooth (Rear Sprocket)

Direction of rotation

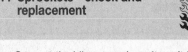

## 11 Sprockets - check and replacement

1   Support the bike securely so it can't be knocked over during this procedure.

2   Whenever the sprockets are inspected, the chain should be inspected also and replaced if it's worn. Installing a worn chain on new sprockets will cause them to wear quickly.

3   Remove the engine sprocket cover **(see illustration 10.3a)**. Check the teeth on the engine sprocket and rear sprocket for wear **(see illustration)**.

4   If the sprockets are worn, remove the chain (see Section 10) and the rear wheel (see Chapter 7).

5   Unbolt the sprocket from the rear wheel hub **(see illustration)**.

6   To remove the engine sprocket, remove two bolts and lift off the retainer plate **(see illustration)**. Lift the sprocket off the transmission shaft.

7   Inspect the countershaft seal behind the engine sprocket. If it has been leaking, thread-in a couple of self-tapping screws (180-degrees apart) and pry on the screws to remove it. Tap in a new seal with a seal driver or a socket with the same diameter as the seal.

8   Installation is the reverse of the removal steps, with the following additions:

a) *Tighten the driven sprocket bolts and nuts to the torques listed in this Chapter's Specifications. Tighten the engine sprocket bolts securely, but don't overtighten them and strip the threads*

b) *Install the master link clip so its opening faces the back of the motorcycle when the master link is in the upper chain run.*

c) *Refer to Chapter 1 and adjust the chain.*

**11.5 Remove the bolts and nuts to detach the driven sprocket from the rear wheel hub**

**11.6 The engine sprocket is secured by two bolts and a plate; the OUT mark on the sprocket faces away from the engine**

# Chapter 7
# Brakes, wheels and tires

## Contents

## Degrees of difficulty

| | | | | | | | | | |
|---|---|---|---|---|---|---|---|---|---|
| **Easy,** suitable for novice with little experience |  | **Fairly easy,** suitable for beginner with some experience |  | **Fairly difficult,** suitable for competent DIY mechanic |  | **Difficult,** suitable for experienced DIY mechanic | 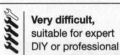 | **Very difficult,** suitable for expert DIY or professional |  |

## Specifications

### Disc brakes

| | |
|---|---|
| Brake fluid type | See Chapter 1 |
| Brake pad minimum thickness | See Chapter 1 |
| Front disc thickness | |
| XL600R, XR600R | |
| 1983 through 1987 | |
| Standard | 3.5 mm (0.14 inch) |
| Limit | 3.0 mm (0.12 inch)* |
| 1988 and later models | |
| Standard | 3.0 mm (0.12 inch) |
| Limit | 2.5 mm (0.10 inch)* |
| XR650L | |
| Standard | 4.0 mm (0.16 inch) |
| Limit | 3.5 mm (0.14 inch) |
| XR650R | |
| All except Australian models | |
| Standard | 2.8 to 3.2 mm (0.11 to 0.13 inch) |
| Limit | 2.5 mm (0.10 inch) |
| Australian models | |
| Standard | 3.3 to 3.7 mm (0.13 to 0.15 inch) |
| Limit | 3.0 mm (0.12 inch) |
| Rear disc thickness | |
| XL600R, XR600R | |
| Standard | 4.5 mm (0.18 inch) |
| Limit | 4.0 mm (0.16 inch)* |
| XR650L | |
| Standard | 5.0 mm (0.20 inch) |
| Limit | 4.0 mm (0.16 inch) |

## Disc brakes (continued)

Rear disc thickness (continued)
XR650R
All except Australian models
Standard............................................................ 3.8 to 4.2 mm (0.15 to 0.17 inch)
Limit................................................................. 3.5 mm (0.14 inch)
Australian models
Standard............................................................ 4.3 to 4.7 mm (0.17 to 0.19 inch)
Limit................................................................. 4.0 mm (0.16 inch)
Disc runout limit
XL600R, XR600R
Front ..................................................................... 0.30 mm (0.012 inch)
Rear ...................................................................... 0.15 mm (0.006 inch)
XR650L
Front ..................................................................... 0.30 mm (0.012 inch)
Rear ...................................................................... 0.40 mm (0.020 inch)
XR650R
Front ..................................................................... 0.20 mm (0.008 inch)
Rear ...................................................................... 0.30 mm (0.012 inch)

*Refer to marks stamped into the disc (they supersede information printed here)*

## Drum brakes

Brake lining minimum thickness................................... See Chapter 1
Brake pedal height ....................................................... See Chapter 1
Drum diameter
XL600R
Standard............................................................ 130 mm (5.12 inches)
Wear limit.......................................................... 131 mm (5.16 inches)*
XR600R
Standard............................................................ 110 mm (4.33 inches)
Limit................................................................. 111 mm (4.37 inches)*

*Refer to marks cast into the drum (they supersede information printed here)*

## Wheels and tires

Tire pressures............................................................. See Chapter 1
Tire tread depth .......................................................... See Chapter 1
Axle runout limit.......................................................... 0.2 mm (0.010 inch)
Wheel out-of-round and lateral runout limit (front and rear).................... 2.0 mm (0.08 inch)

## Torque specifications

**Note:** One foot-pound (ft-lb) of torque is equivalent to 12 inch-pounds (in-lbs) of torque. Torque values below approximately 15 ft-lbs are expressed in inch-pounds, since most foot-pound torque wrenches are not accurate at these smaller values.

Front axle
XL600R, XR600R
1983 through 1987 models..................................... 50 to 80 Nm (36 to 58 ft-lbs)
1988 through 1992 models..................................... 65 Nm (47 ft-lbs)
1993 and later models........................................... 85 Nm (61 ft-lbs)
XR650L ...................................................................... 87 Nm (63 ft-lbs)
XR650R ...................................................................... 88 Nm (65 ft-lbs)
Front axle holder nuts
1983 through 1987 models......................................... 10 to 14 Nm (84 to 120 in-lbs)
1988 and later models ............................................... 12 Nm (108 in-lbs)
XR650L, XR650R ....................................................... 12 Nm (108 in-lbs)
Rear axle nut
XL600R, XR600R
1983 through 1987 models..................................... 80 to 110 Nm (58 to 72 ft-lbs)
1988 and later models........................................... 95 Nm (69 ft-lbs)
XR650L ...................................................................... 90 Nm (65 ft-lbs)
XR650R ...................................................................... 93 Nm (69 ft-lbs)
Front caliper
XL600R
Caliper bracket bolts ............................................ 20 to 30 Nm (14 to 22 ft-lbs)
Lower slider pin-to-bracket .................................. 15 to 20 Nm (132 to 168 in-lbs)
Upper slider pin-to-bracket ................................. 20 to 25 Nm (14 to 18 ft-lbs)
Pad pins................................................................ 15 to 20 Nm (132 to 168 in-lbs)

XR600R (1983 through 1987)
    Caliper bracket bolts .................................................... 20 to 30 Nm (14 to 22 ft-lbs)
    Upper slider pin-to-bracket ......................................... 20 to 25 Nm (14 to 18 ft-lbs)
    Lower slider pin-to-bracket ......................................... 15 to 20 Nm (84 to 168 in-lbs)
    Pad pins................................................................... 15 to 20 Nm (84 to 168 in-lbs)
XR600R (1988 on)
    Caliper bracket bolts
        1988 to 1992 .................................................... 27 Nm (20 ft-lbs)
        1992 and later ................................................. 30 Nm (22 ft-lbs)
    Slider pin-to-caliper.................................................. 23 Nm (17 ft-lbs)
    Slider pin-to-caliper bracket...................................... 13 Nm (120 in-lbs)
    Pad pins.................................................................... 18 Nm (156 in-lbs)
    Pad pin plugs............................................................ 3 Nm (26 in-lbs)
XR650L
    Caliper bracket bolts ................................................. 30 Nm (22 ft-lbs)
    Slider pin-to-caliper.................................................. 23 Nm (17 ft-lbs)
    Slider pin-to-caliper bracket...................................... 13 Nm (120 in-lbs)
    Pad pins.................................................................... 18 Nm (156 in-lbs)
    Pad pin plugs............................................................ 3 Nm (26 in-lbs)
XR650R
    Caliper bracket bolts ................................................. 30 Nm (22 ft-lbs)
    Slider pin-to-caliper.................................................. 23 Nm (17 ft-lbs)
    Slider pin-to-caliper bracket...................................... 23 Nm (17 ft-lbs)
    Pad pins.................................................................... 18 Nm (156 in-lbs)
    Pad pin plugs............................................................ 3 Nm (26 in-lbs)
Rear caliper
  XR600R, XR650L and XR650R
    Allen head slider pin-to-caliper................................. 28 Nm (20 ft-lbs)
    Slider pin-to-bracket................................................. 13 Nm (120 in-lbs)
    Pad pins.................................................................... 18 Nm (156 in-lbs)
    Pad pin plugs............................................................ 3 Nm (26 inch-lbs)
Brake line union bolts
  XL600R ...................................................................... 30 to 40 Nm (22 to 29 ft-lbs)
  XR600R
    1983 through 1987 ................................................. Not specified
    1988 on .................................................................. 35 Nm (25 ft-lbs)
  XR650L, XR650R ....................................................... 35 Nm (25 ft-lbs)
Brake hose to master cylinder (XL600R)................................ 30 to 40 Nm (22 to 29 ft-lbs)
Brake disc-to-wheel bolts
  XL600R, XR650R, front and rear
    1983 through 1987 models..................................... 14 to 16 Nm (120 to 144 in-lbs)
    1988 through 1990 models..................................... 15 Nm (132 in-lbs)*
    1991 and later models ........................................... 20 Nm (168 in-lbs)*
  XR650L
    Front ..................................................................... 37 Nm (27 ft-lbs)*
    Rear ...................................................................... 42 Nm (30 ft-lbs)*
  XR650R, front and rear ............................................. 20 Nm (168 in-lbs)*
Rear drum brake arm pinch bolt ........................................... 8 to 12 Nm (72 to 108 inch-lbs)
Front master cylinder
  Mounting bolts
    1983 through 1987 ................................................. Not specified
    1988 on .................................................................. 27 Nm (20 ft-lbs)
  Pivot bolt locknut
    1983 through 1987 ................................................. Not specified
    1988 on .................................................................. 10 Nm (84 inch-lbs)
  XR650L ...................................................................... 12 Nm (108 in-lbs)
  XR650R ...................................................................... 10 Nm (84 in-lbs)
Rear master cylinder mounting bolts
  XR600R ...................................................................... Not specified
  XR650L ...................................................................... 15 Nm (132 in-lbs)
  XR650R ...................................................................... 13 Nm (108 in-lbs)
Pedal pivot bolt (drum brake models)
  1983 through 1987 .................................................... 35 to 45 Nm (25 to 33 ft-lbs)
  1988 on ..................................................................... 30 Nm (22 ft-lbs)

*Replace the bolts with new ones whenever they're removed.

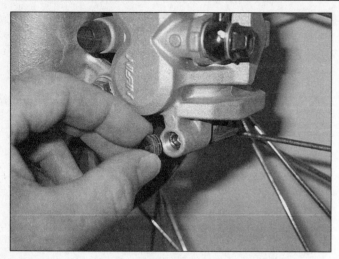

2.5a  Unscrew the pad pin plug; it's at the bottom of the front caliper . . .

2.5b  . . . and at the rear of the rear caliper

## 1  General information

The front wheel on all motorcycles covered by this manual is equipped with a hydraulic disc using a dual-piston pin-slider caliper. The rear wheel on 1983 through 1987 models is equipped with a drum brake. The rear wheel on 1988 and later models is equipped with a hydraulic disc brake using a single-piston pin-slider caliper.

⚠ *Warning: Disc brake components rarely require disassembly. Do not disassemble components unless absolutely necessary. If any hydraulic brake line connection in the system is loosened, the entire system should be disassembled, drained, cleaned and then properly filled and bled upon reassembly. Do not use petroleum-based solvents on internal brake components, as this will cause seals to swell and distort. Use only brake system cleaner, clean brake fluid or rubbing alcohol for cleaning. Use care when working with brake fluid as it can injure your eyes and it will damage painted surfaces and plastic parts.*

## 2  Brake pads - replacement

⚠ *Warning: The dust created by the brake system is harmful to your health. Honda hasn't used asbestos in brake parts for a number of years, but aftermarket parts may contain it. Never blow it out with compressed air and don't inhale any of it. An approved filtering mask should be worn when working on the brakes.*

1    Support the bike securely upright. Push the caliper towards the wheel to depress the piston(s).

### XL600R and 1985 through 1987 XR600R

2    Unscrew the pad pin plugs, then loosen, but do not remove, the pad pins using a hex wrench.
3    Remove the caliper mounting bolts and detach the caliper from the fork.
4    Unscrew the pad pins and remove the brake pads from the caliper.

### 1988 and later XR600R and all 650 models

**Note:** *The caliper doesn't need to be removed for pad replacement.*
5    Unscrew the plug that covers the pad retaining pin (**see illustrations**).
6    Unscrew the pad retaining pin with a hex wrench (**see illustrations**).
7    Pull the pads out of the caliper (**see illustrations**).

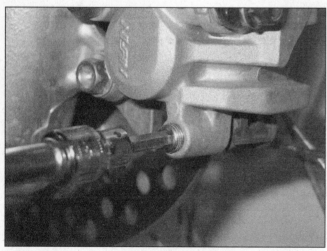

2.6a  Unscrew the pad retaining pin; this is a front caliper . . .

2.6b  . . . and this is a rear caliper

2.7a  Pull out the pad retaining pin and lift out the inner brake pad . . .

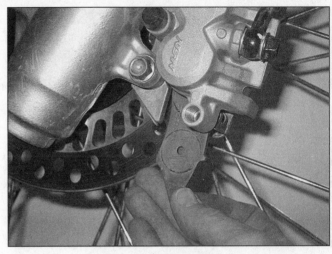

2.7b  . . . then pull the pin out the rest of the way and remove the outer pad

8    Inspect the pad spring **(see illustrations)** and replace it if it's rusted or damaged.

### All models
9    Check the condition of the brake disc (see Section 4). If it's in need of replacement, follow the procedure in that Section to remove it. If it's okay, deglaze it with sandpaper or emery cloth, using a swirling motion.

10   Remove the cover from the master cylinder reservoir and siphon out some fluid. Push the piston(s) into the caliper as far as possible, while checking the master cylinder reservoir to make sure it doesn't overflow. If you can't depress the pistons with thumb pressure, try using a C-clamp. If the pistons stick, remove the caliper and overhaul it as described in Section 3.

11   Install the spring (if removed), new pads and the retaining pin **(see illustrations)**. Tighten the retaining pin to the torque listed in this Chapter's Specifications. Install the plug over the retaining pin and tighten it to the torque listed in this Chapter's Specifications.

12   Operate the brake lever or pedal several times to bring the pads into contact with the disc. Check the operation of the brakes carefully before riding the motorcycle.

**2.8a  The front caliper's pad spring fits under the pad pin like this . . .**

2.8b  . . . and the rear caliper's pad spring fits like this

2.11  Make sure the end of the pad fits into the pad support plate

3.2  Unscrew the union bolt (right arrow) if you're planning to remove the caliper for overhaul; remove the mounting bolts (left arrows) to detach the caliper from the fork leg

3.3  The hose can be left connected if you're removing the caliper for access to other components; on installation, be sure the brake hose fits in the notches

## 3  Brake caliper - removal, overhaul and installation

⚠ **Warning: If a caliper indicates the need for an overhaul (usually due to leaking fluid or sticky operation), all old brake fluid must be flushed from the system. Also, the dust created by the brake system is harmful to your health. Never blow it out with compressed air and don't inhale any of it. An approved filtering mask should be worn when working on the brakes. Do not, under any circumstances, use petroleum-based solvents to clean brake parts. Use brake cleaner or denatured alcohol only!**

**Note:** *If you are removing the caliper only to remove the front forks, or on some models, the swingarm, don't disconnect the hose from the caliper. (On some models, the rear*

*brake hose might not be long enough to allow caliper removal without disconnecting it.)*

### Removal

1    Support the bike securely upright. **Note:** *If you're planning to disassemble the caliper, read through the overhaul procedure, paying particular attention to the steps involved in removing the pistons with compressed air. If you don't have access to an air compressor, you can use the bike's hydraulic system to force the pistons out instead. To do this, remove the pads and pump the brake lever or pedal. If one front caliper piston comes out before the other, push it back into its bore and hold it in with a C-clamp while pumping the brake lever to remove the remaining piston.*

### Front caliper

2    **Note:** *Remember, if you're just removing the caliper to remove the forks, ignore this step.* Remove the brake hose banjo fitting bolt and separate the hose from the

caliper **(see illustration)**. Discard the sealing washers (new ones should be used on reassembly). Plug the end of the hose or wrap a plastic bag tightly around it to prevent excessive fluid loss and contamination.

3    Remove the pad pin plugs and loosen the pad retaining pin(s). Unscrew the caliper mounting bolts and lift it off the fork leg, being careful not to strain or twist the brake hose if it's still connected **(see illustration)**.

### Rear caliper

4    Remove the rear wheel (see Section 11). Remove the caliper shield **(see illustration)**.

5    Remove the caliper guard **(see illustration)**. Remove the brake hose banjo fitting bolt and separate the hose from the caliper. Discard the sealing washers (new ones should be used on reassembly). Plug the end of the hose or wrap a plastic bag tightly around it to prevent excessive fluid loss and contamination.

6    Loosen the caliper mounting bolt and the pad retaining pin (it's easier to loosen them while the caliper is still on the bike).

3.4  Remove the rear caliper shield bolts and lift off the shield for access to the caliper

3.6  If the caliper is being removed for overhaul or replacement, unscrew the Allen-head caliper pin

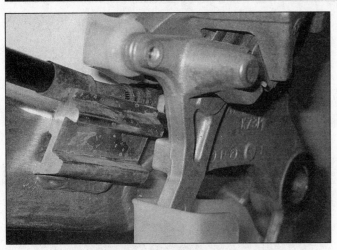

3.7  Slide the caliper and bracket backward off the rail on the swingarm

3.9  Slide the caliper off its bracket (front shown, rear similar)

3.11a  Carefully remove the piston seal from the bore

3.11b  Front caliper piston and seal details (one of two pistons shown); on models so equipped, the metal cap on the end of the piston faces away from the bore (on pistons without a metal cap, the open end of the piston faces out, away from the bore)

7    Slide the caliper and bracket to the rear to disengage it from its mounting rail on the swingarm (see illustration).

## Overhaul

8    Remove the brake pads and anti-rattle spring from the caliper (see Section 2, if necessary). Clean the exterior of the caliper with denatured alcohol or brake system cleaner.
9    Slide the caliper off its bracket (see illustration).
10   Pack a shop rag into the space that holds the brake pads. Use compressed air, directed into the caliper fluid inlet, to remove the piston(s). Use only enough air pressure to ease the piston(s) out of the bore. If a piston is blown out forcefully, even with the rag in place, it may be damaged.

⚠ Warning: Never place your fingers in front of the piston in an attempt to catch or protect it when applying compressed air, as serious injury could occur.

11   Remove the piston seals, being careful

not to scratch the bore or seal groove (see illustrations).
12   Clean the pistons and the bores with denatured alcohol, clean brake fluid or brake system cleaner and blow dry them with filtered, unlubricated compressed air.

13   Inspect the surfaces of the pistons for nicks and burrs and loss of plating. Check the caliper bores, too. If surface defects are present, the caliper must be replaced. If the caliper is in bad shape, the master cylinder should also be checked.

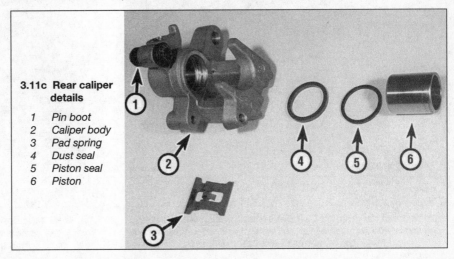

3.11c  Rear caliper details

1  Pin boot
2  Caliper body
3  Pad spring
4  Dust seal
5  Piston seal
6  Piston

3.14 Fit the seals all the way into their grooves

3.17a Install the boot in the front caliper with its wide end facing the same direction as the pistons

14   Lubricate the piston seals with clean brake fluid and install them in their grooves in the caliper bore (see illustration). Make sure they seat completely and aren't twisted.

15   Lubricate the dust seals with clean brake fluid and install them in their grooves, making sure they seat correctly.

16   Lubricate the piston (both pistons on front calipers) with clean brake fluid and install it into the caliper bore. Using your thumbs, push each piston all the way in, making sure it doesn't get cocked in the bore.

17   Pull the old pin boots out of the caliper and bracket. Coat new ones with silicone grease and install them, making sure they seat completely (see illustrations).

18   Make sure the pad springs are in position on the caliper brackets (see illustrations 3.17b and 3.17c).

## Installation

19   Installation is the reverse of the removal steps, with the following additions:

a) Apply silicone grease to the slider pins on the caliper bracket and caliper.
b) Space the pads apart so the disc will fit between them.
c) Use new sealing washers on the brake hose fitting. If you're working on a front caliper, position the brake hose fitting in the caliper notches (see illustration 3.3).
d) Tighten the caliper mounting bolt(s) and brake line union bolt to the torque listed in this Chapter's Specifications.
e) If you're working on a rear caliper, reinstall the wheel (see Section 11) and adjust the chain slack (see Chapter 1). On all except XR650R models, make sure the pin on the rear caliper bracket engages with the hole in the swingarm.

20   Fill the master cylinder with the recommended brake fluid (see Chapter 1) and bleed the system (see Section 10). Check for leaks.

21   Check the operation of the brakes carefully before riding the motorcycle.

## 4   Brake disc - inspection, removal and installation

## Inspection

1   Support the bike securely upright. Place a jack beneath the bike and raise the wheel being checked off the ground, or set the bike on a lift or pit stand. Be sure the bike is securely supported so it can't be knocked over.

2   Visually inspect the surface of the disc for score marks and other damage. Light scratches are normal after use and won't affect brake operation, but deep grooves and heavy score marks will reduce braking efficiency and accelerate pad wear. If the discs are badly grooved they must be replaced.

3.17b Install the boot in the front caliper bracket with its wide end facing the same direction as the pin (right arrow) and install the spring in the bracket notch (left arrow)

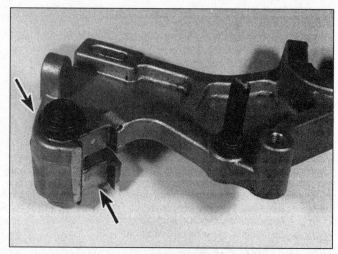

3.17c Install the boot in the rear caliper bracket with its wide end facing the same direction as the pin (left arrow) and install the spring in the bracket notch (right arrow)

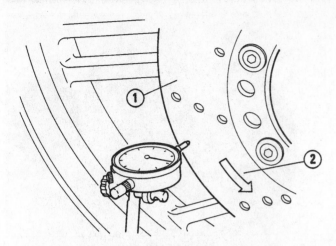

**4.3 Set up a dial indicator against the brake disc (1) and turn the disc in its normal direction of rotation (2) to measure runout**

**4.4 Marks on the disc indicate the minimum thickness (left arrow) and direction of rotation (right arrow)**

3    To check disc runout, mount a dial indicator to the fork leg or the swingarm, with the plunger on the indicator touching the surface of the disc **(see illustration)**. Slowly turn the wheel and watch the indicator needle, comparing your reading with the limit listed in this Chapter's Specifications. If the runout is greater than allowed, check the hub bearings for play (see Section 13). If the bearings are worn, replace them and repeat this check. If the disc runout is still excessive, the disc will have to be replaced.

4    The disc must not be allowed to wear down to a thickness less than the minimum allowable thickness, listed in this Chapter's Specifications. The thickness of the disc can be checked with a micrometer. If the thickness of the disc is less than the minimum allowable, it must be replaced. The minimum thickness is also stamped into the disc **(see illustration)**.

## Removal

5    Remove the wheel (see Section 11).

**Caution: Don't lay the wheel down and allow it to rest on the disc or the sprocket - the disc or sprocket could become warped. Set the wheel on wood blocks or on a five gallon bucket so the disc or sprocket doesn't support the weight of the wheel.**

6    Remove the nuts or Allen head bolts that retain the disc to the wheel **(see illustration 4.4)**. Loosen the bolts a little at a time, in a criss-cross pattern, to avoid distorting the disc.

**Caution: These bolts are coated with a thread-locking agent from the factory and can be very tight. If they don't come loose with moderate effort, apply heat from a heat gun (not a torch), then try loosening them again.**

**Note:** Allen head bolts must be replaced with new ones on installation.

7    Take note of any paper shims that may

be present where the disc mates to the wheel. If there are any, mark their position and be sure to include them when installing the disc.

## Installation

8    Position the disc on the wheel, aligning the previously applied matchmarks (if you're reinstalling the original disc). On models so equipped, make sure the arrow (stamped on the disc) marking the direction of rotation is pointing in the proper direction **(see illustration 4.4)**.

9    If the brake disc is secured by Allen head bolts, use new ones. Apply a non-hardening thread locking compound to the threads of the nuts or bolts. Install the nuts or bolts, tightening them a little at a time in a criss-cross pattern, until the torque listed in this Chapter's Specifications is reached. Clean off all grease from the brake disc using acetone or brake system cleaner.

10    Install the wheel (see Section 11).

11    Operate the brake lever or pedal several times to bring the pads into contact with the disc. Check the operation of the brakes carefully before riding the motorcycle.

## 5  Brake drum and shoes - removal, inspection and installation

**Warning: The dust created by the brake system is harmful to your health (Honda hasn't used asbestos in brake parts for a number of years, but aftermarket parts may contain it). Never blow it out with compressed air and don't inhale any of it. An approved filtering mask should be worn when working on the brakes.**

## Removal

1    Remove the wheel (see Section 11).

2    Lift the brake panel out of the wheel **(see illustration)**.

## Inspection

3    Check the brake drum for wear or damage. Measure the diameter at several points with a drum micrometer (or have this done by a Honda dealer). If the measurements are

**5.2 Lift the brake panel out of the drum**

5.3 The maximum diameter is cast inside the brake drum

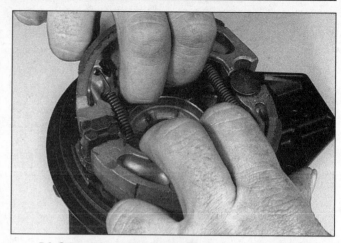

5.6 Spread the shoes and fold them into a V to release
the spring tension

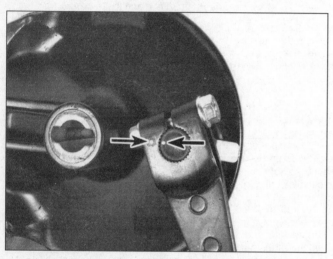

5.9 Look for alignment marks on the brake arm and cam;
make your own marks if you can't see any

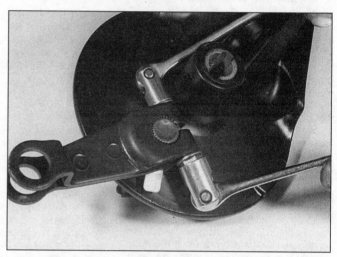

5.10 Remove the pinch bolt and nut and take the brake arm
off the cam

uneven (indicating that the drum is out-of-round) or if there are scratches deep enough to snag a fingernail, replace the drum. The drum must also be replaced if the diameter is greater than that cast inside the drum **(see illustration). Note:** *Honda recommends against machining brake drums.*
4    Check the linings for wear, damage and signs of contamination from road dirt

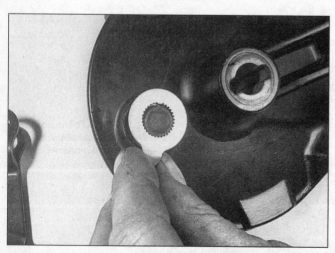

5.11 Remove the wear indicator; the wide spline on the wear
indicator fits into a wide groove in the brake cam

5.12a Replace the brake cam seal if it's worn or damaged

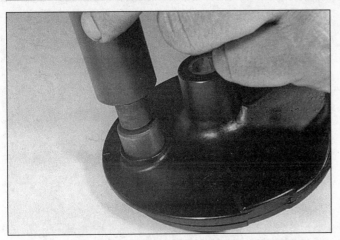

5.12b Pry out the old seal, then press a new one in with a socket the same diameter as the seal

5.16 The assembled brake should look like this

or water. If the linings are visibly defective, replace them.

5    Measure the thickness of the lining material (just the lining material, not the metal backing) and compare with the value listed in the Chapter 1 Specifications. Replace the shoes if the material is worn to the minimum or less.

6    To remove the shoes, fold them toward each other to release the spring tension and lift them off the brake panel (see illustration).

7    Check the ends of the shoes where they contact the brake cam and anchor pin. Replace the shoes if there's visible wear.

8    Check the brake cam and anchor pin for wear and damage. The brake cam can be replaced separately; the brake panel must be replaced if the anchor pin is unserviceable.

9    Look for alignment marks on the brake arm and anchor pin (see illustration). Make your own if they aren't visible.

10   Remove the pinch bolt and nut and pull the brake arm off the cam (see illustration).

11   Lift off the wear indicator (see illustration). Pull the brake cam out of the brake panel.

12   Check the brake cam dust seal for wear and damage (see illustration). To replace it, pry it out of the brake panel and tap in a new one using a socket or seal driver the same diameter as the seal (see illustration).

## Installation

13   Apply high temperature brake grease to the brake cam, the anchor pin and the ends of the springs.

14   Install the cam through the dust seal. Install the wear indicator (see illustration 5.11). Align its wide groove with the wide spline in the cam.

15   Install the brake arm on the cam, aligning the punch marks. Tighten the nut and bolt to the torque listed in this Chapter's Specifications.

16   Hook the ends of the springs to the shoes. Position the shoes in a V on the brake

panel, then fold them down into position (see illustration 5.6). Make sure the ends of the shoes fit correctly on the cam and the anchor pin (see illustration).

17   The remainder of installation is the reverse of the removal steps. Make sure the notch in the brake panel aligns with the boss on the swingarm (see illustration).

### 6    Front brake master cylinder - removal, overhaul and installation

Caution: *Disassembly, overhaul and reassembly of the brake master cylinder must be done in a spotlessly clean work area to avoid contamination and possible failure of the brake hydraulic system components.*

1    If the master cylinder is leaking fluid, or if the lever doesn't produce a firm feel when the brake is applied, and bleeding the brakes doesn't help, master cylinder overhaul is recommended.

2    Before disassembling the master cylinder, read through the entire procedure and

make sure that you have the correct rebuild kit. Also, you will need some new, clean brake fluid of the recommended type, some clean rags and internal snap-ring pliers. **Note:** *To prevent damage to the paint from spilled brake fluid, always cover the gas tank when working on the master cylinder.*

## Removal

3    Place rags beneath the master cylinder to protect the paint in case of brake fluid spills.

### XL600R and XR650L

4    Disconnect the wires from the brake light switch.

5    **XL600R:** Brake fluid will run out of the upper brake hose during this step, so either have a container handy to place the end of the hose in, or have a plastic bag and rubber band handy to cover the end of the hose. Unscrew the flare nut that connects the intermediate metal line to the upper brake hose with a flare nut wrench.

6    **XR650L:** Remove the banjo fitting bolt (see illustration 6.9) and separate the brake hose from the master cylinder. Wrap the end of the hose in a clean rag and suspend the

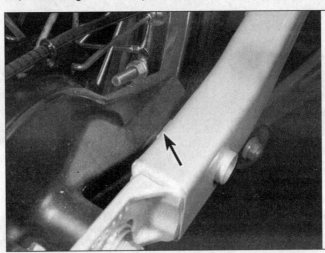

5.17 Be sure the protrusion on the swingarm fits into the notch in the brake panel

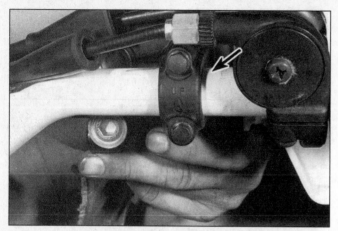

6.8 Remove the clamp bolts and detach the clamp from the handlebar; on installation, make sure the UP mark on the clamp bolt is upright and align the parting line of the clamp and master cylinder with the punch mark on the handlebar

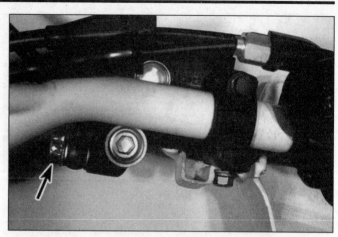

6.9 Remove the union bolt and disconnect the brake line from the master cylinder; use new sealing washers on installation

6.12a Remove the locknut . . .

6.12b . . . and unscrew the pivot bolt to detach the lever

hose in an upright position or bend it down carefully and place the open end in a clean container. The objective is to prevent excess loss of brake fluid, fluid spills and system contamination.

7    If you're planning to remove the rearview mirror from the master cylinder, do it now while the master cylinder is still attached to the handlebar.

8    Remove the master cylinder mounting bolts (see illustration). Take the master cylinder off the handlebar, then, on XL600R

models, unscrew the master cylinder from the brake hose and remove the sealing washer.

### XR600R and XR650R

9    Remove the banjo fitting bolt (see illustration) and separate the brake hose from the master cylinder. Wrap the end of the hose in a clean rag and suspend the hose in an upright position or bend it down carefully and place the open end in a clean container. The objective is to prevent excess loss of brake fluid, fluid spills and system contamination.

10    Remove the master cylinder mounting bolts (see illustration 6.8) and separate the master cylinder from the handlebar together with the hand shield.

### *Overhaul*

11    Remove the master cylinder cover, retainer (if equipped) and diaphragm (see Chapter 1).

12    Remove the locknut and bushing (on models so equipped) from the underside of the lever pivot bolt, then unscrew the bolt (see illustrations). Remove the hand protector (it's held on by the pivot bolt).

6.13a Remove the lever and spring from the master cylinder

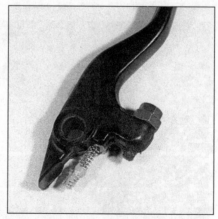

6.13b The spring fits into the lever like this; there's a small steel ball at the end of the spring inside the hole

6.14a Remove the snap-ring from the master cylinder bore

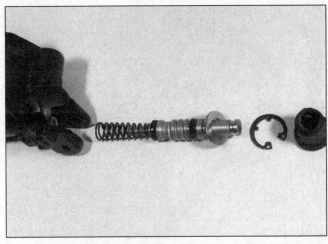

6.14b Remove the piston assembly from the bore

13 The lever on XL600R models is equipped with a cover, small pushrod and a pivot bushing; XR600R and XR650R models have a spring and steel ball (see illustrations). These don't have to be removed to remove the hydraulic components, but make sure they don't get lost.

14 Using snap-ring pliers, remove the snap-ring and slide out the piston assembly and the spring (see illustrations). Lay the parts out in the proper order to prevent confusion during reassembly.

15 Clean all of the parts with brake system cleaner (available at auto parts and motorcycle stores), isopropyl alcohol or clean brake fluid.

Caution: Do not, under any circumstances, use a petroleum-based solvent to clean brake parts. If compressed air is available, use it to dry the parts thoroughly (make sure it's filtered and unlubricated). Check the master cylinder bore and piston for corrosion, scratches, nicks and score marks. If damage or wear can be seen, the master cylinder must be replaced with a new one.

16 Check the baffle plate in the bottom of the reservoir to make sure it's securely held by its retainer (see illustration).

17 Honda supplies a new piston in its rebuild kits. If the cup seals are not installed on the new piston, lubricate them with clean brake fluid and install them, making sure the lips face away from the lever end of the piston (see illustration 6.14b). Use the new piston regardless of the condition of the old one.

18 Before reassembling the master cylinder, soak the piston and the rubber cup seals in clean brake fluid for ten or fifteen minutes. Lubricate the master cylinder bore with clean brake fluid, then carefully insert the piston and related parts in the reverse order of disassembly. Make sure the lips on the cup seals do not turn inside out when they are slipped into the bore.

19 Depress the piston, then install the snap-ring (make sure the snap-ring is properly seated in the groove with the sharp edge facing out) (see illustration 6.14a). Install the rubber dust boot (make sure the lip is seated properly in the piston groove).

20 Install the brake lever (and the hand shield, on models so equipped) and tighten the pivot bolt locknut.

## Installation

21 Installation is the reverse of the removal steps, with the following additions:

a) If you're working on an XL600R, use a new sealing washer at the connection of the brake hose to the master cylinder. Tighten the hose fitting to the torque listed in this Chapter's Specifications.

b) Attach the master cylinder to the handlebar. Align the upper gap between the master cylinder and clamp with the punch mark on the handlebar (see illustration 6.8).

c) Make sure the arrow and the word UP on the master cylinder clamp are pointing up, then tighten the bolts to the torque listed in this Chapter's Specifications.

d) If you're working on an XR600R, XR650L

or XR650R, use new sealing washers at the brake hose banjo fitting. Tighten the union bolt to the torque listed in this Chapter's Specifications.

22 Refer to Section 10 and bleed the air from the system.

## 7 Rear brake master cylinder - removal, overhaul and installation

1 If the master cylinder is leaking fluid, or if the pedal does not produce a firm feel when the brake is applied, and bleeding the brake does not help, master cylinder overhaul is recommended.

2 Before disassembling the master cylinder, read through the entire procedure and make sure that you have the correct rebuild kit. Also, you will need some new, clean brake fluid of the recommended type, some clean rags and internal snap-ring pliers.

3 Caution: Disassembly, overhaul and reassembly of the brake master cylinder must be done in a spotlessly clean work area to avoid contamination and possible failure of the brake hydraulic system components.

6.16 Make sure the baffle plate is securely retained in the bottom of the reservoir

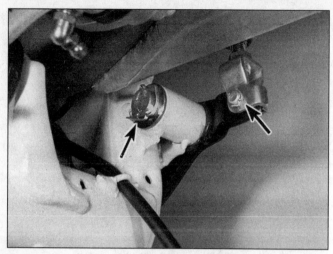

**7.4 Remove the cotter pin and clevis pin (right arrow) to detach the master cylinder from the pedal; the pedal itself is secured by a cotter pin and washer (left arrow)**

**7.6a Remove the mounting bolts to detach the master cylinder from the frame**

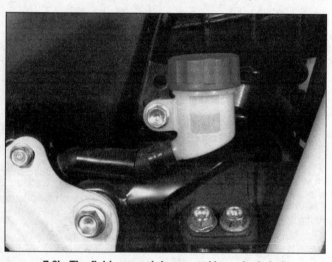

**7.6b The fluid reservoir is secured by a single bolt**

**7.7a Remove the snap-ring . . .**

## Removal

4    Remove the cotter pin from the clevis pin on the master cylinder pushrod **(see illustration)**. Remove the clevis pin.

5    Have a container and some rags ready

**7.7b . . . then work the fluid feed fitting free of its bore and remove the O-ring**

to catch spilling brake fluid. Using a six-point box wrench, unscrew the banjo fitting bolt from the top of the master cylinder. Discard the sealing washers on either side of the fitting.

6    Remove the two master cylinder mounting bolts and detach the cylinder from the bracket **(see illustration)**. Pull the master cylinder out from behind the bracket, squeeze the fluid feed hose clamp with pliers and slide the clamp up the hose. Disconnect the hose from the fitting and take the master cylinder out. If necessary, remove the reservoir mounting bolt and detach it from the frame **(see illustration)**.

## Overhaul

7    Using a pair of snap-ring pliers, remove the snap-ring from the fluid inlet fitting and detach the fitting from the master cylinder. Remove the O-ring from the bore **(see illustrations)**.

8    Count the number of exposed threads on the end of the pushrod inside the clevis

**(see illustration)**. Write this number down for use on assembly. Hold the clevis with a pair of pliers and loosen the locknut, then unscrew the clevis and locknut from the pushrod.

9    Carefully remove the rubber dust boot from the pushrod **(see illustration)**.

10    Depress the pushrod and, using snap-ring pliers, remove the snap-ring **(see illustration)**. Slide out the piston, the cup seal and spring. Lay the parts out in the proper order to prevent confusion during reassembly **(see illustration)**.

11    Clean all of the parts with brake system cleaner (available at motorcycle dealerships and auto parts stores), isopropyl alcohol or clean brake fluid.

**Caution: Do not, under any circumstances, use a petroleum-based solvent to clean brake parts. If compressed air is available, use it to dry the parts thoroughly (make sure it's filtered and unlubricated). Check the master cylinder bore for corrosion,**

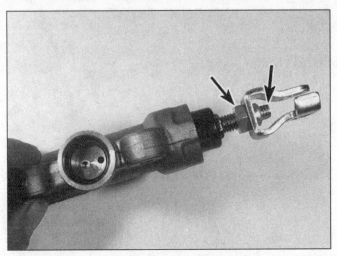

7.8 Write down the number of exposed threads in the clevis (right arrow), then loosen the locknut (left arrow) and unscrew the locknut and clevis from the pushrod

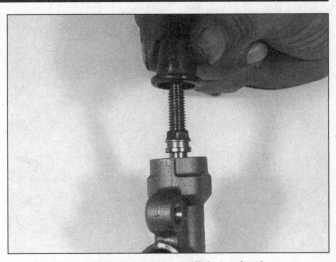

7.9 Take the dust boot off the pushrod

7.10a Remove the snap-ring from the master cylinder bore and withdraw the piston assembly and spring

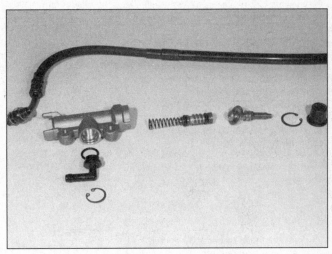

7.10b Rear master cylinder details

*scratches, nicks and score marks. If damage is evident, the master cylinder must be replaced with a new one. If the master cylinder is in poor condition, then the caliper should be checked as well.*

12 Honda supplies a new piston in its rebuild kits. If the cup seals are not installed on the new piston, install them, making sure the lips face the spring end of the piston **(see illustration 7.10b)**. Use the new piston regardless of the condition of the old one.

13 Before reassembling the master cylinder, soak the piston and the rubber cup seals in clean brake fluid for ten or fifteen minutes. Lubricate the master cylinder bore with clean brake fluid, then carefully insert the parts in the reverse order of disassembly. Make sure the lips on the cup seals do not turn inside out when they are slipped into the bore.

14 Lubricate the end of the pushrod with PBC (poly butyl cuprysil) grease, or silicone grease designed for brake applications, and install the pushrod and stop washer into the

cylinder bore. Depress the pushrod, then install the snap-ring (make sure the snap-ring is properly seated in the groove with the sharp edge facing out) **(see illustration)**. Install the rubber dust boot (make sure the lip is seated properly in the groove in the piston stop nut).

15 Install the locknut and clevis to the end of the pushrod, leaving the same number of exposed threads inside the clevis as was written down during removal. Tighten the locknut. This will ensure the brake pedal will be positioned correctly.

16 Install the feed hose fitting, using a new O-ring. Install the snap-ring, making sure it seats properly in its groove.

## Installation

17 Install the fluid reservoir if it was removed. Connect the fluid feed hose to the fitting on the master cylinder and secure it with the clamp.

18 Position the master cylinder on the

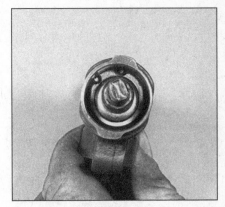

7.14 Make sure the snap-ring is securely seated in its groove

frame and install the bolts, tightening them securely.

19 Connect the banjo fitting to the top of the master cylinder, using new sealing washers on each side of the fitting. Tighten the

8.4 Unhook the pedal return spring

9.4a The front brake hose is secured to the fork leg by a clamp

banjo fitting bolt to the torque listed in this Chapter's Specifications.

20 Connect the clevis to the brake pedal and secure the clevis pin with a new cotter pin.

21 Fill the fluid reservoir with the specified fluid (see Chapter 1) and bleed the system following the procedure in Section 10.

22 Check the position of the brake pedal (see Chapter 1) and adjust it if necessary. Check the operation of the brakes carefully before riding the motorcycle.

## 8  Brake pedal - removal and installation

1 Support the bike securely upright so it can't be knocked over during this procedure.

### Drum brake models

2 Unhook the pedal return spring and the brake light switch spring. Remove the cotter pin, washer and pivot pin and detach the brake rod from the pedal.

3 Unscrew the pedal pivot Allen bolt and detach the pedal from the frame.

### Disc brake models

4 Unhook the pedal return spring from the frame (see illustration).

5 Remove the cotter pin and master cylinder pushrod clevis (see illustration 7.4). Remove the cotter pin and washer from the brake pedal shaft and slide the brake pedal out of the frame.

### All models

6 Inspect the pedal shaft seals (they're in the pedal on drum brake models and in the frame on disc brake models). If they're worn, damaged or appear to have been leaking, pry them out and press in new ones.

7 Installation is the reverse of the removal steps, with the following additions:

a) Lubricate the shaft seal lips, the pivot hole and the bolt shoulder with multi-purpose grease.

b) If you're working on a drum brake model, tighten the pedal pivot bolt to the torque listed in this Chapter's Specifications.

c) Use new cotter pins.

d) Refer to Chapter 1 and adjust brake pedal height.

## 9  Brake hoses and lines - inspection and replacement

### Inspection

1 Before every ride, check the condition of the brake hoses (and the metal line to the front caliper on XL600R models).

2 Twist and flex the rubber hoses while looking for cracks, bulges and seeping fluid. Check extra carefully around the areas where the hoses connect with the metal fittings, as these are common areas for hose failure.

9.4b The rear brake hose is secured to the swingarm by clips

### Replacement

3 The high-pressure brake hoses have banjo fittings on each end of the hose, with the exception of the XL600R hose-to-front master cylinder fitting. The fluid feed hose that connects the rear master cylinder reservoir to the master cylinder is secured by spring clamps.

4 Cover the surrounding area with plenty of rags and unscrew the banjo bolt or flare nut on either end of the hose. Detach the hose or line from any clips that may be present and remove the hose (see illustrations).

5 Position the new hose or line, making sure it isn't twisted or otherwise strained. On hoses equipped with banjo fittings, make sure the metal tube portion of the banjo fitting is located against the stop on the component it's connected to, if equipped. Install the banjo bolts, using new sealing washers on both sides of the fittings, and tighten them to the torque listed in this Chapter's Specifications.

6 On XL600R models, tighten the flare nuts with a flare nut wrench. Where the upper hose joins the master cylinder, use a new sealing washer and tighten the fitting to the torque listed in this Chapter's Specifications.

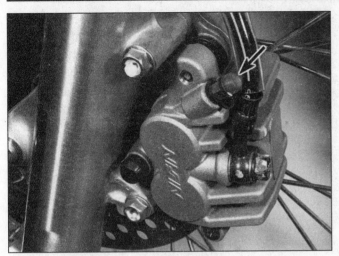

10.5a Pull the rubber cap off the bleeder valve
(front caliper shown) . . .

10.5b . . . and connect a clear plastic hose to the valve
(rear caliper shown)

7   Flush the old brake fluid from the system, refill the system with the recommended fluid (see Chapter 1) and bleed the air from the system (see Section 10). Check the operation of the brakes carefully before riding the motorcycle.

## 10 Brake system bleeding

1   Bleeding the brake system is simply the process of removing all the air bubbles from the brake fluid reservoir, the lines and the brake caliper. Bleeding is necessary whenever a brake system hydraulic connection is loosened, when a component or hose is replaced, or when the master cylinder or caliper is overhauled. Leaks in the system may also allow air to enter, but leaking brake fluid will reveal their presence and warn you of the need for repair.
2   To bleed the brake, you will need some new, clean brake fluid of the recommended type (see Chapter 1), a length of clear vinyl or plastic tubing, a small container partially filled with clean brake fluid, some rags and a wrench to fit the brake caliper bleeder valve.
3   Cover the fuel tank and other painted components to prevent damage in the event that brake fluid is spilled.
4   Remove the reservoir cover or cap and slowly pump the brake lever or pedal a few times, until no air bubbles can be seen floating up from the holes at the bottom of the reservoir. Doing this bleeds the air from the master cylinder end of the line. Reinstall the reservoir cover or cap.
5   Attach one end of the clear vinyl or plastic tubing to the brake caliper bleeder valve and submerge the other end in the brake fluid in the container (see illustrations). Note: Some models have a bleeder valve at the front master cylinder. In this case, start the bleeding procedure at the master cylin-

der bleeder valve, then move to the caliper bleeder valve.
6   Check the fluid level in the reservoir. Do not allow the fluid level to drop below the lower mark during the bleeding process.
7   Carefully pump the brake lever or pedal three or four times and hold it while opening the caliper bleeder valve. When the valve is opened, brake fluid will flow out of the caliper into the clear tubing and the lever will move toward the handlebar or the pedal will move down.
8   Retighten the bleeder valve, then release the brake lever or pedal gradually. Repeat the process until no air bubbles are visible in the brake fluid leaving the caliper and the lever or pedal is firm when applied. Remember to add fluid to the reservoir as the level drops. Use only new, clean brake fluid of the recommended type. Never reuse the fluid lost during bleeding.
9   Be sure to check the fluid level in the master cylinder reservoir frequently.
10  Replace the reservoir cover or cap, wipe up any spilled brake fluid and check the entire system for leaks. Note: If bleeding is difficult, it may be necessary to let the brake fluid in the system stabilize for a few hours (it may be aerated). Repeat the bleeding procedure when the tiny bubbles in the system have settled out.

## 11 Wheels - inspection, removal and installation

### Inspection

1   Clean the wheels thoroughly to remove mud and dirt that may interfere with the inspection procedure or mask defects. Make a general check of the wheels and tires as described in Chapter 1.
2   Support the motorcycle securely upright with the wheel to be checked in the air, then

attach a dial indicator to the fork slider or the swingarm and position the stem against the side of the rim (see illustration). Spin the wheel slowly and check the side-to-side (axial) runout of the rim, then compare your readings with the value listed in this Chapter's Specifications. In order to accurately check radial runout with the dial indicator, the wheel would have to be removed from the machine and the tire removed from the wheel. With the axle clamped in a vise, the wheel can be rotated to check the runout.
3   An alternative, though slightly less accurate, method is to attach a stiff wire pointer to the outer fork tube or the swingarm and position the end a fraction of an inch from the wheel (where the wheel and tire join). If the wheel is true, the distance from the pointer to the rim will be constant as the wheel is rotated. Repeat the procedure to check the runout of the rear wheel. Note: If wheel runout is excessive, refer to Section 13 in this Chapter and check the wheel bearings very carefully before replacing the wheel.

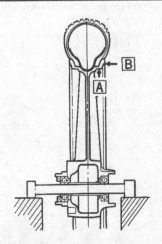

11.2 Check the wheel for out-of-round (A) and lateral movement (B)

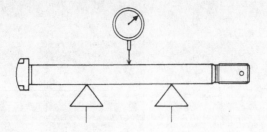

**11.5 Check the axle for runout using a dial indicator and V-blocks - divide the total indicator reading by one-half to obtain the actual runout**

4    The wheels should also be visually inspected for cracks, flat spots on the rim and other damage. Individual spokes can be replaced. If other damage is evident, the wheel will have to be replaced with a new one. Never attempt to repair a damaged wheel.

5    Before installing the wheel, check the axle for straightness. If the axle is corroded, first remove the corrosion with fine emery cloth. Set the axle on V-blocks and check it for runout with a dial indicator **(see illustration)**. If the axle exceeds the maximum allowable runout limit listed in this Chapter's Specifications, it must be replaced.

## Removal
### Front wheel

6    Support the bike from below with a jack beneath the engine, or place the bike on a pit stand or lift.
7    Disconnect the speedometer cable (see Chapter 5, Section 11).
8    If you're working on a 1983 or 1984 XL600R model, remove the guard from the front of the left fork leg.
9    Unscrew the nuts from the axle holder and lift it off the right fork leg **(see illustration)**.
10    Unscrew the axle (it threads into the left

fork) **(see illustration)**. Support the wheel and pull the axle out. Lower the wheel away from the motorcycle, sliding the brake disc out from between the pads. Retrieve the collar from the left side of the wheel hub.

### Rear wheel
11    Support the bike from below with a jack beneath the engine, or place the bike on a pit stand or lift.

### All models except XR650R
12    If you're working on a drum brake model, remove the rear brake adjuster wing-nut from the brake rod (see Chapter 1). Pull the rod out of its pivot and remove the pivot from the brake arm.
13    Record the position of the chain adjusters. Loosen the rear axle nut and back off the chain adjusters all the way (see Chapter 1). Push the wheel forward and disengage the drive chain from the rear sprocket.
14    Hold the axle with a wrench and remove the axle nut, washer, chain adjuster and stopper plate **(see illustrations)**.
15    Support the wheel and slide it back until the axle clears the swingarm, then lower the

**11.9 Remove the axle holder nuts; the UP mark must be upright and the arrow must point upward on installation**

**11.10 Unscrew the axle (it threads into the opposite fork leg)**

**11.14a Remove the axle nut and washer . . .**

**11.14b . . . slide off the chain adjuster . . .**

**11.14c . . . and slide the stopper plate off the pin**

wheel away from the motorcycle. Pull the axle out. Retrieve the collars from each side of the hub, noting their orientations.

### XR650R models

16   Remove the axle nut, washer and block from the right side, then remove the axle **(see illustrations)**. Push the wheel forward and disengage the drive chain from the sprocket, then lower the wheel out of the swingarm.

## Installation

17   Installation is the reverse of the removal steps, with the following additions:

a)   *Make sure the collar(s) is/are returned to their original positions.*

b)   *If you're installing a front wheel, make sure the lugs on the speedometer gear engage with the cutouts in the hub. Also make sure the protrusion fits into the notch in the fork leg (see illustration 11.2 in Chapter 4). Lubricate the end of the speedometer cable with multi-purpose grease.*

c)   *If you're installing a rear wheel on all except XR650R models, make sure the stopper fits over the pin on the swingarm (see illustration 11.14c). On drum brake models, make sure the boss on the swingarm fits into the brake panel notch (see illustration 5.17).*

d)   *If you're working on a front wheel, tighten the axle to the torque listed in this Chapter's Specifications, then install the holder with its UP mark upright and tighten the holder nuts a little, but not completely yet. Pump the forks several times to seat the axle, then tighten the axle holder upper nuts to the torque listed in this Chapter's Specifications, then tighten the axle holder lower nuts to the specified torque.*

e)   *If you're working on a rear wheel, return the chain adjusters to their previous positions (all except XR650R models), then tighten the axle nut to the torque listed in this Chapter's Specifications.*

f)   *Refer to Chapter 1 and adjust the rear brake (drum brake models).*

## 12 Wheels - alignment check

1   Misalignment of the wheels, which may be due to a cocked rear wheel or a bent frame or triple clamps, can cause strange and possibly serious handling problems. If the frame or triple clamps are at fault, repair by a frame specialist or replacement with new parts are the only alternatives.

2   To check the alignment you will need an assistant, a length of string or a perfectly straight piece of wood and a ruler graduated in 1/64 inch increments. A plumb bob or other suitable weight will also be required.

3   Support the motorcycle securely upright, then measure the width of both tires at their

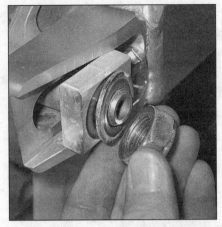

**11.16a  Remove the nut and axle block from the right side of the swingarm . . .**

widest points. Subtract the smaller measurement from the larger measurement, then divide the difference by two. The result is the amount of offset that should exist between the front and rear tires on both sides.

4   If a string is used, have your assistant hold one end of it about half way between the floor and the rear axle, touching the rear sidewall of the tire.

5   Run the other end of the string forward and pull it tight so that it is roughly parallel to the floor. Slowly bring the string into contact with the rear sidewall of the rear tire, then turn the front wheel until it is parallel with the string. Measure the distance from the front tire sidewall to the string.

6   Repeat the procedure on the other side of the motorcycle. The distance from the front tire sidewall to the string should be equal on both sides.

7   As was previously pointed out, a perfectly straight length of wood may be substituted for the string. The procedure is the same.

8   If the distance between the string and tire is greater on one side, or if the rear wheel appears to be cocked, refer to Chapter 6, *Swingarm bearings - check,* and make sure the swingarm is tight.

9   If the front-to-back alignment is correct, the wheels still may be out of alignment vertically.

**11.16b  . . . then pull the axle out, push the wheel forward and disengage the drive chain from the sprocket, then lower the wheel from the swingarm**

10   Using the plumb bob, or other suitable weight, and a length of string, check the rear wheel to make sure it is vertical. To do this, hold the string against the tire upper sidewall and allow the weight to settle just off the floor. When the string touches both the upper and lower tire sidewalls and is perfectly straight, the wheel is vertical. If it is not, place thin spacers under one leg of the centerstand.

11   Once the rear wheel is vertical, check the front wheel in the same manner. If both wheels are not perfectly vertical, the frame and/or major suspension components are bent.

## 13 Wheel bearings - inspection and maintenance

## Front wheel bearings

1   Remove the front wheel (see Section 11).

2   Set the wheel on blocks or on a five-gallon bucket so as not to allow the weight of the wheel to rest on the brake disc.

3   From the right side of the wheel, remove the speedometer drive **(see illustration)**.

**13.3  Lift the speedometer drive out of the wheel; on installation, align the drive lugs with the retainer notches**

13.4a Pry the seal out of the right side . . .

13.4b . . . and remove the speedometer drive

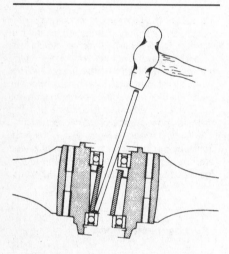

13.6a If there's enough room to tilt a metal rod so it will catch the bearing inner races, drive the bearings from the hub with a metal rod and hammer

4    Pry out the seal from the right side of the wheel (see illustration). Remove the speedometer drive from beneath the seal (see illustration).

5    Turn the wheel over. Remove the cover and pry the grease seal out of the left side.

6    The usual method of removing front wheel bearings is to insert a metal rod (preferably a brass drift punch) through the center of the hub bearing and tap evenly around the inner race of the opposite bearing to drive it from the hub (see illustration). The bearing spacer will also come out. It may not be possible to tilt the rod enough to catch the edge of the opposite bearing's inner race. In this case, use a bearing remover tool consisting of a shaft and remover head (see illustration). These tools are commonly available from aftermarket tool suppliers. The head fits inside the bearing, then the wedge end of the shaft is tapped into the groove in the head to expand the head and lock it inside the bearing. Tapping on the shaft from this point will force the bearing out of the hub.

7    Lay the wheel on its other side and remove the remaining bearing using the same technique. Note: *The bearings must be replaced with new ones whenever they're removed, as they're almost certain to be damaged during removal.*

8    Pack new bearings with grease from the open side. Rotate the bearing to work the grease in between the bearing balls.

9    Thoroughly clean the hub area of the wheel. Install the bearing into the recess in the right side of the hub, with the sealed side facing out. Using a bearing driver or a socket large enough to contact the outer race of the bearing, drive it in until it seats.

10    Turn the wheel over and install the bearing spacer and bearing, driving the bearing into place as described in Step 9.

11    Coat the lip of a new grease seal with grease.

12    Install the grease seal on the right side of the wheel; it should go in with thumb pressure but if not, use a seal driver, large socket or a flat piece of wood to drive it into place.

13    Clean off all grease from the brake disc using acetone or brake system cleaner. Install the wheel.

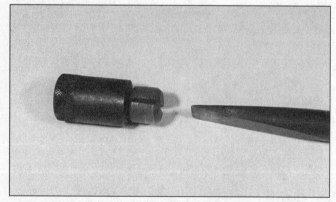

13.6b If you can't position a metal rod against the bearings, this tool can be used instead - place the split portion inside the bearing and pass the wedge through the hub into the split; tapping on the end of the rod will spread the split portion, locking it to the bearing, so the split portion and bearing can be driven out together

13.14 The bearing retainer is staked in place; this makes it impractical to remove it with makeshift tools

13.16  Remove the collar from the disc side of the wheel, then pry out the grease seal

13.17  Turn the wheel over and remove the collar from the sprocket side

## Rear wheel bearings

14   The left rear wheel bearing is held in place by a threaded retainer that is staked in position (see illustration). Removal requires special tools for which there are no good substitutes. Before you try to replace the bearings, read through the procedure. It may be more practical to take the wheel to a Honda dealer and have the bearings replaced.

15   Refer to Section 11 and remove the rear wheel.

16   If you're working on a 1991 or later model, remove the collar from the grease seal on the right side of the wheel, then pry the grease seal out (see illustration).

17   On the other side of the wheel, remove the collar from the bearing retainer and grease seal (see illustration).

18   Insert the shaft of the retainer wrench into the hub from the retainer side. Engage the pins of the wrench with the holes in the retainer, then thread the retainer wingnut onto the shaft (see illustrations). Turn the

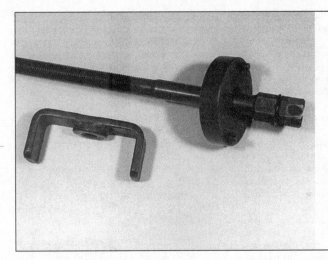

13.18a  These tools are used to remove the bearing retainer; pass the shaft through the hub and fit the pins on the disc into the holes in the bearing retainer

retainer wrench with a socket to unscrew the retainer (see illustration).

19   Remove the bearings with the special tools used for front wheel bearings (see Step 6).

20   Thoroughly clean the hub area of the

13.18b  Thread the nut portion of the tool onto the shaft and tighten it to lock the pins on the disc securely into the holes in the bearing retainer

13.18c  Turn the shaft with a socket or wrench to unscrew the retainer from the hub

**13.20 Drive in the bearing on the sprocket side, using a bearing driver that contacts the outer race (the sealed side of the bearing faces out)**

**13.21 Insert the spacer into the hub, making sure its LH mark is toward the left side of the hub**

wheel. Install the left bearing into the recess in the hub, with the sealed side facing out. Using a bearing driver or a socket large enough to contact the outer race of the bearing, drive it in until it seats **(see illustration)**.

21   Turn the wheel over. Apply a coat of multi-purpose grease to the inside of the spacer and install it in the hub **(see illustration)**. Be sure the LH mark on the spacer is toward the left side of the wheel.

22   Pack the remaining bearing from the open side with grease, then install it in the hub, driving the bearing in with a socket or bearing driver large enough to contact the outer race of the bearing **(see illustration)**. Drive the bearing in until it seats.

23   Pry the grease seal out of the bearing retainer. Place a new one on the retainer, positioned so its lip will face into the hub when the retainer is installed. Tap the seal in, using a bearing driver or socket the same diameter as the seal.

24   Thread the retainer part way into the hub, then install it with the same tools used for removal **(see illustrations 13.18a through 13.18c)**.

25   Install a new grease seal in the right side of the hub **(see illustration 13.16)**. It may go in with thumb pressure, but if not, use a seal driver, large socket or a flat piece of wood to drive it into place.

26   If you're working on a 1991 or later model, install the collar in the right side of the hub. On all models, install the collar in the left side of the hub.

27   Clean off all grease from the brake discs using acetone or brake system cleaner. Install the wheel (see Section 11).

## 14 Tires - removal and installation

1   To properly remove and install tires, you will need at least two motorcycle tire irons, some water and a tire pressure gauge.

2   Begin by removing the wheel from the motorcycle. If the tire is going to be re-used, mark it next to the valve stem, wheel balance weight or rim lock.

3   Deflate the tire by removing the valve stem core. Loosen the rim lock nut. When it is fully deflated, push the bead of the tire away from the rim on both sides. In some extreme cases, this can only be accomplished with a bead breaking tool, but most often it can be carried out with tire irons. Riding on a deflated tire to break the bead is not recommended, as damage to the rim and tire will occur.

4   Dismounting a tire is easier when the tire is warm, so an indoor tire change is recommended in cold climates. The rubber gets very stiff and is difficult to manipulate when cold.

5   Place the wheel on a thick pad or old blanket. This will help keep the wheel and tire from slipping around.

6   Once the bead is completely free of the rim, lubricate the inside edge of the rim and the tire bead with water only. Some manufacturers recommend against the use of soap or other tire mounting lubricants, as the tire may shift on the rim; however, a soapy water solution will greatly ease the removal and installation process, and might even prevent damage to the tire and/or rim. Remove the locknut and push the tire valve through the rim.

7   Insert one of the tire irons under the bead of the tire at the valve stem and lift the bead up over the rim. This should be fairly easy. Take care not to pinch the tube as this is done. If it is difficult to pry the bead up, make sure that the rest of the bead opposite the valve stem is in the dropped center section of the rim.

8   Hold the tire iron down with the bead over the rim, then move about 1 or 2 inches to either side and insert the second tire iron. Be careful not to cut or slice the bead or the tire may split when inflated. Also, take care not to catch or pinch the inner tube as the second tire iron is levered over. For this reason, tire irons are recommended over screwdrivers or other implements.

9   With a small section of the bead up over the rim, one of the levers can be removed

**13.22 Drive in the bearing on the brake disc side, using a driver that contacts the outer race**

and reinserted 1 or 2 inches farther around the rim until about 1/4 of the tire bead is above the rim edge. Make sure that the rest of the bead is in the dropped center of the rim. At this point, the bead can usually be pulled up over the rim by hand.

10   Once all of the first bead is over the rim, the inner tube can be withdrawn from the tire and rim. Push in on the valve stem, lift up on the tire next to the stem, reach inside the tire and carefully pull out the tube. It is usually not necessary to completely remove the tire from the rim to repair the inner tube. It is sometimes recommended though, because checking for foreign objects in the tire is difficult while it is still mounted on the rim.

11   To remove the tire completely, make sure the bead is broken all the way around on the remaining edge, then stand the tire and wheel up on the tread and grab the wheel with one hand. Push the tire down over the same edge of the rim while pulling the rim away from the tire. If the bead is correctly positioned in the dropped center of the rim, the tire should roll off and separate from the rim very easily. If tire irons are used to work this last bead over the rim, the outer edge of the rim may be marred. If a tire iron is necessary, be sure to pad the rim as described earlier.

12   Refer to Section 15 for inner tube repair procedures.

13   Mounting a tire is basically the reverse of removal. Some tires have a balance mark and/or directional arrows molded into the tire sidewall. Look for these marks so that the tire can be installed properly. The dot should be aligned with the valve stem.

14   If the tire was not removed completely to repair or replace the inner tube, the tube should be inflated just enough to make it round. Sprinkle it with talcum powder, which acts as a dry lubricant, then carefully lift up the tire edge and install the tube with the

valve stem next to the hole in the rim. Once the tube is in place, push the valve stem through the rim and start the locknut on the stem.

15   Lubricate the tire bead, then push it over the rim edge and into the dropped center section opposite the inner tube valve stem. Work around each side of the rim, carefully pushing the bead over the rim. The last section may have to be levered on with tire irons. If so, take care not to pinch the inner tube as this is done.

16   Once the bead is over the rim edge, check to see that the inner tube valve stem and the rim lock are pointing to the center of the hub. If they're angled slightly in either direction, rotate the tire on the rim to straighten it out. Run the locknut the rest of the way onto the stem and rim lock but don't tighten them completely.

17   Inflate the tube to approximately 1-1/2 times the pressure listed in the Chapter 1 Specifications and check to make sure the guidelines on the tire sidewalls are the same distance from the rim around the circumference of the tire.

 *Warning: Do not overinflate the tube or the tire may burst, causing serious injury.*

18   After the tire bead is correctly seated on the rim, allow the tire to deflate. Replace the valve core and inflate the tire to the recommended pressure, then finger-tighten the valve stem locknut, install the rubber boot and install and tighten the valve stem cap. **Note:** *Many riders choose to leave off the valve stem locknut. They feel that installing the nut will make the tube more susceptible to failure at the valve stem if the tire happens to shift on the rim while riding.* Tighten the locknut on the rim locknut to the torque listed in the Chapter 1 Specifications.

## 15 Tubes - repair

1   Tire tube repair requires a patching kit that's usually available from motorcycle dealers, accessory stores or auto parts stores. Be sure to follow the directions supplied with the kit to ensure a safe repair. Patching should be done only when a new tube is unavailable. Replace the tube as soon as possible. Sudden deflation can cause loss of control and an accident.

2   To repair a tube, remove it from the tire, inflate and immerse it in a sink or tub full of water to pinpoint the leak. Mark the position of the leak, then deflate the tube. Dry it off and thoroughly clean the area around the puncture.

3   Most tire patching kits have a buffer to rough up the area around the hole for proper adhesion of the patch. Roughen an area slightly larger than the patch, then apply a thin coat of the patching cement to the roughened area. Allow the cement to dry until tacky, then apply the patch.

4   It may be necessary to remove a protective covering from the top surface of the patch after it has been attached to the tube. Keep in mind that tubes made from synthetic rubber may require a special patch and adhesive if a satisfactory bond is to be achieved.

5   Before replacing the tube, check the inside of the tire to make sure the object that caused the puncture is not still inside. Also check the outside of the tire, particularly the tread area, to make sure nothing is projecting through the tire that may cause another puncture. Check the rim for sharp edges or damage. Make sure the rubber trim band is in good condition and properly installed before inserting the tube.

# TIRE CHANGING SEQUENCE - TUBED TIRES

 **1** Deflate the tire and loosen the rim lock nut. After pushing the tire beads away from the rim flanges push the tire bead into the well of the rim at the point opposite the valve. Insert the tire lever adjacent to the valve and work the bead over the edge of the rim.

**2** Use two levers to work the bead over the edge of the rim. Note the use of rim protectors

 **3** Remove the inner tube from the tire

 **4** When the first bead is clear, remove the tire as shown. If the bead isn't too tight, rim protectors won't be necessary

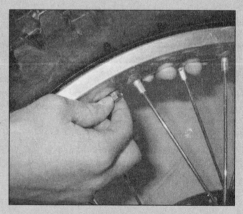

 **5** To install, partially inflate the inner tube and insert it in the tire. Make sure there's a nut on the valve stem

 **6** Work the first bead over the rim and feed the valve through the hole in the rim. Partially screw on the retaining nut to hold the valve in place. (The nut should be removed after the tire has been inflated)

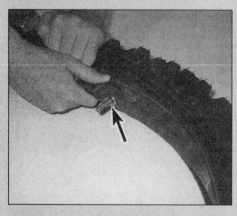

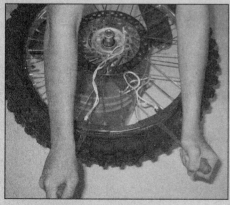 **7** Check that the inner tube is positioned correctly and work the second bead over the rim using the tire levers. Start at a point between the valve stem and the rim lock

 **8** Work final area of the bead over the rim while pushing the valve inwards to ensure that the inner tube is not trapped. Also push the rim lock inwards and, if necessary, pry the tire bead over the rim lock. After inflating the tire, tighten the rim lock nut securely

# Chapter 8
# Frame and bodywork

## Contents

## Degrees of difficulty

| | | | | |
|---|---|---|---|---|
| **Easy,** suitable for novice with little experience  | **Fairly easy,** suitable for beginner with some experience  | **Fairly difficult,** suitable for competent DIY mechanic 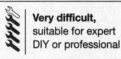 | **Difficult,** suitable for experienced DIY mechanic | **Very difficult,** suitable for expert DIY or professional  |

## Specifications

### Torque specifications

**Note:** *One foot-pound (ft-lb) of torque is equivalent to 12 inch-pounds (in-lbs) of torque. Torque values below approximately 15 ft-lbs are expressed in inch-pounds, since most foot-pound torque wrenches are not accurate at these smaller values.*

| | |
|---|---|
| Seat mounting bolts | |
|   XL600R | 8 to 12 Nm (72 to 108 in-lbs) |
|   All others | Not available |
| Footpeg bolt/nut | |
|   XL600R | 38 to 48 Nm (27 to 35 ft-lbs) |
|   XR600R | |
|     1985 to 1987 models | 50 to 60 Nm (36 to 43 ft-lbs) |
|     1988 and later models | 65 Nm (47 ft-lbs) |
|   XR650L | 65 Nm (47 ft-lbs) |
|   XR650R | 54 Nm (40 ft-lbs) |
| Skid plate/bar | |
|   XL600R | 8 to 12 Nm (72 to 108 in-lbs) |
|   All others | Not available |
| Sidestand | |
|   XL600R and XR600R | 35 to 45 Nm (25 to 33 ft-lbs) |
|   XR650L and XR650R | |
|     Step 1 | Tighten bolt to 10 Nm (84 in-lbs) |
|     Step 2 | Loosen bolt 1/8-turn |
|     Step 3 | Tighten nut to 40 Nm (29 ft-lbs) |
| Sidestand bracket-to-frame bolts (XR650R) | |
|   8 mm bolt | 26 Nm (20 ft-lbs) |
|   10 mm bolt | 36 Nm (29 ft-lbs) |
| Subframe (XR650R) | |
|   Upper bolt | 26 Nm (20 ft-lbs) |
|   Lower bolts | 42 Nm (31 ft-lbs) |

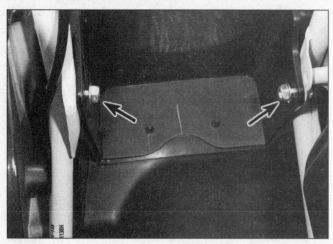

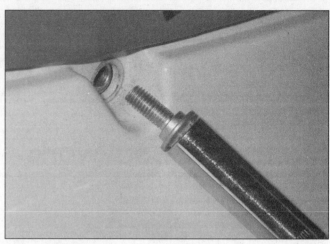

2.2a  Remove the seat mounting bolt on each side of the seat. On 600R models and 650L models the bolts are accessed from underneath

2.2b  On XR650R models the bolts are accessed from the outside. The right-side bolt secures the upper rear of the right side cover (it's longer and has a shoulder)

## 1  General information

This Chapter covers the procedures necessary to remove and install the fenders and other body parts, and the subframe on XR650R models. Since many service and repair operations on these motorcycles require removal of the fenders and/or other body parts, the procedures are grouped here and referred to from other Chapters.

In the case of damage to plastic body parts, it is usually necessary to remove the broken component and replace it with a new (or used) one. The material that the fenders and other plastic body parts are composed of doesn't lend itself to conventional repair techniques. There are some shops that specialize in "plastic welding," but in most cases it is more cost effective to just replace the part. **Note:** *When attempting to remove any body panel, first study the panel closely,* *noting any fasteners and associated fittings, to be sure of returning everything to its correct place on installation. In some cases, the aid of an assistant may be required when removing panels, to help avoid damaging the paint. Once the visible fasteners have been removed, try to lift off the panel as described but DO NOT FORCE the panel - if it will not release, check that all fasteners have been removed and try again. Where a panel engages another by means of lugs and grommets, be careful not to break the lugs or damage the bodywork. Remember that a few moments of patience at this stage will save you a lot of money in replacing broken panels!*

## 2  Seat - removal and installation

1    On all except XR650R models, remove the side covers (see Section 5).

2    Remove the mounting bolt on each side of the seat **(see illustrations)**. If the bike is equipped with a seat strap, remove a bolt from one side of the strap.

3    Pull the seat back to disengage the tang on the front end from the button on the fuel tank or from the frame and lift it off **(see illustrations)**.

4    Installation is the reverse of removal.

## 3  Footpegs - removal and installation

1    To detach the footpeg from the bracket, remove the cotter pin, washer and footpeg pivot pin **(see illustration)**. Separate the footpeg from the motorcycle.

2    On the right side only, the footpeg bracket can be detached from the motorcycle if necessary. Remove the bolts (or bolt and nut, as applicable), then detach the bracket from the frame.

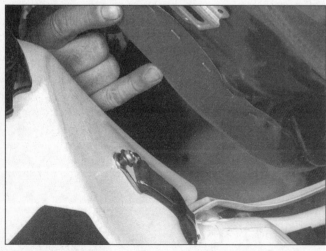

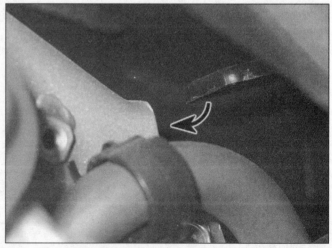

2.3a  Disengage the seat from the screw on the fuel tank . . .

2.3b  . . . or, on XR650L models, from the slot in the top of the rear shock absorber mount

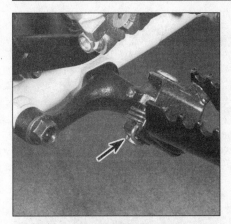

3.1 Remove the cotter pin, washer and pivot pin to detach the footpeg from the bracket

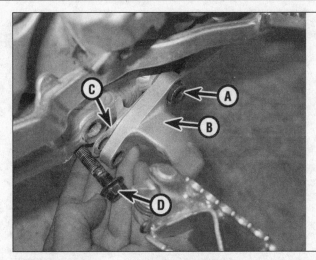

3.3 Right-side footpeg bracket details - XR650R

A   Allen bolt
B   Bracket
C   Shim
D   Hex bolt

4.2 Unhook the sidestand spring from the posts on the sidestand and frame, then remove the locknut and mounting bolt. An automotive brake spring tool, available at most auto parts stores, makes removing and installing the spring easy

4.4 Sidestand bracket-to-frame bolts (XR650R)

3   Installation is the reverse of removal, with the following additions:

a) *If you're working on an XR650R, make sure the shim is installed between the right-side footpeg bracket and the frame, and that the washer on the rear bolt is installed with its sharp side facing the bracket* (see illustration).

b) *Apply a non-hardening thread-locking agent to the threads of the bracket fasteners, then tighten the fasteners to the torque listed in this Chapter's Specifications.*

c) *Use a new cotter pin and wrap its ends around the pivot pin.*

## 4  Sidestand - removal and installation

1   Support the bike securely so it can't be knocked over during this procedure.

2   Unhook the sidestand spring from its posts (see illustration).

3   Remove the self-locking nut and pivot bolt and separate the sidestand from the motorcycle.

4   On XR650R models the sidestand bracket can be unbolted from the frame (see illustration).

5   Installation is the reverse of the removal steps. Tighten the fasteners to the torque listed in this Chapter's Specifications.

## 5  Side covers - removal and installation

### Right side (and left side on XL600R models)

1   Remove the side cover bolt(s) (see accompanying illustration and illustration

5.1a Remove the side cover mounting bolt . . .

2.2b). Pull the cover free of the grommets and take it off the motorcycle (see illustration).

5.1b ... and carefully pull the lugs free of the grommets

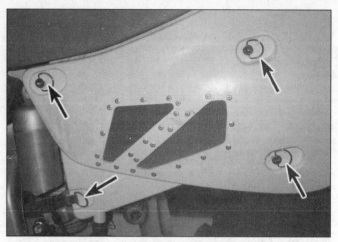

5.3 Twist the retainers counterclockwise to free them (and, on XR650R models, unhook the retainer at the lower front of the panel)

2    Installation is the reverse of removal. Tighten the bolt securely, but don't overtighten it and strip the threads.

### Left side (all except XL600R models)

3    Lift the loops and twist the retainers to free them (see illustration). On XR650R models, also unhook the retainer at the lower front of the panel. Lift the panel off.

4    Installation is the reverse of removal. If you're working on an XR650R, be sure the air filter element is properly seated, and that the panel seals properly with the airbox.

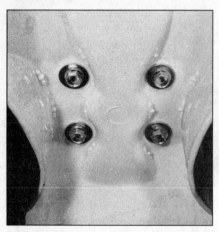

6.1a  The front fender bolts are accessible from below

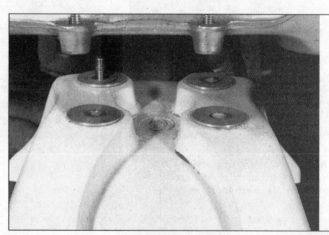

6.1b  Don't forget the washers on top of the fender

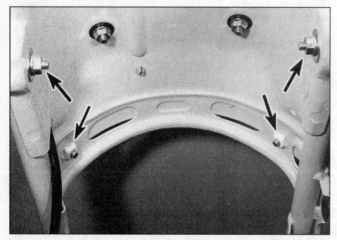

7.2a  Two of the rear fender bolts on XR600R models are accessible from below (upper arrows); two are accessible from above (lower arrows)

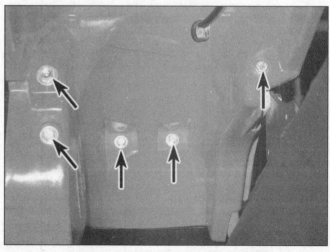

7.2b  Rear fender mounting bolts - XR650R

## 6 Front fender - removal and installation

1 Remove the fender bolts **(see illustration)**. Lower the fender clear of the lower triple clamp and remove the washers **(see illustration)**.
2 Installation is the reverse of removal. Be sure to reinstall the grommets in their correct locations. Tighten the bolts securely, but don't overtighten them and strip the threads.

## 7 Rear fender - removal and installation

1 Remove the seat and both side covers (see Sections 2 and 5). Unplug the electrical connectors to the taillight and, if equipped, the turn signals.
2 Remove the fender mounting bolts (and grommets if equipped) and take the fender off **(see illustrations)**. If you're working on an XR650R, unbolt the rear brake fluid reservoir and set it aside (see Chapter 7).
3 If you're working on an XR600R, unbolt the inner fender and lift it off **(see illustration)**.
4 Installation is the reverse of removal. Tighten the bolts securely, but don't overtighten them and strip the threads.

## 8 Skid plate/bars - removal and installation

1 Support the bike securely so it can't be knocked over during this procedure.
2 If you're working on an XL600R, remove one nut at the front of the skid plate and two

bolts from underneath, then lower the skid plate away from the motorcycle.
3 If you're working on an XR600R or XR650L, remove the bolts at the front and rear of the bars **(see illustrations)**. Lower the bars away from the motorcycle.

4 XR650R models use a plastic skid plate secured by four bolts **(see illustrations)**.
5 Installation is the reverse of removal. Tighten the bolts securely, but don't overtighten them and strip the threads.

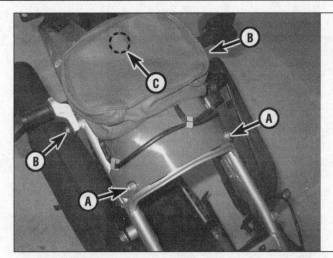

**7.2c Rear fender mounting details - XR650L**

A Fender forward mounting bolts
B Fender rear outer mounting bolts
C Fender rear center mounting bolt (inside tool bag)

**7.3 Remove two bolts to detach the inner fender**

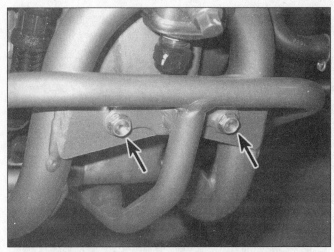

**8.3a Skid bar upper mounting bolts (XR650L shown, XR600R similar) . . .**

**8.3b . . . and lower mounting bolts**

8.4a Skid plate upper mounting bolts . . .

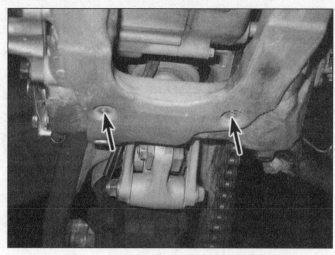

8.4b . . . and lower mounting bolts (XR650R)

## 9 Radiator shrouds/air scoops - removal and installation

1   XR650L: Remove the two bolts from the front and one bolt from the side, then lift the shroud from the fuel tank (see illustrations).
2   XR650R: Remove the three bolts from the side, connecting the shroud to the fuel tank and radiator, then remove the shroud (see illustration).
3   Installation is the reverse of removal. Tighten the bolts securely, but don't over-tighten them and strip the threads.

## 10 Frame - general information, inspection and repair

1   All models except the XR650R use a semi-double cradle frame made of round-section steel tubing. The frame on the XR650R is constructed of aluminum and fea-tures a removable rear subframe.
2   The frame shouldn't require attention unless accident damage has occurred. In most cases, frame replacement is the only satisfactory remedy for such damage. A few frame specialists have the jigs and other equipment necessary for straightening the frame to the required standard of accuracy, but even then there is no simple way of assessing to what extent the frame may have been overstressed.
3   After the motorcycle has accumulated a lot of miles or has seen severe usage, the frame should be examined closely for signs of cracking or splitting at the welded joints. Corrosion can also cause weakness at these joints. Loose engine mount bolts can cause ovaling or fracturing to the mounting bolt holes. Minor damage can often be repaired by welding, depending on the nature and extent of the damage.
4   Remember that a frame that is out of alignment will cause handling problems. If misalignment is suspected as the result of

9.1a Shroud forward mounting bolts - XR650L

an accident, it will be necessary to strip the machine completely so the frame can be thoroughly checked.

9.1b Shroud outer mounting bolt - XR650L

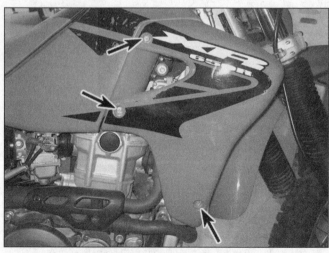

9.2 Shroud mounting bolts - XR650R

11.2  Detach the breather hose from the air filter housing

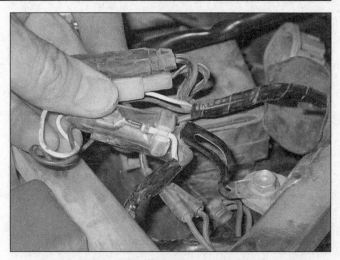

11.4  Pull up this retainer, then disconnect the AC regulator and taillight electrical connectors

11.5  Loosen this bolt and free the rear brake reservoir hose from the clamp

11.6  Loosen the muffler clamp bolt . . .

11.7  . . . and the clamp securing the air filter duct to the carburetor

## 11  Subframe (XR650R) - removal and installation

1    Remove the seat (see Section 2) and the side covers (see Section 5).

2    Detach the breather hose from the air filter housing **(see illustration)**.

3    Remove the ignition control module (see Chapter 5).

4    Pull up the retainer, then disconnect the electrical connectors for the taillight and AC regulator **(see illustration)**.

5    Unbolt the rear brake fluid reservoir from the frame (see Chapter 7). Also loosen the bolt and free the reservoir hose from its clamp on the subframe **(see illustration)**.

6    Loosen the clamp bolt securing the muffler to the exhaust pipe **(see illustration)**.

7    Loosen the carburetor duct clamp screw **(see illustration)**.

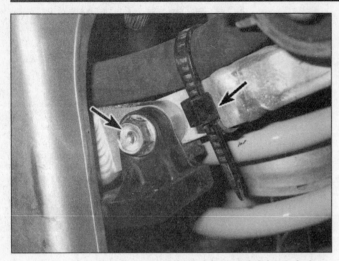

11.8 Remove the wire tie and the subframe's left lower bolt, which also secures the chain slider

11.9 Remove the subframe's right lower bolt . . .

8    Remove the subframe left-lower bolt and the upper chain slider **(see illustration)**.

9    Remove the subframe right lower bolt **(see illustration)**.

10   Remove the subframe upper bolt and detach the subframe **(see illustration)**.

11   Installation is the reverse of the removal procedure. Be sure to tighten the subframe fasteners to the torque listed in this Chapter's Specifications. Tighten the muffler clamp bolt to the torque listed in the Chapter 4 Specifications.

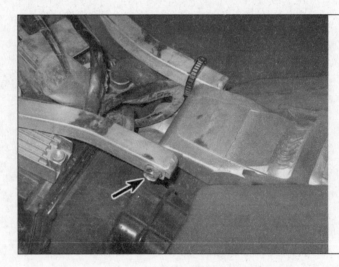

11.10 . . . and the upper bolt, then detach the subframe from the bike

# Wiring diagrams on the following pages

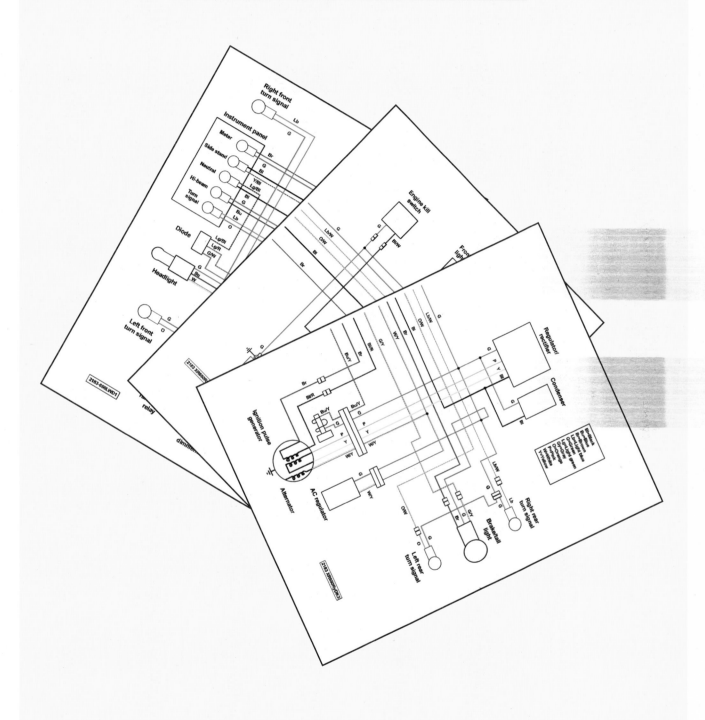

# Notes

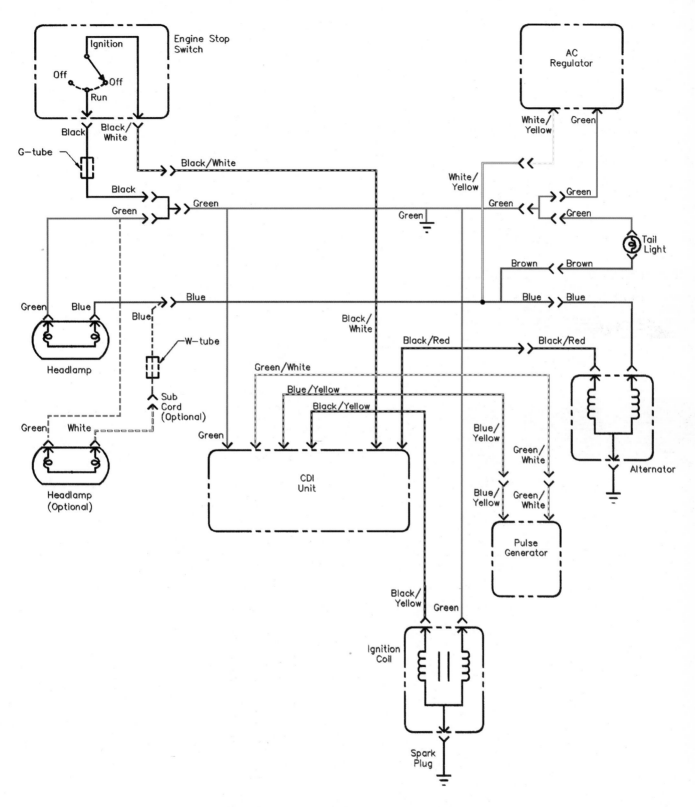

**XR600R wiring diagram - 1985 through 1987 models**

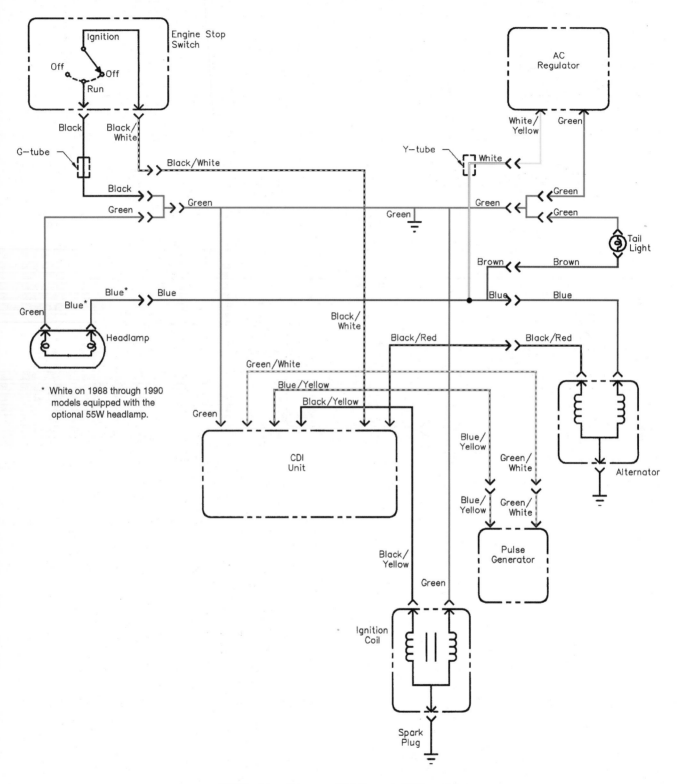

**XR600 wiring diagram - 1988 through 1990 models**

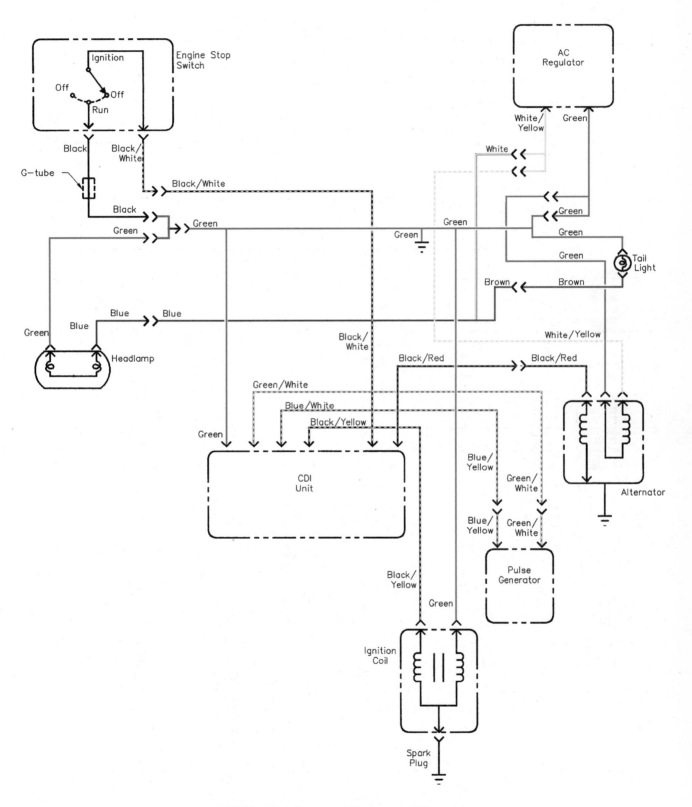

**XR600R wiring diagram - 1991 through 2000 models**

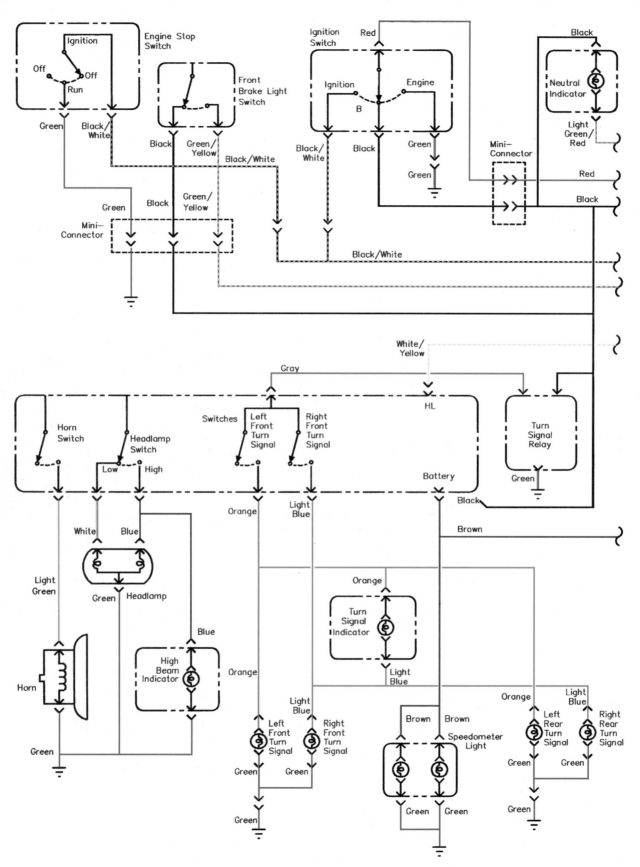

**XL600R wiring diagram (1 of 2)**

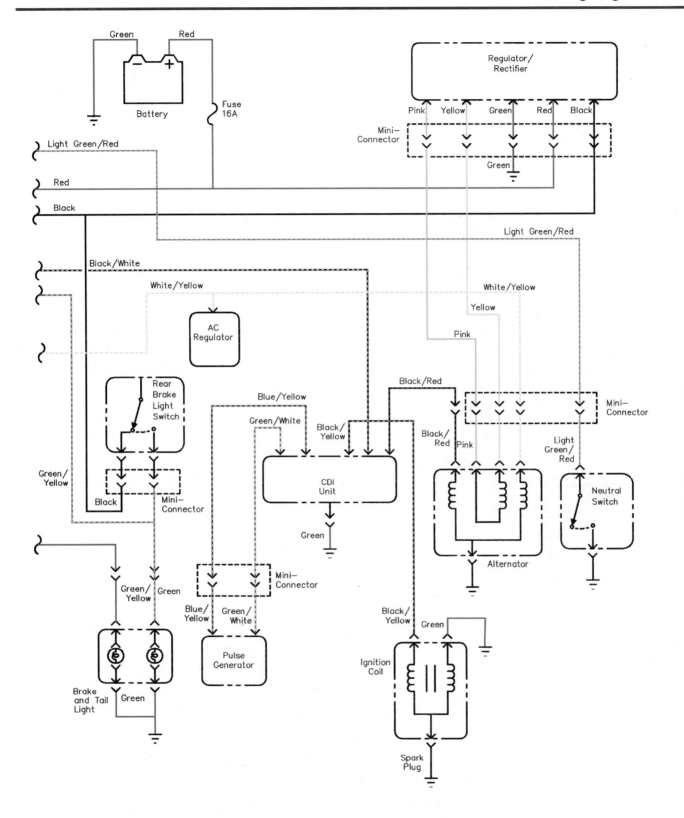

**XL600R wiring diagram (2 of 2)**

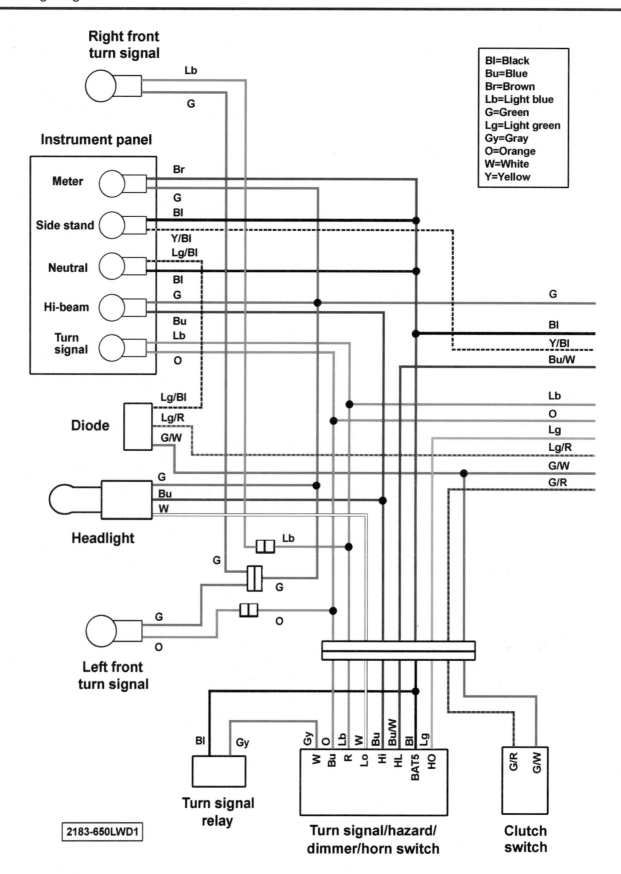

**XR650L wiring diagram (1 of 4)**

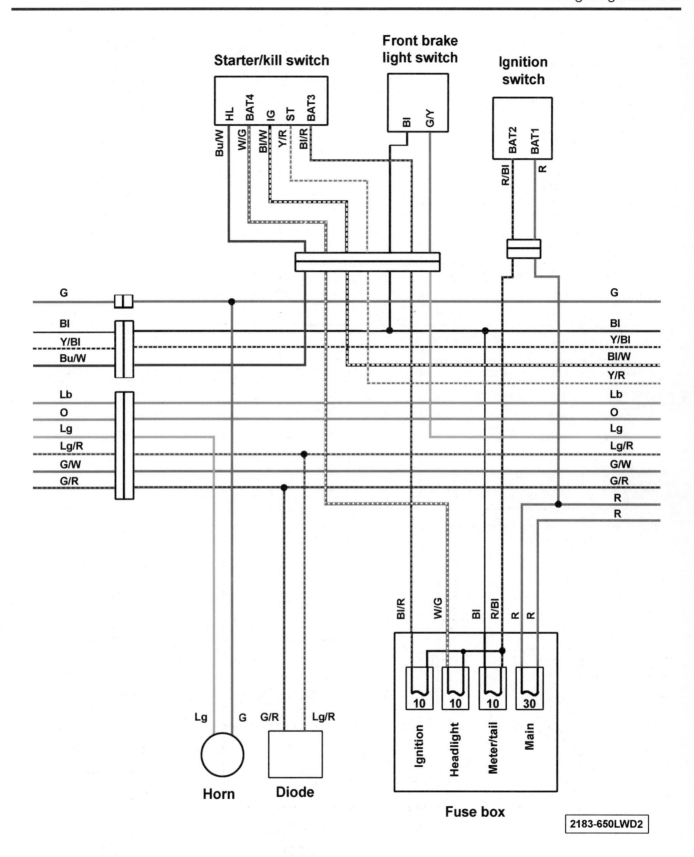

XR650L wiring diagram (2 of 4)

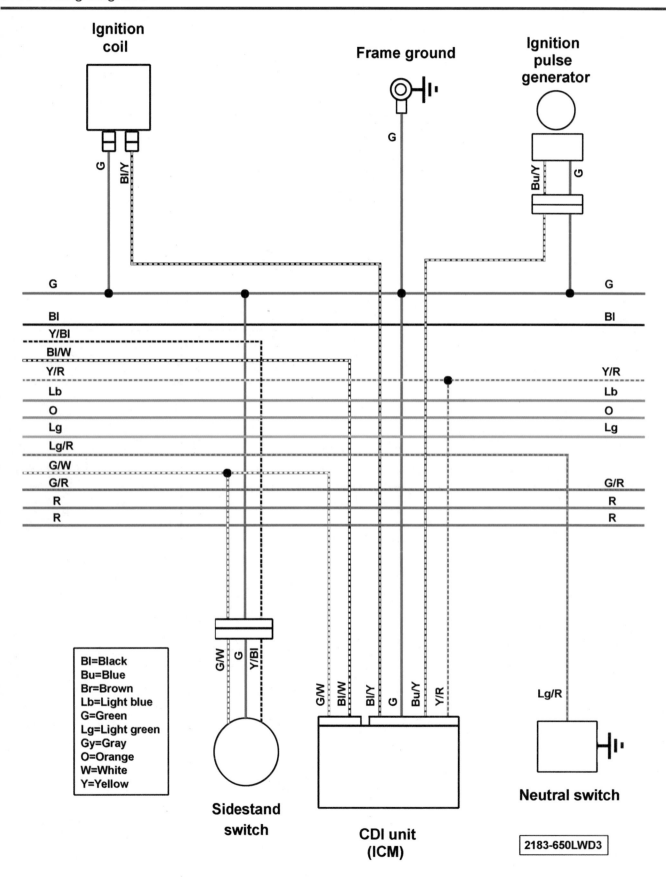

**Ignition coil**

**Frame ground**

**Ignition pulse generator**

G
Bl/Y

G

Bu/Y
G

G          G

Bl          Bl

Y/Bl

Bl/W

Y/R          Y/R

Lb          Lb

O          O

Lg          Lg

Lg/R

G/W

G/R          G/R

R          R

R          R

Bl=Black
Bu=Blue
Br=Brown
Lb=Light blue
G=Green
Lg=Light green
Gy=Gray
O=Orange
W=White
Y=Yellow

G/W
G
Y/Bl

G/W
Bl/W
Bl/Y
G
Bu/Y
Y/R

Lg/R

**Sidestand switch**

**CDI unit (ICM)**

**Neutral switch**

2183-650LWD3

XR650L wiring diagram (3 of 4)

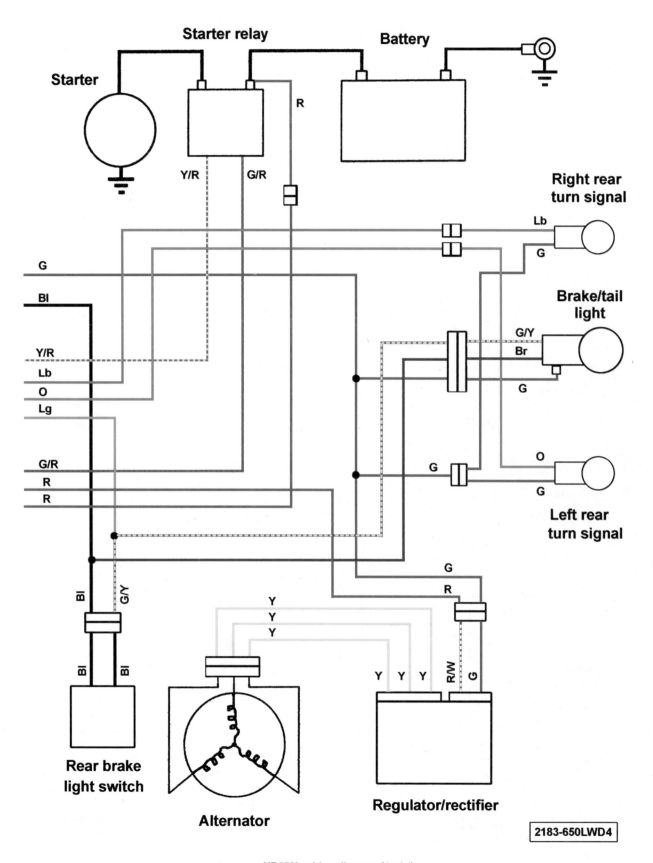

XR650L wiring diagram (4 of 4)

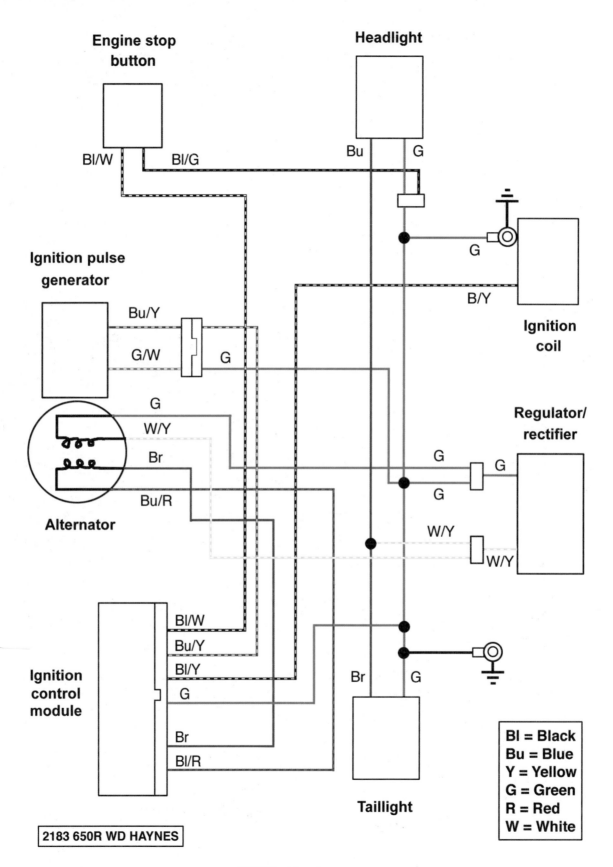

XR650R wiring diagram

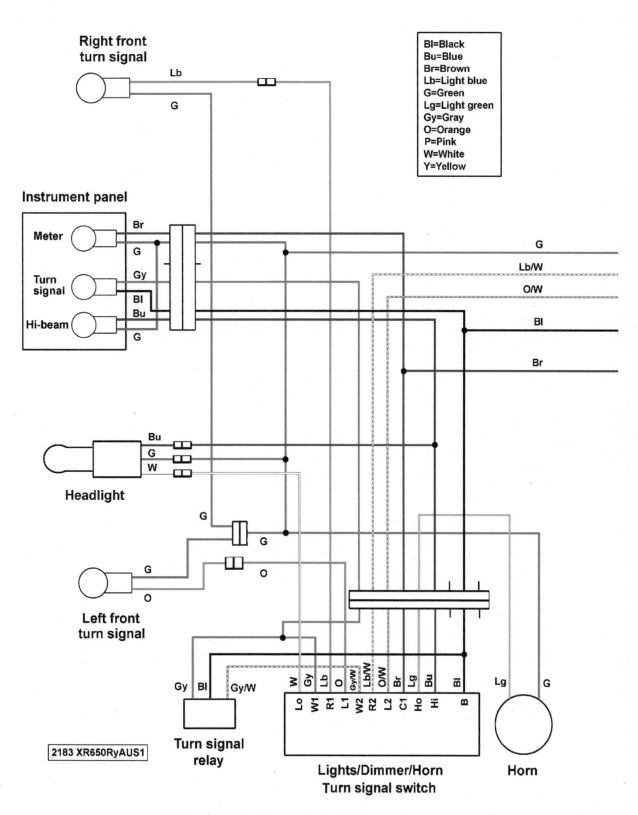

**Right front turn signal**

**Instrument panel**

Meter

Turn signal

Hi-beam

Bl=Black
Bu=Blue
Br=Brown
Lb=Light blue
G=Green
Lg=Light green
Gy=Gray
O=Orange
P=Pink
W=White
Y=Yellow

Headlight

**Left front turn signal**

2183 XR650RyAUS1

Turn signal relay

Lights/Dimmer/Horn
Turn signal switch

Horn

XR650Ry wiring diagram - Australian models (1 of 3)

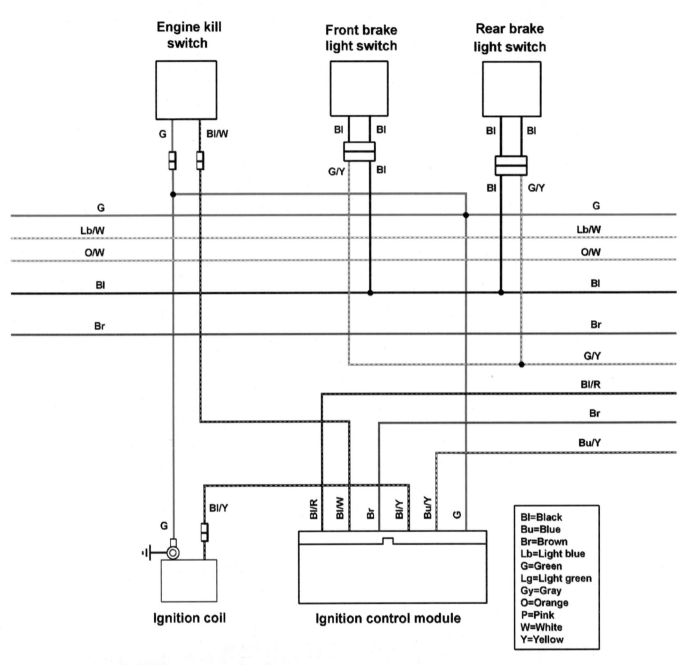

**Engine kill switch**

G    BI/W

**Front brake light switch**

BI    BI

G/Y    BI

**Rear brake light switch**

BI    BI

BI    G/Y

G

Lb/W

O/W

BI

Br

G

Lb/W

O/W

BI

Br

G/Y

BI/R

Br

Bu/Y

BI/Y

G

**Ignition coil**

BI/R    BI/W    Br    BI/Y    Bu/Y    G

**Ignition control module**

BI=Black
Bu=Blue
Br=Brown
Lb=Light blue
G=Green
Lg=Light green
Gy=Gray
O=Orange
P=Pink
W=White
Y=Yellow

2183 XR650RyAUS2

XR650Ry wiring diagram - Australian models (3 of 3)

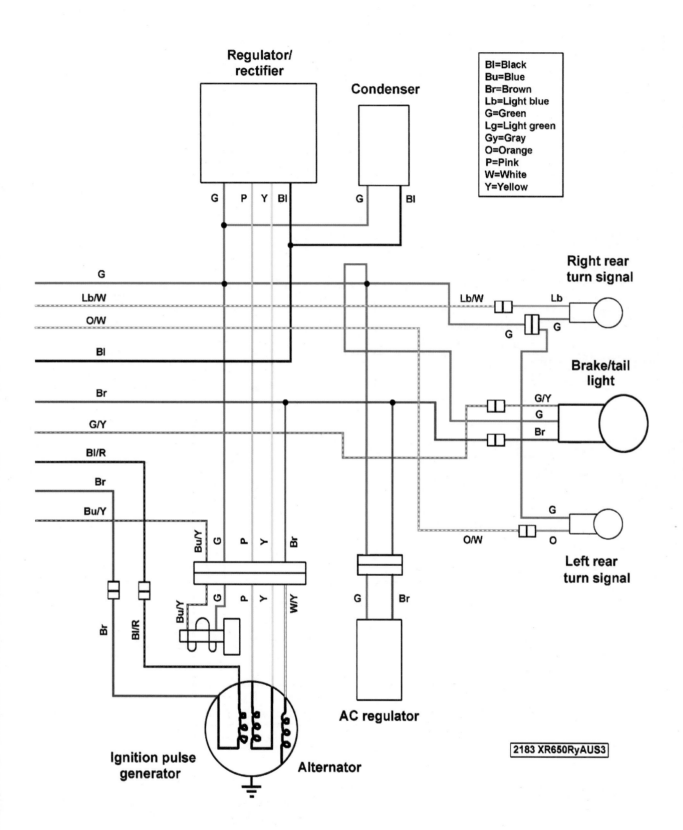

XR650Ry wiring diagram - Australian models (3 of 3)

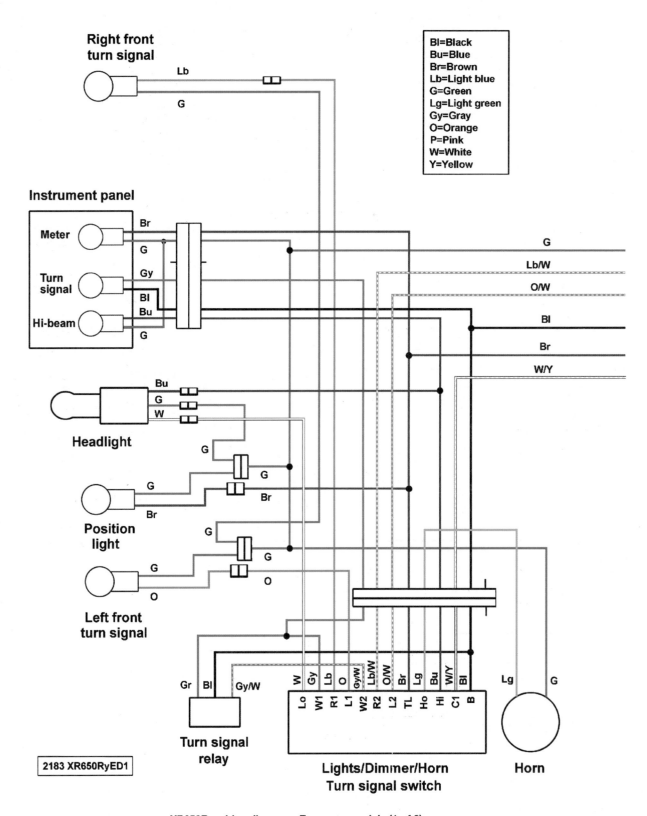

Right front
turn signal

Bl=Black
Bu=Blue
Br=Brown
Lb=Light blue
G=Green
Lg=Light green
Gy=Gray
O=Orange
P=Pink
W=White
Y=Yellow

Instrument panel

Meter

Turn
signal

Hi-beam

Headlight

Position
light

Left front
turn signal

Turn signal
relay

Lights/Dimmer/Horn
Turn signal switch

Horn

2183 XR650RyED1

XR650Ry wiring diagram - European models (1 of 3)

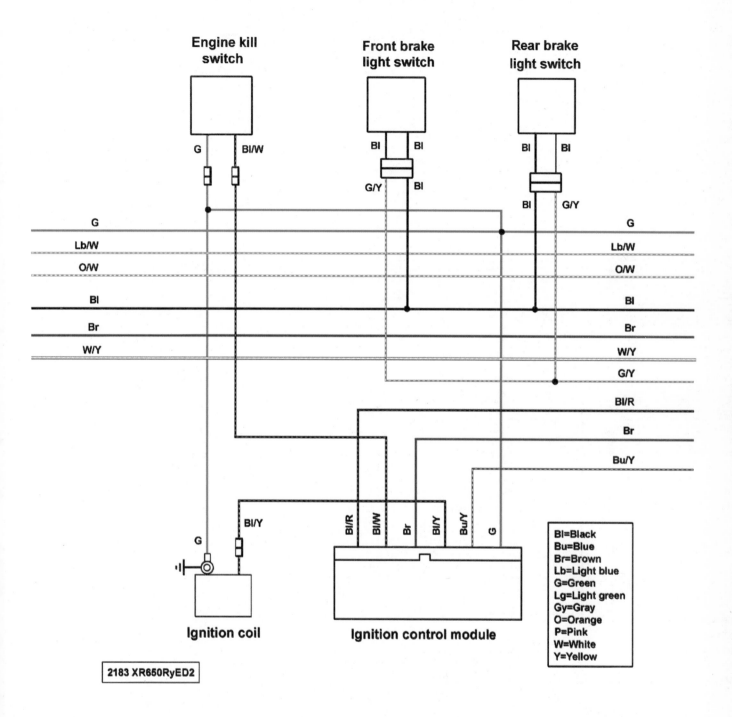

**Engine kill switch**

G    Bl/W

**Front brake light switch**

Bl    Bl

G/Y    Bl

**Rear brake light switch**

Bl    Bl

Bl    G/Y

G

Lb/W

O/W

Bl

Br

W/Y

G/Y

Bl/R

Br

Bu/Y

G

Lb/W

O/W

Bl

Br

W/Y

Bl/Y

G

**Ignition coil**

Bl/R    Bl/W    Br    Bl/Y    Bu/Y    G

**Ignition control module**

Bl=Black
Bu=Blue
Br=Brown
Lb=Light blue
G=Green
Lg=Light green
Gy=Gray
O=Orange
P=Pink
W=White
Y=Yellow

2183 XR650RyED2

XR650Ry wiring diagram - European models (2 of 3)

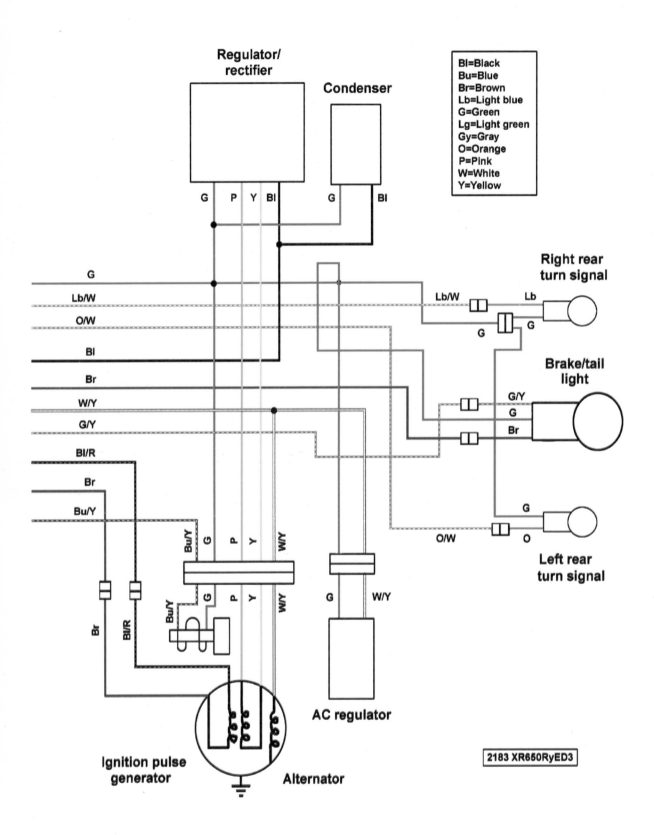

XR650Ry wiring diagram - European models (3 of 3)

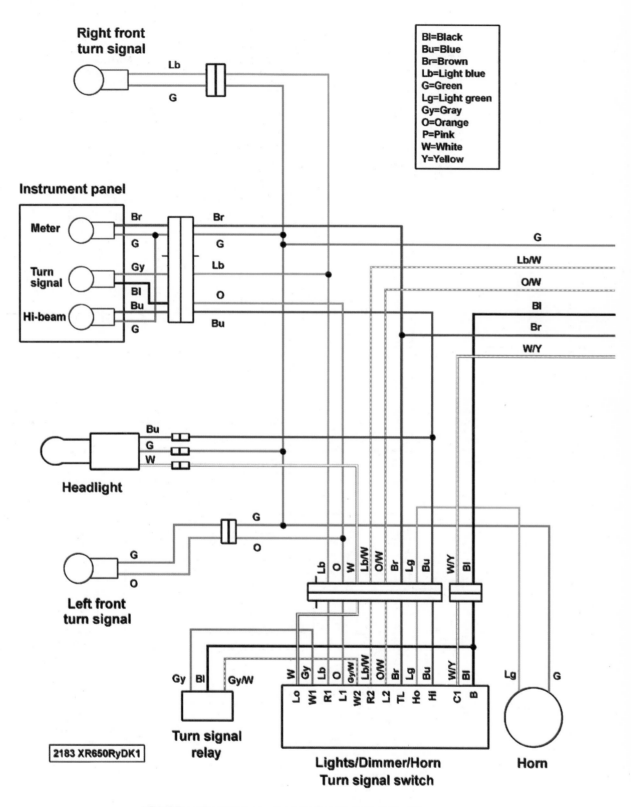

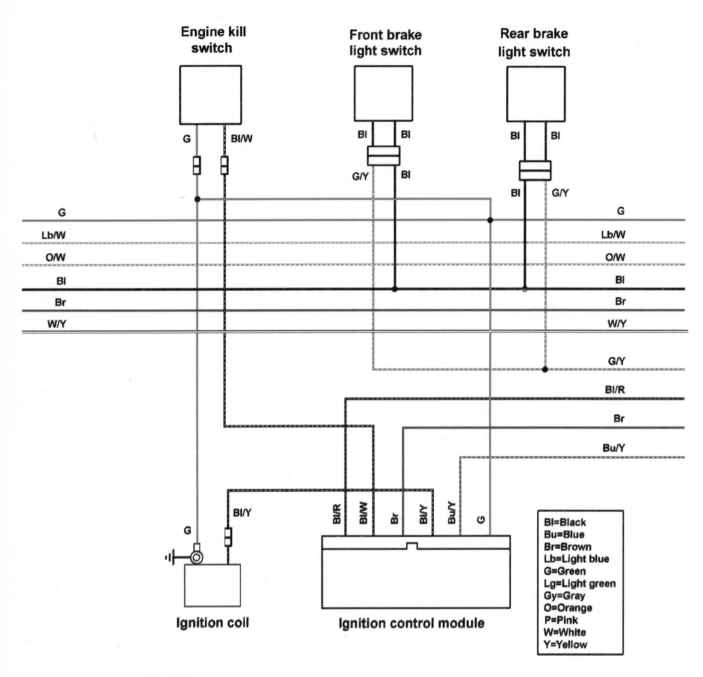

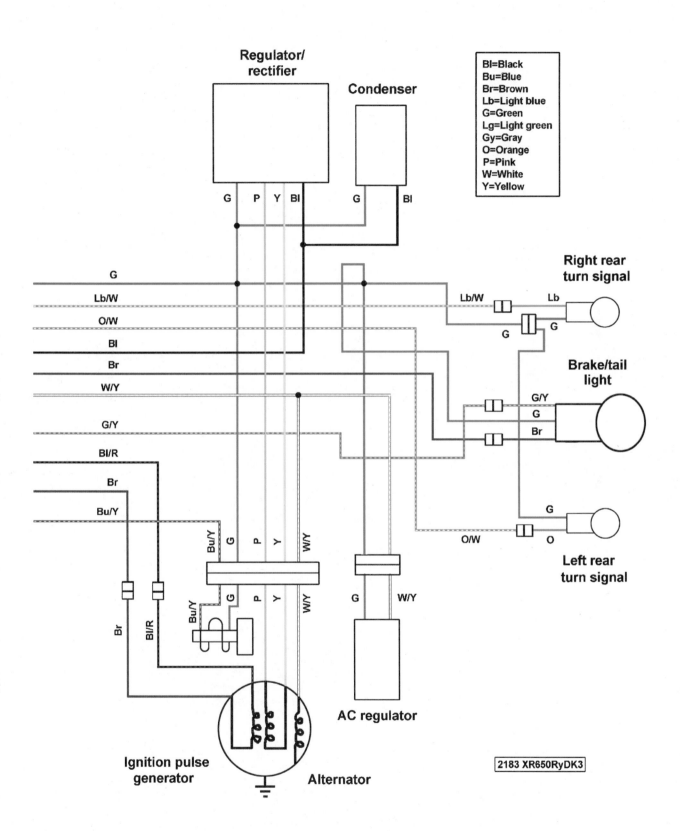

XR650Ry wiring diagram - General Export models (3 of 3)

# Notes

# Reference REF•1

# Dimensions and weights

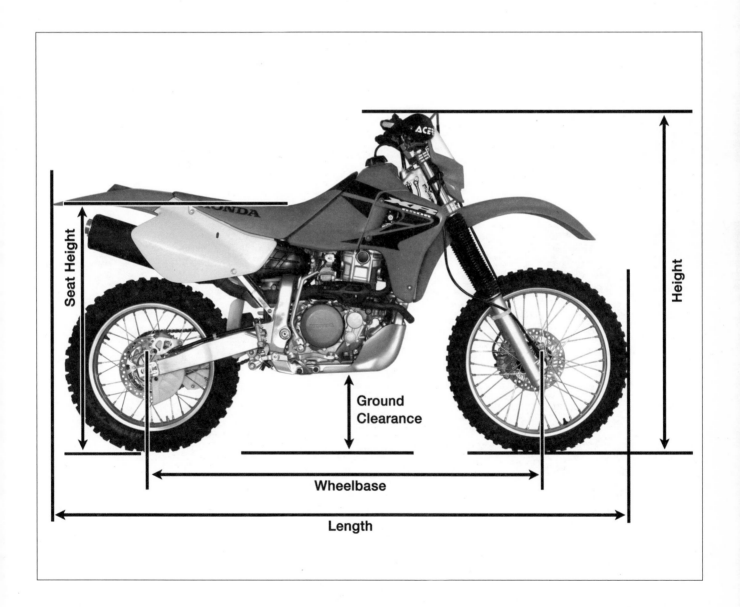

## General specifications

### Bore

XL600R ............................................................... 100.0 mm (3.94 inches)
XR600R ............................................................... 97.0 mm (3.82 inches)
XR650L ............................................................... 100.0 mm (3.94 inches)
XR650R ............................................................... 100.0 mm (3.94 inches)

### Stroke

XL600R ............................................................... 75.0 mm (2.95 inches)
XR600R ............................................................... 80.0 mm (3.15 inches)
XR650L ............................................................... 82.0 mm (3.23 inches)
XR650R ............................................................... 82.6 mm (3.25 inches)

### Compression ratio

XL600R
    1983 and 1984 ........................................................ 8.6 to 1
    1985 on ................................................................. 9.0 to 1
XR600R ............................................................... 9.0 to 1
XR650L ............................................................... 8.3 to 1
XR650R ............................................................... 10.0 to 1

### Horsepower

XL600R ............................................................... 43 at 6000 rpm
XR600R
    1985 through 1987 ................................................. 45 at 6500 rpm
    1988 on ................................................................. not specified
XR650L ............................................................... not specified
XR650R ............................................................... not specified

### Wheelbase

XL600R ............................................................... 1420 mm (55.9 inches)
XR600R
    1985 through 1987 ................................................. 1450 mm (57.1 inches)
    1988 through 1990 ................................................ 1460 mm (57.5 inches)
    1991 on ................................................................. 1455 mm (57.3 inches)
XR650L ............................................................... 1455 mm (57.3 inches)
XR650R ............................................................... 1477 mm (58.1 inches)
XR650Ry
    Europe and General Export ..................................... 1485 mm (58.5 inches)
    Australia ................................................................ 1490 mm (58.7 inches)

### Overall length

XL600R ............................................................... 2170 mm (85.4 inches)
XR600R
    1985 through 1987 ................................................. 2145 mm (84.4 inches)
    1988 on ................................................................. 2160 mm (85.0 inches)
XR650L
    1993 models ......................................................... 2185 mm (86.0 inches)
    1993 and later models ............................................ 2190 mm (86.2 inches)
XR650R ............................................................... 2195 mm (86.4 inches)
XR650Ry ............................................................. 2255 mm (88.8 inches)

### Overall width

XL600R ............................................................... 865 mm (34.1 inches)
XR600R
    1985 through 1987 ................................................. 910 mm (35.8 inches)
    1988 on ................................................................. 900 mm (35.5 inches)
XR650L ............................................................... 955 mm (33.7 inches)
XR650R ............................................................... 827 mm (32.6 inches)
XR650Ry ............................................................. 825 mm (32.5 inches)

## General specifications (continued)

### Overall height
| | |
|---|---|
| XL600R | 1235 mm (48.6 inches) |
| XR600R | |
|   1985 through 1987 | 1205 mm (47.4 inches) |
|   1988 through 1990 | 1220 mm (48.0 inches) |
|   1991 | 1230 mm (48.4 inches) |
|   1992 on | 1215 mm (47.8 inches) |
| XR650L, XR650Ry | 1245 mm (49.0 inches) |
| XR650R | 1239 mm (48.8 inches) |

### Seat height
| | |
|---|---|
| XL600R | 860 mm (33.9 inches) |
| XR600R | |
|   1985 through 1990 | 940 mm (37.0 inches) |
|   1991 on | 955 mm (37.6 inches) |
| XR650L | |
|   1993 models | 950 mm (37.4 inches) |
|   1993 and later models | 940 mm (37.0 inches) |
| XR650R | 935 mm (36.8 inches) |
| XR650Ry | 939 mm (37.0 inches) |

### Ground clearance
| | |
|---|---|
| XL600R | not specified |
| XR600R | |
|   1985 through 1990 | 320 mm (12.6 inches) |
|   1991 on | 345 mm (13.6 inches) |
| XR650L | 330 mm (13.0 inches) |
| XR650R, XR650Ry | 305 mm (12.0 inches) |

### Weight (approximate)
| | |
|---|---|
| XL600R* | 134 kg (295 lbs) |
| XR600R* | |
|   1985 through 1987 | 124 kg (267 lbs) |
|   1988 through 1990 | 119 kg (262 lbs) |
|   1991 | 122 kg (269 lbs) |
|   1992 on (except 1998 and later California models) | 123 kg (271 lbs) |
|   1998 and later California models | 124 kg (273 lbs) |
| XR650L* | |
|   USA models | |
|     1993 | 147 kg (324 lbs) |
|     1994 and later | 149 kg (328 lbs) |
|   All other markets | |
|     1993 | 145 kg (320 lbs) |
|     1994 through 1996 | 148 kg (326 lbs) |
|     1997 and later | 149 kg (328 lbs) |
| XR650R** | |
|   49 states (2006 and earlier models) and Canada | 136 kg (300 lbs) |
|   California and 2007 and later USA models | 138 kg (304 lbs) |
| XR650Ry* | |
|   Europe and General Export | 131 kg (289 lbs) |
|   Australia | 133 kg (293 lbs) |

\* Dry weight
\*\* Wet (curb) weight (dry weight not available)

# Trail rules

Just when you're ready to have some fun out in the dirt you get slapped with more rules. But by following these rules you'll ensure everyone's enjoyment, not just your own. It's important that all off-roaders follow these rules, as it will help to keep the trails open and keep us in good standing with other trail users. Really, these rules are no more than common sense and common courtesy.

• **Don't ride where you're not supposed to.** Stay off private property and obey all signs marking areas that are off limits to motorized vehicles. Also, as much fun as it might be, don't ride in State or Federal wilderness areas.

• **Leave the land as you found it.** When you've left the area, the only thing you should leave behind are your tire tracks. Stay on the trails, too. There are plenty of trails to ride on without blazing new ones. Be sure to carry out all litter that you create (and if you want to do a good deed, pick up any litter that you come across). Be sure to leave gates as you found them, or if the gate has a sign on it, comply with whatever the sign says (some people don't close gates after passing through them. Others may close gates when the landowner actually wants to keep them open).

• **Give other trail users the right-of-way.** There has been an ongoing dispute amongst trail users as to who belongs there and who doesn't. If the off-roading community shows respect and courtesy to hikers and equestrians, we stand a far better chance of being able to enjoy our sport in the years to come, and to keep the trails open for our children. When you ride up behind hikers or horses, give them plenty of room and pass slowly so as not to startle them. When you approach an equestrian from the opposite direction, stop your machine when the horse nears you so it won't get frightened and bolt.

• **Don't scare the animals!** Whether it be horses, cattle or wild animals like deer, rabbits or coyotes, leave them alone. Remember, you're visiting their home, so treat them with respect. Besides, startling animals can be dangerous. Loud noises or your sudden appearance can trigger an animal's defensive instinct, which could mean bad news for you.

• **Don't ride "over your head."** Sometimes the trails start to resemble ski runs, with a few irresponsible riders going so fast that they're barely able to maintain control of their bikes. They'd never be able to stop to avoid another trail user if they had to. Most collisions on the trail are caused by such individuals and the results are occasionally tragic. You should only ride fast in areas where you can clearly see a good distance ahead - never on trails with blind corners or rises high enough that prevent you from seeing what's on the other side.

• **Be prepared.** Carry everything you think you may need to make minor repairs should your machine break down. Know how to make basic repairs and keep your bike in good mechanical condition to minimize the chances of becoming stranded. Always let someone know where you're going, and ride with a friend whenever possible.

# Service record

| Date | Mileage/hours | Work performed |
| --- | --- | --- |
| | | |
| | | |
| | | |
| | | |
| | | |
| | | |
| | | |
| | | |
| | | |
| | | |
| | | |
| | | |
| | | |
| | | |
| | | |
| | | |
| | | |
| | | |
| | | |
| | | |
| | | |
| | | |
| | | |

## Buying tools

A good set of tools is a fundamental requirement for servicing and repairing a motorcycle. Although there will be an initial expense in building up enough tools for servicing, this will soon be offset by the savings made by doing the job yourself. As experience and confidence grow, additional tools can be added to enable the repair and overhaul of the motorcycle. Many of the special tools are expensive and not often used so it may be preferable to rent them, or for a group of friends or motorcycle club to join in the purchase.

As a rule, it is better to buy more expensive, good quality tools. Cheaper tools are likely to wear out faster and need to be replaced more often, nullifying the original savings.

*Warning: To avoid the risk of a poor quality tool breaking in use, causing injury or damage to the component being worked on, always aim to purchase tools which meet the relevant national safety standards.*

The following lists of tools do not represent the manufacturer's service tools, but serve as a guide to help the owner decide which tools are needed for this level of work. In addition, items such as an electric drill, hacksaw, files, soldering iron and a workbench equipped with a vise, may be needed. Although not classed as tools, a selection of bolts, screws, nuts, washers and pieces of tubing always come in useful.

For more information about tools, refer to the Haynes *Motorcycle Workshop Practice Techbook* (Bk. No. 3470).

## Manufacturer's service tools

Inevitably certain tasks require the use of a service tool. Where possible, an alternative tool or method of approach is recommended, but sometimes there is no option if personal injury or damage to the component is to be avoided. Where required, service tools are referred to in the relevant procedure.

Service tools can usually only be purchased from a motorcycle dealer and are identified by a part number. Some of the commonly-used tools, such as rotor pullers, are available in aftermarket form from mail-order motorcycle tool and accessory suppliers.

# Maintenance and minor repair tools

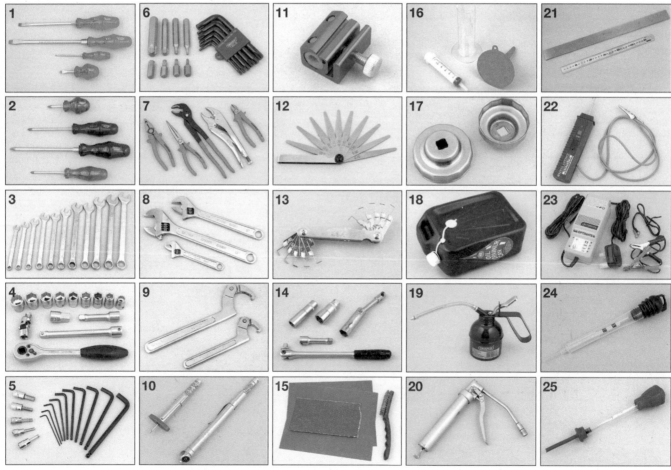

1 Set of flat-bladed screwdrivers
2 Set of Phillips head screwdrivers
3 Combination open-end and box wrenches
4 Socket set (3/8 inch or 1/2 inch drive)
5 Set of Allen keys or bits
6 Set of Torx keys or bits
7 Pliers, cutters and self-locking grips (vise grips)
8 Adjustable wrenches
9 C-spanners
10 Tread depth gauge and tire pressure gauge
11 Cable oiler clamp
12 Feeler gauges
13 Spark plug gap measuring tool
14 Spark plug wrench or deep plug sockets
15 Wire brush and emery paper
16 Calibrated syringe, measuring cup and funnel
17 Oil filter adapters
18 Oil drainer can or tray
19 Pump type oil can
20 Grease gun
21 Straight-edge and steel rule
22 Continuity tester
23 Battery charger
24 Hydrometer (for battery specific gravity check)
25 Anti-freeze tester (for liquid-cooled engines)

## Repair and overhaul tools

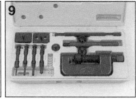

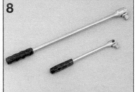

1 *Torque wrench (small and mid-ranges)*
2 *Conventional, plastic or soft-faced hammers*
3 *Impact driver set*
4 *Vernier caliper*
5 *Snap-ring pliers (internal and external, or combination)*
6 *Set of cold chisels and punches*
7 *Selection of pullers*
8 *Breaker bars*
9 *Chain breaking/ riveting tool set*
10 *Wire stripper and crimper tool*
11 *Multimeter (measures amps, volts and ohms)*
12 *Stroboscope (for dynamic timing checks)*
13 *Hose clamp (wingnut type shown)*
14 *Clutch holding tool*
15 *One-man brake/clutch bleeder kit*

## Special tools

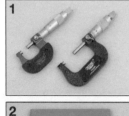

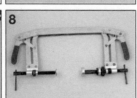

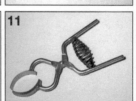

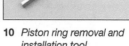

1 *Micrometers (external type)*
2 *Telescoping gauges*
3 *Dial gauge*
4 *Cylinder compression gauge*
5 *Vacuum gauges (left) or manometer (right)*
6 *Oil pressure gauge*
7 *Plastigage kit*
8 *Valve spring compressor (4-stroke engines)*
9 *Piston pin drawbolt tool*
10 *Piston ring removal and installation tool*
11 *Piston ring clamp*
12 *Cylinder bore hone (stone type shown)*
13 *Stud extractor*
14 *Screw extractor set*
15 *Bearing driver set*

## 1 Workshop equipment and facilities

### The workbench

● Work is made much easier by raising the bike up on a ramp - components are much more accessible if raised to waist level. The hydraulic or pneumatic types seen in the dealer's workshop are a sound investment if you undertake a lot of repairs or overhauls (see illustration 1.1).

**1.1 Hydraulic motorcycle ramp**

● If raised off ground level, the bike must be supported on the ramp to avoid it falling. Most ramps incorporate a front wheel locating clamp which can be adjusted to suit different diameter wheels. When tightening the clamp, take care not to mark the wheel rim or damage the tire - use wood blocks on each side to prevent this.
● Secure the bike to the ramp using tie-downs (see illustration 1.2). If the bike has only a sidestand, and hence leans at a dangerous angle when raised, support the bike on an auxiliary stand.

**1.2 Tie-downs are used around the passenger footrests to secure the bike**

● Auxiliary (paddock) stands are widely available from mail order companies or motorcycle dealers and attach either to the wheel axle or swingarm pivot (see illustration 1.3). If the motorcycle has a centerstand, you can support it under the crankcase to prevent it toppling while either wheel is removed (see illustration 1.4).

**1.3 This auxiliary stand attaches to the swingarm pivot**

**1.4 Always use a block of wood between the engine and jack head when supporting the engine in this way**

### Fumes and fire

● Refer to the Safety first! page at the beginning of the manual for full details. Make sure your workshop is equipped with a fire extinguisher suitable for fuel-related fires (Class B fire - flammable liquids) - it is not sufficient to have a water-filled extinguisher.
● Always ensure adequate ventilation is available. Unless an exhaust gas extraction system is available for use, ensure that the engine is run outside of the workshop.
● If working on the fuel system, make sure the workshop is ventilated to avoid a build-up of fumes. This applies equally to fume build-up when charging a battery. Do not smoke or allow anyone else to smoke in the workshop.

### Fluids

● If you need to drain fuel from the tank, store it in an approved container marked as suitable for the storage of gasoline (see illustration 1.5). Do not store fuel in glass jars

**1.5 Use an approved can only for storing gasoline**

or bottles.
● Use proprietary engine degreasers or solvents which have a high flash-point, such as kerosene, for cleaning off oil, grease and dirt - never use gasoline for cleaning. Wear rubber gloves when handling solvent and engine degreaser. The fumes from certain solvents can be dangerous - always work in a well-ventilated area.

### Dust, eye and hand protection

● Protect your lungs from inhalation of dust particles by wearing a filtering mask over the nose and mouth. Many frictional materials still contain asbestos which is dangerous to your health. Protect your eyes from spouts of liquid and sprung components by wearing a pair of protective

**1.6 A fire extinguisher, goggles, mask and protective gloves should be at hand in the workshop**

goggles (see illustration 1.6).
● Protect your hands from contact with solvents, fuel and oils by wearing rubber gloves. Alternatively apply a barrier cream to your hands before starting work. If handling hot components or fluids, wear suitable gloves to protect your hands from scalding and burns.

### What to do with old fluids

● Old cleaning solvent, fuel, coolant and oils should not be poured down domestic drains or onto the ground. Package the fluid up in old oil containers, label it accordingly, and take it to a garage or disposal facility. Contact your local disposal company for location of such sites.

*Note: It is illegal to dump oil down the drain. Check with your local auto parts store, disposal facility or environmental agency to see if they accept the oil for recycling.*

## 2 Fasteners - screws, bolts and nuts

### *Fastener types and applications*

#### Bolts and screws

● Fastener head types are either of hexagonal, Torx or splined design, with internal and external versions of each type (see illustrations 2.1 and 2.2); splined head fasteners are not in common use on motorcycles. The conventional slotted or Phillips head design is used for certain screws. Bolt or screw length is always measured from the underside of the head to the end of the item (see illustration 2.11).

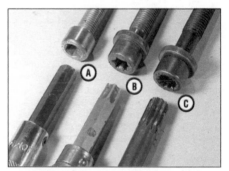

2.1 Internal hexagon/Allen (A), Torx (B) and splined (C) fasteners, with corresponding bits

2.2 External Torx (A), splined (B) and hexagon (C) fasteners, with corresponding sockets

● Certain fasteners on the motorcycle have a tensile marking on their heads, the higher the marking the stronger the fastener. High tensile fasteners generally carry a 10 or higher marking. Never replace a high tensile fastener with one of a lower tensile strength.

#### Washers (see illustration 2.3)

● Plain washers are used between a fastener head and a component to prevent damage to the component or to spread the load when torque is applied. Plain washers can also be used as spacers or shims in certain assemblies. Copper or aluminum plain washers are often used as sealing washers on drain plugs.

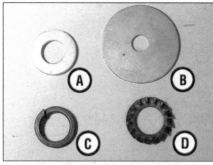

2.3 Plain washer (A), penny washer (B), spring washer (C) and serrated washer (D)

● The split-ring spring washer works by applying axial tension between the fastener head and component. If flattened, it is fatigued and must be replaced. If a plain (flat) washer is used on the fastener, position the spring washer between the fastener and the plain washer.
● Serrated star type washers dig into the fastener and component faces, preventing loosening. They are often used on electrical ground connections to the frame.
● Cone type washers (sometimes called Belleville) are conical and when tightened apply axial tension between the fastener head and component. They must be installed with the dished side against the component and often carry an OUTSIDE marking on their outer face. If flattened, they are fatigued and must be replaced.
● Tab washers are used to lock plain nuts or bolts on a shaft. A portion of the tab washer is bent up hard against one flat of the nut or bolt to prevent it loosening. Due to the tab washer being deformed in use, a new tab washer should be used every time it is removed.
● Wave washers are used to take up endfloat on a shaft. They provide light springing and prevent excessive side-to-side play of a component. Can be found on rocker arm shafts.

#### Nuts and cotter pins

● Conventional plain nuts are usually six-sided (see illustration 2.4). They are sized by thread diameter and pitch. High tensile nuts carry a number on one end to denote their tensile strength.

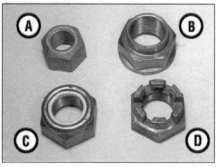

2.4 Plain nut (A), shouldered locknut (B), nylon insert nut (C) and castellated nut (D)

● Self-locking nuts either have a nylon insert, or two spring metal tabs, or a shoulder which is staked into a groove in the shaft - their advantage over conventional plain nuts is a resistance to loosening due to vibration. The nylon insert type can be used a number of times, but must be replaced when the friction of the nylon insert is reduced, i.e. when the nut spins freely on the shaft. The spring tab type can be reused unless the tabs are damaged. The shouldered type must be replaced every time it is removed.
● Cotter pins are used to lock a castellated nut to a shaft or to prevent loosening of a plain nut. Common applications are wheel axles and brake torque arms. Because the cotter pin arms are deformed to lock around the nut, a new cotter pin must always be used on installation - always use the correct size cotter pin which will fit snugly in the shaft hole. Make sure the cotter pin arms are correctly located around the nut (see illustrations 2.5 and 2.6).

2.5 Bend cotter pin arms as shown (arrows) to secure a castellated nut

2.6 Bend cotter pin arms as shown to secure a plain nut

*Caution: If the castellated nut slots do not align with the shaft hole after tightening to the torque setting, tighten the nut until the next slot aligns with the hole - never loosen the nut to align its slot.*

● R-pins (shaped like the letter R), or slip pins as they are sometimes called, are sprung and can be reused if they are otherwise in good condition. Always install R-pins with their closed end facing forwards (see illustration 2.7).

**2.7 Correct fitting of R-pin.
Arrow indicates forward direction**

### Snap-rings (see illustration 2.8)

● Snap-rings (sometimes called circlips) are used to retain components on a shaft or in a housing and have corresponding external or internal ears to permit removal. Parallel-sided (machined) snap-rings can be installed either way round in their groove, whereas stamped snap-rings (which have a chamfered edge on one face) must be installed with the chamfer facing away from the direction of thrust load **(see illustration 2.9)**.

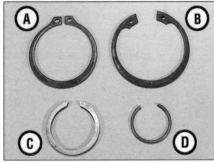

**2.8 External stamped snap-ring (A),
internal stamped snap-ring (B), machined
snap-ring (C) and wire snap-ring (D)**

● Always use snap-ring pliers to remove and install snap-rings; expand or compress them just enough to remove them. After installation, rotate the snap-ring in its groove to ensure it is securely seated. If installing a snap-ring on a splined shaft, always align its opening with a shaft channel to ensure the snap-ring ends are well supported and unlikely to catch **(see illustration 2.10)**.

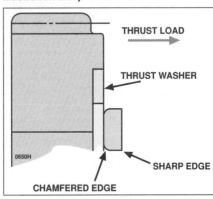

**2.9 Correct fitting of a stamped snap-ring**

THRUST LOAD

THRUST WASHER

SHARP EDGE

CHAMFERED EDGE

0650H

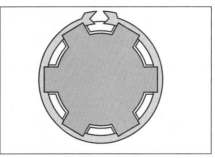

**2.10 Align snap-ring opening
with shaft channel**

● Snap-rings can wear due to the thrust of components and become loose in their grooves, with the subsequent danger of becoming dislodged in operation. For this reason, replacement is advised every time a snap-ring is disturbed.

● Wire snap-rings are commonly used as piston pin retaining clips. If a removal tang is provided, long-nosed pliers can be used to dislodge them, otherwise careful use of a small flat-bladed screwdriver is necessary. Wire snap-rings should be replaced every time they are disturbed.

### *Thread diameter and pitch*

● Diameter of a male thread (screw, bolt or stud) is the outside diameter of the threaded portion **(see illustration 2.11)**. Most motor-cycle manufacturers use the ISO (International Standards Organization) metric system expressed in millimeters. For example, M6 refers to a 6 mm diameter thread. Sizing is the same for nuts, except that the thread diameter is measured across the valleys of the nut.

● Pitch is the distance between the peaks of the thread **(see illustration 2.11)**. It is expressed in millimeters, thus a common bolt size may be expressed as 6.0 x 1.0 mm (6 mm thread diameter and 1 mm pitch). Generally pitch increases in proportion to thread diameter, although there are always exceptions.

● Thread diameter and pitch are related for conventional fastener applications and the accompanying table can be used as a guide. Additionally, the AF (Across Flats), wrench or socket size dimension of the bolt or nut **(see illustration 2.11)** is linked to thread and pitch specification. Thread pitch can be measured with a thread gauge **(see illustration 2.12)**.

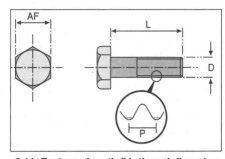

AF

L

D

P

**2.11 Fastener length (L), thread diameter
(D), thread pitch (P) and head size (AF)**

**2.12 Using a thread gauge
to measure pitch**

| AF size | Thread diameter x pitch (mm) |
|---------|------------------------------|
| 8 mm    | M5 x 0.8                     |
| 8 mm    | M6 x 1.0                     |
| 10 mm   | M6 x 1.0                     |
| 12 mm   | M8 x 1.25                    |
| 14 mm   | M10 x 1.25                   |
| 17 mm   | M12 x 1.25                   |

● The threads of most fasteners are of the right-hand type, and they are turned clockwise to tighten, and counterclockwise to loosen. The reverse situation applies to left-hand thread fasteners, which are turned counter-clockwise to tighten and clockwise to loosen. Left-hand threads are used where rotation of a component might loosen a conventional right-hand thread fastener.

### *Seized fasteners*

● Corrosion of external fasteners due to water or reaction between two dissimilar metals can occur over a period of time. It will build up sooner in wet conditions or in areas where salt is used on the roads during the winter. If a fastener is severely corroded it is likely that normal methods of removal will fail, and result in its head being ruined. When you attempt removal, the fastener thread should be heard to crack free and unscrew easily - if it doesn't, stop there before damaging something.

● A sharp tap on the head of the fastener will often succeed in breaking free corrosion which has occurred in the threads **(see illustration 2.13)**.

● An aerosol penetrating fluid (such as WD-40) applied the night beforehand may work its way down into the thread and ease removal. Depending on the location, you may be able to make up a modeling-clay well around the

**2.13 A sharp tap on the head of a fastener
will often break free a corroded thread**

fastener head and fill it with penetrating fluid.

● If you are working on an engine internal component, corrosion will most likely not be a problem due to the well lubricated environment. However, components can be very tight and an impact driver is a useful tool

**2.14 Using an impact driver to free a fastener**

in freeing them **(see illustration 2.14)**.

● Where corrosion has occurred between dissimilar metals (like steel and aluminum alloy), the application of heat to the fastener head will create a disproportionate expansion rate between the two metals and break the seizure caused by the corrosion. Whether heat can be applied depends on the location of the fastener - any surrounding components likely to be damaged must first be removed **(see illustration 2.15)**. Heat can be applied using a paint stripper heat gun or clothes iron, or by immersing the component in boiling water - wear protective gloves to prevent scalding or burns to the hands.

**2.15 Using heat to free a seized fastener**

● As a last resort, it is possible to use a hammer and cold chisel to work the fastener head unscrewed **(see illustration 2.16)**. This will damage the fastener, but more importantly, extreme care must be taken not to damage the surrounding component.

*Caution: Remember that the component being secured is generally of more value than the bolt, nut or screw - when the fastener is freed, do not unscrew it with force, instead work the fastener back and forth when resistance is felt to prevent thread damage.*

**2.16 Using a hammer and chisel to free a seized fastener**

## Broken fasteners and damaged heads

● If the shank of a broken bolt or screw is accessible, you can grip it with self-locking grips. The knurled wheel type stud extractor tool or self-gripping stud puller tool is particularly useful for removing the long studs which screw into the cylinder mouth surface of the crankcase, or bolts and screws from which the head has broken off **(see illustration 2.17)**. Studs can also be removed by locking two nuts together on the threaded end of the stud and using a wrench on the lower nut **(see illustration 2.18)**.

**2.17 Using a stud extractor tool to remove a broken crankcase stud**

**2.18 Two nuts can be locked together to unscrew a stud from a component**

● A bolt or screw which has broken off below or level with the casing must be extracted using a screw extractor set. Centerpunch the fastener to centralize the drill bit, then drill a hole in the fastener **(see illustration 2.19)**. Select a drill bit which is approximately half to three-quarters the diameter of the fastener

**2.19 When using a screw extractor, first drill a hole in the fastener . . .**

and drill to a depth which will accommodate the extractor. Use the largest size extractor possible, but avoid leaving too small a wall thickness, otherwise the extractor will merely force the fastener walls outwards, wedging it in the casing thread.

● If a spiral type extractor is used, thread it counterclockwise into the fastener. As it is screwed in, it will grip the fastener and unscrew it from the casing **(see illustration 2.20)**.

**2.20 . . . then thread the extractor counterclockwise into the fastener**

● If a taper type extractor is used, tap it into the fastener so that it is firmly wedged in place. Unscrew the extractor (counterclockwise) to draw the fastener out.

> ⚠ *Warning: Stud extractors are very hard and may break off in the fastener if care is not taken - ask a machine shop about spark erosion if this happens.*

● Alternatively, the broken bolt/screw can be drilled out and the hole retapped for an oversize bolt/screw or a diamond-section thread insert. It is essential that the drilling is carried out squarely and to the correct depth, otherwise the casing may be ruined - if in doubt, entrust the work to a machine shop.

● Bolts and nuts with rounded corners cause the correct size wrench or socket to slip when force is applied. Of the types of wrench/socket available always use a six-point type rather than an eight or twelve-point type - better grip

**2.21 Comparison of surface drive box wrench (left) with 12-point type (right)**

is obtained. Surface drive wrenches grip the middle of the hex flats, rather than the corners, and are thus good in cases of damaged heads (see illustration 2.21).

● Slotted-head or Phillips-head screws are often damaged by the use of the wrong size screwdriver. Allen-head and Torx-head screws are much less likely to sustain damage. If enough of the screw head is exposed you can use a hacksaw to cut a slot in its head and then use a conventional flat-bladed screwdriver to remove it. Alternatively use a hammer and cold chisel to tap the head of the fastener around to loosen it. Always replace damaged fasteners with new ones, preferably Torx or Allen-head type.

**HAYNES HiNT**

*A dab of valve grinding compound between the screw head and screwdriver tip will often give a good grip.*

## Thread repair

● Threads (particularly those in aluminum alloy components) can be damaged by overtightening, being assembled with dirt in the threads, or from a component working loose and vibrating. Eventually the thread will fail completely, and it will be impossible to tighten the fastener.

● If a thread is damaged or clogged with old locking compound it can be renovated with a thread repair tool (thread chaser) (see illustrations 2.22 and 2.23); special thread

**2.22 A thread repair tool being used to correct an internal thread**

**2.23 A thread repair tool being used to correct an external thread**

chasers are available for spark plug hole threads. The tool will not cut a new thread, but clean and true the original thread. Make sure that you use the correct diameter and pitch tool. Similarly, external threads can be cleaned up with a die or a thread restorer file (see illustration 2.24).

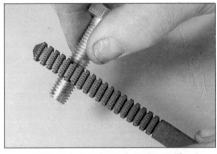

**2.24 Using a thread restorer file**

● It is possible to drill out the old thread and retap the component to the next thread size. This will work where there is enough surrounding material and a new bolt or screw can be obtained. Sometimes, however, this is not possible - such as where the bolt/screw passes through another component which must also be suitably modified, also in cases where a spark plug or oil drain plug cannot be obtained in a larger diameter thread size.

● The diamond-section thread insert (often known by its popular trade name of Heli-Coil) is a simple and effective method of replacing the thread and retaining the original size. A kit can be purchased which contains the tap, insert and installing tool (see illustration 2.25). Drill out the damaged thread with the size drill specified (see illustration 2.26). Carefully retap the thread (see illustration 2.27). Install the

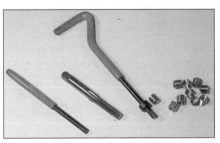

**2.25 Obtain a thread insert kit to suit the thread diameter and pitch required**

**2.26 To install a thread insert, first drill out the original thread . . .**

**2.27 . . . tap a new thread . . .**

**2.28 . . . fit the insert on the installing tool . . .**

**2.29 . . . and thread it into the component . . .**

**2.30 . . . break off the tang when complete**

insert on the installing tool and thread it slowly into place using a light downward pressure (see illustrations 2.28 and 2.29). When positioned between a 1/4 and 1/2 turn below the surface withdraw the installing tool and use the break-off tool to press down on the tang, breaking it off (see illustration 2.30).

● There are epoxy thread repair kits on the market which can rebuild stripped internal threads, although this repair should not be used on high load-bearing components.

## Thread locking and sealing compounds

● Locking compounds are used in locations where the fastener is prone to loosening due to vibration or on important safety-related items which might cause loss of control of the motorcycle if they fail. It is also used where important fasteners cannot be secured by other means such as lockwashers or cotter pins.

● Before applying locking compound, make sure that the threads (internal and external) are clean and dry with all old compound removed. Select a compound to suit the component being secured - a non-permanent general locking and sealing type is suitable for most applications, but a high strength type is needed for permanent fixing of studs in castings. Apply a drop or two of the compound to the first few threads of the fastener, then thread it into place and tighten to the specified torque. Do not apply excessive thread locking compound otherwise the thread may be damaged on subsequent removal.

● Certain fasteners are impregnated with a dry film type coating of locking compound on their threads. Always replace this type of fastener if disturbed.

● Anti-seize compounds, such as copper-based greases, can be applied to protect threads from seizure due to extreme heat and corrosion. A common instance is spark plug threads and exhaust system fasteners.

## 3 Measuring tools and gauges

### Feeler gauges

● Feeler gauges (or blades) are used for measuring small gaps and clearances (see illustration 3.1). They can also be used to measure endfloat (sideplay) of a component on a shaft where access is not possible with a dial gauge.

● Feeler gauge sets should be treated with care and not bent or damaged. They are etched with their size on one face. Keep them clean and very lightly oiled to prevent corrosion build-up.

**3.1 Feeler gauges are used for measuring small gaps and clearances - thickness is marked on one face of gauge**

● When measuring a clearance, select a gauge which is a light sliding fit between the two components. You may need to use two gauges together to measure the clearance accurately.

### Micrometers

● A micrometer is a precision tool capable of measuring to 0.01 or 0.001 of a millimeter. It should always be stored in its case and not in the general toolbox. It must be kept clean and never dropped, otherwise its frame or measuring anvils could be distorted, resulting in inaccurate readings.

● External micrometers are used for measuring outside diameters of components and have many more applications than internal micrometers. Micrometers are available in different size ranges, typically 0 to 25 mm, 25 to 50 mm, and upwards in 25 mm steps; some large micrometers have interchangeable anvils to allow a range of measurements to be taken. Generally the largest precision measurement you are likely to take on a motorcycle is the piston diameter.

● Internal micrometers (or bore micrometers) are used for measuring inside diameters, such as valve guides and cylinder bores. Telescoping gauges and small hole gauges are used in conjunction with an external micrometer, whereas the more expensive internal micrometers have their own measuring device.

### External micrometer

**Note:** *The conventional analogue type instrument is described. Although much easier to read, digital micrometers are considerably more expensive.*

● Always check the calibration of the micrometer before use. With the anvils closed (0 to 25 mm type) or set over a test gauge

**3.2 Check micrometer calibration before use**

(for the larger types) the scale should read zero **(see illustration 3.2)**; make sure that the anvils (and test piece) are clean first. Any discrepancy can be adjusted by referring to the instructions supplied with the tool. Remember that the micrometer is a precision measuring tool - don't force the anvils closed, use the ratchet (4) on the end of the micrometer to close it. In this way, a measured force is always applied.

● To use, first make sure that the item being measured is clean. Place the anvil of the micrometer (1) against the item and use the thimble (2) to bring the spindle (3) lightly into contact with the other side of the item **(see illustration 3.3)**. Don't tighten the thimble down because this will damage the micrometer - instead use the ratchet (4) on the end of the micrometer. The ratchet mechanism applies a measured force preventing damage to the instrument.

● The micrometer is read by referring to the linear scale on the sleeve and the annular scale on the thimble. Read off the sleeve first to obtain the base measurement, then add the fine measurement from the thimble to obtain the overall reading. The linear scale on the sleeve represents the measuring range of the micrometer (eg 0 to 25 mm). The annular scale

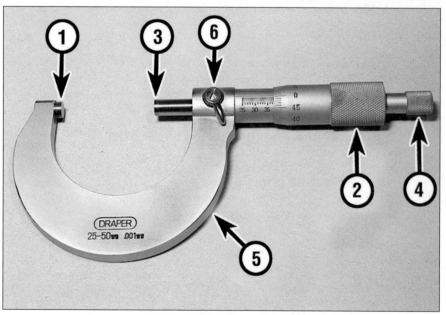

**3.3 Micrometer component parts**

| | | |
|---|---|---|
| 1 Anvil | 3 Spindle | 5 Frame |
| 2 Thimble | 4 Ratchet | 6 Locking lever |

on the thimble will be in graduations of 0.01 mm (or as marked on the frame) - one full revolution of the thimble will move 0.5 mm on the linear scale. Take the reading where the datum line on the sleeve intersects the thimble's scale. Always position the eye directly above the scale, otherwise an inaccurate reading will result.

In the example shown, the item measures 2.95 mm (see illustration 3.4):

| Linear scale | 2.00 mm |
|---|---|
| Linear scale | 0.50 mm |
| Annular scale | 0.45 mm |
| Total figure | **2.95 mm** |

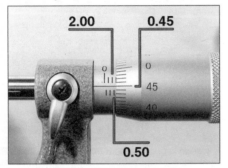

3.4 Micrometer reading of 2.95 mm

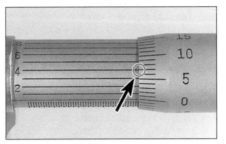

3.5 Micrometer reading of 46.99 mm on linear and annular scales . . .

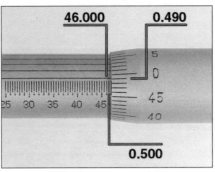

3.6 . . . and 0.004 mm on vernier scale

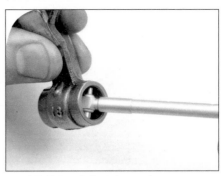

3.7 Expand the telescoping gauge in the bore, lock its position . . .

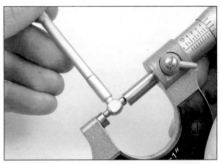

3.8 . . . then measure the gauge with a micrometer

Most micrometers have a locking lever (6) on the frame to hold the setting in place, allowing the item to be removed from the micrometer.
● Some micrometers have a vernier scale on their sleeve, providing an even finer measurement to be taken, in 0.001 increments of a millimeter. Take the sleeve and thimble measurement as described above, then check which graduation on the vernier scale aligns with that of the annular scale on the thimble. **Note:** *The eye must be perpendicular to the scale when taking the vernier reading - if necessary rotate the body of the micrometer to ensure this.* Multiply the vernier scale figure by 0.001 and add it to the base and fine measurement figures.

In the example shown, the item measures 46.994 mm (see illustrations 3.5 and 3.6):

| Linear scale (base) | 46.000 mm |
|---|---|
| Linear scale (base) | 00.500 mm |
| Annular scale (fine) | 00.490 mm |
| Vernier scale | 00.004 mm |
| Total figure | **46.994 mm** |

### Internal micrometer

● Internal micrometers are available for measuring bore diameters, but are expensive and unlikely to be available for home use. It is suggested that a set of telescoping gauges and small hole gauges, both of which must be used with an external micrometer, will suffice for taking internal measurements on a motorcycle.
● Telescoping gauges can be used to measure internal diameters of components. Select a gauge with the correct size range, make sure its ends are clean and insert it into the bore. Expand the gauge, then lock its position and withdraw it from the bore (see illustration 3.7). Measure across the gauge ends with a micrometer (see illustration 3.8).
● Very small diameter bores (such as valve guides) are measured with a small hole gauge. Once adjusted to a slip-fit inside the component, its position is locked and the gauge withdrawn for measurement with a micrometer (see illustrations 3.9 and 3.10).

### Vernier caliper

**Note:** *The conventional linear and dial gauge type instruments are described. Digital types are easier to read, but are far more expensive.*
● The vernier caliper does not provide the precision of a micrometer, but is versatile in being able to measure internal and external diameters. Some types also incorporate a depth gauge. It is ideal for measuring clutch plate friction material and spring free lengths.
● To use the conventional linear scale vernier, loosen off the vernier clamp screws (1) and set its jaws over (2), or inside (3), the item to be measured (see illustration 3.11). Slide the jaw into contact, using the thumb-wheel (4) for fine movement of the sliding scale (5) then tighten the clamp screws (1). Read off the main scale (6) where the zero on the sliding scale (5) intersects it, taking the whole number to the left of the zero; this provides the base measurement. View along the sliding scale and select the division which lines up exactly

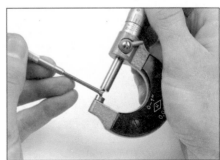

3.9 Expand the small hole gauge in the bore, lock its position . . .

3.10 . . . then measure the gauge with a micrometer

with any of the divisions on the main scale, noting that the divisions usually represents 0.02 of a millimeter. Add this fine measurement to the base measurement to obtain the total reading.

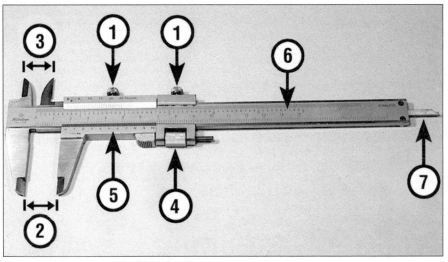

**3.11 Vernier component parts (linear gauge)**

| | | | |
|---|---|---|---|
| 1 *Clamp screws* | 3 *Internal jaws* | 5 *Sliding scale* | 7 *Depth gauge* |
| 2 *External jaws* | 4 *Thumbwheel* | 6 *Main scale* | |

In the example shown, the item measures 55.92 mm **(see illustration 3.12)**:

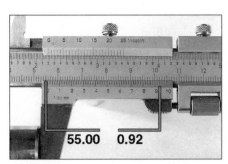

**3.12 Vernier gauge reading of 55.92 mm**

| Base measurement | 55.00 mm |
|---|---|
| Fine measurement | 00.92 mm |
| Total figure | **55.92 mm** |

● Some vernier calipers are equipped with a dial gauge for fine measurement. Before use, check that the jaws are clean, then close them fully and check that the dial gauge reads zero. If necessary adjust the gauge ring accordingly. Slacken the vernier clamp screw (1) and set its jaws over (2), or inside (3), the item to be measured **(see illustration 3.13)**. Slide the jaws into contact, using the thumbwheel (4) for fine movement. Read off the main scale (5) where the edge of the sliding scale (6) intersects it, taking the whole number to the left of the zero; this provides the base measurement. Read off the needle position on the dial gauge (7) scale to provide the fine measurement; each division represents 0.05 of a millimeter. Add this fine measurement to the base measurement to obtain the total reading.

In the example shown, the item measures 55.95 mm **(see illustration 3.14)**:

| Base measurement | 55.00 mm |
|---|---|
| Fine measurement | 00.95 mm |
| Total figure | **55.95 mm** |

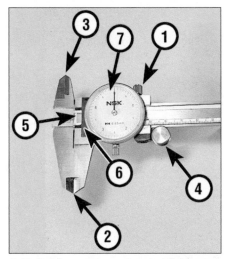

**3.13 Vernier component parts (dial gauge)**

| | |
|---|---|
| 1 *Clamp screw* | 5 *Main scale* |
| 2 *External jaws* | 6 *Sliding scale* |
| 3 *Internal jaws* | 7 *Dial gauge* |
| 4 *Thumbwheel* | |

**3.14 Vernier gauge reading of 55.95 mm**

## *Plastigage*

● Plastigage is a plastic material which can be compressed between two surfaces to measure the oil clearance between them. The width of the compressed Plastigage is measured against a calibrated scale to determine the clearance.

● Common uses of Plastigage are for measuring the clearance between crankshaft journal and main bearing inserts, between crankshaft journal and big-end bearing inserts, and between camshaft and bearing surfaces. The following example describes big-end oil clearance measurement.

● Handle the Plastigage material carefully to prevent distortion. Using a sharp knife, cut a length which corresponds with the width of the bearing being measured and place it carefully across the journal so that it is parallel with the shaft **(see illustration 3.15)**. Carefully install both bearing shells and the connecting rod. Without rotating the rod on the journal tighten its bolts or nuts (as applicable) to the specified torque. The connecting rod and bearings are then disassembled and the crushed Plastigage examined.

**3.15 Plastigage placed across shaft journal**

● Using the scale provided in the Plastigage kit, measure the width of the material to determine the oil clearance **(see illustration 3.16)**. Always remove all traces of Plastigage after use using your fingernails.

> *Caution: Arriving at the correct clearance demands that the assembly is torqued correctly, according to the settings and sequence (where applicable) provided by the motorcycle manufacturer.*

**3.16 Measuring the width of the crushed Plastigage**

## Dial gauge or DTI (Dial Test Indicator)

● A dial gauge can be used to accurately measure small amounts of movement. Typical uses are measuring shaft runout or shaft endfloat (sideplay) and setting piston position for ignition timing on two-strokes. A dial gauge set usually comes with a range of different probes and adapters and mounting equipment.

● The gauge needle must point to zero when at rest. Rotate the ring around its periphery to zero the gauge.

● Check that the gauge is capable of reading the extent of movement in the work. Most gauges have a small dial set in the face which records whole millimeters of movement as well as the fine scale around the face periphery which is calibrated in 0.01 mm divisions. Read off the small dial first to obtain the base measurement, then add the measurement from the fine scale to obtain the total reading.

| Base measurement | 1.00 mm |
|---|---|
| Fine measurement | 0.48 mm |
| Total figure | **1.48 mm** |

**3.17  Dial gauge reading of 1.48 mm**

In the example shown the gauge reads 1.48 mm **(see illustration 3.17)**:

● If measuring shaft runout, the shaft must be supported in vee-blocks and the gauge mounted on a stand perpendicular to the shaft. Rest the tip of the gauge against the center of the shaft and rotate the shaft slowly while watching the gauge reading **(see illustration 3.18)**. Take several measurements along the length of the shaft and record the

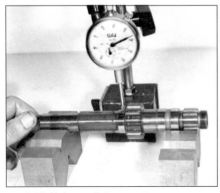

**3.18  Using a dial gauge to measure shaft runout**

maximum gauge reading as the amount of runout in the shaft. **Note:** *The reading obtained will be total runout at that point - some manufacturers specify that the runout figure is halved to compare with their specified runout limit.*

● Endfloat (sideplay) measurement requires that the gauge is mounted securely to the surrounding component with its probe touching the end of the shaft. Using hand pressure, push and pull on the shaft noting the maximum endfloat recorded on the gauge **(see illustration 3.19)**.

**3.19  Using a dial gauge to measure shaft endfloat**

● A dial gauge with suitable adapters can be used to determine piston position BTDC on two-stroke engines for the purposes of ignition timing. The gauge, adapter and suitable length probe are installed in the place of the spark plug and the gauge zeroed at TDC. If the piston position is specified as 1.14 mm BTDC, rotate the engine back to 2.00 mm BTDC, then slowly forwards to 1.14 mm BTDC.

## Cylinder compression gauges

● A compression gauge is used for measuring cylinder compression. Either the rubber-cone type or the threaded adapter type can be used. The latter is preferred to ensure a perfect seal against the cylinder head. A 0 to 300 psi (0 to 20 Bar) type gauge (for gasoline engines) will be suitable for motorcycles.

● The spark plug is removed and the gauge either held hard against the cylinder head (cone type) or the gauge adapter screwed into the cylinder head (threaded type) **(see illustration 3.20)**. Cylinder compression is measured with the engine turning over, but not running - carry out the compression test as described in

**3.20  Using a rubber-cone type cylinder compression gauge**

*Troubleshooting Equipment*. The gauge will hold the reading until manually released.

## Oil pressure gauge

● An oil pressure gauge is used for measuring engine oil pressure. Most gauges come with a set of adapters to fit the thread of the take-off point **(see illustration 3.21)**. If the take-off point specified by the motorcycle manufacturer is an external oil pipe union, make sure that the specified replacement union is used to prevent oil starvation.

**3.21  Oil pressure gauge and take-off point adapter (arrow)**

● Oil pressure is measured with the engine running (at a specific rpm) and often the manufacturer will specify pressure limits for a cold and hot engine.

## Straight-edge and surface plate

● If checking the gasket face of a component for warpage, place a steel rule or precision straight-edge across the gasket face and measure any gap between the straight-edge and component with feeler gauges **(see illustration 3.22)**. Check diagonally across the component and between mounting holes **(see illustration 3.23)**.

**3.22  Use a straight-edge and feeler gauges to check for warpage**

**3.23  Check for warpage in these directions**

● Checking individual components for warpage, such as clutch plain (metal) plates, requires a perfectly flat plate or piece of plate glass and feeler gauges.

## 4  Torque and leverage

### What is torque?

● Torque describes the twisting force around a shaft. The amount of torque applied is determined by the distance from the center of the shaft to the end of the lever and the amount of force being applied to the end of the lever; distance multiplied by force equals torque.

● The manufacturer applies a measured torque to a bolt or nut to ensure that it will not loosen in use and to hold two components securely together without movement in the joint. The actual torque setting depends on the thread size, bolt or nut material and the composition of the components being held.

● Too little torque may cause the fastener to loosen due to vibration, whereas too much torque will distort the joint faces of the component or cause the fastener to shear off. Always stick to the specified torque setting.

### Using a torque wrench

● Check the calibration of the torque wrench and make sure it has a suitable range for the job. Torque wrenches are available in Nm (Newton-meters), kgf m (kilograms-force meter), lbf ft (pounds-feet), lbf in (inch-pounds). Do not confuse lbf ft with lbf in.

● Adjust the tool to the desired torque on the scale (see illustration 4.1). If your torque wrench is not calibrated in the units specified, carefully convert the figure (see Conversion Factors). A manufacturer sometimes gives a torque setting as a range (8 to 10 Nm) rather than a single figure - in this case set the tool midway between the two settings. The same torque may be expressed as 9 Nm ± 1 Nm. Some torque wrenches have a method of locking the setting so that it isn't inadvertently altered during use.

**4.1  Set the torque wrench index mark to the setting required, in this case 12 Nm**

● Install the bolts/nuts in their correct location and secure them lightly. Their threads must be clean and free of any old locking compound. Unless specified the threads and flange should be dry - oiled threads are necessary in certain circumstances and the manufacturer will take this into account in the specified torque figure. Similarly, the manufacturer may also specify the application of thread-locking compound.

● Tighten the fasteners in the specified sequence until the torque wrench clicks, indicating that the torque setting has been reached. Apply the torque again to double-check the setting. Where different thread diameter fasteners secure the component, as a rule tighten the larger diameter ones first.

● When the torque wrench has been finished with, release the lock (where applicable) and fully back off its setting to zero - do not leave the torque wrench tensioned. Also, do not use a torque wrench for loosening a fastener.

### Angle-tightening

● Manufacturers often specify a figure in degrees for final tightening of a fastener. This usually follows tightening to a specific torque setting.

● A degree disc can be set and attached to the socket (see illustration 4.2) or a protractor can be used to mark the angle of movement on the bolt/nut head and the surrounding casting (see illustration 4.3).

**4.2  Angle tightening can be accomplished with a torque-angle gauge . . .**

**4.3  . . . or by marking the angle on the surrounding component**

### Loosening sequences

● Where more than one bolt/nut secures a component, loosen each fastener evenly a little at a time. In this way, not all the stress of the joint is held by one fastener and the components are not likely to distort.

● If a tightening sequence is provided, work in the REVERSE of this, but if not, work from the outside in, in a criss-cross sequence (see illustration 4.4).

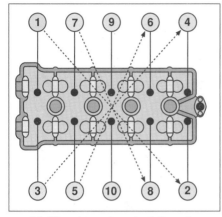

**4.4  When loosening, work from the outside inwards**

### Tightening sequences

● If a component is held by more than one fastener it is important that the retaining bolts/nuts are tightened evenly to prevent uneven stress build-up and distortion of sealing faces. This is especially important on high-compression joints such as the cylinder head.

● A sequence is usually provided by the manufacturer, either in a diagram or actually marked in the casting. If not, always start in the center and work outwards in a criss-cross pattern (see illustration 4.5). Start off by securing all bolts/nuts finger-tight, then set the torque wrench and tighten each fastener by a small amount in sequence until the final torque is reached. By following this practice,

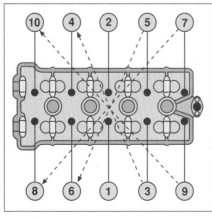

**4.5  When tightening, work from the inside outwards**

the joint will be held evenly and will not be distorted. Important joints, such as the cylinder head and big-end fasteners often have two- or three-stage torque settings.

### Applying leverage

● Use tools at the correct angle. Position a socket or wrench on the bolt/nut so that you pull it towards you when loosening. If this can't be done, push the wrench without curling your fingers around it **(see illustration 4.6)** - the wrench may slip or the fastener loosen suddenly, resulting in your fingers being crushed against a component.

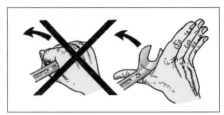

**4.6 If you can't pull on the wrench to loosen a fastener, push with your hand open**

● Additional leverage is gained by extending the length of the lever. The best way to do this is to use a breaker bar instead of the regular length tool, or to slip a length of tubing over the end of the wrench or socket.
● If additional leverage will not work, the fastener head is either damaged or firmly corroded in place (see *Fasteners*).

## 5  Bearings

### Bearing removal and installation

#### Drivers and sockets

● Before removing a bearing, always inspect the casing to see which way it must be driven out - some casings will have retaining plates or a cast step. Also check for any identifying markings on the bearing and, if installed to a certain depth, measure this at this stage. Some roller bearings are sealed on one side - take note of the original installed position.
● Bearings can be driven out of a casing using a bearing driver tool (with the correct size head) or a socket of the correct diameter. Select the driver head or socket so that it contacts the outer race of the bearing, not the balls/rollers or inner race. Always support the casing around the bearing housing with wood blocks, otherwise there is a risk of fracture. The bearing is driven out with a few blows on the driver or socket from a heavy mallet. Unless access is severely restricted (as with wheel bearings), a pin-punch is not recommended unless it is moved around the bearing to keep it square in its housing.

● The same equipment can be used to install bearings. Make sure the bearing housing is supported on wood blocks and line up the bearing in its housing. Install the bearing as noted on removal - generally they are installed with their marked side facing outwards. Tap the bearing squarely into its housing using a driver or socket which bears only on the bearing's outer race - contact with the bearing balls/rollers or inner race will destroy it **(see illustrations 5.1 and 5.2)**.
● Check that the bearing inner race and balls/rollers rotate freely.

**5.1  Using a bearing driver against the bearing's outer race**

**5.2  Using a large socket against the bearing's outer race**

#### Pullers and slide-hammers

● Where a bearing is pressed on a shaft a puller will be required to extract it **(see illustration 5.3)**. Make sure that the puller clamp or legs fit securely behind the bearing and are unlikely to slip out. If pulling a bearing

**5.3  This bearing puller clamps behind the bearing and pressure is applied to the shaft end to draw the bearing off**

off a gear shaft for example, you may have to locate the puller behind a gear pinion if there is no access to the race and draw the gear pinion off the shaft as well **(see illustration 5.4)**.

> *Caution: Ensure that the puller's center bolt locates securely against the end of the shaft and will not slip when pressure is applied. Also ensure that puller does not damage the shaft end.*

**5.4  Where no access is available to the rear of the bearing, it is sometimes possible to draw off the adjacent component**

● Operate the puller so that its center bolt exerts pressure on the shaft end and draws the bearing off the shaft.
● When installing the bearing on the shaft, tap only on the bearing's inner race - contact with the balls/rollers or outer race will destroy the bearing. Use a socket or length of tubing as a drift which fits over the shaft end **(see illustration 5.5)**.

**5.5  When installing a bearing on a shaft, use a piece of tubing which bears only on the bearing's inner race**

● Where a bearing locates in a blind hole in a casing, it cannot be driven or pulled out as described above. A slide-hammer with knife-edged bearing puller attachment will be required. The puller attachment passes through the bearing and when tightened expands to fit firmly behind the bearing **(see illustration 5.6)**. By operating the slide-hammer part of the tool the bearing is jarred out of its housing **(see illustration 5.7)**.
● It is possible, if the bearing is of reasonable weight, for it to drop out of its housing if the casing is heated as described opposite. If

**5.6 Expand the bearing puller so that it locks behind the bearing . . .**

**5.7 . . . attach the slide hammer to the bearing puller**

this method is attempted, first prepare a work surface which will enable the casing to be tapped face down to help dislodge the bearing - a wood surface is ideal since it will not damage the casing's gasket surface. Wearing protective gloves, tap the heated casing several times against the work surface to dislodge the bearing under its own weight **(see illustration 5.8)**.

**5.8 Tapping a casing face down on wood blocks can often dislodge a bearing**

● Bearings can be installed in blind holes using the driver or socket method described above.

## Drawbolts

● Where a bearing or bushing is set in the eye of a component, such as a suspension linkage arm or connecting rod small-end, removal by drift may damage the component. Furthermore, a rubber bushing in a shock absorber eye cannot successfully be driven out of position. If access is available to a hydraulic press, the task is straightforward. If not, a drawbolt can be fabricated to extract the bearing or bushing.

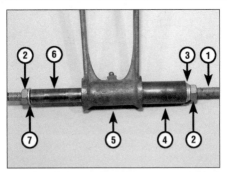

**5.9 Drawbolt component parts assembled on a suspension arm**

1 Bolt or length of threaded bar
2 Nuts
3 Washer (external diameter greater than tubing internal diameter)
4 Tubing (internal diameter sufficient to accommodate bearing)
5 Suspension arm with bearing
6 Tubing (external diameter slightly smaller than bearing)
7 Washer (external diameter slightly smaller than bearing)

**5.10 Drawing the bearing out of the suspension arm**

● To extract the bearing/bushing you will need a long bolt with nut (or piece of threaded bar with two nuts), a piece of tubing which has an internal diameter larger than the bearing/bushing, another piece of tubing which has an external diameter slightly smaller than the bearing/bushing, and a selection of washers **(see illustrations 5.9 and 5.10)**. Note that the pieces of tubing must be of the same length, or longer, than the bearing/bushing.
● The same kit (without the pieces of tubing) can be used to draw the new bearing/bushing back into place **(see illustration 5.11)**.

## Temperature change

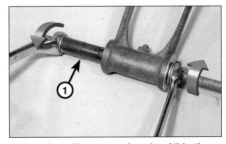

**5.11 Installing a new bearing (1) in the suspension arm**

● If the bearing's outer race is a tight fit in the casing, the aluminum casing can be heated to release its grip on the bearing. Aluminum will expand at a greater rate than the steel bearing outer race. There are several ways to do this, but avoid any localized extreme heat (such as a blow torch) - aluminum alloy has a low melting point.
● Approved methods of heating a casing are using a domestic oven (heated to 100°C/200°F) or immersing the casing in boiling water **(see illustration 5.12)**. Low temperature range localized heat sources such as a paint stripper heat gun or clothes iron can also be used **(see illustration 5.13)**. Alternatively, soak a rag in boiling water, wring it out and wrap it around the bearing housing.
● If heating the whole casing note that

> ⚠ **Warning: All of these methods require care in use to prevent scalding and burns to the hands. Wear protective gloves when handling hot components.**

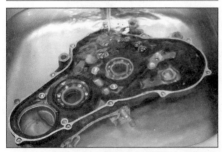

**5.12 A casing can be immersed in a sink of boiling water to aid bearing removal**

**5.13 Using a localized heat source to aid bearing removal**

plastic components, such as the neutral switch, may suffer - remove them beforehand.
● After heating, remove the bearing as described above. You may find that the expansion is sufficient for the bearing to fall out of the casing under its own weight or with a light tap on the driver or socket.
● If necessary, the casing can be heated to aid bearing installation, and this is sometimes the recommended procedure if the motorcycle manufacturer has designed the housing and bearing fit with this intention.

● Installation of bearings can be eased by placing them in a freezer the night before installation. The steel bearing will contract slightly, allowing easy insertion in its housing. This is often useful when installing steering head outer races in the frame.

### Bearing types and markings

● Plain shell bearings, ball bearings, needle roller bearings and tapered roller bearings will all be found on motorcycles (see illustrations 5.14 and 5.15). The ball and roller types are usually caged between an inner and outer race, but uncaged variations may be found.

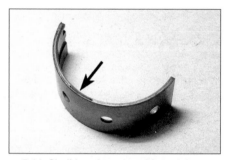

5.14 Shell bearings are either plain or grooved. They are usually identified by color code (arrow)

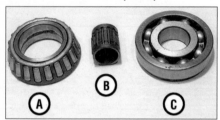

5.15 Tapered roller bearing (A), needle roller bearing (B) and ball journal bearing (C)

● Shell bearings (often called inserts) are usually found at the crankshaft main and connecting rod big-end where they are good at coping with high loads. They are made of a phosphor-bronze material and are impregnated with self-lubricating properties.

● Ball bearings and needle roller bearings consist of a steel inner and outer race with the balls or rollers between the races. They require constant lubrication by oil or grease and are good at coping with axial loads. Taper roller bearings consist of rollers set in a tapered cage set on the inner race; the outer race is separate. They are good at coping with axial loads and prevent movement along the shaft - a typical application is in the steering head.

● Bearing manufacturers produce bearings to ISO size standards and stamp one face of the bearing to indicate its internal and external diameter, load capacity and type (see illustration 5.16).

● Metal bushings are usually of phosphor-bronze material. Rubber bushings are used in suspension mounting eyes. Fiber bushings have also been used in suspension pivots.

5.16 Typical bearing marking

### Bearing troubleshooting

● If a bearing outer race has spun in its housing, the housing material will be damaged. You can use a bearing locking compound to bond the outer race in place if damage is not too severe.

● Shell bearings will fail due to damage of their working surface, as a result of lack of lubrication, corrosion or abrasive particles in the oil (see illustration 5.17). Small particles of dirt in the oil may embed in the bearing material whereas larger particles will score the bearing and shaft journal. If a number of short journeys are made, insufficient heat will be generated to drive off condensation which has built up on the bearings.

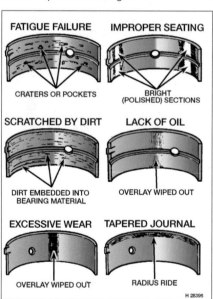

5.17 Typical bearing failures

● Ball and roller bearings will fail due to lack of lubrication or damage to the balls or rollers. Tapered-roller bearings can be damaged by overloading them. Unless the bearing is sealed on both sides, wash it in kerosene to remove all old grease, then allow it to dry. Make a visual inspection looking to dented balls or rollers, damaged cages and worn or pitted races (see illustration 5.18).

● A ball bearing can be checked for wear by listening to it when spun. Apply a film of light oil to the bearing and hold it close to the ear - hold the outer race with one hand and spin the

5.18 Example of ball journal bearing with damaged balls and cages

5.19 Hold outer race and listen to inner race when spun

inner race with the other hand (see illustration 5.19). The bearing should be almost silent when spun; if it grates or rattles it is worn.

### 6 Oil seals

### Oil seal removal and installation

● Oil seals should be replaced every time a component is dismantled. This is because the seal lips will become set to the sealing surface and will not necessarily reseal.

● Oil seals can be pried out of position using a large flat-bladed screwdriver (see illustration 6.1). In the case of crankcase seals, check first that the seal is not lipped on the inside, preventing its removal with the crankcases joined.

6.1 Pry out oil seals with a large flat-bladed screwdriver

● New seals are usually installed with their marked face (containing the seal reference code) outwards and the spring side towards the fluid being retained. In certain cases, such as a two-stroke engine crankshaft seal, a double lipped seal may be used due to there being fluid or gas on each side of the joint.

● Use a bearing driver or socket which bears only on the outer hard edge of the seal to install it in the casing - tapping on the inner edge will damage the sealing lip.

### Oil seal types and markings

● Oil seals are usually of the single-lipped type. Double-lipped seals are found where a liquid or gas is on both sides of the joint.

● Oil seals can harden and lose their sealing ability if the motorcycle has been in storage for a long period - replacement is the only solution.

● Oil seal manufacturers also conform to the ISO markings for seal size - these are molded into the outer face of the seal (see illustration 6.2).

**6.2 These oil seal markings indicate inside diameter, outside diameter and seal thickness**

## 7  Gaskets and sealants

### Types of gasket and sealant

● Gaskets are used to seal the mating surfaces between components and keep lubricants, fluids, vacuum or pressure contained within the assembly. Aluminum gaskets are sometimes found at the cylinder joints, but most gaskets are paper-based. If the mating surfaces of the components being joined are undamaged, the gasket can be installed dry, although a dab of sealant or grease will be useful to hold it in place during assembly.

● RTV (Room Temperature Vulcanizing) silicone rubber sealants cure when exposed to moisture in the atmosphere. These sealants are good at filling pits or irregular gasket faces, but will tend to be forced out of the joint under very high torque. They can be used to replace a paper gasket, but first make sure that the width of the paper gasket is not essential to the shimming of internal components. RTV sealants should not be used on components containing gasoline.

● Non-hardening, semi-hardening and hard setting liquid gasket compounds can be used with a gasket or between a metal-to-metal joint. Select the sealant to suit the application: universal non-hardening sealant can be used on virtually all joints; semi-hardening on joint faces which are rough or damaged; hard setting sealant on joints which require a permanent bond and are subjected to high temperature and pressure. **Note:** Check first if the paper gasket has a bead of sealant

*impregnated in its surface before applying additional sealant.*

● When choosing a sealant, make sure it is suitable for the application, particularly if being applied in a high-temperature area or in the vicinity of fuel. Certain manufacturers produce sealants in either clear, silver or black colors to match the finish of the engine. This has a particular application on motorcycles where much of the engine is exposed.

● Do not over-apply sealant. That which is squeezed out on the outside of the joint can be wiped off, whereas an excess of sealant on the inside can break off and clog oilways.

### Breaking a sealed joint

● Age, heat, pressure and the use of hard setting sealant can cause two components to stick together so tightly that they are difficult to separate using finger pressure alone. Do not resort to using levers unless there is a pry point provided for this purpose (see illustration 7.1), or else the gasket surfaces will be damaged.

● Use a soft-faced hammer (see illustration 7.2) or a wood block and conventional hammer to strike the component near the mating surface. Avoid hammering against cast extremities since they may break off. If this method fails, try using a wood wedge between the two components.

> **Caution: If the joint will not separate, double-check that you have removed all the fasteners.**

**7.1 If a pry point is provided, apply gentle pressure with a flat-bladed screwdriver**

**7.2 Tap around the joint with a soft-faced mallet if necessary - don't strike cooling fins**

### Removal of old gasket and sealant

● Paper gaskets will most likely come away complete, leaving only a few traces stuck

*Most components have one or two hollow locating dowels between the two gasket faces. If a dowel cannot be removed, do not resort to gripping it with pliers - it will almost certainly be distorted. Install a close-fitting socket or Phillips screwdriver into the dowel and then grip the outer edge of the dowel to free it.*

on the sealing faces of the components. It is imperative that all traces are removed to ensure correct sealing of the new gasket.

● Very carefully scrape all traces of gasket away, making sure that the sealing surfaces are not gouged or scored by the scraper (see illustrations 7.3, 7.4 and 7.5). Stubborn deposits can be removed by spraying with an aerosol gasket remover. Final preparation of

**7.3 Paper gaskets can be scraped off with a gasket scraper tool . . .**

**7.4 . . . a knife blade . . .**

**7.5 . . . or a household scraper**

**7.6 Fine abrasive paper is wrapped around a flat file to clean up the gasket face**

**7.7 A kitchen scourer can be used on stubborn deposits**

the gasket surface can be made with very fine abrasive paper or a plastic kitchen scourer **(see illustrations 7.6 and 7.7)**.

● Old sealant can be scraped or peeled off components, depending on the type originally used. Note that gasket removal compounds are available to avoid scraping the components clean; make sure the gasket remover suits the type of sealant used.

## 8 Chains

### Breaking and joining "endless" final drive chains

● Drive chains for many larger bikes are continuous and do not have a clip-type connecting link. The chain must be broken using a chain breaker tool and the new chain securely riveted together using a new soft rivet-type link. Never use a clip-type connecting link instead of a rivet-type link, except in an emergency. Various chain breaking and riveting tools are available, either as separate tools or combined as illustrated in the accompanying photographs - read the instructions supplied with the tool carefully.

> ⚠ **Warning: The need to rivet the new link pins correctly cannot be overstressed - loss of control of the motorcycle is very likely to result if the chain breaks in use.**

● Rotate the chain and look for the soft link. The soft link pins look like they have been

**8.1 Tighten the chain breaker to push the pin out of the link . . .**

**8.2 . . . withdraw the pin, remove the tool . . .**

**8.3 . . . and separate the chain link**

deeply center-punched instead of peened over like all the other pins **(see illustration 8.9)** and its sideplate may be a different color. Position the soft link midway between the sprockets and assemble the chain breaker tool over one of the soft link pins **(see illustration 8.1)**. Operate the tool to push the pin out through the chain **(see illustration 8.2)**. On an O-ring chain, remove the O-rings **(see illustration 8.3)**. Carry out the same procedure on the other soft link pin.

> **Caution: Certain soft link pins (particularly on the larger chains) may require their ends to be filed or ground off before they can be pressed out using the tool.**

● Check that you have the correct size and strength (standard or heavy duty) new soft link - do not reuse the old link. Look for the size marking on the chain sideplates **(see illustration 8.10)**.
● Position the chain ends so that they are

**8.4 Insert the new soft link, with O-rings, through the chain ends . . .**

**8.5 . . . install the O-rings over the pin ends . . .**

**8.6 . . . followed by the sideplate**

engaged over the rear sprocket. On an O-ring chain, install a new O-ring over each pin of the link and insert the link through the two chain ends **(see illustration 8.4)**. Install a new O-ring over the end of each pin, followed by the sideplate (with the chain manufacturer's marking facing outwards) **(see illustrations 8.5 and 8.6)**. On an unsealed chain, insert the link through the two chain ends, then install the sideplate with the chain manufacturer's marking facing outwards.

● Note that it may not be possible to install the sideplate using finger pressure alone. If using a joining tool, assemble it so that the plates of the tool clamp the link and press the sideplate over the pins **(see illustration 8.7)**. Otherwise, use two small sockets placed over

**8.7 Push the sideplate into position using a clamp**

**8.8 Assemble the chain riveting tool over one pin at a time and tighten it fully**

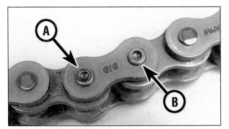

**8.9 Pin end correctly riveted (A), pin end unriveted (B)**

the rivet ends and two pieces of the wood between a C-clamp. Operate the clamp to press the sideplate over the pins.

● Assemble the joining tool over one pin (following the manufacturer's instructions) and tighten the tool down to spread the pin end securely **(see illustrations 8.8 and 8.9)**. Do the same on the other pin.

> ⚠ **Warning: Check that the pin ends are secure and that there is no danger of the sideplate coming loose. If the pin ends are cracked, the soft link must be replaced.**

## Final drive chain sizing

● Chains are sized using a three digit number, followed by a suffix to denote the chain type **(see illustration 8.10)**. Chain type is either standard or heavy duty (thicker sideplates), and also unsealed or O-ring/X-ring type.

● The first digit of the number relates to the pitch of the chain, which is the distance from the center of one pin to the center of the next pin **(see illustration 8.11)**. Pitch is expressed in eighths of an inch, as follows:

**8.10 Typical chain size and type marking**

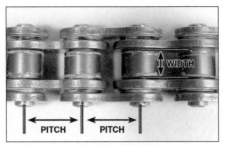

**8.11 Chain dimensions**

| Sizes commencing with a 4 (for example 428) have a pitch of 1/2 inch (12.7 mm) |
| Sizes commencing with a 5 (for example 520) have a pitch of 5/8 inch (15.9 mm) |
| Sizes commencing with a 6 (for example 630) have a pitch of 3/4 inch (19.1 mm) |

● The second and third digits of the chain size relate to the width of the rollers, for example the 525 shown has 5/16 inch (7.94 mm) rollers **(see illustration 8.11)**.

## 9 Hoses

### Clamping to prevent flow

● Small-bore flexible hoses can be clamped to prevent fluid flow while a component is worked on. Whichever method is used, ensure that the hose material is not permanently distorted or damaged by the clamp.

a) *A brake hose clamp available from auto parts stores (see illustration 9.1).*

b) *A wingnut type hose clamp (see illustration 9.2).*

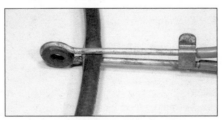

**9.1 Hoses can be clamped with an automotive brake hose clamp . . .**

**9.2 . . . a wingnut type hose clamp . . .**

c) *Two sockets placed on each side of the hose and held with straight-jawed self-locking pliers (see illustration 9.3).*

d) *Thick card stock on each side of the hose held between straight-jawed self-locking pliers (see illustration 9.4).*

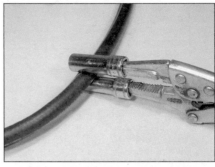

**9.3 . . . two sockets and a pair of self-locking grips . . .**

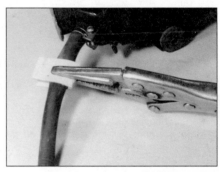

**9.4 . . . or thick card and self-locking grips**

### Freeing and fitting hoses

● Always make sure the hose clamp is moved well clear of the hose end. Grip the hose with your hand and rotate it while pulling it off the union. If the hose has hardened due to age and will not move, slit it with a sharp knife and peel its ends off the union **(see illustration 9.5)**.

● Resist the temptation to use grease or soap on the unions to aid installation; although it helps the hose slip over the union it will equally aid the escape of fluid from the joint. It is preferable to soften the hose ends in hot water and wet the inside surface of the hose with water or a fluid which will evaporate.

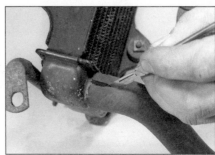

**9.5 Cutting a coolant hose free with a sharp knife**

# Conversion Factors

## Length (distance)

| | | | | |
|---|---|---|---|---|
| Inches (in) | X 25.4 | = Millimeters (mm) | X 0.0394 | = Inches (in) |
| Feet (ft) | X 0.305 | = Meters (m) | X 3.281 | = Feet (ft) |
| Miles | X 1.609 | = Kilometers (km) | X 0.621 | = Miles |

## Volume (capacity)

| | | | | |
|---|---|---|---|---|
| Cubic inches (cu in; in³) | X 16.387 | = Cubic centimeters (cc; cm³) | X 0.061 | = Cubic inches (cu in; in³) |
| Imperial pints (Imp pt) | X 0.568 | = Liters (l) | X 1.76 | = Imperial pints (Imp pt) |
| Imperial quarts (Imp qt) | X 1.137 | = Liters (l) | X 0.88 | = Imperial quarts (Imp qt) |
| Imperial quarts (Imp qt) | X 1.201 | = US quarts (US qt) | X 0.833 | = Imperial quarts (Imp qt) |
| US quarts (US qt) | X 0.946 | = Liters (l) | X 1.057 | = US quarts (US qt) |
| Imperial gallons (Imp gal) | X 4.546 | = Liters (l) | X 0.22 | = Imperial gallons (Imp gal) |
| Imperial gallons (Imp gal) | X 1.201 | = US gallons (US gal) | X 0.833 | = Imperial gallons (Imp gal) |
| US gallons (US gal) | X 3.785 | = Liters (l) | X 0.264 | = US gallons (US gal) |

## Mass (weight)

| | | | | |
|---|---|---|---|---|
| Ounces (oz) | X 28.35 | = Grams (g) | X 0.035 | = Ounces (oz) |
| Pounds (lb) | X 0.454 | = Kilograms (kg) | X 2.205 | = Pounds (lb) |

## Force

| | | | | |
|---|---|---|---|---|
| Ounces-force (ozf; oz) | X 0.278 | = Newtons (N) | X 3.6 | = Ounces-force (ozf; oz) |
| Pounds-force (lbf; lb) | X 4.448 | = Newtons (N) | X 0.225 | = Pounds-force (lbf; lb) |
| Newtons (N) | X 0.1 | = Kilograms-force (kgf; kg) | X 9.81 | = Newtons (N) |

## Pressure

| | | | | |
|---|---|---|---|---|
| Pounds-force per square inch (psi; lbf/in²; lb/in²) | X 0.070 | = Kilograms-force per square centimeter (kgf/cm²; kg/cm²) | X 14.223 | = Pounds-force per square inch (psi; lbf/in²; lb/in²) |
| Pounds-force per square inch (psi; lbf/in²; lb/in²) | X 0.068 | = Atmospheres (atm) | X 14.696 | = Pounds-force per square inch (psi; lbf/in²; lb/in²) |
| Pounds-force per square inch (psi; lbf/in²; lb/in²) | X 0.069 | = Bars | X 14.5 | = Pounds-force per square inch (psi; lbf/in²; lb/in²) |
| Pounds-force per square inch (psi; lbf/in²; lb/in²) | X 6.895 | = Kilopascals (kPa) | X 0.145 | = Pounds-force per square inch (psi; lbf/in²; lb/in²) |
| Kilopascals (kPa) | X 0.01 | = Kilograms-force per square centimeter (kgf/cm²; kg/cm²) | X 98.1 | = Kilopascals (kPa) |

## Torque (moment of force)

| | | | | |
|---|---|---|---|---|
| Pounds-force inches (lbf in; lb in) | X 1.152 | = Kilograms-force centimeter (kgf cm; kg cm) | X 0.868 | = Pounds-force inches (lbf in; lb in) |
| Pounds-force inches (lbf in; lb in) | X 0.113 | = Newton meters (Nm) | X 8.85 | = Pounds-force inches (lbf in; lb in) |
| Pounds-force inches (lbf in; lb in) | X 0.083 | = Pounds-force feet (lbf ft; lb ft) | X 12 | = Pounds-force inches (lbf in; lb in) |
| Pounds-force feet (lbf ft; lb ft) | X 0.138 | = Kilograms-force meters (kgf m; kg m) | X 7.233 | = Pounds-force feet (lbf ft; lb ft) |
| Pounds-force feet (lbf ft; lb ft) | X 1.356 | = Newton meters (Nm) | X 0.738 | = Pounds-force feet (lbf ft; lb ft) |
| Newton meters (Nm) | X 0.102 | = Kilograms-force meters (kgf m; kg m) | X 9.804 | = Newton meters (Nm) |

## Vacuum

| | | | | |
|---|---|---|---|---|
| Inches mercury (in. Hg) | X 3.377 | = Kilopascals (kPa) | X 0.2961 | = Inches mercury |
| Inches mercury (in. Hg) | X 25.4 | = Millimeters mercury (mm Hg) | X 0.0394 | = Inches mercury |

## Power

| | | | | |
|---|---|---|---|---|
| Horsepower (hp) | X 745.7 | = Watts (W) | X 0.0013 | = Horsepower (hp) |

## Velocity (speed)

| | | | | |
|---|---|---|---|---|
| Miles per hour (miles/hr; mph) | X 1.609 | = Kilometers per hour (km/hr; kph) | X 0.621 | = Miles per hour (miles/hr; mph) |

## Fuel consumption*

| | | | | |
|---|---|---|---|---|
| Miles per gallon, Imperial (mpg) | X 0.354 | = Kilometers per liter (km/l) | X 2.825 | = Miles per gallon, Imperial (mpg) |
| Miles per gallon, US (mpg) | X 0.425 | = Kilometers per liter (km/l) | X 2.352 | = Miles per gallon, US (mpg) |

## Temperature

Degrees Fahrenheit = (°C x 1.8) + 32        Degrees Celsius (Degrees Centigrade; °C) = (°F - 32) x 0.56

*It is common practice to convert from miles per gallon (mpg) to liters/100 kilometers (l/100km), where mpg (Imperial) x l/100 km = 282 and mpg (US) x l/100 km = 235

A number of chemicals and lubricants are available for use in motorcycle maintenance and repair. They include a wide variety of products ranging from cleaning solvents and degreasers to lubricants and protective sprays for rubber, plastic and vinyl.

• **Contact point/spark plug cleaner** is a solvent used to clean oily film and dirt from points, grime from electrical connectors and oil deposits from spark plugs. It is oil free and leaves no residue. It can also be used to remove gum and varnish from carburetor jets and other orifices.

• **Carburetor cleaner** is similar to contact point/spark plug cleaner but it usually has a stronger solvent and may leave a slight oily residue. It is not recommended for cleaning electrical components or connections.

• **Brake system cleaner** is used to remove brake dust, grease and brake fluid from the brake system, where clean surfaces are absolutely necessary. It leaves no residue and often eliminates brake squeal caused by contaminants.

• **Silicone-based lubricants** are used to protect rubber parts such as hoses and grommets, and are used as lubricants for hinges and locks.

• **Multi-purpose grease** is an all purpose lubricant used wherever grease is more practical than a liquid lubricant such as oil. Some multi-purpose grease is colored white and specially formulated to be more resistant to water than ordinary grease.

• **Gear oil** (sometimes called gear lube) is a specially designed oil used in transmissions and final drive units, as well as other areas where high friction, high temperature lubrication is required. It is available in a number of viscosities (weights) for various applications.

• **Motor oil** is the lubricant formulated for use in engines. It normally contains a wide variety of additives to prevent corrosion and reduce foaming and wear. Motor oil comes in various weights (viscosity ratings) from 0 to 50. The recommended weight of the oil depends on the season, temperature and the demands on the engine. Light oil is used in cold climates and under light load conditions. Heavy oil is used in hot climates and where high loads are encountered. Multi-viscosity oils are designed to have characteristics of both light and heavy oils and are available in a number of weights from 0W-20 to 20W-50.

• **Gasoline additives** perform several functions, depending on their chemical makeup. They usually contain solvents that help dissolve gum and varnish that build up on carburetor and inlet parts. They also serve to break down carbon deposits that form on the inside surfaces of the combustion chambers. Some additives contain upper cylinder lubricants for valves and piston rings.

• **Brake and clutch fluid** is a specially formulated hydraulic fluid that can withstand the heat and pressure encountered in break/clutch systems. Care must be taken that this fluid does not come in contact with painted surfaces or plastics. An opened container should always be resealed to prevent contamination by water or dirt.

• **Chain lubricants** are formulated especially for use on motorcycle final drive chains. A good chain lube should adhere well and have good penetrating qualities to be effective as a lubricant inside the chain and on the side plates, pins and rollers. Most chain lubes are either the foaming type or quick drying type and are usually marketed as sprays. Take care to use a lubricant marked as being suitable for O-ring chains.

• **Degreasers** are heavy duty solvents used to remove grease and grime that may accumulate on the engine and frame components. They can be sprayed or brushed on and, depending on the type, are rinsed with either water or solvent.

• **Solvents** are used alone or in combination with degreasers to clean parts and assemblies during repair and overhaul. The home mechanic should use only solvents that are non-flammable and that do not produce irritating fumes.

• **Gasket sealing compounds** may be used in conjunction with gaskets, to improve their sealing capabilities, or alone, to seal metal-to-metal joints. Many gasket sealers can withstand extreme heat, some are impervious to gasoline and lubricants, while others are capable of filling and sealing large cavities. Depending on the intended use, gasket sealers either dry hard or stay relatively soft and pliable. They are usually applied by hand, with a brush or are sprayed on the gasket sealing surfaces.

• **Thread locking compound** is an adhesive locking compound that prevents threaded fasteners from loosening because of vibration. It is available in a variety of types for different applications.

• **Moisture dispersants** are usually sprays that can be used to dry out electrical components such as the fuse block and wiring connectors. Some types an also be used as treatment for rubber and as a lubricant for hinges, cables and locks.

• **Waxes and polishes** are used to help protect painted and plated surfaces from the weather. Different types of pain may require the use of different types of wax polish. Some polishes utilize a chemical or abrasive cleaner to help remove the top layer of oxidized (dull) paint on older vehicles. In recent years, many non-wax polishes (that contain a wide variety of chemicals such as polymers and silicones) have been introduced. These non-wax polishes are usually easier to apply and last longer than conventional waxes and polishes.

# Preparing for storage

## Before you start

If repairs or an overhaul is needed, see that this is carried out now rather than left until you want to ride the bike again.

Give the bike a good wash and scrub all dirt from its underside. Make sure the bike dries completely before preparing for storage.

## Engine

● Remove the spark plug(s) and lubricate the cylinder bores with approximately one teaspoon of motor oil using a spout-type oil can (see illustration 1). Reinstall the spark plug(s). Crank the engine over a couple of times to coat the piston rings and bores with oil. If the bike has a kickstart, use this to turn the engine over. If not, flick the kill switch to the OFF position and crank the engine over on the starter (see illustration 2). If the nature of the ignition system prevents the starter operating with the kill switch in the OFF position, remove the spark plugs and fit them back in their caps; ensure that the plugs are grounded against the cylinder head when the starter is operated (see illustration 3).

⚠️ *Warning: It is important that the plugs are grounded away from the spark plug holes otherwise there is a risk of atomized fuel from the cylinders igniting.*

**HAYNES HiNT** *On a single cylinder four-stroke engine, you can seal the combustion chamber completely by positioning the piston at TDC on the compression stroke.*

● Drain the carburetor(s), otherwise there is a risk of jets becoming blocked by gum deposits from the fuel (see illustration 4).

● If the bike is going into long-term storage, consider adding a fuel stabilizer to the fuel in the tank. If the tank is drained completely, corrosion of its internal surfaces may occur if left unprotected for a long period. The tank can be treated with a rust preventative especially for this purpose. Alternatively, remove the tank and pour half a liter of motor oil into it, install the filler cap and shake the tank to coat its internals with oil before draining off the excess. The same effect can also be achieved by spraying WD40 or a similar water-dispersant around the inside of the tank via its flexible nozzle.

● Make sure the cooling system contains the correct mix of antifreeze. Antifreeze also contains important corrosion inhibitors.

● The air intakes and exhaust can be sealed off by covering or plugging the openings. Ensure that you do not seal in any condensation; run the engine until it is hot, then switch off and allow to cool. Tape a

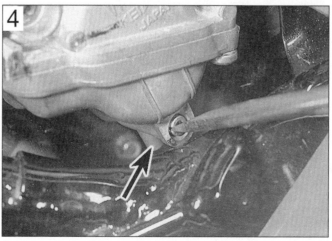

Squirt a drop of motor oil into each cylinder

Flick the kill switch to OFF . . .

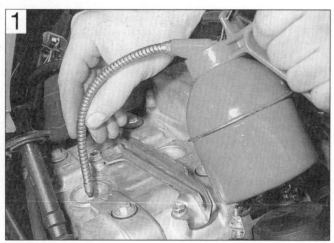

. . . and ensure that the metal bodies of the plugs (arrows) are grounded against the cylinder head

Connect a hose to the carburetor float chamber drain stub (arrow) and unscrew the drain screw

**Exhausts can be sealed off with a plastic bag**

**Disconnect the negative lead (A) first, followed by the positive lead (B)**

piece of thick plastic over the silencer end(s) **(see illustration 5)**. Note that some advocate pouring a tablespoon of motor oil into the silencer(s) before sealing them off.

## Battery
● Remove it from the bike - in extreme cases of cold the battery may freeze and crack its case **(see illustration 6)**.
● Check the electrolyte level and top up if necessary (conventional refillable batteries). Clean the terminals.
● Store the battery off the motorcycle and away from any sources of fire. Position a wooden block under the battery if it is to sit on the ground.
● Give the battery a trickle charge for a few hours every month **(see illustration 7)**.

## Tires
● Place the bike on its centerstand or an auxiliary stand which will support the motorcycle in an upright position. Position wood blocks under the tires to keep them off the ground and to provide insulation from damp. If the bike is being put into long-term

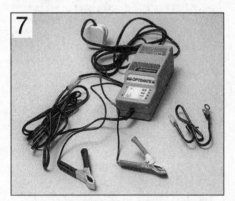

**Use a suitable battery charger - this kit also assesses battery condition**

storage, ideally both tires should be off the ground; not only will this protect the tires, but will also ensure that no load is placed on the steering head or wheel bearings.
● Deflate each tire by 5 to 10 psi, no more or the beads may unseat from the rim, making subsequent inflation difficult on tubeless tires.

## Pivots and controls
● Lubricate all lever, pedal, stand and footrest pivot points. If grease nipples are fitted to the rear suspension components, apply lubricant to the pivots.
● Lubricate all control cables.

## Cycle components
● Apply a wax protectant to all painted and plastic components. Wipe off any excess, but don't polish to a shine. Where fitted, clean the screen with soap and water.
● Coat metal parts with Vaseline (petroleum jelly). When applying this to the fork tubes, do not compress the forks, otherwise the seals will rot from contact with the Vaseline.
● Apply a vinyl cleaner to the seat.

## Storage conditions
● Aim to store the bike in a shed or garage which does not leak and is free from damp.
● Drape an old blanket or bedspread over the bike to protect it from dust and direct contact with sunlight (which will fade paint). Beware of tight-fitting plastic covers which may allow condensation to form and settle on the bike.

# Getting back on the road

### Engine and transmission
● Change the oil and replace the oil filter. If this was done prior to storage, check that the oil hasn't emulsified - a thick whitish substance which occurs through condensation.
● Remove the spark plugs. Using a spout-type oil can, squirt a few drops of oil into the cylinder(s). This will provide initial lubrication as the piston rings and bores comes back into contact. Service the spark plugs, or buy new ones, and install them in the engine.

● Check that the clutch isn't stuck on. The plates can stick together if left standing for some time, preventing clutch operation. Engage a gear and try rocking the bike back and forth with the clutch lever held against the handlebar. If this doesn't work on cable-operated clutches, hold the clutch lever back against the handlebar with a strong rubber band or cable tie for a couple of hours **(see illustration 8)**.
● If the air intakes or silencer end(s) were blocked off, remove the plug or cover used.
● If the fuel tank was coated with a rust

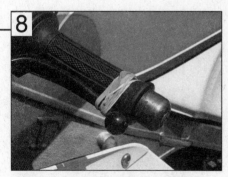

**Hold the clutch lever back against the handlebar with rubber bands or a cable tie**

preventative, oil or a stabilizer added to the fuel, drain and flush the tank and dispose of the fuel sensibly. If no action was taken with the fuel tank prior to storage, it is advised that the old fuel is disposed of since it will go bad over a period of time. Refill the fuel tank with fresh fuel.

## Frame and running gear

● Oil all pivot points and cables.
● Check the tire pressures. They will definitely need inflating if pressures were reduced for storage.
● Lubricate the final drive chain (where applicable).
● Remove any protective coating applied to the fork tubes (stanchions) since this may well destroy the fork seals. If the fork tubes weren't protected and have picked up rust spots, remove them with very fine abrasive paper and refinish with metal polish.
● Check that both brakes operate correctly. Apply each brake hard and check that it's not possible to move the motorcycle forwards, then check that the brake frees off again once released. Brake caliper pistons can stick due to corrosion around the piston head, or on the sliding caliper types, due to corrosion of the slider pins. If the brake doesn't free after repeated operation, take the caliper off for examination. Similarly, drum brakes can stick due to a seized operating cam, cable or rod linkage.
● If the motorcycle has been in long-term storage, replace the brake fluid and clutch fluid (where applicable).
● Depending on where the bike has been stored, the wiring, cables and hoses may have been nibbled by rodents. Make a visual check and investigate disturbed wiring loom tape.

## Battery

● If the battery has been previously removed and given top up charges, it can simply be reconnected. Remember to connect the positive cable first and the negative cable last.
● On conventional refillable batteries, if the battery has not received any attention, remove it from the motorcycle and check its electrolyte level. Top up if necessary, then charge the battery. If the battery fails to hold a charge and a visual check shows heavy white sulfation of the plates, the battery is probably defective and must be replaced. This is particularly likely if the battery is old. Confirm battery condition with a specific gravity check.
● On sealed (MF) batteries, if the battery has not received any attention, remove it from the motorcycle and charge it according to the information on the battery case - if the battery fails to hold a charge it must be replaced.

## Starting procedure

● If a kickstart is fitted, turn the engine over a couple of times with the ignition OFF to distribute oil around the engine. If no kickstart is fitted, flick the engine kill switch OFF and the ignition ON and crank the engine over a couple of times to work oil around the upper cylinder components. If the nature of the ignition system is such that the starter won't work with the kill switch OFF, remove the spark plugs, fit them back into their caps and ground their bodies on the cylinder head. Reinstall the spark plugs afterwards.
● Switch the kill switch to RUN, operate the choke and start the engine. If the engine won't start don't continue cranking the engine - not only will this flatten the battery, but the starter motor will overheat. Switch the ignition off and try again later. If the engine refuses to start, go through the troubleshooting procedures in this manual. **Note:** *If the bike has been in storage for a long time, old fuel or a carburetor blockage may be the problem. Gum deposits in carburetors can block jets - if a carburetor cleaner doesn't prove successful, the carburetors must be dismantled for cleaning.*
● Once the engine has started, check that the lights, turn signals and horn work properly.
● Treat the bike gently for the first ride and check all fluid levels on completion. Settle the bike back into the maintenance schedule.

This Section provides an easy reference-guide to the more common faults that are likely to afflict your machine. Obviously, the opportunities are almost limitless for faults to occur as a result of obscure failures, and to try and cover all eventualities would require a book. Indeed, a number have been written on the subject.

Successful troubleshooting is not a mysterious art but the application of a bit of knowledge combined with a systematic and logical approach to the problem. Approach any troubleshooting by first accurately identifying the symptom and then checking through the list of possible causes, starting with the simplest or most obvious and progressing in stages to the most complex. Take nothing for granted, but above all apply liberal quantities of common sense.

The main symptom of a fault is given in the text as a major heading below which are listed the various systems or areas which may contain the fault. Details of each possible cause for a fault and the remedial action to be taken are given. Further information should be sought in the relevant Chapter.

## 1 Engine doesn't start or is difficult to start

- ☐ Kickstarter or starter motor (XR650L) turns engine over but engine won't start
- ☐ Kickstarter moves but engine doesn't turn over
- ☐ Kickstarter won't move (seized)
- ☐ No fuel flow
- ☐ Engine flooded
- ☐ No spark or weak spark
- ☐ Compression low
- ☐ Stalls after starting
- ☐ Rough idle

## 2 Poor running at low speed

- ☐ Spark weak
- ☐ Fuel/air mixture incorrect
- ☐ Compression low
- ☐ Poor acceleration

## 3 Poor running or no power at high speed

- ☐ Firing incorrect
- ☐ Fuel/air mixture incorrect
- ☐ Compression low
- ☐ Knocking or pinging
- ☐ Miscellaneous causes

## 4 Overheating

- ☐ Engine overheats
- ☐ Firing incorrect
- ☐ Fuel/air mixture incorrect
- ☐ Compression too high
- ☐ Engine load excessive
- ☐ Lubrication inadequate
- ☐ Miscellaneous causes

## 5 Clutch problems

- ☐ Clutch slipping
- ☐ Clutch not disengaging completely

## 6 Gear shifting problems

- ☐ Doesn't go into gear, or lever doesn't return
- ☐ Jumps out of gear
- ☐ Overshifts

## 7 Abnormal engine noise

- ☐ Knocking or pinging
- ☐ Piston slap or rattling
- ☐ Valve noise
- ☐ Other noise

## 8 Abnormal driveline noise

- ☐ Clutch noise
- ☐ Transmission noise
- ☐ Final drive noise

## 9 Abnormal frame and suspension noise

- ☐ Suspension noise
- ☐ Brake noise

## 10 Excessive exhaust smoke

- ☐ White smoke
- ☐ Black smoke
- ☐ Brown smoke

## 11 Poor handling or stability

- ☐ Handlebar hard to turn
- ☐ Handlebar shakes or vibrates excessively
- ☐ Handlebar pulls to one side
- ☐ Poor shock absorbing qualities

## 12 Braking problems

- ☐ Brakes are spongy or weak, don't hold
- ☐ Brake lever or pedal pulsates
- ☐ Brakes drag

## 13 Electrical problems

- ☐ Battery dead or weak
- ☐ Battery overcharged
- ☐ Starter doesn't crank the engine (XR650L models)

# 1 Engine doesn't start or is difficult to start

### Kickstarter or starter motor (XR650L) turns engine over but engine won't start

- ☐ Engine kill switch Off or defective. Check for wet, dirty or corroded contacts. Clean or replace the switch as necessary (Chapter 5)..
- ☐ Fuel tap not turned on or fuel tank empty.
- ☐ Spark plug fouled, or no spark (Section 6).
- ☐ Air filter clogged (Chapter 1).
- ☐ Mixture (pilot) screw dirty. Remove and clean screw tip and its bore with carburetor cleaner spray (see Chapter 4).
- ☐ Carburetor flooded (Section 5).
- ☐ Slow circuit in carburetor clogged. Disassemble and clean carburetor (Chapter 4).
- ☐ Engine compression low (Section 7).
- ☐ Intake air leak. Check for loose carburetor-to-intake joint clamps (Chapter 3).
- ☐ Wiring open or shorted. Check all wiring connections and harnesses to make sure that they are dry, tight and not corroded. Also check for broken or frayed wires that can cause a short to ground (see wiring diagram, Chapter 8).

### Kickstarter moves but engine doesn't turn over

- ☐ Kickstarter mechanism damaged. Inspect and repair or replace (Chapter 2).
- ☐ Damaged kickstarter pinion gears. Inspect and replace the damaged parts (Chapter 2).

### Kickstarter won't move (engine seized)

- ☐ Seized engine caused by one or more internally damaged components. Failure due to wear, abuse or lack of lubrication. Damage can include seized valves, rocker arms, camshaft, piston, crankshaft, connecting rod bearings, or transmission gears or bearings. Refer to Chapter 2 for engine disassembly.

### No fuel flow

- ☐ No fuel in tank.
- ☐ Fuel tap not turned on.
- ☐ Tank cap air vent obstructed. Usually caused by dirt or water. Remove it and clean the cap vent hole.
- ☐ Clogged strainer in fuel tap. Remove and clean the strainer (Chapter 1).
- ☐ Fuel line clogged. Pull the fuel line loose and carefully blow through it.
- ☐ Pilot screw, inlet needle valve or main jet clogged. A very bad batch of fuel with an unusual additive may have been used, or some other foreign material has entered the tank. Many times after a machine has been stored for many months without running, the fuel turns to a varnish-like liquid and forms deposits on the inlet needle valve and jets. Start by removing and cleaning the pilot screw and its bore, and draining the float bowl. If the problem persists, the carburetor should be removed and overhauled.

### Engine flooded

- ☐ Float level too high. Check as described in Chapter 4 and replace the float if necessary.
- ☐ Inlet needle valve worn or stuck open. A piece of dirt, rust or other debris can cause the inlet needle to seat improperly, causing excess fuel to be admitted to the float bowl. In this case, the float chamber should be cleaned and the needle and seat inspected. If the needle and seat are worn, then the leaking will persist and the parts should be replaced with new ones (Chapter 4).
- ☐ Starting technique incorrect. Under normal circumstances (if all the carburetor functions are sound) the machine should start with little or no throttle. When the engine is cold, the choke should be operated and the engine started without opening the throttle. When the engine is at operating temperature, only a very slight amount of throttle should be necessary. If the engine is flooded, turn the fuel tap off and hold the throttle open while cranking the engine. This will allow additional air to reach the cylinder. Remember to turn the fuel tap back on after the engine starts.

### No spark or weak spark

- ☐ Spark plug dirty, defective or worn out. Locate reason for fouled plug using spark plug condition chart and follow the plug maintenance procedures in Chapter 1.
- ☐ Spark plug cap or secondary wiring faulty. Check condition. Replace either or both components if cracks or deterioration are evident (Chapter 5).
- ☐ Spark plug cap not making good contact. Make sure that the plug cap fits snugly over the plug end.
- ☐ Defective alternator (see Chapter 5).
- ☐ CDI models: Defective CDI unit (see Chapter 5).
- ☐ Ignition coil defective. Check the coil, referring to Chapter 5.
- ☐ Kill switch shorted. This is usually caused by water, corrosion, damage or excessive wear. The kill switch can be disassembled and cleaned with electrical contact cleaner. If cleaning does not help, replace the switch (Chapter 5).
- ☐ Wiring shorted or broken between:
  - a) CDI unit and engine kill switch
  - b) CDI unit and ignition coil
  - c) CDI unit and alternator
  - d) Ignition coil and plug
- ☐ Make sure that all wiring connections are clean, dry and tight. Look for chafed and broken wires (Chapter 5).

### Compression low

- ☐ Spark plug loose. Remove the plug and inspect the threads. Reinstall and tighten to the specified torque (Chapter 1).
- ☐ Cylinder head not sufficiently tightened down. If the cylinder head is suspected of being loose, then there's a chance that the gasket or head is damaged if the problem has persisted for any length of time. The head nuts and bolts should be tightened to the proper torque in the correct sequence (Chapter 2).
- ☐ Improper valve clearance. This means that the valve is not closing completely and compression pressure is leaking past the valve. Check and adjust the valve clearances (Chapter 1).
- ☐ Cylinder and/or piston worn. Excessive wear will cause compression pressure to leak past the rings. This is usually accompanied by worn rings as well. A top end overhaul is necessary (Chapter 2).
- ☐ Piston rings worn, weak, broken, or sticking. Broken or sticking piston rings usually indicate a lubrication or carburetion problem that causes excess carbon deposits or seizures to form on the pistons and rings. Top end overhaul is necessary (Chapter 2).
- ☐ Piston ring-to-groove clearance excessive. This is caused by excessive wear of the piston ring lands. Piston replacement is necessary (Chapter 2).
- ☐ Cylinder head gasket damaged. If the head is allowed to become loose, or if excessive carbon build-up on a piston crown and combustion chamber causes extremely high compression, the head gasket may leak. Retorquing the head is not always sufficient to restore the seal, so gasket replacement is necessary (Chapter 2).
- ☐ Cylinder head warped. This is caused by overheating or improperly tightened head nuts and bolts. Machine shop resurfacing or head replacement is necessary (Chapter 2).
- ☐ Valve spring broken or weak. Caused by component failure or wear; the spring(s) must be replaced (Chapter 2).

# 1 Engine doesn't start or is difficult to start (continued)

☐ Valve not seating properly. This is caused by a bent valve (from over-revving or improper valve adjustment), burned valve or seat (improper carburetion) or an accumulation of carbon deposits on the seat (from carburetion or lubrication problems). The valves must be cleaned and/or replaced and the seats serviced if possible (Chapter 2).

### Stalls after starting

☐ Improper choke action. Make sure the choke lever is getting a full stroke and staying in the out position.
☐ Ignition malfunction. See Chapter 5.
☐ Carburetor malfunction. See Chapter 4.
☐ Fuel contaminated. The fuel can be contaminated with either dirt or water, or can change chemically if the machine is allowed to sit for several months. Drain the tank and float bowl and refill with fresh fuel (Chapter 4). The pilot screw might also have deposits on it (especially if the engine runs with the choke on but not after the choke is turned off). See Chapter 4.

☐ Intake air leak. Check for a loose carburetor-to-intake joint connection or a loose carburetor top (Chapter 4).
☐ Engine idle speed incorrect. Turn the throttle stop screw until the engine idles at the specified rpm (Chapter 1).

### Rough idle

☐ Air cleaner clogged. Service or replace the air cleaner element (Chapter 1).
☐ Fuel contaminated or stale. The fuel can be contaminated with either dirt or water, or can change chemically if the machine is allowed to sit for several months. Drain the tank and float bowls (Chapter 4).
☐ Ignition malfunction. See Chapter 5.
☐ Idle speed incorrect. See Chapter 1.
☐ Carburetor malfunction. See Chapter 4.
☐ Idle fuel/air mixture incorrect. See Chapter 4.
☐ Intake air leak. Check for a loose carburetor-to-intake joint connection, a loose or missing vacuum gauge access port cap or hose, or a loose carburetor top (Chapter 4).

# 2 Poor running at low speed

### Spark weak

☐ Spark plug fouled, defective or worn out. Refer to Chapter 1 for spark plug maintenance.
☐ Spark plug cap or secondary wiring defective. Refer to Chapters 1 and 4 for details on the ignition system.
☐ Spark plug cap not making contact.
☐ Incorrect spark plug. Wrong type, heat range or cap configuration. Check and install correct plug listed in Chapter 1. A cold plug or one with a recessed firing electrode will not operate at low speeds without fouling.
☐ CDI unit defective. See Chapter 5.
☐ Alternator defective. See Chapter 5.
☐ Ignition coil defective. See Chapter 5.

### Fuel/air mixture incorrect

☐ Pilot screw out of adjustment (Chapter 4).
☐ Pilot jet or air passage clogged. Remove and overhaul the carburetor (Chapter 4).
☐ Air bleed holes clogged. Remove carburetor and blow out all passages (Chapter 4).
☐ Air cleaner clogged, poorly sealed or missing.
☐ Air cleaner-to-carburetor boot poorly sealed. Look for cracks, holes or loose clamps and replace or repair defective parts.
☐ Float level too high or too low. Check and replace the float if necessary (Chapter 4).
☐ Fuel tank air vent obstructed. Make sure that the air vent passage in the filler cap is open.
☐ Carburetor intake joint loose. Check for cracks, breaks, tears or loose clamps or bolts. Repair or replace the rubber boot and its O-ring.

### Compression low

☐ Spark plug loose. Remove the plug and inspect the threads. Reinstall and tighten it to the specified torque (Chapter 1).

☐ Cylinder head not sufficiently tightened down. If the cylinder head is suspected of being loose, then there's a chance that the gasket and head are damaged if the problem has persisted for any length of time. The head nuts should be tightened to the proper torque in the correct sequence (Chapter 2).
☐ Improper valve clearance. This means that the valve is not closing completely and compression pressure is leaking past the valve. Check and adjust the valve clearances (Chapter 1).
☐ Cylinder and/or piston worn. Excessive wear will cause compression pressure to leak past the rings. This is usually accompanied by worn rings as well. A top end overhaul is necessary (Chapter 2).
☐ Piston rings worn, weak, broken, or sticking. Broken or sticking piston rings usually indicate a lubrication or carburetion problem that causes excess carbon deposits or seizures to form on the piston and rings. Top end overhaul is necessary (Chapter 2).
☐ Piston ring-to-groove clearance excessive. This is caused by excessive wear of the piston ring lands. Piston replacement is necessary (Chapter 2).
☐ Cylinder head gasket damaged. If the head is allowed to become loose, or if excessive carbon build-up on the piston crown and combustion chamber causes extremely high compression, the head gasket may leak. Retorquing the head is not always sufficient to restore the seal, so gasket replacement is necessary (Chapter 2).
☐ Cylinder head warped. This is caused by overheating or improperly tightened head nuts and bolts. Machine shop resurfacing or head replacement is necessary (Chapter 2).
☐ Valve spring broken or weak. Caused by component failure or wear; the spring(s) must be replaced (Chapter 2).
☐ Valve not seating properly. This is caused by a bent valve (from over-revving or improper valve adjustment), burned valve or seat (improper carburetion) or an accumulation of carbon deposits on the seat (from carburetion, lubrication problems). The valves must be cleaned and/or replaced and the seats serviced if possible (Chapter 2).

# 2 Poor running at low speed (continued)

## Poor acceleration

☐ Carburetor leaking or dirty. Overhaul the carburetor (Chapter 4).
☐ Timing not advancing. The CDI unit may be defective. If so, it must be replaced with a new one (see Chapter 5).

☐ Engine oil viscosity too high. Using a heavier oil than that recommended in Chapter 1 can damage the oil pump or lubrication system and cause drag on the engine.
☐ Brakes dragging. Usually caused by a sticking caliper piston (disc brakes) or brake cam (drum brakes), by a warped disc or drum or by a bent axle. Repair as necessary (Chapter 7).

# 3 Poor running or no power at high speed

## Firing incorrect

☐ Air cleaner restricted. Clean or replace element (Chapter 1).
☐ Spark plug fouled, defective or worn out. See Chapter 1 for spark plug maintenance.
☐ Incorrect spark plug. Wrong type, heat range or cap configuration. Check and install correct plugs listed in Chapter 1. A cold plug or one with a recessed firing electrode will not operate at low speeds without fouling.
☐ Spark plug cap or secondary wiring defective. See Chapters 1 and 4 for details of the ignition system.
☐ Spark plug cap not in good contact. See Chapter 5.
☐ CDI unit defective. See Chapter 5.
☐ Ignition coil defective. See Chapter 5.

## Fuel/air mixture incorrect

☐ Air cleaner clogged, poorly sealed, or missing.
☐ Pilot screw out of adjustment. See Chapter 4 for adjustment procedures.
☐ Main jet clogged. Dirt, water or other contaminants can clog the main jets. Clean the fuel tap strainer, the float bowl area, and the jets and carburetor orifices (Chapter 4).
☐ Main jet wrong size. The standard jetting is for sea level atmospheric pressure and oxygen content. See Chapter 4 for high altitude adjustments.
☐ Air bleed holes clogged. Remove and overhaul carburetor (Chapter 4).
☐ Air cleaner-to-carburetor boot poorly sealed. Look for cracks, holes or loose clamps, and replace or repair defective parts.
☐ Float level too high or too low. Check float level and replace the float if necessary (Chapter 4).
☐ Fuel tank air vent obstructed. Make sure the air vent passage in the filler cap is open.
☐ Carburetor intake manifold loose. Check for cracks, breaks, tears or loose clamps or bolts. Repair or replace the rubber boots (Chapter 3).

## Compression low

☐ Spark plug loose. Remove the plug and inspect the threads. Reinstall and tighten it to the specified torque (Chapter 1).
☐ Cylinder head not sufficiently tightened down. If the cylinder head is suspected of being loose, then there's a chance that the gasket and head are damaged if the problem has persisted for any length of time. The head nuts and bolts should be tightened to the proper torque in the correct sequence (Chapter 2).
☐ Improper valve clearance. This means that the valve is not closing completely and compression pressure is leaking past the valve. Check and adjust the valve clearances (Chapter 1).
☐ Cylinder and/or piston worn. Excessive wear will cause compression pressure to leak past the rings. This is usually accompanied by worn rings as well. A top end overhaul is necessary (Chapter 2).
☐ Piston rings worn, weak, broken, or sticking. Broken or sticking piston rings usually indicate a lubrication or carburetion problem that causes excess carbon deposits or seizures to form on the pistons and rings. Top end overhaul is necessary (Chapter 2).
☐ Piston ring-to-groove clearance excessive. This is caused by excessive wear of the piston ring lands. Piston replacement is necessary (Chapter 2).
☐ Cylinder head gasket damaged. If a head is allowed to become loose, or if excessive carbon build-up on the piston crown and combustion chamber causes extremely high compression, the head gasket may leak. Retorquing the head is not always sufficient to restore the seal, so gasket replacement is necessary (Chapter 2).
☐ Cylinder head warped. This is caused by overheating or an improperly tightened head nuts and bolts. Machine shop resurfacing or head replacement is necessary (Chapter 2).
☐ Valve spring broken or weak. Caused by component failure or wear; the spring(s) must be replaced (Chapter 2).
☐ Valve not seating properly. This is caused by a bent valve (from over-revving or improper valve adjustment), burned valve or seat (improper carburetion) or an accumulation of carbon deposits on the seat (from carburetion or lubrication problems). The valves must be cleaned and/or replaced and the seats serviced if possible (Chapter 2).

## Knocking or pinging

☐ Incorrect or poor quality fuel. Old or improper grades of fuel can cause detonation. This causes the piston to rattle, thus the knocking or pinging sound. Drain old fuel and always use the recommended fuel grade.
☐ Spark plug heat range incorrect. Uncontrolled detonation indicates the plug heat range is too hot. The plug in effect becomes a glow plug, raising cylinder temperatures. Install the proper heat range plug (Chapter 1).
☐ Improper air/fuel mixture. This will cause the cylinder to run hot, which leads to detonation. Clogged jets or an air leak can cause this imbalance. See Chapter 4.
☐ Carbon build-up in combustion chamber. Use of a fuel additive that will dissolve the adhesive bonding the carbon particles to the crown and chamber is the easiest way to remove the build-up. Otherwise, the cylinder head will have to be removed and decarbonized (Chapter 2).

## Miscellaneous causes

☐ Throttle valve doesn't open fully. Adjust the cable slack (Chapter 1).
☐ Clutch slipping. May be caused by improper adjustment or loose or worn clutch components. Refer to Chapter 1 for adjustment or Chapter 2 for cable replacement and clutch overhaul procedures.
☐ Timing not advancing due to a faulty ignition control module (Chapter 5).
☐ Engine oil viscosity too high. Using a heavier oil than the one recommended in Chapter 1 can damage the oil pump or lubrication system and cause drag on the engine.
☐ Brakes dragging. Usually caused by debris which has entered the brake piston sealing boot, or from a warped disc or bent axle. Repair as necessary.

# 4 Overheating

## Engine overheats

- ☐ Engine oil level low. Check and add oil (Chapter 1).
- ☐ Wrong type of oil. If you're not sure what type of oil is in the engine, drain it and fill with the correct type (Chapter 1).
- ☐ Coolant level low (XR650R models). Check and add coolant (Chapter 1), then look for leaks (Chapter 3).
- ☐ Radiator cap faulty (XR650R models) (Chapter 3).
- ☐ Stuck thermostat (XR650R models) (Chapter 3).
- ☐ Radiator cooling fins obstructed (XR650R models) (mud, leaves, etc.).
- ☐ Air in cooling system (XR650R models).
- ☐ Radiator(s) clogged internally (XR650R models). Replace radiator(s) (Chapter 3).
- ☐ Defective water pump (XR650R models) (Chapter 3).
- ☐ Air leak at carburetor intake manifold. Check and tighten or replace as necessary (Chapter 4).
- ☐ Air/fuel mixture too lean. Check and adjust if necessary (Chapter 4).
- ☐ Worn oil pump or clogged oil passages. Replace pump or clean passages as necessary.
- ☐ Clogged external oil line. Remove and check for foreign material (see Chapter 2).
- ☐ Carbon build-up in combustion chambers. Use of a fuel additive that will dissolve the adhesive bonding the carbon particles to the piston crown and chambers is the easiest way to remove the build-up. Otherwise, the cylinder head will have to be removed and decarbonized (Chapter 2).
- ☐ Operation in high ambient temperatures and/or low speeds.

## Firing incorrect

- ☐ Air cleaner restricted. Clean or replace element (Chapter 1).
- ☐ Spark plug fouled, defective or worn out. See Chapter 1 for spark plug maintenance.
- ☐ Incorrect spark plug. Wrong type, heat range or cap configuration. Check and install correct plugs listed in Chapter 1. A cold plug or one with a recessed firing electrode will not operate at low speeds without fouling.
- ☐ Spark plug cap or secondary wiring defective. See Chapters 1 and 5 for details of the ignition system.
- ☐ Spark plug cap not in good contact. See Chapter 5.
- ☐ Ignition coil defective. See Chapter 5.
- ☐ CDI unit defective. See Chapter 5.

## Fuel/air mixture incorrect

- ☐ Air filter element clogged, poorly sealed or missing (Chapter 1).
- ☐ Fuel tank air vent obstructed. Make sure that the air vent passage in the filler cap is open.
- ☐ Carburetor intake joint loose. Check for cracks, breaks, tears or loose clamps or bolts. Repair or replace the rubber boot and its O-ring.
- ☐ Air cleaner-to-carburetor boot poorly sealed. Look for cracks, holes or loose clamps and replace or repair defective parts.
- ☐ Pilot screw out of adjustment (Chapter 4).

- ☐ Carburetor jetting or needle clip position incorrect for weather, temperature and track/riding conditions (Chapter 4).
- ☐ Jet or air passage clogged. Remove and overhaul the carburetor (Chapter 4).
- ☐ Air bleed holes clogged. Remove carburetor, clean and blow out all passages (Chapter 4).
- ☐ Float level too high or too low. Check and adjust/replace the float if necessary (Chapter 4).

## Compression too high

- ☐ Carbon build-up in combustion chamber. Use of a fuel additive that will dissolve the adhesive bonding the carbon particles to the piston crown and chamber is the easiest way to remove the build-up. Otherwise, the cylinder head will have to be removed and decarbonized (Chapter 2).
- ☐ Improperly machined head surface or installation of incorrect gasket during engine assembly.

## Engine load excessive

- ☐ Clutch slipping. Can be caused by damaged, loose or worn clutch components. Refer to Chapter 2 for overhaul procedures.
- ☐ Engine oil level too high. The addition of too much oil will cause pressurization of the crankcase and inefficient engine operation. Check the Specifications and drain to the proper level (Chapter 1).
- ☐ Engine oil viscosity too high. Using a heavier oil than the one recommended in Chapter 1 can damage the oil pump or lubrication system as well as cause drag on the engine.
- ☐ Brakes dragging. Usually caused by a sticking caliper piston (disc brakes), brake cam (drum brakes), by a warped disc or drum or by a bent axle. Repair as necessary (Chapter 7).

## Lubrication inadequate

- ☐ Engine oil level too low. Friction caused by intermittent lack of lubrication or from oil that is overworked can cause overheating. The oil provides a definite cooling function in the engine. Check the oil level (Chapter 1).
- ☐ Poor quality engine oil or incorrect viscosity or type. Oil is rated not only according to viscosity but also according to type. Some oils are not rated high enough for use in this engine. Check the Specifications section and change to the correct oil (Chapter 1).
- ☐ Camshaft or journals worn. Excessive wear causing drop in oil pressure. Replace cam or cylinder head. Abnormal wear could be caused by oil starvation at high rpm from low oil level or improper viscosity or type of oil (Chapter 1).
- ☐ Crankshaft and/or bearings worn. Same problems as paragraph 3. Check and replace crankshaft assembly if necessary (Chapter 2).

## Miscellaneous causes

- ☐ Modification to exhaust system. Most aftermarket exhaust systems cause the engine to run leaner, which makes it run hotter. When installing an accessory exhaust system, always rejet the carburetor.

# 5 Clutch problems

## Clutch slipping

☐ No clutch lever freeplay. Adjust freeplay (Chapter 1).
☐ Clutch inner cable sticking. Caused by a frayed inner cable or kinked outer cable. Replace the clutch cable; repair of a damaged cable is not advised.
☐ Friction plates worn or warped. Overhaul the clutch (Chapter 2).
☐ Metal plates worn or warped (Chapter 2).
☐ Clutch spring(s) broken or weak. Old or heat-damaged spring(s) (from slipping clutch) should be replaced with new ones (Chapter 2).
☐ Clutch release mechanism defective. Replace any defective parts (Chapter 2).
☐ Clutch center or housing unevenly worn. This causes improper engagement of the plates. Replace the damaged or worn parts (Chapter 2).

## Clutch not disengaging completely

☐ Clutch improperly adjusted (see Chapter 1).
☐ Clutch plates warped or damaged. This will cause clutch drag, which in turn will cause the machine to creep. Overhaul the clutch assembly (Chapter 2).
☐ Sagged or broken clutch spring(s). Check and replace the spring(s) (Chapter 2).
☐ Engine oil deteriorated. Old, thin, worn out oil will not provide proper lubrication for the discs, causing the clutch to drag. Replace the oil and filter (Chapter 1).
☐ Engine oil viscosity too high. Using a thicker oil than recommended in Chapter 1 can cause the clutch plates to stick together, putting a drag on the engine. Change to the correct viscosity oil (Chapter 1).
☐ Clutch housing seized on shaft. Lack of lubrication, severe wear or damage can cause the housing to seize on the shaft. Overhaul of the clutch, and perhaps transmission, may be necessary to repair the damage (Chapter 2).
☐ Clutch release mechanism defective. Worn or damaged release mechanism parts can stick and fail to apply force to the pressure plate. Overhaul the release mechanism (Chapter 2).
☐ Loose clutch center snap-ring. Causes housing and center misalignment putting a drag on the engine. Engagement adjustment continually varies. Overhaul the clutch assembly (Chapter 2).

# 6 Gear shifting problems

## Doesn't go into gear, or lever doesn't return

☐ Clutch not disengaging. See Section 27.
☐ Shift fork(s) bent or seized. May be caused by lack of lubrication. Overhaul the transmission (Chapter 2).
☐ Gear(s) stuck on shaft. Most often caused by a lack of lubrication or excessive wear in transmission bearings and bushings. Overhaul the transmission (Chapter 2).
☐ Shift drum binding. Caused by lubrication failure or excessive wear. Replace the drum and bearing (Chapter 2).
☐ Shift lever return spring weak or broken (Chapter 2).
☐ Shift lever broken. Splines stripped out of lever or shaft, caused by allowing the lever to get loose. Replace necessary parts (Chapter 2).
☐ Shift mechanism pawls broken or worn. Full engagement and rotary movement of shift drum results. Replace shaft assembly (Chapter 2).
☐ Pawl spring broken. Allows pawl to float, causing sporadic shift operation. Replace spring (Chapter 2).

## Jumps out of gear

☐ Shift fork(s) worn. Overhaul the transmission (Chapter 2).
☐ Gear groove(s) worn. Overhaul the transmission (Chapter 2).
☐ Gear dogs or dog slots worn or damaged. The gears should be inspected and replaced. No attempt should be made to service the worn parts.

## Overshifts

☐ Pawl spring weak or broken (Chapter 2).
☐ Shift drum stopper arm not functioning (Chapter 2).

# 7 Abnormal engine noise

## Knocking or pinging

☐ Carbon build-up in combustion chamber. Use of a fuel additive that will dissolve the adhesive bonding the carbon particles to the piston crown and chamber is the easiest way to remove the build-up. Otherwise, the cylinder head will have to be removed and decarbonized (Chapter 2).
☐ Incorrect or poor quality fuel. Old or improper fuel can cause detonation. This causes the piston to rattle, thus the knocking or pinging sound. Drain the old fuel (Chapter 4) and always use the recommended grade fuel (Chapter 1).
☐ Spark plug heat range incorrect. Uncontrolled detonation indicates that the plug heat range is too hot. The plug in effect becomes a glow plug, raising cylinder temperatures. Install the proper heat range plug (Chapter 1).
☐ Improper air/fuel mixture. This will cause the cylinder to run hot and lead to detonation. Clogged jets or an air leak can cause this imbalance. See Chapter 4.

## Piston slap or rattling

☐ Cylinder-to-piston clearance excessive. Caused by improper assembly. Inspect and overhaul top end parts (Chapter 2).
☐ Connecting rod bent. Caused by over-revving, trying to start a badly flooded engine or from ingesting a foreign object into the combustion chamber. Replace the damaged parts (Chapter 2).
☐ Piston pin or piston pin bore worn or seized from wear or lack of lubrication. Replace damaged parts (Chapter 2).
☐ Piston ring(s) worn, broken or sticking. Overhaul the top end (Chapter 2).
☐ Piston seizure damage. Usually from lack of lubrication or overheating. Replace the pistons and bore the cylinder, as necessary (Chapter 2).
☐ Connecting rod upper or lower end clearance excessive. Caused by excessive wear or lack of lubrication. Replace worn parts.

# 7 Abnormal engine noise (continued)

## Valve noise

☐ Incorrect valve clearances. Adjust the clearances by referring to Chapter 1.
☐ Valve spring broken or weak. Check and replace weak valve springs (Chapter 2).
☐ Camshaft or cylinder head worn or damaged. Lack of lubrication at high rpm is usually the cause of damage. Insufficient oil or failure to change the oil at the recommended intervals are the chief causes.
☐ Valve(s) worn. Replace the valves (Chapter 2).

## Other noise

☐ Cylinder head gasket leaking.

☐ Exhaust pipe leaking at cylinder head connection. Caused by improper fit of pipe, damaged gasket or loose exhaust flange. All exhaust fasteners should be tightened evenly and carefully. Failure to do this will lead to a leak.
☐ Crankshaft runout excessive. Caused by a bent crankshaft (from over-revving) or damage from an upper cylinder component failure.
☐ Engine mounting bolts or nuts loose. Tighten all engine mounting bolts and nuts to the specified torque (Chapter 2).
☐ Crankshaft bearings worn (Chapter 2).
☐ Camshaft chain tensioner defective. Replace according to the procedure in Chapter 2.
☐ Camshaft chain, sprockets or guides worn (Chapter 2).

# 8 Abnormal driveline noise

## Clutch noise

☐ Clutch housing/friction plate clearance excessive (Chapter 2).
☐ Loose or damaged pressure plate and/or bolts (Chapter 2).
☐ Broken clutch springs (Chapter 2).

## Transmission noise

☐ Bearings worn. Also includes the possibility that the shafts are worn. Overhaul the transmission (Chapter 2).
☐ Gears worn or chipped (Chapter 2).
☐ Metal chips jammed in gear teeth. Probably pieces from a broken clutch, gear or shift mechanism that were picked up by the gears. This will cause early bearing failure (Chapter 2).

☐ Engine oil level too low. Causes a howl from the transmission. Also affects engine power and clutch operation (Chapter 1).

## Final drive noise

☐ Dry or dirty chain. Inspect, clean and lubricate (see Chapter 1).
☐ Chain out of adjustment. Adjust chain slack (see Chapter 1).
☐ Chain and sprockets damaged or worn. Inspect the chain and sprockets and replace them as necessary (see Chapter 6).
☐ Sprockets loose (see Chapter 6).
☐ On XL600R models, rubber dampers in the cush drive deteriorated.

# 9 Abnormal chassis noise

## Suspension noise

☐ Spring weak or broken. Makes a clicking or scraping sound.
☐ Steering head bearings worn or damaged. Clicks when braking. Check and replace as necessary (Chapter 6).
☐ Front fork oil level incorrect. Check and correct oil level (see Chapter 6).
☐ Front fork(s) assembled incorrectly. Disassemble the fork(s) and check for correct assembly (see Chapter 6).
☐ Rear shock absorber fluid level incorrect. Indicates a leak caused by a defective seal. Shock will be covered with oil. It may be possible to have the shock overhauled to repair the damage; take the shock to a Honda dealer or motorcycle repair shop for inspection.
☐ Defective shock absorber with internal damage. This is in the body of the shock. It may be possible to have the shock overhauled to repair the damage; take the shock to a Honda dealer or motorcycle repair shop for inspection.
☐ Bent or damaged shock body rod. Replace the shock with a new one (Chapter 6).

## Brake noise

☐ Squeal caused by pad shim not installed or positioned correctly (Chapter 7).

☐ Squeal caused by dust on the brake pads. Usually found in combination with glazed pads. Clean using brake cleaning solvent (see Chapter 6).
☐ Contamination of brake pads. Oil, brake fluid or dirt causing pads to chatter or squeal. Clean or replace pads (see Chapter 7).
☐ Pads glazed. Caused by excessive heat from prolonged use or from contamination. Do not use sandpaper, emery cloth or carborundum cloth or any other abrasives to roughen pad surface as abrasives will stay in the pad material and damage the disc. A very fine flat file can be used, but pad replacement is suggested as a cure (see Chapter 6).
☐ Disc warped. Can cause a chattering, clicking or intermittent squeal. Usually accompanied by a pulsating lever and uneven braking. Replace the disc (see Chapter 7).
☐ Drum brake linings worn or contaminated. Can cause scraping or squealing. Replace the shoes (Chapter 7).
☐ Drum brake linings warped or worn unevenly. Can cause chattering. Replace the linings (Chapter 7).
☐ Brake drum out of round. Can cause chattering. Replace brake drum (Chapter 7).
☐ Loose or worn wheel bearings. Check and replace as needed (Chapter 7).

# 10 Excessive exhaust smoke

## White smoke

☐ Piston oil ring worn. The ring may be broken or damaged, causing oil from the crankcase to be pulled past the piston into the combustion chamber. Replace the rings with new ones (Chapter 2).

☐ Cylinder worn, cracked, or scored. Caused by overheating or oil starvation. If worn or scored, the cylinder will have to be rebored and a new piston installed. If cracked, the cylinder block will have to be replaced (see Chapter 2).

☐ Valve oil seal damaged or worn. Replace oil seals with new ones (Chapter 2).

☐ Valve guide worn. Perform a complete valve job (Chapter 2).

☐ Engine oil level too high, which causes the oil to be forced past the rings. Drain oil to the proper level (Chapter 1).

☐ Head gasket broken between oil return and cylinder. Causes oil to be pulled into the combustion chamber. Replace the head gasket and check the head for warpage (Chapter 2).

☐ Abnormal crankcase pressurization, which forces oil past the rings. Clogged breather or hoses usually the cause (Chapter 2).

## Black smoke

☐ Air cleaner clogged. Clean or replace the element (Chapter 1).

☐ Main jet too large or loose. Compare the jet size to the Specifications (Chapter 4).

☐ Choke stuck open (Chapter 4).

☐ Fuel level too high. Check the float level and replace the float if necessary (Chapter 4).

☐ Inlet needle held off needle seat. Clean the float chamber and fuel line and replace the needle and seat if necessary (Chapter 4).

## Brown smoke

☐ Main jet too small or clogged. Lean condition caused by wrong size main jet or by a restricted orifice. Clean float chamber and jets and compare jet size to Specifications (Chapter 4).

☐ Fuel flow insufficient. Fuel inlet needle valve stuck closed due to chemical reaction with old fuel. Float level incorrect; check and replace float if necessary. Restricted fuel line. Clean line and float chamber.

☐ Carburetor intake tube loose (Chapter 4).

☐ Air cleaner poorly sealed or not installed (Chapter 1).

# 11 Poor handling or stability

## Handlebar hard to turn

☐ Steering stem adjusting nut too tight (Chapter 6).

☐ Steering stem bearings damaged. Roughness can be felt as the bars are turned from side-to-side. Replace bearings and races (Chapter 6).

☐ Races dented or worn. Denting results from wear in only one position (like straight ahead), striking an immovable object or hole or from dropping the machine. Replace races and bearings (Chapter 6).

☐ Steering stem bearing lubrication inadequate. Causes are grease getting hard from age or being washed out by high pressure car washes. Remove steering stem, clean and lubricate bearings (Chapter 5).

☐ Steering stem bent. Caused by a collision, hitting a pothole or by dropping the machine. Replace damaged part. Don't try to straighten the steering stem (Chapter 6).

☐ Front tire air pressure too low (Chapter 1).

## Handlebar shakes or vibrates excessively

☐ Tires worn or out of balance (Chapter 1 or 6).

☐ Swingarm bearings worn. Replace worn bearings (Chapter 6).

☐ Wheel rim(s) warped or damaged. Inspect wheels (Chapter 7).

☐ Wheel bearings worn. Worn front or rear wheel bearings can cause poor tracking. Worn front bearings will cause wobble (Chapter 6).

☐ Handlebar clamp bolts loose (Chapter 6).

☐ Steering stem or triple clamps loose. Tighten them to the specified torque (Chapters 1 and 5).

☐ Engine mount bolts loose. Will cause excessive vibration with increased engine rpm (Chapter 2).

## Handlebar pulls to one side

☐ Frame bent. Definitely suspect this if the machine has been crashed hard. May or may not be accompanied by cracking near the bend. Replace the frame (Chapter 6).

☐ Front and rear wheels out of alignment. Caused by uneven adjustment of the drive chain adjusters (see Chapter 1). May also be caused by improper location of the axle spacers or from a bent steering stem or frame (see Chapter 6).

☐ Forks bent (Chapter 6).

☐ Swingarm bent or twisted. Caused by age (metal fatigue) or impact damage. Replace the swingarm (Chapter 6).

☐ Steering stem bent. Caused by impact damage or by dropping the motorcycle. Replace the steering stem (Chapter 6).

## Poor shock absorbing qualities

☐ Too hard:

a) Damping adjuster set too hard (see Chapter 6).
b) Fork oil level excessive (see Chapter 6).
c) Fork oil viscosity too high. Use a lighter oil (see the Specifications in Chapter 6).
d) Fork tube bent. Causes a harsh, sticking feeling (see Chapter 6).
e) Fork internal damage (see Chapter 6).
f) Shock internal damage.
g) Tire pressures too high (Chapter 1).

☐ Too soft:

a) Damping adjuster set too soft (see Chapter 6).
b) Fork or shock oil insufficient and/or leaking (Chapter 6).
c) Fork oil level too low (see Chapter 6).
d) Fork springs weak or broken (Chapter 6).
e) Shock absorber insufficiently charged (have it serviced by a dealer or other motorcycle repair shop).

# 12 Braking problems

## Brakes are spongy or weak, don't hold

☐ Air in brake line (disc brakes). Caused by inattention to master cylinder fluid level or by leakage. Locate problem and bleed brake (Chapter 7).
☐ Pad or disc worn (Chapters 1 and 6).
☐ Brake fluid leak. See paragraph 1.
☐ Contaminated disc brake pads. Caused by contamination with oil, grease, brake fluid, etc. Clean or replace pads. Clean disc thoroughly with brake cleaner.
☐ Brake fluid deteriorated (disc brakes). Fluid is old or contaminated. Drain system, replenish with new fluid and bleed the system (see Chapter 7).
☐ Master cylinder internal parts worn or damaged, causing fluid to bypass (see Chapter 7).
☐ Master cylinder bore scratched. From ingestion of foreign material or broken spring. Repair or replace master cylinder (see Chapter 7).
☐ Disc warped. Replace disc (see Chapter 7).
☐ Drum brake linings worn (Chapters 1 and 6).
☐ Contaminated drum brake linings. Caused by contamination with oil, grease, etc. Clean or replace linings. Clean drum thoroughly with brake cleaner (Chapter 7).
☐ Drum warped. Replace drum (Chapter 7).
☐ Drum brake cable out of adjustment or stretched. Adjust or replace the cable (see Chapters 1 and 6).

## Brake lever or pedal pulsates

☐ Disc warped. Replace disc (see Chapter 7).
☐ Axle bent. Replace axle (Chapter 7).
☐ Brake caliper bolts loose (see Chapter 7).
☐ Brake caliper shafts damaged or sticking, causing caliper to bind. Lube the shafts or replace them if they are corroded or bent (see Chapter 7).
☐ Wheel warped or otherwise damaged (Chapter 7).
☐ Wheel bearings damaged or worn (Chapter 7).
☐ Brake drum out of round. Replace brake drum (Chapter 7).

## Brakes drag

☐ Master cylinder piston seized. Caused by wear or damage to piston or cylinder bore (see Chapter 7).
☐ Lever or pedal balky or stuck. Check pivot and lubricate (see Chapter 8).
☐ Brake caliper binds. Caused by inadequate lubrication or damage to caliper shafts (see Chapter 7).
☐ Brake caliper piston seized in bore. Caused by wear or ingestion of dirt past deteriorated seal (see Chapter 7).
☐ Brake pad or shoes damaged. Pad or lining material separated from backing plate or shoes. Usually caused by faulty manufacturing process or contact with chemicals. Replace pads (see Chapter 7).
☐ Pads or shoes improperly installed (see Chapter 7).
☐ Cable sticking. Lubricate or replace cable (see Chapters 1 and 6).
☐ Shoes improperly installed (Chapter 7).
☐ Brake pedal or lever freeplay insufficient (Chapter 1).
☐ Drum brake springs weak. Replace brake springs (Chapter 7).

# 13 Electrical problems

## Battery dead or weak (XL600R and XR650L models)

☐ Battery faulty. Caused by sulfated plates which are shorted due to sedimentation or low electrolyte level. Also, broken battery terminal making only occasional contact (see Chapter 5).
☐ Battery cables making poor contact (see Chapter 5).
☐ Load excessive. Caused by addition of high wattage lights or other electrical accessories.
☐ Ignition switch defective. Switch either grounds internally or fails to shut off system. Replace the switch (see Chapter 5).
☐ Regulator/rectifier defective (see Chapter 5).
☐ Stator coil open or shorted (see Chapter 5).
☐ Wiring faulty. Wiring grounded or connections loose in ignition, charging or lighting circuits (see Chapter 5).

## Battery overcharged (XL600R and XR650L models)

☐ Regulator/rectifier defective. Overcharging is noticed when battery gets excessively warm or boils over (see Chapter 5).
☐ Battery defective. Replace battery with a new one (see Chapter 5).
☐ Battery amperage too low, wrong type or size. Install manufacturer's specified amp-hour battery to handle charging load (see Chapter 5)

## Starter doesn't crank engine (XL600R and XR650L models)

☐ Battery voltage low. Check and recharge battery (see Chapter 5).
☐ Fuse blown. Check the fuse (see Chapter 5).
☐ Starter button faulty. Check continuity of starter button (see Chapter 5).
☐ Wiring open or shorted. Check all wiring connections and harnesses to make sure that they are dry, tight and not corroded. Also check for broken or frayed wires that can cause a short to ground.
☐ Clutch switch defective. Check continuity of clutch switch (see Chapter 5).
☐ Starter motor defective. Make sure the starter relay clicks when the start button is pushed. If the relay clicks (and the circuit to the starter motor is OK), the fault is in the starter motor (provided that the battery voltage is adequate) (see Chapter 5).

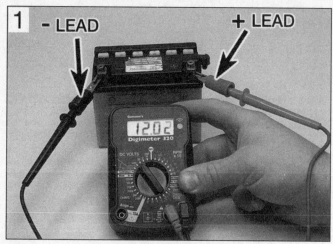

Measuring open-circuit battery voltage

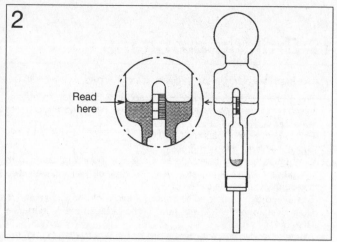

Float-type hydrometer for measuring battery specific gravity

## Checking engine compression

● Low compression will result in exhaust smoke, heavy oil consumption, poor starting and poor performance. A compression test will provide useful information about an engine's condition and if performed regularly, can give warning of trouble before any other symptoms become apparent.

● A compression gauge will be required, along with an adapter to suit the spark plug hole thread size. Note that the screw-in type gauge/adapter set up is preferable to the rubber cone type.

● Before carrying out the test, first check the valve clearances as described in Chapter 1.

● Compression testing procedures for the motorcycles covered in this manual are described in Chapter 2.

## Checking battery open-circuit voltage

⚠ **Warning: The gases produced by the battery are explosive - never smoke or create any sparks in the vicinity of the battery. Never allow the electrolyte to contact your skin or clothing - if it does, wash it off and seek immediate medical attention.**

● Before any electrical fault is investigated, the battery should be checked.

● You'll need a dc voltmeter or multimeter to check battery voltage. Check that the leads are inserted in the correct terminals on the meter, red lead to positive (+), black lead to negative (-). Incorrect connections can damage the meter.

● A sound, fully-charged 12 volt battery should produce between 12.3 and 12.6 volts across its terminals (12.8 volts for a maintenance-free battery). On machines with a 6 volt battery, voltage should be between 6.1 and 6.3 volts.

**1** Set a multimeter to the 0 to 20 volts dc range and connect its probes across the battery terminals. Connect the meter's positive (+) probe, usually red, to the battery positive (+) terminal, followed by the meter's negative (-) probe, usually black, to the battery negative terminal (-) **(see illustration 1)**.

**2** If battery voltage is low (below 10 volts on a 12 volt battery or below 4 volts on a six volt battery), charge the battery and test the voltage again. If the battery repeatedly goes flat, investigate the motorcycle's charging system.

## Checking battery specific gravity (SG)

⚠ **Warning: The gases produced by the battery are explosive - never smoke or create any sparks in the vicinity of the battery. Never allow the electrolyte to contact your skin or clothing - if it does, wash it off and seek immediate medical attention.**

● The specific gravity check gives an indication of a battery's state of charge.

● A hydrometer is used for measuring specific gravity. Make sure you purchase one which has a small enough hose to insert in the aperture of a motorcycle battery.

● Specific gravity is simply a measure of the electrolyte's density compared with that of water. Water has an SG of 1.000, and fully-charged battery electrolyte is about 26% heavier, at 1.260.

● Specific gravity checks are not possible on maintenance-free batteries. Testing the open-circuit voltage is the only means of determining their state of charge.

**1** To measure SG, remove the battery from the motorcycle and remove the first cell cap. Draw some electrolyte into the hydrometer and note the reading **(see illustration 2)**. Return the electrolyte to the cell and install the cap.

**2** The reading should be in the region of 1.260 to 1.280. If SG is below 1.200, the battery needs charging. Note that SG will vary with temperature; it should be measured at 20°C (68°F). Add 0.007 to the reading for every 10°C above 20°C, and subtract 0.007 from the reading for every 10°C below 20°C. Add 0.004 to the reading for every 10°F above 68°F, and subtract 0.004 from the reading for every 10°F below 68°F.

**3** When the check is complete, rinse the hydrometer thoroughly with clean water.

## Checking for continuity

● The term continuity describes the uninterrupted flow of electricity through an electrical circuit. A continuity check will determine whether an **open-circuit** situation exists.

● Continuity can be checked with an ohmmeter, multimeter, continuity tester or battery and bulb test circuit **(see illustrations 3, 4 and 5)**.

● All of these instruments are self-powered by a battery, therefore the checks are made with the ignition OFF.

● As a safety precaution, always disconnect the battery negative (-) lead before making checks, particularly if ignition switch checks are being made.

● If using a meter, select the appropriate

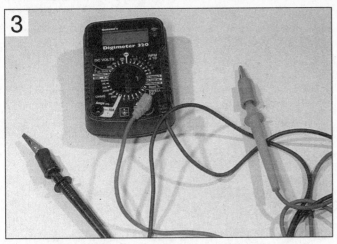

Digital multimeter can be used for all electrical tests

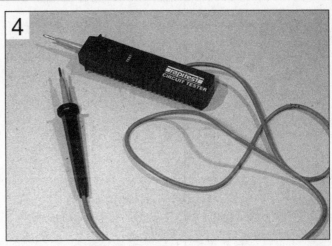

Battery-powered continuity tester

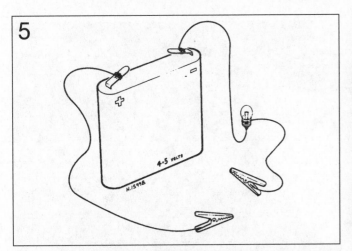

Battery and bulb test circuit

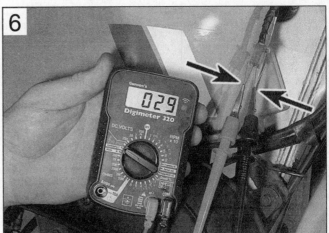

Continuity check of front brake light switch using a meter - note cotter pins used to access connector terminals

ohms scale and check that the meter reads infinity (∞). Touch the meter probes together and check that meter reads zero; where necessary adjust the meter so that it reads zero.

● After using a meter, always switch it OFF to conserve its battery.

## Switch checks

**1** If a switch is at fault, trace its wiring up to the wiring connectors. Separate the wire connectors and inspect them for security and condition. A build-up of dirt or corrosion here will most likely be the cause of the problem - clean up and apply a water dispersant such as WD40.

**2** If using a test meter, set the meter to the ohms x 10 scale and connect its probes across the wires from the switch **(see illustration 6)**. Simple ON/OFF type switches, such as brake light switches, only have two wires whereas combination switches, like the ignition switch, have many internal links. Study

the wiring diagram to ensure that you are connecting across the correct pair of wires. Continuity (low or no measurable resistance - 0 ohms) should be indicated with the switch ON and no continuity (high resistance) with it OFF.

**3** Note that the polarity of the test probes doesn't matter for continuity checks, although care should be taken to follow specific test procedures if a diode or solid-state component is being checked.

**4** A continuity tester or battery and bulb circuit can be used in the same way. Connect its probes as described above **(see illustration 7)**. The light should come on to indicate continuity in the ON switch position, but should extinguish in the OFF position.

## Wiring checks

● Many electrical faults are caused by damaged wiring, often due to incorrect routing or chaffing on frame components.
● Loose, wet or corroded wire connectors

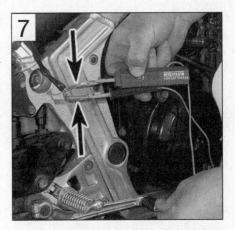

Continuity check of rear brake light switch using a continuity tester

can also be the cause of electrical problems, especially in exposed locations.

**8**

Continuity check of front brake light switch sub-harness

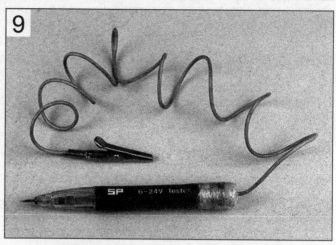

**9**

A simple test light can be used for voltage checks

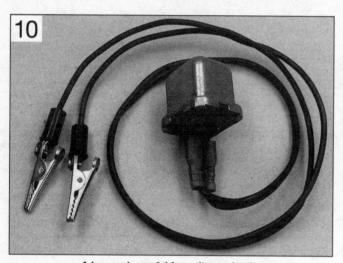

**10**

A buzzer is useful for voltage checks

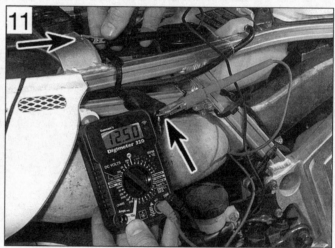

**11**

Checking for voltage at the rear brake light power supply wire using a meter . . .

**1** A continuity check can be made on a single length of wire by disconnecting it at each end and connecting a meter or continuity tester across both ends of the wire **(see illustration 8)**.

**2** Continuity (low or no resistance - 0 ohms) should be indicated if the wire is good. If no continuity (high resistance) is shown, suspect a broken wire.

## Checking for voltage

● A voltage check can determine whether current is reaching a component.

● Voltage can be checked with a dc voltmeter, multimeter set on the dc volts scale, test light or buzzer **(see illustrations 9 and 10)**. A meter has the advantage of being able to measure actual voltage.

● When using a meter, check that its leads are inserted in the correct terminals on the meter, red to positive (+), black to negative (-). Incorrect connections can damage the meter.

● A voltmeter (or multimeter set to the dc volts scale) should always be connected in parallel (across the load). Connecting it in series will destroy the meter.

● Voltage checks are made with the ignition ON.

**1** First identify the relevant wiring circuit by referring to the wiring diagram at the end of this manual. If other electrical components share the same power supply (they are fed from the same fuse), take note whether they are working correctly - this is useful information in deciding where to start checking the circuit.

**2** If using a meter, check first that the meter leads are plugged into the correct terminals on the meter (see above). Set the meter to the dc volts function, at a range suitable for the battery voltage. Connect the meter red probe (+) to the power supply wire and the black probe to a good metal ground on the

motorcycle's frame or directly to the battery negative (-) terminal **(see illustration 11)**. Battery voltage should be shown on the meter with the ignition switched ON.

**3** If using a test light or buzzer, connect its positive (+) probe to the power supply terminal and its negative (-) probe to a good ground on the motorcycle's frame or directly to the battery negative (-) terminal **(see illustration 12)**. With the ignition ON, the test light should illuminate or the buzzer sound.

**4** If no voltage is indicated, work back towards the fuse continuing to check for voltage. When you reach a point where there is voltage, you know the problem lies between that point and your last check point.

## Checking the ground

● Ground connections are made either

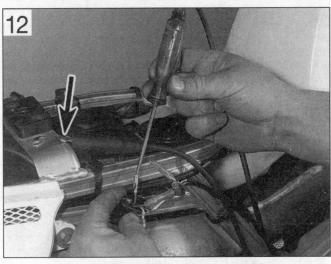

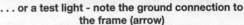

. . . or a test light - note the ground connection to the frame (arrow)

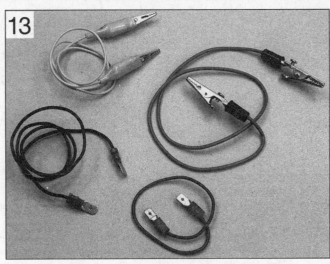

A selection of jumper wires for making ground checks

directly to the engine or frame (such as sensors, neutral switch etc. which only have a positive feed) or by a separate wire into the ground circuit of the wiring harness. Alternatively a short ground wire is sometimes run directly from the component to the motor-cycle's frame.

● Corrosion is often the cause of a poor ground connection.

● If total failure is experienced, check the security of the main ground lead from the negative (-) terminal of the battery and also the main ground point on the wiring harness. If corroded, dismantle the connection and clean all surfaces back to bare metal.

**1** To check the ground on a component, use an insulated jumper wire to temporarily bypass its ground connection **(see illustration 13)**. Connect one end of the jumper wire between the ground terminal or metal body

of the component and the other end to the motorcycle's frame.

**2** If the circuit works with the jumper wire installed, the original ground circuit is faulty. Check the wiring for open-circuits or poor connections. Clean up direct ground connections, removing all traces of corrosion and remake the joint. Apply petroleum jelly to the joint to prevent future corrosion.

## Tracing a short-circuit

● A short-circuit occurs where current shorts to ground bypassing the circuit components. This usually results in a blown fuse.

● A short-circuit is most likely to occur where the insulation has worn through due to wiring chafing on a component, allowing a direct path to ground on the frame.

**1** Remove any body panels necessary to access the circuit wiring.

**2** Check that all electrical switches in the circuit are OFF, then remove the circuit fuse and connect a test light, buzzer or voltmeter (set to the dc scale) across the fuse terminals. No voltage should be shown.

**3** Move the wiring from side to side while observing the test light or meter. When the test light comes on, buzzer sounds or meter shows voltage, you have found the cause of the short. It will usually shown up as damaged or burned insulation.

**4** Note that the same test can be performed on each component in the circuit, even the switch.

## Introduction

In less time than it takes to read this introduction, a thief could steal your motorcycle. Returning only to find your bike has gone is one of the worst feelings in the world. Even if the motorcycle is insured against theft, once you've got over the initial shock, you will have the inconvenience of dealing with the police and your insurance company.

The motorcycle is an easy target for the professional thief and the joyrider alike and the

official figures on motorcycle theft make for depressing reading; on average a motorcycle is stolen every 16 minutes!

Motorcycle thefts fall into two categories, those stolen "to order" and those taken by opportunists. The thief stealing to order will be on the look out for a specific make and model and will go to extraordinary lengths to obtain that motorcycle. The opportunist thief on the other hand will look for easy targets which can be stolen with the minimum of effort and risk.

While it is never going to be possible to make your machine 100% secure, it is estimated that around half of all stolen motorcycles are taken by opportunist thieves. Remember that the opportunist thief is always on the look out for the easy option: if there are two similar motorcycles parked side-by-side, they will target the one with the lowest level of security. By taking a few precautions, you can reduce the chances of your motorcycle being stolen.

# Security equipment

There are many specialized motorcycle security devices available and the following text summarizes their applications and their good and bad points.

Once you have decided on the type of security equipment which best suits your needs, we recommended that you read one of the many equipment tests regularly carried

Ensure the lock and chain you buy is of good quality and long enough to shackle your bike to a solid object

out by the motorcycle press. These tests compare the products from all the major manufacturers and give impartial ratings on their effectiveness, value-for-money and ease of use.

No one item of security equipment can provide complete protection. It is highly recommended that two or more of the items described below are combined to increase the security of your motorcycle (a lock and chain plus an alarm system is just about ideal). The more security measures fitted to the bike, the less likely it is to be stolen.

### Lock and chain

**Pros:** *Very flexible to use; can be used to secure the motorcycle to almost any immovable object. On some locks and chains, the lock can be used on its own as a disc lock (see below).*

**Cons:** *Can be very heavy and awkward to carry on the motorcycle, although some types*

*will be supplied with a carry bag which can be strapped to the pillion seat.*

● Heavy-duty chains and locks are an excellent security measure **(see illustration 1)**. Whenever the motorcycle is parked, use the lock and chain to secure the machine to a solid, immovable object such as a post or railings. This will prevent the machine from being ridden away or being lifted into the back of a van.

● When fitting the chain, always ensure the chain is routed around the motorcycle frame or swingarm **(see illustrations 2 and 3)**. Never merely pass the chain around one of the wheel rims; a thief may unbolt the wheel and lift the rest of the machine into a van, leaving you with just the wheel! Try to avoid having excess chain free, thus making it difficult to use cutting tools, and keep the chain and lock off the ground to prevent thieves attacking it with a cold chisel. Position the lock so that its lock barrel is facing downwards; this will make it harder for the thief to attack the lock mechanism.

Pass the chain through the bike's frame, rather than just through a wheel . . .

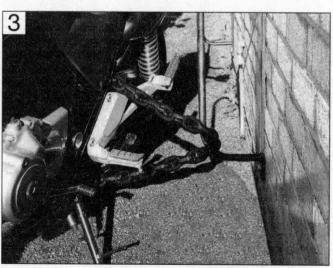

. . . and loop it around a solid object

## U-locks

**Pros:** *Highly effective deterrent which can be used to secure the bike to a post or railings. Most U-locks come with a carrier which allows the lock to be easily carried on the bike.*

**Cons:** *Not as flexible to use as a lock and chain.*

● These are solid locks which are similar in use to a lock and chain. U-locks are lighter than a lock and chain but not so flexible to use. The length and shape of the lock shackle limit the objects to which the bike can be secured **(see illustration 4)**.

**U-locks can be used to secure the bike to a solid object – ensure you purchase one which is long enough**

## Disc locks

**Pros:** *Small, light and very easy to carry; most can be stored underneath the seat.*

**Cons:** *Does not prevent the motorcycle being lifted into a van. Can be very embarrassing if*

**A typical disc lock attached through one of the holes in the disc**

you forget to remove the lock before attempting to ride off!

● Disc locks are designed to be attached to the front brake disc. The lock passes through one of the holes in the disc and prevents the wheel rotating by jamming against the fork/brake caliper **(see illustration 5)**. Some are equipped with an alarm siren which sounds if the disc lock is moved; this not only acts as a theft deterrent but also as a handy reminder if you try to move the bike with the lock still fitted.

● Combining the disc lock with a length of cable which can be looped around a post or railings provides an additional measure of security **(see illustration 6)**.

## Alarms and immobilizers

**Pros:** *Once installed it is completely hassle-free to use. In some cases, insurance companies may give you a discount.*

**Cons:** *Can be expensive to buy and complex to install. No system will prevent the motorcycle from being lifted into a van and taken away.*

● Electronic alarms and immobilisers are available to suit a variety of budgets. There are three different types of system available: pure alarms, pure immobilizers, and the more expensive systems which are combined alarm/immobilizers **(see illustration 7)**.
● An alarm system is designed to emit an audible warning if the motorcycle is being tampered with.
● An immobilizer prevents the motorcycle being started and ridden away by disabling its electrical systems.
● When purchasing an alarm/immobilizer system, check the cost of installing the system unless you are able to do it yourself. If the motorcycle is not used regularly, another consideration is the current drain of the system. All alarm/immobilizer systems are powered by the motorcycle's battery; purchasing a system with a very low current drain could prevent the battery losing its charge while the motorcycle is not being used.

**A disc lock combined with a security cable provides additional protection**

**A typical alarm/immobilizer system**

Indelible markings can be applied to most areas of the bike – always apply the manufacturer's sticker to warn off thieves

Chemically-etched code numbers can be applied to main body panels . . .

. . . again, always ensure that the kit manufacturer's sticker is applied in a prominent position

### Security marking kits

**Pros:** *Very cheap and effective deterrent. Many insurance companies will give you a discount on your insurance premium if a recognized security marking kit is used on your motorcycle.*

**Cons:** *Does not prevent the motorcycle being stolen by joyriders.*

● There are many different types of security marking kits available. The idea is to mark as many parts of the motorcycle as possible with a unique security number **(see illustrations 8, 9 and 10)**. A form will be included with the kit to register your personal details and those of the motorcycle with the kit manufacturer. This register is made available to the police to help them trace the rightful owner of any motorcycle or components which they recover should all other forms of identification have been removed. Always apply the warning stickers provided with the kit to deter thieves.

### Ground anchors, wheel clamps and security posts

**Pros:** *An excellent form of security which will deter all but the most determined of thieves.*

**Cons:** *Awkward to install and can be expensive.*

● While the motorcycle is at home, it is a good idea to attach it securely to the floor or a solid wall, even if it is kept in a securely locked garage. Various types of ground anchors, security posts and wheel clamps are available for this purpose **(see illustration 11)**. These security devices are either bolted to a solid concrete or brick structure or can be cemented into the ground.

Permanent ground anchors provide an excellent level of security when the bike is at home

## Security at home

A high percentage of motorcycle thefts are from the owner's home. Here are some things to consider whenever your motorcycle is at home:

✔ Where possible, always keep the motorcycle in a securely locked garage. Never rely solely on the standard lock on the garage door, these are usual hopelessly inadequate. Fit an additional locking mechanism to the door and consider having the garage alarmed. A security light, activated by a movement sensor, is also a good investment.

✔ Always secure the motorcycle to the ground or a wall, even if it is inside a securely locked garage.

✔ Do not regularly leave the motorcycle outside your home, try to keep it out of sight wherever possible. If a garage is not available, fit a motorcycle cover over the bike to disguise its true identity.

✔ It is not uncommon for thieves to follow a motorcyclist home to find out where the bike is kept. They will then return at a later date. Be aware of this whenever you are returning

home on your motorcycle. If you suspect you are being followed, do not return home, instead ride to a garage or shop and stop as a precaution.

✔ When selling a motorcycle, do not provide your home address or the location where the bike is normally kept. Arrange to meet the buyer at a location away from your home. Thieves have been known to pose as potential buyers to find out where motorcycles are kept and then return later to steal them.

## Security away from the home

As well as fitting security equipment to your motorcycle here are a few general rules to follow whenever you park your motorcycle.

✔ Park in a busy, public place.

✔ Use parking lots which incorporate security features, such as CCTV.

✔ At night, park in a well-lit area, preferably directly underneath a street light.

✔ Engage the steering lock.

✔ Secure the motorcycle to a solid, immovable object such as a post or railings with an additional lock. If this is not possible,

secure the bike to a friend's motorcycle. Some public parking places provide security loops for motorcycles.

✔ Never leave your helmet or luggage attached to the motorcycle. Take them with you at all times.

## A

**ABS (Anti-lock braking system)** A system, usually electronically controlled, that senses incipient wheel lockup during braking and relieves hydraulic pressure at wheel which is about to skid.

**Aftermarket** Components suitable for the motorcycle, but not produced by the motorcycle manufacturer.

**Allen key** A hexagonal wrench which fits into a recessed hexagonal hole.

**Alternating current (ac)** Current produced by an alternator. Requires converting to direct current by a rectifier for charging purposes.

**Alternator** Converts mechanical energy from the engine into electrical energy to charge the battery and power the electrical system.

**Ampere (amp)** A unit of measurement for the flow of electrical current. Current = Volts ÷ Ohms.

**Ampere-hour (Ah)** Measure of battery capacity.

**Angle-tightening** A torque expressed in degrees. Often follows a conventional tightening torque for cylinder head or main bearing fasteners **(see illustration)**.

Angle-tightening cylinder head bolts

**Antifreeze** A substance (usually ethylene glycol) mixed with water, and added to the cooling system, to prevent freezing of the coolant in winter. Antifreeze also contains chemicals to inhibit corrosion and the formation of rust and other deposits that would tend to clog the radiator and coolant passages and reduce cooling efficiency.

**Anti-dive** System attached to the fork lower leg (slider) to prevent fork dive when braking hard.

**Anti-seize compound** A coating that reduces the risk of seizing on fasteners that are subjected to high temperatures, such as exhaust clamp bolts and nuts.

**API American Petroleum Institute**. A quality standard for 4-stroke motor oils.

**Asbestos** A natural fibrous mineral with great heat resistance, commonly used in the composition of brake friction materials. Asbestos is a health hazard and the dust created by brake systems should never be inhaled or ingested.

**ATF** Automatic Transmission Fluid. Often used in front forks.

**ATU** Automatic Timing Unit. Mechanical device for advancing the ignition timing on early engines.

**ATV** All Terrain Vehicle. Often called a Quad.

**Axial play** Side-to-side movement.

**Axle** A shaft on which a wheel revolves. Also known as a spindle.

## B

**Backlash** The amount of movement between meshed components when one component is held still. Usually applies to gear teeth.

**Ball bearing** A bearing consisting of a hardened inner and outer race with hardened steel balls between the two races.

**Bearings** Used between two working surfaces to prevent wear of the components and a build-up of heat. Four types of bearing are commonly used on motorcycles: plain shell bearings, ball bearings, tapered roller bearings and needle roller bearings.

**Bevel gears** Used to turn the drive through 90°. Typical applications are shaft final drive and camshaft drive **(see illustration)**.

**BHP** Brake Horsepower. The British measure-ment for engine power output. Power output is now usually expressed in kilowatts (kW).

Bevel gears are used to turn the drive through 90°

**Bias-belted tire** Similar construction to radial tire, but with outer belt running at an angle to the wheel rim.

**Big-end bearing** The bearing in the end of the connecting rod that's attached to the crankshaft.

**Bleeding** The process of removing air from a hydraulic system via a bleed nipple or bleed screw.

**Bottom-end** A description of an engine's crankcase components and all components contained therein.

**BTDC** Before Top Dead Center in terms of piston position. Ignition timing is often expressed in terms of degrees or millimeters BTDC.

**Bush** A cylindrical metal or rubber component used between two moving parts.

**Burr** Rough edge left on a component after machining or as a result of excessive wear.

## C

**Cam chain** The chain which takes drive from the crankshaft to the camshaft(s).

**Canister** The main component in an evap-orative emission control system (California market only); contains activated charcoal granules to trap vapors from the fuel system rather than allowing them to vent to the atmosphere.

**Castellated** Resembling the parapets along the top of a castle wall. For example, a castellated wheel axle or spindle nut.

**Catalytic converter** A device in the exhaust system of some machines which

Cush drive rubber segments dampen out transmission shocks

**Cush drive** Rubber damper segments fitted between the rear wheel and final drive sprocket to absorb transmission shocks **(see illustration)**.

# D

**Degree disc** Calibrated disc for measuring piston position. Expressed in degrees.

**Dial gauge** Clock-type gauge with adapters for measuring runout and piston position. Expressed in mm or inches.

**Diaphragm** The rubber membrane in a master cylinder or carburetor which seals the upper chamber.

**Diaphragm spring** A single sprung plate often used in clutches.

**Direct current (dc)** Current produced by a dc generator.

**Decarbonization** The process of removing carbon deposits - typically from the combustion chamber, valves and exhaust port/system.

**Detonation** Destructive and damaging explosion of fuel/air mixture in combustion chamber instead of controlled burning.

**Diode** An electrical valve which only allows current to flow in one direction. Commonly used in rectifiers and starter interlock systems.

**Disc valve (or rotary valve)** An induction system used on some two-stroke engines.

**Double-overhead camshaft (DOHC)** An engine that uses two overhead camshafts, one for the intake valves and one for the exhaust valves.

**Drivebelt** A toothed belt used to transmit drive to the rear wheel on some motorcycles. A drivebelt has also been used to drive the camshafts. Drivebelts are usually made of Kevlar.

**Driveshaft** Any shaft used to transmit motion. Commonly used when referring to the final driveshaft on shaft drive motorcycles.

# E

**ECU (Electronic Control Unit)** A computer which controls (for instance) an ignition system, or an anti-lock braking system.

**EGO** Exhaust Gas Oxygen sensor. Some-times called a Lambda sensor.

**Electrolyte** The fluid in a lead-acid battery.

**EMS (Engine Management System)** A computer controlled system which manages the fuel injection and the ignition systems in an integrated fashion.

**Endfloat** The amount of lengthways movement between two parts. As applied to a crankshaft, the distance that the crankshaft can move side-to-side in the crankcase.

**Endless chain** A chain having no joining link. Common use for cam chains and final drive chains.

**EP (Extreme Pressure)** Oil type used in locations where high loads are applied, such as between gear teeth.

**Evaporative emission control system** Describes a charcoal filled canister which stores fuel vapors from the tank rather than allowing them to vent to the atmosphere. Usually only fitted to California models and referred to as an EVAP system.

**Expansion chamber** Section of two-stroke engine exhaust system so designed to improve engine efficiency and boost power.

# F

**Feeler blade or gauge** A thin strip or blade of hardened steel, ground to an exact thickness, used to check or measure clearances between parts.

**Final drive** Description of the drive from the transmission to the rear wheel. Usually by chain or shaft, but sometimes by belt.

**Firing order** The order in which the engine cylinders fire, or deliver their power strokes, beginning with the number one cylinder.

**Flooding** Term used to describe a high fuel level in the carburetor float chambers,

converts certain pollutants in the exhaust gases into less harmful substances.

**Charging system** Description of the components which charge the battery, ie the alternator, rectifer and regulator.

**Clearance** The amount of space between two parts. For example, between a piston and a cylinder, between a bearing and a journal, etc.

**Coil spring** A spiral of elastic steel found in various sizes throughout a vehicle, for example as a springing medium in the suspension and in the valve train.

**Compression** Reduction in volume, and increase in pressure and temperature, of a gas, caused by squeezing it into a smaller space.

**Compression damping** Controls the speed the suspension compresses when hitting a bump.

**Compression ratio** The relationship between cylinder volume when the piston is at top dead center and cylinder volume when the piston is at bottom dead center.

**Continuity** The uninterrupted path in the flow of electricity. Little or no measurable resistance.

**Continuity tester** Self-powered bleeper or test light which indicates continuity.

**Cp** Candlepower. Bulb rating commonly found on US motorcycles.

**Crossply tire** Tire plies arranged in a criss-cross pattern. Usually four or six plies used, hence 4PR or 6PR in tire size codes.

leading to fuel overflow. Also refers to excess fuel in the combustion chamber due to incorrect starting technique.

**Free length** The no-load state of a component when measured. Clutch, valve and fork spring lengths are measured at rest, without any preload.

**Freeplay** The amount of travel before any action takes place. The looseness in a linkage, or an assembly of parts, between the initial application of force and actual movement. For example, the distance the rear brake pedal moves before the rear brake is actuated.

**Fuel injection** The fuel/air mixture is metered electronically and directed into the engine intake ports (indirect injection) or into the cylinders (direct injection). Sensors supply information on engine speed and conditions.

**Fuel/air mixture** The charge of fuel and air going into the engine. See Stoichiometric ratio.

**Fuse** An electrical device which protects a circuit against accidental overload. The typical fuse contains a soft piece of metal which is calibrated to melt at a predetermined current flow (expressed as amps) and break the circuit.

# G

**Gap** The distance the spark must travel in jumping from the center electrode to the side electrode in a spark plug. Also refers to the distance between the ignition rotor and the pickup coil in an electronic ignition system.

**Gasket** Any thin, soft material - usually cork, cardboard, asbestos or soft metal - installed between two metal surfaces to ensure a good seal. For instance, the cylinder head gasket seals the joint between the block and the cylinder head.

**Gauge** An instrument panel display used to monitor engine conditions. A gauge with a movable pointer on a dial or a fixed scale is an analog gauge. A gauge with a numerical readout is called a digital gauge.

**Gear ratios** The drive ratio of a pair of gears in a gearbox, calculated on their number of teeth.

**Glaze-busting** see **Honing**

**Grinding** Process for renovating the valve face and valve seat contact area in the cylinder head.

**Ground return** The return path of an electrical circuit, utilizing the motorcycle's frame.

**Gudgeon pin** The shaft which connects the connecting rod small-end with the piston. Often called a piston pin or wrist pin.

# H

**Helical gears** Gear teeth are slightly curved and produce less gear noise that straight-cut gears. Often used for primary drives.

**Helicoil** A thread insert repair system. Commonly used as a repair for stripped spark plug threads **(see illustration)**.

Installing a Helicoil thread insert in a cylinder head

**Honing** A process used to break down the glaze on a cylinder bore (also called glaze-busting). Can also be carried out to roughen a rebored cylinder to aid ring bedding-in.

**HT (High Tension)** Description of the electrical circuit from the secondary winding of the ignition coil to the spark plug.

**Hydraulic** A liquid filled system used to transmit pressure from one component to another. Common uses on motorcycles are brakes and clutches.

**Hydrometer** An instrument for measuring the specific gravity of a lead-acid battery.

**Hygroscopic** Water absorbing. In motorcycle applications, braking efficiency will be reduced if DOT 3 or 4 hydraulic fluid absorbs water from the air - care must be taken to keep new brake fluid in tightly sealed containers.

# I

**lbf ft** Pounds-force feet. A unit of torque. Sometimes written as ft-lbs.

**lbf in** Pound-force inch. A unit of torque, applied to components where a very low torque is required. Sometimes written as inch-lbs.

**IC** Abbreviation for Integrated Circuit.

**Ignition advance** Means of increasing the timing of the spark at higher engine speeds. Done by mechanical means (ATU) on early engines or electronically by the ignition control unit on later engines.

**Ignition timing** The moment at which the spark plug fires, expressed in the number of crankshaft degrees before the piston reaches the top of its stroke, or in the number of millimeters before the piston reaches the top of its stroke.

**Infinity (∞)** Description of an open-circuit electrical state, where no continuity exists.

**Inverted forks (upside down forks)** The sliders or lower legs are held in the yokes and the fork tubes or stanchions are connected to the wheel axle (spindle). Less unsprung weight and stiffer construction than conventional forks.

# J

**JASO Japan Automobile Standards Organization.** JASO MA is a standard for motorcycle oil equivalent to API SJ, but designed to prevent problems with wet-type motorcycle clutches.

**Joule** The unit of electrical energy.

**Journal** The bearing surface of a shaft.

# K

**Kickstart** Mechanical means of turning the engine over for starting purposes.

Only usually fitted to mopeds, small capacity motorcycles and off-road motorcycles.

**Kill switch** Handebar-mounted switch for emergency ignition cut-out. Cuts the ignition circuit on all models, and additionally prevent starter motor operation on others.

**km** Symbol for kilometer.

**kmh** Abbreviation for kilometers per hour.

# L

**Lambda sensor** A sensor fitted in the exhaust system to measure the exhaust gas oxygen content (excess air factor). Also called oxygen sensor.

**Lapping** see **Grinding**.

**LCD** Abbreviation for Liquid Crystal Display.

**LED** Abbreviation for Light Emitting Diode.

**Liner** A steel cylinder liner inserted in an aluminum alloy cylinder block.

**Locknut** A nut used to lock an adjustment nut, or other threaded component, in place.

**Lockstops** The lugs on the lower triple clamp (yoke) which abut those on the frame, preventing handlebar-to-fuel tank contact.

**Lockwasher** A form of washer designed to prevent an attaching nut from working loose.

**LT Low Tension** Description of the electrical circuit from the power supply to the primary winding of the ignition coil.

# M

**Main bearings** The bearings between the crankshaft and crankcase.

**Maintenance-free (MF) battery** A sealed battery which cannot be topped up.

**Manometer** Mercury-filled calibrated tubes used to measure intake tract vacuum. Used to synchronize carburetors on multi-cylinder engines.

**Tappet shims are measured with a micrometer**

**Micrometer** A precision measuring instru-ment that measures component outside diameters **(see illustration)**.

**MON (Motor Octane Number)** A measure of a fuel's resistance to knock.

**Monograde oil** An oil with a single viscosity, eg SAE80W.

**Monoshock** A single suspension unit linking the swingarm or suspension linkage to the frame.

**mph** Abbreviation for miles per hour.

**Multigrade oil** Having a wide viscosity range (eg 10W40). The W stands for Winter, thus the viscosity ranges from SAE10 when cold to SAE40 when hot.

**Multimeter** An electrical test instrument with the capability to measure voltage, current and resistance. Some meters also incorporate a continuity tester and buzzer.

# N

**Needle roller bearing** Inner race of caged needle rollers and hardened outer race. Examples of uncaged needle rollers can be found on some engines. Commonly used in rear suspension applications and in two-stroke engines.

**Nm** Newton meters.

**NOx** Oxides of Nitrogen. A common toxic pollutant emitted by gasoline engines at higher temperatures.

# O

**Octane** The measure of a fuel's resistance to knock.

**OE (Original Equipment)** Relates to components fitted to a motorcycle as standard or replacement parts supplied by the motorcycle manufacturer.

**Ohm** The unit of electrical resistance. Ohms = Volts ÷ Current.

**Ohmmeter** An instrument for measuring electrical resistance.

**Oil cooler** System for diverting engine oil outside of the engine to a radiator for cooling purposes.

**Oil injection** A system of two-stroke engine lubrication where oil is pump-fed to the engine in accordance with throttle position.

**Open-circuit** An electrical condition where there is a break in the flow of electricity - no continuity (high resistance).

**O-ring** A type of sealing ring made of a special rubber-like material; in use, the O-ring is compressed into a groove to provide the sealing action.

**Oversize (OS)** Term used for piston and ring size options fitted to a rebored cylinder.

**Overhead cam (sohc) engine** An engine with single camshaft located on top of the cylinder head.

**Overhead valve (ohv) engine** An engine with the valves located in the cylinder head, but with the camshaft located in the engine block or crankcase.

**Oxygen sensor** A device installed in the exhaust system which senses the oxygen content in the exhaust and converts this information into an electric current. Also called a Lambda sensor.

# P

**Plastigage** A thin strip of plastic thread, available in different sizes, used for measuring clearances. For example, a strip of Plastigage is laid across a bearing journal. The parts are assembled and dismantled; the width of the crushed strip indicates the clearance between journal and bearing.

**Polarity** Either negative or positive ground, determined by which battery lead is connected to the frame (ground return). Modern motorcycles are usually negative ground.

**Pre-ignition** A situation where the fuel/air mixture ignites before the spark plug fires. Often due to a hot spot in the combustion chamber caused by carbon build-up. Engine has a tendency to 'run-on'.

**Pre-load (suspension)** The amount a spring is compressed when in the unloaded state. Preload can be applied by gas, spacer or mechanical adjuster.

**Premix** The method of engine lubrication on some gasoline two-stroke engines. Engine oil is mixed with the gasoline in the fuel tank in a specific ratio. The fuel/oil mix is sometimes referred to as "petrol".

**Primary drive** Description of the drive from the crankshaft to the clutch. Usually by gear or chain.

**PS** Pferdestärke - a German interpretation of BHP.

**PSI** Pounds-force per square inch. Imperial measurement of tire pressure and cylinder pressure measurement.

**PTFE** Polytetrafluroethylene. A low friction substance.

**Pulse secondary air injection system** A process of promoting the burning of excess fuel present in the exhaust gases by routing fresh air into the exhaust ports.

# Q

**Quartz halogen bulb** Tungsten filament surrounded by a halogen gas. Typically used for the headlight **(see illustration)**.

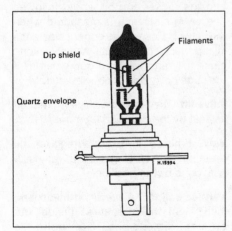

**Quartz halogen headlight bulb construction**

# R

**Rack-and-pinion** A pinion gear on the end of a shaft that mates with a rack (think of a geared wheel opened up and laid flat). Sometimes used in clutch operating systems.

**Radial play** Up and down movement about a shaft.

**Radial ply tires** Tire plies run across the tire (from bead to bead) and around the circumference of the tire. Less resistant to tread distortion than other tire types.

**Radiator** A liquid-to-air heat transfer device designed to reduce the temperature of the coolant in a liquid cooled engine.

**Rake** A feature of steering geometry - the angle of the steering head in relation to the vertical **(see illustration)**.

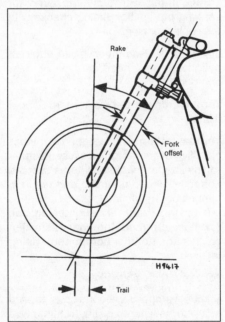

**Steering geometry**

**Rebore** Providing a new working surface to the cylinder bore by boring out the old surface. Necessitates the use of oversize piston and rings.

**Rebound damping** A means of controlling the oscillation of a suspension unit spring after it has been compressed. Resists the spring's natural tendency to bounce back after being compressed.

**Rectifier** Device for converting the ac output of an alternator into dc for battery charging.

**Reed valve** An induction system commonly used on two-stroke engines.

**Regulator** Device for maintaining the charging voltage from the generator or alternator within a specified range.

**Relay** A electrical device used to switch heavy current on and off by using a low current auxiliary circuit.

**Resistance** Measured in ohms. An electrical component's ability to pass electrical current.

**RON (Research Octane Number)** A measure of a fuel's resistance to knock.

**rpm** revolutions per minute.

**Runout** The amount of wobble (in-and-out movement) of a wheel or shaft as it's rotated. The amount a shaft rotates "out-of-true." The out-of-round condition of a rotating part.

# S

**SAE (Society of Automotive Engineers)** A standard for the viscosity of a fluid.

**Sealant** A liquid or paste used to prevent leakage at a joint. Sometimes used in conjunction with a gasket.

**Service limit** Term for the point where a component is no longer useable and must be replaced.

**Shaft drive** A method of transmitting drive from the transmission to the rear wheel.

**Shell bearings** Plain bearings consisting of two shell halves. Most often used as big-end and main bearings in a four-stroke engine. Often called bearing inserts.

**Shim** Thin spacer, commonly used to adjust the clearance or relative positions between two parts. For example, shims inserted into or under tappets or followers to control valve clearances. Clearance is adjusted by changing the thickness of the shim.

**Short-circuit** An electrical condition where current shorts to ground bypassing the circuit components.

**Skimming** Process to correct warpage or repair a damaged surface, eg on brake discs or drums.

**Slide-hammer** A special puller that screws into or hooks onto a component such as a shaft or bearing; a heavy sliding handle on the shaft bottoms against the end of the shaft to knock the component free.

**Small-end bearing** The bearing in the upper end of the connecting rod at its joint with the gudgeon pin.

**Snap-ring** A ring-shaped clip used to prevent endwise movement of cylindrical parts and shafts. An internal snap-ring is installed in a groove in a housing; an external snap-ring fits into a groove on the outside of a cylindrical piece such as a shaft. Also known as a circlip.

**Spalling** Damage to camshaft lobes or bearing journals shown as pitting of the working surface.

**Specific gravity (SG)** The state of charge of the electrolyte in a lead-acid battery. A measure of the electrolyte's density compared with water.

**Straight-cut gears** Common type gear used on gearbox shafts and for oil pump and water pump drives.

**Stanchion** The inner sliding part of the front forks, held by the yokes. Often called a fork tube.

**Stoichiometric ratio** The optimum chemical air/fuel ratio for a gasoline engine, said to be 14.7 parts of air to 1 part of fuel.

**Sulphuric acid** The liquid (electrolyte) used in a lead-acid battery. Poisonous and extremely corrosive.

**Surface grinding (lapping)** Process to correct a warped gasket face, commonly used on cylinder heads.

# T

**Tapered-roller bearing** Tapered inner race of caged needle rollers and separate tapered outer race. Examples of taper roller bearings can be found on steering heads.

**Tappet** A cylindrical component which transmits motion from the cam to the valve stem, either directly or via a pushrod and rocker arm. Also called a cam follower.

**TCS** Traction Control System. An electron-ically-controlled system which senses wheel spin and reduces engine speed accordingly.

**TDC** Top Dead Center denotes that the piston is at its highest point in the cylinder.

**Thread-locking compound** Solution applied to fastener threads to prevent loosening. Select type to suit application.

**Thrust washer** A washer positioned between two moving components on a shaft. For example, between gear pinions on gearshaft.

**Timing chain** See **Cam Chain**.

**Timing light** Stroboscopic lamp for carrying out ignition timing checks with the engine running.

**Top-end** A description of an engine's cylinder block, head and valve gear components.

**Torque** Turning or twisting force about a shaft.

**Torque setting** A prescribed tightness specified by the motorcycle manufacturer to ensure that the bolt or nut is secured correctly. Undertightening can result in the bolt or nut coming loose or a surface not being sealed. Overtightening can result in stripped threads, distortion or damage to the component being retained.

**Torx key** A six-point wrench.

**Tracer** A stripe of a second color applied to a wire insulator to distinguish that wire from another one with the same color insulator. For example, Br/W is often used to denote a brown insulator with a white tracer.

**Trail** A feature of steering geometry. Distance from the steering head axis to the tire's central contact point.

**Triple clamps** The cast components which extend from the steering head and support the fork stanchions or tubes. Often called fork yokes.

**Turbocharger** A centrifugal device, driven by exhaust gases, that pressurizes the intake air. Normally used to increase the power output from a given engine displacement.

**TWI** Abbreviation for Tire Wear Indicator. Indicates the location of the tread depth indicator bars on tires.

# U

**Universal joint or U-joint (UJ)** A double-pivoted connection for transmitting power from a driving to a driven shaft through an angle. Typically found in shaft drive assemblies.

**Unsprung weight** Anything not supported by the bike's suspension (ie the wheel, tires, brakes, final drive and bottom (moving) part of the suspension).

# V

**Vacuum gauges** Clock-type gauges for measuring intake tract vacuum. Used for carburetor synchronization on multi-cylinder engines.

**Valve** A device through which the flow of liquid, gas or vacuum may be stopped, started or regulated by a moveable part that opens, shuts or partially obstructs one or more ports or passageways. The intake and exhaust valves in the cylinder head are of the poppet type.

**Valve clearance** The clearance between the valve tip (the end of the valve stem) and the rocker arm or tappet/follower. The valve clearance is measured when the valve is closed. The correct clearance is important - if too small the valve won't close fully and will burn out, whereas if too large noisy operation will result.

**Valve lift** The amount a valve is lifted off its seat by the camshaft lobe.

**Valve timing** The exact setting for the opening and closing of the valves in relation to piston position.

**Vernier caliper** A precision measuring instrument that measures inside and outside dimensions. Not quite as accurate as a micrometer, but more convenient.

**VIN** Vehicle Identification Number. Term for the bike's engine and frame numbers.

**Viscosity** The thickness of a liquid or its resistance to flow.

**Volt** A unit for expressing electrical "pressure" in a circuit. Volts = current x ohms.

# W

**Water pump** A mechanically-driven device for moving coolant around the engine.

**Watt** A unit for expressing electrical power. Watts = volts x current.

**Wet liner arrangement**

**Wear** limit see **Service limit**

**Wet liner** A liquid-cooled engine design where the pistons run in liners which are directly surrounded by coolant **(see illustration)**.

**Wheelbase** Distance from the center of the front wheel to the center of the rear wheel.

**Wiring harness or loom** Describes the electrical wires running the length of the motorcycle and enclosed in tape or plastic sheathing. Wiring coming off the main harness is usually referred to as a sub harness.

**Woodruff key** A key of semi-circular or square section used to locate a gear to a shaft. Often used to locate the alternator rotor on the crankshaft.

**Wrist pin** Another name for gudgeon or piston pin.

# Notes

**Note:** *References throughout this index are in the form, "Chapter number"•"Page number"*

# Haynes Automotive Manuals

*NOTE: If you do not see a listing for your vehicle, consult your local Haynes dealer for the latest product information.*

## ACURA
| | |
|---|---|
| 12020 | **Integra** '86 thru '89 & **Legend** '86 thru '90 |
| 12021 | **Integra** '90 thru '93 & **Legend** '91 thru '95 |
| | **Integra** '94 thru '00 - *see HONDA Civic (42025)* |
| | **MDX** '01 thru '07 - *see HONDA Pilot (42037)* |
| 12050 | **Acura TL** all models '99 thru '08 |

## AMC
| | |
|---|---|
| | **Jeep CJ** - *see JEEP (50020)* |
| 14020 | **Mid-size models** '70 thru '83 |
| 14025 | **(Renault) Alliance & Encore** '83 thru '87 |

## AUDI
| | |
|---|---|
| 15020 | **4000** all models '80 thru '87 |
| 15025 | **5000** all models '77 thru '83 |
| 15026 | **5000** all models '84 thru '88 |
| | **Audi A4** '96 thru '01 - *see VW Passat (96023)* |
| 15030 | **Audi A4** '02 thru '08 |

## AUSTIN-HEALEY
| | |
|---|---|
| | **Sprite** - *see MG Midget (66015)* |

## BMW
| | |
|---|---|
| 18020 | **3/5 Series** '82 thru '92 |
| 18021 | **3-Series** incl. Z3 models '92 thru '98 |
| 18022 | **3-Series** incl. Z4 models '99 thru '05 |
| 18023 | **3-Series** '06 thru '10 |
| 18025 | **320i** all 4 cyl models '75 thru '83 |
| 18050 | **1500 thru 2002** except Turbo '59 thru '77 |

## BUICK
| | |
|---|---|
| 19010 | **Buick Century** '97 thru '05 |
| | **Century** (front-wheel drive) - *see GM (38005)* |
| 19020 | **Buick, Oldsmobile & Pontiac Full-size (Front-wheel drive)** '85 thru '05<br>**Buick** Electra, LeSabre and Park Avenue; **Oldsmobile** Delta 88 Royale, Ninety Eight and Regency; **Pontiac** Bonneville |
| 19025 | **Buick, Oldsmobile & Pontiac Full-size (Rear wheel drive)** '70 thru '90<br>**Buick** Estate, Electra, LeSabre, Limited, **Oldsmobile** Custom Cruiser, Delta 88, Ninety-eight, **Pontiac** Bonneville, Catalina, Grandville, Parisienne |
| 19030 | **Mid-size Regal & Century** all rear-drive models with V6, V8 and Turbo '74 thru '87<br>**Regal** - *see GENERAL MOTORS (38010)*<br>**Riviera** - *see GENERAL MOTORS (38030)*<br>**Roadmaster** - *see CHEVROLET (24046)*<br>**Skyhawk** - *see GENERAL MOTORS (38015)*<br>**Skylark** - *see GM (38020, 38025)*<br>**Somerset** - *see GENERAL MOTORS (38025)* |

## CADILLAC
| | |
|---|---|
| 21015 | **CTS & CTS-V** '03 thru '12 |
| 21030 | **Cadillac Rear Wheel Drive** '70 thru '93<br>**Cimarron** - *see GENERAL MOTORS (38015)*<br>**DeVille** - *see GM (38031 & 38032)*<br>**Eldorado** - *see GM (38030 & 38031)*<br>**Fleetwood** - *see GM (38031)*<br>**Seville** - *see GM (38030, 38031 & 38032)* |

## CHEVROLET
| | |
|---|---|
| 10305 | **Chevrolet Engine Overhaul Manual** |
| 24010 | **Astro & GMC Safari Mini-vans** '85 thru '05 |
| 24015 | **Camaro V8** all models '70 thru '81 |
| 24016 | **Camaro** all models '82 thru '92 |
| 24017 | **Camaro & Firebird** '93 thru '02<br>**Cavalier** - *see GENERAL MOTORS (38016)*<br>**Celebrity** - *see GENERAL MOTORS (38005)* |
| 24020 | **Chevelle, Malibu & El Camino** '69 thru '87 |
| 24024 | **Chevette & Pontiac T1000** '76 thru '87<br>**Citation** - *see GENERAL MOTORS (38020)* |
| 24027 | **Colorado & GMC Canyon** '04 thru '10 |
| 24032 | **Corsica/Beretta** all models '87 thru '96 |
| 24040 | **Corvette** all V8 models '68 thru '82 |
| 24041 | **Corvette** all models '84 thru '96 |
| 24045 | **Full-size Sedans** Caprice, Impala, Biscayne, Bel Air & Wagons '69 thru '90 |
| 24046 | **Impala SS & Caprice and Buick Roadmaster** '91 thru '96<br>**Impala** '00 thru '05 - *see LUMINA (24048)* |
| 24047 | **Impala & Monte Carlo** all models '06 thru '11<br>**Lumina** '90 thru '94 - *see GM (38010)* |
| 24048 | **Lumina & Monte Carlo** '95 thru '05<br>**Lumina APV** - *see GM (38035)* |
| 24050 | **Luv Pick-up** all 2WD & 4WD '72 thru '82<br>**Malibu** '97 thru '00 - *see GM (38026)* |
| 24055 | **Monte Carlo** all models '70 thru '88<br>**Monte Carlo** '95 thru '01 - *see LUMINA (24048)* |
| 24059 | **Nova** all V8 models '69 thru '79 |
| 24060 | **Nova and Geo Prizm** '85 thru '92 |
| 24064 | **Pick-ups** '67 thru '87 - Chevrolet & GMC |
| 24065 | **Pick-ups** '88 thru '98 - Chevrolet & GMC |
| 24066 | **Pick-ups** '99 thru '06 - Chevrolet & GMC |
| 24067 | **Chevrolet Silverado & GMC Sierra** '07 thru '12 |
| 24070 | **S-10 & S-15 Pick-ups** '82 thru '93, **Blazer & Jimmy** '83 thru '94, |
| 24071 | **S-10 & Sonoma Pick-ups** '94 thru '04, including **Blazer, Jimmy & Hombre** |
| 24072 | **Chevrolet TrailBlazer, GMC Envoy & Oldsmobile Bravada** '02 thru '09 |
| 24075 | **Sprint** '85 thru '88 & **Geo Metro** '89 thru '01 |
| 24080 | **Vans - Chevrolet & GMC** '68 thru '96 |
| 24081 | **Chevrolet Express & GMC Savana** Full-size Vans '96 thru '10 |

## CHRYSLER
| | |
|---|---|
| 10310 | **Chrysler Engine Overhaul Manual** |
| 25015 | **Chrysler Cirrus, Dodge Stratus, Plymouth Breeze** '95 thru '00 |
| 25020 | **Full-size Front-Wheel Drive** '88 thru '93<br>**K-Cars** - *see DODGE Aries (30008)*<br>**Laser** - *see DODGE Daytona (30030)* |
| 25025 | **Chrysler LHS, Concorde, New Yorker, Dodge Intrepid, Eagle Vision**, '93 thru '97 |
| 25026 | **Chrysler LHS, Concorde, 300M, Dodge Intrepid**, '98 thru '04 |
| 25027 | **Chrysler 300, Dodge Charger & Magnum** '05 thru '09 |
| 25030 | **Chrysler & Plymouth Mid-size** front wheel drive '82 thru '95<br>**Rear-wheel drive** - *see Dodge (30050)* |
| 25035 | **PT Cruiser** all models '01 thru '10 |
| 25040 | **Chrysler Sebring** '95 thru '06, **Dodge Stratus** '01 thru '06, **Dodge Avenger** '95 thru '00 |

## DATSUN
| | |
|---|---|
| 28005 | **200SX** all models '80 thru '83 |
| 28007 | **B-210** all models '73 thru '78 |
| 28009 | **210** all models '79 thru '82 |
| 28012 | **240Z, 260Z & 280Z** Coupe '70 thru '78 |
| 28014 | **280ZX** Coupe & 2+2 '79 thru '83<br>**300ZX** - *see NISSAN (72010)* |
| 28018 | **510 & PL521 Pick-up** '68 thru '73 |
| 28020 | **510** all models '78 thru '81 |
| 28022 | **620 Series Pick-up** all models '73 thru '79<br>**720 Series Pick-up** - *see NISSAN (72030)* |
| 28025 | **810/Maxima** all gasoline models '77 thru '84 |

## DODGE
| | |
|---|---|
| | **400 & 600** - *see CHRYSLER (25030)* |
| 30008 | **Aries & Plymouth Reliant** '81 thru '89 |
| 30010 | **Caravan & Plymouth Voyager** '84 thru '95 |
| 30011 | **Caravan & Plymouth Voyager** '96 thru '02 |
| 30012 | **Challenger/Plymouth Saporro** '78 thru '83 |
| 30013 | **Caravan, Chrysler Voyager, Town & Country** '03 thru '07 |
| 30016 | **Colt & Plymouth Champ** '78 thru '87 |
| 30020 | **Dakota Pick-ups** all models '87 thru '96 |
| 30021 | **Durango** '98 & '99, **Dakota** '97 thru '99 |
| 30022 | **Durango** '00 thru '03 **Dakota** '00 thru '04 |
| 30023 | **Durango** '04 thru '09, **Dakota** '05 thru '11 |
| 30025 | **Dart, Demon, Plymouth Barracuda, Duster & Valiant** 6 cyl models '67 thru '76 |
| 30030 | **Daytona & Chrysler Laser** '84 thru '89<br>**Intrepid** - *see CHRYSLER (25025, 25026)* |
| 30034 | **Neon** all models '95 thru '99 |
| 30035 | **Omni & Plymouth Horizon** '78 thru '90 |
| 30036 | **Dodge and Plymouth Neon** '00 thru '05 |
| 30040 | **Pick-ups** all full-size models '74 thru '93 |
| 30041 | **Pick-ups** all full-size models '94 thru '01 |
| 30042 | **Pick-ups** full-size models '02 thru '08 |
| 30045 | **Ram 50/D50 Pick-ups & Raider and Plymouth Arrow Pick-ups** '79 thru '93 |
| 30050 | **Dodge/Plymouth/Chrysler RWD** '71 thru '89 |
| 30055 | **Shadow & Plymouth Sundance** '87 thru '94 |
| 30060 | **Spirit & Plymouth Acclaim** '89 thru '95 |
| 30065 | **Vans - Dodge & Plymouth** '71 thru '03 |

## EAGLE
| | |
|---|---|
| | **Talon** - *see MITSUBISHI (68030, 68031)*<br>**Vision** - *see CHRYSLER (25025)* |

## FIAT
| | |
|---|---|
| 34010 | **124 Sport Coupe & Spider** '68 thru '78 |
| 34025 | **X1/9** all models '74 thru '80 |

## FORD
| | |
|---|---|
| 10320 | **Ford Engine Overhaul Manual** |
| 10355 | **Ford Automatic Transmission Overhaul** |
| 11500 | **Mustang '64-1/2 thru '70 Restoration Guide** |
| 36004 | **Aerostar Mini-vans** all models '86 thru '97 |
| 36006 | **Contour & Mercury Mystique** '95 thru '00 |
| 36008 | **Courier Pick-up** all models '72 thru '82 |
| 36012 | **Crown Victoria & Mercury Grand Marquis** '88 thru '10 |
| 36016 | **Escort/Mercury Lynx** all models '81 thru '90 |
| 36020 | **Escort/Mercury Tracer** '91 thru '02 |
| 36022 | **Escape & Mazda Tribute** '01 thru '11 |
| 36024 | **Explorer & Mazda Navajo** '91 thru '01 |
| 36025 | **Explorer/Mercury Mountaineer** '02 thru '10 |
| 36028 | **Fairmont & Mercury Zephyr** '78 thru '83 |
| 36030 | **Festiva & Aspire** '88 thru '97 |
| 36032 | **Fiesta** all models '77 thru '80 |
| 36034 | **Focus** all models '00 thru '11 |
| 36036 | **Ford & Mercury Full-size** '75 thru '87 |
| 36044 | **Ford & Mercury Mid-size** '75 thru '86 |
| 36045 | **Fusion & Mercury Milan** '06 thru '10 |
| 36048 | **Mustang V8** all models '64-1/2 thru '73 |
| 36049 | **Mustang II** 4 cyl, V6 & V8 models '74 thru '78 |
| 36050 | **Mustang & Mercury Capri** '79 thru '93 |
| 36051 | **Mustang** all models '94 thru '04 |
| 36052 | **Mustang** '05 thru '10 |
| 36054 | **Pick-ups & Bronco** '73 thru '79 |
| 36058 | **Pick-ups & Bronco** '80 thru '96 |
| 36059 | **F-150 & Expedition** '97 thru '09, **F-250** '97 thru '99 & **Lincoln Navigator** '98 thru '09 |
| 36060 | **Super Duty Pick-ups, Excursion** '99 thru '10 |
| 36061 | **F-150 full-size** '04 thru '10 |
| 36062 | **Pinto & Mercury Bobcat** '75 thru '80 |
| 36066 | **Probe** all models '89 thru '92<br>**Probe** '93 thru '97 - *see MAZDA 626 (61042)* |
| 36070 | **Ranger/Bronco II** gasoline models '83 thru '92 |
| 36071 | **Ranger** '93 thru '10 & **Mazda Pick-ups** '94 thru '09 |
| 36074 | **Taurus & Mercury Sable** '86 thru '95 |
| 36075 | **Taurus & Mercury Sable** '96 thru '05 |
| 36078 | **Tempo & Mercury Topaz** '84 thru '94 |
| 36082 | **Thunderbird/Mercury Cougar** '83 thru '88 |
| 36086 | **Thunderbird/Mercury Cougar** '89 thru '97 |
| 36090 | **Vans** all V8 Econoline models '69 thru '91 |
| 36094 | **Vans** full size '92 thru '10 |
| 36097 | **Windstar Mini-van** '95 thru '07 |

## GENERAL MOTORS
| | |
|---|---|
| 10360 | **GM Automatic Transmission Overhaul** |
| 38005 | **Buick Century, Chevrolet Celebrity, Oldsmobile Cutlass Ciera & Pontiac 6000** all models '82 thru '96 |
| 38010 | **Buick Regal, Chevrolet Lumina, Oldsmobile Cutlass Supreme & Pontiac Grand Prix** (FWD) '88 thru '07 |
| 38015 | **Buick Skyhawk, Cadillac Cimarron, Chevrolet Cavalier, Oldsmobile Firenza & Pontiac J-2000 & Sunbird** '82 thru '94 |
| 38016 | **Chevrolet Cavalier & Pontiac Sunfire** '95 thru '05 |
| 38017 | **Chevrolet Cobalt & Pontiac G5** '05 thru '11 |
| 38020 | **Buick Skylark, Chevrolet Citation, Olds Omega, Pontiac Phoenix** '80 thru '85 |
| 38025 | **Buick Skylark & Somerset, Oldsmobile Achieva & Calais and Pontiac Grand Am** all models '85 thru '98 |
| 38026 | **Chevrolet Malibu, Olds Alero & Cutlass, Pontiac Grand Am** '97 thru '03 |
| 38027 | **Chevrolet Malibu** '04 thru '10 |
| 38030 | **Cadillac Eldorado, Seville, Oldsmobile Toronado, Buick Riviera** '71 thru '85 |
| 38031 | **Cadillac Eldorado & Seville, DeVille, Fleetwood & Olds Toronado, Buick Riviera** '86 thru '93 |
| 38032 | **Cadillac DeVille** '94 thru '05 & **Seville** '92 thru '04 **Cadillac DTS** '06 thru '10 |
| 38035 | **Chevrolet Lumina APV, Olds Silhouette & Pontiac Trans Sport** all models '90 thru '96 |
| 38036 | **Chevrolet Venture, Olds Silhouette, Pontiac Trans Sport & Montana** '97 thru '05<br>**General Motors Full-size Rear-wheel Drive** - *see BUICK (19025)* |
| 38040 | **Chevrolet Equinox** '05 thru '09 **Pontiac Torrent** '06 thru '09 |
| 38070 | **Chevrolet HHR** '06 thru '11 |

## GEO
| | |
|---|---|
| | **Metro** - *see CHEVROLET Sprint (24075)*<br>**Prizm** - '85 thru '92 see CHEVY (24060), '93 thru '02 see TOYOTA Corolla (92036) |
| 40030 | **Storm** all models '90 thru '93<br>**Tracker** - *see SUZUKI Samurai (90010)* |

## GMC
| | |
|---|---|
| | **Vans & Pick-ups** - *see CHEVROLET* |

## HONDA
| | |
|---|---|
| 42010 | **Accord CVCC** all models '76 thru '83 |
| 42011 | **Accord** all models '84 thru '89 |
| 42012 | **Accord** all models '90 thru '93 |
| 42013 | **Accord** all models '94 thru '97 |
| 42014 | **Accord** all models '98 thru '02 |
| 42015 | **Accord** '03 thru '07 |
| 42020 | **Civic 1200** all models '73 thru '79 |
| 42021 | **Civic 1300 & 1500 CVCC** '80 thru '83 |
| 42022 | **Civic 1500 CVCC** all models '75 thru '79 |

*(Continued on other side)*

Haynes North America, Inc., 861 Lawrence Drive, Newbury Park, CA 91320-1514 • (805) 498-6703 • http://www.haynes.com

# Haynes Automotive Manuals (continued)

*NOTE: If you do not see a listing for your vehicle, consult your local Haynes dealer for the latest product information.*

**42023** Civic all models '84 thru '91
**42024** Civic & del Sol '92 thru '95
**42025** Civic '96 thru '00, CR-V '97 thru '01,
Acura Integra '94 thru '00
**42026** Civic '01 thru '10, CR-V '02 thru '09
**42035** Odyssey all models '99 thru '10
Passport - see ISUZU Rodeo (47017)
**42037** Honda Pilot '03 thru '07, Acura MDX '01 thru '07
**42040** Prelude CVCC all models '79 thru '89

## HYUNDAI
**43010** Elantra all models '96 thru '10
**43015** Excel & Accent all models '86 thru '09
**43050** Santa Fe all models '01 thru '06
**43055** Sonata all models '99 thru '08

## INFINITI
G35 '03 thru '08 - see NISSAN 350Z (72011)

## ISUZU
Hombre - see CHEVROLET S-10 (24071)
**47017** Rodeo, Amigo & Honda Passport '89 thru '02
**47020** Trooper & Pick-up '81 thru '93

## JAGUAR
**49010** XJ6 all 6 cyl models '68 thru '86
**49011** XJ6 all models '88 thru '94
**49015** XJ12 & XJS all 12 cyl models '72 thru '85

## JEEP
**50010** Cherokee, Comanche & Wagoneer Limited
all models '84 thru '01
**50020** CJ all models '49 thru '86
**50025** Grand Cherokee all models '93 thru '04
**50026** Grand Cherokee '05 thru '09
**50029** Grand Wagoneer & Pick-up '72 thru '91
Grand Wagoneer '84 thru '91, Cherokee &
Wagoneer '72 thru '83, Pick-up '72 thru '88
**50030** Wrangler all models '87 thru '11
**50035** Liberty '02 thru '07

## KIA
**54050** Optima '01 thru '10
**54070** Sephia '94 thru '01, Spectra '00 thru '09,
Sportage '05 thru '10

## LEXUS
ES 300/330 - see TOYOTA Camry (92007) (92008)
RX 330 - see TOYOTA Highlander (92095)

## LINCOLN
Navigator - see FORD Pick-up (36059)
**59010** Rear-Wheel Drive all models '70 thru '10

## MAZDA
**61010** GLC Hatchback (rear-wheel drive) '77 thru '83
**61011** GLC (front-wheel drive) '81 thru '85
**61012** Mazda3 '04 thru '11
**61015** 323 & Protegé '90 thru '03
**61016** MX-5 Miata '90 thru '09
**61020** MPV all models '89 thru '98
Navajo - see Ford Explorer (360?
**61030** Pick-ups '72 thru '93
Pick-ups '94 thru '00 - see Ford R
**61035** RX-7 all models '79 thru '85
**61036** RX-7 all models '86 thru '91
**61040** 626 (rear-wheel drive) all mode
**61041** 626/MX-6 (front-wheel drive
**61042** 626, MX-6/Ford Probe '93 thr
**61043** Mazda6 '03 thru '11

## MERCEDES-BENZ
**63012** 123 Series Diesel '76 thru '8
**63015** 190 Series four-cyl gas mod
**63020** 230/250/280 6 cyl sohc mod
**63025** 280 123 Series gasoline mod
**63030** 350 & 450 all models '71 thr
**63040** C-Class: C230/C240/C280/C320/

## MERCURY
**64200** Villager & Nissan Quest '93
All other titles, see FORD L

## MG
**66010** MGB Roadster & GT Coupe '6
**66015** MG Midget, Austin Healey S

## MINI
**67020** Mini '02 thru '11

## MITSUBISHI
**68020** Cordia, Tredia, Galant, Pre
Mirage '83 thru '93
**68030** Eclipse, Eagle Talon & Ply. L
**68031** Eclipse '95 thru '05, Eagle Talc
**68035** Galant '94 thru '10
**68040** Pick-up '83 thru '96 & Monte

## NISSAN
**72010** 300ZX all models including Turbo '84 thru '89
**72011** 350Z & Infiniti G35 all models '03 thru '08
**72015** Altima all models '93 thru '06
**72016** Altima '07 thru '10
**72020** Maxima all models '85 thru '92
**72021** Maxima all models '93 thru '04
**72025** Murano '03 thru '10
**72030** Pick-ups '80 thru '97 Pathfinder '87 thru '95
**72031** Frontier Pick-up, Xterra, Pathfinder '96 thru '04
**72032** Frontier & Xterra '05 thru '11
**72040** Pulsar all models '83 thru '86
Quest - see MERCURY Villager (64200)
**72050** Sentra all models '82 thru '94
**72051** Sentra & 200SX all models '95 thru '06
**72060** Stanza all models '82 thru '90
**72070** Titan pick-ups '04 thru '10 Armada '05 thru '10

## OLDSMOBILE
**73015** Cutlass V6 & V8 gas models '74 thru '88
*For other OLDSMOBILE titles, see BUICK,
CHEVROLET or GENERAL MOTORS listing.*

## PLYMOUTH
*For PLYMOUTH titles, see DODGE listing.*

## PONTIAC
**79008** Fiero all models '84 thru '88
**79018** Firebird V8 models except Turbo '70 thru '81
**79019** Firebird all models '82 thru '92
**79025** G6 all models '05 thru '09
**79040** Mid-size Rear-wheel Drive '70 thru '87
Vibe '03 thru '11 - see TOYOTA Matrix (92060)
*For other PONTIAC titles, see BUICK,
CHEVROLET or GENERAL MOTORS listing.*

## PORSCHE
**80020** 911 except Turbo & Carrera 4 '65 thru '89
**80025** 914 all 4 cyl models '69 thru '76
**80030** 924 all models including Turbo '76 thru '82
**80035** 944 all models including Turbo '83 thru '89

## RENAULT
Alliance & Encore - see AMC (14020)

## SAAB
**84010** 900 all models including Turbo '79 thru '88

## SATURN
**87010** Saturn all S-series models '91 thru '02
**87011** Saturn Ion '03 thru '07
**87020** Saturn L-series models '00 thru '04
**87040** Saturn VUE '02 thru '07

## SUBARU
**89002** 1100, 1300, 1400 & 1600 '71 thru '79
**89003** 1600 & 1800 2WD & 4WD '80 thru '94
**89100** Legacy all models '90 thru '99
**89101** Legacy & Forester '00 thru '06

## SUZUKI

## TRIUMPH
**94007** Spitfire all models '62 thru '81
**94010** TR7 all models '75 thru '81

## VW
**96008** Beetle & Karmann Ghia '54 thru '79
**96009** New Beetle '98 thru '11
**96016** Rabbit, Jetta, Scirocco & Pick-up gas
models '75 thru '92 & Convertible '80 thru '92
**96017** Golf, GTI & Jetta '93 thru '98, Cabrio '95 thru '02
**96018** Golf, GTI, Jetta '99 thru '05
**96019** Jetta, Rabbit, GTI & Golf '05 thru '11
**96020** Rabbit, Jetta & Pick-up diesel '77 thru '84
**96023** Passat '98 thru '05, Audi A4 '96 thru '01
**96030** Transporter 1600 all models '68 thru '79
**96035** Transporter 1700, 1800 & 2000 '72 thru '79
**96040** Type 3 1500 & 1600 all models '63 thru '73
**96045** Vanagon all air-cooled models '80 thru '83

## VOLVO
**97010** 120, 130 Series & 1800 Sports '61 thru '73
**97015** 140 Series all models '66 thru '74
**97020** 240 Series all models '76 thru '93
**97040** 740 & 760 Series all models '82 thru '88
**97050** 850 Series all models '93 thru '97

## TECHBOOK MANUALS
**10205** Automotive Computer Codes
**10206** OBD-II & Electronic Engine Management
**10210** Automotive Emissions Control Manual
**10215** Fuel Injection Manual '78 thru '85
**10220** Fuel Injection Manual '86 thru '99
**10225** Holley Carburetor Manual
**10230** Rochester Carburetor Manual
**10240** Weber/Zenith/Stromberg/SU Carburetors
**10305** Chevrolet Engine Overhaul Manual
**10310** Chrysler Engine Overhaul Manual
**10320** Ford Engine Overhaul Manual
**10330** GM and Ford Diesel Engine Repair Manual
**10333** Engine Performance Manual
**10340** Small Engine Repair Manual, 5 HP & Less
**10341** Small Engine Repair Manual, 5.5 - 20 HP
**10345** Suspension, Steering & Driveline Manual
**10355** Ford Automatic Transmission Overhaul
**10360** GM Automatic Transmission Overhaul
**10405** Automotive Body Repair & Painting
**10410** Automotive Brake Manual
**10411** Automotive Anti-lock Brake (ABS) Systems
**10415** Automotive Detailing Manual
**10420** Automotive Electrical Manual
**10425** Automotive Heating & Air Conditioning
**10430** Automotive Reference Manual & Dictionary
**10435** Automotive Tools Manual
**10440** Used Car Buying Guide
**10445** Welding Manual
**10450** ATV Basics
**10452** Scooters 50cc to 250cc

## SPANISH MANUALS
**98903** Reparación de Carrocería & Pintura
**98904** Manual de Carburador Modelos
Holley & Rochester
**98905** Códigos Automotrices de la Computadora
**98906** OBD-II & Sistemas de Control Electrónico
del Motor
**98910** Frenos Automotriz
**98913** Electricidad Automotriz
**98915** Inyección de Combustible '86 al '99
**99040** Chevrolet & GMC Camionetas '67 al '87
**99041** Chevrolet & GMC Camionetas '88 al '98
**99042** Chevrolet & GMC Camionetas
Cerradas '68 al '95
**99043** Chevrolet/GMC Camionetas '94 al '04
**99048** Chevrolet/GMC Camionetas '99 al '06
**99055** Dodge Caravan & Plymouth Voyager '84 al '95
**99075** Ford Camionetas y Bronco '80 al '94
**99076** Ford F-150 '97 al '09
**99077** Ford Camionetas Cerradas '69 al '91
**99088** Ford Modelos de Tamaño Mediano '75 al '86
**99089** Ford Camionetas Ranger '93 al '10
**99091** Ford Taurus & Mercury Sable '86 al '95
**99095** GM Modelos de Tamaño Grande '70 al '90
**99100** GM Modelos de Tamaño Mediano '70 al '88
**99106** Jeep Cherokee, Wagoneer & Comanche
'84 al '00
**99110** Nissan Camioneta '80 al '96, Pathfinder '87 al '95
**99118** Nissan Sentra '82 al '94
**99125** Toyota Camionetas y 4Runner '79 al '95

Over 100 Haynes
motorcycle manuals
also available

7-12

Haynes North America, Inc., 861 Lawrence Drive, Newbury Park, CA 91320-1514 • (805) 498-6703 • http://www.haynes.com